SOCIOLOGY: *CULTURAL DIVERSITY IN A CHANGING WORLD*

George J. Bryjak
University of San Diego

Michael P. Soroka
University of San Diego

Allyn and Bacon

Boston   London   Toronto   Sydney   Tokyo   Singapore

Why should there be one empty belly in the world when the work of one man can feed a hundred? What if my brother be not as strong as I? He has not sinned. Wherefore should he hunger—he and his sinless little ones? Down with the old law. There is food and shelter for all, therefore let all receive food and shelter.

From "Wanted: A New Law of Development," Jack London, 1902

Senior Editor: Karen Hanson
Developmental Editor: Hannah Rubenstein
Executive Editor: Susan Badger
Editorial Assistant: Laura Lynch
Production Administrator: Susan McIntyre
Editorial-Production Service: Sally Stickney
Photo Researcher: Sharon Donahue
Cover Administrator: Linda Dickinson
Manufacturing Buyer: Megan Cochran

This book is printed on recycled paper.

Library of Congress Cataloging-in-Publication Data

Bryjak, George J.
    Sociology : cultural diversity in a changing world / George J. Bryjak,
Michael P. Soroka.
        p.   cm.
    Includes bibliographical references and indexes.
    ISBN 0-205-13101-8
    1. Sociology. I. Soroka, Michael P. II. Title.
HM51.B896   1991
301 — dc20   91-29769
                                                                        CIP

Printed in the United States of America

10 9 8 7 6 5 4 3   96 95 94 93

Photo Credits

Abbreviations: Gamma-Liaison Network (GLN); Michael Freeman (MF); Doranne Jacobson (DJ); Picture Group (PG); Stock, Boston (SB); Woodfin Camp & Associates (WCA).
Ch. 1: 1: Lisl Dennis/The Image Bank. 5 (left): Dallas & John Heaton/(SB). 5 (right): Karen Kasmauski/ (WCA). 17: (MF). 20: John Arthur/Impact/(PG). *Ch. 2:* 37: Cary Wolinsky/(SB). 41: (DJ). 47: Kaku Kurita/(GLN). 52: Bob Daemmrich/(SB). 55: Dallas & John Heaton/(SB). *Ch. 3:* 71: (MF). 77: Dilip Mehta/Contact/(WCA). 83: (MF). 84: Dick Luria/Photo Researchers, Inc. 95: Alon Reininger/Contact/ (WCA). *Ch. 4:* 103: (DJ). 106: (MF). 112: Nathan Benn/(WCA). 118: (MF). 129: Peter Menzel/ (SB). *Ch. 5:* 135: David Austen/(SB). 140: Chris Brown/(SB). 148: Dean Abramson/(SB). 154: Shawn Henry/(PG). 160: Steve Benbow/(PG). *Ch. 6:* 167: J. Kyle Keener/*Philadelphia Inquirer*/Matrix. 174: Nathan Benn/(WCA). 179: Terry Eiler/(SB). 187: Lester Sloan/(WCA). 190: David Harvey/(WCA). *Ch. 7:* 199: Sudhir/(PG). 207: Cary Wolinsky/(SB). 214: (DJ). 218: Alexis Duclos/(GLN). 230: Nishiyama/ Japho/(PG). *Ch. 8:* 235: Matthew Neal McVay/(SB). 237: P. Piel/(GLN). 246: Lawrence Migdale/Photo Researchers, Inc. 271: Peter Menzel/(SB). *Ch. 9:* 277: Dallas & John Heaton/(SB). 278: Andy Levin/Photo Researchers, Inc. 290: (DJ). 301: Chip Hires/(GLN). 314: Matthew Naythons/(SB). 320: Dallas & John Heaton/(SB). *Ch. 10:* 325: Author's photo. 330: Wendy Stone/(GLN). 335: Tony O'Brien/(PG). 355: Michael Springer/(GLN). 359: Kim Newton/(WCA). *Ch. 11:* 363: (MF). 367: Courtesy, Toronto Convention & Visitors Association. 377: Cradoc Bagshaw/(GLN). 390: (MF). 393: Allen Russell/(PG). *Ch. 12:* 401: (MF). 404: Nubar Alexanian/(SB). 417: Leong Kai-Tai/(WCA). 425: Charlie Cole/(PG). 431: Chip Hires/(GLN).

MAP 1   The Modern World

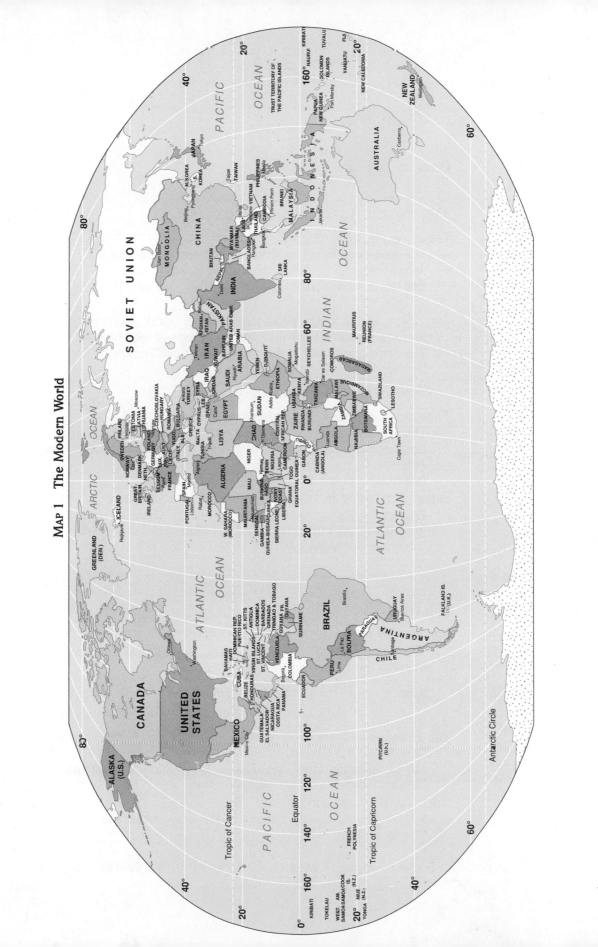

Contents

Preface

THEMES AND RATIONALE

In some respects, trying to sell sociologists on the merits of a new introductory textbook could be compared to arguing on behalf of additional shopping malls in southern California or a few more inches of snow in northern Maine. We have so many already—is there really any need for more?

It is true that many useful and successful texts are available for the introductory course, with more seeming to arrive each month. However, our many years of combined experience teaching introductory sociology have led us to conclude that existing texts do not completely fulfill our vision of what a first course in the field ideally could and should accomplish.

The primary objective of any introductory course is to infuse students with the sociological perspective—to help them develop, in C. Wright Mills's famous phrase, a "sociological imagination." In this regard, introductory texts (including this one) commonly expose students to the theoretical and methodological tools of the discipline, using them to interpret the students' surrounding social environment. But though a thorough understanding of one's own society may be a necessary condition for attaining a sociological imagination, it is not a sufficient condition. To comprehend and fully appreciate the dynamics and effects of social and cultural forces in the contemporary world, students must be provided with a far broader perspective than is typically offered in existing texts.

A Cross-Cultural Perspective

It is becoming increasingly clear that the forces affecting our lives are not confined to the internal dynamics of the United States. International trade agreements and political alliances influence more than just the cost of many consumer goods. They also partially determine the nation's employment picture as well as the rate and consequences of some forms of criminal behavior (such as the use of illegal drugs). Although factors in the global marketplace and political arena have always had some effect on people in the United States, the frequency and magnitude of changes in the "global village" have never been greater. The ascendancy of newly industrialized nations like South Korea, Taiwan, Singapore, and Hong Kong; the recent war in the Persian Gulf; and sweeping changes in the Soviet Union and the Eastern European countries have already influenced and will continue to have a pronounced effect on our lives.

One of the goals of this text is to acquaint students with the concept of modernization—the ongoing process of change that transforms traditional agricultural or pastoral societies into industrial (and now, postindustrial) nation-states. Although modernization cannot explain all the momentous events and processes occurring in the world today, it is a useful—and in introductory texts, overlooked—perspective for examining these phenomena.

Because modernization significantly affects virtually all aspects of contemporary societies, we believe an understanding of this concept is vital to developing a sociological imagination. Today, the first course in sociology is an appropriate setting for introducing students to this key force in our world. We are convinced that students will intuitively recognize that in addition to core sociological concepts such as culture, social structure, socialization, and stratification, the process of modernization plays a central role in their lives.

An exploration of this key social process obviously calls for a cross-cultural framework, and this text is replete with examples and statistics from numerous countries, especially developing nations. However, we have attempted to avoid the danger of presenting a bewildering array of "strange but true" facts drawn from too large an assortment of societies and cultures from around the world. Such a display may make for entertaining reading, but it can confuse rather than enlighten students taking their first course in sociology.

Thus, to provide integration, depth, and continuity, we have placed, at the end of chapters 2–12, extended discussions of Mexico and Japan, two countries vital to the interests of the United States—and to today's students' lives. Mexico, a rapidly modernizing nation, is the United States' nearest southern neighbor; Japan, the post–World War II "economic miracle," has become our major competitor in the economic arena. The Focus on Mexico and Focus on Japan sections provide both historical background and contemporary analyses of some significant aspects of these two societies as they relate to core concepts introduced in the respective chapters. For instance, in chapter 2 on culture we explore the paramount value of harmony (*wa*) to the Japanese and describe the central role of the family, *machismo* (manliness), and religion in Mexican culture (for a complete listing of topics, see the Contents). By utilizing the Mexican and Japanese societies to provide a consistent basis for cross-cultural comparisons rather than the more common smorgasbord approach, we feel this text is more likely to enlighten than to confuse. At the conclusion of this book, in addition to having a greater appreciation of both the continuities and variations of cultural views and social practices across the United States and different societies, students will have a basic understanding of Mexico and Japan from a sociological perspective.

To provide students with insight into the workings of other societies as they relate to one or more of the central themes developed within chapters, chapters 2–12 also contain a cross-cultural feature entitled Ourselves and Others. The endless bureaucratic structure that comprises the government of the People's Republic of China, for instance, is the subject of this feature in chapter 3 on groups and social structure; in chapter 7, "Growing Up Female in Bangladesh" investigates the impact of gender stratification on women's lives in one of the world's poorest societies. Other countries featured in these boxes include Brazil, Canada, France, India, Poland, and the Soviet Union (for a complete listing of topics, see the Contents).

An Exploration of Cultural Diversity in U.S. Society

In addition to devoting a significant portion of the text to the people, processes, and structures of other societies, *Sociology: Cultural Diversity in a Changing World* consistently explores the many social groups and cultural patterns coexisting within contemporary U.S. society. The social, economic, and political consequences of the rapidly changing composition of the U.S. population and changing conceptions of gender roles are examined throughout. In chapter 2 on culture, for example, we explore the influence of race, ethnicity, and social class on "traditional" core values of U.S. society. What constitutes the essence of being an American? The attempt by members of the majority group to preserve "American" culture through legislating English as the official language of the United States is one facet of this controversial question explored in the chapter. In chapter 7 on gender, we investigate subgroup memberships and the effects of racial, ethnic, class, and sexual-orientation differences on the experiences of women in the economic and political realms. The theme of cultural diversity is similarly threaded through separate chapters on stratification, race and ethnicity, three key social institutions (marriage and family, politics, and religion), population, and urbanization.

A Basic Foundation

Notwithstanding the important themes introduced above, the primary function of any introductory text in sociology must be the clear and theoretically balanced presentation of the discipline's most important core concepts. *Sociology: Cultural Diversity in a Changing World* is first and foremost a sound introduction to the discipline of sociology. Theory, culture, socialization, groups and social structure, stratification, race and ethnicity, gender, and deviance and social control are presented in a lively and comprehensive manner. Separate chapters on population, urbanization, and modernization build upon core concepts and inform students about critical areas of sociological study. The twelve-chapter format allows instructors the option of supplementing the text with other readings; *Sociology:*

Cultural Diversity in a Changing World was created, however, to stand alone as a firm foundation for the introductory course.

FEATURES OF THE TEXT

Focus on Mexico and Focus on Japan

As described above, these sections provide students with an in-depth look into many significant aspects of the Mexican and Japanese societies. Each "Focus on" section investigates how the core concepts introduced in that chapter manifest themselves in these societies. Questions at the end of each "Focus on" section give readers a consistent basis for making intelligent comparisons and contrasts with the United States.

Ourselves and Others

Cross-cultural boxes in chapters 2–12 provide students with another basis for comparing their own society with others. "Why France Outstrips the United States in Nurturing Children," in chapter 4, compares U.S. socialization practices with those of France. A surge in crime following the collapse of communism in Warsaw is the subject of this feature, "Fighting Crime Just Doesn't Pay. Ask a Policeman," in chapter 8 on crime and deviance (see the Contents for a complete listing of Ourselves and Others boxes).

Other Pedagodical Features

Questions to Consider   Directly following each chapter's brief introductory overview, students are presented with focusing questions to alert them to the important concepts and issues to be introduced and developed in the chapter. These questions have been created to develop students' analytical skills by encouraging them to critically evaluate, rather than simply memorize, what they are learning.

Key Terms   Key terms are defined throughout the text in boldface, easily identifiable type. These terms provide students with a working definition of the most important sociological concepts as they are introduced and applied.

Extensive Chapter Summaries   Numbered chapter summaries review, highlight, and reinforce the most important concepts and issues discussed in each chapter. They are linked to the chapter opening Questions to Consider.

Comprehensive Glossary   A comprehensive glossary brings together all important concepts and terms introduced throughout the text into a single, accessible format.

FEATURES OF THE SUPPLEMENTS PACKAGE

Allyn and Bacon/CNN Sociology Video Connection

In keeping with our cross- and multi-cultural focus, a fully integrated 120-minute video program consisting of thirty-four film segments drawn from recent CNN programming from the United States and around the world accompanies this text. These film segments, which range in length from two to ten minutes, address timely and important topics that illustrate key text issues or concepts. There are an average of three film segments per chapter; each chapter's films are introduced by a narrator who alerts the students to what they are about to see and describes the significance of the film clips to the concepts discussed in the chapter. Among the thirty-four topics explored in this video program are "Changing U.S.

Composition and Bilingual Education" (culture); "The 'Brown Tide': Growing Hispanic Population in U.S." and "Racism on Campus" (race and ethnicity); "Women's Rights in Kenya: A Case of Cultural Lag" (gender); and "Deforestation of the Amazon—Dilemma of Development" (modernization). An accompanying *Video Guide* provides a description of each segment and keys each film to the appropriate text section.

A wide variety of other videos are also available from the Allyn and Bacon Video Library.

Ourselves and Others: The Washington Post *Sociology Companion*

By exclusive arrangement with the *Washington Post,* Allyn and Bacon is publishing an integrated collection of ninety-six recent articles on sociology, each of which illustrates and amplifies important concepts in *Sociology: Cultural Diversity in a Changing World.* This timely multicultural reader contains articles examining sociological issues in the United States and worldwide and is organized to match the contents of this text.

Instructor's Manual/Testbank

This combination manual offers a complete instructor's section and testbank to accompany each text chapter. The *Testbank* includes over 1,100 questions (40 multiple-choice questions, 30 true-false questions, 15 fill-in questions, and 5 essay questions per chapter) all page referenced to the text. The *Instructor's Manual* includes teaching objectives, annotated chapter outlines, a list of key terms, a list of key people, class-discussion questions, in-class exercises, film and video listings, guest speaker suggestions, essay/applications, pop quizzes, and transparency masters.

Computerized Test Banks

The Allyn and Bacon *Test Manager* (for IBM-PC) is a convenient, two-part software package accompanied by a disk containing all items in the printed testbank. The *Test Manager* allows the instructor to add questions, edit all items from the *Testbank,* and construct multiple versions of the same test. The *Grade Manager* allows the instructor to record and compute grades for an unlimited number of students and classes.

Micro Test III (for Macintosh) is an easy-to-use software program that provides instructors with a multitude of options in formulating tests, including creating multiple versions of tests, customizing headings to aid student instruction, and assigning difficulty levels to questions. Full customer support is available.

Call-in and Fax Testing Services

Allyn and Bacon's testing center can process and send finished tests, ready for duplication, within forty-eight hours. Fax service of hardcopy is available on a same-day basis.

Study Guide Plus: Language and Multicultural Enrichment

Written by Professor Diana Kendall, Austin Community College, the *Study Guide* contains chapter overviews, learning objectives, annotated chapter outlines, key terms to define (with answers), key people, self-tests (with answers and explanations), multiple-choice questions, true-false questions, fill-in questions, matching questions, and essay questions.

Coordinated by Professor Louis Clunk of Golden West College, in conjunction with the Golden West Student Multicultural Center, each chapter also provides a glossary in which potentially confusing idioms, colloquial expressions, and vocabulary are identified and translated.

Thinking Sociologically

Thinking Sociologically: A Critical Thinking Activities Manual, by Josephine A. Ruggiero of Providence College, offers students eight sets of short exercises designed to sharpen critical thinking skills. Through examples and questions, the exercises guide students through a three-step process in which they must think critically about an issue or problem, consciously reflect on the thought processes involved, and apply this skill to other issues and contexts.

SocScience Software

Ten interactive modules present simulated research and other demonstrations on topics such as AIDS, economic development, social deviance, education, and cultural values. Each module is designed to be completed in one class period.

Custom Published Ancillaries

Allyn and Bacon can customize supplements packages to meet instructors needs more closely. For example, an instructor may wish to add a course syllabus or additional study and test questions. For more information on custom publishing or any of the above supplemental materials, please contact your local Allyn and Bacon representative.

ACKNOWLEDGMENTS

Many people have given generously of their time and talents in the preparation of this book. We are especially grateful to Series Editor Karen Hanson and Developmental Editor Hannah Rubenstein. We would be hard pressed to find more competent, professional individuals. They guided us through the difficult periods of this endeavor and gave us constant encouragement. Karen provided the general direction and overall scope of this project, and Hannah helped us refine our ideas and writing. Without their expertise, this would have been a much different (and poorer) text. Sally Stickney, production coordinator, did a great job integrating all the various elements of the text into its final form. Other members of the Allyn and Bacon staff, including Laura Lynch and Susan McIntyre, were most helpful.

Colleagues at the University of San Diego and other institutions read portions of this manuscript and gave us useful comments and valuable insights. We would like to thank Judy Liu, Gene Labovitz, Kathy Grove, Judy McIlwee, Frank Young, Gary Macy, and Allen Wittenborn, all of the University of San Diego. Harold Grasmick of the University of Oklahoma, and Howard Daudestil and Malcolm Holmes of the University of Texas, El Paso, also read portions of the manuscript. Yoshio Ikeda of the Aichi Institute of Technology provided us with material from Japan. Librarian Devin Milner, now of San Diego Mesa College, helped us locate some hard-to-find sources of information. Research Assistant Amy Kupic spent many hours digging through the stacks at university libraries in and around San Diego tracking down books and journal articles. Thanks, Amy. Ron Pajak and Ted Swiatek—the Buffalo Connection—also contributed to this project.

The following reviewers made important comments, especially in the early stages of the project: Maxine Baca Zinn, Michigan State University; Howard C. Daudistel, University of Texas at El Paso; Ramona L. Ford, Southwest Texas State University; Kay Gillespie, Weber State College; Paul S. Gray, Boston College; Dennis E. Hoffman, University of Nebraska at Omaha; Barbara Johnson, Augsburg College; Thomas Keil, University of Louisville; Diana Kendall, Austin Community College; Laura O'Toole, University of Delaware; Larry Perkins, Oklahoma State University; Virginia Powell, Beloit College; Michele L. Rollins, California State University; Robert J. S. Ross, Clark University; Allan Schaffer, Texas A & M; and Theodore C. Wagenaar, Miami University. Many of their responses have been incorporated into the final draft. We thank them for their time and effort.

Finally, we acknowledge our significant others, Diane Kulstead and Gaye Soroka. They endured a neverending work schedule and our often less than cheerful dispositions during the preparation of this text, especially the last six months of work. Their understanding, support, and love are most appreciated.

1

THE WORLD ACCORDING TO SOCIOLOGY

Sometime between the end of summer and the end of November (the exact time seems to creep up each year) retail stores throughout the United States undergo a remarkable transformation. Outside, display windows suddenly become enchanted winter wonderlands of bright packages beneath beautifully decorated trees. Inside, traditional Christmas songs replace the vaguely identifiable music normally piped in over public address systems, and hordes of wide-eyed children line up to plead their cases to Santa. As Labor Day gives way to Halloween and then to Thanksgiving, a growing sense of excitement and anticipation begins to infuse the shoppers who crowd the malls looking for gift ideas and bargains. Later, as early and mid-December shade into the last few shopping days before the big event, this sense of excitement may be replaced by a growing sense of frustration and desperation. Tempers flare as mall parking lots fill to capacity by 10 A.M. and the perfect gift remains unfound. Even in southern California, where one-horse open sleighs seldom go dashing through the snow, it is that time of year again.

A few miles south, on the other side of the U.S.-Mexican border, the people of Baja California are also preparing for Christmas. But here, in cities like Tijuana, stores are

1

much less enchanted, preparations much more subdued. Greetings of "*feliz Navidad*" may sound through the air as family members and friends pass one another on the crowded streets, but Christmas shows considerably less of the glitter and the gift giving that most Americans may be used to. Given the massive poverty of the residents in the *colonias* that dot the hillsides surrounding the city, it is impossible for most parents to plan much of a material holiday celebration for their families. It is equally difficult for children to entertain any visions of sugarplums dancing in their heads. Their most pressing thoughts may be of food and warm clothing to protect them from the cold winds shaking the ramshackle building that serves as home. A traditional "Christmas with all the trimmings" is reserved for members of the comfortable middle and affluent upper classes, and most Mexican people simply do not fall into those categories. For the bulk of the population, Christmas is hardly a time of comfort or joy. If gifts are exchanged at all, they may be objects made by hand, donated by a public or private agency, or salvaged from other people's cast-offs.

Several thousand miles west of both southern and Baja California, December also brings lavish window displays and crowds of shoppers hurrying into department stores in Tokyo's Ginza district and in most other Japanese cities as well. But the frenetic gift buying and selling that take place in these stores have almost nothing to do with Christmas as we know it. Most Japanese are not Christians and do not acknowledge December 25 as a significant date. Rather, this period marks the *oseibo*, the end of the year. It is one of two established seasons during which gift giving takes place in Japan on a societywide basis (the other period, *ochugen,* occurs from mid-July to mid-August and is the celebration of the midyear). Like its Western Christmas counterpart, *oseibo* once was primarily a religious celebration. But like Christmas (in the United States, at least), it has become highly commercialized, an opportunity to affirm social relations and to satisfy social obligations. Gifts often are selected on the basis of the respective social standings of the giver and the receiver, as well as their value. The actual properties of the items themselves—their beauty or utility—may be of little or no importance to any of those concerned, especially in the corporate or business context.

These three patterns are obviously and significantly different from one another, yet in a certain respect they are quite similar. Although no doubt strange and incomprehensible to a foreign observer (e.g., a U.S. tourist visiting Mexico City or Tokyo for the first time), each is recognizable and understandable to someone who is involved in it. That is because the behaviors of all participants are patterned, organized according to a logical system that is known and makes sense to the members of the local population.

In this text we will examine a variety of human activities through the perspective of **sociology,** the academic discipline that attempts to describe, explain, and predict human social patterns from a scientific orientation. Several other fields known collectively as the social sciences (including anthropology, economics, political science, and psychology) also study human social behaviors scientifically. But sociology is different in focusing on the ways in which the organization and operation of the groups that make up societies affect the members of those societies. In keeping with this tradition, our attention throughout the book will be on recognizable groups or types of people—college students, women, and religious fundamentalists, for example—rather than on individual persons. Our primary goal is to bring you to some understanding of how human social patterns are established, maintained, and changed over time. We also explore the differences that particular patterns make in the lives of the people who carry them out. In most cases, these differences are of greater importance than the numbers and kinds of gifts people give and receive during holiday seasons.

QUESTIONS TO CONSIDER

1. What is the subject matter of sociology?
2. When did the two phases of modernization begin?
3. In what sense is sociology a debunking science?
4. What is positivism?
5. What are social facts and how do they differ from individual/psychological phenomena?
6. What is a theory? What is the difference between grand theories and middle-range theories?
7. What is the problem of order and how is it solved, according to functionalist sociologists?
8. What are the functional requirements that all societies must meet if they are to survive?
9. What are manifest and latent functions?
10. What basic assumptions do conflict sociologists make about the nature of society?
11. Can conflict be beneficial for society?
12. According to symbolic interactionism, in what sense do people create the world they live in?
13. What is the difference between the independent and dependent variables in a scientific experiment?
14. What is survey research and what are some of the problems associated with this investigative technique?
15. What is participant observation and what are some of the problems surrounding this strategy?

THEME OF THE TEXT

The Modernization of Sociology: A Growing International Perspective

When we think of social scientists doing **cross-cultural research,** that is, gathering comparable data from different human populations, the discipline of anthropology usually comes to mind. As a result of watching Indiana Jones–type movies, people often think of cross-cultural research as a continuing adventure with investigators studying strange and sometimes dangerous people in the far reaches of the globe. **Cultural anthropologists** typically study the social organization and patterns of behavior of premodern people throughout the world, but their days are more likely to be filled with hard work and careful observation than with adventure.

A sister discipline of anthropology, sociology focuses on the social organization and patterns of behavior in large, complex, modern, industrial societies. Although interested in modern societies as a whole, sociologists have traditionally attempted to understand and explain social phenomena in their own countries, and have not spent as much time carefully examining patterns of behavior in other nations. For example, to the extent that American and French sociologists have looked beyond their own borders, they have been inclined to see if what was happening in the United States and France was similar to the social structures and patterns of behavior in other industrial nations as a whole.

This tendency to peer inward at one's own society as well as to look outward at the broader picture can be traced to sociology's inception in mid-nineteenth-century Europe. By this time the Industrial Revolution was well under way, and societies that had been relatively stable for hundreds of years were changing rapidly. As new machines and sources of power enhanced humans' ability to produce a growing list of products, people left farms and small towns by the tens of thousands and moved to the cities for a life of factory work. This heretofore unprecedented rural-to-urban migration resulted in the growth of hundreds of cities in Europe and in North America. With this growth came many of the social problems (like higher rates of violent crime) that accompany urbanization and that increasingly plague cities today. Population increase, the beginning of mass education, and the fall of aristocracies in favor of increasingly democratic forms of government were transforming the face of Europe. The old rural, feudal, agrarian way of life was giving way to urban, capitalist, industrial societies.

Some intellectuals of this period realized that although the disciplines of psychology and economics helped them understand these changes, their focus of study was too narrow. Psychologists studied individual behavior and were more likely to shed light on how people were affected by these changes than on what brought the changes about in the first place. Economists studied the production, distribution, exchange, and consumption of goods and services in society. Although the transformation of economies was a vital component of the Industrial Revolution, societies are composed of other critical institutions like the family, religion, and government. A new science that would take into account the interrelation and interdependence of all the institutions in society was required to explain the scope, direction, and duration of these changes. French philosopher Auguste Comte (1798–1857) coined the term *sociology* for the discipline he believed would eventually become the "queen of the sciences."

The question of how and under what conditions societies change has been the most important sociological question since the days of Comte over 150 years ago. In the post–World War II era more and more sociologists have attempted to understand the process of modernization, or Second Industrial Revolution, as developing nations attempt to abandon traditional institutions and emulate societies like the United States and Japan. Today, sociologists from many nations study the interrelation of political and economic institutions of societies that make up the so-called global village. They also are taking a closer look at the day-to-day lives of people who live in these nations. The proliferation of social science research in many countries and the amount of this material available in English and other international languages make in-depth, cross-cultural research possible today.

In this book we attempt to draw from the rich store of cross-cultural sociological data that have greatly enhanced our discipline's understanding of human social phenomena. Not only does this research strategy enable us to comprehend better the workings of other societies, it gives us a look at ourselves from another vantage point. This view of the United States from the outside looking in could provide us with additional insights as we assess the strengths and weaknesses of this society and attempt to correct the latter.

The Modernization of the World

You don't have to be a seasoned traveler to realize that a country like the United States is more prosperous than Mexico, and thousands of times wealthier than some of the poorest nations in Africa and Asia. Not only is the United States more economically advanced than these nations, the people in this and other rich countries have a different world view or mind-set, than individuals who struggle to survive on a day-to-day basis. To alleviate the suffering and misery that affect 80 percent of the earth's population, almost every poor nation is attempting to increase its economic productivity, reduce death and disease, and improve the quality of life for its citizens. They are all trying to leave the world of the "have nots," and join the world of the "haves." In short, they desperately want to modernize. Millions of people in poor countries realize that to date they have been left out of the modernization process (see Table 1.1 for terminology used in this section) and want to acquire a share of the planet's wealth before they are left hopelessly behind.

At the risk of an oversimplification, we may think of modernization as occurring in two broad stages. The first stage began with the Industrial Revolution and resulted in the modernization of numerous European countries, the United States, Canada, Australia, and New Zealand. The second phase started in the aftermath of the Second World War and continues to unfold at different speeds and under widely different circumstances in the Third World.

Social scientists use a classification scheme to categorize nations as to their degree of modernity. Although these systems are quite useful and permit us to speak in general terms of now rich countries and less developed countries, in reality the approximately 175 nations of the world cannot be so neatly divided. More accurately, they may be thought of as falling along a lengthy continuum from very poor to very rich, all at various stages or levels of development. It is also somewhat misleading to speak of stages of development, since there is no single path to modernization with a specified number and sequence of stages that all nations will inevitably follow. For example, First

Virtually all large societies are a combination of modern and traditional characteristics. In a technologically advanced society such as Japan, bullet-trains reach speeds in excess of 125 miles per hour while some people engage in physically demanding labor much as they have for centuries.

TABLE 1.1 Modernization Terminology

Term	Definition
First World	The modern, industrial, capitalist countries of North America, and Europe. Japan, Israel, Australia, New Zealand, and South Africa are also in this group. Almost all of these nations have democratic political institutions.
Second World	Until events beginning in 1989–1990, this term referred to the totalitarian, socialist, industrial countries of Eastern Europe and the Soviet Union. However, most East European nations and the U.S.S.R. are currently in the process of changing to capitalism and more democratic political institutions. These countries are moving toward capitalism or possibly a mixed (socialist and capitalist) economic system with more political freedom and less government control over the day-to-day lives of their citizens. It remains to be seen how long this transformation will take and how successful it will be.
Third World	Coined by the French intellectual Alfred Sauvy in 1952, Third World is a translation of the expression, *le tiers monde.* Sauvy made a comparison between the inhabitants of poor, post–World War II nations struggling to rid themselves of colonial rule, and the common people in France—the Third Estate—at the time of the French Revolution. This term is widely used to refer to the poor nations of the world collectively. A problem with this categorization is that it includes desperately poor countries like the Sudan and Bangladesh as well as modestly rich nations like Argentina and South Korea.
Less developed countries (LDCs)	This term refers to the less *economically* developed countries of the world and is often used interchangeably with Third World and traditional societies. Typically, between 40 and 90 percent of the labor force in LDCs work in agriculture. As Toffler (1990) noted, *less developed* is really an "arrogant misnomer" inasmuch as many LDCs including Mexico, India, and China have highly developed cultures dating back hundreds (and in some cases, thousands) of years.
Now rich countries (NRCs)	The rich, modern, industrial countries of the world taken as a whole. This includes societies in the First and Second Worlds as well as those with mixed (capitalist and socialist) economies.
Modernization	This rather slippery, often vague concept is used by journalists, politicians, and social scientists to describe the transformation from a traditional, usually agrarian, society to a contemporary, industrially-based state. According to Black (1966), modernization is the general process of change across five major dimensions of society: intellectual, political, economic, social, and psychological. In this text, the terms modernization and development are used synonymously.

World countries like the United States and Japan developed with capitalist economic systems, whereas the Soviet Union, until recently a Second World nation, industrialized under a socialist system. Each country, because of its own history and culture, takes a somewhat different path. However, a set of problems shared by most Third World nations (rapidly increasing populations, food shortages, large foreign debt, etc.) allows us to think of them as a whole to a certain extent. Regardless of which path of

MAP 2 First, Second, and Third World Countries

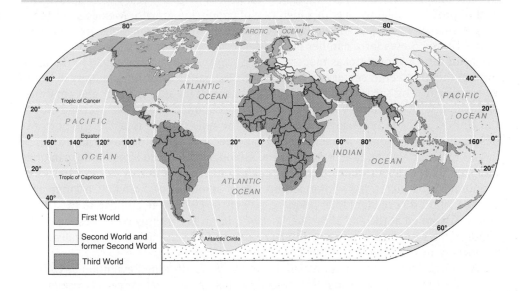

Legend:
- First World
- Second World and former Second World
- Third World

development individual nations follow, they will have to solve these problems, and the range of possible solutions may be quite limited.

The study of modernization, according to Paul Harrison (1984, p. 17), is the "central story of our time," a story affecting the lives of more than three-fourths of humanity. Social scientists began studying modernization seriously in the years after World War II, when people in now rich countries became aware of the enormous discrepancies of wealth between rich nations and poor nations (Larkin and Peters, 1983). This was also a period of revolutionary activity as many Third World, colonial nations demanded and fought for independence. As an increasing number of poor countries were successful in their struggle for freedom, statesmen watched and waited to see if they would align themselves with the communist world or the "free" world, and what impact these new countries would have on Cold War politics. In the aftermath of the Second World War, policy-oriented researchers were primarily interested in how to increase the economic output of poor nations. As a result, they measured modernization almost exclusively in terms of economic indicators such as the gross national product and per capita income.

Today, modernization is a much broader concept that focuses on the positive social changes accompanying industrialization and economic growth. Some researchers assert that, ideally, modernization should include an equitable distribution of the wealth that comes from economic progress. As a result, people in Third World nations will share a "higher standard of living in terms of income, food and other forms of consumption, health, housing, education, and increased freedom of choice in all aspects of life" (Welsh and Butorin, 1990, p. 310).

Mexico and Japan: Two Societies in Transition

Most introductory sociology texts use cross-cultural examples from many different societies to give students a taste of the often vast cultural and social differences between the United States and other nations. This book continues in that tradition. In addition, we focus on two societies, Mexico and Japan, that are at different points on the modernization continuum. The Japanese economic miracle produced a societal transformation few would have thought possible less than fifty years ago. Faced with a host of problems beginning with a high rate of population growth, Mexico's economic progress has been slower and much more erratic. Both of these nations are important to the United States for a number of political, economic, and social reasons.

Japan can be thought of as modernizing in two stages. The first began in the latter third of the nineteenth century and ended with the nation's crushing military defeat in World War II. The second stage commenced in the years after the war and continues to this day, with the country now a financial and economic superpower, second only to the United States in productivity and wealth. The only country to suffer the horror of destruction from atomic weapons, Japan may become the most powerful economic nation in history by the turn of the century. Although the United States and Japan often disagree sharply about trade policies (especially quotas and access to markets), their economies are increasingly intermeshed. Japan is our largest trading partner after Canada, and 34 percent of total Japanese exports in 1989 were shipped to the United States. Disarmed at the end of the war in 1945, Japan is currently being pushed by the United States to take a stronger military posture for the defense of capitalism and democracy in the Middle and Far East.

Although Mexico began industrializing in the years after the Revolution of 1910, it was not until the post–World War II period that modernization really accelerated. Currently, Mexico can be thought of as somewhere in the middle of the continuum, much farther along economically than the poorest nations of Africa and Asia, but lagging behind rich nations like the United States and Japan. In the past twenty years, relations between the United States and Mexico have become more complex and increasingly important for both countries. Politically, Mexico is viewed as an ally in Central America, a region that recent administrations have viewed as a jumping-off point for the spread of communism in the Americas. Washington, D.C. and Mexico City do not always see eye to eye on the solution to problems in Central America. But these disagreements are overshadowed by a commitment the United States has to a politically stable Mexico, if for no other reasons than to protect existing U.S. investments and to ensure a safe haven for future economic endeavors. Between 1983 and 1989, exports from the United States to Mexico increased from $17 billion to almost $28 billion. During that same period, however, the value of Mexican goods sent to the United States jumped from $9 billion to almost $25 billion.

There can be little doubt that increasing the value of exports to the United States fits prominently in Mexico's plans for economic development. If a North American economic community composed of the United States, Mexico, and Canada becomes a reality, trade among these three nations will increase dramatically. Mexico also stands to benefit from disruptions in the worldwide supply of oil. The volatile and unpredictable political situation in the Middle East, coupled with American dependence on foreign oil, means that Mexico's huge off-shore oil reserves (by some estimates the largest in the world) are potentially important to the economic well-being of the United States. It appears that economic ties between the United States and Mexico will only become stronger in coming years.

The Debunking Science

Before proceeding with our introduction to the science of sociology and subsequent examination of the United States and other societies, a few words about the sociological perspective are in order. It is the nature of sociology to look at the various structures and patterns of behavior with a critical eye. One aspect of this critical examination is what sociologist Peter Berger (1963) referred to as **debunking**—looking for levels of reality other than those given in the official interpretations. However, this unmasking of the hidden but very real facets of societal life is in no way meant to denigrate or belittle those people and institutions that are the subjects of inquiry. As Danish criminologist Karl Otto Christiansen (1977) stated, "It is the object of criminology to describe and explain criminality, not to condemn it or defend it." We take the same position in this book. Like most sociologists, we are attempting to explain what is, and not what should or ought to be; and we are not passing judgment on the values and behavior of others.

It is imperative that students keep this perspective in mind, especially when reading the sections devoted to Mexico and Japan. For example, like other modernizing nations, Mexico is faced with a host of social, political, and economic problems, problems on which we focus a great deal of attention in this book. However, our critical analysis of these difficulties should not be construed as an indictment of the Mexican people. On the contrary, during the course of our research it soon became apparent that they are an extremely proud, hard-working people who will do just about anything for the well-being of their families. In a typical year, over one and a half million Mexicans seeking employment in the United States will be caught illegally crossing the border. Many of them will try again and again until they are successful. The mostly young males who make up this growing "army of the poor" are not headed for high-paying jobs. Typically, and for extremely low wages, they do the dirty, boring, backbreaking, and sometimes dangerous work that other people will not even consider. So much for the stereotypical lazy Mexican. Millions of poor people in Mexico and hundreds of millions of impoverished individuals throughout the developing world live with the physical hardships and psychological pain of poverty each and every day of their existence. The overwhelming majority do so with courage and dignity. They are worthy of our understanding and compassion. Most of all, they deserve our respect.

We hope our presentation of Mexico and Japan gives students an accurate, albeit limited, view of these societies. Many who have written about Japan are often characterized as being either pro- or anti-Japanese. Commentators on Mexico could be similarly categorized. As sociologists, we do not intend to wave the flags of these nations or to tear them down. Rather, our goal is to introduce students to these and other countries, and examine these nations from the debunking stance inherent in the science of sociology.

 The Sociological Style: Unraveling Human Social Patterns

Prescientific and Nonscientific Interpretations of Social Reality

The development of the scientific perspective has given humans the tools to analyze their world in a comprehensive way. Long before there were sciences and scientists, however, large numbers of thoughtful people had tried to make sense out of the natural and social realities that surrounded them. Some, political rulers, for example, did so for practical reasons. The physical survival of the people under their leadership depended on their ability to read the world correctly and adjust to it accordingly. Others, theologians and philosophers, for instance, perhaps did so for less tangible reasons. Their attempts to explain the world were reflections of the same intellectual curiosity that led them into their respective lines of work in the first place. In any event, a variety of world interpretations predated scientific models by thousands of years and guided the social behaviors of the millions of humans who lived during those times.

Auguste Comte, the founder of sociology, claimed that the method employed by people to understand their world was perhaps the single most significant factor shaping the course of societal development. Different kinds of knowledge systems, he posited, did a better or worse job of providing an accurate picture of how the world worked. In turn, people's ability to know the true nature of reality was critical to their collective well-being. It determined whether or not they could organize social and cultural patterns that would promote their survival and comfort. The better the understanding of the world provided by the available knowledge base, the more elaborate and successful the social structure that was possible.

According to Comte (1877), societies evolved through three historical stages or epochs, each of which was characterized by a distinctive way of explaining the world. In the theological stage, *imagination* dominated as the principle of understanding. People interpreted events in terms of supernatural beings (spirits of good and evil) and their activities. Social patterns consequently were structured to reflect these relations and obligations to the supernatural world, and the patterns remained very simple. For example, in a traditional farming society, crop failure might be interpreted as a sign of the gods' displeasure with the people. The required response would be an appropriate sacrificial offering to atone for the offense and restore the gods' good will.

As time passed and humans began to exercise their capacity for abstract thought, societies advanced into what Comte called the metaphysical stage of development. *Observation* of specific events led to rational *speculation* as to the nature of general events. Through the power of the mind and the application of accepted principles of logic, people could derive sophisticated theoretical explanations of real-world phenomena. They no longer had to rely on imagined supernatural forces to interpret what was happening around them. The enhanced grasp of reality that was made possible by this change in their way of knowing allowed for the development of larger and more sophisticated social arrangements.

One example of this type of prescientific knowledge comes from historical attempts to explain social deviance. During the Middle Ages, Europeans believed that people who engaged in behaviors that violated established moral or legal rules were possessed by evil spirits (a theological explanation). However, with the age of enlightenment that swept through European societies during the eighteenth century, philosophers and other intellectuals began to reject this doctrine. Instead, they developed what has since become known as the classical perspective or model of crime and deviancy (Pfohl, 1985).

According to this interpretation, criminal and deviant behaviors, like other kinds of human behaviors, represented the outcome of rational calculation and free decision. People chose to break the law and violate social rules when they believed it was in their best interest to do so. For example, a student confronted by a surprise sociology examination and the likelihood of a failing grade might decide to copy answers from a classmate who seemed to be prepared, even though such cheating was a violation of university policy. In this case (at least from the cheating student's standpoint) the cost of failing the examination would be greater than any benefit to be derived from taking the test honestly.

The only way that people like the student might be deterred from rule-breaking behaviors was to make the costs of those actions so high that they would outweigh any potential benefits. The penalty for cheating on college examinations is almost always a failing grade in the course, and often expulsion as well. In modified form, this principle still underpins the criminal justice system in this society in the 1990s (crime and deviance are examined in chapter 8).

Despite the ability of rational, calculated thought to provide people a more successful interpretation of the world, Comte believed that metaphysical knowledge still was not a satisfactory basis for societal development. Complex social and cultural arrangements, he theorized, could be created and sustained only by the kind of understanding generated through the adoption of the scientific method of analysis and the movement of society into the final, positivistic stage of development. To this end, he sought to create a new field of inquiry that would be devoted specifically to the *scientific analysis* of the human social world.

The Sociological View of the World: Comte and Durkheim, and the Development of Scientific Sociology

Auguste Comte Auguste Comte believed the task of his new discipline was to discover the underlying forces in society responsible for *social statics* (stability) and *social dynamics* (change and progress). He argued that just as natural laws governed the biological and physical world, social laws were responsible for the patterns of social integration and change present in all human societies. The philosophical foundation of sociology is based on a way of understanding the social and physical environment called **positivism**— the belief that knowledge can be derived only from people's sensory experience. In other words, human beings can only know something of the world to the extent that they can see, hear, feel, touch, and taste it. Positivism is a rejection of intuition, speculation, or any purely logical analysis for attaining knowledge (Theodorson and Theodorson, 1969).

Influenced by the success of the natural sciences (biology, chemistry, etc.), Comte introduced the methodology of these disciplines to his scientific analysis of society (Coser, 1971). Guided by theory, sociologists would observe social facts in the environment, determine how these facts are related to one another, and explain their meaning. Whenever possible, some form of experimentation would be used to test these explanations. Next, sociologists would engage in cross-cultural research and compare societies at different stages of their evolutionary development. Finally, Comte called for an overarching historical analysis that would put the evolution of societies in their proper chronological context. The father of sociology believed that historical comparison was at "the very core of sociological inquiry" (Coser, 1971, p. 6).

This emphasis on observation and experimentation was an important step in establishing sociology as the scientific study of society. As such, it was distinct from the writings of social philosophers who speculated on the nature of society and the causes of human behavior without conducting any firsthand, systematic research in the social world. However, Comte's belief that social laws determined the inevitable progression of human societies through a number of stages was erroneous and unwarranted. This evolutionary theory contributed to sociology's misunderstanding of societal change and modernization for over a hundred years. Collins and Makowsky (1984) noted that sociologists are finally beginning to realize "the so-called developing nations show few signs of creating our kind of politics, stratification, or even economy in the foreseeable future . . ." (p. 29). Ironically, the man who emphasized the collection, organization, and comparison of facts in his new science of society could not himself overcome speculation and conjecture in his theories of social change.

Emile Durkheim   For most of his career, the great French sociologist Emile Durkheim (1858–1917) defended sociology against the reductionism of psychologists (especially) and biologists who claimed that any social phenomena could ultimately be reduced to, and explained in, psychological and biological terms. Reductionists stated that although society is a collection of interacting individuals, in the final analysis any form of social behavior is individual behavior, and can be explained only in terms of each person's personality, motivation, and overall state of consciousness. Therefore, the emerging science of sociology is basically irrelevant.

Durkheim countered by persuasively arguing that social phenomena exist *sui generis* (in and of themselves) and cannot be reduced, effectively studied, or interpreted at the individual level of analysis. He presented a "definitive critique of reductionist explanations of social behavior" by demonstrating that social facts were the primary subject matter of sociology (Coser, 1971). According to Durkheim (in Johnson, 1981, pp. 172–173), social facts have three characteristics that distinguish them from individual and psychological phenomena: (1) they exist *external* to individuals (e.g., language, laws, and institutions such as the family), (2) they *constrain* or influence a person independent of his or her will, and (3) they are *shared* by a significant number of people.

Let's examine a social fact that Durkheim considered to be of upmost importance, the collective conscience—those beliefs and sentiments common to the average member of a group or society. The collective conscience is easily recognized and experienced by members of emotionally charged groups. As Collins and Makowsky (1984) stated, "It is a feeling of contact with something outside yourself that does not depend precisely on any one person there, but which everyone participates in together" (p. 108). For example, consider the sentiments and excitement at a big football game just before kickoff as the crowd anticipates a close, competitive match—and a victory. The excitement in the air is external to individuals and independent of any individual who moves in or out of the stadium. The sentiment of the crowd would no doubt change dramatically if the home team were losing by forty-two points at halftime. Some disgruntled fans could become rowdy and start picking fights. The majority, however, would resist any temptation to engage in violence, being *constrained* by *shared* rules of civility, as well as by the sight of security personnel with nightsticks. (Social facts can have physical consequences.)

Durkheim argued that social facts could be explained only in terms of other social facts. To do otherwise was to slide back into reductionism. He used a basic research strategy still widely practiced in sociology—*controlled comparison.* To determine the cause of something, "look for *the conditions under which it occurs* and compare them with *the conditions under which it does not occur*" (Collins and Makowsky, 1984, p. 110). Durkheim used this method effectively in his study of suicide.

Emile Durkheim almost single-handedly made Comte's dream of a legitimate science of society a reality. Whereas Comte struggled for recognition most of his life, Durkheim had a long and fruitful career in the French university system. In 1913 sociology was formally recognized at the Sorbonne (University of Paris), the most prestigious university in France. The title of Durkheim's academic chair was changed to Science of Education and Sociology.

Suicide: The Sociology of Self-Destruction

Suicide is the final act of people who have decided they must end their lives. Since self-destructive behavior is committed by individuals, suicide is typically analyzed from a psychological or psychiatric perspective. Its cause(s) are thought to be lodged in the depths of the individual's personality. However, nineteenth-century statisticians discovered that these were not purely individual events, randomly distributed in the population. On the contrary, suicides followed predictable patterns. For example, Durkheim found the following in his examination of suicide rates in France and some central European countries in the 1800s:

1. Soldiers have a higher suicide rate than civilians.
2. Protestants have higher rates than Catholics.
3. The rate is higher among single, widowed, and divorced persons than among the married.
4. Older people have a higher rate than younger people.
5. Rates rise in times of economic crisis and fall during times of political crisis.

In *Suicide* (1951, original 1897), Durkheim argued that these patterns of behavior clearly indicate that the root causes of the "intensely individual" act of suicide must be external to the individual (Douglas, 1967). For each group in society a "collective force of a definite amount of energy" (Durkheim, 1951, p. 299) impels people to self-destruction. In other words, although the individual pulls the trigger of the gun that ends his life, a number of social factors determine the likelihood of his putting the gun to his head.

Durkheim theorized that there were four types of suicide in society. *Altruistic* and *egoistic suicides* are one related pair, and *anomic* and *fatalistic suicides* form another. **Altruistic suicide** is committed by individuals who are overinvolved in and therefore overcommitted to a particular group or society as a whole. Durkheim subdivided this category into two types, *obligatory altruistic* and *optional altruistic*. In obligatory altruistic suicide, the self-destructive act is viewed as an obligation or duty. Failure to perform it results in dishonor or punishment. This form of suicide can be institutionalized, as it was in Japan during World War II when *kamikaze* pilots and *raiden* (suicide submarines) crashed

their vessels into American ships. These acts were redefined so that individuals who committed them considered their behavior "other-destructive" and not "self-destructive" (Lebra, 1976).

In optional altruistic suicide, society does not demand that the individual take his or her life, although social prestige is often attached to doing so. For example, in feudal Japan the *samurai* (warrior class) code of honor stated that it was honorable for an individual to kill himself rather than run the risk of being captured and disgraced by the enemy. Durkheim concluded that, as a whole, soldiers tend to have high suicide rates because they are taught to devalue their sense of self and think in terms of the group. Life itself becomes less important to them, and suicide no longer has the same meaning that it does for civilians. Consequently, it becomes easier for military personnel to take their own lives.

Psychologist Takie Sugiyama Lebra (1976) stated that suicide notes in Japan (at least in the past) typically ended with a statement of self-accusation and an apology. The victims were sorry for causing trouble and not being good sons or daughters. These suicides can be interpreted as optional altruistic in that individuals were overly involved with family and groups, and felt they had to kill themselves for not living up to the expectations of others, or for disgracing them in some way.

Whereas altruistic suicide is a function of over-involvement and commitment to the group, **egoistic suicide** is caused by lack of involvement and commitment to others. If individuals do not share beliefs common to a social group, they will not be integrated into that body, or be involved regularly with people who share a common world view. Durkheim (1951) argued that a strongly integrated group or society "holds individuals under its control" (p. 209) and forbids them from taking their own lives. Conversely, when people are not well integrated into groups, they cannot help but realize that all of their efforts in life will finally end in nothingness, since they will die and disappear—alone.

Durkheim reasoned that Protestants have a higher suicide rate (egoistic) than Catholics because they are less integrated and involved in group activity. For Catholics, salvation comes through the church, which serves as an intermediary between the individual and God. In Protestant sects individuals have a more direct relationship with God, and the church is a less necessary link between the two.

Married individuals are less likely to take their own lives than nonmarried individuals because they become involved in a family network. This network gives additional meaning to their lives and binds them to spouses and children both emotionally and by way of mutual obligations. Elderly people have higher suicide rates than younger individuals because they are not as involved in groups as a result of retirement, death of a spouse, and physical impairments that prevent them from fully participating in group activities.

Group involvement (but not overinvolvement) binds people together, provides a system of shared beliefs, and as such, tends to protect them from suicide. Conversely, lack of shared beliefs and social attachments increases the likelihood of suicide. For Durkheim, the level of association or involvement people have with groups like the church and family are social facts available for positivistic, sociological analysis.

Anomic and fatalistic suicides are polar opposites on a continuum of social regulation. Durkheim observed that people cannot be happy unless their desires and the means for achieving these desires are in harmony. Since human beings have no natural "psychological constitution," these desires are held in check by society. For example, during periods of economic stability means and ends (desires) are in balance as people keep their wants in line with existing mechanisms for satisfy them. In times of economic prosperity, however, desires increase to the point that they are unlimited and, by definition, cannot be satisfied. During periods of rapid economic growth people often move from one economic class to another in a short period of time, but even this new-found wealth fails to satisfy them. "Inextinguishable thirst is constantly renewed torture" (Durkheim, 1951, p. 247) and leads to **anomic suicide.**

The "torture" of never having one's escalating desires satisfied is complicated by the fact that people are now in social positions unfamiliar to them. Norms and rules that formerly regulated their behavior have been replaced by rules they do not understand or accept. These individuals are free floating in society, devoid of regulations that might anchor them in a familiar social reality. This lack of stability also contributes to anomic suicide.

Durkheim found that people in less developed countries tend to have lower suicide rates than those in developed nations. He observed that poverty protects against suicide because it is a restraint in and of itself. Prolonged poverty keeps people's longing for wealth, status, and power in check. Individuals do not passionately desire those things they have virtually no chance of acquiring.

Whereas economic upheavals increase the rate of suicide, political crises such as wars tend to reduce the number of self-destructive acts. During periods of external conflict, society is more integrated as the population stands behind an effort to survive and defeat a common enemy. They also may experience a shift away from personal troubles, as they increasingly focus on the nation's war effort. One's individual problems may appear rather insignificant in comparison to the fighting and dying taking place on the battlefield.

At the other end of the social regulation continuum, people's desires can be choked off by excessive control. Their lives are so closely regulated they have little if any freedom to do even the most basic things in life. Durkheim suggested that excessive restraint results in the **fatalistic suicide** committed by slaves. Farberow (1989) noted that thousands of Indians in Mexico and Central America enslaved by Spanish conquistadors took their own lives. More recently, an Indian-rights group in Brazil reported seventy-four suicides over a two-year period on the Guarani-Kaiowa reservation. Anthropologists said the victims—all between fourteen and twenty-one years of age—took their lives as a result of the loss of tribal identity and land to white cattle ranchers. Depressed by the destruction of their culture, these young suicide victims get drunk on sugar cane rum before hanging themselves (Kepp, 1991). According to Durkheim (1951), victims of moral and physical despotism chose to die rather than lead lives over which they had no control.

In Durkheim's fourfold typology, each of the forms of self-destructive behavior is associated with a different state of mind (Madge, 1962). The altruistic suicide has strong inner convictions, and death by one's own hand is in line with them. The egoistic suicide is in a state of resignation, having made the choice to opt out of society. The anomic suicide is a person whose desire for pleasure is out of control. Finally, the fatalistic suicide's passion for life has been crushed by overregulation.

While *Suicide* is a complex and valuable piece of research, it does not fully explain self-destructive behavior. As Collins and Makowsky (1984) pointed out, not everyone who is elderly, unmarried, and Protestant commits suicide. To determine why many people who fit into Durkheim's classification do not kill themselves, psychological factors would have to be taken into consideration. However, Durkheim was not particularly interested in psychology; rather, he wanted to account for varying rates of suicide in different groups over time, and toward this end he was quite successful. Although the official statistics he used were not completely reliable, as they are not completely reliable today (Douglas, 1967), and he made analytical mistakes, his theory is still a powerful tool for understanding different rates of suicide both within and among countries.

Suicide Rates in Mexico and Japan

Suicide rates in the United States (medium), Mexico (low), and Japan (high) are considerably different. Like other developing nations, Mexico has a young population and as we have seen, older people have a higher rate of suicide than younger people. The emphasis on family relations, combined with a population that is almost overwhelmingly Catholic, would explain the low rates of egoistic suicide in Mexico. Poverty in that developing nation accounts for the low frequency of anomic suicide. As modernization continues, however, the rate of population growth will stabilize, with more people reaching an advanced age. These factors, combined with the increased passions of a growing middle class as the nation develops economically, will drive Mexico's rate of suicide up.

In Japan, the suicide rate began to fall in 1936, the year a coup d'etat (political crisis) pushed the country down the road to militarism. Just as Durkheim predicted, the country's suicide rate hit an all-time low (12 per 100,000) in the middle of World War II. With rapid economic recovery in the postwar period, it rose to a high of 25.7 in 1958 (Fuse, 1983). The "graying" of Japan (one of the world's oldest populations) partially explains that country's currently high suicide rate, and will contribute to the number of self-inflicted deaths for many years to come.

Lebra (1976) commented on a common form of suicide in Japan resulting from the "compulsive identification with or commitment to the status and role to which one aspires" (pp. 198–199). In a society where people typically are very involved in and highly integrated into groups, failure to achieve one's goals is not only an individual shortcoming, it is failure to live up to group expectations. Lebra spoke of the suicidal tendencies of these "status dropouts," especially young Japanese who are under so much pressure to get into the best schools and eventually obtain high-paying, prestigious jobs. From a Durkheimian perspective, the self-destruction of these people could be seen as optional altruistic suicide. In recent years the Japanese, especially those in their twenties and thirties, have been increasingly preoccupied with making money and acquiring material goods, an attitude associated with anomic suicide. Collective forces "impelling" people to suicide in Japan are facilitated by a traditional cultural ethos that views taking one's life as heroic, romantic, and aesthetic (Lebra, 1976).

Suicide in the United States

In the United States the suicide rate is at the low end of the continuum of now rich countries, although much higher than the rates of poorer nations like Egypt and the Philippines. The national rate in 1986 was 12.8 (per 100,000), a relatively low figure that included data for African Americans (approximately 6), and Hispanic Americans (approximately 7.5), whose rates were in line with some developing nations. Kastenbaum (1989) believed the rate for black Americans is low because historically this group has been the target of systematic discrimination in the marketplace. As a result, their desire for economic success has been held in check. Hence, they have a low rate of anomic suicide. Strong support from the family, church, and black community means that egoistic suicide would be low. Similar arguments could be made for the low rate of Hispanic suicide in the United States. We would predict that economic and social equality for these groups will be accompanied by higher rates.

The suicide rate for teenagers between 15 and 19 years of age (especially white males) increased sharply between 1960 and 1980, when it leveled off at that high plateau. Psychiatrist Keith Hawton (1986) associated the loss of family support systems resulting from a high rate of divorce with the trend for young people to face the pressures involved with assuming adult roles earlier in life. "Evidence is accumulating concerning the importance of supportive relationships at such times, and how, if they are lacking, depression is a likely consequence" (p. 44). This may be a major cause of teenage suicide, in view of the "well-established link between depression and suicide" (p. 44). The loss of religious faith that leads to the abandonment of church-affiliated groups may be another contributing factor. These phenomena would promote egoistic suicide.

Durkheim's contribution to our understanding of suicide is that he focused on the individual's decision to forfeit life (arguably the most agonizing decision anyone ever makes) and demonstrated that it was in some way the result of *social* factors (Douglas, 1967). His book also helped put sociology on the academic and intellectual map in Europe. If something as seemingly personal and individual as suicide could be explained in part by sociology, then virtually any aspect of human behavior could be analyzed from a sociological perspective.

 ## Thinking Sociologically: Theoretical Paradigms

Theories and Science

In everyday conversation, *theory* is used synonymously with the words *guess* or *hunch*. For example, when someone says, "My theory is that John just doesn't like Marsha," he or she usually means "My guess is that . . . ." Theory also is thought of as something at a high level of abstraction not grounded in observation and factual experience. "Don't give me your theories, I just want the facts," and "Theories are one thing, the real world is something else" are typical reactions to the word.

For a scientist, a **theory** is a set of logically coherent, interrelated concepts that attempts to explain some observable phenomena or group of facts. As such, it is not a wild, off-the-cuff guess, but rather a carefully thought-out explanation grounded in observable (and usually repeatable) phenomena. In sociology there are two types of theories. A **grand theory** deals with universal aspects of social life and is usually grounded in basic assumptions (as opposed to data) concerning the nature of humans and society. The grand theories of Comte and Karl Marx explained the workings of all types of societies as they progressed through evolutionary stages. These theories tend to be at a rather high level of abstraction and are difficult, if not impossible, to test. They could be considered world views from a sociological perspective.

Middle-range theories focus on relatively specific problems in the social world. For example, in the United States, the rate of divorce tends to be higher in the lower classes than in the upper classes. Also, people who marry at an early age have higher divorce rates than those who marry when they are older. A theory of the middle range would explain these specific, observable facts of one component of social life—marriage and divorce. Ultimately, a number of middle-range theories could be incorporated into some larger theoretical framework (Johnson, 1981), perhaps a grand theory.

Theories are necessary because facts do not speak for themselves. Knowing that as social class goes up divorce goes down is very different from knowing why this relationship exists. In a sense a theory is like a story, weaving together all the available data about a particular phenomenon, forming a coherent, integrated explanation. Without theory, science would be nothing more than an ever-increasing mass of facts completely devoid of any understanding of how and why those facts are related. Theory is the life blood of science. In the case of sociology, it organizes and explains observable facts and relationships, as well as guides the course of research.

The Organic Analogy: Classic and Contemporary Functionalist Theory

Pioneer sociologists such as Comte and Herbert Spencer (1820–1903) constructed theories on a grand scale. They wanted to explain the structure, internal dynamics, and historical development of societies. As previously noted, Comte was heavily influenced by the success of the natural sciences, especially biology. He believed that biology and sociology were similar in that both had living beings as their focus of study. Just as a human organism was made up of a number of systems, organs, and tissues, the social organism was made up of various parts. Societies had institutions (e.g., the family), classes, and cities that were interrelated and interdependent. Turner and Maryanski (1979) noted that this vision of society as a complex social body with numerous parts contributing to the well-being and survival of the whole was an important moment in sociological theorizing: "When society is seen as an organism, it is a short analytical step to asking: What does this or that structure 'do for' or 'contribute' to the society" (p. 7). In other words, what is the function of each of the constituent parts for the whole? This is the beginning of functional analysis, and *functionalist* theories of society.

Early functionalist sociologists were concerned with the problem of order. Recall that sociology was born in the midst of major social, economic, and political transformations sweeping across Europe as a result of the Industrial Revolution. The question of how societies endure and maintain order even though they were changing rapidly was uppermost in the minds of these theorists. For that matter, what keeps societies from breaking up into thousands of groups or hundreds of thousands of families with everyone behaving in their own self-interest even during periods of

These students preparing to be Buddhist monks are taking examinations in a temple school. A literate population, able to communicate effectively and to access information, is an important component of the modernization process.

tranquility? For both Comte and Durkheim, the answer was the same—the foundation of society and social stability is moral order (Collins and Makowsky, 1984). People reach a consensus on laws, religious beliefs, and the basic rules that govern everyday life. This consensus makes for a shared world view that binds people to their families and various communal organizations, as well as to larger economic and political institutions. Governments exist because individuals agree to the principles they are founded on; people even agree to the manner in which those governments resort to force when necessary. Social solidarity and stability are impossible without this shared moral order.

Durkheim described this communal moral order or collective conscience as taking two different forms. For example, in traditional agricultural societies, where most people did the same type of work, had the same system of beliefs, and had common everyday experiences, the collective conscience was a powerful force providing for order and stability. The social cohesion in societies of this type is called **mechanical solidarity.** As societies modernize and specialization in the workplace increases, however, people are much less likely to have common experiences and beliefs. Then the individual conscience resulting from a complex division of labor takes precedence over the collective conscience. Social solidarity is now more a function of mutual dependence; that is, people with a wide variety of occupations need each other to survive. Influenced by the work of Comte and others, Durkheim called social cohesion based on interdependency **organic solidarity.** Although qualitatively different, both mechanical and organic solidarity serve a common function in that they provide for order, integration, and the overall stability of society.

Twentieth-century functionalist theorists have been interested in more than the problem of order and social solidarity. Talcott Parsons (1902–1979) outlined four basic functional requirements that all social systems (from small groups to societies) must meet if they are to survive.

Adaptation   Social systems must adapt to their social and physical environment. For example, modern societies are choking (figuratively and literally) as a result of the wholesale pollution of their air and water. If significant changes are not made, failure to adapt to the natural environment could result in the deaths of millions of people worldwide, as well as the production of a greenhouse effect threatening the entire planet.

Goal Attainment   All social systems must provide their members with goals (or ends) and the means necessary to achieve them. If instructors were not motivated to teach and pursue knowledge, and the public did not see fit to fund schools, the entire system of education would collapse.

Integration   Like their nineteenth-century predecessors, modern functionalists realize that all of the components of society must be integrated if the social system is to function effectively.

Pattern Maintenance   Members of a social system must be provided with occasional periods of rest. This is especially true in fast-paced, modern societies where people are subject to considerable pressure and tension. However, rest periods cannot result in reduced commitment to one's duties. The current emphasis on engaging in regular exercise and sports provides people with a psychological break from work, helps keep them in physical shape, yet reinforces basic values such as working hard, getting ahead, and continually striving to better oneself.

Sociologist Robert Merton (1968) refined the tools of functional analysis by introducing concepts that permitted investigators to examine the *multiple consequences* of patterns of behavior and institutions. Manifest functions are consequences that contribute to the system, and are intended and recognized by participants in the system. Latent functions are consequences that are neither intended nor recognized. For example, let's look at the manifest and latent functions of professional basketball in the United States. Owners of teams in the National Basketball Association (NBA) became involved in this enterprise to make money by way of providing entertainment to the American public. Because of the popularity of the sport, the average NBA player earns almost $1 million a year, with superstars like Michael Jordan and Larry Bird making much more between their salaries and lucrative commercial endorsements. The *intent* of the owners was to make money (for themselves) and the *consequence* of their efforts is a financially successful business for all concerned.

However, the latent function or unintended consequences of their action was to provide unrealistic career goals in the form of rich role models for tens of thousands of adolescent males. Collectively, the teams in the NBA employ no more than 350 players. But in 1986–1987 approximately 516,000 boys played high school basketball. To the extent that many high school athletes devote most of their time and effort to the sport at the expense of being successful academically, they are severely limiting their chances for earning more than the minimum wage when they fail to make it to college, much less to the professional ranks. This is especially problematic for African American, inner-city youths who already have a more limited opportunity structure. A nationwide poll (*Los Angeles Times,* 1990c) found that 43 percent of black high school athletes surveyed said they could make it in professional sports. The corresponding number for white high school athletes was 16 percent. Sport sociologist Jay J. Coakley (1990) said that the odds of a black male between the ages of twenty and thirty-nine years becoming a professional basketball player are 1 in 153,800.

The latent (unintended) function of a successful sports league is a decline in academic motivation and in eventual economic success for a significant number of young men. Whereas the existence of the NBA is beneficial (functional) for owners, players, and most fans, it is dysfunctional for thousands of high school student athletes. As you no doubt imagine, dysfunctional pertains to any phenomenon that undermines the stability or survival of the system.

Contemporary functionalism has been criticized for being ahistorical, concentrating on how present-day events are functional in helping to maintain the social system. As we will see in the next section, conflict theorists (especially Marxists) argue that any form of social theorizing and analysis that ignores the social, political, and economic forces instrumental in creating any society is all but useless. Critics also contend that inasmuch as functionalism focuses on integration, stability, and consensus, it is inherently conservative and supportive of the status quo. They contend that competition, conflict, and social change are almost totally ignored by functionalist theory and analysis. According to Turner and Maryanski (1979), although much functional analysis has been ahistorical, conservative, and tending to ignore conflict and change, it is inherently none of these. There is a difference between what a theory is capable of and how it is used.

Conflict Sociology: The Zero-Sum Game

Whereas functionalist sociologists view society as a rather harmonious, well-integrated social system held together by shared values and common goals, conflict theorists look at the social world and see strife at virtually every level of group existence. For them, society is not held together by value consensus but by the exercise of power. Institutions, organizations, and individuals simply force people with less power than themselves to conform to their values and standards of conduct.

For conflict theorists, dissension (and sometimes open combat) is everywhere. Examples in the United States include blacks versus whites, labor versus management, students versus faculty and administrators, pro-choice versus pro-life groups, and gangs versus the community, the police, and other gangs. Even the sacred institution of the family is not immune from strife. The United States has one of the highest rates of divorce in the world, and each year records hundreds of thousands of cases of spousal

As nations develop, competing political, economic, and religious perspectives may lead to violence, as various groups and classes within society vie for supremacy. Belfast, Northern Ireland, has repeatedly been the scene of such violence.

and child abuse. For some sociologists, conflict is as much a part of social life as breathing is a part of our physical existence. To be alive is to struggle and fight. Although the roots of conflict sociology can be traced back to many theorists, the most influential writer in this tradition was Karl Marx (1818–1883). Keep in mind that although all Marxists are conflict theorists, not all conflict theorists are Marxists. As we will see, the world of conflict sociology is quite diverse.

Like other evolutionary thinkers, Marx believed that societies progress through various stages. The driving force in history (the force responsible for movement from one stage to another) is the way people relate to one another in the workplace. Some individuals own and control the means of production—those things used to create material objects and wealth—and others have only their labor to trade for wages. In an industrial society, the means of production include land, machines, buildings, and technological know-how. Under capitalism, these resources are used to further the private fortunes of their owners.

The owners of the means of production in a capitalist society are the **bourgeoisie**, and those who exist by selling their labor power in the market Marx called the **proletariat.** The bourgeoisie systematically exploit the proletariat, and in doing so become increasingly wealthier and more politically powerful. Meanwhile, the lives of the working class become more and more wretched. However, in time, the significantly more numerous proletariat realize that liberty, justice, and equality are nothing more than empty words, and stage a successful revolution against their bourgeoisie masters. With class conflict between the haves and have nots at an end, capitalism gives way to socialism, an economic system in which the means of production are owned by all the people and the wealth is distributed equitably. For Marx, the end of capitalism was also the end of centuries of class conflict in the historical stages preceding and including capitalism. Socialism signaled the final stage of our economic evolution, where class conflict ceased and humans could realize their maximum potential.

Ralf Dahrendorf   German sociologist Ralf Dahrendorf constructed a theory of conflict that is more general than the Marxist perspective. According to Dahrendorf, conflict is not limited to the dispute between the bourgeoisie and the proletariat regarding ownership of the means of production. In more advanced capitalist states, ownership is no longer a crucial factor in disputes between the haves and the have nots, but centers around who should *control* the means of production. The conflict is now between managers and executives (who are not owners) and workers. As such, this is not a struggle over possession but over authority—who will make and implement policy. Dahrendorf posited that virtually all social conflict is a struggle between those who exercise authority and those who are subject to that authority.

These struggles can be intense and are often violent because authority (and power) relationships are examples of a zero-sum game. This means that in any relationship there is a fixed amount of power (100 percent), and that any increase in power made by some individuals comes at the expense or loss of this commodity on the part of others. For example, four production managers in an aircraft company supervise 250 employees and have total power regarding the day-to-day operation of their department. In other words, they have 100 percent of the authority and power. If the employees go on strike and eventually win the right to participate in decision making, the managers will no longer have total control. A gain of power of 25 percent by the employees would translate to a loss of 25 percent on the part of the managers, who now have 75 percent of the decision-making power.

For Dahrendorf (1959), authority relations exist wherever people are subject to legitimate sanctions that originate *outside* of themselves but *inside* a social structure. For example, on entering college you became subject to the rules of that institution, rules over which you had absolutely no input. A moment's reflection will reveal that most people are in a number of such authority relations at school, at work, and in voluntary organizations such as clubs. It is important to note that the conflict between those with and those without authority is rooted in the "very nature of the authority structure" (Johnson, 1981, p. 472), and is not a consequence of individual personalities. Working in the Durkheimian tradition, Dahrendorf argued that the ubiquitous conflict over authority is a social fact, and as such cannot be explained by psychological variables like anger or aggression.

Lewis Coser   The word *conflict* typically brings to mind thoughts of a struggle or battle, perhaps a violent confrontation between opposing parties. In this sense, it is to be avoided or entered into with extreme care inasmuch as the consequences can be dysfunctional and deadly. However, Lewis Coser (1964) maintained that conflict both *internal* and *external* to the group can have positive benefits. At Marine Corps boot camp in Parris Island, South Carolina, a drill instructor tells recruits, "I want you to dedicate all this training to one very special person. To your enemy: the reason being so he can die for his country. So who are we going to dedicate all this training to, privates?" And the recruits shout enthusiastically, "The enemy sir! The enemy sir!" (Dyer, 1985, p. 124). The threat of the enemy (in peacetime or during war) is continually held up to the recruits, binding them together and reinforcing their commitment to each other, their unit, and, in this example, the Marine Corps. As Coser (1964) described it, " 'searching for the outside enemy' (or exaggeration of the danger which an actual enemy presents) serves not only to maintain the structure of the group, but also to strengthen its cohesion when threatened by a relaxation of energies or by internal dissension" (p. 106). Conflict within a group can act as a safety valve when the differences and hostilities between members are openly expressed and then negotiated. If these feelings are suppressed, they can intensify, to explode at some later date and seriously damage or destroy the group. This is especially true of groups such as the family that are characterized by strong emotional feelings.

Conflict theorists are criticized by functionalists for viewing the world almost entirely in terms of strife and disorder. They are preoccupied with class antagonisms and the struggle for wealth, status, and power, and thus fail to recognize the harmonious, integrative, and stabilizing aspects of group life that are a product of shared religious, moral, and political values. Although Dahrendorf (1968) believed that neither conflict theory or functionalist theory can make a "claim to comprehensive and exclusive applicability. . . . As far as I can see we need both models for the explanation of social problems . . . one of stability, harmony, and consensus, and one of change, conflict, and constraint" (p. 128).

"Are You for Real?" Symbolic Interactionism and the Subjectivist Approach

As we have seen, functionalist and conflict theorists stand poles apart in their portrayals of social groupings and interactions. Functionalists focus on what might be called the up side, stressing the cohesiveness and collective benefits of organized social life. In sharp contrast, conflict proponents seem to stress the down side, focusing on the power struggles and other forces that pull people apart and create exploitive social relations. In at least two respects, however, the approaches share common ground.

First, structural-functional theory and conflict theory represent what are called **macrolevel** paradigms or models (Collins, 1988b). They both are concerned primarily with large-scale social phenomena such as societies (e.g., Mexico) and the major structural elements within those societies (e.g., the Mexican political system). Their analyses of social processes also are directed at assessing the impact of various forces on maintaining or changing the structures and operations of these units.

Second, both approaches are essentially **objectivistic** in orientation; that is, they start from the assumption that the tangible, objective facts of social reality, such as the structure of the political system in Mexican society, are of primary importance in shaping events and lives within that society. Both perspectives then proceed to identify and examine those objective social phenomena from substantially different viewpoints.

In contrast, a third major sociological paradigm, **symbolic interactionism,** takes a quite different approach. It is concerned primarily with small-scale, **microlevel** social phenomena, and analyzes them from what amounts to a **subjectivistic** perspective (Collins, 1985a). In these respects, symbolic interactionism represents more of a social psychological rather than a purely sociological perspective.

Cooley, Mead, and Thomas Although the term *symbolic interactionism* did not appear until 1937 (Collins, 1985b), the roots of this approach can be traced to the work of a trio of scholars at the University of Chicago in the beginning of this century. Charles H. Cooley and George Herbert Mead (whose works are examined in detail in chapter 4) were both concerned with the process by which individuals acquire a set of human personal and social characteristics, especially a self-identity. They concluded that people are not born with this sense of self, but it is a social product, created and maintained through the individual's interaction with other human beings. Mead went even further, arguing that the human mind itself was a product of the same social interaction, as was the language that provided the mind with the means to think.

William Isaac Thomas, the third member of this founding trio, perhaps is best known in sociology for his massive study (conducted with a colleague, Florian Znaniecki) of the adjustment of Polish peasant immigrants to big-city life in the United States of the early 1900s. From this work, he derived his assertion that human behavior ultimately is subjective. Before people respond to an objective event, Thomas (1967) claimed that they engage in what he called a **definition of the situation,** a personal interpretation. They then respond in terms of this subjective reading, whether or not it is accurate and valid. In Thomas's famous and often-quoted words, "If men define situations as real, they are real in their consequences" (Thomas and Thomas, 1928, p. 572).

Social patterns, in other words, can be understood only in terms of people's subjective picture of their world, and not by examining that world's objective properties. For example, someone dying of cancer but not aware of the seriousness of her disease may act carefree, as though she had all the time in the world to live, when in fact she may have only six months. Conversely, someone who is quite healthy but is convinced she has an advanced terminal illness may begin to give away prized possessions and otherwise close out her affairs, even though in fact she has all the time in the world. In each case, knowledge of the objective health of the person, terminally ill or healthy, would not help us explain or understand the behavior. Rather, we would have to know what the individual thought about her state of health in order to make sense out of her behavior.

Together, the contributions of these three men formed the foundation for the modern symbolic interactionist perspective. This particular way of looking at social relations focuses on the millions of small-scale social encounters or interactions that take place between individuals every single day and that are the building blocks for larger-scale social units. It attempts to understand the process by which the participants are able to structure these interactions in a way that allows them normally to take place without great friction or conflict. As part of this effort, symbolic interactionists are led to examine the role of human communication in the construction of the subjective meanings that shape people's responses to their world.

Symbolic interactionists argue that human communication is unique among the animal world because of its use of **significant symbols** or stimuli that have attached meanings and values. These meanings and values are created through social interaction, and people respond to objects in terms of their symbolic content rather than their physical properties (Blumer, in Collins, 1985b).

The recent uproar over legislation concerning the desecration of the U.S. flag, for instance, has nothing at all to do with the fact that an inexpensive, multicolored cloth rectangle is being burned, ripped, or otherwise mutilated. The real source of the controversy is symbolic. One side sees the flag's destruction as a desecration of the United States, an assault on American beliefs and values. The other side views the same behavior as an expression of one of our most cherished values, the freedom of speech. For this group, the burning of the American flag is an affirmation of what the United States and its flag represent.

Social patterns, therefore, must be understood in terms of the symbolic contexts in which they occur, and these contexts are always subject to negotiation. For symbolic interactionists, human societies are continuing processes rather than finished structures. They are always dependent on the subjective perceptions and interpretations of their members, and these subjective readings are never simply automatic or permanent responses to objective conditions in the external world. Herbert Blumer, the sociologist generally credited as being the creator of contemporary symbolic interaction theory, summarized what he called the basic ideas or "root images" of the perspective (Blumer, 1969; in Collins, 1985b):

1. People respond to things (objects, events, actions, other people, circumstances) on the basis of the meanings those things have for them.
2. These meanings do not exist in the things themselves, but are created through the process of social interaction.
3. Individuals interpret these meanings as they apply in specific circumstances. The assignment of meaning to a given thing by a particular individual can and will vary with the situation.

In its more extreme versions, symbolic interactionism denies the existence of any sort of recognizable objective social reality, effectively making integration of this approach with either functionalism or conflict theory impossible. In more moderate form, however, this perspective complements and supplements these other theories. It permits sociologists to understand the linkage between external social realities and human social patterns that may vary significantly from one group to another (each of these groups is interpreting the objective event in a different way, attaching a different subjective meaning to it). Like each of the other two perspectives, symbolic interactionism provides a different and productive view of our social world. As in the case of the functionalist and conflict models, however, that view, by itself, is incomplete.

DOING SOCIOLOGY: IS THERE A METHOD TO THIS MADNESS?

Problems in Social Scientific Research

Comte and other early sociologists believed that it was possible and desirable for this new field to duplicate the methodology of the natural sciences in its study of social patterns. Contemporary sociologists, however, are more likely to acknowledge that whereas the employment of scientific methodology in sociological analysis might be desirable (although not all sociologists would agree on this point), it is not really possible. The differences between the natural and the social worlds make such a simple one-to-one translation out of the question.

As applied to the study of the natural physical world, the scientific approach is characterized by a number of distinctive features that set it apart from other possible techniques for understanding and explaining reality (see Table 1.2 for some important methodological terminology). Scientific research begins with the systematic observation of empirical phenomena of some sort, and the formulation of a problem or question for study. This problem is stated as one or more hypotheses about how two or more variables are related to each other. Generally, these hypotheses are offered in the form

---

TABLE 1.2 Important Methodological Terms

Term	Definition
Empirical	Existing in or relating to the physical world.
Variable	An empirical object or phenomenon that can assume a number of different values; individual yearly income, for example.
Independent variable	A factor that is assumed to be responsible for causing or bringing about the value of some other factor. For example, the number of hours worked by a person in a given year might be a major factor shaping that individual's income for the year.
Dependent variable	A factor whose value is assumed to be caused or brought about by the operation of an independent variable. Yearly income, in the example above, is dependent on the number of hours worked during the year.
Hypothesis	The statement of a relationship between independent and dependent variables. The greater the number of hours worked during the year, the higher the yearly income level.
Reliability	The ability of a measurement instrument to give the same results when repeated; that is, its consistency. The time clock in a factory would be a reliable measure of the passage of units of work time.
Validity	The ability of an instrument to measure what it is supposed to. The use of time-card records is likely to be a valid measure of the number of hours worked by a person in a factory.

---

of **causal relationships,** asserting that one of the factors under examination (the independent variable) somehow is responsible for bringing about the observed value of the other factor (the dependent variable). These hypotheses must be stated in such a way as to allow for the possibility of empirical disconfirmation; that is, it must be possible to find physical evidence that would disprove the hypotheses. This requirement means that the phenomena under study must be capable of being measured accurately. Scientific research thus is restricted to verifiable phenomena in the empirical world.

Scientific testing of hypotheses ideally involves some sort of experiment in which the variables are subjected to a series of controlled conditions according to a systematic plan developed by the researcher. The objective of these controlled experiments is to observe whether changes in the value of the independent variable from one experimental condition to another will lead to changes in the dependent variable as predicted or implied by the hypothesis. If the predicted changes in fact do take place, the hypothesis can be accepted tentatively (subject to further empirical testing). If the predicted changes do not occur, the hypothesis will be rejected.

If all of this sounds a little too abstract, consider the following example. Suppose that, after hearing the weather forecast on five successive days call for hot and humid conditions, I begin to wonder if the two phenomena, temperature and humidity, somehow are linked together in a causal relationship. Believing that they are, and that the former (heat) causes the latter (humidity), I construct an experiment in which I artificially manipulate the temperature in a sealed room whose humidity level has been carefully measured and recorded prior to the start of the research. I raise the temperature level, expecting the humidity level to increase similarly (after all, who ever heard of cold and humid weather?). Much to my surprise, nothing happens. I raise the temperature again, but again nothing happens to the humidity level. Suddenly, the suppressed memory of long-past New York winters with their cold and damp weather conditions hits me. So much for that hypothesis.

Although this procedure—the example notwithstanding—might sound fairly straightforward, several inherent features of the social world prevent its direct implementation in the realm of the social sciences.

Nonempirical Variables   One basic problem involves the fact that the social world inhabited by human beings is not simply or entirely empirical. It also consists of many significant nonphysical components including religious beliefs (a supreme being), political values (individual freedom), and emotional states of being (love) that reflect our human characteristics and capacities. Scientists refer to these nonempirical components as **constructs** (Black and Champion, 1976). Because constructs are not directly measurable they are not, strictly speaking, proper subjects for scientific inquiry. But because they are so significant and so distinctively human, they cannot be ignored by any discipline such as sociology that hopes to understand social realities.

The attempted solution to this problem involves social scientists in the creation and application of often ingenious (and sometimes bizarre) **operational definitions** that specify how a phenomenon that has no direct empirical basis (e.g., intelligence) is to be measured empirically: intelligence is that which is measured by an intelligence test. The question of how validly or correctly these operational definitions capture the commonly accepted idea of a phenomenon is a critical one in the social sciences. Very often, social and political policies have been constructed on the basis of scientific measures of human characteristics that did not at all accomplish what they claimed.

According to some observers, this is especially true of traditional intelligence tests, which have incorrectly defined particular groups of people as mentally inferior to others and thus deserving of unequal treatment. Stephen Jay Gould (1981) called these tests "the mismeasure of man" (p. 25).

Ethical Constraints   A second basic impediment to the direct application of the scientific method to the study of social patterns lies in the nature of sociology's subject matter—human beings. For a number of reasons, we just do not make ideal subjects for scientific research.

People have basic moral and legal rights that include the recognition and protection of their physical and psychological well-being. Consequently, they cannot be used as guinea pigs in a sociological experiment in the same way that real guinea pigs could be used in a natural experiment. For example, earlier in this chapter we examined a theory of suicide developed by Durkheim. Durkheim was able to find support for his hypotheses by observing specific social circumstances in which suicide rates were unusually high or unusually low. To test his theory, however, he would have had to conduct controlled experiments in which groups of people otherwise equal in all important respects were subjected to different social pressures structured to generate suicidal forces (the independent variable). If people exposed to these experimental conditions then committed suicide (the dependent variable), and those not exposed did not, the theory would have received very strong empirical support. But you can imagine the justifiable public outrage and the deep trouble that Durkheim would have been in once the nature of this research became known.

Social scientists must take great care not to jeopardize in any way the people who serve as the subjects in their research efforts, and this often means that critical kinds of analyses have to be abandoned. Recognizing this obligation, most universities and research organizations maintain a research subjects committee that evaluates proposed studies involving humans to ensure that no harm comes to them. As the authors of this text can verify from personal experience, such committees take their work very seriously and scrutinize research proposals rigorously. Even apparently harmless attitude surveys may have to be redesigned or scrapped if they contain any hint that certain questions will result in any psychological, social, or economic harm to respondents. These committees may be discouraging to researchers, but they are essential to speak up for people whose rights and needs otherwise might be ignored or compromised.

The Hawthorne Effect   An additional difficulty presented by the use of human beings in social science research lies in the fact that these subjects often react to the study itself in ways that nonhuman subjects of natural science experiments cannot. Knowing that they are participating in a scientific investigation, subjects may change their behaviors or attitudes in ways not fully known to the researcher, thus invalidating the results of the study. Known as the **Hawthorne effect** after the 1930s-era study of an industrial plant where the phenomenon was first documented, this response most often involves attempts by individuals to be "good" subjects, that is, to live up (or down) to the researcher's expectations. Efforts by social scientists to deal with this problem led to the creation of "unobtrusive measures" (Webb et al., 1966) that allow researchers to study people without the subjects being aware they are being studied. Even so, the problem remains serious in many types of sociological research. Sociologists and other social scientists must work hard for their money, but with persistence and creativity they can and do get the job done.

Nonexperimental Research Designs in Sociology

A large number of sociological studies involve what is called **nonexperimental or descriptive research.** They follow some format other than the controlled experiment and normally are not concerned with trying to establish the existence of causal relationships among a specific set of variables. Rather, their primary objective is to provide accurate information about some aspect of social reality that can be used as the basis for more elaborate research or for policy development. Imagine that you are the head of the sociology department in a large university and are trying to put together a long-range plan for your department. As part of the preparation stage, you may want to assess how well your department is doing. To do this, you have to know how many students currently are enrolled in sociology courses, and which specific courses are drawing the largest (and smallest) numbers of students. You may also want to examine how current enrollment figures compare to past years' numbers, and whether there has been any significant increase or decrease over some specified time period. You may even want to gain some sense of how students in your department's courses feel about those courses and their instructors. Before you can begin to plan effectively for the future, you must know the present, and this is what descriptive or nonexperimental research is all about.

To gather this necessary information, you will probably take advantage of an assortment of data-collection techniques at your disposal. For instance, it is likely that other departments in your university already possess information about current and past course enrollments. A telephone call or visit to the Registrar's Office may give you a set of course-by-course figures from which you can calculate trends. In the larger world of sociological research, many private and public organizations collect such information as part of their daily activities and routinely make it available to social scientists. The U.S. Bureau of the Census, for example, is a gold mine of such data, and you will note the many references to its publications throughout this text.

Whereas the use of existing data (information collected by some group or agency other than oneself) has many appealing advantages, the technique has one serious potential problem. Information is only as good as the methods used to gather it, and using data that were collected and analyzed by someone else does not usually allow the researcher direct assessment of its validity or reliability. This is especially true when the information comes from a society or culture other than one's own.

For example, in the course of gathering materials for this book, the authors were struck by the fact that both descriptive and explanatory data relating to Mexico are more often notable for their absence than for their abundance. Unlike developed nations such as Japan and the United States that have been the subjects of extensive and rigorous research efforts by scholars from many different fields, developing societies like Mexico more often have been overlooked and underexamined (by Western social scientists, at least). Social science research in universities in these societies also tends not to have the same level of priority as research in business and in natural sciences, whose findings perhaps have more direct applications to the immediate needs and concerns of the society. Consequently, nonacademic sources often must be consulted and used, as in the case of this text.

Two of our most heavily used resources for descriptive data about Mexico were books written by professional journalists who spent time living and working in that country (Patrick Oster's *The Mexicans: A Personal Portrait of a People,* and Alan Riding's *Distant Neighbors: A Portrait of the Mexicans*). Although these books contain many important insights drawn from intimate contact with the people (Oster and

Riding) as well as extensive background research into the country's history and institutions (Riding), they must be treated with a certain degree of caution. Neither work was written by someone trained and well-versed in sociological methods or theories.

Sociological Research Methods   Sociologists do not claim to have a monopoly when it comes to perceptive and accurate understanding of social realities. But we do claim a special way of conceptualizing and examining human social relations that sensitizes us to certain phenomena that may be missed or dismissed by observers employing different perspectives. One certainly can acquire a store of valuable knowledge by direct experiences such as living in another culture and talking extensively with local people who have an insider's knowledge of it. But these experiences are not really complete substitutes for the basic world view that one develops through deep immersion and involvement in a particular discipline. For these reasons, sociologists prefer, whenever possible, to gather information themselves or, if necessary, to use data collected by other social scientists. Fortunately, a number of ways exist in which this can be accomplished.

One such method involves what is called **survey research.** In this technique, the social scientist attempts to learn about people's behaviors or attitudes (or some other social phenomenon) by asking them to respond to a series of questions. These questions may be asked verbally in the course of an **interview,** or posed in writing in a **questionnaire.** In some cases, it will be possible to survey the entire **population** (all the members of the particular group being studied). More often, however, the sociologist will have to limit the survey to a smaller segment or **representative sample** that is assumed to be reflective of the larger population (all the members of the target population must have an equal chance of being selected for the sample).

If you are still holding on to the thought of being the head of that large university's sociology department, consider how you might apply survey research techniques to find out how students think about your courses and your instructors. If your resources permit, and you do not have too many students enrolled in your courses, you might ask every sociology student to stop by the office for a brief interview. More likely, though, you and your colleagues will put together a series of questions to be distributed in all the current semester's classes. These questions will be designed in such a way as to elicit students' feelings about the subject matter of the courses, the teaching styles and abilities of the instructors, and other relevant issues.

If you do find that you have too many students in your classes to make this feasible (a condition comparable to being too rich), you might select a representative sample of both lower-division and upper-division courses to respond to the questionnaires. This sample can be constructed to ensure that every departmental instructor has at least one course at each level included in the survey. In this way, you are maximizing the likelihood that the responses you receive will be typical of those that students not included in the sample also would give if asked the same questions.

Survey research is probably the most popular and widespread form of nonexperimental methodology in sociology today. It is a straightforward technique, not expensive, and relatively easy to conduct, and the large amount of data generated can be coded and computer-analyzed very quickly. However, a number of problems are inherent in this type of research that can often limit its utility to social scientists.

Some of these problems are mechanical; that is, they revolve around the technical difficulties in drawing samples that really are representative of larger populations and developing questions that ask what they are supposed to while being clear enough for respondents to understand. Although troublesome, these problems can be resolved, if necessary, through simple trial and error. But a deeper problem in survey research is not mechanical or so easily resolved. That is the problem of truthfulness.

The logic of survey research is based on the assumption that people know why they are behaving (or thinking) in a certain way, and that they are willing to share that knowledge with the researcher. Very often, however, this assumption turns out to be invalid. Subjects in both oral and written surveys can and do provide less than truthful information with great frequency. The researcher who is not careful can be duped by respondents (Douglas, 1976).

Sometimes this lack of truthfulness reflects the fact that respondents are asked to admit to illegal or deviant behaviors; for example, questions about spouse abuse or "abnormal" sexual practices. At other times, the behaviors being studied are not in themselves illegal or deviant, but nonetheless embarrassing, such as failing to vote in a society like the United States where that right is considered a central value. Finally, respondents might hedge on their answers if they feel that what they say could jeopardize them. In our continuing example, you as department chair have assured students that their survey responses will be kept completely confidential. However, you may feel that they still might hesitate to make negative statements about their sociology instructors for fear that those instructors would retaliate against them through low grades. For whatever reason, the fact remains that responses to survey questions cannot and should not be taken at face value.

Observation Studies   Faced with these difficulties, many sociologists prefer to conduct a more immediate form of research, known as the **observation study.** As the name might imply, the technique involves the researcher directly observing the subjects' behaviors or expressions of attitudes, rather than relying on their reporting of what they do or think. The principle might be summed up as "believe as I do, not as I say." The two main varieties of these studies are distinguished from one another on the basis of the degree of the researcher's involvement with the observed groups.

In the **neutral observation** study the researcher remains removed from the group being studied, in terms of participation in group activities if not in actual physical distance, while the subjects go about their normal activities. As the chair of sociology, for instance, you might observe a class through a one-way mirror or an audio-video device installed in a classroom for that purpose. In other instances, you might attend class and observe events from a seat in the back row. However, either case, especially the latter, is likely to generate the Hawthorne effect discussed earlier. Students (and instructors) may be on their best behaviors if they know or suspect they are being observed and perhaps evaluated by a higher power.

A possible solution to this problem lies in what is termed **participant observation** research. Here, the researcher does not remain an outsider but joins the group being studied and participates in its activities. In some cases the researcher's identity may be known to the group members (overt participant observation), but more commonly the researcher engages in covert observation; that is, the researcher is not known as such to group members. As far as they are concerned, the researcher is one of them.

You, our hypothetical department head (surely by now you must be a tenured chair), for example, are probably too well known to at least some sociology majors—and possibly are too old — to be able to go undercover as an undergraduate student. But you may bring in a sociology graduate student or some other trained, trustworthy person to conduct the observations from the inside by enrolling in several classes. Not being known to either students or instructors, this observer could look at the classes as they really are conducted. By being part of the group's activities, the observer could also develop a greater sense of why the group engages in certain behaviors and not others. Such close involvement allows for an understanding of the group's definition of its circumstances and its consequent subjective structuring of the world. Participant observation, in fact, is a favored research technique of sociologists in the interactionist theoretical perspective.

Problems in Observation Studies   Significant problems are associated with this type of research strategy, especially with the covert variety. To maintain cover, the researcher must deceive or lie to the subjects, thus robbing them of the option of choosing not to participate in the study, or what social scientists call informed consent. This can become especially problematic if the research could in any way cause harm to the subjects as a result of something they did or said in the presence of the researcher whose existence was unknown to them.

Suppose, for instance, that some sociology students made negative comments about the department chair (i.e., you) while having coffee with the covert observer, and those comments were later reported to you. Or imagine what might happen if an untenured junior faculty member made the same kind of offhand remarks to the observer outside of class. This is roughly equivalent to having someone tape your telephone conversation without your knowledge. Believing that you are speaking in confidence, you might say things that could prove highly embarrassing and possibly damaging if they were to go beyond that time and place.

In this society, at least, people in the ordinary social world now are legally required to inform others that their conversation is being taped. In similar fashion, social scientists are required by human subjects protection committees to acquire the informed consent of subjects prior to the start of the research. The objective, of course, is to avoid these kinds of compromising conditions. Although the restrictions accomplish that objective, they also place severe limits on the possibility of successfully conducting this type of research. Sociologists who do covert participation observation argue that, without this technique, we would never be able to study deviant and criminal subcultures, or any organization that for some reason or other does not want to be scrutinized.

By this time, we hope that the message is clear. Sociologists have a variety of descriptive research techniques to draw on in their attempts to understand the human social world. Whereas most of these procedures can generate important information when and if properly employed, none of them is cost free or without significant weaknesses. For this reason, it is always a wise move not to rely on any one methodology in carrying out even descriptive research in this field. Whenever and wherever possible, sociologists try to cross-check the results of any single piece of research with another, different technique. Survey results, for example, may be verified through a series of observational studies. Observational studies may be compared to results of research conducted by other social scientists or sources outside academia. If the results of these different procedures are consistent, we have some assurance that our descriptions of that portion of the social world under study are accurate. If they are not consistent, we have a problem whose resolution may require more sophisticated types of analyses.

Experimental Research Designs in Sociology

Whereas the purpose of nonexperimental research in sociology is to describe social patterns, the objective of **experimental research** is to *explain* these observed patterns or *predict* future ones. To put it a little differently, nonexperimental research generates the information to construct hypotheses, and experimental research provides the data to test hypotheses. These research designs can take a large variety of different forms (Campbell and Stanley, 1963), but several common elements cut across individual versions.

All true experimental designs involve the systematic comparison of at least two groups of subjects who initially are equivalent in all characteristics relevant to the study, especially the dependent variable. The **control group** consists of subjects who will not be exposed to the experimental condition (some deliberate change in the independent variable). This group essentially serves as the baseline against which the second or **experimental group** will be measured. Members of the latter group will be exposed to the experimental condition that is the focus of the research. After that exposure, the two groups again will be measured on the dependent variable. Any changes that now are observed between them will be attributed to the effects of the experimental condition, since that is the only characteristic of the groups that now is different.

For example, suppose that Professor X has developed a hypothesis that students' performances on introductory sociology examinations can be improved by the application of what behavioral psychologists call a "negative reinforcement agent," in this case, physical pain. To test her hypothesis, she sets up an experiment using the students in her freshman Sociology 101 classes. These students all complete one ordinary midterm examination and then are grouped on the basis of their test scores into different pools—A students, B students, C students, and so on. From within each pool, students are randomly assigned to either the control group or the experimental group. After the second midterm exam has been given, individual members of each group meet with their instructor to go over the test answers. Members of the control group will be advised of their correct and their incorrect answers, receive their grade, and be sent on their way.

For members of the experimental group, however, the experience will be a bit different. They will be seated in a special chair and have electrodes attached to their wrists and ankles. The other end of the electrodes will be attached to a portable generator. As long as the students' exam answers are correct, nothing happens. The first time an incorrect answer is detected, however, they receive a negative reinforcement (15 volts of electric shock). The second incorrect answer prompts a second reinforcement (30 volts this time). The application of these reinforcement stimuli continues until the entire examination has been scored. The students then are allowed to go.

At the end of the semester, the third and final examination is given, and the scores of the control and the experimental groups are compared. The performance of each student on the third test also is compared to his or her performances on the previous two, so that the improvement (or lack of it) can be charted. The scores of the experimental group—those who received the electric shocks—show a dramatic rise between the second and third exams. They also are substantially higher than both the scores and the increase in scores of the control group. The researcher thus concludes that the application of the negative reinforcers had the predicted effect. On the basis of her findings, Professor X submits a large grant application to her university's research and development department.

The Milgram Experiment If this example sounds a bit farfetched, you might be surprised to learn that it is based loosely on a real social science experiment that took place a number of years ago (Milgram, 1963, 1965), although nobody actually received electric shocks. The study generated the same type of response from the academic community as the above example perhaps did from you when you read it.

In this experiment, Stanley Milgram, a psychologist at Yale University, placed an ad in the local newspapers requesting paid volunteers for participation in the study of a new learning technique. When the people who answered the ad arrived at the psychology labs, they joined a group of other people who they thought also were there in response to the ad. In fact, this other group consisted of people who were working for Milgram.

The group was split up into smaller groups of two, a "teacher" and a "student." In each case, the real subjects of the experiment served as the teachers, and the researcher's assistants were the students. The instructions called for the application of electric shocks to students who were unable to repeat a sequence of words after learning them from the teacher. Each additional incorrect response, or a refusal by the student to respond, called for a higher level of electric shock. Milgram had instructed his assistants to give incorrect responses (and had disconnected all the electrical wiring), since the true purpose of the experiment was to discover the extent to which the real subjects would be willing to comply with an order to administer what they might think was a dangerous electric shock to a stranger. As the experiment progressed, Milgram was surprised and disturbed to discover that a large number of subjects were so willing, although many did so under protest.

When Milgram published the results of his study of "obedience," he was criticized severely (for a review of some of these criticisms, see Miller, 1986). Among other things, he was accused of causing harm to his research subjects; not to the "students" (remember, they did not really receive any electric shocks), but to the "teachers" who were the real subjects. At the end of the experiment, Milgram explained the study to them, and assured them that his assistants ("students") had not been hurt in any way. Nonetheless, the subjects had discovered something very disturbing about themselves during this experiment. They had learned that they were capable of doing harmful things to other humans just because they had been ordered to do so by someone in authority who had agreed to take responsibility for the consequences. Critics claimed that, without being fully aware of what he had done, Milgram perhaps had caused these subjects psychological trauma by forcing them to see a side of themselves they would prefer not to know. It was partially because of controversies like the one generated by this experiment that such great concern is expressed today for the rights of human research subjects. Like the covert participation study, the possibility of conducting experiments in sociology has been greatly reduced by the restrictions on social science currently in place.

Even without these considerations, a number of other factors limit the application of the experimental method in sociology. This particular type of research is suitable only for microlevel social phenomena, that is, for small-group research. It would be impossible, for instance, to assign entire societies to control or experimental groups and then manipulate their environments in order to test the validity of some hypothesis. In addition, most social phenomena occur in a real-world setting where the simultaneous effects of what may be hundreds of individual variables make systematic control and manipulation all but impossible.

Nevertheless, experimental methodologies have contributed a significant body of information to the store of sociological knowledge, particularly in that subfield known as group dynamics. A great deal of what sociologists know about the formation and development of small social groups, friends or co-workers, for example, has come from experimental studies. These findings perhaps are not directly transferable to larger, macrolevel social phenomena, but they often have served as the starting point for that type of larger-scale research.

Chapter Summary

1. Sociology is the academic discipline that attempts to describe, explain, and predict human social patterns from a scientific orientation. It is one of the social sciences—disciplines that study human behavior scientifically. Other social sciences are anthropology, psychology, political science, and economics.

2. Sociology typically focuses on the social organization and patterns of behavior of large, complex, modern industrial states. However, in recent years sociologists have started investigating patterns of behavior and change in developing or Third World nations.

3. Sociology originated in the mid-nineteenth century when the Industrial Revolution was rapidly transforming European societies. Early sociologists attempted to understand the cause of these changes, and the consequences they had on societies' major institutions as well as on people's behavior.

4. Sociology is a debunking science; that is, it looks for levels of reality other than those presented in official interpretations of society and people's "common sense" explanations of the social world. Sociologists attempt to understand and explain what is, and are not interested in passing judgment on people, their behavior, or entire societies.

5. Auguste Comte, the founding father of sociology, believed that some nations were moving into the positivistic stage, the third and final phase of societal development. Positivism is the belief that reliable knowledge of the world can be gained only through people's five senses. Scientific analysis, with its emphasis on observation and experimentation, is grounded in positivism.

6. Emile Durkheim argued against the reductionist position that social phenomena could be reduced or explained in biological and psychological terms. According to Durkheim, social facts exist *sui generis* (in and of themselves) and cannot

be interpreted at the individual psychological level. Social facts such as laws exist external to the individual, constrain or influence a person's behavior, and are shared by a significant number of people.

7. A theory is a set of logically coherent, interrelated concepts that explains some observable phenomenon or group of facts. Grand theories explain "the big picture," that is, the progression or development of societies over long periods of time. Middle-range theories focus on a much narrower range of events in the social world; for example, Durkheim's explanation of suicide in different social groups and societies.

8. Influenced by the biological sciences, early functionalist theorists thought of society as a social organism made up of interrelated and interdependent parts or institutions. Each of these parts performed a certain useful function for society. Modern functionalists like Talcott Parsons examined the functional requirements that all societies must fulfill if they are to survive.

9. Robert Merton introduced the concepts of manifest and latent functions. Manifest functions are those recognized and intended consequences of a group or organization. For example, a manifest function of universities is to provide young adults the skills necessary for productive employment. However, in the 1960s universities became recruiting grounds and headquarters for a significant amount of antiestablishment behavior. This was a latent or unintended consequence of higher education.

10. As opposed to the group consensus orientation of functionalist theorists, conflict sociologists see turmoil as the fundamental reality of social life. Karl Marx argued that capitalist societies like the United States consist of two classes locked in struggle. The ruling class, or bourgeoisie, own and control the means of production—land, factories, machinery, and capital. With few if any resources,

the proletariat must sell their labor (for whatever the ruling class will pay them) in order to survive. This struggle between the haves and have nots will eventually give way to revolution and a socialist society.

11. Symbolic interactionists focus on microlevel as opposed to macrolevel social phenomena, and reject the objectivist approach of both functionalist and conflict sociologists. From this perspective, sociologists must strive to understand the world from the individual's subjective point of view. People define a particular situation and then act on the basis of that subjective definition. Symbolic interactionists maintain that human beings communicate by significant symbols to which they have attached meaning.

12. Much scientific research is an attempt to determine if there is a causal relationship between variables. The independent variable is the factor that is thought to be a cause of, or bring about change in, something. The dependent variable is a measure of the observed change caused by the independent variable.

13. A scientific problem is usually stated in terms of a hypothesis—an educated guess concerning the relationship between two or more variables. An example of a hypothesis would be as education goes up (independent variable), racial prejudice goes down (dependent variable). To test this hypothesis the researcher would devise some way of measuring each of the variables.

14. Using survey research, sociologists ask people a series of questions regarding their attitudes and behavior. This may be done directly, during the course of an interview, or indirectly with a questionnaire. Sociologists rarely survey all of the members of a given population. Rather, they take a representative sample of the population and generalize their findings to this larger group. For a sample to be truly representative, all members of the population must have an equal chance of being represented or selected.

15. One type of observational study frequently used by sociologists is participant observation. In overt participant observation, the researcher informs members of the group being observed that he or she is a sociologist. In covert studies, group members do not realize they are being observed. Rather, they believe the researcher is one of them.

16. A true experiment involves the comparison of at least two groups of subjects who are identical across all characteristics that are relevant to the study. One or more experimental groups receives or is exposed to the independent variable. The control group does not receive the independent variable and is used as a baseline or comparison group to the experimental group(s). In the absence of a control group we would not know if changes in the experimental group (dependent variable) were caused by the independent variable or were the result of some other factor.

2

CULTURE

In 1880 an English visitor to the United States noted that American women lived in fear of being too thin. "They are constantly having themselves weighed," he noted, "and every ounce of increase is hailed with delight . . . . When I asked a beautiful Connecticut girl how she liked the change, 'Oh immensely,' she said, 'I have gained eighteen pounds in flesh since last April' " (Banner, 1983, p. 107). Until the turn of the century, women on the covers of magazines, the burlesque stage, and chorus lines were all "plump," or by today's standard of beauty, fat. By the early 1900s, however, changing ideas in the scientific, medical, and fashion communities ushered in an era that redefined the nation's concepts of health and beauty and began to view overweight (especially in women) as both a physical liability and character impairment.

Prosperity and what might be called a short-lived women's movement of the Roaring Twenties intensified the notion that slimness was the feminine ideal. Women gained the right to vote in 1920, had more personal freedom, were participating as never before in the work force, and attended high schools, colleges, and universities in record numbers. They also learned that having a slender body was a way of disassociating themselves from "the plump Victorian matron and her old-fashioned ideals of nurturance, service, and self-sacrifice" (Brumberg, 1989, p. 244). The Great Depression of the 1930s put an end to the youthful, skinny, breast-binding, flapper look, and gave way to a more sophisticated image in the 1940s and 1950s. Slender not skinny was the current ideal, with the emphasis on a fuller, more rounded physique à la Rita Hayworth and Betty Grable (Boskind-White, 1985).

In 1966 a lanky, 5-foot, 6-inch, 97-pound British model nicknamed Twiggy began appearing on the covers of magazines like *Seventeen* and *Vogue*. Clothes draped over Twiggy's 31-22-32-inch frame set the new fashion standard, with hundreds of thousands of young American females trying to model themselves after her. With the tight jeans and no-bra look of the late 1960s and early 1970s, the "liberated" female body was on display as never before. The beautiful, well-dressed American woman at work or at play was portrayed as thin and getting thinner. A number of studies found that, beginning in the late 1950s, the weight of fashion models, Miss America contestants, and *Playboy* centerfolds continually decreased (Brumberg, 1989).

This brief survey of feminine beauty as it relates to body weight in the United States not only illustrates how quickly standards can change, it also indicates how culturally defined values of what is desirable and undesirable can affect people's lives. In the 1990s losing weight continues to be a major concern for millions of American women. Approximately 50 percent of them are on some calorie-reducing regimen at any given time. This obsession with dieting and thinness not only causes millions of women untold mental and physical anguish (low self-esteem and being hungry much of the time), it also has serious health implications. An estimated 10 percent suffer from eating disorders—roughly 20 percent of college females have these same afflictions.

One of the most serious disorders, anorexia nervosa, is undoubtedly related to a culture's definition of beauty in terms of appropriate body weight. Virtually unknown in developing countries, this malady overwhelmingly afflicts middle- and upper middle-class females in affluent, Western industrialized nations and Japan. Anorexics can literally starve to death in their quest for a more perfect (slimmer) body. Although family and friends tell them they resemble concentration camp inmates, anorexics see themselves as fat and continue to eat minimum amounts of food.

The fact that 95 percent of anorexics are female, and no sex-linked, physiological explanation for this disorder has been put forth, indicates what a powerful influence cultural factors have on people's lives. But cultural definitions of beauty and desirability that affect behavior are not limited to one sex. While women are risking their health to be thin, young males in the United States are putting their health on the line to develop muscular bodies. A 1988 study by William E. Buckley et al. of forty-six private and public high schools across the country found that one of every fifteen twelfth-grade males admitted using or having used anabolic steroids. Some of them were taking steroids to enhance athletic performance, although the majority just wanted to "get big" and look better physically.

At this moment in our history young men are taking extremely dangerous drugs to conform to one cultural ideal, and women are starving themselves and taking weight-reducing drugs to conform to another arbitrary value. Body weight not only determines the number of people in our pool of potential marriage partners, it is also a factor in the extent to which people believe and trust us (Dion, 1979; Hatfield and Sprecher, 1986; Feingold, 1988).

Culture is a people's way of life or social heritage that includes values, norms, institutions, and artifacts that are passed from generation to generation by learning alone (Hoult, 1974). Culture provides a "world-taken-for-granted" that most people accept most of the time. As we have seen, it sets boundaries for behavior and provides standards for good and bad, right and wrong, beauty and ugliness, and so on. However, it would be a serious mistake to view culture as some all-powerful, irresistible force that compels people to conform slavishly to an ideal standard of behavior. Culture not only helps determine and shape our behavior, but in turn is altered by human beings as they adapt to a changing social and physical environment.

Questions to Consider

1. To paraphrase Margaret Wolfe Hungerford, in what sense is beauty in the eyes of a culture?
2. Is human behavior a function of instincts, biological drives, or both?
3. What are the main arguments of the proponents and opponents of sociobiology?
4. What is language and how does it differ from nonverbal communication?
5. What is the relation between material and nonmaterial culture?
6. What is popular culture and why do sociologists study this aspect of culture?
7. What are some of the core values of American society? Are they changing?
8. What are mores and why must they be obeyed? What are some mores in American society?
9. What is the difference between ethnocentrism and cultural relativism?
10. What is the difference between subcultures and countercultures? Are countercultures always destructive elements in society?
11. What is cultural lag? Is cultural lag inevitable in modern industrial societies? In Third World societies?

 ## The Roots of Human Culture

The Biological Basis

In everyday explanations of behavior, the term "human nature" is often mentioned or alluded to. This catch-all phrase has been used to explain everything from a mother's love for her child to a group of adolescent males fighting. As we will see in chapter 7, many of the attributes and patterns of behavior we associate with men are thought of as natural, or somehow rooted in the male physiology. Biological explanations for female behavior are just as common in hundreds of societies. The question of whether human behavior as a whole, as well as more gender-specific acts, are a function of "nature or nurture" is one of the oldest and most controversial riddles in the biological and social sciences. Are human cultures a result of some biological programming that predisposed our species to act and evolve socially in a certain way, or are they a function of our ability to learn and adapt to a varied and changing environment?

By the 1920s this question was answered in terms of **instincts**—biologically inherited predispositions that impel most members of a species to react to a given stimulus in a specific way. Almost every aspect of human behavior was thought to be the result of some instinct or other. However, as scientists began to realize that they were not coming any closer to explaining the tremendous diversity in human behavior and cultural variation by labeling everything an instinct, this line of research was abandoned. But failing to discover a core group of instincts responsible for much if not most of our behavior does not mean that human beings are free of biological constraints.

Many social scientists are of the opinion that human beings have **biological drives** experienced as a bodily imbalance or tension leading to activity that restores balance and reduces tension. For example, drives such as hunger, thirst, and sex are influenced by stimuli that originate inside the body. The fact that drives can be satisfied in a variety of ways makes cultural variation possible. Consider for a moment the sex drive and the myriad ways in which it can be satisfied: males with females, males with males, females with females, males and animals, females and animals, males and inanimate objects, females and inanimate objects, males by themselves, and females by themselves. This list not only demonstrates the malleability of the human sex drive, but illustrates that important cultural values (especially religious values) are associated with sexual behavior. In our society, all but "normal" male and female sexual relations are considered wrong, and even unnatural, by tens of millions of people.

Biological drives influence our behavior in yet another important way. For example, human beings have to eat and drink on a regular basis, optimally a number of times each day. This means that hunting, gathering, fishing, and cultivating various forms of food are essential activities in every human society. Since we cannot fly or run as fast as a cheetah, and lack innate, predatory skills, we had to learn to acquire food and adapt to a changing environment. This satisfaction of biological drives through learned behavior not only permitted our species to survive and prosper, but also accounts for human cultural diversity. Humans have successfully adapted to a changing physical and social world because they are flexible and "not pre-programmed to a particular way of life" (*Economist,* 1987, p. 83).

In the 1970s some researchers in the new discipline of *sociobiology* stated that although human beings did not have instincts, some forms of behavior like altruism, aggression, and homosexuality were biologically based and transmitted genetically from one generation to another. Sociobiologists reasoned that because these behaviors are found in virtually every human society they must have a biological base. They argued that just as our bodies prohibit us from flying, for example, our genetic makeup predisposes us to various types of behaviors that we simply cannot escape. Even though we have highly developed brains and are capable of an almost endless assortment of behavior, we are still prisoners of our physiology and heredity.

Pioneer sociobiologist Edward O. Wilson (1978a) noted that whereas we do not inherit an instinct that directs us to engage in specific types and quantities of aggression, our capacity and tendency to engage in violent behavior is hereditary. Wilson (1978b) argued further "that it is entirely possible for all known components of the mind, including will, to have a neurophysiological basis subject to genetic evolution by natural selection" (p. 13). Although humans are highly adaptable creatures, learning and adaptability evolved and were naturally selected. The flexibility that distinguishes us from other animals is part of our genetic makeup.

Although sociobiology has its adherents, most scientists are hostile to the biological determinism that is such an important component of this perspective. Paleontologist Stephen Jay Gould (1976) believes that sociobiologists have overstated the biological

As members of a given culture, we become aware of standards of behavior—including appropriate attire for different occasions—at an early age. This Indian girl is being outfitted in a ceremonial costume.

basis of human behavior. For Gould, the fact that human beings are animals "does not imply that our specific patterns of behavior and social arrangements are in any way directly determined by our genes" (p. 12). He believes that sociobiologists have erred by confusing the concepts of "potential" and "determinism." The "brain's enormous flexibility" gives us the potential to engage in a wide variety of behavior but directs us toward none in particular. Leeds and Dusek (1981–1982, pp. xxxv) stated that some critics of sociobiology deny any biological component to human behavior beyond "eating, sleeping, and defecating." When pressed by their adversaries, sociobiologists claim that culture is 10 percent biological and 90 percent social, "which is hardly informative." Critics note that because biological constraints on culture are too weak to be significant, "models of genetic evolution will be of little use in understanding variation in human behavior" (Rogers, 1988, p. 819).

Anthropologist Ashley Montagu (1980) argued that above all, human beings are creatures of learning: "If there is one trait more than any other that distinguishes *Homo sapiens* from all other living creatures it is educability . . . the species trait of mankind. Humans are polymorphously educable, which is to say they are capable of learning everything it is possible to learn" (p. 11). For Montagu and others, we are not predisposed to any type of behavior, and we have the capacity to make and continually change our cultures virtually without limit. Biological drives require that we continually satisfy a number of bodily needs and functions, but the fact that we choose how to meet these drives is what distinguishes us from the other animals. Although the sociobiological position cannot be dismissed, it has yet to demonstrate that there is a link between some aspect of our genetic endowment and significant specieswide patterns of behavior.

By way of summary, although sociologists do not deny that biological processes (drives) affect human conduct, they stress that these processes *interact* with social and cultural forces to produce behavior. What is not completely understood, however, is where biological factors end and sociocultural forces begin.

Language, Thought, and Culture

As linguists Fromkin and Rodman (1988) pointed out, language more than anything else separates humans from the other animals. According to the philosophy, myths, and religions of numerous cultures, it is the source of our humanity and power. The spoken language developed approximately 40,000 years ago, and a written form of symbolic communication is about 4,000 years old. The written word, coupled with the language-assisted ability for more complex thought, was a crucial feature in human evolution and is closely linked to our modern "cultural takeoff" (Harris, 1983, p. 29).

The development of language was important for at least three reasons. First, human beings acquired the ability to transmit culture from one generation to another. This meant that much information gained from experience would not be lost, making it unnecessary for subsequent generations to learn these things anew. Second, language makes possible an ever-expanding repository of knowledge and tradition. It has been estimated that in the modern world the accumulated knowledge of our species doubles approximately every ten years, with much of this information stored in written form. Finally, with language we have achieved what Greenberg (1968) called semantic universality, the ability to transcend the here and now and speak of people, places, and events in the past, present, and future, be they near or far, real or imaginary.

This last aspect of language is a major difference between human and nonhuman communication. Other animals communicate by sound, odor, movement, and touch, with these signals having meaning for their immediate environment or emotional state. Some species are also capable of communicating aggressiveness, and superordination and subordination, especially as it relates to sexual activity. Inasmuch as the basic vocabulary of animals is limited to the present, however, communication is primarily an emotional response to particular situations (Fromkin and Rodman, 1988). In other words, animals have no way of relating the hunger they felt the day before yesterday, or expressing anticipation for next week's hunt.

By contrast, human communication relies to a great extent on sounds that have *arbitrary* meanings and can be arranged into an almost infinite number of combinations to convey information about any subject imaginable. For example, by age three years, speakers of English generally know what the word *cat* signifies. But cat is an arbitrary sound with no inherent meaning. Children in Mexico learn the furry little animal that goes "meow" is a *gato,* whereas speakers of Japanese call the same creature a *neko.* Speaking a language, therefore, means knowing that particular sounds signify specific meanings.

There are a number of theories of how children learn to speak (Fromkin and Rodman, 1988). According to the **imitation perspective,** children simply repeat what they hear spoken by those around them. No doubt imitation is involved in language acquisition to some extent, but from whom would a child hear, "boat big wow uh-huh," or "Mommy already eated"? The **reinforcement theory** suggests that children are positively reinforced when they say something correctly, and negatively reinforced when they say something wrong. However, one study indicated that when children are corrected it is usually for pronunciation or the incorrect reporting of facts, and not for ungrammatical sentences (Brown, 1973). Even if they are corrected for grammatical mistakes, children do not know what they are doing wrong and are typically unable to make appropriate changes.

Linguist Noam Chomsky offered an explanation of language acquisition that has been labeled the **innateness hypothesis.** Human beings learn to speak because our brains are biologically constructed or "prewired" to acquire language. In other words, the ability to speak is a physiological component of our species. We learn it naturally with little if any formal instruction because we inherit a deep-seated universal grammar that serves as the foundation, or underlies the grammar of all other languages (Chomsky, 1965). The innateness hypothesis may explain why all of the attempts to teach other primates language have resulted in only limited success, and why no animal has acquired the linguistic skills normally found in a three-year-old human (Harris, 1983).

Recent evidence that babies begin learning the language they will speak even before birth lends support to the argument that human beings are prewired to acquire linguistic skills. Anthony DeCasper asked a group of women whose fetuses were in their thirty-second week to recite a particular paragraph of a children's story three times in a row every day until birth. Approximately two days after birth, researchers gave the babies a special nipple and earphones. By altering their rate of sucking the babies could choose to hear the story their mothers read or other stories. The babies chose to listen to the familiar stories (*San Diego Union,* 1990i).

The Sapir-Whorf Hypothesis   As noted, acquisition of language was the key ingredient in humankind's cultural takeoff. Although it is easy to see how language unleashed our creative abilities in virtually every human endeavor, we do not usually think of it as something that limits our ability to think and therefore to act. However, anthropologist Edward Sapir and his student, linguist Benjamin Whorf, argued that language is more than just a means of communication. Languages are like so many pairs of colored glasses, and the people who wear these glasses see and interpret the world around them differently; that is, they furnish the categories by which we think, divide up, and make sense of the social world.

For example, in the English language the color black has more negative connotations and associations than positive ones. It represents death, sickness, evil, villains, crime, gloom, and despair. It is also associated with the occult, devils, and vampires. We have expressions such as "Black Death," "black arts," "black magic," "black-listed," "black mark," "blackmail," "black market," "black cat," "black sheep," and "black heart." Conversely, white is associated with birth, purity, holiness, goodness, and innocence. This linguistic color coding of things and attributes as either good and desirable (white) or bad and undesirable (black) may function as a cultural backdrop in which racial prejudice can thrive.

The Sapir-Whorf hypothesis goes beyond suggesting that language merely influences the way people relate to the world around them. Rather, it functions as a kind of mental straitjacket that actually forces people to perceive the social and physical environment in terms that are built into it (Howard and McKim, 1986). For example, in English the two major classifications of words are nouns and verbs, which leads to a bipolar view of nature. People, animals, and plants (nouns) run, walk, and grow (verbs). Lightning, flame, waves, and a puff of smoke are events (nouns). In the Hopi language, however, lightning, flame, and so on are verbs, "events of brief duration cannot be anything but verbs" (Whorf, 1939, in Carroll, 1961, p. 44). In other words, the Hopi language uses what we would call events (nouns) as verbs, and classifies them by their duration, from short to long. Whereas English draws our attention to the thing or event (e.g., flame), the Hopi language focuses on motion and change.

Language also reflects the orientation and world view of a particular group of people. For example, the use and number of personal pronouns in the Japanese language indicates the importance of status and hierarchical arrangements. It uses a number of first-person pronouns—*watakushi, boku, ore,* and the like—that help distinguish power differences and gradations of social distance between the speaker and the person being addressed. Suzuki (in Lebra and Lebra, 1986, pp. 142–157) referred to this process as "speaker's linguistic self-identification" and noted that in Japanese "one actually alters the linguistic definition of self to accord with changed conditions." As you might expect, a number of second-person pronouns are also used on the basis of power differences and social distance. Conversely, in languages like English and Spanish the speaker uses only one personal pronoun to identify herself or himself (I and *yo*). Spanish uses the formal (*usted*) and informal (*tú*) second-person pronouns, but speakers of English employ the pronoun "you" regardless of whether they are speaking to a dog or to the president of the United States.

Language as Social Control From the example of pronoun usage in Japan, we can see that language can be a continuing and not very subtle mechanism of social control. Superordinate and subordinate positions in virtually every aspect of Japanese society are verbalized and reinforced hundreds of millions of times each day. British novelist and social critic George Orwell was deeply concerned with how language can be used not only to influence but also to diminish people's thought processes. Recall the basic premise of the Sapir-Whorf hypothesis, that the structure of language determines how people view the world around them. In Orwell's most famous novel, *1984,* the totalitarian government of Big Brother invented a language called Newspeak with a very limited vocabulary. The idea behind Newspeak was that the fewer words and categories people had at their disposal, the less capable they were of complex, abstract thought and, therefore, the easier they would be to control. Words such as honor, justice, democracy, and science were abolished and replaced by the single word crimethink.

Although words in American English have not disappeared as a result of some sinister plot, government officials and other bureaucrats routinely use *doublespeak* to convey messages. Doublespeak is a combination of Orwell's Newspeak and "doublethink." According to William Lutz (1989, p. 1), it is "language which pretends to communicate but really doesn't. It is language which makes the bad seem good, the something negative appear positive, something unpleasant appear positive (or at least tolerable). It is language which avoids responsibility. . . ." Doublespeak illustrates how the use of language is shaped by power relations in society. Those in power invent a distorted language that obscures reality. From a conflict perspective, doublespeak keeps the masses ignorant and confused, less likely to understand that they are being exploited by the ruling class.

As these examples illustrate, language can be used to influence how people perceive the world, the way they think, and ultimately, how they behave. It is also important because it is a central component of a people's identity, and is often linked with intense feelings of patriotism and nationalism. Prior to gaining independence from England in 1947, the leaders of the Indian Congress Party promised that when the British finally quit India, the country would be reorganized along linguistic lines. What the leaders failed to consider is that in a country with 200 languages and 630 local dialects, regional loyalties would severely weaken nationalism. With the Constitution of 1950, the new Indian government changed course and said that local languages would be used until 1965, when Hindi was to become the national language. The plan was scrapped, however, after language riots broke out in many parts of the country as the deadline approached (Warshaw, 1988a).

Language can also help preserve a group's identity under the most difficult circumstances. Partitioned by Prussia, Austria, and Russia in the latter part of the eighteenth century, Poland disappeared from the map of Europe until the Treaty of Versailles redrew its borders after World War I. For over one hundred years Polish identity persisted because people tenaciously held onto their culture primarily through the use of their language. Linguistic pride also may prove to be a key issue in the partition of Canada. Since the 1960s, Canada has been trying to deal with the conflict between its English- and French-speaking citizens and the possible independence of the province of Quebec. Although many of the problems between Quebec and the rest of the country revolve around economic and political issues, the future of the French language and culture is a key component. A people's cultural heritage anchored in their language will stir the passions and give them the will and energy to fight like few other things in this world.

A battle of language has also been taking place in the United States. Two groups, U.S. English and English First, want English to be the official language of this country. As of 1989, twelve states have such legislation in place and thirty-seven of the remaining thirty-eight states were considering English-only laws. Advocates of this position argue that in a society as pluralistic as ours, the government should do everything possible to unite the many diverse segments and thus foster a national identity. These groups also believe that candidates for U.S. citizenship should be required to have knowledge of the English language in addition to a basic understanding of the nation's system of government (Imhoff, 1990). Such advocates typically oppose bilingual education in schools, arguing that these programs are supported primarily by Hispanic organizations whose power depends on "strong ethnic support and separatism and defining Hispanic Americans as a minority rather than an immigrant group" (Imhoff, 1990).

Opponents argue that the English-only movement plays into deeply held fears of the majority population—fears of minority groups and of change. Arturo Madrid (1990) argues that the imposition of an official English-only policy will limit "civic assimilation and participation" (p. 62) of non-English-speaking people. Just as so-called literacy tests were used to keep many nonwhites from voting until the Voting Rights Act of 1963, English-only laws would effectively disenfranchise hundreds of thousands of people. Madrid noted that the framers of the Declaration of Independence and Constitution "wisely chose not to single out English as the national or official language" (p. 62). For him, the real linguistic problem in the United States is literacy. Currently we have twenty-five million illiterates, the vast majority of whom speak only English. He advocates a national language policy emphasizing both literacy and multilingual skills.

Material and Nonmaterial Culture

The concept of culture comes from anthropology and is that discipline's most important contribution to the social sciences. Whereas culture represents the complete social heritage and way of life of a society or group of people, sociologists generally make a distinction between its material and nonmaterial parts. **Material culture** comprises those things people make and use. In other words, features of the material culture have our handprint since they were created and fashioned by human beings. The building you are sitting in, the clothes on your back, as well as computers, airplanes, and the Styrofoam box hamburgers used to come in are all examples of material culture.

Nonmaterial culture does not have physical substance, although it, too, was created by human beings. Ideas, religions, beliefs, customs, laws, and economic systems such as capitalism and socialism are all examples.

As you may have guessed, aspects of material and nonmaterial culture are almost always intertwined, as the latter give meaning to the former. Consider an airplane loaded with baseball bats that crashes in a country where nobody ever heard of the infield fly rule. The bats are likely to be thought of as fence posts, clubs, fancy firewood, or whatever, but not as implements with which Babe Ruth, Hank Aaron, and Sadaharu Oh hit home runs. In the absence of knowledge of baseball and the rules of the game (nonmaterial culture), bats are just so many evenly proportioned pieces of timber. Children in any society spend a good deal of time learning how features of their material and nonmaterial cultures fit together. One of the questions most frequently asked by two-, three-, and four-year-olds is, "What's this?" Older siblings and adults then name the object and give some explanation regarding how, when, and why the thing is used.

Material Culture and Technology   Material culture is also indicative of a society's technological sophistication and its values regarding technology. For example, nomadic food collectors have simple tool kits that are limited to those items they can carry. People in the group are usually given access to the tools of others (Ember and Ember, 1988). On the other end of the spectrum, the Japanese now have fully automated factories where robots make other robots twenty-four hours a day (Tasker, 1987). As of 1986 they had 41,265 robots in industry, whereas the United States had 9,400. Japanese corporations not only have more robots than U.S. firms, they also seem to have the upper hand in integrating these machines into the workplace while maintaining the loyalty and trust of their employees. The movement of robots into the factory has not been resisted by workers, who are given other jobs when their former positions are rendered obsolete by automation. By contrast, in the United States unions have been vocal opponents of robotization of the workplace because jobs are so likely to be eliminated when this occurs. Different levels of robotization (material culture) may well be linked to management styles and business ethics (nonmaterial culture) in the two countries.

In the years after the Mexican Revolution (1910–1920) the government funded artists for painting and sculpting works of art that celebrated the revolution and glorified some key political themes. Artists hailed Mexico's Indian roots, blasted the nation's prerevolutionary corrupt officials, and helped forge a new national identity. This use of material culture in the form of art to further the nonmaterial political values of the state is certainly nothing new. Both democratic and totalitarian societies have long attempted to create powerful symbols and portraits of leaders that would unify people and enhance values such as loyalty, solidarity, and discipline. During the Persian Gulf conflict we saw that pictures and statues of Saddam Hussein were ubiquitous in Iraq. In the United States portraits of important political leaders adorn our currency. Monuments like the Lincoln memorial and Marines planting the American flag in Iwo Jima symbolize prominent values such as freedom and courage.

A society's material and nonmaterial cultures are not limited to economic, political, and religious spheres of life. Much that we see, hear, appreciate, and become obsessed with is part of **popular culture;** that is, the culture of everyday life as expressed through sport, music, hobbies, television, movies, books, magazines, comic books, and so on. Popular culture is also a vehicle for connecting with our past and helps people hang on to and celebrate a time, place, person, or thing that is important to them. For example, Elvis Presley was a prominent and successful entertainer. Since his death in 1977, not only have people continued to buy his records, but tens of thousands of individuals see him as a personification of a romanticized, more carefree, rock-and-roll era of their youth.

Popular culture reflects many of the values and patterns of behavior in contemporary society, and can also be an influential factor in shaping those values and behavior. For example, television programs like "The Cosby Show," with an all-black cast, are indicative of changing values concerning race relations in the United States. Although watching blacks on television may or may not make white America less prejudiced, evidence shows that viewing violence night after night on various programs does lead to aggressive behavior.

Popular culture is the vehicle of mass consumption by which we continually reinterpret the past, evaluate the present, and speculate on the future. For example, black Americans were rarely featured in motion pictures between 1920 and 1950. When

In an age of almost instantaneous communication, many aspects of popular culture (especially entertainment and food) rapidly cross international borders. Pluto is as easily recognizable to these visitors at Disneyland, Tokyo, as he is to people in the United States.

OURSELVES AND OTHERS

Soviet "Vanna White" Casts Own Spell: Smiles, Prizes, and Miniskirt

Moscow—She fumbles the plastic letters. She doesn't walk like a star. And she never heard of Vanna White.

But like Vanna, Natasha Chistyakova has her fans. She is the letter lady on "Magic Field," the Soviet Union's copy of the American TV game show "Wheel of Fortune."

"Magic" is far from the staid, doctrinaire fare that once dominated state-run television. Glasnost and the switch to a free-market economy have resulted in 50 minutes of Hollywood-style glitter, smiles and commercials.

But it is not the only game show in town. Others on TV here include "What, Where and When?," "Club of the Witty and Jolly," a Soviet version of "The Dating Game" titled "Find Me," and a Soviet video adaptation of the board game "Trivial Pursuit."

(The non-game TV fare includes PBS' "Adam Smith's Money World," dubbed in Russian; "Adam's Apple," a program for men that has featured topless women; and "Walt Disney Presents," featuring the best of Mickey, Donald and Goofy.)

"Magic Field" is less flashy and has a slower-moving wheel than its American cousin. But it's more colorful and upbeat than other Soviet TV shows. Everyone seems to be smiling.

Not quite the same "lots of cash and an assortment of fabulous and exciting prizes" that "Wheel" offers, "Magic Field" does tantalize with Soviet-style treasures: hard-to-buy items such as vacuum cleaners and cars.

Chistyakova, the letter lady, is a slender blonde who wears a tight black miniskirt and sparkling white blouse. During a recent taping, she dropped a pile of plastic letters and walked on the set without the elegance of her American counterpart.

When she's not on the set at the Ostankino Soviet TV studios in north Moscow, the 22-year-old is in a booth editing the program or studying French at Moscow State University.

Unlike her American counterpart, who gets equal billing with host Pat Sajak, Natasha does not even get introduced. Her name appears only in the ending credits, listed only as an editor.

And she only earns what Vanna White might consider spare change—200 rubles a month ($320) and a royalty of $40 a show.

Vladislav Listiev, a witty former journalist, is her on-air partner—the Soviet Pat Sajak, if you can imagine a mustachioed, brown-haired Sajak. "Magic Field" is not his wheel of fortune, either. He earns just $592 a month.

"I am very rich person," he sarcastically says, "so rich I have to live in a hotel."

Despite the obvious similarities with the "Wheel of Fortune," Listiev insists he has never seen the American program and traces "Magic Field" to the children's game "Hangman."

With a once-taboo combination of commercialism and capitalism, the show manages to offer highly coveted items in this consumer's wasteland of shortages. One recent show ended with a contestant winning a bottle of perfume and a samovar, a Russian urn for brewing tea.

The show receives 2,000 letters a day from fans and applicants to be contestants.

One mendicant was so eager she called show administrator Julia Logovaya and offered her about $7,500 and a house on the beach if she put him on as a contestant. The offer and its maker were turned down.

Contestants represent a broad cross section of Soviet society. One recent program featured the head of the housewares section of the Central Department Store in the Siberian village of Yaya, a student of the Moscow Water Transport Institute, a naval officer from the northern port of Murmansk and a dairy engineer.

The show's creators don't try to foster "socialist construction" and do not seek to provide a "serious organ of economic education" of the communist masses, as Lenin envisioned the media's role.

The creators of "Magic Field" just want to draw a large audience.

Source: Andrew Katell, Associated Press, *San Diego Union*, May 15, 1991, E-7. Reprinted by permission.

they did appear, they were typically stereotyped as happy-go-lucky, simple-minded servants, and occasionally, musicians or dancers. They were portrayed as childlike individuals, completely dependent on good, benevolent white folk for their well-being. By the 1960s and the civil rights movement, films often featured independent, nononsense tough guys in the *Super Fly* mold. By the 1980s and 1990s, blacks on television ("The Cosby Show," "The Jeffersons," "The Heat of the Night") were portrayed as upwardly mobile, successful professionals in a more racially tolerant America.

THE NORMATIVE ORDER

Core Values and National Character

Every society has a set of values that establishes which forms of behavior and beliefs are desirable and what are undesirable. In the United States cleanliness is an important part of our culture (Spradley and McCurdy, 1989). As children we are taught to bathe regularly, practice personal hygiene, and wash our hands before every meal. However, cleanliness is valued to some extent in virtually every modern society. On the other hand, **core values** are especially promoted by a particular culture (Haviland, 1990) and are often important identifying characteristics of that culture. They provide the basis for social behavior and some of the goals pursued by members of society (Howard and McKim, 1986).

Based on core values, anthropologists and sociologists sometimes generalize about the personality characteristics and patterns of behavior of an entire tribe or society. Critics of this approach believe it is impossible to assess accurately the national character of a group in this manner. But anthropologist Francis Hsu (1979) maintained that studies of national character are important if we are to understand what motivates the leaders and civil servants of nations in the modern world. This is especially true of developing nations.

Virtually every society, however, places some value on duty, loyalty, honor, and the like. Our discussion focuses on the relative importance of these concepts and how they shape a people's national character.

American Values

Sociologist Robin M. Williams (1970) attempted to identify the major values in American society. Although he listed twenty core values, twelve appear to be the most important. They are placed in groups of four, including the identifying value of that cluster.

Certainly one of the cornerstones of American life is the tremendous emphasis placed on *success* and related values of work, achievement, and material comfort. Success and upward mobility have been part of both the fact and fiction of life in the United States since the days of the founding fathers. The dream of making it big has attracted millions of people, beginning with the huge migration of European settlers in the middle of the nineteenth century. In a society that placed much more emphasis on what an individual can do as opposed to who one is or where one comes from, for many people the dream came true.

Rags to riches stories were celebrated in the nation's popular culture as early as the nineteenth century. Young boys read the adventures of Horatio Alger's (1834–1899) heroes as they overcame poverty and adversity on the road to fame and fortune. Sports have come to reflect the hard work–achievement–success theme, and movies such as *The Knute Rockne Story* and *The Lou Gehrig Story* reinforced the idea that anyone can have success if they want it badly enough. More recently, films such as *Rocky, The Natural,* and *Field of Dreams* have done much the same. Television has also been an important vehicle for the success motif. Todd Gitlin (1985, pp. 268–269) noted that many programs, especially the soap operas, feature characters who are preoccupied with ambition. "Personal ambition and consumerism are the driving forces of their lives. The sumptuous and brightly lit settings of most series amount to advertisements for a consumption-centered version of the good life. . . ." For those whose achievements fall short of their goals, the medium offers a glimpse of the grand life. Harris and Yankelovich (1989, pp. 36–39) stated, "TV's 'Lifestyles of the Rich and Famous' captivates the masses just as the penny-dreadful details of Mr. Cornelius Vanderbilt's latest bash once did."

If the quest for success has been a prime ingredient in this country's economic achievements, hard work has always been viewed as the road to prosperity. Williams (1970) noted that work has been a core value in American culture for at least three reasons. First, in the days of frontier settlements and westward expansion, work was necessary for group survival. Second, the majority of people who initially came to this country were from the working classes in Britain and Europe. We might add the experience of blacks from the earliest days of slavery was certainly one of hard physical labor. Hispanics, Chinese-Americans, and other non-European minorities also have a history of very demanding work. Finally, the Puritan ethic linked work and success with a state of grace and eternal salvation. Robert Bellah et al. (1985) stated that work is not only the basis for success, but for self-esteem as well. In a society that measures people in terms of what they do, what they have, and what they have accomplished, unemployment is particularly painful.

Studies have reported that Americans may be starting to reject money as the sole motivator for work. The Daniel Yankelovich group found that 53 percent of Americans now work for money plus "challenge, identity, collegiality, power, the chance to learn, new skills, creativity, and growth" (Harris and Yankelovich, 1989, p. 37). A poll of working Americans between the ages of twenty-five and forty-nine years reported that 75 percent of respondents would like to return to a simpler lifestyle with less emphasis on money. Work, however, is still vitally important to Americans. A 1988 Gallup poll asked people if they would welcome less emphasis on working hard. Seventy percent responded no, up 1 percent from 1978.

Although Americans may want to see the emphasis on money reduced, financial success is still a core value in the United States. It is also the principle mechanism by which we evaluate and score the general success of ourselves and others (Harris and Yankelovich, 1989). Above all, money leads to material comfort in a material world, and Americans continue to consume goods and services at one of the highest rates on earth, often in a highly conspicuous manner.

A second cluster of values revolves around *progress,* efficiency, rationality, and applied science. Since Alexis de Tocqueville visited this country in the 1830s, foreign observers have been impressed with America's faith in progress and high expectations of the future. A fundamental component of progress is the acceptance of change for the good of society. For generations of Americans the benefits of technological change surrounded them as they lived longer, more prosperous lives. There was nothing that ingenuity and hard work could not accomplish. Even failures were viewed as temporary setbacks. When the Soviet Union sent Sputnik to orbit around the earth in 1956, the

United States space program went into high gear and put a man on the moon by 1969. In the 1940s and 1950s outbreaks of poliomyelitis crippled and killed thousands of children. The disease was almost wiped out by the development of the Salk and Sabin vaccines.

Progress is closely linked to our belief and faith in *technology* and *applied science.* Whereas most people may be indifferent to science as it relates to questions concerning the origin of life or understanding black holes in deep space, they are enthusiastic about scientific applications that will make their life easier, healthier, and longer. Williams (1970) noted that Americans are much more receptive to events in the here and now that make an immediate impact in our lives. As a nation, we are more "manipulative than contemplative" (p. 502). Applied science is so highly valued because it permits us to control nature to a significant degree.

Science and progress also go hand in hand with *efficiency* and *practicality.* They are important in a society concerned with getting things done quickly and economically, with a minimal amount of wasted time, energy, and money. People oriented toward these values are constantly looking to the future, searching for time- and labor-saving means for doing more things faster. Traditionalism and a strong attachment to the past are the antithesis of a "let's do it better, cheaper, and faster" ethos. For example, although France is a modern industrial state, practicality and efficiency are not nearly as important to the French as they are to Americans. Most shops and government offices in France are closed from noon until 2:00 or 3:00 P.M.—precisely the time when people on lunch breaks could use their services. The majority of stores are closed on Sundays and holidays, and the nation's economy shifts into low gear during August, when a significant number of French people are on vacation. It is still quite common for people to spend an hour or two eating the evening meal, whereas Americans are more likely to be hurrying through supper and mentally preparing for some upcoming activity.

The final cluster of core American values is *freedom,* individualism, equality, and patriotism. Bellah et al. (1985) argued that freedom is perhaps the most deeply held American value. To be free "is not simply to be left alone by others; it is also somehow to be your own person . . . free as much as possible from the demands of conformity to family, friends, or community" (p. 23). Freedom gives each person a sense and a measure of power to strive for whatever he or she desires.

A corollary of freedom is individualism, which "lies at the very core of American culture" (Bellah et al., 1985, p. 142). The dignity of the individual is sacred, and any threat to limit a person's right to act and think for himself or herself is sacrilegious. The Bill of Rights outlines more individual safeguards than perhaps any other political document in the world. We enjoy thinking of ourselves as a nation of rugged individuals, made from the same mold as the pioneers who tamed the land on their own initiative without the help or hindrance of the government or anybody else. Americans have had a continuing love affair with the mythical individual hero—the cowboy—since at least the turn of the century. Be it Alan Ladd in the classic movie *Shane* or the Lone Ranger (Bellah et al., 1983), the cowboy-hero saves the town from some terrible injustice, kisses his horse, and rides off into the sunset. Private detectives, loner cops, and people who persevere and win against all odds possess the unconventionality, stubbornness, and personal toughness that Americans associate with success and moral righteousness.

Fairness and equality, especially equality of opportunity, have been persistent themes in this society for most of our history as a nation (Williams, 1970). If a person's eventual success or failure is to be a function of his or her abilities and hard work, then society must provide an opportunity structure free of any individual or group favoritism or discrimination. It is precisely at this juncture of freedom, individualism, and equality that inconsistencies related to these values as they are translated into behavior by both individuals and institutions have been the most evident. The history of the United States is rife with examples of discrimination based on race, ethnicity, gender, religion, sexual preference, age, and language that have effectively prohibited people from participating politically, economically, and socially to one degree or another.

The final value in this cluster is patriotism. Despite the waning confidence Americans express in their elected officials and public institutions, they have a "degree of patriotism that is remarkable when compared to most other industrial societies" (Bellah et al., 1985, pp. 221–222). We continue to rally around the flag even though the percentage of people voting in local and national elections is low and dropping in many parts of the country. President Carter's inability to free the American hostages in Iran may have cost him the 1980 election, as a significant number of voters interpreted this crisis as indicative of the country's political and military decline. The ensuing military buildup in the Reagan years occurred with the support of much of the nation.

It would be naive to think that everyone in the United States accepts and adheres to these values with the same level of intensity. The extent to which core values are held is related to a number of factors, including race, ethnicity, and social class, and the experiences people have had as individuals and in groups as a result of these factors. Madsen and Meyer (1978, p. 244) argued that the "central character of the value system" of Mexican Americans "comes from their long history of feudalism from Spain,

Some symbols are capable of eliciting powerful emotional responses. National flags embody the values and ideals people associate with their society, as well as a nation's history. Symbols such as flags and military insignia establish group solidarity and a strong sense of one-ness.

oppression in Mexico, and discrimination in the United States." William Madsen (1964) noted that Mexican Americans temper the core value of progress with an acceptance and understanding of things as they are. He summarized this aspect of the Mexican American world view as follows:

> We are not very important in the universe. We are here because God sent us and we must leave when God calls us. God has given us a good way to live and we should try to see the beauty of His commands. We often fail for many are weak but we should try. There is much suffering; we should accept it for it comes from God. Life is sad but beautiful. (p. 17)

If Madsen is correct, Mexican Americans are not interested in progress and change in the sense that these terms mean a mastery of the physical environment, and a better life through science and technology. Because God controls events, they plan less for the future than do people in Anglo cultures; one cannot control or predict what is ultimately in God's hands.

In the months prior to the Persian Gulf War of 1991, blacks appeared more willing to rely on sanctions to force Iraqi strong man Saddam Hussein out of Kuwait than whites, who were more likely to support a military option (Helm, 1991). Does this mean that black Americans are less patriotic or less courageous than white Americans? A closer examination of this issue reveals that if anything, blacks are more patriotic and courageous. They also are disproportionately represented (high) in the armed forces as a whole (and in combat units), just as they were during the Vietnam War. Rates of unemployment in the inner cities that can exceed 50 percent for young black males suggest the "patriotic" act of joining the armed forces can also be interpreted, at least in part, as motivated by economic survival and thoughts of upward mobility on discharge.

Culture of Poverty   The culture of poverty thesis put forth by anthropologist Oscar Lewis (1966) and others states that the core values of poor people are different from those of more economically successful individuals. These values are passed down from generation to generation and contribute to a cycle of poverty from which they cannot escape. The poor are thought to lack the drive, desire, and discipline to be successful, as well as to condone a good deal of deviant behavior the rest of society regards as deviant. Hyman Rodman (1963) rejected this interpretation, arguing that lower-status people develop an alternative set of values without abandoning the core value of success. They "stretch" these values so that lesser degrees of success become desirable—and attainable. For example, whereas middle-class families simply assume their children will finish high school and go on to college or find good jobs, families living in poverty have internalized the core value of success, but have scaled it down so as to be realistic and therefore attainable. For them, having their children finish high school and gain steady employment in neighborhoods with high rates of unemployment is considered a success.

In a participant observation study of working and nonworking black men who frequented a local bar and liquor store, Elijah Anderson (1978) found that these men did not stretch a set of given values as much as they created their own standards of social conduct in line with the opportunities available to them. When certain individuals could not find jobs and conduct their lives on values based on decency, they could gain the esteem of their peers by being "good" hoodlums.

Although core values are not likely to be completely abandoned, they can be modified. Heightened awareness of environmental pollution and destruction has already called into question fundamental values of progress in a society that has come to realize the affluence of a throw-away industrial society. Antiwar movements in both the Vietnam and Persian Gulf wars indicate that patriotism can be expressed in numerous ways. Finally, core values are affected by one's position in the social system, as well as racial-ethnic identity and experience.

Norms, Folkways, Mores, and Laws

Every society has codes of conduct that regulate the behavior of its members. These standards tell what demeanor is appropriate in the classroom, in the boardroom, and even in the bedroom. In other words, in no society are individuals completely free to do whatever they please, whenever they please. **Norms** are rules that state "what human beings should or should not think, say or do under given circumstances" (Blake and Davis, 1964, p. 456). Marshall Clinard (1974) observed that people are not usually aware of the arbitrary nature of the norms they live by, as these rules of conduct become part of an individual's world-taken-for-granted from an early age. A moment's reflection will reveal that we are bound by norms virtually every time we interact with other people. We are also subject to the normative standards of various organizations and institutions to which we belong. Not all norms are of equal importance, however, or carry equal punishment or reward. The hierarchy of rules from least to most important is usually defined as folkways, mores, and laws (Wickman, 1974).

Coined by the American sociologist and anthropologist William Graham Sumner (1840–1910), **folkways** refer to the customary, habitual way a group does things; simply stated, the ways of the folks. Folkways should be followed because they represent proper etiquette, manners, and the generally acceptable and approved way that people behave in social situations. For example, in the United States, as in most other countries, people eat soup with a spoon or drink it out of a cup or bowl. Someone dining in a restaurant who dipped his hands in a soup bowl and then slurped it out of his palms would probably be stared at in amazement (and disgust), laughed at, and possibly asked to leave. People who violate folkways may be thought of as immature or strange, but they are not considered evil or wicked. Similarly, if your sociology instructor came to class wearing a tuxedo and a top hat, or a flowing formal evening gown, he or she would probably get some stares and no doubt would be greeted with a good deal of laughter. Such outrageous attire, totally inappropriate to the college classroom, would be a clear violation of folkways.

Whereas the folkways of a group or larger society should be followed, **mores** must be obeyed. Continuing with the preceding example, if a male sociology instructor began wearing an evening gown to class on a regular basis he would have to deal with more than laughter. In many institutions he would surely be dismissed. Mores are important because they are grounded in deep-seated cultural values. People are likely to believe (rightly or wrongly) that if they are violated something bad will happen to the group. In this instance many individuals would be incensed because in their view a man wearing a dress is condoning or flaunting a deviant sexual lifestyle and poses a serious threat to the morality of students.

Incest taboos (from the Polynesian *tapu*) are good examples of mores. No society permits either marriage or sexual intercourse between mother and son, father and daughter, or brother and sister. Anthropologist Bronislaw Malinowski (1927) believed that these liaisons were forbidden and punished because they would produce so much tension, rivalry, and competition that the family could not function and might even be destroyed (Ember and Ember, 1988). Evidence from psychologists and family therapists suggests that family harmony and stability are certainly threatened where incest exists.

As societies modernize, some of the most important norms are codified, or formally written into a legal code. They become **laws** and are legally binding for people who reside in a specific political jurisdiction. **Proscriptive laws** state what behavior is prohibited or forbidden. Laws against taking another's life, robbing people, or burglarizing their homes are proscriptive and carry some form of punishment administered by the state. **Prescriptive laws** spell out what must be done. Income tax laws, traffic laws, draft registration laws, and licensing laws require people to do things at specific times, places, and under given circumstances. These two types of laws are not limited to the legal system. The Ten Commandments are predominantly proscriptive rules ("Thou shall not . . ."), and rules mandating church attendance are mostly prescriptive.

When people violate norms and their nonconforming behavior is observed or later discovered, they are likely to be punished or sanctioned for their transgression. This sanction can be either mild or severe, formal or informal. An informal sanction may be administered by a relative or friend by way of a frown, an angry word, or even a slap in the face. Some occasions of child abuse and wife beating can be thought of as severe informal sanctions. Formal sanctions are handed out by organizations and institutions when rules (usually written ones) are violated. These groups typically have specific procedures for determining that a rule has been broken and what sanction applies in a given situation.

As nations modernize, many people, including this newly married Chinese couple, choose to maintain their ties with traditional customs, especially those marking significant life transitions such as births, marriages, and deaths. These customs provide a link with the past and give additional meaning to the present event.

In one sense, norms (and their implementation) constitute the backbone of society. Without them, human groups would fly apart or degenerate into a kind of free-for-all in which everyone did as he or she pleased and the powerful ravaged the powerless. Most people would agree that norms and laws are necessary to maintain stability; however, many questions remain concerning a society's normative order. Who should make and administer the laws? Should everyone in society have input into the formation of group norms, or should this important job be left to a select few "wise" individuals? Should a society's laws be grounded in religious "truths" or secular values? Should laws be designed to safeguard individual freedoms, or be made with the welfare of the group in mind, even if individual freedoms are jeopardized?

Functionalist and conflict theorists disagree sharply concerning the manner in which norms are created and implemented (social control). The former are more likely to see norms originating as a result of group consensus, and the latter argue that laws are a product of power relations. For example, in a society like the United States the capitalist class (bourgeoisie) makes laws to exploit and control the proletariat or working class. We will have more to say about norms and social control in the chapters on socialization and deviance.

Ethnocentrism and Cultural Relativism

The world-taken-for-granted that culture provides is often synonymous with the view that one's way of life is best. **Ethnocentrism** is the tendency to believe that the norms and values of one's own culture are superior to those of others, and use these norms as a standard when evaluating all other cultures. The "ugly American" tourist in another country who continually notes that in the United States everything is bigger, better, and more expensive, and cannot figure out why the natives act the way they do, is being ethnocentric.

It is commonplace for people to believe their way of life is of value, and a certain amount of ethnocentrism is, in fact, beneficial, as it facilitates social cohesion and a sense of "we-ness." Solidarity and pride in one's group are necessary if an organization or political state is to survive and prosper. More extreme levels, however, result in the unwarranted rejection and condemnation of other people and their way of life. When expressed in terms of fanatical patriotism and nationalism, ethnocentrism can set the stage for war.

People can be ethnocentric and not even realize they are offending another group. Residents of the United States think of themselves as, and call themselves, Americans. This term is used by the person in the street, news commentators, and the authors of this text with no intention of slighting or demeaning anyone. Unfortunately, in the eyes of Canadians, Mexicans, and Latin Americans, that is exactly what we are doing. Residents of these nations are quick to point out that they too are Americans, and resent the fact that people from the United States reserve this term exclusively for themselves (Broom and Selznick, 1970). They refer to us, and wish we would call ourselves, North Americans. Because we have been using the word Americans for over 200 years, and there is no identifiable, easily used alternative, this form of self-identification will no doubt remain.

As one might expect, people in Japan are proud of their accomplishments and way of life. Peter Tasker (1987) noted that they refer to all other countries as *mukoz,* a vague term meaning "over there," and their inhabitants as *gaijin* ("foreigners"). The Japanese see themselves as a unique people and routinely phrase things when speaking to a *gaijin* in terms of "We Japanese think/like/dislike . . ." (Tasker, 1987, p. 33). Bookstores typically have large sections devoted to *Nihonjin-ron* ("Japanese theory") that catalogue the special characteristics of Japanese (both positive and negative) in pseudo-scientific terms. Some people in Japan see themselves as not only culturally but physically distinct. They believe that Japanese think with a different side of their brain than do people in the rest of the world.

Views concerning the superiority of one's group leads to stereotyping the values, attitudes, and behavior of others. A **stereotype** is a preconceived (not based on experience), standardized, group-shared idea about the alleged essential nature of a whole category of persons without regard to individual differences within the category (Hoult, 1974). Stereotypes often focus on the supposed negative or humorous attributes of a group. In the nineteenth century they were routinely used by businesses to sell products to largely Anglo American consumers. Advertising stereotypes consisted of "lively Latins, thrifty Scots, clean Dutch, Italian fruit peddlers, Mexican bandits, and pigtailed Chinese" (Westerman, 1989, p. 29). Blacks were subservient domestics and "hired help," like the Cream of Wheat Chef and plantation mammy, Aunt Jemima.

Since the mid-1970s or so, stereotyping on the part of the business community has disappeared to a significant extent. Unfortunately, this practice did not subside because people realized it was often harmful and cruel, and categorized entire groups of people as one dimensional, but for political and economic reasons. The civil rights movement of the 1950s and 1960s resulted in more minorities voting, thus creating a political pressure group. More sophisticated marketing research indicated that minorities had increasing amounts of buying power. For example, in 1988 blacks spent $218 billion on goods and services, and Mexican Americans were "worth $134 billion" in 1989 (Westerman, 1989). It appears the days of the Pancho Villa look-alike Frito Bandito are just about over. However, stereotypes are still firmly rooted in the nation's humor, as is evidenced by the number of jokes about Italians, Poles, Jews, Mexicans, Irish, and every other nationality and cultural group under the sun.

Whereas ethnocentrism is the practice of using one's culture as a basis for judging the way of life of others, **cultural relativism** is the belief that there is no universal standard of good and bad or right and wrong, and that an aspect of any given culture can be judged only within its own context. In other words, the values, laws, and religious practices of society A cannot be evaluated using the standards of society B. Every culture is a special entity and must be dealt with as such. For example, Mexicans seem to have a preoccupation with death (see the Mexico box at the end of chapter 3) that culminates with a celebration on November 2, the Day of the Dead. Although children playing with death-related toys and people eating cookies shaped like skulls may seem bizarre and macabre to an outsider, within the context of the Mexican value system this behavior loses its sinister connotations and makes sense.

When the Japanese women's volleyball team was defeated at the Tokyo Olympics in 1964, the athletes all burst into tears. From a Western perspective this could easily be interpreted as poor sportsmanship on the part of an immature group of sore losers. But the Tokyo Olympics marked Japan's return to respectability in the aftermath of World War II, and the crying women were expressing a profound sense of shame after failing to win a gold medal in front of their fellow citizens (Tasker, 1987). In the context of a so-called shame culture, this incident can be understood for what it really meant.

The problem with cultural relativism is that any behavior can be accepted, rationalized, and justified. Amnesty International reports that human rights violations and torture occur in over fifty countries. Under the Pol Pot regime in Kampuchea (formerly known as Cambodia) in the 1970s, one million or more people were murdered by the state or died from hardships inflicted by the government. Idi Amin's reign of terror in Uganda in the 1970s resulted in the brutal deaths of approximately 300,000 people. Few individuals would condone this behavior or accept cultural relativism as a justification for torture and murder. The question, therefore, is how far can we push the cultural relativism perspective? Is behavior always "relative" to the situation, or is there some absolute standard of right and wrong? If so, what is it, and how do we know this value system is correct? For Klaus-Friedrich Koch (1974), the answer to these questions are simple and straightforward: "Notions of dignity, honor, and cooperation are as universal as the taboo against indiscriminate killing of fellow men, notwithstanding cultural differences in the definition of these ideas" (p. 67).

Culture Shock

In the popular television program "Star Trek: The Next Generation," the crew of the *USS Enterprise* travels to distant galaxies on its mission to "seek out and explore" new civilizations. Often these beings from alien societies engage in a wide variety of behavior that leaves crew members bewildered and confused. **Culture shock** is the experience of encountering people who do not share one's world view that leads to feelings of disorientation, frustration, and, on some occasions, revulsion.

It is unlikely that any of us will experience culture shock at the intergalactic level, but the emotional upheaval of observing and dealing with people from other nations (and even different parts of our own country) can be profound. The greater the difference between our way of life and that of the people we are interacting with, the more intense the shock is likely to be.

For example, while walking down a busy street in Bombay, one of us suddenly came upon an old blind beggar with no arms and legs, lying on a tattered old blanket in the middle of the sidewalk. Some of the many passersby gave him a few coins, although most adroitly stepped around the pitiful figure without looking at the man. On another occasion, a woman whose face, arms, and hands were grotesquely disfigured by leprosy was also asking for money. Coming from a society where people with such deformities are institutionalized (some would say warehoused), we found seeing people in this condition, struggling to survive, quite disturbing. So too was the fact that the majority of people paid no attention to these individuals.

This apparent callousness was even more of a shock than the sight of disease and dismemberment. On reflection, however, it became clear that in a country as populated as India, with so many suffering and needy people, one could not possibly give even a meager amount of money to the hundreds of beggars likely to be encountered every day. The shock of gross disfigurement began to wear off, in the same way that one is less likely to be frightened by even the scariest movie after seeing it three or four times.

 CULTURAL DIVERSITY AND CHANGE

Subcultures and Countercultures

What do a Polish American steelworker in Pittsburgh, a Vietnamese American fisherman in Galveston, Texas, a Mexican American cattle rancher in Colorado, and a Japanese American computer operator in San Francisco have in common? Outside of the fact that they all live and work in the United States, and share some of the core values discussed earlier, the answer probably is little or nothing, because they come from different cultural traditions. All of us belong to numerous **subcultures**—groups that hold norms, values, and patterns of behavior in common with the larger society, but also have their own design for living and world view.

Subcultures are especially numerous in heterogeneous societies like the United States, a nation settled by people from all over the world. In fact one might argue that we have no dominant culture, inasmuch as we are a nation of such diverse racial and ethnic backgrounds. From this perspective the country is a collection of racial and ethnic groups sharing a geographic location, living in a loosely agreed-upon political state. Subcultures are comprised not only of people from various racial and ethnic groups, but also individuals from different religions, geographical locations, occupations, political affiliations, and recreational interests.

For example, soldiers have specialized training in the use of sophisticated weapons, wear distinctive uniforms, and have jobs as well as a set of values and norms that requires them to kill people and give up their own lives if necessary. They are typically young males known for their he-man attitudes and frequent use of profanity. There are even subcultures within subcultures. The life of an infantryman is different from that of someone in an armored division. These individuals train and fight with different technologies and have their own work-related language or argot.

Perhaps the most culturally diverse society in the world, India is made up of people from 3,000 *jati,* or subcastes, who speak almost 200 languages and 630 regional dialects (Warshaw, 1988a). India's Hindu majority (83 percent) has been at odds with people from different religious subcultures for hundreds of years. Since group identification and pride are so often rooted in language, religion, and geographical residence, societies with subcultural divisions along these lines are prone to conflict and violence.

Subcultures like those consisting of people who share the same hobby (e.g., stamp or coin collecting) may have little impact on any group or institution in society. Others, however, have significant consequences for a nation's political, economic, and social institutions. Hundreds of thousands of military men and women served in Vietnam during the 1960s. On returning to the United States, thousands of them joined the Vietnam Veterans Against the War, a subculture committed to pressuring the government to end the fighting in Southeast Asia. In the past few years, subcultures of individuals for and against the right of women to legally have an abortion have clashed (often violently) over this important and deeply emotional issue.

Although a much more racially and ethnically homogeneous country than either the United States or Mexico, Japan is also comprised of hundreds of subcultures. One of the more interesting of these groups is the *onedan,* the organized cheering section of baseball fans found at any stadium in the country. *Onedan* exist at every level of sport in Japan, having originated in the nineteenth century when they were a major presence at college baseball and football games (Whiting, 1989). Unlike more reserved fans, they are veritable wild people, yelling and screaming, banging on drums, and blowing horns and whistles nonstop for nine innings. One American observer characterized them as lunatics making more noise than is heard at the World Series and Army-Navy games combined. A Japanese social scientist argued that *onedan* serve an important psychological function: "Japanese work too hard. Traditionally, it has only been at *matsuri* (festival) time each year that we lose our inhibitions and let our hair down. These days, however, a trip to the ballpark has become a good substitute for the *matsuri*" (Oda, in Whiting, 1989, p. 117).

Some subcultures are not only different from, but also in opposition to, mainstream society. **Countercultures** are groups whose members share values, norms, and ways of life that contradict the fundamental beliefs and lifestyle of the larger, more dominant culture. These members reject some or all of the core values and institutions of society, and may or may not engage in criminal behavior. For example, founded in Tennessee just after the Civil War, the Ku Klux Klan (KKK) rejects the core values of freedom, liberty, and justice for all, and has engaged in violent behavior against African Americans, Hispanics, Asians, Catholics, and Jews. In the late 1980s young males with shaved heads calling themselves Skinheads began harassing and beating up some of the same people the KKK targeted. On the other end of the political spectrum (the extreme left), the Symbionese Liberation Army and the Students for a Democratic Society were hostile to the government and big business—"the establishment"—during the 1960s and 1970s.

Occasionally a counterculture is incorporated into the larger society. In Poland during most of the 1980s the Solidarity Union was considered a counterculture from the point of view of the ruling Communist Party. Solidarity demanded better pay for workers and wanted an open, more democratic government. Union members engaged in demonstrations, work stoppages, and prolonged strikes in an effort to realize their goals. Their leaders were routinely harassed, jailed, and tortured by a government that refused to make major concessions. With the collapse of the communist regime in Poland, however, Solidarity and its members became part of the legitimate power structure. In a somewhat similar but less successful manner, the African National Congress (outlawed for many years by the South African government) was recognized by the government in the months after the release of Nelson Mandela from prison.

Inasmuch as countercultures are in opposition to some of society's core values, they often clash with a nation's ruling government. A poll in Japan found that a small minority of people (approximately 2–3 percent) still considered the late emperor Hirohito to be "something like a god" (Smith, 1990, pp. 10–11). No doubt a significant number of the nation's 120,000 right-wing political radicals are drawn from this group, and approximately 5,000 of these individuals are affiliated with extremist paramilitary organizations (Maulain, 1987). In January 1990 the mayor of Nagasaki narrowly missed being killed after he was shot by a member of the *Seikijuku* ("Righteously Minded Academy"). The mayor had remarked that the late Emperor Hirohito bore some responsibility for World War II.

In the months before the 1968 summer Olympics in Mexico City, opposition to the games was voiced by students and thousands of middle-class sympathizers. Members of this counterculture opposed the government's decision to spend millions of dollars on what they considered a frivolous activity when the country was beset by so many social and economic problems. The students were also critical of a government that was much more democratic in theory than in practice. On October 2, 1968, just ten days before the games began, 10,000 people were jammed into the *Zocalo*—the "plaza of the three cultures." Suddenly shots rang out from an undetermined location and the police and army units surrounding the crowd opened fire. A government report stated that twenty-two people were killed, although unofficial estimates placed the number of deaths in the hundreds. During the night, soldiers carried away bodies and cleansed the square of blood (Riding, 1989). The short-lived student protest had come to a tragic end. Although the government was never threatened by a movement that did not include peasants or organized labor, Mexican officials acted quickly and decisively to rid the nation of what they considered a dangerous counterculture.

It is not unusual for countercultures to be associated with violence. Sometimes, as is the case with the KKK, members victimize people they define as standing between their organization and its stated goals. At other times, members are targets of violence by the government (as happened in Mexico City in 1968), or even rival countercultures (militant Hindus and Muslims fighting each other in India).

Integration and Change

To a certain extent all cultures are integrated, meaning that the major material and nonmaterial components of a society fit together and form a consistent, workable whole. Japanese society is geared toward economic expansion, with the nation's major institutions, values, and patterns of behavior supporting the financial success of Japan "Inc." However, no society is completely integrated, and Japan's strong emphasis on academic achievement and hard work has resulted in internal strains. The rate of premature death among businessmen is rising (according to one estimate, 10,000 in 1989) as is the number of children with chronic exam anxiety. Parent-child relationships are also strained as a result of the intense pressure to be accepted by the nation's best universities (van Wolferen, 1990). Japanese *sararimen* (salarymen), who work long hours and are often obliged to spend additional time eating, drinking, and carousing with co-workers and superiors, are little more than part-time family men. Japanese males have excluded females from the more important decision-making positions in society and thus have deprived the nation of the energy and talent of half the population.

One reason cultures are not completely integrated is that they are constantly changing. Change occurs because societies must adapt to the internal and external demands of the social, political, and physical environment. Change can be either fast or slow and accepted or resisted by various groups. For example, the way of life of some Australian Aborigines has changed relatively little over hundreds of years. On the other hand, both the material and nonmaterial cultures of the United States changed rapidly in the 1960s and 1970s. One need only consider the impact of organizations like the Civil Rights Movement, Women's Movement, Gay Liberation Movement, the drug culture, and rise of Christian fundamentalists to realize the tremendous changes that occurred during this period.

Rapid and continuing cultural change can put enormous pressure on people who are trying to determine to what extent they should modify their values and behavior in accord with such transformations. Young people in the 1960s and 1970s raised in conservative, religious families saw friends and classmates experiment with drugs and casual sex. They had to decide whether to accept the values and standards of behavior they had been taught, or go along with the new lifestyle of an emerging youth culture.

Technological Change The impact of technological change on society has been monumental in the twentieth century. Automobiles, airplanes, computers, medical science, telephones, and television, to name only a few things, have altered the lives of hundreds of millions of people around the world. One area of cultural change, the technological evolution of weapons, resulted in "modern" warfare and has been a crucial factor in geopolitical politics since World War I. The development of weapons such as bombs, tanks, poison gas, and machine guns meant that people could kill each other faster and at a greater distance. Beginning with World War I casualties were no longer measured in the thousands or even hundreds of thousands, but in the millions. With the ability to drop bombs from planes and sink ships with torpedoes, war was turned into depersonalized mass destruction. This spatial separation of killer and victim reduced the psychological cost of killing increasingly large numbers of people. It is much easier to take the life of a faceless enemy miles away than it is to destroy a living, breathing human being on the battlefield (Milgram, 1963; Zimbardo, 1969). Speaking of remote-control weapons used in modern warfare, Konrad Lorenz (1971) stated, "The man who presses the releasing button is so completely screened against seeing, hearing, or otherwise emotionally realizing the consequences of his action, that he can commit it with impunity—even if he is burdened with the power of imagination" (p. 234).

Cultural Lag Whereas technology has developed at an extremely rapid pace in the twentieth century, not all aspects of culture change at a steady pace over the same period of time. Sociologist William Ogburn (1950) referred to this phenomenon as **cultural lag**—the process whereby one aspect of culture changes faster than another aspect of culture to which it is related. Ogburn noted that the social customs, patterns of organization, and levels of technology that exist within a given society change at different rates. In modern societies, material culture (especially technology), typically changes faster than associated values, norms, and laws (nonmaterial culture).

This lag or gap means that modern humans live in a state of perpetual "maladjustment" (Ogburn, 1950). For example, medical technology now makes it possible for people to remain alive indefinitely, although they may have been pronounced "brain dead" with no hope of recovery. This has resulted in a number of complex legal and ethical questions. Who should decide if and when the "plug is pulled" from a life support system? The family? Doctors? One's church? The state? The fact that people are just now beginning to make living wills covering such an eventuality, as well as leaving instructions regarding the giving and receiving of vital human organs, is indicative of the lag time between technological change and our adaptation to it.

With the increasing pace and sophistication of advances in medicine, genetic engineering, and other areas of applied science, we can expect to see more examples of nonmaterial culture (law, values, ethical and religious systems) lagging behind. The maladjustment Ogburn spoke of appears to be a permanent condition of modern industrial societies.

Human ingenuity has been responsible for advances in technology from the introduction of stone tools to the launching of space probes that explore distant planets. Within the context of various political, economic, and social institutions, people ultimately decide how that technology is to be used. However, we tend to view some of these inventions as things beyond our control. In a sense, they have a life of their own, with human beings *reacting* to them rather than *determining* how they will be used. Many people seem to have accepted the notion that an unfortunate (yet inevitable) consequence of modernization is environmental pollution. Politicians typically speak in terms of economic growth (jobs) versus environmental protection, as though the two were inherently mutually exclusive.

Since the creation of modern armies and the invention of sophisticated and deadly weapons in the World War I era, global powers have acted as though a lasting peace could be achieved only by having more weapons than one's enemy. With the proliferation of nuclear arms since the 1940s, these weapons have been accepted by world leaders as an unfortunate but real fact of geopolitics. Not only does humanity have to live with the fear of a nuclear confrontation, but the worldwide expenditure for armaments is approximately $1 trillion a year. In a period of rapid population growth and monumental economic and social problems (especially in the developing nations) that desperately need financing, we seem to be trapped by a technological monster of our own creation.

FOCUS ON
MEXICO

MEXICAN VALUES: ALL IN THE FAMILY

Three of the most important core values in Mexican society are related to the family, *machismo* (manliness), and religion. Although analytically distinct, they are interrelated and interdependent, and serve as a bedrock for a significant amount of behavior in Mexico. Even a superficial study will reveal how important the family is in everyday life. What is more, this fundamental social institution is considered near sacred, and Riding (1989) noted that "for most Mexicans the family remains the pivot of their lives" (p. 239). So much of an individual's social life and psychological support come from interacting with relatives that people need few friends.

Celia Falicov (1982) made the following observations about the rural, semirural, and working-class families that comprise a majority of Mexico's people. The nuclear family (mother, father, children) is embedded in an extended family that includes close relationships with cousins, aunts, uncles, and grandparents. Sibling relationships are very close, with the strong bond an ideal that parents instill in their offspring from an early age. As a result of their parents' close sibling ties, children are also very close with their *primos hermanos* (first cousins).

Falicov (1982) saw *compadrazgo,* the custom that defines certain familial relationships, as an especially important aspect of Mexican family life. As a result of this custom, two sets of relationships are established: "one is between *padrinos y ahijados* (godparents and their godchildren); the other is between the parents and the godparents who become *compadres* (coparents)" (pp. 142–143). The majority of Mexicans and Mexican Americans have *compadres* living in the same city or town. Godparents not only serve

as surrogate parents in the event of an emergency, they also help their godchildren in a variety of ways. Parents may choose *compadres* with an eye toward how they will be able to help their children (Falicov, 1982). "Poor families may seek a wealthier family; rural families may choose a city family; others may have political favors in mind . . ." (p. 143). According to Mexican sociologist Fernando Penalosa (1968), however, in the lowest socioeconomic classes the extended family network and the practice of *compadrazgo* has all but been destroyed. The rural-to-urban migration of so many poor people in search of employment and a better life may be responsible for the eventual demise of this tradition, a victim of Mexico's modernization.

Individual achievement is not particularly emphasized in working-class Mexican families, although honesty and the preservation of one's *dignidad* ("dignity") are. Falicov and Karrer (1988) noted that the family in Mexico protects and helps the individual but demands allegiance to itself. In other words, people trade (or sacrifice) a certain amount of individuality and personal freedom for the support and protection familial bonds provide. Choosing a husband or wife not entirely satisfactory to one's family is something most Mexicans would never seriously consider. A similar situation may prove to be difficult in a society like the United States, but in Mexico a person risks being alienated from his or her entire family-support group.

Macho or *machismo* is the cult of masculinity in Spanish America and can be traced back to the days of the conquistadors. Nobel Prize winner Octavio Paz (1985, pp. 29–46) said, "It is impossible not to notice the resemblance between the figure of *macho* and the Spanish conquistador. This is the model—more mythical than real—that determines the images the Mexican people have of power. . . ." According to Marvin Goldwert (1983, p. vii) *machismo* has been and continues to be an especially "potent and historical force in Mexico," and regardless of his social position, "the macho is admired for his sexual prowess, action-orientation (both physical and verbal), and aggressiveness."

The concept of *macho* serves as a backdrop for male-female and family relations. Males are assumed to be biologically, intellectually, and socially superior to females. Although the latter are sometimes put on a pedestal (e.g., the woman during courtship, a man's mother), they are less valued (Goldwert, 1983). Anthropologist Oscar Lewis (1961) related *macho* behavior to social class. In the middle classes it is typically expressed in terms of sexual conquest and the Don Juan complex, whereas in the lower class it is more often manifested in terms of heroism and the absence of physical fear.

The feminine counterpart to *machismo* is *hembrismo,* the amplification and exaggeration of traits associated with women such as weakness and passivity in dealing with men (Bermudez, in Penalosa, 1968). Another manifestation is the "undercover power" of the self-sacrificing woman who does everything for her family. In this case, power in Mexican families may be shared more equitably, or the scales may even be tipped in favor of the wife. So while men are undoubtedly and overwhelmingly the dominant gender, they are not always undisputed masters of the household.

In 1975 Hawkes and Taylor examined the familial power structure of seventy-six Mexican and Mexican American farm labor families living in California-operated migrant camps. In 62 percent of marriages power was shared equitably between husband and wife and in 20 percent the wife was semidominant (17 percent) or dominant (3 percent). Either *machismo* had been mitigated by "changing human conditions" without "public and scientific awareness" (p. 811), or it is not as pervasive or strong in these families as previously believed.

Mexico is overwhelmingly a Roman Catholic country, and the Church has played an important role in its history since the colonial period when it owned as much as one-third of the country's land. "Catholicism was the very bone and marrow of the emerging Mexican nation" (Whalen, 1971, p. 353), and continues to be an important influence for individuals as well as in local and national politics. Alan Riding (1989) noted that although the people in general are not devout Catholics (particularly in urban areas where church attendance is falling), most still have strong religious beliefs, customs, and superstitions. In rural areas the local priest, often referred to as *el padrecito* ("the little father"), is a powerful figure influencing women who seek his advice and men in the orchestration of local religious festivals.

The Church is important also because it continues to foster a traditional male-female relationship that endorses *machismo* (Riding, 1989). Males are dominant and to be obeyed, whereas females are expected to be modest and gentle in the image of Mexico's patron the Virgin of Guadalupe. Church teachings function to legitimate male authority: "an obedient woman is a good woman, while an independent woman must somehow be motivated by some sinful intention" (Riding, 1989, p. 242). Women's indifference to the Church is evident, however, in the number who practice birth control and the thousands who have abortions each year.

Values concerning the family, *machismo,* and religion are rooted in Mexico's colonial past and have had a profound effect on the daily life of its people for almost 500 years. But societies are not static. Rather, they are dynamic entities continually changing as a result of both internal and external pressure. History suggests that as Mexico modernizes the extended family will become less important, *machismo* will be challenged by women seeking gender equality, and the role of the Catholic Church will diminish as a more urban, industrial society becomes increasingly secular in its world view.

These changes will also affect the country's political and economic institutions. A decline in *machismo* coupled with a push toward gender equality means that more women would receive an education and eventually compete for jobs with men in a country that has high unemployment. As more women vote, the traditionally male-dominated power structure in all of the nation's political parties would have to reassess their policies as they affect women, as well as incorporate more females into the political system. As we will see in chapter 10, as the education of women increases, the number of children they have decreases. Coupled with the declining influence of a conservative Catholic Church, the move toward gender equality could help reduce Mexico's rate of population growth.

DISCUSSION QUESTIONS

1. Why is the family so important in Mexico?
2. What is the custom of *compadrazgo*? Has this practice been affected by modernization? Explain.
3. What is *machismo*? What effect does it have on family life and relationships? Is there a "cult of masculinity" in the United States as well? What forms does it take?
4. What is *hembrismo*? Is there a counterpart to this phenomenon in the United States? Explain.
5. How does the Catholic Church affect life in Mexico?
6. You are a foreign correspondent living and working in Mexico City in the year 2000. Write a *brief* article evaluating the current state of machismo and the family in Mexican society. (Speculate on the changes that will take place affecting people's behavior.)
7. A person traveling in Mexico or any other foreign nation for the first time is likely to experience some level of culture shock. Give an example of culture shock you have experienced, or relate an incident of this phenomenon you saw in a movie or have read about.

FOCUS ON
J A P A N

JAPANESE VALUES: YOU GOTTA HAVE *WA*

The most salient values in Japanese society are hard work, *wa* (harmony), and a "shame" culture. These values in and of themselves are not unique to Japan. However, the combination of the three as they are believed and practiced by the Japanese has led to a distinct national character, a character largely responsible for the nation's postwar economic success.

In her classic work *The Chrysanthemum and the Sword*, anthropologist Ruth Benedict (1946) characterized Japan as a shame culture. People do their *giri* ("duty") and meet their *on* ("obligations") not only because they believe it is right and proper to do so, but also because they fear being dishonored and disgraced. Failure to comply with the norms of a given situation may subject one to embarrassment and the loss of face, and in a society as group-oriented and status conscious as Japan, the almost ever-present threat of loss of face can be a powerful mechanism of social control. Takie Sugiyama Lebra (1976) argued that the more status conscious a person is, the more vulnerable he or she is to shame. This concern for not acting in a dishonorable way partially explains why relatively little intragroup conflict exists in Japan. According to Lebra (1976, p. 220), "it is just as shameful to embarrass another person as to be embarrassed by one."

In Western societies like the United States, where children are more likely to be taught absolute standards of morality (e.g., the Ten Commandments), people learn to feel guilty if they fail to do what is expected of them. Benedict (1946) noted that in a "guilt culture" a person "can get relief by unburdening himself" of wrongdoing. By literally confessing one's sins (for Catholics), seeing a therapist, or talking to a friend, an individual can remove the accumulated guilt of sinning or breaking the rules.

Where shame is the major sanction, however, a person does not experience any relief when faults are confessed. On the contrary, confessing only increases the chances that word of one's transgression will be made public. Shame cultures like Japan rely on the threat of external sanctions for nonconforming behavior, whereas guilt cultures are geared to an internalized notion of sin.

After the publication of the *The Chrysanthemum and the Sword,* Benedict was severely criticized both inside and outside Japan for labeling that nation a shame culture. Many Japanese believed her characterization of them was untrue and were highly insulted. Psychologist Lebra (1976) defended Benedict by stating that labeling is a first step in understanding anything at all: "The question What is X? can begin to be answered only by giving X a name" (p. 1). He found no evidence to indicate Benedict used shame culture to denigrate the Japanese intentionally. It is also important to note that Benedict never considered shame and guilt to be mutually exclusive concepts in Japan or any other society. She stated, "Shame is an increasingly heavy burden in the United States," whereas people in Japan "sometimes react as strongly as any Puritan to a private accumulation of guilt." In Japan, however, the emphasis "falls on the importance of shame rather than on the importance of guilt" (Benedict, 1946, p. 222).

A second core value in Japan involves the related concepts of hard work, self-discipline, and diligence. The emphasis on individual drive and hard work is something the Japanese share with other peoples of East Asia, the Chinese, Koreans, and Vietnamese. The Japanese are proud of their diligence and consider it one of their most outstanding virtues (Reischauer, 1988). This cluster of virtues related to effort and achievement is especially evident in the way they play baseball, which was introduced to the islands by an American missionary in 1873. They have a passion for the game on both the amateur and professional levels. Over the past few years baseball has showcased important cultural differences between that country and the United States. Robert Whiting (1989) argued that Americans play baseball but the Japanese work at it, approaching the game as if it were an assembly-line job at an automobile factory.

Suishu Tobita, "the god of Japanese baseball," who died in 1965 stated, "If the players do not try so hard as to vomit blood in practice, then they cannot hope to win games" (Whiting, 1989, p. 38). Not surprisingly Tobita's system is known throughout the country as "death training." Whereas American clubs prepare for the season in the spring sunshine of Florida and Arizona, Japanese professional teams typically start training in the snow and cold of mid-January. The players practice seven hours a day, then run ten miles, and finish the day with evening meetings. One American who played in Japan for five years said that spring training "makes boot camp look like a church social." During the season practice is cut to only four hours a day. People in the West are likely to view these practices as excessive, if not fanatical, but the Japanese believe that "only through endless training can one achieve the unity of mind and body necessary to excel" (Whiting, 1989, p. 60).

In the United States we tend to approach a task or game with the idea of working hard and gradually acquiring proficiency. In Japan people think more in terms of conquering self as a precondition to success. This can be accomplished by pushing oneself to the limits of mental and physical endurance. In a country where passing a nationwide entrance exam and getting into the best universities is the goal of millions of students (and their parents), one piece of folk wisdom states, "Sleep five hours, pass. Sleep six hours, fail." Another saying advises, "Sleep four hours, pass. Sleep five hours, fail" (Bonhaker, 1990, p. 189).

Pushing oneself to the limit is not confined to athletes and students. Thomas Rohlen (1986) participated in a training program—boot camp for 120 new bank employees. Training sessions were carried out six days a week, for ten to sixteen hours a day, and lasted three months. Another Japanese company sends its recruits on a four-day survival test in which young men and women dropped off on an uninhabited island with limited amounts of food must endure cool spring nights without tents and sleeping bags (Nishimura, 1991).

Once on the job, young company workers must learn to toil long hours for extended periods of time if they are to be considered *kaisha senshi* ("corporate warriors"). To be able to work sixty-hour weeks all year long (often with no vacation), Japanese employees drink vitamin mixtures laced with caffeine and nicotine. One ad for such a product in this $700 million a year business asks, "Can you keep fighting for twenty-four hours?" (Helm, 1991).

Karoshi ("death from overwork") is a hot social and political issue in Japan. Victims of overwork, the number of whom some believe may run into the thousands annually, are typically managers and supervisors in their forties and fifties. They are known in their companies as *sha-fa* ("fanatical workers") and *yoi kigyo senshi* ("good company soldiers") (Yates, 1990). In one well-publicized case a *karoshi* victim worked one hundred hours of overtime each month for a year. The week of his death he worked eighty-nine hours, including thirty-five and a half hours in the final forty-eight hours of his life (Yates, 1990).

Like other Asian people, the Japanese are concerned with maintaining harmony, or *wa,* in social relations and minimizing conflict and disruption. This is one reason why their baseball teams often play for ties rather than victories. The president of the Pacific League stated that ties were "suited for the Japanese character. That way nobody loses" (in Whiting, 1989, p. 25). *Wa* is often disrupted by American athletes in Japan who bring their "bad" habits with them. When calls go against American players they often scream and kick dirt at the umpire, and throw bats and helmets on the field. The Japanese find this "let it all hang out" and "do your own thing" mentality highly offensive and disruptive of a team's *wa* (Whiting, 1989, p. 85). In 1988 an American player left the Hanshin Tigers to be with his son who was undergoing an operation for a brain tumor in San Francisco. When the player postponed his return for a month the Tigers released him, saying he would no longer be of use to the team after a prolonged absence. From a Western perspective such drastic action seems insensitive and heartless. But no Japanese player would have abandoned his teammates and disturbed their *wa.* "In the corporate nation that is Japan, the company always comes first, even before a family crisis" (Whiting, 1989, pp. 302–303).

The emphasis on harmony is one of the reasons so few disputes end up in Japanese courts. The United States has approximately twice the population of Japan and thirty times as many lawyers. Taking someone to court is absolutely the last resort in a society where social harmony is so important; litigation is viewed as a breach of a community's *wa* (Christopher, 1983). This reluctance to be involved in civil suits is also held by companies in Japan, many of which do not even have corporate attorneys. In the United States it would be virtually impossible to engage in business without lawyers. This cultural difference causes problems between American and Japanese executives. In the United States business deals are negotiated, or "hammered out," with both parties signing on the dotted line. In Japan business is more personal, and deals are concluded after lengthy sessions when individuals get to know each other and establish rapport. Reischauer (1988, pp. 338–339) noted that the "importance of personal respect and trust cannot be overemphasized in any explanation of how Japanese big business works." Personal relationships "precede legally binding agreements which merely spell out the details." Whiting (1989) captured this attitude in the title of his book on Japanese baseball, *You Gotta Have* Wa.

Karel van Wolferen (1990) was highly critical of the cultural values explanation of Japanese behavior. Values such as *wa* and hard work are often excuses for the systematic exploitation of people throughout society. He rejected the notion that the Japanese have no motives other than those implanted in them by their culture, as if they were all enslaved by some "national autonomous nervous system" (p. 246). For example, the fact that people routinely settle disputes among themselves as opposed to going to court has much more to do with the Justice Ministry strictly limiting the number of judges and lawyers in the country than the nation collectively holding *wa* in high regard. As a result, litigation can drag on for years, and in some cases decades. The legal system also appears to be stacked against plaintiffs, whether they are suing a government agency or a giant corporation. When men work so long and hard that they only see their children on weekends and die prematurely, explanations are typically given in terms of cultural values such as loyalty and duty. In reality, a significant number of these long hours and the amount of hard work (be they in the office or on a baseball diamond) are a function of the tremendous power gap between employers and employees. The latter have little choice but to do as they are told.

Regardless of whether Japan's economic success is the result of a strong work ethic or the product of forty-five years of systematic exploitation, how much longer can this prosperity continue in a nation beginning to feel the pain of *karoshi?* This issue could be a turning point in a more affluent, relaxed era, when young people are somewhat less inclined to believe that any obstacle can be overcome if only one works hard enough. Some older Japanese feel values like hard work and self-discipline that made the nation strong are already beginning to erode (Reischauer, 1988). The stage may be set for intergenerational as well as political conflict as young people become just as dedicated to spending money as they are to making it . Although maintaining *wa* may be a core value of considerable importance in Japan, demonstrations, strikes, and even violent confrontations between police and protesters are hardly unknown. The central question is whether a change in these values will result in behavioral alterations that transform Japan's economic and political institutions.

Discussion Questions

1. What is a shame culture and how does it apply to Japan?
2. Are shame cultures more effective than guilt cultures in controlling people's behavior? Explain.
3. Compare and contrast the work ethics in Japan and the United States. What would motivate you to work one hundred hours of overtime each month? Money? Status? Fame?
4. What is *wa* and what part does it play in both personal and business relationships in Japan?

5. Karel van Wolferen was highly critical of *wa* as an all-encompassing explanation for hard work, dedication, and harmony in Japanese society. Explain the basis of his criticism.
6. Go to the library and gather material on the core values of one of the newly industrializing Asian countries: South Korea, Hong Kong, Singapore, and Taiwan. Compare and contrast these core values with those of Japan and the United States.

Chapter Summary

1. Culture is a people's way of life or social heritage that includes values, norms, institutions, and artifacts that are passed from generation to generation by learning alone. Culture provides members of a society with a world-taken-for-granted.

2. Instincts are biologically inherited predispositions that cause members of a species to react to a given stimulus in a given, specific way. Human beings have biological drives that are experienced as bodily tensions leading to activity that restores balance. These drives can be satisfied in a variety of ways, which makes cultural diversity possible and inevitable.

3. Sociobiologists argue that although human beings do not have instincts, some forms of behavior like altruism and aggression are transmitted genetically from one generation to another.

4. Human beings communicate through language—a set of sounds and symbols that have arbitrary meanings. These meanings can be arranged into an almost infinite number of combinations to convey information.

5. The three major theories of how children learn to speak are the imitation perspective, the reinforcement theory, and the innateness hypothesis.

6. According to the Sapir-Whorf hypothesis, language furnishes the categories by which people interpret and make sense of the physical and social world in which they live.

7. Language also reflects and helps reinforce power relationships in society. George Orwell noted that it can diminish people's thought processes by hiding and misinterpreting information. In this sense language is an important mechanism of social control in society.

8. Popular culture is the culture of everyday life as expressed through sport, movies, television, books, magazines, and so on. Sociologists use it as a vehicle for understanding the values, norms, and patterns of behavior of subcultures and the larger society. Popular culture also reflects a society's changing values and attitudes.

9. Core values are values especially promoted by and central to the life of a given culture. Some of the most important ones in the United States are success, progress, freedom, and patriotism. The extent to which people adhere to these values is a function of race and ethnicity, social class, and individual experience. People in the lower class may stretch or modify success values so they can be more easily achieved.

10. All societies regulate people's behavior through a system of norms. The hierarchy of norms from least to most important is folkways, mores, and laws. Whereas folkways should be followed, mores must be obeyed.

11. Functionalist sociologists see norms originating as a result of group consensus, whereas conflict theorists think that norms are created by the most powerful groups in society and used to dominate politically and exploit economically the lower classes.

12. Ethnocentrism is the tendency to view one's group and way of life as superior to the values and behavior of others. Ethnocentrism promotes social cohesion and a sense of "we-ness." In extreme forms it can result in prejudice, discrimination, and even war. According to cultural relativism, any aspect of a culture can be judged only within the context of that culture. The problem with this perspective is that any behavior (genocide, for example) can be rationalized and justified.

13. Culture shock is the experience of initially encountering people who do not share one's core values and overall world view. The shock of such an experience is usually a painful reminder that values and norms can vary considerably from one culture to another.

14. All of us belong to a number of subcultures, groups that have norms and values in common with the larger society, but also have some of their own patterns of behaviors. Countercultures reject some or all aspects of the larger, more dominant culture. Because they are opposed to some core values of the larger society, they are often associated with violence either as perpetrators or victims.

15. The values, norms, patterns of behavior, and institutions of individual societies are integrated to a certain extent. However, this integration is far from complete, as societies are continually changing and often experience internal strife.

16. Some primitive groups change very slowly, whereas modern, industrial states do so much more rapidly. Change is typically uneven in industrial nations as some aspects of a society (such as technology), develop at a faster rate than people's values and behavior. According to William Ogburn, cultural lag is the process whereby one aspect of the culture changes faster than another aspect of the culture to which it is related.

3

GROUPS AND SOCIAL STRUCTURE

Anyone who has ever had the pleasure of attending a plastic-wares or laundry products party hosted by a friend or relative is familiar with a concept known as "the ice-breaker." This little device is some exercise or game, often a silly one, designed to loosen people up and get them in the mood for the important events (the selling of products) that will follow.

Experienced instructors of introductory sociology sometimes start off a new semester, especially in freshman-level classes, with their own version of the ice-breaker. In this case, the exercise is designed to give students an opportunity to learn something about each other and the content of the course, and to get them used to participating in class discussions. It provides a gentle mechanism for easing students into the sometimes abstract work to come throughout the term.

Although not originally developed for this particular purpose, one ice-breaker that has proved useful is a questionnaire entitled "Who Am I?" Students are given a sheet of paper with twenty statements, each beginning with the phrase "I am . . . ." They are instructed to complete each of the statements with some piece of important information describing themselves. When everyone has finished, they share the descriptions with their classmates who, with the guidance of the instructor, discuss and interpret the meanings of specific responses.

Assuming that they take the exercise seriously, students' responses to these statements are predictable. One major category of replies, for instance, consists of personal characteristics relating to individual identity or state of being—"I am female"; "I am twenty years old"; "I am usually very happy." A second typical response involves what could be called social attributes, that is, characteristics that define the individual in relation to other individuals: "I am a sociology major"; "I am the oldest of three children"; "I am a single parent." It is this kind of response that is of particular interest to sociologists.

Most individuals respond to the "Who Am I?" exercise with a large proportion of these social attribute descriptions, thus reflecting a basic observation of sociology: *human beings are social creatures who lead their lives in the company of other humans.* Whether by nature or necessity, for better or worse, most people spend each day eating, drinking, studying, working, playing, praying, and in general being with other people.

Sociologists take this observation one step further. We maintain that the affiliations and relationships individuals develop with others play a critical part in their respective lives. Most individuals are part of larger groups such as families, work teams, and religious congregations. In turn, these groups are part of larger social organizations such as clans, corporations, and religions that, together, form a social structure. These groups and structures are tremendously important in shaping not only the conditions of our individual everyday lives, but the outlines of our personal identities. In large measure, they provide the answers to the question of who and what we are.

Questions to Consider

1. What is the role of culture in the creation of human social structure?
2. How do social groups differ from aggregates and categories?
3. What is the difference between formal role and role performance?
4. How does role strain differ from role conflict?
5. What is the difference between a membership group and a reference group?
6. Why do primary groups have such a lasting impact on their members?
7. What factors make the social dyad the most fragile of all human social groups?
8. How does increasing group size affect relations among group members?
9. What is the difference between a utilitarian organization and a coercive organization?
10. According to Max Weber, what are the distinguishing features of bureaucratic organization?
11. What is an informal organization?
12. In what ways does the Japanese formal organization differ from the traditional bureaucracy?
13. What are gemeinschaft and gesellschaft?
14. According to Lenski, how have changes in productive technology affected human-societal organization?

THE CONCEPT OF SOCIAL STRUCTURE

As we observed in chapter 1, human social life in general is organized rather than chaotic, just as individuals' behaviors are stable rather than random. In every population, daily events seem to follow some pattern that is logical (i.e., makes sense) to the members of the particular society. This makes it possible for people to predict and anticipate what others are likely to do or say in a given situation. Using these predictions, individuals can plan their own actions accordingly.

What makes for the possibility of an organized social life in which the behaviors of millions of individuals coordinate smoothly is a shared way of looking at the world. As we tried to demonstrate in the last chapter, over a period of time the members of all human populations develop sets of values, beliefs, and norms that reflect their common experiences with the surrounding world. These cultural systems give people a framework for observing and interpreting reality, and a foundation for successfully dealing with one another. Within a given population, the formation of groups of different kinds, as well as the various patterned relationships that take place within and among these groups—what we term **social structure**—reflects the presence of an underlying, unifying culture.

Social structure represents the attempts of a population to translate its particular view of the world into concrete terms. For example, in a culture whose beliefs define anatomical differences as insignificant, social practices encourage both women and men to pursue occupations according to their individual interests and abilities, without regard to their sex. Female police officers and male airline flight attendants may be just as common as male construction workers and female nurses. However, cultures whose beliefs define females and males as intellectually, mentally, and morally different are likely to exhibit occupational structures in which women and men are channeled into different kinds of jobs on the basis of their sex. In these societies, preserving law and order may be a man's job, and serving coffee, tea, and milk a woman's.

Whereas culture provides the members of a population with a blueprint for reality, social structure represents the rendering of that blueprint into some sort of inhabitable residence. The linkage between culture and social structure is much more complex than a simple one-way cause-and-effect relationship. Culture supplies the important backdrop against which organized social life is constructed. It lays out the pattern for assembling the different groups that will form the building blocks of social structure.

GROUPS AND OTHER COLLECTIVITIES

In ordinary language usage, the word "group" conjures up an image of numbers. We talk about such things as a group of pedestrians waiting to cross a busy intersection, the particular group of taxpayers who will benefit the most from recent tax law changes; the group of friends with whom we share a summer rental house at the beach. In each case, what we have in mind is some situation with several people. The specific numbers can vary anywhere from two (a couple in love) to more than 250 million (the estimated population of the United States in 1990). However else these groups may differ from one another, they all include more than one person.

As we have already seen, the study of human groups is the central focus of sociology; however, when sociologists talk of groups, we use the word in a much more restrictive way than other people. The term that would properly apply to the three examples described above, as well as any general circumstance featuring more than one person, is **social collectivity.** From the sociological perspective, all social groups are examples of collectivities, but not all collectivities are groups.

For example, the collection of pedestrians waiting to cross a busy intersection represents an **aggregate.** Members of social aggregates share the same physical space at a particular time, but not necessarily anything else. As in the case of pedestrians in a crowded city, the individuals who make up an aggregate may be very different from one another in terms of race, gender, religion, age, social class, personality, and other characteristics. They may have little or nothing in common besides their physical proximity. They constitute a social collectivity only for as long as they remain bunched together at that intersection. When the light changes and the individuals disperse, the aggregate ceases to exist.

In a similar way, the taxpayers who benefit the most from some new provision in the income tax laws do not constitute a group in the sociological sense of the word. Rather, they make up what is called a **category,** a number of people who share some common characteristic(s). In this example, they share a particular income level—and perhaps skilled tax accountants. By itself, the fact that these people have a similar economic background tells us nothing at all about whether they ever did or ever will occupy the same physical space at the same time. They exist as a collectivity on paper only, that is, as a statistical cluster based on one particular attribute. If we were to focus our attention on some other attribute (e.g., religious affiliation), the category would dissolve as its members were sorted into new statistical clusters.

Of the three examples given above, only the third, the collection of vacationing friends, represents a group in the sociological sense. **Group** refers to a number of people who possess a feeling of common identity and who interact in a regular, patterned way. To the extent that these friends think of themselves as a group and do things together (eat, party, pay the rent), they form an authentic social group. Social groups display the characteristics of both aggregates and categories; their members often share space and time, and usually share attributes or interests as well. As their members continue to interact with one another, groups develop additional traits that distinguish them from either aggregates or categories. Over time, these relationships come to form an organization or structure involving statuses and roles.

Status and Role

Status is another concept that sociologists employ in a different way than nonsociologists. In ordinary usage, status implies some sort of social ranking or level of prestige. For example, we speak of high-status cars, or of certain people as being very status conscious. In making these statements, what we really are saying is that such and such an automobile is associated with wealth and power. The people who drive this make of car are important and "classy." Someone who is known to be status conscious is perceived as being very concerned with money, fame, or other trappings of social rank. (Social class and rank are discussed in chapter 5.)

In sociological usage, however, status simply means any defined or recognized position within a group or society. For example, an individual's status in the corporation that employs her may be that of accounts payable officer; some other person's status may be that of customer relations specialist. When used this way, the word does not carry any connotations that one position is higher or better than the other. All that really is being implied is that one position is different from the other.

What makes one defined status different from another is the role—the set of expected behaviors and attitudes—associated with them. The **role** (or **formal role**) defines what it is that someone who occupies a particular position is supposed to do. For example, because you are a student, you are expected to attend classes, complete reading and writing assignments on time, take examinations, and do the other things that make up student life. Your instructor, on the other hand, is expected to perform the duties of a professor: to offer interesting and informative lectures, construct equitable examinations, grade students objectively and fairly, be available for student advising during office hours, and so on. Whereas status indicates the different recognized positions within a group or larger social body, role defines how and why these positions are different from one another.

Of course, the fact that people are supposed to behave a certain way doesn't necessarily guarantee that they will or can. In an imperfect world, not everyone can be the perfect student or the perfect professor. Sociologists recognize that formal roles define "the best of all possible worlds" with respect to what the holders of individual statuses should be like. We use the concept of **role performance** to indicate an individual's actual behaviors and attitudes in response to expectations. For a number of reasons, some of which are discussed in detail in chapter 8, these everyday behaviors of real people may not always resemble the idealized actions specified by their social roles.

Formal role expectations often require behaviors that are complex and difficult enough so that carrying them out becomes problematic. For example, in this culture, prevailing beliefs define adult married males as "the breadwinners" in their families, even if their spouses also are working full time. For any number of reasons, however, some men are not able to find the kind of employment that would allow them to provide a comfortable life for their families. To the extent that they have accepted and internalized the assumption that they should be the ones to take care of their wives and children, they likely will experience what sociologists call **role strain**—inability to meet successfully all the expectations attached to a particular social role. Even if their unemployment or underemployment is the result of factors beyond their personal control (e.g., a factory shutdown, job discrimination against their particular racial or ethnic group) the men may feel ashamed that they are letting their families down.

Individuals also can experience difficulty in meeting role requirements by virtue of the fact that they occupy several different statuses at the same time, and may be expected to perform behaviors that are incompatible. For example, one of the things you are at this point in your life is a student, but it is not the only thing you are. You also may be a full-time employee, a spouse, and a parent. Your professor expects you to be a good student and be well prepared for next Tuesday night's midterm examination, and your employer expects you to be a good worker and put in overtime hours taking stock inventory that same night. Just to make life even more complicated, you may find that your husband and kids expect you to be a good wife/mother and be home for the special birthday celebration they have planned for Tuesday evening.

Congratulations! You have just experienced **role conflict,** being caught in the middle of the clashing role expectations that often accompany the multiple group memberships and statuses we hold in our social world. Unless you have mastered the art of being in several different places at the same time, you will have to violate one or more sets of expectations in order to satisfy the other. It is probably not a very comforting thought to know that, in a complex, modern society like the United States, many other people also find themselves between this proverbial rock and a hard place.

The moral of this story is that organized social life is much more than merely a case of individual persons being plugged into statuses and then carrying out the directives of the associated roles. People's actual behaviors represent attempts to negotiate a working relationship with the demands of the larger structure of which they are a part. Statuses and roles may outline the structure of our social world, but they do not absolutely determine it. Groups envelop individuals but normally do not smother them. As we will see, many groups both permit and encourage the free expression of individuality by their members. Even in the most highly structured and depersonalized groups, the possibilities for human individuality are not altogether stifled.

 ## TYPES OF SOCIAL GROUPS

Modern societies like the United States and Japan are characterized by complex, highly differentiated structures as well as populations numbering in the tens or hundreds of millions. They also display an astonishingly large variety of social groups. Trying to understand the nature and workings of these groups on a case-by-case basis would be impossible. Consequently, sociologists have attempted to simplify the task by simplifying the social world.

Rather than treating each group as a specific entity, we employ typologies that allow us to focus our attention on different kinds of groups. These **typologies** are ordering systems that sort and classify individual groups on the basis of distinguishing characteristics. In effect, they create groups of groups, permitting us to examine both the common and the uncommon denominators of group life. Several of these typologies are of particular significance in the analysis of groups.

Membership Groups and Reference Groups

One way of distinguishing among the various groups that make up our social environment is the nature of our involvement with them. The term **membership group** or "ingroup" (Sumner, 1960, original 1906) refers to a specific group in which certain individuals belong and participate as members. For example, the softball team on which a person plays third base is, for that person, a membership group. The members of the team meet on a regular basis for batting and fielding practice and, of course, for games against other teams in the same league. Over the course of the season, the members of the team likely will come to develop a sense of group identity and a feeling of belonging based on their shared experiences. They may begin to think of themselves as "we" and the rest of the world—what Sumner (1960/1906) called "outgroups"—as "they."

Sociologists regard these membership groups as important because they help us understand and perhaps predict people's behaviors and attitudes. All groups establish some pattern of norms, values, beliefs, and behaviors, and they expect and demand that their members will follow it. Individuals' membership group affiliations thus provide us with a great deal of information about what they will be like. Within limits, people will do and be what the important membership groups in their life specify. For example, the knowledge that a particular young man is a Bible College student, a charismatic Chris-

Members of groups interact in a regular, patterned way and come to consider themselves a unit. For the Soviet Olympic gymnastics team pictured here, this sense of identity and belonging may be a necessary condition for the successful attainment of group goals.

tian, and a founder of his school's "Robertson for President in 1992" chapter tells us something. It gives us the ability to construct a behavioral and attitudinal profile that will capture the spirit of who and what this individual is, even though we might not know him individually and personally. In this particular case, the experienced sociologist could safely discount the possibility that he would stop by the local topless bar for a few cold beers after marching in the afternoon lesbian and gay-rights parade.

Sometimes, however, even experienced sociologists are fooled. People can and do often act in ways that are unexpected, given their membership group affiliations. For instance, the Christian student could well have a very liberal attitude regarding differences in sexual preference, despite his otherwise conservative credentials. We might discover that he is a war veteran whose life was saved during combat by a fellow soldier who happened to be gay. Astonished to learn of his rescuer's "deviant" sexual orientation but knowing him to be a decent human being, our student had done some homework on the question. The result was a reexamining of his own prejudices and actions toward homosexuals.

The hypothetical student's surprising attitude could not be explained in terms of his membership group linkages alone. On the contrary, if anything, knowing his objective group ties would lead to the opposite conclusion. His feelings about gay people could be understood only by recognizing his subjective identification with those elements of society who believe that people should be treated equally and judged individually, rather than by categorical labels such as "sexual deviant." Although not himself a member of any liberal group like the American Civil Liberties Union, the student perhaps is using this organization as a **reference group,** whose values, norms, beliefs, and behaviors serve as the basis for one's daily life.

For the most part, individuals' membership groups and reference groups are one and the same. As we have already stated, all groups exert pressure on their members to conform to their norms and values. As we will see in the next chapter, most individuals internalize their membership groups' perspectives, incorporating them into their own developing world views. However, on many occasions membership groups and reference groups are not the same entities. For example, people who are in the process of preparing for some future social status often adopt the perspective and behaviors of this sought-after group before they actually gain admission to it, a phenomenon known as **anticipatory socialization.** In the law school parking lot at a certain local university, for instance, is a car that has both a student parking sticker and a personalized license plate adorning the rear bumper. The license plate—SUE THEM—indicates that at least one aspiring lawyer has started to think the part. Similarly, some students in the university's NROTC program have been known to sport "top gun" flight jackets and sunglasses well before their graduation and commissioning.

At any given moment, then, individuals' behaviors and attitudes reflect the perspectives both of the groups in which they participate objectively as members, and the reference groups with which they identify subjectively, perhaps as would-be members. As we will see, the nature of these objective and subjective groups has a great deal to do with the resulting orientations and actions of their respective members.

Primary Groups and Secondary Groups

Although it may be true, as the U.S. Constitution states, that all people are created equal, the same thing cannot be said of social groups. From your own experiences you may realize that some groups (the friends with whom you picnic on the weekend) are occasions for unwinding and just being yourself. Others (your community's town or city council) are no-nonsense vehicles for getting some specific job done. Some groups (the people who show up on Saturday morning for a game of pickup basketball) just seem to develop or happen over time; others (the Board of Directors of the International Widgit Corporation) are deliberately and carefully created. Some groups (the regular Monday night football and pizza crew) are enjoyable and fun to be part of; others (a jury in a prolonged criminal trial) may represent nobody's idea of a good time.

One of the first sociologists to draw these kinds of distinctions was Charles Horton Cooley, an important figure at the University of Chicago during the first few decades of this century. As we saw in chapter 1, Cooley was interested in the process of human social interaction and its effects on individuals' perceptions of reality. He regarded involvement in group relations as a critical mechanism for the social learning that gives humans a sense of their world and of their own humanity.

In looking at the connection between group involvement and human social learning or socialization (discussed in chapter 4), Cooley (1909) focused on the impact of what he called **primary groups.** These are groups like the family in which individuals typically have their first social experiences and receive their first important lessons about social reality. Primary groups also are essential in the formation of individual self-identity. It is through continuous and close interaction with primary groups that individuals begin to develop a self-concept, a notion of who and what they are in relation to the world.

Cooley determined that primary groups have such an important and lasting impact on their members because of the nature of the relationships that occur within them (see Table 3.1). The members, like families, are bound together in warm emotional

TABLE 3.1 Characteristics of Primary and Secondary Group Relationships

Primary Group (families, close friends)	Secondary Group (tax accountant, clients)
Total personality involvement	Segmented personality involvement
Emotional warmth	Emotional coolness
Spontaneity, informality	Patterning, formality
Direct (face-to-face) contact	Indirect (non-face-to-face) contact
Smaller size	Larger size
Valued as end (intrinsic rewards)	Valued as means to end (extrinsic rewards)

relations. They interact as total or complete personalities, bringing with them to the relationship everything that is important about them. Families and other primary group members (e.g., close friends) know and care about each other as individuals, and identify strongly with one another. Their interactions often tend to be spontaneous, and usually involve face-to-face contact. Because of their emotionally supportive and satisfying atmosphere, these groups become valued by their members as ends in themselves. Families and friends seek each other out for the intrinsic or internal reward of being together.

In contrast, **secondary groups** (a term implied but not used by Cooley himself) are less inclusive, less emotional, more formalized groupings created and organized for some specific purpose. A certified public accountant and his clients is a good working illustration of this concept.

In this particular relationship, the members of the group are directed to some defined goal; the preparation of people's income tax returns, for example. Their interactions are limited to the issue at hand and typically follow established routines. The accountant may have a series of standard questions concerning expenses and deductions to ask the clients; the clients will have sets of financial documents and receipts to give to the accountant. Some appropriate pleasantries ("Nice to see you, how are you doing?") may be exchanged, but the real focus of the meeting is the exchange of information necessary to complete the client's tax return. The general subject of income tax liability and tax laws may generate any number of emotional responses from people, but the exchange of information between the accountant and the client will be done impersonally and factually, as will the eventual planning and preparation of the tax return.

To a large extent, members of secondary groups are interchangeable. They are not so much individuals as they are role players. Within limits, all properly trained tax accountants are capable of producing approximately the same tax return document. Within limits, all individual clients fall into some recognizable category of taxpayers, based on income level, job, mortgage expenses, and other relevant factors. The clients may choose from among any number of certified public accountants simply by paging through a telephone directory; accountants will deal with any given number of different clients during a busy income tax–preparation season.

Although the members of a secondary group may come to value their group experiences, the value lies in the group's utilitarian function, not in the relationship itself; that is, people find the group to be an important means to some other goal. Neither the tax accountant nor the client may like each other personally or care to be in one another's company for any length of time, but each benefits from their interaction. The client receives a tax return that minimizes income tax liability; the accountant earns a healthy fee for his professional services. These external or extrinsic rewards may be enough to bring the group members together again the same time next year.

Such formulations of primary and secondary groups represent what sociologists call **ideal types**—logical constructions that present, in exaggerated and idealized form, the distinguishing features of some phenomenon. In the real social world, groups exist as combinations of both primary and secondary group characteristics. Even in such primary groups as friends and lovers, relationships can take a more formalized, depersonalized turn (perhaps an indication that the relationship is cooling), and relationships in such secondary groups as large-scale formal organizations often become highly personal. In this context, the words *primary* and *secondary* should be thought of as representing the end points on a range of possibilities for social group relations, rather than valid empirical descriptions of specific groups.

Thus, we could envision a continuum or array, with different groups located along the continuum in terms of how "primary-like" or "secondary-like" their atmosphere and members' interactions appeared to be (see Figure 3.1). At one extreme, we might list groups such as parent and child, or lover and lover, that come very close to approximating the ideal formulation of primary groups. Here, individual identities and complete, emotion-based interactions reach their maximum level.

Moving over a bit, we might list groups such as first- or second-grade school classes. They manage to retain much of their personal, emotional atmosphere while introducing specifically defined goals and more formalized, secondary relationships.

Continuing, we might recognize larger groupings created for a specific purpose and exhibiting clearly defined status and role structures, but retaining something of a scaled-down, homey atmosphere. Small, family-owned businesses that pride themselves on their "friendly and personalized service" might be located here.

FIGURE 3.1 The Primary–Secondary Group Continuum

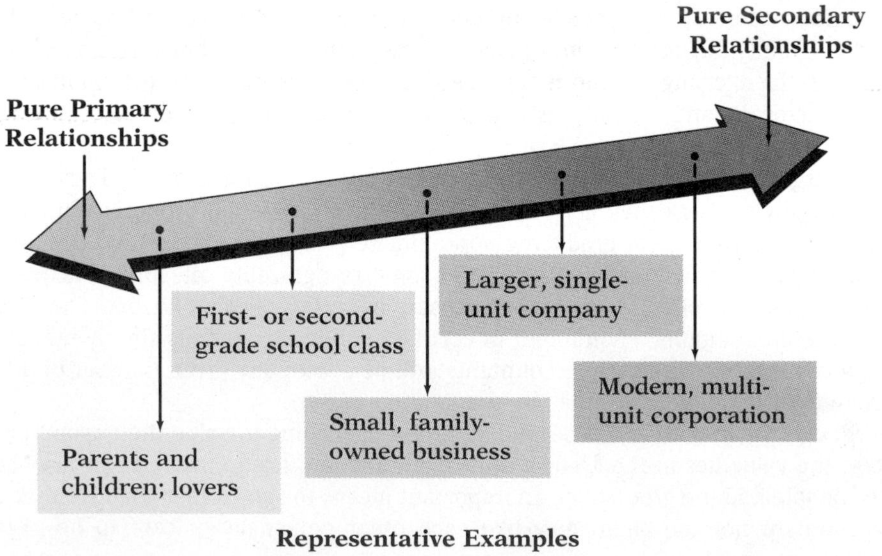

Pure Secondary Relationships

Pure Primary Relationships

Larger, single-unit company

First- or second-grade school class

Small, family-owned business

Modern, multi-unit corporation

Parents and children; lovers

Representative Examples

The larger, single-unit business firm might be our next stopping point, as we begin to move well into secondary group territory. With staff and employees numbering into the hundreds, workers can become interchangeable units, names rather than faces, and numbers rather than names.

Finally, at the other extreme, we might identify bodies such as modern multiple-unit corporations that seem to exhibit nothing but secondary group characteristics. These entities clearly exist for specific and defined objectives that are impersonal (economic profits). Interaction patterns are established through a set of corporate policies and directives, and individuals become and remain members on the basis of measurable skills, rather than personal identities or qualities. Participation is instrumental ("it's a job") and will end under clearly defined conditions (a better job offer, retirement, dismissal for a specified cause). However, as we will see shortly, even these gigantic groupings are not entirely devoid of primary undercurrents.

The Effects of Group Size   Although the relationship is far from perfect, sociologists have long noted a significant association between group size and the likelihood of primary-like or secondary-like relations. The classic work in this area is that of Georg Simmel (1858–1918), a German sociologist whose analysis of two-person and three-person social groups (1950, original 1908) triggered interest in what is now called group dynamics, or the sociology of small groups. Simmel was particularly interested in the effects of group size on the nature and the strength of the social bonds that formed between members.

According to Simmel, the **dyad,** or two-person group, is the most basic and intimate of all possible human groupings. It is in the dyad (e.g., that formed by married couples, two siblings, or two best friends) that personal identities and emotional relations are maximized, since only one linkage is possible between the members. The dyad is also special in the sense that it is the most fragile of social groups. Since it depends so heavily on the particular characteristics of the two people, if either one leaves the relationship the character of that group will be destroyed. Replacing one member with another creates an entirely new dyadic group, rather than a continuation of the old group. The dyad thus is the most mortal type of social group, existing only as long as its original members.

The addition of a third person to a dyadic relationship creates what Simmel termed a **triad.** The social triad marks the beginning of more complex social interaction patterns and the development of an identifiable group structure. Three relationships now are possible, and the addition of the newcomer qualitatively alters the previous direct bond that may have existed between the original pair. Think, for instance, of the effect that a developing love interest between one of two siblings or best friends and a third person would have on the original relationship. Very often, it seems, one of the parties begins to feel like the proverbial third wheel, experiencing a distinct change in the previous relation. Simmel in fact noted a strong tendency for triads to reform into a coalition of two members against the third, an observation that was confirmed by Theodore Caplow (1968). However, Simmel also examined other possible roles of the third person, including that of a mediator when relations between the other two became strained.

The addition of other members dramatically increases the number of linkages within the group. In turn, the rapidly expanding linkages create strong pressures to decrease personal relations and a movement toward more formal, role-defined, secondary involvement patterns. Larger group size makes it increasingly difficult to form primary-like relations with all the other members. A likely consequence is thus the creation of smaller, more intimate groups within groups. As we will see in the remaining sections of this chapter, the increasing size and complexity of societal populations has been linked historically to the qualitative change from primary to secondary relations at nearly all levels of group life.

Formal Organizations

In our everyday lives we routinely deal with a variety of special-purpose groups created to provide us with essential products and services. Our breakfast food probably came from the neighborhood branch of a regional or national supermarket chain. We prepare it using conventional, microwave, or toaster ovens manufactured by an electrical appliances company, as we watch the morning news on network television. Hopping into a vehicle mass-produced by one of the major domestic or foreign automobile companies, we head to our jobs in one of the large downtown firms that make up the local business sector. After work we may rush to our classes at the community college where we are completing general education courses before transferring to State University. As we drive along a freeway built and maintained by our state's transportation department, we are careful to keep an eye peeled for highway patrol or local police radar checks. No sense ending up in traffic court or traffic safety school again because of another speeding ticket!

These **formal organizations** are large, deliberately planned groups with established personnel, procedures, and rules for carrying out some particular objective or set of objectives (Scott, 1987). Producing reliable consumer goods, communicating important information, educating young adults, and developing mass transit systems are only a few such possible goals. In modern societies like the United States, formal organizations have come to dominate the social landscape. They absorb the time, energy, and resources of countless millions of individuals who interact with them as employees, clients, regulators, or competitors. Formal organizations are both indicators and consequences of the increasing rationalization and elaboration of contemporary social life.

Types of Formal Organizations

In an attempt to make their analytic tasks more feasible, students of formal organizations have constructed typologies of the various kinds found in modern societies. One of the best known of these classification systems was developed by sociologist Amitai Etzioni (1975), who distinguished among normative, coercive, and utilitarian organizations on the basis of their members' motives for participation.

Normative Organizations   Sometimes also referred to as voluntary associations, **normative organizations** include charitable and community service groups, as well as other public interest associations (e.g., United Way/CHAD, Rotary Club, Girl Scouts or Boy Scouts, youth sports leagues). People join them because they perceive their goals as being socially or morally worthwhile. The satisfaction they receive from participation is the sense of contributing to a good cause, rather than financial or other material payoffs. In this society, churches, schools, hospitals, and a host of other important social groupings historically have depended on the volunteer activities of their members.

Coercive Organizations   By way of contrast, this type of organization might be termed an involuntary association. **Coercive organizations** are formal organizations that force people to join and typically remove them from normal contact with the larger society for the duration of their membership. They also were described by Erving

Members of normative organizations, such as this group of Thai Boy Scouts, typically derive satisfaction from their sense of participating in socially or morally worthwhile activities. These voluntary associations are an important component of contemporary societies.

Goffman (1961) under the term "total institutions." Prisons and military boot camps are examples. As we will see in the next chapter, these organizations often are settings for a dramatic kind of adult social learning called resocialization.

Utilitarian Organizations   Etzioni's third type of formal organization, the **utilitarian organization,** attracts members who are seeking some sort of tangible, material benefit from their participation. People go to work for businesses, banks, or other corporations in order to make a living. Students enroll in universities to earn the degrees that will allow them to make a better living. Factory workers join labor unions to protect their rights and to give them better bargaining positions in their negotiations with management. Strictly speaking, membership in utilitarian organizations is voluntary rather than coerced. However, in modern societies in which most major societal activities have become specialized and elaborated, these organizations may be "the only game in town." People who want or need a job, an education, or protection of their interests may have little choice but to join one of the many economic, educational, political, or other utilitarian organizations that have come to define and dominate the social structure.

Bureaucratic Organization

The German sociologist Max Weber (1864–1930) was one of the first social scientists to offer a detailed analysis of formal organizations. He argued that the increasing complexity and division of labor in modern societies stimulates the development of patterned, formalized administrative procedures. These structures are necessary to coordinate the activities of the large groups that constitute the personnel in specialized units such as governments and businesses. Weber's systematic presentation of the principles and practices of administration (1946, original 1919) became a classic in the

The separation of complex activities into more specialized individual tasks is a hallmark of bureaucratic organization. Specific functions are assigned to designated bureaus or offices whose members are selected on the basis of technical expertise. Sometimes, however, the resulting compartmentalization can lead to a sense of isolation and a decrease in organizational efficiency.

field of formal organizational research not only in sociology, but in business management, education, and other related fields as well.

According to Weber, bureaucratic organization is the tool that promotes successful administration in modern society. He saw **bureaucracy** as a device for maximizing human efficiency through the logical, orderly structuring of individual behaviors within a particular setting. Reduced to its essentials, bureaucratic organization is a set of principles for matching people, procedures, and circumstances to produce the highest level of productivity possible. In its pure or ideal form, bureaucracy involves several elements.

1. The different jobs necessary to fulfill organizational goals are identified, and objective, standard procedures are established for each. Specific jobs are assigned to designated positions, which are grouped in offices or "bureaus." Each bureau is responsible for completing the set of tasks assigned to it.

2. Each bureau is provided with the authority, personnel, and other resources required to meet its assigned jobs. Positions are filled on the basis of talent and ability rather

than subjective, personal characteristics, and individuals are promoted on the basis of performances.

3. Individual bureaus are linked to one another through an established hierarchy of communications and decision-making channels. Each bureau is under the authority of, and reports to, the next higher bureau in the structure. The hierarchy defines the areas of responsibility and authority for each position in the organization.

4. Organizational norms govern interactions among members of the bureaucracy, as well as those between bureaucrats and the organization's clients or customers. All such interactions involve objective and impartial secondary relationships in which all members of a given category are treated alike.

5. A clear distinction is made between organizational life and personal life. Bureaucrats do not "own" their positions or the resources associated with them, nor do officials have authority over their subordinates in matters not related to organizational activities. Great care is taken to divorce objective, rational, goal-directed organizational concerns from the subjective, personal, and often emotional concerns of individuals.

In modern societies whose large populations are linked together in a variety of complex networks, many activities are too important to be left to chance. They require intelligent planning and coordination, and this is what bureaucracy is all about. It is hardly a coincidence that the overwhelming majority of our government, military, business, and most other private and public sector organizations are established and run according to the principles of bureaucratic organization. In a society that values and requires rational efficiency, bureaucracy can fill the bill.

Bureaucratic Shortcomings

If you have been reading this description of bureaucracy with a growing amount of skepticism, you are not alone. In the experience of many people, bureaucratic organization is associated with anything but smooth, efficient activity. Very often, it seems that little or nothing of substance actually is accomplished. Wheels spin, people move, memos fly, but nothing seems to come out the other end. Somewhere along the way, the theory of bureaucratic organization seems to have lost something in translation as it moved from the logical realm of the ideal-type formulation to the less than ideal realm of the empirical world.

For example, as part of his government's effort to secure the capital investments required to build economic stability in his country, Mexican President Carlos Salinas de Gortari has begun to slash some of that country's bureaucratic red tape. In the past, according to the chief financial executive of the Ministry of Commerce and Industrial Development, even relatively simple business transactions became hopelessly bogged down in the government bureaucracy. Starting up a business required 103 steps and, "The bureaucrats always hid the forms. Or they'd give out one form today, one the next day, and one the next. You never knew how many you needed" (in Lindquist, 1991, p. D-1).

Bureaucracies often seem slow and unable to respond to novel situations demanding rapid action. Because they view the world in terms of well-defined categories with clear-cut boundaries, they appear to grind to a halt when they are faced with people, things, or circumstances that don't fit recognized patterns. When certain phenomena do not clearly fall into any one office's area of responsibility they often become no one's responsibility. They can get lost—and stay lost—in the bureaucratic cracks. Bureaucrats

OURSELVES AND OTHERS
Bound by Red Tape

China's bureaucracy is easily the world's largest. Of the country's 543.3 million workforce, 9.71 million were classified as state and party officials at the end of 1988. By China's broad definition of a bureaucrat, or *guan*—someone with an administrative title who manages people or property on the state's behalf—there are 24 million state cadres—groups of bureaucrats—according to local press reports, which is an amazingly high ratio of bureaucrats to civilians.

The reach of the state today is more extensive than at any other time in Chinese history. As recently as the Qing dynasty in the late 19th century, some 2,000 civil and military officials governed a population of 450 million, albeit supported by a vast class of local gentry who acted as intermediaries between the government and the populace.

For much of China's imperial history, the civil administration consisted of six ministries. Today, the 50,000-staff state council—the government's nerve centre—employs three vice premiers, nine state councillors and a secretary-general and controls 41 ministries and commissions. There are also 19 "administrations," five "offices," 16 state bureaus, five institutes and 43 non-standing bodies. A similar, scaled-down organizational structure is replicated at the provincial, municipal, county and district levels.

Binding the millions of bureaucrats together is an elaborate ranking system based on the grade of salary and the housing, official limousines, access to classified information and even funeral services an official is entitled to receive. Within a ministry there are, in the formal order of rank, the grades of a general bureau, bureau, division and section. In a province or a municipality, grades descend from commission, provincial and prefectural departments.

Ministries and provinces are of equal rank, as are ministerial bureaus and provincial departments. Peking, Tianjin and Shanghai are the only municipalities which fully enjoy the rank of a province; others may be regarded as the equivalent of prefectural, county or sub-county units.

Most high officials have three formal ranks indicating their status—their formal government and party title, their position within the party and their civil service grade. Often, the party status is more significant than government rank as an indicator of real power.

In one sense, the entire society is organised as an enormous bureaucracy. Those without an administrative title or not attached to an administrative unit cannot hope to gain much access to information, material supplies and other resources. In order to set up a company, for example, the venture must be "hooked," as the Chinese say, to a *danwai* or unit. Free agents cannot ascend far up the social and economic ladder.

Aware of the drain on resources needed to support this vast bureaucracy, paramount leader Deng Xiaoping in the early 1980s set the goal of reducing its size by several million people, a third at the central levels and by more than a third at lower levels. But without equally attractive alternative channels for mobility, and with no proper retirement system until recently, officials continue to cling stubbornly to their positions. As a result, the state apparatus has undergone endless "streamlining and re-expansion." Between 1982–1988, China's workforce grew by 20%, from 453 million to 543 million, while the number of state and party officials climbed by 59%, from 6.1 million to 9.71 million, according to the state statistical bureau.

China's bureaucracy remains a vast iron-rice bowl system, breeding laziness, inefficiency and mediocrity. Few officials are dismissed or demoted, even for committing serious offences. Overstaffing is worst where officials are least needed, notably the day-to-day running of the economy. About half of all government officials are involved in implementing the state economic plan, which has diminished in scope since 1978.

In Jiangsu, for example, a major industrial enterprise has at least six layers of bureaucratic leadership overseeing its operation, according to one press report. They are, in order of importance, the provincial industrial bureau, the local planning commission, the provincial party committee's economic section, the governor's office, the party's financial leadership group and the provincial party committee. In other areas, such as taxation, law enforcement and auditing, by contrast, the bureaucracy is thin and overstretched. In general, govern

seem unable or unwilling to interpret events and assume responsibility on their own
(Silver and Geller, 1978). Things must be clarified and authorized by some higher-
ranking office, and while this process is taking place, they are left in a state of limbo.
"No action is better than the wrong action" seems to sum up the operating philosophy
of many career bureaucrats.

Bureaucratic Ritualism

Bureaucracies frequently give the impression of being more concerned with following
rules to the letter rather than doing a job or solving a problem. This phenomenon has
been described as **goal displacement** or **bureaucratic ritualism** and is widely recognized both in the sociological literature (Blau and Meyer, 1987; Merton, 1968) and in
popular literature. Anyone who has read Ken Kesey's powerful novel *One Flew Over
the Cuckoo's Nest* (1962) will not easily forget "the Big Nurse," the perfect bureaucrat
who was so consumed with maintaining order in her mental hospital ward that none
of her patients ever received any genuine rehabilitative care. The activities that would
have helped them therapeutically might have threatened the carefully created routine
that she had worked so hard to establish. It was only after the hero, McMurphy, had
completely disrupted Miss Ratched's mind-numbing ward pattern that any effective
therapy occurred. But McMurphy's eventual fate at the hands of the Big Nurse demonstrated chillingly what can happen to those who dare to challenge the bureaucratic
machinery. In the entrenched ritualistic worlds of bureaucracies, messengers of change
are not normally welcomed with open minds or open arms.

If these popular perceptions of bureaucratic inefficiency are even partially valid,
how is it that they are able to accomplish as much as they seem to? After all, U.S.
political, military, and corporate organizations could not have been so successful if they
were subject only to the sorts of pathologies described above. Somehow, someone must
be doing something right.

The Informal Organization

One answer lies in the existence of what often is called the informal organization that
develops in the shadow of, and in response to, the formal bureaucratic structure. The
informal organization can be thought of as the actual set of relationships developed by
the real people who are the nameless, faceless officeholders plotted on organizational

charts. If the formal structure exists in the diagrams that hang on executives' office walls or that appear in the company's annual stockholder report, the informal structure exists in the minds and in the actions of the company's staff. In their daily activities, these flesh-and-blood people translate the generic procedures defined by bureaucratic principles into specific behaviors required to fit immediate needs. Their friendships (and antagonisms) for one another fill in the emotional vacuum created by impersonal organizational rules, and may help close gaps or loopholes in the formal structure that could cause severe difficulties for the organization.

For example, secretaries in corporations or universities, and company clerks in military units, typically establish primary group relations with other secretaries or clerks. They take coffee breaks together, have lunch together, swap war stories together (figuratively or literally), and do things for each other. These personal networks often can transmit information and supply (or acquire) necessary resources much faster and more efficiently than established bureaucratic channels. Information or materials that are required in a hurry can be received in a hurry. Activities that may be impeded by bureaucratic policies and channels can be facilitated by stepping outside the established structure. In an ironic way, ignoring the formal structure can help preserve it. Since the members spend a significant portion of their daily lives within these structures, they invariably attempt to make their "organizational homes" as comfortable as possible. In the process, they may strengthen and stabilize the structures.

It would be incorrect and rash to assume that informal structures always work to the formal organization's advantage, however. In cases where the personnel see their best interests being threatened by the imposed official pattern, they may use informal, primary group networks to resist or sabotage bureaucratic goals (Gouldner, 1954a, 1954b). When formal and informal organizational demands or expectations conflict, those of the informal structure may prevail for many individuals. They arise from primary group relations that may be more satisfying and meaningful to participants than the depersonalized, secondary formal structure.

The Japanese Corporation

At any given moment, the harmony between formal and informal structures is contingent on a number of factors whose fluctuations could generate deep antagonisms between the official and the unofficial faces of organizational life. If formal organizations are to be successful over the long run, they must address and maximize the satisfaction of human, as well as organizational, needs and goals. Since, in many critics' opinion, bureaucracies seem unable to accomplish a compatible alliance of this sort, alternative forms of formal organizational structuring have been explored. In particular, the amazing and apparently continuing success of Japanese businesses has focused a great deal of attention on the potential merits of Japan's answer to Western-style bureaucracy.

Compared to bureaucratic organization as described by Max Weber, the Japanese formal organization is an interesting (and, to Western eyes, curious) mixture of more authoritarian and more democratic elements; of rational, goal-directed, and emotional people-directed relations. The structure of the Japanese corporation was described in detail by William Ouchi (1981) in his analysis of "Theory Z."

According to Ouchi, the typical Japanese organization differs from the U.S. corporation in several major respects. First, in Japan, employees' relationships with the organization are more long lasting. Although not exactly the cradle-to-grave association sometimes portrayed, it often comes close. Japanese workers are not nearly as prone to employer changes as their U.S. counterparts. For the majority, occupational careers unfold within a single organization.

Second, Japanese hiring, promotion, and pay practices emphasize groups, rather than individuals. The cohort of employees initially hired together move through the ranks of the organization together. This practice is in contrast to that in the United States, where individuals compete against one another for advancement in what amounts to a zero-sum game.

Third, unlike U.S. organizations, which encourage and demand a high level of specialized expertise, the Japanese corporation stresses a more generalized sphere of knowledge. Employees often are rotated through a series of different positions to give them a more complete picture of the various facets of the organization. This practice gives workers a greater understanding of the company's overall operations and objectives.

Fourth, the Japanese corporation is much more involved in the personal lives of its workers; that is, their activities outside the company, and many of their behaviors within the organization that Americans might regard as private matters. A number of Japanese companies, for example, begin the work day with mandatory group calisthenics for all workers. As a result of this holistic orientation, primary-like ties form between companies and workers. Thus, the company assumes the status of a second family.

Finally, decision making in the Japanese organization is far less centralized and less "top-down" than in the typical U.S. bureaucracy. Workers are given opportunities to participate in a far wider and more significant range of work-related decisions. Through the medium of "quality control (QC) circles" that meet on a weekly or more frequent basis, Japanese employees can exercise meaningful input into the conditions of their jobs (Cole, 1979). Such participation gives them a sense of compatibility and harmony between their personal interests and goals and those of the company.

Whereas the Japanese model of formal organization seems to have worked remarkably well in that society, it is doubtful that the same principals could be applied to the United States with equal effect. As Ouchi (1981) was quick to note, the Japanese corporate structure is a product of the very group-centered social and cultural philosophy that emphasizes belonging, duty, and obligation to a collectivity outside oneself. In a much more individual-centered culture with primary emphasis placed on personal autonomy and democracy, the Japanese system would be perceived as authoritarian and heavy-handed, and likely resisted very strongly.

The plot of director Ron Howard's 1986 film *Gung Ho* revolved around the (friendly) takeover of a U.S. automobile plant by a Japanese firm and the attempt of the Japanese to implement their style of management on American assembly-line workers used to a different way of life. Although meant as a comedy and working to a "together, we can learn from each other and find a better way" ending, the film expressed what may be a widespread belief on the part of workers in the United States that the vaunted Japanese organization is little more than a slave labor camp in disguise. The fact that at least one major study has indicated that job satisfaction and job commitment in Japan actually are lower than that among U.S. plant workers (Lincoln and Kalleberg, 1985) does little to curb these feelings. Thus far, the actual experiences of real U.S. auto workers in Japanese-managed plants have not been nearly as friction free or ultimately as successful as those depicted in *Gung Ho.* The Japanese corporation may be an idea whose time has yet to come in this society.

It may be impossible to transplant an organizational structure developed in a radically different cultural setting to our own place and time, but there is no reason to assume that the traditional bureaucratic organization is the only way to skin a cat. In recent years, many U.S. companies (e.g., Apple Computers) have begun to experiment with more human-oriented, flexible administrative structures. These arrangements attempt to capture some of the family atmosphere of the Japanese system while recognizing domestic cultural beliefs and priorities for individual expression. Research by sociologist Rosabeth Moss Kanter (1983, 1985) indicated that companies that have been able to humanize their administrative structures are more profitable than those adhering to more traditional bureaucratic procedures. With the U.S. economy in a slump and rapidly being overtaken by the still-booming Japanese economic miracle, success in finding a newer and better way of organizing and encouraging the productive efforts of the workforce may become a matter of survival.

SOCIETIES AND SOCIETAL DEVELOPMENT

As discussed in chapter 1, human societies were the focal point for the earliest sociologists, and still are the basic unit of analysis for functionalists and other macro-level theorists. **Societies** can be defined as self-perpetuating groups of people who occupy a given territory and interact with one another on the basis of a shared culture. Having said that, we now can backtrack a bit to add on the limiting and qualifying phrases for which sociological definitions have become famous.

Like other groups (e.g., families, friends, neighbors, work associates), societies consist of some number of people whose patterned social interactions are based on a common definition of reality. In this instance, however, a society can be envisioned as the largest group of individuals within a specified territory who share the same world view. A group of friends share common beliefs and values, but those same beliefs and values may be held by people who are not part of that particular friendship; in fact, even people who are enemies may have much the same world view. Thus, societies are more encompassing than other types of human groups in the sense that they include many more individuals than any other group in the same geographical area.

Societies also differ from other social groups by virtue of the fact that they are self-perpetuating; that is, unlike the smaller groups contained within them, societies provide all the necessary resources and services to sustain their members over time, and to replace the members who die or otherwise leave over the course of time. City councils and Girl Scout troops normally do not reproduce themselves biologically. New members for these groups must be recruited from the outside society. A family group may (and usually does) perpetuate itself through biological reproduction, but even that process requires other families to provide appropriate reproductive partners. Neither city councils, Girl Scout troops, nor families normally are capable of fulfilling all the economic, recreational, medical, nutritional, and other life-sustaining needs of their respective members. To accomplish this, they have to interact with other groups within the larger society.

Sociologists have made the study of human societies the central focus of their discipline. In fact, the literal (i.e., dictionary) definition of sociology is "the science of society." It was the massive changes sweeping through eighteenth-century European societies that triggered the creation of this field. Since that time, sociologists have continued their efforts to describe, explain, and predict how and why societies change over time. Their analyses have led to the development of a variety of typologies and models of societal structures.

Durkheim and Tonnies

The French sociologist Emile Durkheim, as you may recall from the discussion in chapter 1, saw the development of human societies as tied up with twin processes he called the division of labor and the specialization of function. Over the passage of centuries, human societies have grown progressively larger. As populations increased, what had been a simple but workable arrangement in which everyone participated in all necessary jobs became too inefficient to meet growing needs. It was refined into a more elaborate system in which specific individuals and groups began to specialize in particular tasks. As occupational structures became more complex, the members of societies became more and more unlike one another by virtue of their specialized roles and social functions. The mechanical solidarity of a community held together by common values and beliefs began to be replaced by an organic solidarity grounded in the interdependency and interlocking of these differentiated statuses. Societies that had been anchored by the sameness of their people now began to be united by their members' differences (Durkheim, 1966, original 1893).

A similar theme had been developed a few years earlier by the German sociologist Ferdinand Tonnies (1855–1936). Tonnies (1963, original 1887) saw traditional human societies as organized along the lines of what he called **gemeinschaft** ("communal") relations among population members. In these societies, people interacted with one another on the basis of long-standing customs, and with personal emotions. Kinship and friendship groupings were of great importance, and people were known for who they were. In short, this type of society was premised on what we would call primary group relations.

As societies increased in size and became more highly differentiated, however, the quality of social relations changed dramatically. Interactions among individuals became more formal, impersonal, calculated, and directed to particular goals. For example, whereas people in traditional societies might exchange or barter goods and services with their neighbors, members of modern societies shop at food, clothing, hardware, and other specialized stores. They are not known as individuals, but rather are customers, paying a predetermined sum of money to an unknown clerk in exchange for items that were mass-produced by still other strangers in a factory located perhaps hundreds of miles away. Tonnies argued that, in this type of **gesellschaft** ("association") society, secondary group relations dominate people's daily lives, just as large-scale formal organizations dominate all spheres of societal activity. Everyday life is more rational, efficient, and, perhaps, alienating. People who once had been oriented and integrated into emotional, cohesive groupings now are self-oriented and individualistic. For many members of societies that are in passage from gemeinschaft to gesellschaft forms of organization, the change can be troublesome.

For example, as a developing nation, Mexico is now going through the same kinds of structural and relational changes described a century ago by Tonnies and Durkheim. Many observers have commented on the apparent deep feelings of distrust, alienation, and hostility that rural peasants and many members of the urban lower and working classes display toward the large bureaucracies that define Mexican politics and business. The popular classes perceive these governmental and economic bodies as increasingly uninterested in and removed from the concerns and needs of a large majority of the people. In many cases, they have responded by retreating into the relative security of family relations.

Alan Riding (1989) speculated that the high walls that surround many houses even in poor neighborhoods in Mexican cities may be deeply symbolic as well as architecturally functional. They offer their inhabitants at least temporary refuge from an outside world grown increasingly bewildering and hostile. However, past experience indicates that the changes wrought by societal modernization do not bypass the family. As we will see in chapter 9, family units and kinship structures in developing societies are profoundly affected by these massive social and cultural changes. As buffers between individuals and societies, primary groups such as the family must absorb a great deal of pressure coming from both directions. Their ability (or inability) to do so is a matter of utmost significance for the individual population members who are forced to go along for the ride as their society jumps—or is pushed—into the modern world.

Lenski's Evolutionary Theory of Societal Development

A more recent attempt to catalogue the developmental changes that have characterized human societies from the past to the present has been offered by U.S. sociologist Gerhard E. Lenski. Over the past twenty-five years Lenski (1966; Lenski and Lenski, 1987) has refined an evolutionary model of human development that links societal change to changes in economic technology. In his view, economic surpluses created through improvements in productive technology have been the catalyst for changes ranging from population size to the number and content of organized religions.

According to Lenski, for well over 90 percent of our history as a species, humans existed in scattered nomadic groups that survived on the hunting and gathering skills of their members. Small in size and simple in organization, these early societies embodied the essence of primary group relations. Family and kinship groups were about the only recognized social units, and group ties were close and personal. Showing little social differentiation, these hunter-gatherer bands practiced a "primitive egalitarianism" in which hierarchical property, power, and prestige differences among individuals were minimal. The need to be able to follow food supplies, as well as the absence of any real economic surplus, prevented the development of any significant or permanent social differences.

As our ancestors learned the rudiments of simple farming, things began to change significantly. With the advent of settled horticultural villages and the creation of food surpluses, populations began to increase and a division of labor began. The presence of surplus goods permitted some members of the village to be freed from actual participation in food growing or hunting. Full-time noneconomic positions and roles were established (most notably, political and religious leaders), and these functions came to be performed by designated kinship groups. These leaders were able to acquire larger than average shares of social resources, and to pass these advantages along to their descendants. Simple equality began to give way to simple inequalities.

The development of metal tools and other farming technologies led to the creation of agrarian societies with populations numbering into the tens of thousands, true urban settlements, complex divisions of labor, and large political, economic, and military bureaucracies. The needs of these bureaucracies and of the sometimes empires they served stimulated increasing specialization and rational planning of many societal activities. Objective, impersonal relations began to compete with more subjective and emotional primary relations in everyday life. As productive surpluses grew, so did the differential distribution of these resources to various segments of the population. Simple social inequalities began to develop into complex and significant inequalities.

Finally, in the past 300 years the era of agrarian empires was eclipsed and replaced by the age of industrial societies. The development and harnessing of mechanical power sources led to a dramatic shift from agriculture to manufacturing (and, later, to servicing and administration) as the major productive sources of economic wealth, power, and prestige. Societal populations now were extremely large, and thoroughly urbanized, rationalized, educated, differentiated, and stratified. Most areas of societal activity came under the influence of the large, specialized formal organizations that made up the framework of governmental, economic, educational, and other major institutions. In response to the increasing rationalization of human efforts, deliberate and impersonal secondary relationships began to characterize most spheres of social life. The modern age had arrived.

Durkheim, Tonnies, and Lenski differed in their terminology and specific focus, but all were in agreement about the general course of societal development. Over time, we have gone from small to immensely large, from simple to enormously complex, from passive responders to active planners of events. In the process, much has been gained, but perhaps something has been lost as well. In the chapters that follow we address some of the benefits and costs of the different forms of social organizations that distinguish human life in the contemporary world.

FOCUS ON
MEXICO

MEXICAN SOCIETY: WHO AM I?

In many ways, the people, culture, and society of Mexico not only differ from, but are the complete opposite of those of Japan. Whereas approximately 95 percent of Japan's population share a 1,000-year-old racial, ethnic, and cultural heritage, most Mexicans are *mestizaje,* or of mixed-blood heritage. Ninety percent of the population are part Indian and part Spanish. As one writer put it, *"No somos espanoles, ni criollos, ni indios . . . somos puro mexicanos . . . el pueblo mexicano que es el Mexico de hoy"* ("We are neither Spanish nor Creole [Spaniards born in Mexico] nor Indians; we are pure Mexicans, the Mexican people which is the Mexico of today" (in Elizondo, 1983, p. 13). The combination of two cultures and a unique historical experience has resulted in a people that Alan Riding (1989, p. 31) believed are still searching for their identity, "hovering ambivalently between ancient and modern, traditional and fashionable, Indian and Spanish. . . ."

Many writers have attempted to define or capture the essence of "Mexicanness." According to Riding (1989), Mexicans are basically distrustful, fiercely proud, and consumed by questions of honor. A strong religious tradition and the "accumulated customs and passions of centuries" give Mexicans "enormous internal strength" (p. 5). Unlike the Japanese, who are group centered and concerned about where individuals belong and what they do in society, the opposite is true in Mexico. "What counts to the Mexican is what he is rather than what he does, the man rather than the job: he works to live and not the inverse" (Riding, 1989, p. 5). In other words, Mexicans emphasize what Chie Nakane (1984, pp. 1–22) calls *attribute,* a characteristic a person is born with, such as race, gender, or membership in a specific descent group or caste. This is in contrast to the Japanese, who are much more concerned with *frame,* one's place in an institution "or a particular relationship which binds a set of individuals into one group" (p. 1).

The Japanese spend much of their work and leisure time in groups, but Mexicans are not team players, and find it difficult to conform to the demands of highly structured organizations. The planning and implementation of a strategy toward some future goal that form the essence of formal organization run counter to a fatalistic world view Mexicans are likely to hold. If the course of events is predetermined and beyond human control, it makes little sense to plan for the future and lead a disciplined, routine life

(Riding, 1989). The future will take care of itself, for it can be no other way. Therefore, the *manana* ("tomorrow") syndrome is not a function of laziness, but a component of a world view with a different conception of time than our own.

The renowned Mexican poet and writer Octavio Paz (1961) characterized Mexicans as people who live behind masks and shut themselves off from the outside world. The ideal of manliness in a male-dominated society "is never to 'crack,' never to back down. Those who 'open themselves up' are cowards. Unlike other people, we believe that opening oneself up is a weakness or betrayal. The Mexican can bend, bow humbly, even stoop, but he cannot back down, that is he can never allow the outside world to penetrate his privacy. The man who backs down is not to be trusted, is a traitor or person of doubtful loyalty" (p. 30). For Paz, the heart of Mexican *macho* is not the aggressive, swaggering male looking for a fight, but the defensive man capable of guarding himself and whatever is confided in him.

Samuel Ramos (1962) also commented on the lack of cooperative action and collective discipline that undermines social solidarity in Mexico. He viewed the Mexican character as an array of different and often contradictory traits, although he claimed the common denominator included distrust, resentment, deception, and timidity. These traits can be traced back to the Colonial Era, when *mestizos* were subject to injustice at the hands of Spaniards. These "old attitudes" (distrust, resentment, etc.) returned as a result of the turbulence leading up to and including the Mexican Revolution (1910–1920) and its aftermath. Ramos took issue with Paz and argued that solitude and life behind a mask are not born of choice, but rather come from a history of disruptive elements "that makes human character anti-social" (1962, p. 175). However, in spite of his critical analysis of the Mexican national character, Ramos reminded us that many Mexican people have been successful and have made significant contributions to their society. "They are men whose natural superiority leaves no room for an inferiority complex" (1962, p. 180).

As is the case in Japan, Mexicans are very concerned about face and public image. They may hide behind their masks, as Paz and Ramos suggested, but the mask has to be polished and put on correctly in front of a watchful audience. Riding (1989, p. 10) noted that "status and appearance" are crucial components of Mexican society. For example, poor people typically spend what little money they have and go into debt for village fiestas, weddings, birthday parties, and funerals. A young man will spend his last peso to impress the girl he is courting, and at restaurants men argue for the privilege of paying the bill. The common U.S. practice of "going Dutch" is considered rude and offensive.

The occasion of encountering a superior in public can lead to either a boost or an embarrassing cutting of one's social esteem. Males engage in a mutual greeting that follows a strict sequence. "First comes the handshake, followed by the *abrazo* ("embrace") and two hearty coordinated back slaps and, finally, a second handshake and shoulder slap" (Riding, 1989, p. 10). To receive a voluntary *abrazo* from one's boss or a political figure in public is something to be celebrated. However, if the *abrazo* is resisted by the higher-ranking person, the lower-status individual is humiliated.

Chilangos

One of the most pronounced socially and culturally recognized divisions in Mexico today is that between *chilangos* and everybody else. "*Chilango*" is slang for someone who comes from Mexico City. In recent years, it has become a dirty word, with residents of the nation's capital being blamed for many of the country's current problems. *Chilangos* are thought to be pushy, arrogant, and rude, and to have a condescending attitude toward nonresidents of Mexico City—people who live in "the provinces" (Gross, 1990).

According to political scientist Samuel Schmidt (in Gross, 1990), *chilangos* are hated because Mexicans have been distrustful of outsiders (even regional ones) since the Spanish Conquest. Today, as the center of a powerful federal government, Mexico City controls the nation's political and financial affairs. With the biggest, best, and most expensive opera houses, theaters, art galleries, and university, the capital city also dominates the country culturally.

Although "chilangophobia" exists throughout Mexico, it is especially strong in the north. *Nortenos* (people from the northern states) dislike Mexico City because the federal government draws so much tax revenue from these prosper-

Organized group living requires people to play many different roles—in effect, to wear a variety of social masks and to assume various social identities. Individuals may sometimes wonder just who and what they are beneath these socially mandated exteriors.

ous states. Northerners feel they are paying more than their fair share of the bill for the nation's modernization and its social and economic ills. What's more, many people from this region believe the federal government is totally corrupt and incompetent, doing little more than wasting their money. This disdain for *chilangos* is particularly intense in the city of Tijuana on the United States–Mexican border. In past years, posters and bumper stickers reading "Serve the motherland. Kill a *chilango*" could be seen in Baja California's largest city (Gross, 1990). This sentiment may reflect the anger and confusion of the members of a gemeinschaft community over the erosion of a personal, traditional way of life in the face of modernization and its accompanying depersonalized gesellschaft social organization.

Fiestas

At least one aspect of Mexican society is especially well known and enjoyable to people in the United States—the fiesta. The Mexican Tourist Bureau, as well as breweries on both sides of the border, promote an image of Mexico as one non-stop party with music, food, *cerveza* ("beer"), and people wearing colorful native costumes dancing in the streets. Although this portrayal of party time no doubt is exaggerated for the benefit of *gringo* (people from the United States) tourists, the Mexican calendar, as Octavio Paz (1961, pp. 47–64) noted, is crowded with fiestas. Days such as September 16 (Mexican Independence) and December 12 (the feast of the Virgin of Guadalupe) are national holidays celebrated throughout the country. On any given day, some Mexican village or city is having a fiesta in honor of a saint or local hero.

Paz believed that these celebrations perform an important function in a relatively poor (although developing) country. They are a momentary escape from poverty, and from too hard or too little work; a luxury for people who can't leave town for long weekends, take vacations, or run up big credit card bills. In his words, "their brilliance and excitement, the enthusiasm with which we take part, all suggest that without them we would explode" (1961, pp. 52–53). In this sense, fiestas are safety valves that allow people's frustrations, disappointment, tension, and anger to be drained off in a socially acceptable manner. The more physical and mental energy expended preparing for, participating in, and recovering from a fiesta, the less people have for deviant and revolutionary behavior. In a similar vein, fiestas may be seen as institutionalized "time outs" during which the norms governing everyday conduct are temporarily suspended. According to Paz, one can "leap over the wall of solitude that confines him during the rest of the year" (1961, p. 49). Individuals can remove the masks, show their true faces, and together "get drunk on noise, people, colors" (p. 49). People who normally confine their intimate feelings within their own families can achieve, at least momentarily, primary group solidarity outside that small circle.

If fiestas serve as a vehicle for increasing social cohesion among the living in Mexico, they can also promote solidarity between the living and the dead. One of the most important days on the Mexican calendar is November 2, *el Dia de los Muertos* ("the Day of the Dead"). Whereas death is not a polite or frequent topic of conversation in the United States because it "burns the lips," the Mexican "is familiar with death, jokes about it, caresses it, sleeps with it, celebrates it; it is one of his favorite toys and most steadfast loves" (Paz, 1961, p. 57). Death is a common theme in virtually all forms of artistic expression, and "Mexican folk artists represent death with humor, affection, charm, satire . . ." (Wilcox, 1984, pp. 40–41). The Day of the Dead culminates preparations that have been taking place for weeks. It marks the nation's fascination and "sophisticated acceptance" of death, as well as one's bonds with family, both past and present. In the weeks prior to November 2, bakeries, shops, and markets are filled with candies, breads, and toys symbolic of death, most notably, skeletons. Breads are baked in human forms and sweets shaped into skulls.

In rural Mexico and in many small cities, mourners carry a coffin to the cemetery on *el Dia de los Muertos* when graves are repainted, replanted, and redecorated. Shrines made out of fruits, vegetables, jewelry, clothing, and paper cut-outs are constructed (Wilcox, 1984), and the favorite food of the dead is placed on their tombs. People believe that the deceased return to visit their families, eat the spirit of the food, and leave. The next day, the living come back to eat and drink what they have prepared (Foster and Foster, 1986), a communion with the dead and with the still-living past (Riding, 1989).

This annual confrontation with death is an important symbolic reaffirmation of perhaps the most basic and enduring of all Mexican groups—the family. The family provides a sense of refuge and continuity in a world that otherwise might be experienced as being completely out of one's control. As noted earlier, however, the same societal changes responsible for the proliferation of more formalized and depersonalized secondary groups in other spheres of life also are known to place great pressures and stress on the family as well. As the traditional family is increasingly subjected to the forces of societal development, it will be interesting to see if the fiestas that unite Mexicans in communal celebration of their family ties will also become victims of the country's march toward modernization.

DISCUSSION QUESTIONS

1. What are *chilangos*? Why are they regarded negatively by many Mexicans?
2. To modernize its economy successfully, Mexico is introducing rational planning and bureaucratic organization in what had been a highly personalized social structure. What particular obstacles do you think the government will face from its citizens as it attempts to implement a more formalized, goal- and future-oriented system of social relations?
3. Fiestas and celebrations often have a much deeper and more important significance beyond being an excuse to party. Go to the library and read about one of the developing nations of Africa. Does this particular country have any festivals that resemble those found in Mexico? What role or function do you think such festivals play in these types of societies?

JAPANESE SOCIETY: WHERE DO YOU BELONG?

"So, what do you do?"

"I'm a sociology major at State."

During the course of a lifetime, we meet hundreds of people, and one of the first pieces of information we exchange concerns our present occupation or major activity. In Japan, however, neither the question nor answer above would be appropriate or make much sense. Rather, the conversation would go like this:

"*Dochira desuka?*" "Where is it [that you work or belong]?"

"I am at the University of Tokyo studying sociology."

Do you see the difference between the two? The first question and answer emphasize *attribute,* whereas the second emphasize *frame.*

In Western societies the emphasis is on attribute: "I am a sociology major. . . ." However, in Japan, frame is more important: "I am at the University of Tokyo. . . ." In other words, we emphasize who people are and what they do in life; for the Japanese, this information is of secondary importance. What really matters is where an individual belongs. Nakane noted that some frames can be even more significant than blood ties. For example, in Japan, relationships within the home are thought to be of utmost importance. Therefore, wives and daughters-in-law who come to the household from the outside are much more important than one's own sisters and daughters who have married and now are members of other households. In this example, sister and daughter are characteristics of who an individual is, or attributes. Wives and daughters-in-law, on the other hand, are now part of the household frame. According to Nakane, the emphasis on frame has contributed to the weakening of kinship ties in Japan: "A married sibling who lives in another household is considered a kind of outsider" (1984, p. 6).

This emphasis on frame or "belongingness" characterizes what many scholars believe is the most distinctive feature of Japanese social structure compared to Western societies. Not only do the Japanese place tremendous emphasis on group membership, they also stress the individual's willingness to fulfill all of the obligations attached to his or her membership in the group.

The word *bun* ("portion," "share," "part," or "fraction") is a central component of this group-centered orientation. Anthropologist Takie Sugiyama Lebra (1976) noted that *bun* has three related meanings. First, a person is thought of as a fraction, a part of the whole. The individual is a "nobody but becomes a somebody" (p. 68) when he or she contributes to the group or the larger society. Second, the individual is not self-reliant, but part of interdependent organizations as well as the larger society. The awareness of one's self-*insufficiency* is a central component of the *bun* concept. Finally, every member of society is supposed to be a *bun* holder. The fact that an individual depends on people, and those people in turn depend on her, makes life meaningful. The Japanese feel that everyone ought to have *bun.* If they don't, something is wrong with society.

At first glance, it appears that *bun* is merely the Japanese equivalent of the sociological terms status and role. However, it is a central concept in the Japanese world view, bound up with values about how people should lead their lives and how society should be structured.

The importance of group membership and the willingness to fulfill one's obligations within the organization are directly related to how the Japanese raise their children. Ian Burma (1984, p. 20) noted, "Being a Japanese child, especially a boy, and most of all the eldest son, is as close as one can get to being a God." Babies and small children are indulged and treated quite permissively. They are nursed for a relatively long time, and constantly held and fondled by their mothers. It is not uncommon for children to sleep with their parents until they (the children) are quite large (Reischauer, 1988).

As a result of these child-rearing practices, Japanese children are accustomed to being the center of attention and having their needs promptly met. This attitude is called *amae,* the noun form of the verb *amareau*—"to depend and presume upon the benevolence of others" (Doi, 1956, p. 90). Children learn quickly that parents (especially mothers) are the source of all their physical and psychological support. They also learn to be compliant and to accept their mother as an authority figure. "In time this attitude becomes expanded into an acceptance of authority of the surrounding social milieu and a need for and dependence upon this broader social approval" (Reischauer, 1988, pp. 144–146).

Amae is closely associated with *on*—the debt of gratitude or lasting obligation one has to an individual (e.g., a boss) who has provided a favor. In addition, the concept of *giri* is a moral imperative to perform one's assigned duties toward other members of the group. These firmly held notions of duty and obligation, coupled with child-rearing practices that foster dependence and obedience, help explain the significance of group membership and a good deal of social behavior in Japan.

From a Western perspective, the Japanese appear to be a nation of sheep, quietly and obediently doing what they are told when they are told to do it. More often than not, this conformity is interpreted as a sign of personal weakness. In our eyes, people who do not think for themselves lack the courage and inner strength to do what they want, regardless of the opinions of others. However, the Japanese view their behavior in a much different light. Rather than weak-willed conformists, they see themselves as possessed of tremendous self-control. It takes discipline to curb one's feelings, desires, and needs for the good of the group. Following the rules and doing one's duty (*giri*) is nothing to be ashamed of. On the contrary, conformity is the product of inner strength (Reischauer, 1988).

A Hierarchical Society

Japanese society is not only group-centered, but hierarchical as well. Lebra (1976, pp. 72–73) stated that the Japanese are very status conscious and have a tendency to "differentiate ranks infinitesimally" based on criteria such as age, the date of graduation from school, and the date of entry into one's company. These distinctions are manifested overtly through clothing and accessories, which most often reflect social position rather than individual fashion tastes. For example, Japanese scholars who visit the United States are often shocked to find that so many American professors dress as casually as their students. Also, inasmuch as red is a feminine color, a Japanese man would sooner get drenched than carry a red umbrella in the rain. Even the style of wristwatch, fountain pen, and briefcase a person has should be commensurate with one's rank. Since most people conform to these "status-corresponding codes" of attire, it is relatively easy to determine a stranger's social rank with no more than a casual glance. On introduction, should there be any uncertainty about someone's status and how he or she must be treated, the mandatory exchange of *meishi* ("calling card") will clear things up. Virtually all Japanese above the blue-collar level carry *meishi*, which present the two most important pieces of information necessary to conduct business and engage in social interaction: one's group affiliation, and position within that group (Christopher, 1983).

In a hierarchical society like Japan, one would expect to find tough, no-nonsense leaders who routinely impose their wills on subordinates. In fact, just the opposite is true. A good leader is not domineering or forceful, but sensitive to the feelings and needs of others. Ideally, consensus through prolonged consultation leads to a decision (Reischauer, 1988). A major advantage of this approach is that it significantly reduces the chances of interpersonal conflict. No matter how competitive they may be with foreigners, among themselves the Japanese play by a set of rules that states, "a resort to confrontation tactics automatically signals that you have lost the game" (Christopher, 1983, p. 54). The much more confrontational, decisive, autocratic style of leadership characteristic of the Western world causes suspicion and resentment in Japan (Reischauer, 1988). Japanese businessmen who have spent a prolonged period of time in the West may find that their opportunities for advancement are not as good as those of their colleagues who stayed home, as too many months or years dealing with argumentative foreigners calls into question their ability to fit once again into a more tranquil society.

Social Exchange Model

So far, we have been looking at Japan from what Moeran (1986, pp. 62–79) called the "group model." According to this view, people think and act within the framework of a hierarchically organized group that is headed by a benevolent leader. However, the weakness of this perspective is that it doesn't account for the competition, conflict, and crime that exist in Japanese society. Harumi Befu (in Moeran, 1986) offered an exchange model for understanding Japanese behavior. He believes it is less ideological and more practical than the often-cited group perspective. According to the model, individuals have resources such as knowledge, expertise, and influential friends that they exchange within the group for resources they do not possess, most notably, money. The benevolent attitudes and dutiful behavior typically associated with the Japanese do not fit into the equation.

Moeran argued that rather than being mutually exclusive, the group model and the exchange model actually complement each other. For example, a company can act in a benevolent manner toward its employees as long as it is making a profit, and workers will be loyal to their employers until they receive an offer of more money from another organization. In other words, the group model focuses on altruism, duty, and obligation to explain Japanese behavior, whereas the social exchange perspective sees action motivated by self-interest.

By focusing on self-interest, the social exchange model opens the door for the often ignored or downplayed notion of individualism in Japanese society. Although the expression, "The nail that sticks out gets hammered down" emphasizes the fact that Japan is much more group-oriented than the United States, a conflict between individuality and conformity exists in Japan, as it does in all societies (Reischauer, 1988). For example, the wandering, masterless *samurai* is the subject of numerous films. Although this cultural antihero exhibits values and behavior that run counter to tradition in Japan, the lone *samurai* is to be admired for his independence. Audiences also identify with the nonconforming behavior of the *yakuza* ("gangster") because he, too, is a solitary figure. Japanese literature in the form of the "I novel" is a search for the ultimate truth of one's existence. Psychiatrist L. Takeo Doi (1973) noted that the Japanese are quite concerned about individuality and use the expressions *jibun ga aru* ("having self") and *jibun ga nai* ("lacking the self"). People often take pride in the freedom of *jibun* and their ability to resist social pressure. The struggle for individuality and introspection may be one reason why keeping a diary is so popular in Japan (Lebra, 1976).

Japan's postwar economic success propelled the country into the ranks of the world's modern superpowers, but many Japanese seem to be unsure of how to deal with economic prosperity and the changes it has brought to their society. Although they are earning more money than people in the United States for the first time in history, material success alone is apparently not enough for an increasing number of people, as evidenced by the proliferation of neoreligions.

By the end of the American occupation in 1952 there were an estimated 700 new religions in Japan. In 1990 the Ministry of Culture reported 23,000 registered religions, with the number increasing at the rate of one every two and a half days (*San Diego Union,* 1990f). The strong attraction neoreligions have for so many people may be indicative of a deep reservoir of dissatisfaction that is currently gripping the country in spite of its material success. In the counterculture years of the 1960s and early 1970s, the sons and daughters of affluent Americans were well represented in neoreligions (e.g., Hare Krishna, Rev. Moon's Unification Church, etc.) that were taking hold in the United States. Perhaps a similar form of uneasiness, boredom, or longing for additional meaning in one's life is occurring among the Japanese. Japan's economic growth may well be adversely affected if this wave of religious seekers becomes preoccupied with finding new spiritual meaning in life, and less concerned with where they belong, as well as traditional notions of *on* ("obligation") and *giri* ("duty").

Discussion Questions

1. What is the difference between "attribute" and "frame" as ways of distinguishing people in a given society?

2. Imagine that you are an American business executive who has been sent to manage a factory your company has opened in Tokyo.

What do you think you would find most difficult or frustrating about supervising Japanese workers? How do you think you might deal with the problems you will face in your new position?

3. Japan is not the only Asian society with a strong group-orientation and a highly developed sense of knowing one's proper place. Go to the library and read about the social structure and social relations in the People's Republic of China. How do relations between individuals and the larger society there differ from those in Japan? How are they similar?

CHAPTER SUMMARY

1. Human beings typically spend most of their lives doing things and being with other humans. Their social lives are structured, showing order and predictability rather than chaos and randomness. This social structuring is made possible through a shared culture that gives the members of a population a common world view.

2. In describing populations and their activities, sociologists distinguish among several different types of collectivities or situations involving more than one person. Aggregates are made up of people who occupy the same physical space at the same particular time. Categories are distinguished by common or shared characteristics of their members. The people who constitute a given category may or may not ever be physically present with one another. Social groups are made up of people who interact with one another in a regular, patterned way and who come to form a sense of common identity.

3. Group patterns are established by the statuses or recognized positions within the group, and the formal roles or expected behaviors and attitudes associated with them. People's role performances or actual behaviors in response to expectations may depart significantly from formal requirements, resulting in role strain. Individuals also may experience role conflict as they find themselves caught between the contradictory demands of two or more statuses occupied at the same time.

4. There are many different types of social groups in modern societies. Membership groups are those in which a given individual objectively belongs and participates. Reference groups are those with whom a given individual affiliates subjectively, and whose beliefs, norms, values, and behaviors become the frame of reference for his or her personal life. Whereas people's membership groups and reference groups ordinarily will coincide, individuals who are going through a process of anticipatory socialization may identify with and imitate groups to which they do not yet belong.

5. Primary groups such as families and close friends display total personality involvement, warm personal relations, and informal interactions among their members. Because they are satisfying to their members, primary groups are valued as intrinsic ends in themselves. Secondary groups such as customers and clerks are characterized by more formal, less emotional, more deliberate social interactions. Their value lies in being means to some important end for their members.

6. Group size appears to be an important factor in shaping the likelihood of primary or secondary relations among members. The two-member social dyad is the most basic and intimate type of group. Its continued existence rests entirely on both members' participation in the relationship. Triads or three-person groups mark the beginning of groups with an identifiable structure. They often re-form into a coalition of two against one. Increasing population size in societies historically has been associated with the movement from primary to secondary relations at all levels of group life.

7. Formal organizations—large, deliberately planned groups designed to carry out some specific objectives—have come to characterize most important activities in modern societies. Etzioni's typology distinguishes among normative, coercive, and utilitarian organizations on the basis of their members' motivations for participation. Max Weber's description of bureaucracy as the logical, rationally planned administration of people and ac-

tivities within a particular setting showed the bureaucratic organization to be a device for maximizing human productivity and efficiency. However, observations of bureaucracies in action suggest that ritualism and rigidity often make these organizations less than ideal vehicles for accomplishing complex objectives.

8. The informal organization of social relations and practices that invariably develops among the people within bureaucratic organizations often can enhance the formal organization's effectiveness by complementing and supplementing official rules and procedures. But if employees perceive the formal organization's goals or activities as being opposed to their own personal best interests, they may use the informal organization against the bureaucracy. In the long run, the best solution may be the development of a very different type of formal organizational structure.

9. Much of modern Japan's economic success has been attributed to the family style of Japanese formal organization. The Japanese company represents a near life-long commitment for many workers, whose personal lives merge with and often are regulated by the corporation. Such organizations are far less centralized in decision making than their counterparts in the United States, and their workers are able to participate more extensively in policy and procedure formation through quality control circles and other mechanisms. It is unclear if the Japanese style of organization could be implemented fully in the United States, whose culture is far less group oriented and much more individualistic. Research by Kanter and others seems to indicate that a more flexible, humanized administrative structure may prove to be more efficient and more profitable than the traditional bureaucratic model.

10. Societies are self-perpetuating groups of people who occupy a given territory and share a common culture. The study of societies was a major focus of early sociologists and remains so for macro-level researchers. Emile Durkheim, Ferdinand Tonnies, and Gerhard Lenski developed typologies of human societies in order to examine important developmental changes and trends over time. Durkheim argued that increasing population size, division of labor, and specialization of function led to the end of mechanical solidarity structures whose members formed cohesive bonds because of their shared social attributes and cultural world view, and the development of organic solidarity systems whose cohesiveness rested on the functional interdependency created as a consequence of increasing dissimilarities among members.

11. German sociologist Tonnies viewed societal change as a movement away from traditional gemeinschaft organization based on personal, primary group relations toward gesellschaft organization — formal, impersonal, and rational interaction typical of secondary groups. For Lenski, changes in productive technology created larger economic surpluses as societies developed from hunting and gathering bands through settled horticultural and then agrarian groups, and finally into modern industrial systems. These increasing surpluses permitted greater population sizes, which in turn fostered increasingly specialized social roles and greater societal complexity. Like Durkheim and Tonnies, Lenski saw human social history as the increasing movement from primary to secondary relations.

4

SOCIALIZATION

In the winter of 1973–1974 millions of motorists in the United States awoke to an unfamiliar and unfriendly world of gasoline shortages, gas station lines, and gasoline rationing. Pricing and production strategies implemented by the members of the OPEC (Oil Producing and Exporting Countries) cartel had removed from the marketplace many of the automotive fuels, lubricating oils, and other petroleum-based products that powered the U.S. economic machine. Drivers who once filled up on thirty-cents-a-gallon gasoline found the price of gas doubling and tripling—when they could find it at all. People used to cruising around in their cars with no place in particular to go now found this pleasurable pastime much more expensive; some even considered such driving unpatriotic. A society that for decades had been hooked psychologically on cars and structured socially around the unlimited use of personal vehicles suddenly had a critical part of its automotive "fix" cut off at the pump.

Drivers, of course, were not the only ones affected by this change. Dwindling petroleum supplies drove up the price of heating fuels, siphoning off increasingly larger portions of individual, family, and business budgets. Consumer prices for many other goods and services also began to escalate, as an economy largely based on petroleum-dependent industries started to feel the full effects of the OPEC cutbacks. As people began to realize that the wide variety of oil-related products they had always taken for granted someday might dry up, a population that had been raised with a throw-away, disposable mentality began to rethink, retrench, and recycle. Energy conservation became the new order of the day.

Nearly twenty years after that first energy crisis, people in the now-rich countries still face a world of depleted resources and rapidly decaying natural environments. That is the bad news. The good news is that, even though the problem itself remains, people's perceptions of it and their responses to it have changed significantly. Once seen as the exclusive interest of hippies and nature freaks, environmentalism is now a mainstream political issue. People from all social classes and all walks of life increasingly are becoming involved in a wide range of environmental concerns. Even corporate America has begun to examine its social responsibility to help restore and maintain the planet, although its motives for doing so often have been challenged as being driven more by profits than by genuine concern. For example, responding to public pressure (and perhaps sensitive to public relations), fast-food restaurants have phased out Styrofoam containers in favor of paper wrappers that require less energy to produce and are more biodegradable. Once scorned as scavenging and left to those desperate souls who needed money, recycling now occupies the attention of everyone from preschool children to retired business executives. It has become a symbol of the new environmental awareness sweeping across this society.

The ability of people in contemporary societies to reshape their daily activities and values so dramatically to meet the demands of changed environmental and energy realities illustrates the basic theme of this chapter. Most human behaviors, including those we might regard as natural, in fact are acquired through **socialization,** the social learning process we all experience from the day we are born until the day we die.

People in what had been traditional societies once treated their physical environments with respect, because they relied on those environments for their continued survival. They developed a cautious orientation to the earth that eventually became a part of what we referred to in chapter 2 as their world-taken-for-granted. As many societies modernized, however, their populations started to view the physical environment in a very different way. They began to treat nature as a wilderness to be tamed for social and economic expansion, a storehouse of resources to be exploited for personal gain. Over time, this new orientation became incorporated into the modern world-taken-for-granted that, until very recent years, was characteristic of most industrialized societies.

Today, those same populations find themselves having to abandon that mentality. They are adopting a radically different perspective, one that emphasizes the fragile, limited nature of the planet, and a "reuse it" rather than "trash it" environmental ethos. Although this process of unlearning and relearning has not been easy or painless, it nonetheless is occurring. As the tens of millions of people who gathered across the United States and the world for Earth Day 1990 clearly demonstrated, old dogs could be (and were being) taught new tricks. Perhaps in the near future, this "new" environmental ethic once again will form a central component of people's world-taken-for-granted. The populations of future societies then may well wonder how their ancestors ever could have been so primitive and unnatural as to treat the earth like a giant dumpster.

QUESTIONS TO CONSIDER

1. How are human social behaviors different from the behaviors of nonhuman beings?
2. Why is early contact with other humans so important for the social development of children?
3. How does increasing involvement in social group life affect individual personality development?
4. Why is successful socialization an important objective in all human societies?
5. Why is the family such a critical socialization agent in most societies?
6. What is the role of formal education in the socialization process of modern societies like the United States and Japan?
7. Why do peer groups have such a significant influence on their members, especially among adolescents?
8. Why have mass media such as television become critical agents of social learning in modern societies?
9. What has led to the increasing amount of adult socialization that occurs in contemporary societies?
10. How does the process of resocialization differ from other forms of socialization?

 ## ON BEING HUMAN: BIOLOGY AND HUMAN NATURE

As we saw in chapter 2 on culture, although human beings may be biological creatures, we do not show evidence of being biologically *determined*. Scientists' long search for a set of specific instincts that form the core of human nature has failed to demonstrate the existence of any such biologically grounded patterns. What this research does indicate is that biological factors form an important set of resources and limitations for humans. They significantly affect, but don't absolutely determine, the behaviors of human beings as a species and as individuals. For example, the fact that all the readers of this book are humans means that every so often they have to eat food to satisfy their biological need for nourishment. The fact that I am a large, tall person also means that typically I will have to eat more food than will a smaller, shorter individual. But the biological drive for nourishment that we all experience as hunger does not tell us what to eat or how to eat it. Many Americans' idea of the perfect meal may be a well-done cheeseburger and an order of crispy french fries. Samoans may favor fish and breadfruit, and the Ngatatjara aborigines of western Australia dine on fruit and lizard meat (Ember and Ember, 1988). The question of how hunger is to be resolved is primarily a matter of cultural preferences (as well as the availability of different food resources) rather than of human instinct. Biological drives may compel us to engage in certain common types of behaviors like eating, drinking, and sleeping; but social and cultural considerations specify how, when, what, and where we should eat, drink, or sleep.

If there is such a thing as human nature, it defines only general behavioral possibilities (and impossibilities) rather than specific behaviors. Instead, culture provides the set of specific behavioral responses to the world that instincts supply for nonhumans. Since culture represents a human creation rather than an inherited biological program, it must be learned by the individuals who live under its influence. This learning normally occurs as a by-product of the close and sustained contact with other human beings that all individual humans require (and most will experience) by virtue of their biological makeup.

ON BEING HUMAN: SOCIAL LEARNING AND HUMAN NATURE

Human beings are vastly superior to most other living creatures in a variety of important ways, but biological superiority does not appear to be one of them. Many mammals (e.g., horses) are able to walk, feed, and otherwise fend for themselves within a short time after their birth. Human infants, however, are so biologically helpless that they must depend entirely on other humans for their physical survival. Newborn humans cannot open bottles or cans of baby formula, change their soiled diapers, find shelter against wind and snow, or even roll out of the way of approaching danger. They require the physical assistance of others of their kind if they are to have their basic biological

Sociologists argue that most human behaviors reflect the results of social learning rather than inherited biological or psychological drives. This Pakistani father is teaching his son the proper use of one modern instrument of violence.

needs met. This physical dependency not only is complete, but also lasts for several years.

Sociologists argue that the resulting prolonged physical contact between human infants and their caretakers creates an environment of close social interaction that is essential to the development of attributes we normally think of as human. These traits include verbal and written language, rational thought, and the formation of a self-concept. The basic premise is that biological inheritance provides all humans with a pool of behavioral potentials. It is the quality and quantity of individuals' social and cultural experiences that largely decide which of these potentials will be actualized. Biology supplies the necessary raw materials that go into the creation of the finished human product. Through the socialization process, society and culture provide the necessary machinery through which the transformation of those raw materials takes place.

The Effects of Isolation: The Cases of Anna, Isabelle, and Genie

Compelling evidence to support this assertion has been provided by several documented cases of children who were raised in apparent isolation from other humans (Curtiss, 1977; Davis, 1940, 1947; Pines, 1981). The experiences of Anna, Isabelle, and Genie were remarkably similar in many respects. All were relatively young girls (ages five, six, and thirteen, respectively, when discovered by authorities) who had been subjected to extreme social deprivation from the first year or two of their lives. Anna and Genie had been shut away in closetlike rooms and had almost no interaction with other human beings outside of the occasional physical contact required to provide for their minimal physical needs. Isabelle was somewhat more fortunate in the sense that she at least had been hidden away with her mother, who was deaf and mute. When discovered, none of these girls could talk, feed or dress herself, or otherwise demonstrate an ability to interact with other human beings in a normal manner. Each gave the physical and behavioral appearance of being in an arrested infantile stage, unable to maintain appropriate and expected standards of cleanliness or self-control.

After being removed from her captivity and receiving a great deal of attention from psychologists and social welfare workers, Isabelle was able to make extraordinary social and intellectual progress. Within a few years she had acquired written and verbal language skills typical for other children her age, and seemed to be well on her way to a normal life. The intensive remedial efforts of the concerned authorities apparently were enough to offset the effects of her prolonged social deprivation. The fact that she had remained in contact with her mother also may have played a crucial part in her successful entry into the social community, even though the two had not been able to communicate verbally (Davis, 1947).

Anna and Genie did not fare nearly as well. From the time of her discovery until she died some four years later, Anna did not make any substantial progress toward becoming a full-fledged human being. Although finally able to take care of her own physical needs and to follow simple instructions, she never really developed more than the simple rudiments of verbal language. At the time of her death she remained intellectually and socially far behind other children of the same chronological age (Davis, 1947).

Like Anna, Genie never was completely able to develop normal human language skills or social behaviors appropriate for a person her age during the time of her attempted rehabilitation (Curtiss, 1977; Pines, 1981). Since her mother later acquired custody of Genie and removed her from the therapy program, we cannot determine just how much developmental progress she eventually would have been able to make. However, her general lack of improvement, despite the intensive attention she received, suggested that she had suffered irreversible damage as a result of being isolated during a critical period of her life. Apparently, involvement in human social interaction must occur early in our lives if we ever are to become fully human. Unlike other animals, our biology represents possibility rather than destiny. As the unusual and tragic cases of Anna and Genie demonstrate, that possibility can become actuality only through the teaching of other human beings. This social learning comes in the course of sustained interaction with family, friends, and those others who make up our surrounding social world.

 ## THEORIES OF SOCIALIZATION AS HUMAN DEVELOPMENT

Most social scientists agree that social learning experiences are critical to creating beings who are truly human. Their specific visions of how this process occurs have been influenced greatly by their respective intellectual and academic backgrounds. Psychologists, for example, typically have stressed the interplay between internal conscious or unconscious personality forces and external social factors. The work of Freud is illustrative of this perspective.

The psychiatrist and psychoanalyst Sigmund Freud (1854–1939) developed what amounts to a conflict interpretation of the human socialization process. In this view, the objective of important **socialization agents**—parents, teachers, and other important groups involved in the socialization of individual societal members—is to create within individuals a sense of moral right and wrong, as these matters are defined by cultural values, beliefs, and norms. Freud (1930) maintained that such a social conscience or **superego** was necessary to counteract the antisocial impulses of the **id,** the bundle of unconscious aggressive and sexual drives inherited by all individuals from their prehuman ancestors. The imposition of such societal restraints on the individual and pleasure-directed id creates a series of conflicts within the developing personality structure. These conflicts ultimately will be negotiated by the **ego,** the conscious mechanism by which individuals are able to engage in deliberate decision making and other behaviors. The socialization process consists of the progressive development of the superego, and the increasing submission of individual impulses to societal wishes and requirements.

Socialization as Self-Development: Cooley and Mead

In contrast to the biological focus of most psychological theories of human development, sociological approaches emphasize the social contexts within which this phenomenon occurs. The classic interpretations were offered by two men who taught at the University of Chicago in the early decades of this century. Both models stress the creative interplay between the developing person and the **significant others**—people who are important in establishing an individual's self-concept—who make up his or her immediate social world. These people play a primary role in creating the sense of **self** (one's awareness and concept of personal identity) that is a characteristic of true human beings.

Charles Horton Cooley (1864–1929) argued against the then-prevailing belief that humans are creatures whose basic nature is determined by genetic heritage and activated through biological maturation. Taking the opposite view, Cooley (1902) proposed that human development, including the critical ability to experience oneself objectively as well as subjectively, is a product of interaction with other humans in social groups. It is our close involvement with others that provides us with what he termed a **looking-glass self**—an impression of who and what we are that mirrors others' images of us. As he envisioned it, the formation of the looking-glass self is a three-step process.

In the first step, the reaction of these other people to us leads us to imagine how we must appear to them. Suppose, for example (in what is obviously a hypothetical illustration), after ten minutes of lecturing to an introductory sociology class one morning I notice that many students are yawning and sitting slumped over with their eyes closed. I might interpret their responses to my presentation as a sign that I am boring them.

In the second step, we imagine what sort of judgment these other people are making about us. To continue with the example, the fact that I have been around college students for about twenty years, and was once a college student myself, leads me to recognize that boring professors are not regarded highly. I can anticipate some hard times on my course evaluations at the end of the semester. If student comments are sufficiently negative, I may even get some raised eyebrows from my departmental colleagues and my academic dean.

Finally, in the third step of the process we experience some sort of self-feeling reflecting our perception of how these other people have seen and judged us. Having always thought of myself as a charismatic, dynamic lecturer, I now am more than a little embarrassed by the fact that I have just sent a room full of freshmen into a deep coma. I may begin to question or doubt my competency as an instructor and, as a result, may experience a reduction in self-esteem. Perhaps I should have become an anesthetist after all; at least in that line of work successfully putting people to sleep is regarded as a job well done.

Silly examples aside, Cooley's basic assertion that the development of human attributes is contingent on social experiences remains profound and important. His seminal analysis of the relationship between group interaction and personal development reshaped social scientists' thinking on this crucial phenomenon. It remained for one of Cooley's colleagues to clarify and expand upon his initial description of this vital aspect of the human socialization process.

George Herbert Mead (1863–1931) was a social philosopher who made a number of important contributions to the discipline we now call social psychology. In particular, he was interested in the process by which the human mind and sense of self developed. His own observations, as well as the work of his colleagues in the fields of psychology and sociology, led him to conclude (1934) that both mind and self are social products. They represent the outcomes of the individual's interactions with others in social situations rather than the outcomes of biological inheritance. Mead also argued that language, involving the use of **significant symbols** (physical stimuli with associated socially created, culturally defined meanings and values) is fundamental to the entire developmental sequence. In the absence of language skills, individuals cannot interact with others in such a way as to fashion a human personality. The cases of Anna and Genie seem to provide tragic support for this thesis.

Mead interpreted the socialization process that humanizes children as a series of increasingly complex interactions with a variety of significant others, including parents, siblings, peers, and teachers. Initially, the child's contact with parents and other people in his environment is primarily a physical and one-way process. As a helpless and dependent organism, the newborn requires and receives a great deal of physical attention from those responsible for his care. Children at this age act on the basis of physical stimuli (they cry when they are hungry, wet, or in pain) and react to the actions of other people (they calm down after they have been changed, fed, and had the open diaper pin that was sticking them refastened). But they cannot yet initiate deliberate, meaningful interaction.

As physiological and neurological maturation proceeds, the growing child becomes able to move under her own power and to explore her world. With time, she is able to distinguish herself as a physical being distinct from other beings and objects in the environment. The child also begins to engage in an important type of nonverbal communication with others through gestures, sounds, and facial expressions. In the process, she begins to associate certain physical stimuli (a smile) with specific meanings (happiness), and to experiment with such stimuli to express herself to others.

As the child continues to mature, he becomes capable of exercising verbal language skills requiring an understanding and manipulation of symbols. Direct verbal communication with other people who form the child's social world opens the door to a wide variety of learning experiences. It also makes possible a form of activity with significant consequences for the child's developing awareness of himself in relation to the world: play.

As Mead described the concept, **play** refers to that type of behavior in which the child pretends to be some specific person (typically, mommy or daddy) going about some specific task (preparing for a sales presentation to a client or shopping for tonight's dinner). In this way the child acts as she has seen that person act (perhaps in previous trips to the office with mommy or to the supermarket with daddy). The actions of these people whom the child is pretending to be are in fact role behaviors defined by those others' statuses—mommy is getting ready for the big meeting because she is the sales manager for her company; daddy is going shopping because he is a house husband. Thus, without any real awareness by the child of what is taking place, play becomes an exercise in **role taking** and **role playing.** In the course of replicating the behaviors of mommy or daddy (role playing), the child begins to view and to evaluate the world, and herself as an element of that world, from that other person's frame of reference (role taking).

Increasing maturation and exposure to the organized social world expand the child's play activities. More people become the objects of pretend behavior, and more details of their roles become incorporated into play. The child's frame of reference for seeing and assessing things (including himself) also expands. The child now is ready to participate in more complex game activities.

As employed by Mead, the word **game** applied to any organized group behavior. Although he happened to use the example of a genuine game (baseball) in his analysis, he just as easily could have talked about a cub scout den meeting or a brownie troop overnight campout. Whatever the particular circumstance, participation in the game demands new abilities and new levels of understanding not required for successful play behavior.

The teams (groups) involved in game activities consist of a number of individuals linked together as a set of interdependent positions governed by rules. Each position has its own associated role, and to participate successfully in the game the child must be aware of what is expected of her as an individual team member. Would-be pitchers must understand what it is that pitchers do, and would-be catchers must know what it is that catchers do. In addition, pitchers and catchers must understand each other's roles, and those of the other seven team members on the field, if either is to perform successfully.

Continued experience with the game brings the child a growing awareness of the concept of group structure and a group perspective. As this understanding develops, the child begins to use the group's frame of reference as his own in analyzing the world and himself. Little League baseball players adopt an athletic view of the world and define themselves in terms of athletic prowess. Members of scout troops begin to see the world in terms of wood craft and public service issues, and define themselves in terms of merit badges.

Mead asserted that as children begin to participate in a growing number of game situations, they discover that the individual games and teams in which they are involved are linked through common beliefs, values, and norms as parts in a larger structure. This larger structure, or **generalized other,** as Mead called it, is the surrounding cultural and social community of which the child is a member. With increased exposure to this larger entity, the child comes to adopt the perspective of the generalized other—the entire sociocultural system—as her own. Society's interpretation of the world and of the child becomes the child's interpretation of the world and of herself.

The result of this lengthy, complex interactive process is a human personality structure (termed by Mead the **social self**) that incorporates both a collective group dimension and an individual personal dimension. The "me" component of the social self is the objective, status-holding, role-playing aspect of the person. It reflects internalized cultural views and societal practices. Me represents that aspect of the self that the individual can step outside of and evaluate from an outsider's perspective.

The "I" component, on the other hand, is the subjective, creative, individual aspect of the person. It is that part of each of us that is not so immediately observable or predictable to others who do not know us well. Although Mead was not entirely clear on this point, it seems that the I represents a personal assessment of our own social statuses and social roles, and the resulting relationship we develop to ourselves as a result of that assessment.

Because one's social statuses and their associated roles are subject to change throughout the entire life cycle, the social self is never a final, completed product. Rather, the sense of self-identity, the concept of who and what one is, always remains in process, a continuing dynamic interplay between the individual and the larger society. In a very real sense, as long as the individual remains alive, the process of human self-development remains alive. It does not cease to exist until the individual ceases to exist.

SOCIALIZATION AS SOCIAL LEARNING

Although socialization itself is a lifelong experience, we do not generally experience it in the same way across our entire lifetime. Depending on prevailing cultural beliefs and social practices within a given population, people of various age groups may be exposed to different kinds of messages from an assortment of socialization agents. Several important organizations and groups are involved in the social learning process. Collectively, they help ensure the continuity of the established social system by converting newborn organisms into functioning societal members whose daily lives reflect and reinforce current cultural and social arrangements.

The Family

For most individuals in premodern societies, the family was the single most important source of information and learning about the surrounding world. This largely remains the case in developing nations today. It was from an extended family group, which typically included a variety of relatives in addition to parents and siblings, that new members received their introduction to social realities. This **primary socialization** entailed the establishment of one's initial societal position, the internalization of proper cultural values and beliefs, and the learning of appropriate communication and social interaction patterns. It even included preparation for later adult marital and occupational roles. As the all-encompassing, multipurpose group that formed the central axis of social organization, the family enjoyed a near monopoly as *the* agent of socialization for members of these traditional societies.

In modern societies like the United States and Japan, the differentiation and elaboration of more specialized social units have eroded much of the family's traditional role as the exclusive source of social learning. Young children in these societies now spend a considerable amount of time outside the family. At the same time, the family itself has changed considerably. The extended kin structure of the past has given way to the **nuclear family** composed of two spouses and their children. Changing gender roles (discussed more fully in chapter 7) and increasing financial demands also have led to the rapid expansion of two-career families and a resulting child-rearing vacuum (Tobin et al., 1989). In a growing number of cases, this streamlined, modern family

In virtually all contemporary societies, the family remains a critically important agent of socialization. Our sense of self, knowledge of our cultural world, and initial social position all are shaped strongly by our family experiences. For many people in modern societies, the family may be one of the few remaining settings for primary group relations.

structure has shrunk even further, as increasing numbers of divorces create more and more single-parent households.

Despite these significant changes, the family remains a critically important agent of socialization for most people. It still constitutes the initial setting of social interaction for newborn individuals, and is likely to be the major source of the child's contact with the world over an extended period of time. The family also provides the first experiences most of us have with primary group relations. As a result, in most cases its impact on the child's developing self-concept (in Cooley's terminology, the child's looking-glass self) is enormous. By acting as the first medium for the introduction of accepted cultural and social wisdom, it becomes a vehicle for their incorporation into the child's developing world view. For example, it is in the family that children begin to acquire a gender identity and a sense of what a girl or boy generally is like. This knowledge, of course, is a translation of cultural beliefs and values as mediated through the family unit (the process of socialization into a gender identity is discussed in more detail in chapter 7).

Finally, the family continues to function as the initial and continuing determinant of the individual's social class position. Its beliefs, values, and behaviors reflect its own position within the societal hierarchy. In teaching these patterns to its members, the family thus operates as the continuing mechanism for socializing them into the existing stratification system of the larger society (we explore this topic in greater detail in chapter 5).

The School

Formal education was virtually unknown to most individuals in traditional societies, but it has become a fact of life for most members of modern social systems. The sophisticated economic, political, and social structures that distinguish these societies are dependent on individuals who possess both a body of technical knowledge and the ability to think. Formal education for the masses through some sort of public (i.e., state-run) school system now is the norm in modern societies. Advanced education, provided through either public or private universities and colleges, is pursued by most middle- and upper-class members.

Compared to their counterparts of less than half a century ago, individuals in societies like the United States and Japan enter the world of formal education at a much earlier age. First grade once was the initial point of exposure to formal education. Today, it is not unusual for children as young as two or three to have some sort of preschool experience (Tobin et al., 1989). Whereas the curricula of these preschools hardly could be described as academic, children who attend them nevertheless receive an important education. They learn self-control, good work habits, and correct ways of interacting with other children and with teachers. These skills are necessary to their later formal education and instrumental in shaping their chances of success in those later school experiences (Gracey, 1977; Tobin et al., 1989). By the time many children do enter first grade, they already are seasoned veterans of the educational system.

At the other end of the formal educational stream, growing numbers of people are exiting the system at a much later age than ever before. As the body of general cultural knowledge continues to expand, individuals must spend a significantly longer amount of time in school simply to get some degree of exposure to existing information. The rapid development of knowledge in specific academic areas similarly necessitates an extended period of study to gain an in-depth knowledge of one's chosen field. Diplomas and advanced degrees have increasingly become a critical requirement for higher-status, higher-rewarded jobs in an increasingly credentialled society (Collins, 1979).

OURSELVES AND OTHERS

Why France Outstrips the United States in Nurturing Children

Paris—In a contest between child care in France and the United States, American children are the losers.

"Why don't you change it? It is incredible for a large rich country to accept the terrible infant-mortality rate. It's crazy."

That was how a woman who helps oversee child-care and preschool education in France reacted to the way the United States treats its infants and children. The official, Solange Passaris, special counselor on early childhood and motherhood to the Ministry of Health and Social Protection, said in an interview that because Europe was no longer in economic crisis it could now deal with children's welfare as part of a country's economic well-being.

She said she did not understand how the United States could accept ranking 19th in the world in the prevention of infant deaths while France ranked fourth.

National commitment may be at the heart of the matter. Even discounting the French passion for dramatic style, there is a political message in President François Mitterrand's statement that "France will blossom in its children." Or, as the president of the French-American Foundation, Edward H. Tuck, said more prosaically in a recent report by the foundation, "A Welcome for Every Child," France's success is attributable to "national policies focused on children, highly trained staffs, clearly defined responsibilities among agencies and a committed leadership at all levels of government."

Child care in France enjoys strong support from business and industry. "We try to create a partnership between business, the unions and government," Mrs. Passaris said.

Maternal leaves with pay begin six weeks before birth and continue for 10 weeks after delivery. Corporate leaders do not appear to be concerned over any possible negative effect on productivity and profits.

By contrast, American business interests lobbied so successfully against legislation that would have provided 10 weeks of *unpaid* maternity leaves that President Bush vetoed it.

To strengthen the family, French parents may take off two years without pay after a child's birth, knowing that their jobs remain protected.

On major issues, this is truly a tale of two countries.

Pre- and postnatal health care, lacking for so many poor women and their babies in the United States, is firmly anchored in French national policy. So is immunization, which in the United States has become increasingly erratic, leading to the revival of children's diseases that had been considered virtually extinct.

French educators, health experts and politicians appreciate the close link between preventive health care and children's future success in school and in life.

In the United States, millions of children are exposed to unlicensed day care. In high-quality centers, the cost is high. That creates great disparities in the lives of rich and poor children.

In France, the cost of care for children up to the age of 3 ranges from $195 a year for the poorest families to a maximum of $4,700 for the wealthiest.

Preschool for 3-to-5-year-olds is free, and 98 percent of the children attend it, more than three times the American percentage. Safe and nurturing places for young children of working parents are available from early morning to late afternoon.

In the United States, low pay and low status severely hamper the staffing of child-care centers. According to a recent report by the General Accounting Office, 40 percent of the workers in child-care centers in the United States leave each year.

French preschool teachers hold the equivalent of a master's degree in early childhood and elementary education. The directors of child-care centers are pediatric nurses, with additional training in public health and child development. Staff members have the equivalent of two years of college plus a two-year course in child development and early childhood education.

As an incentive, France offers students of preschool education free college tuition plus a stipend in return for a pledge to work in the field for at least five years after graduation.

Home care, which allows families to take in three children in addition to their own, is also licensed. In addition to daily compensation, family day-care providers are covered by Social Security, disability and unemployment insurance.

The home-care system is augmented with small-group centers to allow the children to mingle with others once a week.

A look at child care in industrial societies suggests that under regulated capitalism, as in France, or in social democracies, as in Scandinavia, children's welfare is protected because it is viewed as crucial to the children's and the nations' futures.

By contrast, leaving child care exposed to the uncertainties of a largely unregulated free market, as in the United States and Britain, has created conditions that Mrs. Passaris calls crazy. The practice leaves many children with inadequate care and permanently damaged, a costly liability to society.

Source: Fred M. Hechinger, *The New York Times,* August 1, 1990, B8. Copyright © 1990 by The New York Times Company. Reprinted by permission.

Individuals pursuing these occupations find it necessary to continue their training well beyond the baccalaureate level. Thus, for many of them, schools of one kind or another have become important and constant agents of socialization from shortly after birth to well into adulthood. Board-certified physicians in California, for example, are required to take formal classes each year in their areas of specialization regardless of how many years they have been in practice.

This educational system provides individuals with several different kinds of learning experiences. At the manifest level (discussed in chapter 1), the formal objective of primary, secondary, and postsecondary education is to create and transmit academic skills and cultural knowledge. As individuals progress through higher levels, they are exposed to more sophisticated bodies of thought and thought processing. These experiences teach them the general outlines and specific details of the world as viewed by their culture. They also prepare people to enter the occupational system of their society by providing training in important job-related skills.

Manifest objectives, however, are only half the story. The formal educational system also generates a number of other important consequences for the individuals traveling through it and for the society in which it is embedded. These less recognized effects constitute what might be termed the informal or hidden curriculum.

For many individuals, entering school marks the beginning of sustained social interaction outside the sphere of the immediate family. In the classroom, students must adjust their individual needs and whims to fit the requirements of the teacher and the school. They also must accept the fact that now they are being defined as members of some larger category and evaluated according to criteria that apply equally to all members of that category. Final spelling grades are determined by scores on tests and quizzes, not by virtue of being mommy and daddy's cute little Bobby or Bonnie. This experience may come as a real shock to children used to being the center of their families' universe. It represents the beginning of the individual's socialization into a large-scale, depersonalized structure that evaluates and places its members on the basis of performance criteria rather than personal identities. In this respect, the school may be viewed as an important instrument of **anticipatory socialization**— the early learning of attitudes and behaviors that will be required for some future social role. The everyday routine allows and requires students to practice behaviors they will be expected to display as functioning adults.

In modern societies, formal education also contains a political agenda—the promotion and legitimation of the societal status quo as the best of all possible worlds (Bowles and Gintis, 1976). We normally think of political socialization as indoctrination taking place in countries like the Soviet Union or China. In school children, however, it takes place to one degree or another in virtually every industrial nation (Hess and Torney, 1967). In fact, a good deal of this activity is designed deliberately and overtly into the formal curriculum. It is reflected through such devices as civics classes, the celebration of patriotic holidays (e.g., Presidents' Day in the United States; the Emperor's birthday in Japan; September 16th—the beginning of the War of Independence from Spain—in Mexico), and the pledge of allegiance to the flag. Much of it also occurs in more subtle ways.

Textbooks in history, literature, and other academic fields may be chosen by federal, state, or local boards of education as much on the basis of their political content as on their pedagogical merit. For example, until recently, most history texts used in elementary and secondary schools in the United States presented an Anglocentric, whitewashed picture of U.S. westward expansion during the nineteenth century. The wholesale destruction of indigenous Native American cultures was seldom discussed. Most often, "Indians" were depicted as temporary problems encountered in the process of fulfilling our manifest destiny of taming the frontier and developing the continent from sea to shining sea. Similarly, the Japanese Ministry of Education continues to approve only history textbooks that present a sanitized account of that country's military aggression in Asia throughout this century, especially during the invasion of China in the 1930s and World War II. Critics of this political editing of historical facts have been charged with dishonoring the nation, threatened with death, and physically assaulted (Inoue, 1990).

Finally, the school itself can be viewed as a microcosm of the society that envelops it. Like that larger society, the school has its own set of values, beliefs, and norms; that is, its own culture. It also possesses a social stratification system, a political apparatus, and established networks of primary and secondary groups that figure heavily in everyday student life. Whereas it may not be a mirror image of its surrounding society, it nonetheless is founded on the same principles that drive that larger system. The process of becoming integrated into the world of the school thus prepares the student to accept the basic premises of the larger society. By legitimizing existing social and cultural arrangements, the school functions as an important agent of political socialization.

Peer Groups

The term **peer group** or **peers** refers to people of approximately the same social position and age as oneself. Our peers typically form what we described in the last chapter as reference groups—people whose beliefs and behaviors serve as guidelines for our own personal orientation to the world. By definition, we might expect peers to be important agents of socialization for individuals. By observation and experience, this expectation has been validated, especially for adolescents in modern societies like the United States.

For someone still in the fairly early stages of socialization, peers are buffers between the individual and the larger society (Berndt and Ladd, 1989). Adolescents are being introduced to the confusing expectations and demands of an age-stratified world in which their own status has not been defined clearly. Peer groups provide them at least temporary breathing space and a measure of freedom from adult control. They also give adolescents an opportunity to explore aspects of life (e.g., smoking, drinking, sexual activity) normally discouraged and punished by parents or other authority figures. To those who experience the larger society as formalized and depersonalized, peers may represent genuine communities whose members are bound together in personalized, primary group relations. It is no wonder that these groups exert profound social learning effects on adolescents (Coleman, 1961, 1975). Adolescent peer groups can demand — and get — conformity to their values and standards of behavior.

Adolescents are by no means the only ones who are subject to important peer group influence, although pressures to conform to peer group norms may not be felt as intensely or responded to as fully by older, more established individuals. Adult workers in this society, for example, typically structure their own labor pace and productivity levels to conform to the informal expectations of their co-workers, a phenomenon first documented decades ago in the now classic Hawthorne studies (Roethlisberger and Dickson, 1964, original 1939). The original research dealt with industrial blue-collar workers, but any college or university faculty member can attest readily to the fact that informal collegial pressures operate just as effectively in academic departments as on factory assembly lines.

As we progress through the life cycle, we move into and out of a succession of age, occupational, marital, class, and other socially defined groups. At every step along the way we form important social relationships with others like ourselves. These peers serve as our immediate connecting links to the larger world. We never really outgrow our peer group affiliations, and our peer groups never really stop educating us about the social world and our places in it. They provide us with the standards we use to measure our success or failure, our happiness or discontent. We tend to think of peer groups as being significant elements only in the lives of children and adolescents, but they remain important forces in all our lives, throughout our lives.

The Mass Media

Few of the many changes associated with the modernization process have had the same kind of far-reaching impact on social and cultural organization as those in the area of communications. The transformation of communication patterns from traditional to modern societies could well be called revolutionary. Mass communications systems make possible the rapid transmission of information, attitudes, and ideas over great distances to enormous audiences (Wilson, 1989). They form a taken-for-granted but critical component of modern life. In a very real sense, mass communication creates and sustains societal life as we know it.

Modern societies depend on the smooth, continuous flow of information. In the absence of accurate, up-to-the-minute data, for example, government leaders could not possibly make effective or intelligent decisions relating to events halfway around the world (e.g., the Persian Gulf War of 1991). Economic planning by multinational corporations requires reliable financial statistics from many different areas of the world. In the case of both political and economic policy making, even this morning's news is old, and old news is worse than useless. The mass media make such communications flow possible.

It is difficult to visualize life without television and radio programs, films, newspapers, magazines, and books. Without these avenues of information and entertainment, we would remain disconnected and fragmented, unable to comprehend or respond appropriately to the world around us. For example, think of the various kinds of reports—traffic, weather, stock market—that reach us over television and radio each day. They allow us to plan our commute to work or school, our activities for the weekend, and perhaps our investment futures.

In modern societies the mass media play a multifaceted and profound role in the human social learning process. Employed as tools by recognized socialization agents such as the school, their obvious contribution lies in being the backdrop through (or on) which important information is presented to students. Your reading this textbook is a perfect illustration. In this context, the primary significance of the printed, visual, and audio media may lie in the sheer number of individuals who can be reached and affected by their messages at the same time. Simply stated, the mass media make mass formal education possible.

Mass media play critical roles in both the developed and the developing nations. A large variety of international newspapers and magazines link customers at this Indian newsstand with events and people around the world, creating a true global village.

But the socialization role extends well beyond media's utility as audiovisual resources in public and private schools. As conduits of information and entertainment between individuals and the larger society, the mass media, television in particular, are important agents of social learning in their own right.

Our involvement with the media is staggering. On average, American adults spend more than half of their waking lives with some form of them. They watch four hours of television and listen to three hours of radio each day, and read nine magazines each month; two-thirds read at least one newspaper each day (Biagi, 1990). These media serve as important windows on the world, providing people with significant information. In turn, this information can become a major basis for the formation of an individual's orientation to the world. A critical question, then, concerns the accuracy and validity of this media-provided information.

Adults who can distinguish between programs meant to entertain and those meant to inform understand that the former may take liberties with the facts in order to create a more interesting show. They expect that the latter will present a truthful portrayal of reality; however, their expectations often do not reflect what actually occurs. Studies of newspaper and television news reporting (Gans, 1980; Tuchman, 1978) indicate that, contrary to popular belief, news facts usually do not speak for themselves. Like other aspects of perceived reality, the news is a social construct. In deciding such issues as how much air time or column space will be allocated to a particular story, or what angle the story will receive, reporters and editors bend and shape events to fit their own requirements or priorities (Rosenberg, 1991). Even when this recasting of facts is done without any deliberate attempt to deceive or mislead, it nonetheless can have exactly that effect. Mass media news is not so much an act of reporting events as it is an act of filtering and interpreting those events for the audience (Tuchman, 1978).

Children and the Media If adults sometimes have a difficult time sorting out media facts from media fiction, children can find it impossible. Since young children ordinarily do not read, their contact with mass media largely comes through watching television. They have no systematic interaction experience with the larger social world to serve as a reality check on what they see, however. Consequently, they are susceptible to accepting everything that is portrayed as the truth (Dorr, 1986). This vulnerability, and the potential consequences of extensive, uncritical viewing, have served as the bases of a heated controversy concerning the effects of television on children.

One major area of criticism revolves around the effects of televised violence on children's developing personalities and social behaviors. At issue is the question of whether acts of aggression on the screen generate similar acts in reality. A large body of studies indicates that such an association does exist and may constitute a cause-and-effect relationship (National Institute of Mental Health, 1982). The issue is far from settled, however. Later studies (Josephson, 1987) suggested that the relationship may be weaker and more complex than first believed.

Whether or not television viewing is directly responsible for acts of aggression (or any other specific behaviors), it is evident that the medium is an important element of children's social learning experience. Many children spend as much time with it as they do in school or interacting with parents and other traditional socialization agents. They incorporate what they see into their growing understanding of the world and, to some extent, interpret the world in light of it. Later, as they become exposed to other media such as films, music, and books, these factors are added to children's developing world view.

In a mass society whose members share in a mass culture, mass media add an important element to childhood and adolescence social learning being shaped by family, schools, and peers. But socialization does not end with adulthood, and no single group or organization is likely to have the only word or the last word in determining the final outcome of the individual's socialization. The interplay of diverse and sometimes conflicting forces may help people retain their individuality throughout the learning process. It keeps them from becoming clonelike beings stamped out in their society's image.

Adult Socialization and Resocialization

Freud claimed that the essential details of personality are established through experiences occurring within the first five or six years of life. Perhaps influenced by this view, for a long period of time social scientists and lay people alike regarded socialization as primarily a childhood phenomenon. As children, individuals are taught the important facts of life they will need to know as adults. As adults, they behave according to the accepted patterns they learned as children.

Such a picture of socialization may have been remotely true for slow-changing traditional societies, but it is not an accurate portrayal of the process that occurs in most societies of the contemporary world. In both modern and developing societies, a great deal of socialization takes place after individuals have passed through childhood and adolescence and have entered the adult world. Such **secondary socialization,** as it is sometimes called, is especially likely in the face of the rapid, significant changes that characterize contemporary life. In many instances, traditional values, beliefs, and practices taught to children bear little resemblance or relevance to the realities confronting them as adults. As we saw in the introduction to this chapter, in such instances the survival of both the individual and the society demands that people remain flexible enough to learn new life patterns, as well as to unlearn old ones.

For most people, adult socialization occurs in the context of marriage and work. As we will discuss in greater detail in chapter 9, traditional conceptions of marriage and family life have changed drastically. Dramatic increases in both the number of divorces and the number of women entering the workforce as full-time employees have created new marital and familial arrangements (dual-career couples, single parenthood) as well as new problems (finding day-care services for young children, structuring so-called quality time into parent-child interactions) that often were not anticipated or covered during childhood. Adults who find themselves in family circumstances outside established cultural frames of reference have to rethink their roles as spouses and parents. Since they may have little or nothing in the way of existing knowledge to fall back on, this often takes the form of on-the-job training. The proliferation of self-help counseling groups for single parents, spouses of workaholics, and other nontraditional role players may be indicative of this trend.

Like marriage and family, occupational roles also have changed considerably. Unlike "the old days" when parents taught children the occupational skills they would require, most children now do not learn specific occupation-related behaviors from their parents. Children of attorneys or physicians or accountants may follow those occupational footsteps, but they learn the tricks of their respective trades in graduate or professional schools—law school, medical school, business school. However, even these training centers do not prepare their students for the specifics of the jobs they will be performing after graduation. Newly minted tax law specialists or surgeons or certified public accountants still must learn how things are done in the individual organizations that employ them. In addition, to the extent that people change organizations or professions in the course of their lives, they will encounter new socialization experiences throughout their adult years.

Sometimes adult socialization involves rapid and dramatic social learning in which old, established attitudes or behaviors are removed and new patterns are implanted; the process is known as **resocialization.** It often entails the construction of new personal and social identities for individuals, and occurs within the confines of what sociologist Erving Goffman (1922–1982) called total institutions.

Goffman (1961) described **total institutions** as places where large numbers of people who are cut off from the larger society live and work for an extended period of time in a carefully controlled atmosphere. Examples include army barracks, convents, orphanages, mental hospitals, and prisons. Individually, they serve a variety of social purposes; collectively they involve attempts to remake individuals in a new mold. Personal identities and differences, as symbolized by such things as individual clothing and hair styles, are stripped away and replaced with a new, categorical identity— common uniforms and numbers rather than names. The attempt is to break down individual resistance to the important learning of new, mandated behaviors and attitudes. Given the almost complete control such institutions exercise over their inmates' lives, such resocialization efforts frequently are highly successful. People leave these centers prepared and knowing how to lead more moral lives (in the case of monasteries and convents) or how to put an end to those who lead less moral lives (in the case of military boot camps).

SOCIALIZATION, OVERSOCIALIZATION, AND SOCIAL CONTROL

We began this chapter with an examination of the argument that humans are biologically determined creatures whose basic nature has been shaped by forces outside their control. Rejecting that claim, we attempted to construct a case for the opposite assertion. We are social creatures whose human thoughts and actions represent the consequences of lifelong socialization. As far as we can tell, we do not enter the world programmed by instincts or other inherited factors to develop in any sort of automatic fashion. Rather, the traits we normally associate with being human must be acquired from others through intensive and extensive interaction. In the absence of such interaction (as in the cases of Anna and Genie) individuals may remain prehuman— biologically equipped to become human, but unable to complete the process on their own.

The critical importance of social learning becomes even more evident as we examine the manner in which the members of a given population develop a sense of their surrounding social and cultural world. As we saw in the two preceding chapters, cultural and social structures are human creations that vary significantly over time and space. A quick look at any standard cultural anthropology textbook will verify the fact that humans have an amazing ability to interpret their world and then to build on that interpretation in an almost endless variety of ways. That same textbook could also verify the fact that the members of these different sociocultural systems invariably come to view their own particular arrangement as being right and natural. Ethnocentrism, as we tried to demonstrate in chapter 2, appears to be a near-universal human phenomenon.

The fact that one has been born into a particular society in a given historical period might be interpreted either as blind chance or individual karma. The fact that the individual ordinarily comes to accept that society's basic cultural premises and to follow its basic rules should be interpreted as a matter of deliberate design. Every society has a fundamental interest in ensuring that its members internalize its established patterns. Its continued survival depends on the successful transmission of those patterns to each new generation. Important primary and secondary groups such as families, schools, peers, and the mass media cooperate (or conspire) to carry out this objective. So also (as we will see in chapter 8 on crime and deviance) do larger organizations and institutions such as law and government. Fitting individuals into the surrounding sociocultural order is a crucial task, one on which socialization agents expend a great deal of time and effort.

Social systems have a need to direct and control the actions of their members, and most succeed in doing so to a large extent. Incidents of crime and deviance in modern societies often appear numerous, but the ratio of such acts to the entire body of social interactions that occur in a given day, week, month, or year is small. Every day of our lives, each of us has the opportunity to violate our society's informal norms or established laws hundreds of times. However, most of us do not do so, and the fact that we do not has little to do with being monitored by police or other agents of social control threatening severe punishments if we step out of line. For the most part, we act as our own agents; we choose not to break the rules because to do so would be "wrong." For example, the feeling that taking another student's sociology textbook would be morally wrong illustrates the fact that we have accepted and internalized our society's view regarding theft of someone else's property. In Mead's terminology, we have taken the perspective of the generalized other and made it our own. As Mead suggested, this phenomenon is both normal and, from the standpoint of societal continuity, necessary.

We should not rush to the conclusion that the social learning of accepted values, beliefs, and behaviors is equivalent to social programming, however. Most people accept and follow their society's rules most of the time. But as any student who has ever left a textbook sitting unattended too long has learned the hard way, many do not; and most people break some rules at least some of the time. Even when we follow the established norms we often do so only after a painful internal struggle between our individual desire and our social conscience.

In a famous and often-cited article, sociologist Dennis H. Wrong (1961) cautioned social scientists against accepting what he termed an **oversocialized conception of human beings.** By oversocialized, he meant a portrayal of people as puppets who have been manipulated by their society to believe everything they have been taught and to act blindly on the basis of these beliefs. In any given society, he stated, attempts to socialize individual members into complete knowledge and acceptance of the system invariably will fall short of perfection. The fact that modern societies are heterogeneous structures with racial, ethnic, class, religious, and other subcultural groups means that, in fact, no single integrated world view will be shared by all their members. The picture of the world that one is likely to receive will be a function of the values, beliefs, and experiences of one's subculture. Even if the social learning process worked exactly as intended, individuals still would exhibit different attitudes and social behaviors to the extent that their particular subculture differed from that of others. Societies may control their members, but they do not own them.

THE MEXICAN FAMILY: ANCHORING THE PAST, HARBORING THE FUTURE

From the time of the Spanish Conquest to the economic and political uncertainties of the 1990s, the majority of Mexican people have had to adjust to circumstances not of their own making but nonetheless of fundamental significance in shaping their daily lives. The fact that they have been able to do so with relatively few episodes of widespread social upheavals is, according to Riding (1989), a tribute to the strength of their families. The traditional Mexican family, he noted, mirrors the operating principles and structural atmosphere of Mexican society at large. In teaching individual members their proper roles in what amounts to a paternalistic, authoritarian structure, it prepares them to assume their proper roles in the surrounding hierarchically arranged social system. Through childhood experiences in family affairs, individuals acquire the personality traits and world view necessary for successful adaptation to a reality where planning is impossible, and events are controlled by forces outside one's own limited sphere of influence.

Family Structure

As was typical in most other not-yet-developed societies, the normative and most prevalent type of family structure in prerevolutionary Mexico was a version of the **extended family**. In its pure form, this arrangement is characterized by several generations of blood-related individuals of the same sex, and their spouses and offspring, who occupy a single household and who are under the authority of a household head (Nanda, 1987). It never was true that all families, or even all rural families, in traditional societies followed this pattern (Brydon and Chant, 1989), but the extended family unit provided a number of important benefits to its members that made it a logical and functional choice in this type of society. These included pooled financial resources (including the labor of household members) and shared, primary relationships that helped shield family members from economic and social impoverishment in the outside world. In most respects, the family was all that mattered to individuals in not-yet-developed societies, and it was all that was necessary to satisfy most of their pressing daily needs.

In Mexico, the most common form of the extended family was a **patriarchal family** in which males dominated females, married couples resided with the husband's parents, and family descent was traced through the male lineage (Lewis, 1960). This particular pattern was (and to an extent still is) prevalent in most Latin American societies. It may reflect a common heritage of Spanish and Indian cultures, the influence of the Roman Catholic Church, primarily rural and semirural residential backgrounds, and generally low socioeconomic status among these populations (Falicov and Karrer, 1988).

The beginning of economic and social modernization in the early decades of this century led to a streamlining of the Mexican family structure, as it did in many other societies undergoing the same developmental process. The nuclear family consisting of a married couple and their immediate offspring living in a separate household now became the most prevalent unit. In Mexico, however, the nuclear family remained strongly connected to a larger network of extended family groupings. Relations within the nuclear family also retained much of their traditional character, with a clearly defined, gender-based division of labor (discussed in greater detail in chapter 7). The male husband-father still assumed primary economic and decision-making responsibilities for the family. The female wife-mother remained responsible for childbearing, child rearing, and other domestic household activities. This traditional role complex has operated in conjunction with long-standing cultural belief in the natural superiority of males over females. Together, according to a number of observers (Diaz-Guerro, 1975; Oster, 1989;

Penalosa, 1968; Riding, 1989), they have fostered a family environment that has been largely responsible for perpetuating a kind of societywide personality neurosis among the Mexican people.

The *Machismo* Complex

As we saw in chapter 2, one paramount value in Mexican culture is *machismo*, the cult of masculinity that presumably dominates the male psyche and permeates all social relationships between men and women. The original basis for the creation of *machismo* (a topic that is examined in chapter 7) is still a matter of debate. So, too, is the question of contemporary forces that help sustain this belief, and the resulting complex of highly unequal male-female interactions that follow from it.

According to the authors cited above, the early socialization that occurs within the typical Mexican family plays a critical role in the *machismo* phenomenon. They view the rearing of children as an attempt by women to shield themselves and their families from the social and psychological voids created by their husbands' behaviors. However, in what may be a classic illustration of the concept of latent dysfunction discussed in chapter 1, the mothers' subsequent relationships with their children—especially their sons—implant the *machismo* ideology firmly in the minds of those children. In this sense, the primary socialization that takes place within the family is pathological. It almost guarantees the replication of personality profiles and social relationship patterns that are inherently dysfunctional for all involved.

The only party that may receive any tangible benefits from this situation is the Institutional Revolutionary Party (PRI) that has controlled Mexican politics for well over sixty years. Its rule has depended on a docile population resigned to accepting its designated place in the social hierarchy, more interested in matters of honor than in matters of politics.

According to this Mexican family as pathology perspective, all essential relations within the family structure bear the twisted imprint of the *machismo* complex. The heart of this complex is the male's need to validate his masculine superiority and virility, as well as his tendency to divide the female world into "good" women (who are pure and motherly) and "bad" women (who are sexually promiscuous and responsive).

Relations between husbands and wives thus are characterized by dominance and ambiguity by the men, and resentment and frustration by the women. Having a love-hate orientation to a wife who is mother to his children but also partner to his sexual lust, the husband often is absent from the family, out either with male friends or with mistresses. The wife often is frustrated by her husband's lack of sexual or other interests in her, and resents both his interest in other women and his attempts to control the household in which he may spend little actual time.

To compensate for this unsatisfying relationship, the wife adopts a long-suffering martyr role—the *marianismo* complex—that has become institutionalized as a type of feminine cultural ideal (Escobar et al., 1987). She lavishes great love and attention on her children, particularly her sons, cultivating their devotion to her. She also acts as a buffer between her sons and their father, who most often is emotionally distant and not involved to any significant extent in raising his children.

Because she herself has been socialized to accept the culture's definition of men as naturally superior, the mother also socializes her sons into that role. She gives them privileges denied their sisters (especially in matters of personal independence) and encourages them to demonstrate manliness in their behaviors. On the other hand, mothers teach their daughters to be pure and good, to develop an interest in "feminine" skills (especially motherhood), and to put up with the natural shortcomings of men. That is, females are taught to accept their society's traditional gender role.

The result of this complex, mother-dominated socialization process is a set of personality types that create a self-fulfilling prophecy in shaping future male-female relations. Supposedly, Mexican boys move into adolescence with ambiguous feelings toward both their father and their mother. Sons admire their father's *machismo* as expressed in his domination of internal family affairs and his outside sexual affairs; but they despise him for his betrayal and abandonment of the saintly mother to whom they are devoted. They love and revere the mother who has sacrificed so much for them; but they cannot respect her weakness in allowing herself to be used and abandoned by her husband. When they marry, they will end up treating their own wives as their father treated his, while they remain devoted and attached to their mothers.

Mexican girls, too, presumably emerge from childhood with confused and contradictory images of male and female social roles. They have been taught to devote their lives to men, but also have learned important lessons about the untrustworthiness of men from observing their mother's life. From their mothers, they also have learned to define their own future roles primarily in terms of motherhood, as well as to anticipate apathy, abuse, or abandonment from the fathers of their children. Thus, the stage is set for a recurring dysfunctional family cycle that will duplicate, in the next generation, the same personality traits and social climate that were inherited by the present generation.

This Freudian-like interpretation of Mexican family socialization dynamics has not gone unchallenged. Although a critique of what is essentially a psychological thesis is beyond the scope of a sociology text such as this, a number of comments are in order.

Public versus Private Realities

Celia Falicov (1982) stated that broad cultural-psychological explanations or interpretations such as the one above run the risk of ignoring significant differences in Mexican family structures and dynamics. These differences reflect important variations in social class, regional, residential, and other family living circumstances, and often are overlooked by researchers in their efforts to provide a global view of the phenomenon. What is presented as a universal cultural pattern in fact may be unique to a particular subgroup within the larger society.

Similarly, Falicov cautioned against confusing public and private realities. Public realities are the cultural norms that specify ideal family behaviors or values. Private realities are the actual behaviors or values that govern a particular family group. Although they may be based on prevailing cultural norms, private realities seldom are identical to those expressed cultural ideals. More specifically, Falicov and Karrer (1988) maintained that the presumption that all Mexican families are composed of *machismo* husbands and *marianismo* wives is a form of ethnic stereotyping. The moral is that sociological realities often (or usually) are more complex than psychological or cultural paradigms.

Nonetheless, there may be some validity to the argument that existing cultural (*machismo* complex) and social (male-headed nuclear family) structural factors have combined to create widespread dysfunctional relationships between men and women (Cubitt, 1988). If so, a number of recent changes in Mexican society may signal the beginning of the end of those relations. These changes are linked to economic opportunities and migration patterns, which have had important consequences for both the composition of the family and the ways in which children are socialized.

As we will see in later chapters, population migration is a widespread and significant phenomenon in developing countries like Mexico. In these societies it takes two major forms. **External migration** involves the movement of people out of the society; for example, tens of thousands of Mexicans cross the border into the United States each month. **Internal migration** is the movement of people from one area to another within the same society. In the developing nations, internal migration most often means people moving from rural into urban areas; for example, thousands of Indian and *mestizo* peasants move to Mexico City, Guadalajara, and other large Mexican cities each month. In both cases, the primary factors underlying migration are economic. The migrants generally come from lower socioeconomic classes, and they move for job- and income-related reasons (Brydon and Chant, 1989).

The wholesale internal and external migration of Mexican people during the past several decades is associated with major economic changes linked to modernization. Specifically, it appears to be a corollary of the capitalization of agriculture in the rural areas of the country, and of many industries in urban areas. In both instances, the result has been growing unemployment and underemployment for a large segment of the population (Massey, 1987). A second result has been a redistribution of males and females within the population and a corresponding change in family household composition (Brydon and Chant, 1989).

Mexican migration patterns show a distinct structuring by gender. Internal migration from rural areas to cities has been primarily a female phenomenon (Brydon and Chant, 1989). As a result of the general lack of agricultural work opportunities, large numbers of young women move to cities to find employment. There they work either as maids in the households of middle- and upper-class families, or as laborers in the growing number of *maquiladoras* (factories in which finished products are assembled from imported parts and then exported for final sale). Whereas they may retain ties with their rural families for a time, many eventually take up permanent residence in the city, establishing their own family there. In a large number of cases, these households will be headed by the woman herself. The prevailing *machismo* mentality creates a pattern in which individual men may father children with a number of different women and then leave the children to be raised by their mothers. In a growing number of cases, women may deliberately choose to dissociate themselves from abusive men and establish their own households. In either event, more than one-fifth of all urban households throughout the country now are female headed (Brydon and Chant, 1989).

In contrast to this internal migration pattern, external migration tends to be primarily a male phenomenon (Massey, 1987). Men by the tens of thousands cross into the United States to work in low-paying agricultural jobs or as unskilled laborers as a means of supporting their families who remain in rural Mexico (Conover, 1987). Many eventually rejoin their families, but many others do not. In their absence, the running of the family household may fall on their wives.

Through a combination of internal and external population migration patterns, more Mexican women thus are gaining a larger measure of economic and social independence from men. As they begin to experience a more autonomous lifestyle, they may begin to rethink and reevaluate traditional gender roles, and to raise their children in nontraditional beliefs and values.

At the same time that the number of households headed by women has been growing, the exclusive control of childhood socialization by these women has been decreasing. Typically, Mexican employers do not provide child-care facilities. However, the low wages they pay means that mothers generally cannot afford the cost of hiring someone to watch children during the long hours they must spend at work. Mexican factory pay is one of the lowest in the world, averaging only $1.57 an hour and ranking below

average salaries of workers in Hong Kong, Singapore, and South Korea (*Los Angeles Times,* November 4, 1990).

Working mothers have attempted to solve this problem in a number of ways. One strategy has been to create an extended family network involving siblings, cousins, and other kin who live together, pooling financial and child-care resources. Brydon and Chant (1989, p. 143) estimated that such family units make up about 25 percent of all households in lower-income Mexican urban communities.

A second strategy is to leave children with state-licensed orphanages, hoping that their daily needs will be met, and visiting them whenever possible. According to one recent estimate, over 90 percent of the children in Baja California orphanages come from single-parent households in which the mother is working but simply cannot afford to raise her children or pay for their day care (Briseno, 1990b). The number of available spaces in these orphanages is nowhere near the number needed, however.

Perhaps the most frequent response adopted by these women is simply to leave their children at home while they are at work. In all likelihood, Mexican cities had large numbers of latch-key children long before that term was coined. Like their counterparts in the United States, these children acquire much of their knowledge of the world through television. Mexico boasts the largest television production company in the world, and is becoming one of the fastest growing television markets in the world (Calderon, 1990). So pervasive has been the impact of the medium that it was described as "the country's Ministry of Culture, its Ministry of Education and its Ministry of Information" (Riding, 1989, pp. 311–312).

For Mexican viewers, especially those living in the northern states bordering on the United States, television has become the main window of access to a way of life very different from their own. As in the United States, a great deal of debate is being conducted concerning the potential negative effects of television on its viewers and in particular, on the children who are the country's future. However this debate may turn out, one thing seems clear. The generation currently coming of age will be the first in that country's long history to be socialized in nontraditional family settings by nontraditional agents.

The effects of these changes cannot be predicted with certainty, but it does seem likely that the world this new generation of Mexican children inherits and eventually passes along to their children will not be their father's world.

DISCUSSION QUESTIONS

1. What have been the major effects of the *machismo* complex on the socialization of children in the Mexican family?
2. You are a poor peasant thinking about migrating to Mexico City in search of a job. You do not want to leave your spouse and children behind, but you are concerned about what they might face in the big city. What factors do you think would be most important in your final decision either to leave them behind or to take them with you in your search for a better life?
3. The number of young children being left unattended at home by working parents is increasing not only in Mexico but in many other developing societies as well. Go to the library and read about day care provisions in the People's Republic of China. How is that country dealing with the potential problem of large numbers of unsupervised latch-key children?

FOCUS ON
JAPAN

THE JAPANESE SCHOOL: READING, WRITING, AND REGIMENTATION

Next to the family, the primary school is probably the most important agent of socialization for preadolescent children in modern societies. For the majority of these children, it is their introduction to the world of academic education. It is here that children get their first exposure to basic factual knowledge and knowledge-building skills. High-tech industrial and postindustrial social systems assume some minimal level of literacy from all their members, and also demand very high levels of intellectual competency from many. The school plays a critical role in helping to ensure that these needs and expectations are met. Primary schools, in particular, instill in their young students the fundamental academic abilities on which all other, more advanced knowledge acquisition depends.

Because formal education is so critical, the leaders of these societies place great emphasis on creating efficient, effective educational structures. Nowhere has this been more true than in Japan.

Formal Schooling in Japanese History

Official Japanese government interest in developing widespread formal schooling dates from the 1700s and the Tokugawa Period (1603–1867). During the eighteenth century, according to Fewster and Gorton (1987), three different types of schools were formed to meet the respective needs and interests of the different levels of Japanese society. Sons of the *samurai* class attended elite schools that taught warrior and administrative skills and a classical, Chinese-model education. Private academies based on European models and Western ideas tended to focus on members of a growing middle class. Finally, for the common people, temple schools stressed basic reading, writing, and mathematics, as well as moral education.

Within the first five years of the Meiji Restoration (1868–1912) the Japanese government established a Ministry of Education and mandated compulsory primary education for all children between six and fourteen. Although this move was resisted by peasants in the countryside, by the end of the 1880s a societywide system of education was in place. It featured centralized control by the state, a core of prestigious universities, and a strong element of patriotic loyalty and moral correctness (Fewster and Gorton, 1987). A network of "ordinary" and "higher" middle schools fed students into elite academic universities, whereas a series of vocational schools stressed more practical knowledge and skills developed at the secondary level. Throughout the early decades of the 1900s, the curricular content of Japanese schools at all levels became increasingly patriotic and militaristic, culminating with Japan's wars against China in the 1930s and against the Western nations in the 1940s.

World War II led to the destruction of much of the physical infrastructure of the educational system and a need to rebuild the facilities from the ground up. It also led to reconstruction of curricula at all levels by the Allied Occupational authorities, who purged Japanese education of its ultranationalistic, aggressive foundation and its strong centralized control (Buckley, 1990). At first under Allied control, then increasingly under the direction of the postwar Japanese government, the educational system has exploded since 1945. As we move into the 1990s Japan has, arguably, the most comprehensive and organized system of formal education among the modern societies of the world. It certainly produces students who outscore their counterparts from other industrialized societies in virtually every measure of academic performance.

Japanese Education Today

Japanese education is structured according to a six-three-three-four model. All Japanese children must complete six years of primary education (ages six through twelve) and three years of lower or ordinary secondary education (the equivalent of junior high school in the United States) (ages thirteen through fifteen). The three-year higher secondary school education that follows (the equivalent of senior high school in the

United States) is voluntary, as are the final four years of college or university study. Most students (about 95 percent) who complete lower secondary education continue to the higher secondary level, and about 40 percent of those graduates proceed to a college or university (Fewster and Gorton, 1987). In theory, education at the compulsory primary and lower secondary school levels is democratic and egalitarian. All children are accepted for admission, and all are promoted from one level to another at the end of each year, regardless of academic performance. Selection for admission to the higher secondary school level, and from there to college or university, is hierarchical and inegalitarian. Students enter and are promoted through these advanced levels on the basis of individual merit, as displayed through performances on entrance examinations prior to admission, and in subject area exams after admission (Hendry, 1987, pp. 88–91). Spaces in these higher level secondary schools and universities are limited, and competition for them has become fierce. As discussed in more detail in chapter 5, the entrance examinations for university acceptance have become an institutionalized ordeal for students and their parents, and the subject of a great deal of public debate and controversy.

The Japanese are well aware of the critical role of university and college education in providing graduates with the proper credentials for occupational mobility and social success (Vogel, 1979). They also are well aware of the equally critical role played by primary and even preprimary (nursery and kindergarten) schools in providing their graduates with the proper interpersonal skills to fit into the highly structured and group-oriented society (Simons, 1987). To a degree far greater than that found in the United States, what we described earlier in this chapter as a hidden curriculum of culturally approved values and beliefs and socially mandated patterns of interaction permeates the early levels of Japanese formal education. Schools have become crucial vehicles for socializing new members of the society into the world view necessary to guarantee the orderly flow of daily life.

The Role of the Group

As we saw in chapters 2 and 3, Japanese cultural values and social organization revolve around the group rather than the individual. The concept of individualism is by no means entirely absent, but it is not the type of rugged individualism so highly prized in the United States. In the Japanese world view, individual identity more often is understood in terms of the nature of the person's connections and obligations to the larger collectivity of the household, the school, the company, or the nation itself.

From the Japanese standpoint, individualism represents a residual component of the self. It is that which remains after one's status commitments and role obligations have been attended to, rather than that which selects those commitments and directs the carrying out of those obligations. If we were to frame the difference using Mead's terminology, we might state that the me element of the social self clearly and ordinarily dominates the I. For people in the United States, the me and the I more often are coequal partners in the individual's conception of self and conduct of social life; the statement "free to be you and me" expresses the cultural ideal. In Japan, "the nail that protrudes will be hammered down" (Simons, 1987, p. 52).

Given this cultural orientation and a social system whose operating principle is individual submission to the expectations and needs of larger social entities, it is imperative that children learn quickly and effectively not to protrude. In most cases, this critical socialization begins with the mother. Mother-child relations are intense and long lasting. Close physical bonding creates in the child a sense of dependency and obligation to the family, the first in the long line of groups that will be encountered throughout life. Given changing social, economic, and demographic conditions in the country, however, many mothers' traditional direct involvement in the child's socialization is being shifted into the hands of preschools. Today, more than 95 percent of all Japanese children experience some sort of preschool training. Some of these schools

As this group of preschoolers illustrates, the development of a strong sense of group identity and conformity is a major objective of the Japanese educational system. Although people in an individually oriented society such as the United States might find such a group-centered focus overly regimented and repressive, it apparently has contributed greatly to the post-war Japanese economic "miracle."

(*hoikuen*) may enroll children as young as six months of age and retain them until they are ready for primary education at age six years (Tobin et al., 1989).

The preschool represents the first group experience that most Japanese children have outside the immediate family. From the day they first enter one of these schools, they are introduced to the importance of these larger groups and of defining their own place in the world through them. By the design of their creators and with the approval of their students' parents, preschools begin a regimen that leads the child to identify with the other children in his or her class, who now are his or her status equals. Children dress alike and are given the same type of equipment to work with. Each day they are moved as a group through a series of carefully planned activities that stress cooperation and interdependence. For example, physical training exercises emphasize team activities like tug-of-war or marching in formation that promote the sense of being an integral and important part of the group (Hendry, 1987).

At the same time, preschool children are encouraged by their teachers to become more and more aware of the feelings and expectations of their fellow students. They also are led to increasing dependency on those others' feelings of approval or disapproval in structuring and evaluating their own behaviors. In Cooley's terms, the preschool class forms the basis for the looking-glass self. In the case of a student whose actions disrupt the classroom routine or ruin some class activity, for instance, teachers often allow the children themselves to deal with the event and the offender. Individual children thus are moved to look at themselves from the standpoint of their class (*mina-san*) and to conduct themselves with an eye toward what is best for the group (Hendry, 1987).

Peer Group Pressures

We in the United States may think of peer groups and peer group pressure as adolescent phenomena that operate primarily in junior and senior high schools, and this in spite of school officials' best efforts to eliminate them. This conception views peer groups as subcultures or perhaps even countercultures whose values and practices may mock and defy those of the larger sociocultural order. In Japan, however, preschool children are encouraged and guided to form strong peer group bonds before they enter the first grade and then, throughout their formal education, to rely on their peers for support in dealing with the larger society. The social organization of formal education at all levels has been designed to maximize the likelihood of these strong allegiances developing. There is a method to this madness.

As we saw earlier in this chapter, peers serve as important buffers between individuals and social systems. When they can be pressed into service on behalf of the established order, they become powerful and effective mechanisms for ensuring individual compliance with larger societal objectives. Like other, more official agents of socialization, they promote the stability of the status quo by directing their members' loyalties to the established order. Three-year-old preschoolers practice their marching lessons for long hours and try their hardest so that they won't let their classmates down or embarrass them. In the process, they are developing the self-discipline and sense of obligation that in future years will best serve the needs of their society's economic and occupational system.

The practice of using peer groups to further officially defined societal interests has been raised to a form of fine art. The country's rebuilding from the ashes of World War II and emergence as an economic superpower was made possible largely through the creation of highly disciplined, goal-directed workers who were willing and able to sacrifice individual interests and needs to those of the collective enterprise. To this end, the Japanese have been able to use a school system mandated by their conquerors and turn it into an impressive vehicle for social and cultural expansion.

An Educational Miracle—At a Price

The Japanese are perhaps the most educated and literate population in the modern world. The curriculum they have mastered is very demanding by U.S. standards and requires student commitments unheard of in most U.S. schools. Japanese students put in more school days each year (240 versus 180) and longer school work days (an average of two hours of homework each day versus thirty minutes), a phenomenon that manifests itself in their superior academic accomplishments compared to U.S. students (Barrett,

1990). However, this educational miracle carries a hefty price tag that few people in this society—students, their parents, their teachers, or their future employers—would be willing to pay.

In the United States, parents and professionals involved in preschool education were asked to name two of the most important things children can learn in preschool; the answer was self-reliance and self-confidence. Educating students to *think* and to trust their thinking abilities is evident in the fairly open structure of preschools and in teachers' encouragement of students' questions and independent work projects. In contrast, when asked the same question, only one-third as many Japanese respondents gave the same answer (Tobin et al., 1989). Over six times as many Japanese described "sympathy, empathy, and concern for others" as the most important educational learning objective at this level (p. 44). This orientation is evidenced in the more closed and regimented structure of Japanese preschools.

The theme of regimentation and group-oriented performance is carried through successive levels of the school system. As students move from preschool to primary to lower secondary and then higher secondary school ranks, the process of socializing them to centrally imposed standards accelerates and intensifies. Those in higher secondary school, especially, are instructed to memorize facts rather than process ideas, and to accept all they are exposed to. As one critic, an Englishman living and teaching in Japan for over thirty-five years, commented, "The whole Japanese system of education is geared to the formation of willing slaves in a vast slave-state" (Milward, 1990, p. 11). In the judgment of another observer, "Japanese school rules make English 'public schools' of forty years ago look like hippy colonies" (*Economist,* April 21, 1990, p. 21).

Whereas these lurid charges might sound like the words of ethnocentric (and perhaps worried) foreigners, similar critiques are starting to appear from the Japanese themselves. As the economy begins to move away from manufacturing jobs into service and administrative positions, some business leaders have expressed doubt that the current educational system can produce creative thinkers rather than well-trained doers (Smith, 1987). Faced with the shortage of home-grown innovators, some firms have begun to establish research ties with universities in the United States, touching off waves of controversy in both countries (Watanabe, 1990). Skyrocketing education costs, especially the cost of special "cram" schools for students facing university entrance exams, have begun to put a real burden on many families already strained to the hilt by the high cost of living (*Japan Times,* July 21, 1990, p. 3). Students themselves are starting to vote with their feet. A growing number of university students are choosing to study abroad (often in U.S. schools) or to attend one of the increasing number of branch campuses operated by foreign universities in cities like Tokyo (*Economist,* April 21, 1990).

Parents also have begun to speak out against the traditionally harsh treatment of students, treatment that includes physical punishment as well as psychological humiliation of students judged to be out of harmony with the school philosophy (*San Diego Union,* July 28, 1990). In one case that achieved national and international notoriety, a high school teacher in Kobe was fired and then later indicted for professional negligence after closing an iron gate and accidentally crushing to death a fifteen-year-old student arriving a few minutes late for classes (*Japan Times,* September 24–30, 1990). The teacher's intention had been to teach students a moral lesson about the importance of coming to school on time.

So far, the conservative Ministry of Education that retains full and final control over education has been reluctant to make any significant changes in the system. Under the apparent belief that schools have done an admirable job of preparing both individuals and the society to meet the challenges of the times, the ministry has adopted what amounts to a hands-off policy. Japan is well on the way to the number one position in the international economic sphere and is making significant strides in the international political community as well. It remains to be seen if the educational system that has taken the nation so far can adapt to the reality of the country's new superpower status. Given long-standing educational traditions in this tradition-conscious culture, such changes will not come quickly or easily. But even the most deeply embedded nails can be removed if the right kind of force is applied.

CHAPTER SUMMARY

1. Unlike other creatures whose behaviors are shaped largely by instincts, most human behaviors are learned through a process called socialization. This learning occurs as a by-product of the close social interaction young children have with parents and other important socialization agents.

2. Several case studies of young children who were isolated from normal social contact shortly after birth suggest that early socialization is critical for the development of language skills and other human characteristics.

3. Whereas psychological interpretations of socialization such as Sigmund Freud's focus on the interplay of conscious and unconscious personality forces, sociological approaches examine the impact of group experiences on individual personality development. Two important theorists in this tradition are Charles Horton Cooley and George Herbert Mead.

4. Cooley argued that humans are able to form a self-concept, a sense of individual identity, only through contact with other humans. He described a looking-glass self process in which the responses of other people to a particular individual give that person critical information for forming a set of beliefs and feelings about his or her personal attributes.

5. Mead portrayed socialization as a process in which increasing social contact between the individual and others creates role-playing and role-taking activities. In the play stage, young children pretend to be specific other people such as mother or father, learning something about the roles of parents in the process. In the game stage, the child interacts with others in group activities, developing a sense of social structures and the relationships among different statuses and roles. In the generalized other stage, the child comes to form a sense of self based on the whole system of social groups of which he or she is an acting part.

6. Mead claimed the sense of self-identity, or what he termed the social self, is composed of two related elements. The "me" is the objective, predictable part, reflecting the individual's involvement in social roles and role playing. The "I" is the subjective, creative, unpredictable part, reflecting the person's individual attributes. Mead argued that the self is never fully finished. Rather, it is subject to significant modification throughout one's lifetime, as one's social statuses and relationships change over time.

7. In modern societies, large numbers of groups and agents are involved in the socialization process. For most individuals, the family remains the single most important social learning influence. For a growing number of people, an educational system that takes students at earlier ages and keeps them for a longer time than ever before also has become a critical source of social learning.

8. For adolescents in particular, peer groups made up of people of the same age and social status are significant agents of socialization. Peers are buffers between the individual and the larger society, and create communities in which they can experiment with behaviors prohibited by parents and other adult authorities.

9. In contemporary societies, mass media such as television have become important sources of knowledge and social learning. A large amount of controversy exists over charges of distortion of factual news by the media, as well as the alleged effects of televised violence on young viewers. However, a simple one-to-one relationship between such programs and acts of violence by children has yet to be confirmed empirically.

10. A great deal of the socialization that occurs in contemporary societies involves adult learning of marital and occupational roles in a changing social and cultural world. In some cases this includes rapid and dramatic attempts to replace existing attitudes and behaviors with new patterns, a process known as resocialization. Resocialization often occurs within total institutions such as prisons, convents, and monasteries, where all aspects of people's lives are controlled and directed by agents of the organization.

11. Although socialization agents in all societies greatly shape the lives of their members, they never control them completely. Compliance with norms and values may be widespread, but such conformity is never automatic or achieved without difficulty. Sociologists must be careful not to develop an oversocialized concept of human beings.

5

SOCIAL STRATIFICATION

As a little exercise in mental gymnastics, close your eyes for a moment and try to imagine the world around you as a place in which all people are defined and treated as complete social equals. There are no significant differences in wealth or power or prestige among people. Skin color, age, gender, ethnic background, and religion make no real difference in shaping the quality of people's lives.

If you find yourself having a difficult time picturing such a world, you are by no means alone. Although complete social equality may be an idea with a long history in human philosophical thought, it so far has remained an idea whose time has yet to come. Despite a variety of efforts to create true egalitarian social structures, most societies throughout the world remain characterized by **social stratification**—the systematic division of a population into categories in which they are defined and treated as unequals. Populations are structured into layers or ranks that often show startling differences in **property** (income, wealth, other material resources), **prestige** (reputation, social honor), and **power** (the ability to accomplish desired objectives even in the face of opposition) (Weber, 1946). Such unequal systems apparently have been a persistent fact of life since the formation of settled, horticulture-based societies thousands of years ago (Lenski and Lenski, 1987). Whereas the amount or degree of stratification varies significantly from one society to another, structured inequalities are a fact of life in virtually all contemporary societies (Tumin, 1985).

The continuing and seemingly universal presence of such inequalities has made the study of social stratification a basic part of sociological concern since the field began. Given the existence of a number of competing theoretical paradigms, stratification has been subject to a variety of competing and often conflicting explanations. Several important interpretations have guided sociological research (and often social and political policies) over the past two centuries.

QUESTIONS TO CONSIDER

1. Some theorists argue that social stratification is natural in human societies. In what way is such inequality thought to be natural?
2. Functionalists such as Davis and Moore argued that if all social inequalities were eliminated, the survival of societies would be jeopardized. Why did they feel this way?
3. How do conflict theorists like Marx explain the existence of stratification in most human societies?
4. Why was Max Weber so critical of Marx's class conflict theory of stratification?
5. What major approaches have been employed to study social class in contemporary societies like the United States?
6. What major features distinguish open-class stratification systems from closed-caste structures?
7. How does structural mobility differ from voluntary mobility?
8. What is the relationship between position in the inequality hierarchy and physical or mental health?
9. Why does formal education play such an important role in the social stratification systems of modern societies?
10. How does social class affect people's educational experiences in societies like the United States?

EXPLANATIONS AND INTERPRETATIONS OF STRATIFICATION

Natural Superiority Theory

The approach embodied by natural superiority theory was in existence in popular thought long before the advent of the discipline of sociology. It found early sociological expression in the writings of Herbert Spencer and William Graham Sumner. Both men were important figures in the history of **Social Darwinism,** a social and political philosophy that believed in the existence of natural laws of social evolution and argued for a hands-off approach to human social affairs (Bryjak and Soroka, 1985).

Although never really fully developed and stated as a formal theory, the natural superiority perspective was an influential part of European and U.S. social thought in the late nineteenth and early twentieth centuries. It maintained that the *social* inequalities found in all human societies reflect underlying and fundamental *natural* inequalities among population members. For example, differences in people's wealth and privilege are the result of individual differences in physical strength, mental agility or intellectual capacity, or some other natural human trait.

Proponents of the approach viewed social life as a competitive struggle for existence among individual human beings. In this game of life, it was only natural that some would win and some would lose. Individuals who were better equipped mentally or physically would emerge as winners, and those who were more poorly equipped would end up as the losers. "Survival of the fittest" (a phrase coined by Spencer) was the harsh but very real fact of life. It might seem unfortunate that some people would experience great misery and distress while others around them prospered, but it would be even more unfortunate to intervene artificially on behalf of the losers. To do so would be to interfere with the natural cleansing process that strengthened societies by purging them of their unfit members.

By the same token, it would be an equally serious mistake to restrict in any way the activities or lives of the prosperous. They, too, were part of the larger natural plan for the improvement of human societies. Since inequalities were grounded in natural human differences, any action taken to eliminate them through social means (e.g., welfare programs for the poor funded through taxation of the rich) was doomed to failure. The best and only viable policy was that of a laissez-faire approach to social activities (for what is probably the classic statement of the natural superiority–based, Social Darwinist approach, see Sumner, 1883).

The natural superiority argument originally was intended as an explanation of social differences among individuals. However, it was adapted rather easily to be an explanation — and justification — as to why certain kinds of people might be expected to occupy superior or inferior positions in a given society. Given the assumed superior natural abilities of males as compared to females, of whites as compared to nonwhites, and of Anglo-Saxons as compared to non-Anglos, it was only "natural" that U.S. society would be dominated by white Anglo-Saxon males over the past two centuries. Given their assumed inferior natural abilities, it was only "natural" that females, nonwhites, and certain white ethnic people would be relegated to the lower positions. Historically, such arguments, as advanced by early sociologists such as Edward Alsworth Ross (1922), became a basis for a series of immigration quota laws first enacted during the 1920s. These laws were designed to halt or limit the flow of "inferior," undesirable people into the United States and thus prevent the ultimate catastrophe of (in Ross's words) "race suicide."

Empirical studies of human populations have failed to support the basic assumption that any specific class, gender, racial, ethnic, or age group is naturally superior or inferior to any other such groups. Thus this approach largely has been discredited as a valid *scientific* explanation of social inequality. However, natural superiority interpretations of social stratification continue to exert significant influences over cultural beliefs, social actions, and political policies in many societies. As we will see in the next two chapters, African Americans in the United States, blacks in South Africa, Indians in Mexico, Koreans in Japan, and women throughout the world are denied full access to social opportunities because of their presumed "natural" deficiencies. Natural superiority theory remains alive and well in the modern world.

Functionalist Theory

As discussed in chapter 1, structural-functional theory represents an attempt to explain certain patterns of organized social action (social structures) by examining their contributions to the survival of the social system (their social functions) over time. The classic functionalist statement concerning the question of social inequality was made by Kingsley Davis and Wilbert E. Moore (1945). It has been a source of great debate and controversy within the field of sociology for the past forty-five years.

The functionalist theory of stratification, or, as it is often called, the **Davis-Moore theory,** seems to share some of the basic assumptions of the natural superiority approach. It asserts that social stratification is a natural and perhaps inevitable part of the human condition, a part of life that in fact may be necessary for the continued survival of society.

Davis and Moore began with the observation that virtually all human societies in the past and in the present have been characterized by differentiated social positions that receive unequal amounts of property, power, and prestige rewards. They then sought to explain these systems in terms of a basic survival problem (a "functional requisite") common to all societies.

In every society, they claimed, people with unequal kinds and amounts of talent somehow must be encouraged to assume and to perform various social tasks. These tasks differ in a number of significant respects, including required skills and impact on societal well-being. For example, Supreme Court justices have a much more important effect on U.S. life than dog trainers. Although dog trainers may perform a positive function, its importance pales in comparison with that of the justices, who define the laws that govern our social relations. A successful career in dog training does not require formal educational credentials or an exhaustive knowledge of legal precedents; a successful court career requires both.

Davis and Moore argued that, to meet the challenge of matching talented people to critical social roles, all societies have developed reward systems that offer individuals property, power, and prestige incentives proportional to the skill requirements and the functional importance of the positions they fill. The more important the task and the smaller the number of people with the abilities to perform it, the higher the reward level. The less important the task and the larger the number of people with the abilities to perform it, the lower the reward level.

The underlying assumption appears to be that humans can be motivated best—or only—by appealing to their individual desires for prestige, fortune, and power. At the same time, the collective actions of individuals who pursue their own self-interests create effects that promote the well-being of the larger society. For example, some people may enter the legal profession to acquire the finer things in life this line of work typically offers. If some of these lawyers turn out to be inspiring defenders of justice, the fact that they were working just for the material rewards becomes irrelevant. What is important is that, without the tangible incentives, society would have been deprived of activities important for the continuity of the system.

This argument amounts to a social version of the "invisible hand," which Adam Smith claimed guided human economic systems. Presumably, if talented individuals were not offered these reward incentives, they would not undertake difficult, demanding, but important roles, since it would not be in their best self-interest to do so. Because critical social positions then would go unfilled, or would be filled by unqualified, incompetent people, tasks necessary for social survival would remain undone. The preservation of the system then would be jeopardized.

According to the functionalist approach, some of the effects of social stratification might be dysfunctional for particular individuals or groups whose rewards did not permit them any level of material comfort. But stratification itself was functional and necessary for the continued well-being of the society at large. Like that of the natural superiority approach, the functionalist argument could be translated into a hands-off, nonintervention social policy (although Davis and Moore themselves never suggested such a practice).

Critics of the functionalist model such as Melvin Tumin (1953a, 1953b) claimed it is impossible to assess validly the exact levels of difficulty various work entails and the actual functional importance of specific social statuses. These critics also argued that stratified reward systems do not work in practice the way they are supposed to in theory.

In what he termed the "strangulation of talent" effect, Tumin argued that any system of stratification created to promote the search for individual ability and talent ultimately will have the opposite consequence. Offering different levels of rewards to different social statuses initially may encourage open competition in which the most qualified people will win the most desirable (and important) social positions. But over time, the competition becomes less and less open. Children born to successful parents will have an advantage over children born to less successful parents, even where ability levels are identical. For example, the likelihood that the talents of a gifted ghetto child will be discovered and developed by teachers is far less than that for a gifted child from the affluent suburbs. Individual social identity and background, rather than personal talents, eventually become the primary criteria for filling social positions. Over the space of several generations, Tumin stated, what began as a mechanism for identifying and promoting talented people becomes a device for ignoring and stifling them. In the long run, therefore, stratification systems are dysfunctional for societal preservation.

Perhaps the most serious charge against the Davis-Moore interpretation of stratification is that it ignores the role of power in creating and maintaining social inequality systems. Critics (Dahrendorf, 1959; Lenski, 1966; Tumin, 1985) claimed that Davis and Moore treated power solely as a type of reward attached to individual social statuses, but failed to recognize its potential as a resource employed to establish which specific positions will be defined as most important for societal survival. In addition, Davis and Moore did not investigate the use of power by individuals or groups to restrict access to highly valued, highly rewarded statuses (Tumin, 1953a). For example, in the United States, powerful professional organizations like the American Medical Association and the American Bar Association have been able to set limits or quotas for openings in medical and law schools. Some critics of these associations have interpreted such actions as an attempt to keep the supply of professionals artificially low, thus increasing the demand (and the fees) for their services.

Davis and Moore apparently viewed the structure of unequally rewarded positions as forming a free market system in which people competed for specific statuses on the basis of their individual talents and abilities. Conflict theorists, on the other hand, take a dramatically different approach. They see a social world where individuals and groups use their power to manipulate economic, social, and political markets to their own best advantage. Although it predated the Davis-Moore statement by decades, Karl Marx's work in many ways represents the antithesis of the functionalist approach.

Marxist Class Conflict Theory

Karl Marx (1818–1883) focused on the phenomenon of social power. For him, the system of stratification was rooted in people's relationship to the economic process, a relationship that was central to all societies. Marx regarded the power struggles that inevitably ensued between the stratified groups in all societies—that is, **class conflicts**—as the driving force of human social history (Marx and Engels, 1955, original 1848).

This theory represents an example of materialistic determinism, the claim that all aspects of human social life are determined by the material or physical conditions of the given time and place. For Marx, the single most important fact of life for every human population was its **mode of production,** the mechanism by which wealth was produced in the given society. This economic **substructure** shaped all other significant material and nonmaterial aspects of societal life. Politics, law, religion, and even cultural forms were **superstructures** derived from and reflective of this economic foundation.

For individuals, the single most important fact of life was their position in the "relations of production"; that is, whether they were owners whose living was derived from the use of their property resources, or nonowners whose living had to come from the sale of their labor to others. Ultimately, Marx argued, societies would polarize into two distinct **objective classes** (in modern industrial societies, bourgeoisie and proletariat) along the lines of this basic economic distinction.

The fundamental interests of these two classes—maximum profit for owners, maximum wages for workers—are inherently incompatible. This conflict of interests puts

According to Marxist interpretations of social stratification, the impoverished conditions of some societal members are the result of exploitation by the powerful property-owning classes. Marxists would view this Haitian scene as reflective of the inherently unequal economic system in that country.

OURSELVES AND OTHERS

Rio Slum Children Find Death in "City of God"

Rio de Janeiro—The sounds of children happily chasing a soccer ball came in an open window, but Maria Teresinha Justo's mind was on the street children who never made it to her drop-in center.

"Fifteen children were exterminated here since June," she said, referring to a nearby slum of 180,000 called the Cidade de Deus, or City of God.

Brazil does not have capital punishment. But the social worker said that in the warren of muddy alleys and shanties that make up the City of God, military policemen routinely act as self-appointed executioners. Their victims are usually teen-agers who have fallen into a life of petty crime.

The Brazilian practice of treating homelessness and juvenile delinquency with bullets was snapped into sharp focus in September by a report from Amnesty International.

"At least one child a day is killed by death squads," the human-rights group said. "Daily, children are being ill treated, tortured, mutilated and killed."

The report was based on a yearlong survey of crime coverage in newspapers in three of Brazil's largest cities, Rio, Recife and São Paulo.

"We counted 424 violent deaths of children and adolescents," said Rosana R. Heringer, a sociologist who conducted the survey for the Brazilian Institute for Social and Economic Research, a private group here. "Undoubtedly, there were a lot more."

About half of the killings studied in the survey appeared to be the work of death squads. Victims were overwhelmingly black, male and poor.

Only 10 years old and small for his age, António Carlos da Silva would fit the survey's profile of a potential child victim.

When an abusive stepfather moved into his family shanty, António moved out. "I lived in the streets," the slender boy said as he fidgeted behind a large table at the shelter run by the Children's Crusade, a private aid group.

António said he had started earning spare change watching parked cars. He then moved on to serving as a courier for drug dealers. Then, before

António learned to write his name, he learned to handle a gun.

"The kids are in the street trying to survive," said Belmiro Carlos Nunes, general superintendent of the Children's Crusade. "Their parents' money doesn't go far enough and there is a lack of family planning."

Brazil's grinding poverty makes boys grow up fast, and the legal system makes minors useful for criminal gangs: it is rare that a judge will lock up a youth under 17. Youths walk away in droves from low-security reform schools, institutions that rarely reform.

The military police, who operate in a similar atmosphere of impunity reinforced by the indifference of the middle and upper classes, frequently act as judge, jury and executioner.

The attitude of people in Brazil's small middle and upper classes to these killings is due to several factors, sociologists and social workers say.

These people are overwhelmingly of European or Asian origin. Brazil's poor are heavily of African origin. In addition to racial prejudice, rising urban crime has caused a further closing of minds.

In a measure of the hardening of attitudes here toward crime, Rio voters easily elected to the State Legislature in October a retired policeman who campaigned under the slogan, "A safe Rio—the only good bandit is a dead bandit."

But there are also signs of a different, more generous kind of reaction to the problem of homeless and wayward youths.

In October, a group of tourist hotels on Rio's Atlantic beaches started a program to provide food, showers, schooling and a drop-in center for the roughly 500 children who live by their wits on the streets of Brazil's affluent southern zone. Also in October one of the city's top samba choreographers opened a samba school for street children.

On the Government side, President Fernando Collor de Mello declared in September that he was "appalled by the Amnesty report of the child killings, and the Justice Ministry is developing a human rights course for police cadets and police officers.

them into continuing opposition with one another. The owners possess great economic, political, social, and other power resources. They also exist as a **subjective class,** conscious and aware of their own collective position and interests in the mode of production. Together, these factors give this class an overwhelming advantage in its relations with workers.

Workers generally lack effective economic, political, and social power, as well as the ability to recognize their historical role in the economic productive process. Consequently, they are dominated and exploited by the superior powers of the owners. They will remain so until their objective living conditions deteriorate to the point at which they are unable to maintain even minimum survival standards. Only then will they begin to recognize their plight as a collective problem, and identify the source of the problem as the self-seeking policies of the owning class. At this point they finally will begin to take collective, conscious, revolutionary action to end their exploitation.

Human social history is a series of such revolutionary conflicts, and it is exactly as a result of these class upheavals that social and cultural change occurred. Past class revolutions succeeded only in replacing one ruling class with another. However, in industrial society, the proletarian revolution that was to come would end this changing of the palace guard history for good. Modern workers would recognize private property as the ultimate source of class divisions and antagonisms, and act to abolish it. With the elimination of private property, the basis for human social inequalities would be removed, and social stratification itself would become a thing of the past.

Marx believed that social stratification was neither natural nor inevitable; nor did it serve the best interests of societal survival. The interests of human populations were far better served by systems of social equality. He argued strongly for interventionist, indeed, revolutionary, action to create and maintain such egalitarian systems.

Thus far, history has failed to verify Marx's predictions. A worldwide proletarian revolution resulting in the destruction of private property–based economic systems and the elimination of social stratifications as a basic component of social life has yet to materialize. If anything, recent events in Eastern bloc socialist societies would seem to signal the kiss of death for Marxist class conflict theory. In these societies, capitalist-flavored economics are being reintroduced to bolster political regimes besieged by popular cries for democracy.

Conflict interpretations since the time of Marx (Collins, 1975; Dahrendorf, 1959; Wright, 1985) modified and broadened his original formulations to reflect the complexities of modern stratification structures. Marx's image of a society fundamentally divided along economic property lines may have been rendered obsolete. But a model depicting societies stratified into opposing groups, whose memberships change with shifting interests and issues, remains a powerful analytic tool for the study of stratification in the contemporary world. Sociologists owe a large debt to Marx for his outlining the basic concepts and premises of the conflict interpretation of social stratification. They owe a similar debt to one of Marx's critics, Max Weber. Weber's **multidimensional model** of modern stratified societies became the basis for a great deal of stratification research in the United States and in other contemporary societies as well.

Weberian Multiple-Hierarchies Model

Perhaps the most widely known and frequently applied model of stratification in modern societies is that of the great German sociologist Max Weber (1864–1920). His explanation of social inequality systems was developed as a rebuttal to Marx's economic-based class conflict theory. Weber believed that Marx's analysis of social stratification was dangerously simplistic. He also regarded Marx's call for a proletarian revolution as an essential violation of the principle of "value-free" inquiry in the search for sociological truths.

Although he himself was a conflict theorist, Weber rejected Marx's materialistic determinism and exclusive focus on economic stratification. He argued instead that in modern, complex societies, individuals and groups are ranked in hierarchies across a number of important dimensions. These inequality hierarchies might overlap, but they are at least partially independent in their effects on both individuals and the social structure (Weber, 1946).

Weber acknowledged that economics were an important part of the system of inequality in any society, but rejected the claim that economic-based inequalities were the only significant component. It was not ownership of private property, but the level of **life chances**—access to basic opportunities and resources in the marketplace—that defined the individual's **class** position within the larger society. Further distancing himself from Marx on this issue, Weber asserted that economic classes were not responsible for significant social or cultural changes in human societies. Instead, the important societal changes that Marx had interpreted as the result of class dynamics were brought about by the actions of groups stratified socially or politically.

For Weber, two other dimensions of inequality were crucial to understanding modern stratification structures and processes. In the **social hierarchy,** individuals were ranked according to the level of prestige or honor accorded them by others. People came to occupy a particular level, or **stratum,** in this hierarchy by virtue of a certain **lifestyle,** a distinctive orientation or relationship to the social world. Various lifestyles (whether of the rich and famous, or the poor and obscure) were reflected in artistic tastes, leisure pursuits, fashion styles, and—significantly—the company one kept. Unlike economic classes, the members of specific social strata were self-conscious communal groups. Their relationships with one another and with members of other strata were grounded in considerations of prestige and reputation.

In the **political hierarchy,** individuals were ranked as **parties** by virtue of their different abilities to mobilize and employ power. Such power was a function of the degree and type of organization developed by individuals in groups. For example, in most societies, bureaucracies have come to dominate in government and business sectors because of their success in organizing and coordinating the activities of large numbers of people. Weber claimed that power was sought deliberately as a means to influence and structure societal activities on behalf of the particular party. Like strata (but unlike classes), parties were self-conscious, organized groups.

Power-seeking groups might be drawn from particular classes or strata, from a specific set of classes and strata, or from sources completely unrelated to the economic and social hierarchies. In the United States, for example, economic and social position typically is a major shaper of political party affiliation. Generally speaking, Democrats draw their strength from the lower and working classes, and Republicans appeal primarily to middle, upper middle, and upper-class groups. However, there are occasions on which specific issues relating to race, gender, age, and morality (abortion, gay rights, etc.) create coalitions that have little or nothing to do with socioeconomic position (this may be the origin of the old notion that "politics makes strange bedfellows"). For Weber, Marx's assertion that economic position and political power were one and the same was false.

Weber saw the connections among economic, social, and political hierarchies as flexible and changing over time. For example, whereas prestige and power generally are associated with economic wealth, the relationship does not always hold. In Ireland and in many South American countries, Roman Catholic priests have little in the way of personal wealth, but exercise considerable power over their congregations and are highly respected by the faithful. To comprehend the realities of social stratification in the modern world, one must understand the workings of the many inequality systems.

As already stated, Weber's interpretation has become the fundamental model for much of the enormous body of stratification research generated during the past half-century. Individual sociologists might disagree on such matters as the relative importance of economic, social, or political inequality factors in a given society at a given time. Others might question the appropriateness of a specific empirical measure of these inequalities. Nevertheless, a majority of contemporary sociologists are committed solidly to Weber's model of a complexly stratified world as providing the most accurate and productive portrait of human social inequality.

 METHODS AND ISSUES IN STRATIFICATION ANALYSIS

If you were to ask half a dozen sociologists for a precise picture of *the* stratification system of the contemporary United States or even of one of its larger communities, you might receive as many as six different snapshots of the same social landscape. It would then be your task to select the one that you found to be of greatest interest or usefulness.

To some degree, this lack of agreement reflects the fact that social stratification in the United States is a complex and ambiguous phenomenon that defies precise description and measurement. Unlike the more clearly bounded and recognizable groupings found in some other societies, social classes in the United States are hazy, shifting entities. Their exact boundaries often remain unknown to their inhabitants, much less to outside observers.

To a significant extent, however, the confusion also reflects the fact that stratification has been studied from several different theoretical perspectives by researchers employing a variety of methodological techniques. To the degree that the phenomenon has been conceptualized, operationalized, and measured in different ways, several different pictures of the stratification system have resulted. These images often have mirrored the nature of the sociologists' research tools as much as the social reality being studied. Three such tools are **objective class analysis, subjective self-placement,** and **subjective reputation.**

Objective Class Analysis

The objective class analysis method has its conceptual underpinnings in the writings of both Marx and Weber. Marx described class in terms of the objective facts of property ownership and power (class in itself) that exerted important effects on individuals whether they recognized it or not. Along those same lines, Weber described classes as groups of individuals possessing similar levels of objective life chances.

In the objective approach, a given population is divided into hierarchies of income and occupational, educational, or other objectively defined categories. The cutting points or boundaries for these groupings typically are established by the researcher on the basis of either observed or predicted significant differences in attitudes or behaviors among the categorized groups. Figure 5.1 shows the distribution of family incomes in the United States for 1988, with families broken into seven income-receiving classes.

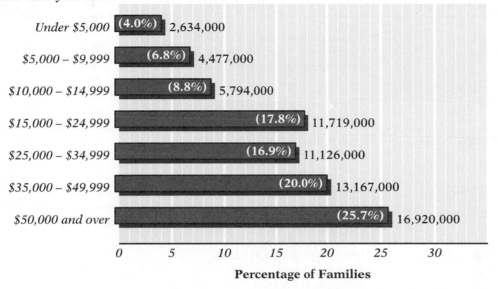

FIGURE 5.1   U.S. Family Incomes, 1988

Total Yearly Income

Income	Percentage	Number of Families
Under $5,000	(4.0%)	2,634,000
$5,000 – $9,999	(6.8%)	4,477,000
$10,000 – $14,999	(8.8%)	5,794,000
$15,000 – $24,999	(17.8%)	11,719,000
$25,000 – $34,999	(16.9%)	11,126,000
$35,000 – $49,999	(20.0%)	13,167,000
$50,000 and over	(25.7%)	16,920,000

Percentage of Families

Note: Numbers to the right of the bars indicate the number of families in this income category; the percentage of the total population they comprise is indicated within the bars. The total number of families — 65,837,000.

Source: U.S. Bureau of the Census, *Statistical Abstracts of the United States, 1990,* p. 450.

Do these data indicate that there are, in fact, seven economic classes in this society? Probably not, since a different set of cutting points would have resulted in a larger or a smaller number of income categories.

Voting, childrearing practices, preferred forms of leisure activities, and other behaviors associated with socioeconomic status do not show any clear natural breaking points with respect to income, education, or occupational level. For example, no single yearly income figure marks the precise boundary line between those who vote and those who don't. In general, higher-income groups have higher rates of voting and lower-income groups have lower rates, but not all high- and middle-income people vote, and not all lower-income people fail to vote. Because of the overlapping of these behavior patterns, the number and location of objective class boundaries always represent a decision made and imposed by the researcher.

Studies of stratification that use the objective method often present their findings in the form of a composite portrait of the U.S. social class structure (see Table 5.1 for some examples). In these composites, the researchers have tried to simplify a complex reality for the sake of clarity. Like other such abstractions, they should be treated as useful analytic devices rather than mirror images of social reality.

Subjective Class Analysis: Self-Placement

The subjective self-placement approach to stratification analysis also owes its conceptual foundation to Marx and to Weber. Recall Marx's description of a subjectively aware, class-conscious *group* standing in opposition to its counterpart on the other side of the

TABLE 5.1   Composite Portraits of the U.S. Class Structure

Class According to Gilbert and Kahl	Class Features	Class According to Rossides
Capitalist (1%)	Very high income (over $500,000) Elite/prestige university degree Executive/professional occupations	Upper (1–3%)
Upper middle (14%)	High income ($50,000 plus) Elite college/graduate training Upper manager/professional occupations	Upper middle (10–15%)
Middle (60%)	Modest income (about $30,000) High school/some college training Lower manager/semiprofessional/sales occupations	Lower middle (30–35%)
Working	Low income (about $20,000) High school/ Grade school/some high school Skilled/unskilled/service labor	Working (40–50%)
Working poor (25%)	Low income (below $15,000) Some high school Service work/laborers	
Underclass	Poverty income (below $10,000) Illiteracy/primary school Unemployed/surplus labor	Lower (20–25%)

Sources: Adapted from Dennis Gilbert and Joseph A. Kahl, *The American Class Structure: A New Synthesis,* 3rd ed. (Chicago: Dorsey Press, 1987), p. 332; and Daniel W. Rossides, *Social Stratification: The American Class System in Comparative Perspective* (Englewood Cliffs, NJ: Prentice-Hall, 1990), pp. 406–408.

property ownership line. Recall, also, Weber's depiction of self-conscious *individuals* forming status communities or strata on the basis of lifestyle and prestige.

Sociologists operating within this perspective treat social class as a subjective self-identification with some particular socioeconomic grouping. These affiliations presumably have significant consequences for personal values, beliefs, and behaviors (recall our discussion of membership and reference groups in chapter 3).

Researchers in this tradition seek to describe the stratification system of a specific society by asking members to locate themselves within a class. In some instances, respondents are given complete freedom to choose their own terminology to describe both the class structure and their own location within it. They may be asked if they ever think of themselves as being a member of some social class, and, if they answer yes, to name the social class they belong to.

In other instances, respondents may be asked to select their own appropriate group from among a set of such groups provided by the researcher. They may be given a listing of different names (upper class, middle class, lower class, etc.) and asked which term best describes their own social class position. In either case, the assumption is that the individual's self-perception is the true measure of his or her social class (Centers, 1949). After all, it is subjective perception and interpretation of reality that shape one's dealings with reality. Situations that people define as real, as

W. I. Thomas (Thomas and Thomas, 1928) noted in his classic "Thomas Theorem," are real in their consequences.

The additional assumption that seems present in this line of research is that individuals can and will locate themselves accurately within the inequality system. That is, respondents are presumed to be capable of validly reading the indicators that would in fact make them members of some particular group. In practice, this assumption sometimes has proved problematic. Respondents at times will place themselves within a social class that seems inappropriate for their actual socioeconomic characteristics. For example, a $20,000-a-year, high school–educated factory worker might describe herself as upper middle class.

At times, self-placements appear to be more a result of the number and names of class choices provided by the researcher than of any deeply held identification by the individual (Hodge and Treiman, 1968). For example, when given a choice of lower, middle, and upper categories, three-fourths or more of respondents typically choose middle as their class affiliation. When given a choice among lower, working, middle, and upper categories, an approximately equal percentage (about 40 to 45 percent) select working- and middle-class affiliations.

Despite the limitations of this approach, however, it continues to be used routinely in large-scale, cross-sectional studies of the U.S. population. It is a major source of much interesting and important information concerning people's beliefs and behaviors across a wide range of class-related issues.

Subjective Class Analysis: Reputation

In the reputational approach, social class positions are defined on the basis of evaluations made by people (e.g., friends and neighbors) who are in a position to know individuals well enough to make such a judgment. That is, people are located on the basis of their social reputations. The overall structure of such reputation-based placements constitutes the stratification hierarchy of that population group.

The reputational approach is clearly linked to Weber's depiction of social strata. It has led to a portrayal of social class (in U.S. society, at least) as primarily a matter of status or prestige. The classic and continuing inspiration for sociologists operating within this framework was the landmark series of studies conducted by W. Lloyd Warner and his associates (Davis et al., 1941; Warner and Lunt, 1941; Warner, 1960).

Warner viewed social classes as self-aware groups whose structure and relationships were central to the daily life of the typical American community. He also held that social class in the United States is largely a matter of inequality of status rather than of economics. Such inequality is created by community members through a subjective process of perceiving, evaluating, and responding to the life conditions of other members—what Warner called the "evaluated participation" of individuals in the daily life of their communities. In turn, these subjective evaluations were grounded in income, wealth, occupation, and other objective factors. As Warner stressed, however, they were not just a function of material resources (life chances, in Weber's terminology) but also of what one made, or failed to make, of them (lifestyle considerations).

Warner conducted his studies in relatively small communities and employed panels of residents who were knowledgeable about local affairs and people. He portrayed the U.S. stratification system as a hierarchy of six social class groups (upper-upper, lower-upper, upper-middle, lower-middle, upper-lower, and lower-lower) whose members were known to each other. These classes, according to Warner, served as perhaps the single most important principle for structuring interactions and relationships of all types within the community.

Although they had certain objective characteristics in common (e.g., wealth, education, etc.), what members of a given class really shared was a certain level of reputation among their peers. Warner claimed that it was not the possessed objective socioeconomic traits per se that defined who was and who was not a member of a particular group. Rather, the evaluations made of individuals and the reputations generated by them were the critical factors. Once made, class designations shaped virtually all other significant aspects of people's lives.

As might be anticipated, a number of difficulties are associated with the reputational approach to class analysis. One such problem relates to the settings within which reputational studies can be done with confidence.

Warner's studies originally were conducted in communities of about 20,000 or fewer people. People in these communities most often were long-time residents who knew each other well enough to make the detailed status observations that formed the basis of Warner's research methodology. However, in contemporary industrial societies like the United States, most people live in large cities with populations numbering upwards of 100,000. They are a great deal more geographically mobile than those people who were interviewed and observed by Warner a half-century ago. This means that many people just don't have the opportunity to get to know their neighbors well enough to make accurate evaluations of their social positions. By the requirements and assumptions of the approach, reputational studies would seem to be limited to the

Developed and refined by W. Lloyd Warner and his associates over fifty years ago, the reputational approach to social class analysis relies on the judgments of community members about their neighbors to form a picture of the social class structure. Although this technique has a long history in U.S. stratification research, it is best suited for smaller-sized communities such as this town in Maine.

kinds of communities that do not reflect the residential conditions of most people in contemporary society.

This may not prove to be a fatal or inevitable shortcoming of the approach, however. Using a combination of detailed interviews, survey research instruments, and observational techniques, several stratification researchers have been able to modify and adapt Warner's methods to examine successfully the social class structures of large urban areas (see, for example, Coleman and Rainwater's 1978 study of Kansas City and Boston).

What may be a more serious flaw is the fact that respondents who are located at different levels in the class hierarchy tend to perceive and evaluate the stratification structure in very different ways. In his original research, Warner noted that respondents higher in the class structure gave detailed descriptions of the overall structure, especially of those groups relatively near their own. Respondents located at lower levels presented a much simpler picture. They made fewer and less-detailed judgments of the number, names, and characteristics of the various classes, especially those much higher than their own.

Warner had to reconcile these different perceptions of stratification and of the criteria for placement in one class or another. In trying to do so, he seemed to have accepted an upper-middle-class view of the stratified world, perhaps with its associated upper-middle-class biases and distortions. This particular group's vision of social class became Warner's vision of class. The problem of what to do in the (likely) event of different perceptions and evaluations of social class by different groups of respondents remains a very real one.

The moral of this story is that there is no single best or error- and problem-free method for examining a phenomenon so basic, so pervasive, yet so complex and so difficult to pin down as social stratification. The fact that the structures and dynamics of inequality in many modern societies are difficult to isolate and analyze clearly may be good news for the members of these groups, however. It may point to the relative openness and flexibility of the systems and thus to the real possibility of movement and advancement for individuals and groups within them.

 ## OPEN AND CLOSED STRATIFICATION SYSTEMS: CLASS, CASTE, AND SOCIAL MOBILITY

In attempting to study social stratification across different societies and different time periods, sociologists have had to deal with hundreds of specific inequality systems. To help make sense out of what otherwise might be an impossibly complex task, these researchers have employed a number of devices to simplify and organize their observations. One such device is the construction of ideal types of stratified societies.

As you may remember from our discussion of ideal types in chapter 3, the word "ideal" as used here does not mean "best." Rather, it refers to logically extreme forms of social inequalities that may be thought of as the end points in a continuum of such inequalities. By elaborating the structural features that characterize such polar opposite types, the researcher can locate a specific society along the continuum in terms of its amount and kind of inequality (see Figure 5.2).

At one end of this hypothetical inequality continuum is the minimally stratified society, an attempt to approximate social equality. At the other end is the maximally stratified society, an embodiment of extreme inequality.

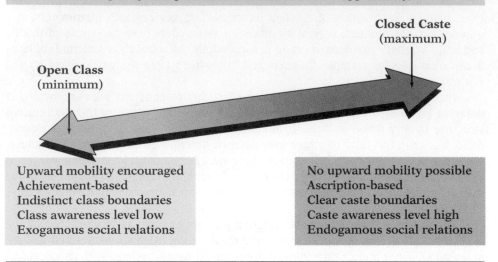

FIGURE 5.2   Ideal-Type Formulation of Stratification Systems (amount of social inequality: inequalities of condition and of opportunity)

Closed Caste
(maximum)

Open Class
(minimum)

Upward mobility encouraged
Achievement-based
Indistinct class boundaries
Class awareness level low
Exogamous social relations

No upward mobility possible
Ascription-based
Clear caste boundaries
Caste awareness level high
Endogamous social relations

In the first hypothetical system, minimal inequalities of condition (differences in Weber's life chances) are combined with maximum equality of opportunity. All members of society have the same chance to attain any given level of life conditions. In the second system, profound inequalities in condition are present. They are reinforced and preserved by great disparities in opportunities for different individuals and groups within society. For some members, wealth and power are almost certainties; for others, poverty is inevitable.

The first case describes what sociologists call an **open-class society,** and the second a **closed-caste structure.** Although many significant discrepancies exist between the society and the model (discussed below, and in chapters 6 and 7), the contemporary United States is often cited as the working example of an open-class society in action. Traditional (i.e., pre-twentieth-century) India, with its thousands of caste and subcaste groups, most often provides the working illustration of the closed-caste society.

The Open-Class System: (Nearly) All Things Are Possible

As used to describe societies such as the contemporary United States, "open" means that the stratification system allows for the possibility of individuals' **social mobility**— movement from one level or rank to a different level or rank within the social hierarchy, in this case, from a lower level to a higher one. No formal organizational arrangements, laws, customs, or cultural traditions deliberately bar or significantly restrict the free circulation of people up (or down). Such movements are in fact common and widespread.

What makes such social movements possible is the fact that, in the open-class system, positions at all levels are filled on the basis of achievement. Abilities and performances—what people can do—are the keys to location. A number of alternative routes to social success are present, so that individuals who somehow may be deficient in one particular area can compensate through accomplishments in another. Social mobility also is assisted by the vague and overlapping nature of class boundaries, as well as the relatively low levels of class awareness among people in most levels in the hierarchy. In combination, these factors make the transition from one level to another relatively free of culture shock, and permit socialization to new class behaviors and attitudes to proceed smoothly. Finally, relations among people are characterized by **exogamy,** the freedom to engage in secondary and primary relationships outside one's own group. Thus social interactions across class and status boundary lines are not formally restricted or limited in any way (Tumin, 1985, provides a more detailed description of the characteristics of the open-class system).

In the United States, most people occupy a specific rung on the social ladder by virtue of income, prestige, and power derived from their occupation. In turn, occupation is most often a function of one's level of formal education. Since people presumably attain education on the basis of academic abilities and performance, anyone with talent is capable of earning advanced university degrees. Theoretically, race, sex and social class do not aid or interfere with one's educational accomplishments.

Armed with the proper credentials, individuals can acquire good jobs that will give them access to a better life. They can purchase a dream house in the suburbs, join the local country club, and send their children to quality private or public schools. Perhaps a son or daughter will meet, fall in love with, and marry someone from an affluent family. This pattern obviously is not likely for everyone, but it is at least possible for some. That is the point of the open-class system: such things are possible.

The Closed-Caste System: Stay Where You Were

The systems of contemporary class-stratified societies such as the United States, Canada, and Japan presumably promote the open and free movement of individuals through the various ranks. In contrast, the caste structures of traditional societies such as nineteenth-century India captured individuals and froze them in social space.

What little social movement between ranks existed was of the downward variety; an individual might lose caste, but could not gain it. For all practical purposes, upward mobility into a higher caste was impossible within a given lifetime. (In the context of the Hindu religious belief in reincarnation and multiple existences, people thought it was possible to attain upward mobility across different lifetimes.) Socialization practices operated in such a way as to discourage the very thought of upward movement, as individuals were taught to accept their positions and to carry out assigned roles with dignity. An imposing array of established social, cultural, religious, and other institutional barriers effectively thwarted any misguided individual attempts at upward movement.

Caste positions in these societies were assigned to individuals on the basis of **ascription,** that is, personal characteristics (e.g., sex, race, age) over which one had no control. In the case of traditional India, the caste of one's parents, acquired from them at birth, was the critical factor. No accomplishments in economic, educational, or occupational arenas were sufficient to offset the overriding effect of birth caste. Caste behaviors and boundaries were clearly defined and understood by all members of society, and caste awareness was a central part of individual and collective identities. Virtually all important social relations were governed by **endogamy,** the principle of restricting and limiting everyday social interactions to other people in one's own membership group.

In short, one's life was spent within the physical and social confines of a particular inherited position, carried as a burden (or privilege) throughout life, and bequeathed to

MAP 3 World Economic Inequality as Measured in U.S. Dollars (1989)

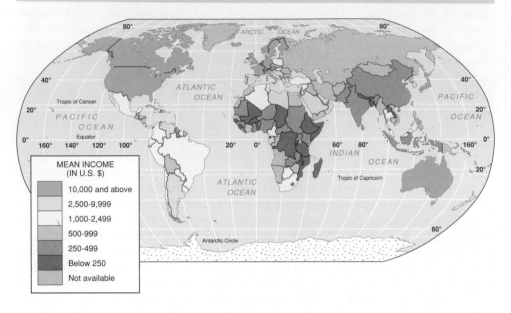

MEAN INCOME
(IN U.S. $)

10,000 and above
2,500-9,999
1,000-2,499
500-999
250-499
Below 250
Not available

one's children. Caste identity was the paramount fact of life in a society that was minutely and rigidly structured to emphasize the disparities and inequalities of human social life (Tumin, 1985).

Social Mobility Principles and Patterns

As previously discussed, social mobility refers to the movement of individuals and groups through social space within stratification systems. Historically, great differences in social mobility patterns distinguished between open and closed societies. Such differences also served as important indicators of various amounts of inequality among given types of societies. Comparative studies of contemporary class-stratified systems, for example, invariably use social mobility data to draw some conclusion about whether one particular society is "more equal" or "less equal" than another.

Some of these studies focus on what sociologists call **horizontal mobility**—the movement of people within a given level of the hierarchy. Most, however, focus on **vertical mobility,** the movements of people from one level of the social hierarchy to a different level. Such movements may be either upward or downward. In the United States, upward mobility (social climbing) is the American dream. Downward mobility (skidding) is the American nightmare.

Although sociologists talk of social class mobility in their studies, often what they are actually examining is occupational mobility. Ambiguities in the conceptualization and measurement of social class make its use in mobility research problematic. If we don't know exactly how many different social classes there really are in a given society, or what their precise boundaries are, we are not in a very good position to examine the movements of people from one of these classes to another.

On the other hand, occupations can be defined more clearly and measured more easily. In addition, they show fairly significant and consistent linkages to education and income, as well as to prestige and power factors. Thus they can serve as an (imperfect) operational measure of social class without doing serious injustice to the spirit of the concept.

Typically, studies of social mobility rates and patterns examine one or both of two different types of occupational movement. **Intergenerational mobility** studies chart the movements of people within the social structure across several different generations. The social positions of individuals at a particular point in their careers (e.g., age thirty-five) are compared to the corresponding positions of the individuals' fathers and grandfathers at the same time in their respective careers. (The use of masculine examples here is deliberate. Most such studies to date have examined the movement of males in the occupational structure, a fact that reflects the continuation of traditional sex role typing in most societies.)

Intragenerational mobility refers to the extent of social movement experienced by individuals within their own occupational careers. People are examined at a variety of significant points for evidence of upward or downward movement (or no movement). For example, we might track a graduating college class, beginning with the new graduates' first full-time jobs. We would return to see how our graduates, now preparing for their fifteenth college reunion, are doing. Then we might look in at our alumni, now pushing age fifty, to see how things have gone. Finally, we might attend their retirement ceremonies to see what positions they are retiring from. In a related vein, studies of what has been termed the status attainment process have focused on factors that, singly and in combination, influence and shape people's occupational careers (Blau and Duncan, 1967; Featherman and Hauser, 1978).

Several major studies of social mobility in the United States have indicated that both intergenerational and intragenerational mobility are widespread in modern industrial societies. In most cases, however, the movement is rather modest—short steps rather than system-jumping rags-to-riches leaps. In addition, research suggests that this pattern may be slowing down or even reversing itself (Blumberg, 1981). As accumulating data point to the growth of the bottom layers of the social hierarchy and a growing distance between top and bottom segments, researchers have begun to raise questions about the erosion and eventual disappearance of the middle class (Newman, 1988).

In attempting to understand and interpret mobility patterns, analysts make a further distinction between what is called voluntary (or exchange or individual) mobility and structural (or demand) mobility. **Voluntary mobility** represents the effects of individual efforts in propelling people up the social structure. The ambitious person who holds two jobs, takes courses in night school, and sees her hard work rewarded with a vice presidency in the corporation that once employed her as a secretary is an example.

Structural mobility represents the effects of significant changes in, for example, a society's economic system on the social movement of large numbers of people. The experience of Irish immigrants to the United States illustrates this type of mobility. Many of these people arrived in the country at a time when the rapid change from a small-town, agrarian system to an urban-based, industrial economy created a need for huge numbers of laborers to fill mills and factories and to build railroads. It even created a need for a smaller number of supervisors to direct and oversee this work. Thus, many immigrants who otherwise might have remained frozen in place at the bottom of an agrarian class hierarchy were pulled up into higher-level and higher-paying jobs by the needs of the new industrial order.

Historically, it appears that the relatively high rates of mobility experienced by various immigrants to this society during the nineteenth century, and by their descendants during the twentieth century, were related primarily to such demand mobility factors (Levy, 1988). Comparable patterns and rates observed in many other modern societies may also stem from the same structural sources; that is, systemic changes associated with the modernization process itself.

These observations are not meant to downplay or demean the role of individual effort in achieving mobility. In expanding, receptive economic structures in which many people are moving up the social ladders, the hard-working, committed individual will move up farther and faster. In fixed or shrinking, nonreceptive economic structures in which few people are moving up, perhaps only the hard-working, committed individual will experience upward mobility.

The Consequences of Social Stratification

Physical and Mental Health

Prestige, power, and fortune do not necessarily guarantee happiness, but they do seem to foster levels of physical and psychological well-being that may make happiness more likely. People from higher socioeconomic groups become ill less often and less seriously than members of lower socioeconomic groups (U.S. Department of Health and Human Services, 1989). When they are ill they can avail themselves of some of the finest medical and health care facilities in the world. These facilities are beyond the reach of people in the lowest social classes, who cannot afford the often extraordinarily high financial cost of getting well. Members of the lower classes must then pay the cost of staying ill.

Although upward social mobility remains the American Dream, the reality is quite different for many people in the United States. It is unlikely this resident of the Rio Grande Valley, the poorest region in the country, will experience significant opportunities for moving up the socioeconomic status ladder.

Like physical well-being, psychological or mental health seems to be distributed differentially among the various social classes. People in higher classes are far less likely than those in the lowest classes to experience serious psychological disturbances or impairments (Kessler and Cleary, 1980). When they are in need of mental health treatment, they have access to individual therapists or private psychiatric care. When psychiatric care is available at all to members of lower classes, it most often takes the form of state mental hospitals in which drug-based and other, less gentle treatments are widely employed. More often than not, however, serious psychological problems among members of the lower class remain untreated (Hollingshead and Redlich, 1958; Kohn, 1976).

Political Involvement

In democratic political systems, participation in the electoral process represents perhaps the most significant way for average people to influence their society. This is especially true if that society does not seem to be operating in their best interests. To the extent that government decisions and policies set the course of economic, social, and even cultural patterns, individuals can influence these patterns by selecting those who will serve in the government.

However, data from a wide variety of studies (Conway, 1991; Marger, 1987; U.S. Bureau of the Census, 1990) clearly indicate that members of the lower classes in this and other democratic societies have opted out of the electoral process. Compared to members of the higher strata, lower-class and working-class people display much less interest in and knowledge of political issues or political actors. They have significantly lower rates of voter registration and correspondingly low rates of actual voting among those who are registered (O'Connell, 1990). Participation beyond the act of casting a vote, such as becoming involved in campaign activities or running for elected office, is even more uncommon for these individuals.

In the absence of widespread participation from lower-class and working-class levels, upper middle- and upper-class groups can maintain control of the political structure. Once in command, they can set policies and make decisions in accordance with their own best interests and their own view of the world. Given the generally more conservative, status quo social and economic orientations of these higher-strata groups, both domestic and foreign societal policies typically end up supporting and maintaining the existing social system (Dye, 1990).

Crime and Criminal Justice

People from all classes face the possibility of some contact with crime, whether as victims or as perpetrators. Members of the lower rungs on the social ladder have a much higher probability of both types of contacts than do those situated above them. Lower-class people often are the victims of various street crimes, especially those involving violence, such as aggravated assault and homicide. In many instances, these crimes are committed by members of the same social group, perhaps by members of the same family.

There seems to be a widespread pattern of family violence among lower-class groups, especially within the "underclass" of racial minorities at the very bottom of the income structure (Wilson, 1987, 1989). At the present time, for example, murder is the single most frequent cause of death among young African American males in the lower classes of U.S. society. Enormous financial pressures and the general lack of economic resources to deal successfully with them that are characteristic of lower-class conditions may be important factors in the origin of homicidal and other violence.

International comparisons of homicide rates in societies at different levels of economic development suggest that this pattern holds among poorer societies as well. Mexico, with a significant proportion of its population near or at poverty existence, in 1981 had a homicide rate of 17.7 per 100,000. Japan, with a large and relatively affluent middle class and a much smaller segment of impoverished citizens, had an amazingly low rate of 0.9 homicides per 100,000 in 1984. Although the rates for other industrialized societies were not quite as low as Japan's, they averaged below 3.0 per 100,000 in most cases. Even the United States, an affluent but murderous (compared to other economically advanced nations) society, had a rate of 9.5 homicides per 100,000 in 1982. This figure was well below that of Mexico and other developing nations (Little, 1989).

Compared to members of higher social classes, lower-class people also are perpetrators of crime more often, at least according to official crime statistics, and with respect to conventional or street crimes. While middle- and upper-class members are involved in significant and socially costly amounts of criminal activity, these white-collar, corporate, and elite offenses often go unrecognized and unpunished. Crimes committed by lower-class people receive more attention from police and court agencies, and lower-class people receive more frequent and more serious punishments for their offenses (Rossides, 1990).

Education

In contemporary societies, formal education is both an indicator of current social position and an important resource for attaining future higher positions. Modern societies are "credential" systems (Collins, 1979) that feature occupations that increasingly demand formal certification of competency. Higher education, especially at the college level, provides the certification necessary to gain entry to high-status–high-salary jobs. Cross-cultural studies clearly indicate the critical role of formal education in attaining status, a role well recognized by members of society themselves.

Realizing the value of formal schooling, immigrants to the United States in the past and present have taken advantage of available public education to begin their climb up the ladder of their adopted society. In contemporary Latin American countries in which a grade school education often is the national average, members of the developing urban middle classes are aware of the many advantages of being a university graduate. Their eventual goal is a career in the business and government bureaucracies that dominate these societies and provide individuals a means of economic and social success. In Asian countries such as Korea, formal education and educational achievement have almost become something of a fetish to people hungry for advancement and a taste of the good life offered by modernized, industrialized social systems.

Historically, formal education has been an escape mechanism for many members of the lower classes who otherwise would have remained stuck at the bottom of the social hierarchy. At the same time, the historical experience is one of formal education playing an important role in preserving existing hierarchies.

In traditional societies, such formal education as existed was reserved solely for the use of the nobility and other privileged classes. There was no need for literacy among peasants or serfs, who were believed to be too intellectually inferior to qualify for or benefit from formal education. In developing societies where only the established upper classes can appreciate and afford it, education again is reserved for elites. Even in modern societies like the United States where free public education exists as a reality as well as a concept, the system of higher education continues its close association with the class system.

In the United States, upper-middle- and upper-class children are far more likely to attend a college or university than their counterparts in the working and lower classes. This holds true even when individual ability levels are held constant (Sewell and Shah, 1967). These young people also are far more likely to attend an elite, prestigious university, one of the Ivy League schools, for example. The financial and other admissions requirements of these universities lie beyond the means of most lower- or working-class families, effectively putting the benefits of graduating from one of them out of their reach. The academic currency value of degrees from such schools tends to be much higher than that of degrees from lesser-known institutions. In a society in which a college-level education is becoming more commonplace, the source of one's degree becomes increasingly important in shaping occupational and other career lines (Useem and Karabel, 1986).

Close linkages to the stratification system also exist at the other end of the educational structure (entry-level primary schools). Children from high-status families often attend private boarding or "country day" schools that serve as important agents of class socialization (Baltzell, 1958; Levine, 1980). In addition to the more standard educational components found in public schools, the curricula in these schools include cultural values and social behaviors appropriate for their particular social class.

Within the public school system, children from the middle classes fare better academically than lower-class students, in part because the latter are much less likely to have had the benefit of one or more years of prior education (nursery school, prekindergarten). Whereas children may not actually learn a great deal in the way of academic information in prekindergarten classes, what they do learn are the behaviors and attitudes appropriate for school. They also learn important lessons in student-teacher and student-student interactions. By the time they arrive in kindergarten where it counts (they will be formally evaluated, graded, and either promoted to or held back from the next formal grade level), middle-class children know the educational ropes (Gracey, 1977).

Having no such prior experience, lower-class children entering school for perhaps the first time in kindergarten have to start from scratch to learn the rules in what is basically a system structured along the lines of middle-class values and norms. They find themselves at an immediate and continuing disadvantage, in which their normal behaviors and beliefs from outside the classroom setting may be held and used against them inside the classroom. Daily confrontations with the educational system, coupled with a less education-oriented home environment and real pressures from the economic environment (the need to get a job), create high dropout rates both before and during high school. Formal education is an important resource for securing jobs and money in contemporary societies, and, like other important societal resources, it tends to be distributed unequally along established class lines.

Although hardly a comprehensive or exhaustive review of the consequences of social stratification, this brief discussion should make one thing perfectly clear. Whether or not you or I believe in the reality of structured social inequality, we all are members of groups occupying some level within the hierarchies of our respective societies. The nature of these hierarchies and the social level of one's specific membership group are possibly two of the most important facts in individuals' lives. What people are, what they can be, what they will be, will be determined largely by the system of social inequality. Social stratification is much more than just a fact of life. It often can be a matter of life and death.

FOCUS ON

MEXICO

MEXICAN STRATIFICATION: SOMETHING OLD, SOMETHING NEW, SOMETHING BORROWED

Gerhard E. Lenski, one of the most prominent contemporary scholars in the field of stratification, developed a sophisticated and wide-ranging evolutionary theory of human social inequality (Lenski, 1966; Lenski and Lenski, 1987). The theory represents an attempt to reconcile and synthesize the major propositions of the functionalist and the conflict interpretations of stratification. It investigates social inequality from historical, comparative, and macrolevel perspectives.

In this model, Lenski argues that technological change has been perhaps the single most important driving force in human social history. It has revolutionized economic productivity systems and thus generated fundamental social, political, cultural, and other societal-level developments.

Lenski viewed societal-level phenomena such as stratification as being shaped by the level of economic development. He constructed a typology of societies—hunting and gathering, horticultural, agrarian, and industrial—based on the kind and level of economic system of a particular society (see chapter 3). His basic argument was that the general shape and level of stratification was primarily a function of the level of economic development in that society. According to the logic of this theory, societies of a given type (e.g., two industrial societies such as the United States and Japan) should resemble one another in terms of social inequality structures. Societies of different types (e.g., a modern industrial society like Japan and a developing, not yet industrialized society like Mexico) should display significant differences in social inequality from one another.

Within a given type of society, variations in the stratification systems of individual societies, Japan and the United States, for instance, could

be explained by other factors. These would include the age of the economic development level (early industrial systems versus mature industrial systems) and variations in political, religious, and cultural institutions. However, Lenski asserted that the overall level or type of economic system remained the primary explanatory variable.

Lenski noted that the "primitive egalitarianism" found in the earliest hunting and gathering groups represented perhaps the closest that humans have ever come to attaining true social equality due to their small population size, simple social structure, and nomadic lifestyle. As technological advances moved these societies through horticultural and into agrarian stages of development, simple equality had begun to give way to primitive, and then sophisticated, inequalities.

Traditional agrarian systems represented perhaps the zenith or high point of structured social inequality. These societies displayed great disparities in power, prestige, and privilege among different hereditary class or caste groups. The stratification system was shaped like an elongated pyramid, with the overwhelming bulk of the population (peasants or serfs) forming the impoverished, uneducated, and menially employed (or unemployed) wide base of the pyramid. The very small group of successful landowners and merchants formed the narrow middle, and the even smaller group of land-rich, enormously wealthy and powerful elites served as the tiny apex.

The development and harnessing of mechanical power (e.g., the steam engine), which ushered in the Industrial Age, radically transformed established agrarian empires. As these economies industrialized, new types of social, political,

158   Chapter 5 Social Stratification

cultural, and even personality structures emerged. The "age-old evolutionary trend toward ever increasing inequality" (Lenski, 1966, p. 308), which had been a feature of societies since the days of the horticultural settlements, finally was halted.

Modern technologically sophisticated societies emphasize and depend on principles of achievement to fill occupational positions requiring technical expertise. They institute mass educational structures to ensure a steady supply of workers who possess such competencies. Through the higher salaries that accompany such technical occupations, industrial societies generate a higher general standard of affluence. Finally, the combination of increasing education, higher income, and material well-being creates widespread democratic ideologies among population members. The result, according to Lenski, is that the industrialization and modernization of agrarian systems has led to a general flattening out of the stratification pyramid and a significant movement toward social equality.

A Case Study of Lenski's Model

Contemporary Mexican society provides an interesting case study of Lenski's evolutionary model of stratification. For the first several hundred years of its existence, Mexico was ruled politically and dominated economically, socially, and culturally by Spain. Its society represented a transplanted version of traditional Spanish society. It was stratified into a very small, extraordinarily well-situated group of landowners of pure Spanish extraction and a gigantic, extraordinarily poorly situated group of Indians and Africans (and later, mixed-race *mestizos*). These groups formed, respectively, the top and bottom rungs of the social ladder in what was then called New Spain.

In 1821 the Mexican people revolted and broke from Spanish rule, establishing the society as an independent nation. However, this revolt was not much more than a changing of the palace guard. Political rule was now Mexican rather than Spanish, but the economic and social structures remained as before. A tiny cadre of landholding elites controlled most of the agricultural resources of the country, and a large mass of landless, impoverished peasants eked out a minimal existence working the fields of the elites' *haciendas.* In 1895 over 90 percent of the Mexican population were members of the country's lower class (Granato and Mostkoff, 1989).

During the latter part of the nineteenth century, Mexico moved increasingly into a position as an exporter of agricultural products in the growing international market economy. This movement led to the creation of urban-based working- , middle- , and even upper-middle-class groups of business and government employees and managers as the country began to modernize. These groups, however, still represented a distinct numerical minority in what remained a society stratified along agrarian lines. In 1910, on the eve of the revolution that was to be the single most important event in twentieth-century Mexican history (Riding, 1989), the social disparities remained striking. One percent of the population owned 85 percent of the land, and 95 percent of the peasants owned no land at all (Huntington, 1968). It was these great disparities that led to revolution, which was an attempt to give land back to the people, to establish social and economic opportunities for the sizeable Indian population of the country, and to establish a more egalitarian system.

As political and social revolutions are measured, Mexico's was not a raging success in accomplishing its objective of a radical, or even a moderate, restructuring of the social order. It was followed by protracted civil war and the gradual formation of single-party political rule by the **Institutional Revolutionary Party (PRI).** Although economic development proceeded into and through the decades of the 1920s, 1930s, and 1940s, the social inequality structure remained largely unchanged. By 1950 the country possessed a fairly large middle class of educated business and government technocrats, but the distribution of income among the population remained highly unequal. In that year, the bottom one-fifth of the population received 6.1 percent of the total income, whereas the top one-fifth received 60 percent. Eighty percent of the population still were members of the lower class (Granato and Mostkoff, 1989).

Twenty-five years later, even after Mexico had begun to industrialize more heavily, the distribution of income was even more skewed. The bottom one-fifth of the population received only 2.6 percent of the total income and the top one-fifth's share had increased to 66 percent (Felix, 1977). This persistent growth of economic inequality

Once seen as the country's ticket to economic success, the Mexican oil boom has failed to live up to its early promises. A depressed international oil market has left the country saddled with huge foreign debts and a host of other social and economic problems that could threaten Mexico's political stability.

was linked to what appeared to be the absence of an overall economic development policy on the part of the succession of presidents who governed during this time, and the absence of necessary capital to undertake massive industrial development and expansion. It may also have been related to the apparent use of government office for self- rather than societal enrichment.

During the 1970s the government, encouraged by discoveries of massive oil deposits and by the demand for petroleum in the international market, began to solicit large loans. The money from these loans was to be invested in the development of the domestic petroleum industry. The belief and expectation was that the resulting great wealth generated by oil could then be employed to bring about essential economic and social development. (Mexico's population had been expanding rapidly, and had been racked by high inflation and deteriorating living condi-

tions.) In the early 1980s, however, the international petroleum market became oversaturated. Oil prices collapsed, and the government found itself in the position of not only having to meet the daily survival needs of its growing population, but also owing some $100 billion in loan debts.

Today, the country's leaders recognize and concede the fact that continuing social inequality remains one of the most serious and pressing problems. Nonetheless, at this point, the government has little chance to do very much to attack that problem as long as it has a more immediate economic crisis to worry about.

It has been over eighty years since the political revolution that was supposed to end drastic inequalities in Mexico, and nearly thirty years since a burst of economic development that, at the time, was seen as a textbook example of societal modernization. The bulk of the population remains impoverished, uneducated, and facing a marginal and uncertain future. Whereas many Mexicans have opted to seek a better way of life as documented or undocumented workers in the United States, others have responded by challenging the sixty-year rule of the PRI. The election of Carlos Salinas de Gortari, the PRI candidate, in the 1988 presidential election is regarded by many observers as a function of the party's control over the electoral process, and not necessarily of the will of the people. The first real PRI loss in state elections occurred in 1989, as the governorship of Baja California went to the opposition National Action Party (PAN).

Lenski's evolutionary model of stratification predicted increasing political instability of "perhaps revolutionary magnitude" in the event that economic development was impeded or that egalitarian trends failed to follow in the wake of economic development in a given society. The apparent break-up of the Soviet bloc in Eastern Europe would seem to verify the power of that prediction. It remains to be seen if it will come true in Mexico.

DISCUSSION QUESTIONS

1. In Lenski's view, what specific factors associated with economic development are responsible for the high levels of social equality in modern industrial societies?
2. If you were the president of Mexico and concerned about the possibility of another revolution, what steps would you take to deal with the great social and economic inequalities in your country? What difficulties do you think you would encounter in carrying out your plan?

3. Mexico's history as a colony of Spain shaped the country's social stratification system in many important ways. Go to the library and read about one of the modern African nations that also was a former colony of one of the European powers. In what ways has the colonial status of this country affected its current system of social inequality?

FOCUS ON
JAPAN

LAND OF THE RISING SONS

Many people living in the United States look on their society as the exemplar of a true egalitarian system, a free and open society. Empirically, however, that reputation is not entirely deserved. The United States has been and continues to be a society characterized by deep (if not always immediately obvious) social and economic inequalities. As we will see in the next two chapters, these inequalities often are embedded in widespread beliefs about supposed "natural" differences that distinguish members of various racial, ethnic, and gender groups. Such racist and sexist beliefs create radically different opportunities and social paths for members of these specific groups.

Compared to traditional agrarian societies of the past or to present-day developing societies like Mexico, the United States is certainly much more egalitarian. This holds true whether we measure equality in terms of the way resources are dis-tributed among socially stratified groups, the distances separating such groups in the hierarchy, or the patterns of individual movement up and down the hierarchy. However, this should not be surprising, given the different levels of economic development of these societies. As we saw in the preceding Focus on Mexico, Lenski's evolutionary theory predicted exactly these kinds of stratification differences between industrial and nonindustrial societies.

Greater Relative Egalitarianism

Compared to other modern, industrialized societies, however, the U.S. egalitarian score may not be quite as high as we might imagine it to be or want it to be. This would appear to be the case when the comparison base is modern Japan.

The spectacular development experienced by the Japanese since the end of the Second World War has been described as nothing short of an economic miracle. Next to the United States, Japan has become the most productive economy in the world. Like their counterparts in the United States, Japanese people enjoy a relatively high per capita income. Unlike the United States, however, overall income in Japan is distributed in a much more egalitarian fashion. The total income share of the bottom one-fifth of families in Japan is nearly twice that of the comparable group in the United States (8.8 percent versus 4.7 percent). At the opposite end of the income structure, the top one-fifth of Japanese income-receiving families command a smaller share of total societal income than their U.S. counterparts (37.6 percent versus 42.9 percent). This flatter Japanese income distribution, according to Johnson (1982), is accomplished through a salary structure much less skewed than that in the United States. Japanese workers receive a larger share of economic profits than do workers in the United States, and business executives' salaries typically are far less than those of U.S. executives.

The greater relative egalitarianism of Japanese society is further reflected in patterns of social mobility. In one early study, Fox and Miller (1965) examined inflow and outflow patterns of sons in five occupationally defined social classes in each society: elite, middle, skilled, semiskilled, and unskilled. Compared to the United States, Japan had more mobility into the elite class, especially in terms of movement from semiskilled and unskilled class groups. In both societies, mobility from middle to elite classes was about the same. These patterns are indicative of a greater amount of inheritance of elite status in the United States, and a greater amount

of achievement in Japan. The essential vehicle by which this Japanese achievement is accomplished is formal education.

Education-Based Mobility

Like other Asian peoples, the Japanese traditionally have placed a high cultural value on education and on educational achievement. Compared to the public educational system in the United States, that in Japan involves a good deal more seriousness and rigor. The school calendar is longer, curricula are more structured, homework assignments more lengthy, and required study time much longer. Students typically outperform their American counterparts in a variety of subject areas, especially mathematics (Barrett, 1990). Whereas most Japanese students can do quite well in the U.S. educational system at almost any level, few American students fare equally well in Japanese schools. This has led to fears of an "educational exchange gap" (Schoenberger, 1990) between the two countries.

In Japan, student efforts and achievements are strongly supported by the family, especially by mothers. Recognizing that a high level of formal education is a critical necessity in their technologically advanced economy, the mothers assist and encourage their children's (especially their sons') school achievement. Some of these *kyoiku-mamas* ("education mamas") devote their waking lives to these efforts. They often begin laying the groundwork for their children's eventual high school and college or university education while the children are still in kindergarten or prekindergarten (Garfinkel, 1983; Simons, 1987). They prepare the students' lunches and snacks, take them to and from classes, monitor their progress, create a quiet study space for them at home, and in general do the hundreds of little things that make school work easier for their children. According to some observers (Garfinkel, 1983), many *kyoiku-mamas* also attempt to browbeat their children to excel academically through a mixture of threats and guilt feelings. There is a good reason why these *kyoiku-mamas* make such extraordinary efforts.

Formal education is a mixture of ascription and achievement principles. All children must complete nine years of mandatory schooling, and during these years they are moved up through the grades as a group, without much attention paid to individual differences in academic performances. After high school, however, students are admitted to university-level study only if they successfully pass a series of nationwide placement examinations administered by the Ministry of Education. A high score on these examinations is absolutely essential for acceptance to one of the more prestigious universities (e.g., University of Tokyo) whose diplomas are necessary entry cards to top-echelon corporate positions. Consequently, competition for these limited number of university positions is intense.

In many cases, Japanese families make great financial and other sacrifices to send their sons to tutoring schools (*juku*) to increase their chances of success. A similar phenomenon appears to be developing in the United States, as competition among high school students for acceptance into elite universities is creating a whole private tutoring and placement industry. But such tutoring efforts begin at a much earlier age and level in Japan. About one-sixth of elementary school students, one-half of junior high students, and virtually all high school students are enrolled by their families in these *juku*. For Japanese high school students, not to have such extra input is almost tantamount to failure on the university placement exams; and such failure is the kiss of death as far as mobility into higher-echelon occupations is concerned. It is no wonder that for the students and their families the formal educational experience is a time of great turmoil and stress, an "examination hell" (*juken jigoku*) (Rohlen, 1983). Cases of stress-induced illnesses, breakdowns, and even suicides are not unknown (Kitsuse and Murase, 1987). Thus, although educational achievement can yield great rewards, it often exacts a high price from those pursuing it.

Work-Based Mobility

For students who are successful in winning a slot in one of the universities and entry into salaried corporate work, the battle is far from over. In many ways, the fight for social success has just begun.

White-collar workers (*sararimen*) are expected and required by their companies to put in very long work days, often without financial compensation. Men who are unwilling or unable to do so often find their positions terminated and themselves out of a job. Faced with this prospect, most middle-class men work exceptionally long hours compared to their Western counterparts, often accepting long separations from their families. In recent years, a growing number of these salaried workers have begun to experience what the Japanese call *karoshi*—"death from overwork" (Fujimoto, 1991). The government has been reluctant to investigate these instances of *karoshi,* but public opinion has forced them to do so. In several cases, companies have been ordered to pay death benefits to surviving family members of employees who died as a result of long work hours. A growing amount of concern has been expressed about this feature of the workplace, but so far it has not changed a great deal. Most Japanese corporate men still have too little time to enjoy the fruits of their labors.

As already discussed, income distribution in Japan is more egalitarian than in the United States in terms of the percentage of overall income going to each income-receiving population segment. But this fact does not necessarily translate into a high level of economic affluence for the average Japanese wage earner. In 1989 the average earnings of Japanese workers was $30,769, and the average worker's income tax bill was only $1,763 (*Parade,* January 20, 1991). However, the average price for consumer goods in Japan was 40 percent higher than that in the United States (*U.S. News & World Report,* November 20, 1989).

In particular, land and real estate prices are extraordinarily high compared to those in the United States (*San Diego Union,* October 21, 1990). Housing prices in Tokyo, for example, average from $700 to $1,500 per square foot, putting home ownership effectively beyond the reach of anyone who is not a millionaire (Cook, 1990). Faced with these mind-boggling prices, many people are beginning to speak of their country and their situation as "rich Japan, poor Japanese" (Miller, 1990) and to put aside personal dreams of economic affluence.

In an article that first appeared over thirty years ago, Melvin Tumin (1957) challenged the prevailing cultural belief and popular sentiment that widespread and rapid social mobility—the American dream and the Japanese miracle—was desirable and beneficial in modern societies. He examined a number of negative or "unapplauded" individual and social consequences that seemed to be linked to such vertical social movements. These effects included the weakening of social bonds as people moved into and out of groups on their way up or down the social ladder, as well as widespread insecurity among people whose primary concern was to move up in the social world. In examining these and other less obvious effects of mobility in modern open-class systems, Tumin was led to the conclusion that unlimited mobility in fact may lead to personal dysfunction and be harmful to both individuals and the larger social collectivity. His observations, and observations of the Japanese experience, seem to lend support to the adage that more—in this case, more mobility—is not necessarily better.

DISCUSSION QUESTIONS

1. What is the meaning of the phrase "rich Japan, poor Japanese"?
2. In Japan, as in the United States and Mexico, getting ahead is an important and widespread goal. If you were a brand-new parent in Japan and wanted to plan for your baby's future, what specific things would you do now to give your child the best possible chance for success in a highly competitive society?

3. Like Japan, Germany has become a major economic power since the end of the Second World War, and like the Japanese, the Germans have a reputation for seriousness and efficiency. Go to the library and read about formal education and corporate life in modern Germany. In what ways are the two countries alike? How do they differ?

CHAPTER SUMMARY

1. Social stratification refers to the division of a population into categories in which they are defined and treated as social unequals. Virtually all human societies have had some type of stratification system.

2. Different theories have offered a variety of explanations for social stratification. Natural superiority approaches interpret social inequalities in wealth, power, and prestige as reflections of natural inequalities in mental and physical abilities among individuals. Functionalist theorists like Davis and Moore view systems of unequally rewarded positions as incentives motivating talented people to perform important social tasks.

3. Critics of functionalism claim that this theory ignores the role of power in the creation and preservation of stratification systems. Conflict theorists like Karl Marx focused on power factors to explain inequality structures. For Marx, differences in property ownership created objective classes whose opposed interests put them into conflict with one another. As these classes (owners and nonowners) became subjectively aware of their respective circumstances, the class struggle would lead to a revolution by the workers and the violent overthrow of the property-based, capitalist system.

4. Max Weber criticized Marx's theory for its oversimplicity and for ignoring important noneconomic inequality dimensions. According to Weber, modern stratification systems rank people socially and politically as well as economically. Strata and parties often are more significant than classes in bringing about social and cultural changes. Weber's multiple-hierarchy approach has guided a great deal of stratification research over the past fifty years.

5. Stratification systems have been studied in a number of ways. In objective class analysis, groups within the hierarchy of social inequality are defined on the basis of differences in such factors as income, education, and occupation. Subjective class analyses define the various stratified groups on the basis of either individuals' self-perceptions

of their own position, or other people's judgments of the individuals' class. Each of these approaches has serious shortcomings, and can lead to different portrayals of stratification in a given society or community.

6. Sociologists often distinguish between two logically extreme, ideal types of stratified systems in order to locate specific societies on a continuum of social inequality. The open-class system represents minimal social inequality. It is marked by free movement among social ranks, achievement-based criteria for filling positions, indistinct class boundaries and low levels of class consciousness, and exogamous social relations across class boundaries. The closed-caste system represents maximum social inequality. People are born into groups that are characterized by great differences in life conditions, and remain there throughout their lives. Boundaries between the stratified groups are distinct, and awareness of caste membership is high. All important relationships are confined within individuals' caste.

7. Social mobility refers to movements of people through social space within stratification systems. Most mobility research has focused on movements within the occupational structures of societies. Intergenerational studies analyze patterns of mobility across several generations, and intragenerational studies focus on mobility patterns within a given generation. Both indicate that a great deal of social mobility in modern societies is the result of the significant structural changes brought about by modernization. Successful mobility also reflects the result of individual or voluntary efforts.

8. Social stratification generates many significant consequences for members of human societies. People who occupy the higher rungs in their social hierarchy enjoy better mental and physical health. They are more likely than the members of lower-ranked groups to be involved in political activities and less likely to be victims of violent crimes. If accused of criminal activities, members of higher-ranking groups are less likely to be convicted and punished for their actions.

9. In modern societies, formal education is a critical resource for economic and occupational success. It is an important vehicle for upward social mobility for many people, and is also a primary means of preserving the existing system of social inequality in a given society. Children of higher social classes in the United States are much more likely to get a college education, especially from a prestigious university. They also may attend elite boarding schools that socialize them into appropriate class behaviors, and are far more likely than lower-class children to have gone to nursery or prekindergarten schools. Such early schooling gives them an edge in their competition for formal educational credentials.

6

RACIAL AND ETHNIC MINORITIES

According to a story that was widely circulated at the time (1972), Spiro T. Agnew, then vice president of the United States, was involved in a last-minute, whirlwind campaign tour to promote the reelection of the Nixon-Agnew ticket. Having already addressed a series of different racial and ethnic groups whose votes were being sought by the Republican party, the vice president was asked if he wanted to schedule one final trip to speak to one last ethnic group and to hear their concerns. "What's the point?" he is supposed to have replied. "If you've seen one slum, you've seen them all."

Mr. Agnew's alleged remark was both politically insensitive and sociologically ignorant of the empirical realities of racial and ethnic groups in the United States. Members of these groups differ greatly from one another not only in terms of residential living arrangements, but also with regard to numerical representation in the population, physical and cultural attributes, education, and other important characteristics. In one sense, however, members of many racially and ethnically distinct groups in the United States do resemble one another sociologically. They frequently constitute **minority groups**—recognizable groups occupying subordinate positions in the social structure. Lacking important social, political, and economic power resources, they are subject to unequal treatment at the hands of powerful **majority groups**—those in dominant positions in the society. Denied equal access to educational, occupational, and other opportunity structures, minorities often are relegated to the lowest rungs of the stratification ladders in their respective societies. This holds true even when pure achievement criteria presumably serve as the formal mechanism for allocating people to social roles.

A minority is a group of people who possess (or who are thought to possess) physical, cultural, mental, lifestyle, or other characteristics that are valued negatively in a given society. Because of these negative or stigmatizing traits, members of minority groups are believed to be inferior to the dominant societal group and thus somehow deserving of unequal treatment.

As we saw in the preceding chapter, minority group stratification represents a prime example of the continued existence of natural superiority thinking, with its emphasis on ascribed, personal qualities as the basis for social placement. In the particular case of minorities, these personal qualities often are presented as **stereotypes**—categorical portrayals of all members of a specific group as being essentially identical to one another and essentially unlike all members of other groups. Differences in attributes among individual members of the group are discounted or ignored altogether, and traits (real or imagined) common to all members are emphasized as the basis for social relations with the societal majority. For example, all members of one racial group may be pictured as lazy and sneaky, and the members of another as industrious and honest.

Stereotyping of minorities appears to be a basic and recurring theme in intergroup relations. These portrayals ignore the actual differences that exist among people, and in doing so, they greatly oversimplify and distort reality. The social world is defined (in this case, perhaps literally) in terms of black and white.

Stereotypes foster a climate that encourages the development of **prejudice**—irrational, negative beliefs and feelings about members of certain groups based on generalizations about the characteristics of those groups. Such prejudicial beliefs are rigid and inflexible. Whereas they do not absolutely guarantee that **discrimination**—unequal and unfair treatment of a given group—will follow automatically, they none-theless make such behaviors toward minority group members highly likely (Wagley and Harris, 1964; Vander Zanden, 1983).

Before proceeding with the discussion of race and ethnicity, we must define these concepts. The terms often are confused in people's minds, and are used interchange-ably and inconsistently in social relations as well as in social policies. We must also examine the many forms that racial and ethnic group relations have assumed through-out human social history, ranging from complete and open acceptance of differences within a given society to attempts to eliminate such differences through a policy of systematic extermination.

Questions to Consider

1. What is the difference between a racial minority and an ethnic minority?
2. In what ways does prejudice differ from discrimination?
3. Why do members of racial or ethnic minorities occupy subordinate positions in the larger society?

4. Why do functionalists regard assimilation as a desirable form of racial and ethnic intergroup relations?
5. What were the major differences between "melting pot" and "Anglo-conformity" immigration philosophies in the United States?
6. From a Marxist conflict perspective, why have racial and ethnic minorities been the objects of continued subjugation in societies like the United States?
7. In what ways does de facto racism differ from de jure racist practices?
8. How has the experience of slavery affected relations between whites and African Americans in the contemporary United States?
9. What factors account for the high levels of poverty and low levels of education among many Hispanic American groups?
10. What is meant by the word "superminority"?
11. How does relative poverty differ from absolute poverty?
12. What is the relationship between minority group status and absolute poverty in the contemporary United States?

 RACE AND ETHNICITY

Race Defined

In the history of human social interaction, few concepts have been so widely misunderstood as race. The word has been widely misapplied in social relations, with a host of significant consequences. In different times and places, people have believed that race is the single most important determinant of individual mental, physical, emotional, and moral capacities, and they developed drastic and tragic policies toward millions of fellow human beings purely on that basis. The subjugation of blacks by whites in the South African system of racial segregation known as **apartheid,** and the "final solution" to the Jewish "problem" in Nazi Germany are two blatant examples that come readily to mind, but they hardly exhaust the supply of historical cases. Ironically, as with Hitler's answer to the Jewish "racial" issue, these social policies often were constructed on a fundamental distortion of what race and membership in a particular racial group really mean.

From a strictly scientific standpoint, **race** refers to a classification of human beings that is based on biological attributes. Specifically, Webster's Dictionary defines it as "a population that differs from others in the relative frequency of some gene or genes" (1983, p. 1484). These gene differences are hereditary, and may manifest themselves as observable differences in skin color, body shape, hair texture, and other physical characteristics (Schaefer, 1990).

Although this definition seems straightforward, attempts to translate the concept into empirical terms have not been successful. The question of which specific biological characteristics are of most importance in defining the various human races has not yet been answered. Nor has the related question of how many different races there really are.

Ethnologists (scholars who study races and their origins) often speak of three major racial groups: **Caucasoid** or "white"; **Negroid** or "black"; and **Mongoloid** or "yellow." This classification scheme is imprecise and inaccurate, however. Variations in physical and other characteristics, including skin color, among individuals of a given racial group often are greater than the variations of these same characteristics across different racial groups (Gould, 1981). Further adding to the confusion is the fact that, throughout the long course of human history, there has been a tremendous amount of **amalgamation**, that is, biological reproduction across various racial group lines. The notion that any sort of pure races may still exist in the contemporary world is extremely naive.

Objective truths have seldom been the only determinants of human social beliefs and actions, however, and nowhere is this more evident than in the case of race. It is inherently difficult, if not impossible, to establish definitive boundaries to distinguish human races clearly. It is equally difficult to chart the psychological and other consequences of membership in a particular racial group. Nonetheless, people in many societies have acted toward one another as though it were possible to do so, and as though race per se were of fundamental importance in shaping individual abilities and disabilities.

Ethnicity Defined

Race represents a way of classifying people based on biological differences. In contrast, ethnicity represents a way of classifying or grouping people based on cultural differences. **Ethnic groups** consist of people who share a common orientation toward the world, who thus have developed a sense of "peoplehood" or identification with one another, and who are perceived by others as possessing and sharing a distinctive culture (Bahr et al., 1979).

In this sense, there is no such thing as a "Jewish race," that is, a population sharing a set of specific genes. Rather, Jews represent an ethnic group based on a set of religious and cultural traditions. To the extent that they lack effective power and are the targets of prejudice and discrimination, Jewish Americans would represent a minority ethnic group in the United States. Similarly, the Irish are an ethnic group, not a race. Irish Americans represent a recognizable ethnic group to the extent that their common ancestry and cultural traditions make them identifiably different from the majority or dominant Anglo-Saxon Protestant group. Since Irish Americans generally are no longer the objects of prejudice and discrimination, they no longer constitute a minority in this society.

As is true with race, the concept of ethnicity has been subjected to misunderstanding and misapplication in social relations in many societies. Although ethnicity itself has nothing to do with biological differences among people, many ethnic groups in fact possess specific physical characteristics that differentiate them from others. For example, many Mexican Americans display a number of features including hair color and skin tone that distinguish them from their Anglo neighbors. These physical features sometimes lead them to embarrassing and volatile interactions with U.S. Border Patrol agents, who mistake them for undocumented Mexican nationals attempting to enter into the United States illegally.

By the same token, people who appear indistinguishable on the basis of physical characteristics may be members of vastly different ethnic groups. For example, in those regions of the United States having large Southeast Asian immigrant populations, many Anglos simply lump the newcomers together under the generic title "Indochinese." In the process, they ignore important cultural distinctions that Vietnamese, Laotians, Cambodians, and Thais make among themselves.

In similar fashion, although ethnic groups often are defined at least partially on the basis of common ancestry or nationality, ethnicity is not equivalent to common political or geographic background. Throughout the last part of the nineteenth and early part of the twentieth centuries, immigrants to the United States from any part of what was then Russia were listed officially as being of "Russian" origin. It was only later that specific ethnic groups from within the geographic boundaries of what is now called the Soviet Union were recognized (e.g., Lithuanians, Latvians, Ukranians, Georgians). Switzerland is a recognized political entity, yet there is no Swiss ethnic group per se. Rather, that country is made up of three recognizable and different ethnic populations, German, Italian, and French, each of which maintains its own identity and sense of peoplehood. On the other hand, many of the formerly hyphenated-American ethnic groups (e.g., Irish American, Polish American) can trace their ancestors to a common geographic or political area (e.g., Ireland, Poland). Given these complexities, perhaps it is no wonder that we have such a difficult time making sense out of the distinctions among racial, ethnic, political, and other groups.

In the United States, at least, it appears that "ethnic group" has become something of a blanket or umbrella term. It includes groups that are recognizably different on the basis of cultural or physical characteristics, or some combination of the two. This might not reflect a great deal of scientific or objective validity, but it does seem to reflect common social practices, as well as people's apparent need for some way of classifying themselves and others in their social relations (Bahr et al., 1979).

PATTERNS OF RACIAL AND ETHNIC GROUP RELATIONS

As discussed in chapter 3, virtually all human societies have developed over time in the direction of larger, more heterogenous (differentiated) populations. Compared to societies that existed 10,000, 1,000, or as recently as 200 years ago, contemporary societies are much larger in population. Many now number into the tens of millions of inhabitants. Most also are composed of people who in many ways, including biological and cultural features, have become more and more unlike one another.

Whereas most societies have followed the same developmental pattern, they have not all been alike with respect to relations among these recognized racial and ethnic subgroups. Racial and ethnic intergroup relations have taken different forms from one place or time to another.

Sociologists George Simpson and J. Milton Yinger (1985) described six distinct patterns of majority-minority racial and ethnic group relations. These patterns—assimilation, pluralism, legal protection of minorities, population transfer, continued subjugation, and extermination—are not mutually exclusive; nor do they necessarily follow any invariable or natural sequence. They represent dominant or majority group policies toward minorities in the given society.

Assimilation

Assimilation is the process in which minority groups become absorbed or incorporated into the majority's sociocultural system, thereby eventually losing their individual cultural and physical identities. Milton Gordon (1964) identified several different types or stages of assimilation, indicative of progressive entry into the mainstream of societal life.

Cultural assimilation (acculturation) involves changes in behaviors, beliefs, values, and attitudes among minority group members to approximate more closely the patterns of the dominant societal group. In the language of symbolic interaction theory, incoming ethnic groups are resocialized into a new set of symbols — a cultural world view — necessary for successful everyday interaction in their adopted society. For example, in the United States, non-English-speaking immigrants surrender (or at least are expected to surrender) their native tongues in favor of the English language.

Structural assimilation involves the gradual acceptance and admittance of minority group members into secondary and, later, primary relationships with members of the dominant societal group. As foreign-born immigrants to the United States became more Americanized and less culturally distinct, they were more acceptable as friends and neighbors to dominant group members, and gradually were drawn into more intimate interaction networks. This was especially true as the immigrants' income, educational, and occupational statuses began to improve toward middle-class level.

Finally, **marital** or **physical assimilation** (amalgamation) involves large-scale intermarriage and biological reproduction across majority-minority group lines, resulting in the gradual decline of distinctive physical features that may have been associated with particular minority groups. In the continuing illustration of foreign-born immigrants to the United States, marital assimilation occurred between, for example, Polish Americans and **WASP**s (white Anglo-Saxon Protestants, generally regarded as the dominant or majority group in U.S. society), or between Jamaican Americans and Chinese Americans.

For almost two centuries, one of the most enduring images of American (i.e., United States) society has been that of the **melting pot**. According to this metaphorical portrayal of the immigration experience, the great experiment that attracted so many diverse groups of people to the New World in search of a better way of life also had created a new breed of person. The "American" was a distinctive physical and cultural type born of a hundred Old World heritages and representing the very best that each had to contribute. Melting pot theory envisioned the assimilation of individual immigrant groups into American society as an amalgamation of cultural and physical traits. It offered a model of intergroup relations that stressed each group's surrendering of individual ethnic or national identity on behalf of an end product that was unique unto itself. "Americans" might be of English and French and Dutch and Italian and Polish and Greek and other origin (Figure 6.1), but they were much more than any or all of these individual strains. They were, in effect, the best of all possible cultural and physical blends (Parrillo, 1990).

The reality of the U.S. immigration experience was quite different from this highly idealized portrait, however. White ethnics of both the Old Wave (northern and western European) and the New Wave (central, southern, and eastern European) immigrants were expected to assimilate into their new society, but it was to be a one-way process. From the early days of this society, the United States has been characterized by a high degree of **ethnocentrism** — the belief in the superiority of one's own way of life, and a corresponding belief in the inferiority of others' ways of life. For the dominant host group, the established Anglo-Saxon cultural pattern already represented the best of all worlds and was a pattern to which arriving ethnic immigrants must learn to adapt. **Anglo conformity**, as this belief was known, became the actual policy throughout the nineteenth and early twentieth centuries.

In practice, becoming an American meant becoming as much like the dominant Anglo-Saxon group as was possible. Immigrant groups were to give up their existing systems of meanings and values (i.e., their cultural world views) and replace them with the "correct" (dominant group's) frame of reference. Whereas white ethnic immigrants might hope to become fully Americanized in this sense, this was impossible for

FIGURE 6.1   U.S. Population by Selected Ancestry Group, 1980

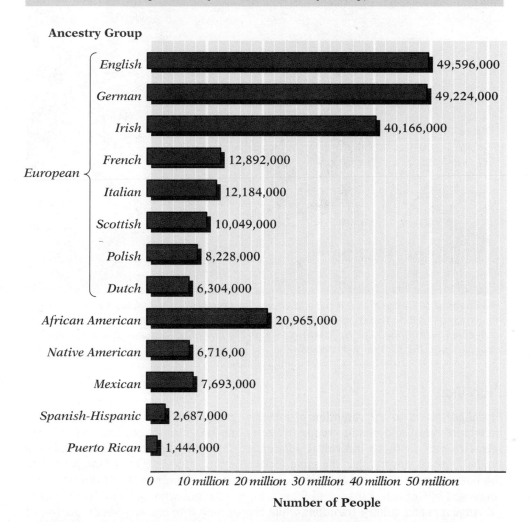

Ancestry Group

English	49,596,000
German	49,224,000
Irish	40,166,000
French	12,892,000
Italian	12,184,000
Scottish	10,049,000
Polish	8,228,000
Dutch	6,304,000
African American	20,965,000
Native American	6,716,00
Mexican	7,693,000
Spanish-Hispanic	2,687,000
Puerto Rican	1,444,000

European {

0   10 million   20 million   30 million   40 million   50 million

Number of People

Note: Numbers to the right of the bars indicate actual numbers of people in each ancestry group.

Source: U.S. Bureau of the Census, *1980 Census of the Population, Supplementary Report,* series PC80-S1-10.

nonwhites. The combination of their overt physical differences from the majority group and prevailing racist notions of the innate inferiority of people of color branded them as foreign. As an ideological symbol, the melting pot was a tremendous success. As a statement of historical reality, it is a complete myth.

Sociologists operating within the structural functional theoretical perspective have tended to regard assimilation as the most desirable form of intergroup relations. In their view, successful assimilation of population subgroups promotes social and cultural unity and thus is functional for the social system as a whole. At the same time it is functional for the subgroups themselves. It provides them with the means for economic advancement and success, as well as other group goals. For these reasons, functionalists view assimilation as the preferred and ideal pattern for ethnic and racial groups.

The image of U.S. society as a racial and ethnic "melting pot" is historically inacurrate. As this group of Hasidic Jewish men in New York City illustrates, different cultural groups have been able to retain their unique identities even in the face of often tremendous pressures to assimilate into the societal mainstream.

Pluralism

Pluralism refers to the retention of minority group identities and diversities, with individual racial and ethnic groups (majority and minorities) accommodating themselves to one another's individual differences. It entails the acceptance of different symbolic world views within the same social structure. Modern Switzerland is perhaps the best example of successful pluralism in action. As discussed earlier, the nation is composed of German, Italian, and French subpopulations who maintain their individual languages and cultural traditions while cooperating with one another on matters or issues of mutual importance.

Legal Protection of Minorities

As the name might imply, **legal protection of minorities** refers to a variety of legal-political actions designed to establish or maintain the civil and other rights of recognized minority groups. In the United States, the thirteenth, fourteenth, and fifteenth amendments to the Constitution, various civil rights laws passed during the past three decades, and, more recently (and more controversially), affirmative action directives are indicative of this particular pattern of majority-minority group relations.

Population Transfer

The voluntary or involuntary movement of minority group members from contact with other specific groups to a different geographic area is called **population transfer**. The relocation of Native American tribes to reservations during the nineteenth century, and the relocation of Japanese American U.S. citizens to internment camps during the Second World War are examples of involuntary population transfers. The large-scale, illegal immigration of poverty-stricken Mexicans into U.S. cities, especially in the southwestern part of this country, is an example of voluntary population transfer.

Continued Subjugation

Continued subjugation refers to a variety of formal or informal practices that are undertaken by the dominant group to maintain the powerless and subservient position of some particular minority group(s) in a given society. The system of apartheid in South Africa is perhaps the most obvious illustration. In the United States, such racial separation is no longer the law of the land (**de jure**) as it once was in certain southern states. Nevertheless, many civil rights leaders, social scientists, and politicians maintain that a large number of **de facto** (in practice) racist patterns still present in this society have had the effect of continuing a 300-year legacy of exploitation and subjugation of African Americans.

Just as functionalist sociologists find the assimilation model compatible with their view of the social world, so do conflict sociologists with the subjugation model. As discussed in the last chapter, the conflict theory of social inequality focuses on the different power resources of various groups, and the use of power by some to exploit and subordinate others. According to sociologists like Blauner (1972), the subjugation and exploitation of racial and ethnic minorities by powerful majority groups remains a continuing part of the history of the United States and other modern societies. Although assimilation may be the stated or formal goal, the actual social and political policies have been to dominate minorities, to keep them in their proper place.

For many years, social scientists interested in the dynamics of racial and ethnic intergroup behaviors have examined the role of economic factors in what have so often been conflict relations. Marxian conflict theorists in particular advanced the argument that majority-minority conflicts ultimately are a subset of class conflicts. Prejudice and discrimination against some specific racial or ethnic group are motivated by the economic exploitation of the group and the need to legitimize its subordination. A racist ideology that defines the subjugated group as somehow inferior to the majority (and thus undeserving or incapable of equal treatment) serves this purpose well. It takes the burden of responsibility for the minority group's subordinate social position off of the shoulders of the dominant group and transfers it to the minority. The subordinate group then is seen as the cause of its own inferior status. Thus, the position of African Americans in the United States was explained (Cox, 1948) as a continuing consequence of a white belief in the inherent inferiority of black people. This doctrine was developed over 200 years ago to support and justify the plantation system of the South, which required a large, cheap workforce for the labor-intensive agrarian economy. Similarly, the current positions of Native Americans and Mexican Americans were interpreted as consequences of the internal colonial policies of the dominant Anglo group in U.S. society (Blauner, 1972).

The race as class hypothesis is far from being universally accepted among sociologists, but ample empirical evidence supports the argument that economic factors are an important contributing element to the development of prejudice and discrimination against racial and ethnic minorities. One version of this line of reasoning argues that direct competition between members of the majority group and a specific minority for such rewards as jobs, education, and housing creates hostilities. These hostilities are expressed through prejudicial attitudes and acts of discrimination against the threatening minority group. This would explain, for instance, white lower-class and working-class racism, as well as similar patterns often displayed by minorities toward other minorities. These groups are in direct competition with one another for the meager rewards to be found in their segment of what Edna Bonacich (1972) termed a "split labor market" created and maintained by the dominant group to further its own advantaged social position.

A second version of this economic-based argument views the economic decline of the majority group (or of some segment of the majority group) as the underlying source of prejudice and discrimination against minority group members. Here, minorities are made into **scapegoats**, innocent targets for the majority group's frustration and aggression, even though they may be blameless for the dominant group's perceived deprivation. In this instance, the minority group's primary failing is its lack of power and its high visibility. Minority people are powerless and therefore a safe target. They are made to bear the brunt of dominant group members' frustrations with a larger and perhaps not fully understood world (Allport, 1958).

If this argument has any validity, the opposite also should be true. That is, if times are good and the presence of minorities would not pose an economic threat to the majority group, levels of prejudice and discrimination should decrease. Events in contemporary Japan may permit an empirical test of this proposition.

From the standpoint of symbolic interaction theory, the power struggles that are so characteristic of majority-minority interactions might be interpreted as an outgrowth of the different world views of these groups. To the extent that people who share the same societal space do not share a common symbolic (cultural) perspective, divergent values and meanings might set them on a collision course that finds expression in economic and political conflicts. In this interpretation, conflict resolution involves the development of a new world view acceptable to all parties (as in the melting pot model) or the triumph of one world view over its competitors (the Anglo conformity model).

Extermination

Extermination refers to attempts to destroy physically or annihilate members of particular minority groups. For members of the majority group, intergroup relations problems are solved by eliminating the offending minority group(s). **Genocide**, as this practice is called, has had a long history in human intergroup relations. Hitler's mass murder of some six million Jews during the Second World War, and the systematic killing of one and a half million Cambodians by the Khmer Rouge in Southeast Asia, are twentieth-century examples of this extreme policy.

 RACIAL AND ETHNIC INTERGROUP RELATIONS IN THE UNITED STATES

Throughout the history of racial and ethnic majority-minority group relations in the United States, virtually all of the policies discussed above have been attempted by dominant societal groups. A complete discussion of the many racial and ethnic groups that make up the contemporary U.S. population would be well beyond the scope of this text. But even a brief overview of some of the more visible or more important minority groups will illustrate the point (for a more comprehensive review, see Parrillo, 1990; Schaefer, 1990).

African Americans

It has been 130 years since the Emancipation Proclamation formally ended slavery in the United States, and nearly 30 years since the passage of landmark civil rights laws designed to fulfill the promise of the Emancipation Proclamation. In 1990, however, the *New England Journal of Medicine* carried a disturbing article concerning high mortality rates among African American men living in Harlem, New York: their death rates were more than double those for U.S. whites and 50 percent higher than those for African Americans as a whole. For this group the mortality rates were actually higher than those for men in Bangladesh, a society generally considered to be among the most poverty-stricken of the developing countries. These figures and their implications were so shocking that the authors of this study (McCord and Freeman, 1990) were led to the conclusion that Harlem and other inner-city areas with largely African American populations warranted "special consideration analogous to that given to natural-disaster areas" (p. 173).

The United States has one of the highest average standards of living in the contemporary world. Yet a sizeable portion of its largest racial minority group (African Americans constitute approximately 12 percent of the total U.S. population) simply is not making it on a long-term basis. Despite a series of economic gains during the 1960s and 1970s, living conditions for African Americans in the 1980s remained substantially below those of their white counterparts (Table 6.1). This fact is reflected in significant differences in median incomes between African American and white families ($19,329 vs. $33,915 in 1988) and in the proportion of African American families living below the government-established survival-level income or poverty line (28 percent, compared to 8 percent of white families in 1988). It is also manifested in substantially higher rates of unemployment for African Americans (12 percent in 1988, vs. 5 percent for whites) and in significantly higher rates of homicide (approximately four times higher than those for whites in 1987). On average, in 1988 African Americans had a life expectancy six years shorter than whites (U.S. Bureau of the Census, 1990).

To understand both the creation and the persistence of these conditions over such a long period of time, it is necessary to remember one critical fact. African Americans

TABLE 6.1 Selected Quality-of-Life Indicators for Whites and African Americans, 1988

Indicator	Whites	African Americans
Life expectancy at birth	75.5	69.5
Homicide rate (1987, for males, per 100,000)	7.9	53.3
Percentage below poverty level	10.5	33.1
Median yearly income, males	$28,262	$20,716
Median yearly income, females	$18,823	$16,867
Median yearly income, families	$33,915	$19,329
Percentage with less than twelve years of school	22.3	36.7
Percentage female-headed households	12.9	42.8
Percentage who own homes	67.2	42.7

Source: U.S. Bureau of the Census, *Statistical Abstracts of the United States, 1990.*

originally were brought to this society involuntarily, to work as slaves in the southern plantation economy. During nearly 250 years of slavery they endured incredibly demeaning and dehumanizing conditions. At the same time, many whites developed a set of attitudes and beliefs justifying the buying and selling of human beings as property. These beliefs involved the basic and deep-rooted feeling that black-skinned people somehow are naturally and profoundly inferior to whites.

The system of slavery was formally destroyed by the Civil War. However, the reconstruction of the South after the war led to the development of a set of segregation laws—the so-called Jim Crow laws—that effectively barred the newly freed slaves from any real participation in the social, political, and economic order on a par with whites. In effect, these laws locked them into a subservient social position.

The U.S. Supreme Court's historic 1954 *Brown* v. *Board of Education* decision declared racially segregated school facilities unconstitutional and opened the assault on the southern Jim Crow system. The often heroic efforts of civil rights leaders such as Dr. Martin Luther King, Jr., during the 1950s and 1960s led to the passage of sweeping legislation during the 1960s and 1970s that dismantled the formal, de jure segregation system. However, this legislation did not really eliminate prejudice and discrimination against African Americans in U.S. society.

What had been formal and legally supported mechanisms of repression now became informal, de facto practices. These were often embedded within established institutional structures (e.g., the neighborhood school system), a pattern sociologists call **institutionalized racism**, and seemed immune to attempts to correct them through legislative action. If anything, attempts to legislate racial equality through measures designed to deal with the subtle but persistent consequences of such institutionalized practices seem to have had an opposite effect. In some instances, these efforts increased feelings of antagonism against African Americans and other minorities, who were seen as undeserving beneficiaries of government intrusion at the expense of innocent majority group members. Many whites have come to see affirmative action and preferential treatment directives as reverse discrimination against their own group.

Reflecting this development is a series of Reagan-era Supreme Court rulings that effectively narrowed the scope of previous minority rights legislation. The Civil Rights Act of 1990 that would have reversed these Supreme Court decisions was vetoed by President Bush on the grounds that it would have required minority hiring quotas, thus destroying the principle of merit in employment. Whether other civil rights legislation can pass in the near future is not clear at this time. What is clear is the fact that, after a nearly 400-year history in this society, African Americans remain second-class citizens.

Native Americans

If African Americans were among the earliest arrivals to the United States from foreign shores, Native Americans were the indigenous peoples who were here to greet them. Their ancestors apparently migrated to the North American continent some 30,000 years ago from Asia. By the time of their first contact with Europeans, North American "Indians," as they were incorrectly called by Columbus, numbered several million people (estimates of exactly how many millions vary widely) divided into a very large number of tribal groupings and speaking over 300 languages (Schaefer, 1990).

The facts of first arrival and large numbers, however, did not give Native Americans a superior advantage over the European settlers who arrived in ever increasing numbers to the North American continent. The Europeans' advanced military technology gave them the mechanism for successful domination. As colonial settlements developed and expanded, Native American tribes were forced either to move aside or to submit to the whites.

Cultural and physical conflicts were characteristic of the early period of Native American–European contact, a pattern that persisted throughout much of the subsequent history of the United States after the Revolutionary War. Native American tribes were viewed as foreign nations by the U.S. government. In many cases, relations between the government and specific tribes took on the character of foreign wars. Given their superior firepower, the whites won nearly all of these wars.

By the mid-nineteenth century, all Native American tribes living in the United States had been forcibly relocated west of the Mississippi River. Their collective numbers had been reduced to an estimated 250,000. This dramatic decrease largely was a result of dwindling food resources and the effects of previously unknown diseases brought by European settlers. Further conflicts with white settlers followed the opening of the western frontier after the Civil War. Native Americans were simply swept aside by the tide of expansion that brought whites across the Mississippi in search of land, gold, and other dreams.

Because of Native Americans' inability to adjust to the white man's way of life, that is, to assimilate to Anglo culture, and their perceived threat to settlers, they were once again forcibly relocated. This time they were removed to reservations that were typically on land that was so resource poor as to be of no interest to whites. Here they languished, their lives structured and controlled by the U.S. government's Bureau of Indian Affairs (BIA).

Subject to population transfer and long-term discrimination, life for Native Americans in the United States has proven to be plagued by both spiritual and material hardships.

For most Native Americans, life under the BIA has been a disaster. The bureau's policies seem to have been directed to forcing the assimilation of these people to white cultural patterns, and to breaking up tribal groupings. These policies have left many Native Americans in desperate straits. Their ways of life have been destroyed and their tribal resources squandered or sold away by their so-called guardian.

Fed up with their status as legal wards of the federal government, in the 1960s and 1970s Native American groups began a series of acts of protest to focus public attention on their plight. These included the occupation of Alcatraz Island in 1969 and the seizure of Wounded Knee, South Dakota, site of an 1890 massacre of 300 Sioux by U.S. Army troops. They also began to organize a **pan-Indian movement**, a coalition of individual tribal groups united in common cause to pursue common interests against a common enemy (the federal government).

Schaefer (1990) noted some of the successes of pan-Indianism in securing tribal rights from the U.S. government and in pursuing several successful court cases against the government and other white groups. Overall, however, its success has been mixed. Despite the efforts of groups such as the American Indian Movement (AIM), Native Americans remain today perhaps *the* most disadvantaged American minority group, whether measured in terms of economic, educational, physical and mental health, or other quality-of-life factors. It is both ironic and tragic that the group that was first in this land in the past is last in this land in the present.

Hispanic Americans

The term Hispanic Americans (or, more simply, Hispanics) refers to a variety of ethnic groups who can trace their ancestry to Old World Spanish or New World Latin American societies. In the contemporary United States, Hispanic Americans include such large and recognized groups as Mexican Americans in the Southwest, Puerto Rican Americans in the Northeast, and Cuban Americans in the Southeast, as well as less visible groups such as Nicaraguans and Argentines.

Collectively, Hispanic Americans represent a sizeable portion of the U.S. population—approximately twenty million people in 1988. They are also one of the fastest-growing racial or ethnic minorities in this society, evidencing a growth pattern of 34 percent during the 1980s (Savage, 1990). In some portions of the country, most notably south Florida and southern California, they already constitute a numerical majority, and their population in these areas continues to grow.

For many Anglos, Hispanics form a perceived threat to the economic well-being of U.S. workers through the massive inflow of documented and undocumented workers who often are hired at wages substantially lower than those paid to Anglos. They are also perceived as a threat to the cultural well-being of U.S. society because of their refusal to abandon the Spanish language in favor of English and to become Americanized. Consequently, Hispanics have assumed the proportions of a problem or question for many members of the dominant Anglos.

In 1986 Californians voted to make English the official state language, joining twelve other states with similar laws. Nationally, the USA English movement represents a similar attempt to legislate the use of English as the official language of the United States. According to their supporters, both efforts represent attempts to preserve an individual and fundamental aspect of U.S. culture—its grounding in a common language.

In Texas and California, unions and other organized labor groups have sought to have local, state, and federal governments address the problem of illegal aliens. They contend that their livelihoods are being destroyed by the tide of immigrants from south of the border who take jobs and social welfare benefits that should more properly belong to tax-paying U.S. citizens. In response to their complaints, in 1986 Congress passed the Simpson-Mazzolli Law aimed at curbing the hiring of illegal aliens. This law has had the effect of lessening the hiring both of Mexican nationals and of U.S. citizens of Hispanic ancestry by employers in the Southwest. In these geographic areas, relations between Anglos and Hispanics remain extremely volatile.

Like those of African Americans and Native Americans, the life circumstances of many Hispanics in this country are characterized by significantly lower economic, educational, occupational, housing, and other quality-of-life standards (Table 6.2). Although not quite as low as those for African Americans or Native Americans, Hispanic family median income levels are still substantially lower than those of Anglos ($22,769 vs. $33,915 in 1988). These families are overrepresented below the poverty line (24 percent compared to 8 percent of Anglos in 1988), and have significantly lower levels of formal educational attainment. Approximately 51 percent of Hispanics twenty five years of age or over had a twelfth-grade (high school graduate) or higher level of education as of 1988, compared to approximately 77 percent of Anglos (U.S. Bureau of the Census, 1990).

Many of these disparities can be explained by the fact that a substantial proportion of the Hispanic American population consists of recent immigrants (legal or illegal) to the United States from Mexico and from Central American countries such as El Salvador, Guatemala, and Nicaragua. These people fled economic or political disasters in their home countries. Very often, they came to *El Norte* with little more than the clothes on their backs. Once here, their lack of education and occupational skills held them back. Their tenuous status as undocumented (i.e., illegal) aliens consigned them to low-paying domestic, service, and manual labor jobs that make up the bottom sector of what has been described as the "dual labor market" (Baron and Bielby, 1980; Lord and Falk, 1982).

Trapped in jobs that often pay below minimum wages, these immigrants often must settle for what little housing they can afford. Often, this takes the form of more or less permanent camps in fields and canyons near sources of employment. In recent years, the camps have become an increasing irritant to Anglos living in nearby (and often upscale) neighborhoods. The result has been that in many areas of southern California

TABLE 6.2   Selected Quality-of-Life Indicators for Whites and Hispanic Americans, 1988

Indicator	Whites	Hispanic Americans
Percentage below poverty level	10.5	28.2
Percentage children below poverty level (1987)	15.0	39.3
Median yearly income, males	$28,262	$18,190
Median yearly income, females	$18,823	$15,201
Median yearly income, families	$33,915	$21,769
Percentage with eight or fewer years of school	11.2	34.8
Percentage female-headed households	12.9	23.4
Percentage who own homes	67.2	40.2

Source: U.S. Bureau of the Census, *Statistical Abstracts of the United States, 1990.*

OURSELVES AND OTHERS

Brazil's Idol Is a Blonde, and Some Ask "Why?"

Rio de Janeiro, July 30 — When Rosane Collor, the wife of Brazil's President, wanted to collect food for children's nurseries in Rio, she turned to Xuxa.

Maria da Graca Meneghel, a children's television host who goes by the stage name Xuxa (pronounced SHOO-shuh), agreed to help. Turning the opening night of her latest movie into a benefit, she declared that admission would be several pounds of nonperishable food.

At the end of the gala here last month, weary volunteers declared that had they collected 69 tons in aid.

Once bowled over by Carmen Miranda, Brazil is now entranced by a rosy-cheeked 27-year-old singer with flaxen hair and blue eyes. Her performing retinue features the Paquitas, seven girls with golden tresses.

The Fruits of Success

A descendant of Italian, Polish and German immigrants, Xuxa has become the nation's most successful performing artist. At last count, her four records had sold 12 million copies. Her eight movies have done equally well, with the last one, "Princess Xuxa," selling four million tickets. Her comic book is now Brazil's best-selling one, with 400,000 copies printed daily. Children (and their parents) are bombarded by more than 40 Xuxa-endorsed products.

Politicians court her. Last year, presidential candidates sought unsuccessfully to win her endorsement. José Sarney, the President at the time, presented her with a medal honoring her work against polio.

This year, with an eye to Xuxa's morning audience of tens of millions of children and adults, Alceni Guerra, Brazil's Health Minister, visited the star at her home here to win support for campaigns against drugs, smoking and meningitis.

Having conquered Portuguese-speaking Brazil, Xuxa is studying Spanish to extend her entertainment empire to the rest of Latin America. Recent appearances in Los Angeles, Miami, Mexico City and Viña del Mar, Chile, helped push sales for her record "Xuxa en Español" to more than 300,000 copies.

"Profoundly Racist" Culture

"When I go to an airport and am not mobbed by children, I get worried," the entertainer said during a break in taping at her studio here.

But in a land largely populated by people of African, Indian and Latin stock, some chafe at the idea that Brazil's idol looks as if she just stepped off a jet from Frankfurt.

"You have a nation that is half brown or black, and the national symbol is blond," said Herbert de Souza, a sociologist here. "Our culture is profoundly racist."

Abdias do Nascimento, a leader in the United Black Movement, said: "It's very negative for children. It makes people despise themselves because they don't have the same model of beauty. You have little black girls who only want blond dolls."

Indeed, the blond image that Xuxa projects runs counter to racial trends here.

Last month, a survey of Brazil's racial composition indicated that "browns and blacks" made up 43 percent of the population of 140 million.

Positive Roles for Asians

Demographers who studied the survey, prepared by the Brazilian Institute for Geography and Statistics, forecast that by the turn of the century Brazil would return to its historic makeup of a black and brown majority. A century of European and Asian immigration, which ended in the 1960's, put blacks and browns in the minority.

Some say the Xuxa phenomenon is part of a preference for racial stereotypes often associated in this third-world nation with first-world success.

The race survey found that Brazilians of Asian origin had the highest incomes of all racial groups in the nation. With the rise of the million-strong Japanese-Brazilian minority here, Asian faces have started appearing in positive roles in advertisements here.

"Before they only wanted Japanese for the roles of laundryman, cookie maker or Buddhist monk," said Luis Nobuki Morisawa, who recently opened an agency in São Paulo specializing in Asian models. "Today the face of an Oriental on TV is synonymous with competence, seriousness and the future."

"Children's Choice"

Xuxa says her all-blond cast responds to the "children's choice."

"Children like Snow White, Cinderella, Barbie," she said. "When they see me close to them, it's as if the mythical person has become reality."

On the rare occasion that the race issue is raised, Xuxa's defenders note that she first achieved prominence in the early 1980's when she dated Pelé, the soccer player who is Brazil's most prominent black citizen.

Others speculate that Brazil's infatuation with Xuxa merely reflects a universal premium—rarity.

Oba Oba is a Rio night club that features samba dancers of the Afro-Latin type that foreigners traditionally associate with Brazilian beauty.

"In January alone, I lost three dancers to marriages with Europeans, largely Germans," Elias Abifadel, the club's manager, said in a recent interview.

This summer, the winner of the annual "Girl From Ipanema" contest was Carla Henker, a 20-year-old dentistry student. The daughter of German immigrants, Miss Henker was glowingly described in Rio's press as "extremely blond with blue eyes."

To compete with Xuxa's wildly successful program, on the Globo network, a rival network, Manchet, recently launched Angélica Ksyvickis as host of a children's program. Promotional photographs invariably stress her enormous head of blond hair.

But Angelica's competition is tough. During a 39-city tour of Brazil last year, an estimated two million children and their parents paid to see Xuxa perform live.

When the show came to Salvador, often called the capital of black Brazil for its majority Afro-Brazilian population, 10 children were hurt in a mad scramble to get closer to Xuxa.

Source: James Brooke, *The New York Times*, International, July 31, 1990. Copyright © 1990 by The New York Times Company. Reprinted by permission.

and elsewhere, undocumented workers' camps have been closed down by local law enforcement officials or by informal actions by concerned local citizens.

Not all Hispanic groups, of course, fit this description. Descendants of the old Spanish elite in New Mexico, for instance, continue to enjoy high social and economic status. Middle-class Cubans who fled Castro's regime during the 1960s have income, occupational, and educational profiles that match or even exceed those of Anglos.

In recent years, Hispanic groups in this society have attempted to organize what amounts to a pan-Hispanic coalition in an effort to strengthen their political power position vis-à-vis the dominant Anglos (Briseno, 1990b). Although they have made some modest gains, their effort has been hampered by the continuing diversities and disagreements among the various groups that make up this segment of the U.S. population (*San Diego Union*, 1991). Although Hispanic Americans may be a numerical majority in some parts of U.S. society, they remain very much a sociological minority.

Asian Americans

Asian American is a collective term that refers to a number of individual ethnic minority groups, including Filipinos, Chinese, Japanese, Koreans, and various Indochinese groups (e.g., Vietnamese, Laotians, Cambodians, Thais). In all, Asian Americans today number some six and a half million U.S. citizens. Since the late 1980s, social scientific and public attention has been drawn to the economic, educational, and occupational accomplishments of these individuals. Their often-startling successes rival the best stories in the rags to riches tradition, and have earned them the designations "superminority" (Schwartz, 1987) and "model minority" (McBee, 1984; McLeod,

1986). Asian Americans have the highest median family incomes of all ethnic groups in the United States, as well as the highest average level of formal education of any group in this society, including whites. Thirty-three percent have completed college, compared to 17.5 percent of whites. As Schaefer (1990) cautioned, however, these overall profiles may be more than a little misleading.

Asian Americans have very high proportional representation among high-status, highly compensated managerial and professional occupations. They also have very high proportional representation among low-status, poorly compensated service occupations (e.g., restaurant help). They seem to enjoy the best and the worst of the dual labor market. In addition, although they may be the most highly educated group in all of U. S. society, they have begun to experience prejudice and discrimination from top-rung universities and colleges. Admissions committees apparently have begun to fear that too many Asian students are being accepted at the expense of whites (Biemiller, 1986; Lindsey, 1987; Salholz, 1987).

High numbers of Asian Americans have been able to fulfill the American dream of upward mobility and success. Numerous recently arrived immigrants, who have contributed to the explosive growth of the Asian American community in the past several years, have sunk to the bottom with respect to occupation and income. Unfortunately, the persistence of the superminority image might blind the government and the larger majority community to the plight of these refugees (Shaw, 1990).

Despite the sometimes phenomenal success of many Asian Americans (or perhaps because of it), members of this group still are subjected to a variety of negative responses from the dominant majority group. Such responses are by no means new from this group.

Chinese Americans were the victims of violent attacks in California during the mid-1800s. They were also the first group to be specifically targeted for immigration restriction later in that same century through the Chinese Exclusion Act of 1882. During the Second World War era, Japanese Americans were subjected to forced relocation and internment in special camps, even though there was no objective evidence that they posed a threat to national security. The hostile treatment received by both of these groups at the hands of the larger white society seems to have been part of a much larger "yellow peril" stereotype. This involved the deep-seated belief by whites in a worldwide plot by Orientals to overthrow their civilization and take over the world (Hoppenstand, 1983).

Fear of the yellow peril has been rekindled, one major source being the flood of political and economic refugees from war-torn Southeast Asia. The Vietnam War deeply divided the U.S. population as no previous military conflict had. It was also the first war that the United States lost. The second source of this fear is the increasing economic "war" with Japan, which the United States again is perceived to be losing. It remains to be seen to what extent this growing tide of resentment will erode the gains made by this highly visible minority group.

 ## Minorities and Poverty in the United States: A Declining Significance of Race?

With few exceptions, the pattern of racial and ethnic minority group linkages to the social stratification system in the United States has remained remarkably stable over time. More than fifty years ago, pioneer social class researcher W. Lloyd Warner and his associates (Davis, Gardner, and Gardner, 1941; Warner and Srole, 1945) noted that two separate paths were followed by or available to minorities in this society.

For white ethnics (European-born immigrants who physically resembled the dominant WASPs) the pattern was one of initial rejection by and subjugation to the majority group. Dominant group prejudices and discriminatory acts were reflected in restricted economic, educational, occupational, and other opportunities for the ethnics. As their cultural assimilation progressed, however, the groups were able to take advantage of rapidly expanding social, economic, and political structures to move up in the social class structure. Improved status in turn led to their increased acceptance by the dominant societal group. The resulting structural and marital assimilation finally created a condition in which the distinctive cultural and physical traits of the ethnics all but vanished. Original ethnic group membership then ceased to be an important factor in the shaping of social class.

The course was different for racial minority groups, however. Unlike white ethnics who could physically blend in with the majority group after reaching a certain level of cultural assimilation, people of color remained physically distinctive even after full cultural assimilation had occurred. Prevailing racist ideologies of the dominant societal group continued to associate skin color and other physical characteristics with intellectual and moral inferiorities. Thus, racial minorities' physical visibility meant that they would be the objects of continued prejudice and discrimination. For them, race would remain a critically important determinant of position in the stratification hierarchy, and that position would be on the bottom rungs of the ladder. Caste rather than class factors characterizes relations between the racial majority and minority groups.

Poverty

Data relating to income distribution and patterns of economic poverty in the United States during the past three decades certainly seem to verify the validity of this argument. As already discussed, median yearly incomes for African Americans, Native Americans, and many Hispanic American groups are substantially below comparable figures for non-Hispanic whites. So, also, are occupational and educational profiles. This pattern is even more pronounced when the issue being considered is poverty.

Poverty, or economic deprivation, is a politically and socially sensitive issue. It is also a concept that lends itself to a variety of interpretations. Relative poverty definitions compare various groups in order to draw conclusions about the economic circumstances of one group relative to others. In this instance, **relative poverty** is the situation of being economically deprived compared to some other particular group. Relative to the middle class, for example, the life of the working class may be described as involving relative poverty or deprivation. Typical working-class incomes do not permit the same types and levels of material goods as do middle-class incomes. Working-class people may have all the material necessities of life, but they do not possess the same level of material comfort as do middle-class people. In this sense, they are poor.

In contrast, absolute poverty definitions measure economic deprivation in terms of an objective, fixed standard. In this case, **absolute poverty** refers to the inability to maintain physical survival on a long-term basis. Conceptualized in this manner, poverty can be measured as incomes that fall below the amount of money needed for a minimally adequate supply of material resources such as food, clothing, and shelter.

For more than a quarter-century the federal government has used just such a measurement to define poverty and to examine its prevalence in this society (Figure 6.2).

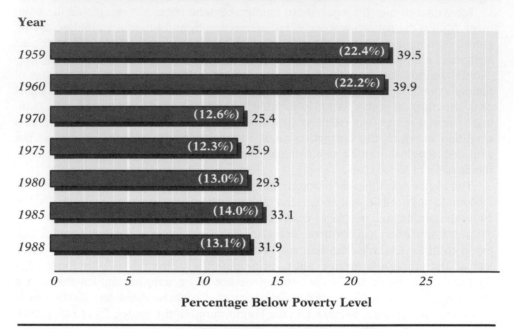

FIGURE 6.2 Persons Below Poverty Level, 1959–1988

Year

Year		
1959	(22.4%)	39.5
1960	(22.2%)	39.9
1970	(12.6%)	25.4
1975	(12.3%)	25.9
1980	(13.0%)	29.3
1985	(14.0%)	33.1
1988	(13.1%)	31.9

Percentage Below Poverty Level

Note: Numbers to the right of the bars indicate actual numbers of persons below the poverty level (in millions); numbers within bars indicate the actual percentage of the population they represent.

Source: U.S. Bureau of the Census, *Current Population Reports,* series P-60, no. 166.

The **poverty line,** as this index is called, represents the yearly income required to provide a nutritionally adequate diet for a typical nonfarm family of four people, assuming that one-third of the total income is used for food. In 1988 the poverty line was set at $12,092. In that year, approximately 13.1 percent of the U.S. population, representing nearly thirty-two million people, were officially defined as poor (U.S. Bureau of the Census, 1990). Whether or not these figures are an accurate assessment of real poverty in the United States is controversial. Like other official government statistics, they are subject to political as well as mathematical manipulation and interpretations. Incumbent administrations have a vested interest in minimizing the extent of reported poverty, as figures that are too large may be read as a failure of governmental economic policies and used by the out-of-power party to make political hay.

Who are the poor in the United States and how does minority group status affect the likelihood of being poor? Contrary to prevailing stereotypes, poverty is an overwhelmingly white phenomenon, at least in terms of sheer numbers. In 1988 whites constituted 65 percent of all persons living in poverty. Another 29 percent were African Americans, and the remainder were "other" nonwhite racial groups, including some Hispanics (U.S. Bureau of the Census, 1988).

These figures might appear to disconfirm the hypothesis that racial minority group status is a significant factor in the experience of poverty. They are more than a bit misleading, however, since whites make up the overwhelming numerical majority within the United States. A more accurate measurement would be the proportional representation of the various races among the poverty population, that is, the percentage of each racial group that falls below the poverty line.

The question of whether racial discrimination or class-related factors are of greater importance in the perpetuation of poverty among people of color in the United States is a subject of dispute among social scientists. Although causal factors may be a source of contention, no one disputes the need for creative solutions to the cycle of poverty.

Looked at from this perspective, the picture appears substantially different. Whereas 65 percent of all poor people may be white, only 10 percent of all whites are poor. Whereas only 29 percent of all poor people are African American, over 31 percent of all African Americans are poor. Whereas Native Americans make up part of the approximately 6 percent of all poor people who are of "other" racial background, 40 percent of all Native Americans are poor (U.S. Bureau of the Census, 1988).

Clearly, race is a major factor in the phenomenon of U.S. poverty. This is evident especially when attention is directed to what has been called "the American under-class" (Wilson, 1987). This group consists of the hardcore poor for whom poverty has become a permanent way of life, and who increasingly are becoming separated and isolated from mainstream American life. What is not entirely clear is exactly how much race contributes to creating and maintaining this truly disadvantaged group compared to the effects of social class factors.

Wilson on Race, Class, and Poverty   Sociologist William Julius Wilson (1978) offered a highly controversial hypothesis with respect to this issue. He acknowledged that racial factors may have once been important in originally pushing many minority people into poverty. However, it is class-related factors of occupational skills and educational levels, not racial group status, that now keep some people trapped in poverty over the long run. To make his point, Wilson cited the growing number of African Americans who have moved into middle-class and upper middle-class occupations and income levels. He argued that such upward mobility patterns demonstrate the fact that white prejudices and discriminatory actions no longer operate in such a way as to suppress all African Americans uniformly on the basis of race.

What these data show, according to Wilson, is that race per se has declined as an important determinant of socioeconomic status. What has caught and trapped some African Americans in underclass life is a series of occupational and other structural changes in the United States. These changes include a decline in the types of unskilled, semiskilled, and service jobs that in the past provided employment opportunities for people with lower levels of education and few occupational skills. They also include the geographical relocation of many industries and businesses that in the past provided local employment opportunities for residents of inner-city areas. Wilson concluded that if racism were still a paramount factor in the determination of socioeconomic situation, no (or only a very few) African Americans would have achieved middle-class and upper middle-class status.

Wilson's hypothesis was criticized sharply by a number of analysts (Willie, 1978, 1979). They challenged his assertion that race and racism no longer are significant factors in the structuring of African Americans' stratification. In fact, they and other people of color still face daily instances of prejudice and discrimination regardless of their socioeconomic status. Firsthand accounts of otherwise successful African American professionals and managers who have experienced such subtle and often nonsubtle forms of racial hostility would seem to lend support to Wilson's critics (Benjamin, 1991).

Whereas racist patterns may have declined and racial relations may have improved during the past several decades, race-related problems in the United States are far from being resolved. In a number of important respects, the situation may have begun to deteriorate over the space of the past few years. A rapidly accumulating body of reports testifies to a significant increase in hate crimes and other racial incidents in local communities and on college campuses since 1985.

 ## THE FUTURE OF MINORITY GROUP RELATIONS IN THE UNITED STATES

The objective lives of many racial and ethnic groups have improved significantly during the past forty years. The civil rights of minorities now are protected by laws that prohibit discrimination against them. Various affirmative action directives and court decisions also have served the advancement of these racial and ethnic groups. Substantial gains in minority group education, income, and occupational opportunities were made during this time. That's the good news.

The bad news is that many of these gains are more apparent than real, and even these may have begun to deteriorate (*San Diego Union*, 1989b). For example, more African Americans and Hispanic Americans are enjoying middle-class incomes, but the ratios of these groups' incomes to those of Anglos have remained the same over the past thirty years: 58 percent for African Americans, and 70 percent for Hispanics. Many members of both of these minority groups have been able to advance to higher educational and occupational status, but many more have not. Recent figures indicate dramatic declines in the percentages of low-income and middle-income African Americans and Hispanics entering college after high school during the past decade—from 40 percent to 30 percent for African Americans, and from 50 percent to 35 percent for Hispanics (*San Diego Union*, 1990b).

In the case of both Hispanics and Asian Americans, large numbers of recent immigrants have increased poverty and unemployment rates in these groups dramatically. These immigrants frequently have put the groups on a direct collision course with majority group members whose jobs and economic well-being appear threatened by these newcomers. Acts of violence directed against Asians and Hispanics in California and Texas attest to the fact that economic conflicts can generate or aggravate conflicts in intergroup relations.

During the eight years of the Reagan administration, executive and judicial actions (and nonactions) had the overall effect of eroding many gains won through legislation enacted during administrations that were kinder and gentler to minority group concerns. The United States currently is engaged in intense head-to-head economic and trade competition with Japan. The perception that the Japanese are winning this competition has begun to generate increasing expressions of frustration by many Americans. Increasingly, stereotyping, prejudices, and overt discriminatory acts have been directed not only against the Japanese, but also against many other Asian American groups (Lau, 1990). For example, one widely publicized anecdote reported a frustrated New York restaurant owner's response to a group of Japanese tourists seeking directions to a popular department store: "You people had no trouble finding Pearl Harbor, so you should be able to find Bloomingdale's on your own."

On a less humorous note, Asian Americans who were mistaken for Japanese have been physically attacked and, in at least one instance, killed (Schaefer, 1990). Their attackers were whites angered and frustrated by growing Japanese economic presence and influence in the United States. As minority group pressures continue to increase, it is likely that race and ethnic relations will continue to unravel. Majority group members increasingly see themselves under seige from minority group members who, in turn, view themselves as victims. Although the future of these intergroup relations cannot be predicted with certainty, it does seem fairly certain that this future will be less than rosy.

FOCUS ON
MEXICO

FROM SONS OF DONS TO JUANS OF BRONZE

As we have seen, the image of the United States as a great melting pot of ethnic and racial immigrants is more of a cultural myth than a statement of historical reality. However, the model would seem to apply to one American immigrant experience, that of Mexico. According to sociologist Pierre L. van den Berghe (1978), since the time of its original conquest by Spain in the early sixteenth century, Mexico has become a homo-geneous society. Racial and ethnic group consciousness is low, and racist ideology and racial-ethnic conflicts are practically nonexistent.

A Nation of Bronze
Mexican revolutionary and postrevolutionary ideology depicted the society as "a nation of bronze." Mexicans are a racial and ethnic alloy that was forged from the amalgamation of Span-

Even though most modern Mexicans can trace at least some of their ancestry to the Indian groups who populated the country at the time of the Spanish Conquest, prejudice and discrimination against "pure" Indians in Mexico remain strong. Like their counterparts in the United States, Mexican Indians are severely disadvantaged in terms of most quality-of-life indicators.

ish, Indian, and African groups who formed the major population elements over the nearly 500-odd years since the Spanish Conquest and colonization. In this particular case, according to van den Berghe, the melting pot was created as a byproduct of the brutality and excesses of the Spanish colonial period. It represents a forced homogeni-zation of what had been a culturally and racially diverse population. The twin processes by which this blending of the Mexican population occurred were **Hispanization** (adoption of Spanish culture) of the Indian and African population segments and the **mestizoization** (biological-genetic mixing) of Spanish, Indian, and African elements.

Successful Hispanization was accomplished by the superior power of the Spanish *conquistadores* (conquerors) who simply imposed their cultural patterns on the much less powerful Indians and Africans. Mestizoization represented a biological success for the Indian population segment, who by virtue of their vast numerical superiority were able to impose their physical pat-

terns on the Spanish and the African subgroups with whom they reproduced.

In the early days of the colonial period, Mexico was characterized by a racially and ethnically stratified estate system of five *castas*. At the apex of the system stood the racially pure, white European Spaniards. This group controlled political, religious, and military positions and owned the bulk of the land. Below them stood the American Spaniards, or Creoles. They represented the legitimate offspring of European Spaniards and indigenous Indians. They owned substantial lands and occupied high-level positions within the economy. Next came mestizos, the illegitimate offspring of Spaniards and Indians or of Indians and Africans. Status within this group was often determined by skin tone and other physical features. An elaborate taxonomy of terms was developed over time to reflect the many genetic combinations represented in this residual group. Below mestizos stood Indians, by far the largest group, who became peasants on the *haciendas* of the land-owning *castas*. Finally, at the bottom of the system, came African and mulatto (mixed-race) slaves. Like the mestizos, mulattos were subject to numerous skin tone and other physical variations. A large taxonomy also was developed to express these variations and to establish relative status within the group.

As Hispanization progressed, the population became increasingly culturally homogeneous. As members of the different *castas* reproduced across the generations, a bewildering number of physical and racial combinations developed. Ultimately, it became impossible to establish specific racial or ethnic identities with any sort of accuracy. The result, supposedly, was a dramatic decline in racial and ethnic considerations in modern-day social relations. Such has been the effect of the Mexican melting pot that race and ethnicity have become obsolete as factors relevant to everyday life. Social status still is an important force in shaping formal and informal social relationships, but it is determined by social class factors such as occupation, income, and education, and not by racial and ethnic subgroup identities.

This benign analysis of a society untroubled by racial or ethnic tensions as the result of a true melting or blending of subgroups has not gone unchallenged. Two recent ethnographic portraits of Mexican society and people (Oster,

1989; Riding, 1989) offered interpretations of the consequences of the forced melting pot that differ substantially from van den Berghe's. They would seem to offer a plausible alternative explanation for observed social and cultural patterns.

A Malignant Result?

In these somewhat less kindly interpretations, the amalgamation phenomenon is depicted as a primary causal factor in what amounts to a love-hate relationship the Mexican people have with themselves. This relationship presumably is reflected in the operations of their social institutions, and in their cultural beliefs and values.

According to these analyses, the melting of the individual cultural and racial population strains during the periods of conquest and colonialism resulted in a cultural-racial amalgam featuring distinguishing traits that are inherently incompatible. The forced Hispanization of Indian and African subgroups destroyed these groups' own cultural patterns. The *conquistadores* made it quite clear that Spanish culture was infinitely superior, and they had the political muscle to make that definition stick. They effectively dominated all major social institutions and processes during the colonial period. Even though the Spanish may have been quite able to differentiate between the cultural and the racial components of Indian and African subgroups, however, an obvious association still existed between the superior cultural pattern and a distinctive racial pattern. White people were the possessors of the superior and preferred cultural pattern. Dark-skinned Indian and African peoples were the possessors of inferior cultural patterns.

At the same time, the mestizoization of the developing population created a new physical-racial type in which Indian features predominated. These physical traits had been associated with inferior cultural and social patterns from the time of the Spanish Conquest. The end product of this imposed blending process, then, was a people who represented simultaneously both the best of all possible worlds (the culture of the Spanish) and the worst of all possible worlds (the physical characteristics of the Indians) (Oster, 1989; Riding, 1989). Contemporary Mexican society, in this respect, might be visualized as a macro-level case of what has been termed **social marginality**.

That concept was first introduced over a half-century ago under the rubric of "the marginal man." It refers to individuals who share important characteristics of two or more defined social groups but are unable to identify fully with, or be accepted fully by, either group. Rather, they find themselves poised or torn between the groups and must perform a delicate and difficult balancing act between what are often conflicting expectations and demands.

Regardless of the specific term employed, the phenomenon appears to generate a number of significant social consequences. One such effect is increased prejudice and discrimination against individuals and groups perceived to be lower than oneself on the social hierarchy. A second consequence is the development of feelings of self-hatred. Evidence of both exists in modern Mexico.

In a society where poverty, unemployment, illiteracy, and depressed living conditions in general are widespread, conditions are most desperate for surviving groups of pure Indians. They typically display the lowest amounts of economic, employment, educational, housing, health, and other critical resources within the population. In states like Chiapas, Guerrero, Oaxaca, and Puebla, Indians have mortality and alcoholism rates that are staggeringly high compared to the population at large. This pattern is reminiscent of that among Native Americans in the United States; as is also the case for them, conditions for Indians in Mexico seem strongly linked to racist attitudes and practices on the part of the larger society. In Mexico, open disdain for Indians and a special respect for *gueros* (whites) are widespread (Riding, 1989). A more subtle form of racism is that displayed by the numerically dominant mestizos against themselves.

One of the more tragic consequences of stereotyping, prejudice, and discrimination is the fact that the targets often come to accept the majority group's definition of them as valid. They then begin to treat themselves as inferiors, setting in motion a vicious circle of action that serves to confirm and reinforce the original negative stereotypes. In the United States, for example, this pattern was reflected in the preference of many African Americans for lighter-skin spouses or children. It also was expressed in the attempts of some African Americans to "whiten" themselves by using any number of skin bleaches, hair straighteners, and other products designed specifically for this purpose.

The Black Pride movement of the 1970s tried to combat this insidious trend of self-hatred by providing African Americans with positive group images with which they could identify and from which they could develop healthy self-images. Slavery itself, which had been a source of continuing shame, was portrayed as a setting for daily acts of heroism and courage in Alex Haley's enormously successful book and television miniseries, *Roots*.

In modern Mexican society, where negative feelings and actions against Indians are widespread among the larger mestizo population, members of that population find themselves faced with a serious dilemma. Despite their feelings of superiority over Indians, based on their white, Spanish background, they overtly resemble the stigmatized Indian group. Their physical appearance clearly serves as a continuing reminder of their close historical linkage to the Indian population, and thus, continuing evidence of their own inferiority. This problem may be compounded by Mexico's nearest northern neighbor. The United States is a society with a long-standing history of discrimination against people of color. It also is a society in which Mexican Americans are perceived as a racial, rather than ethnic, group and treated as nonwhite (i.e., racial inferiors) by many Anglos.

Although the Mexicans' dilemma conceivably could be resolved by identifying more closely with the Indian groups, this solution is highly unlikely. Beliefs about the profound cultural inferiority of Indians are strongly entrenched, and they are reinforced by Indians' obvious inferior and depressed living conditions. While the dilemma also might conceivably be resolved by identifying more closely with the white group, the Mexicans' obvious nonwhite physical features, and, perhaps, the prejudices of their Yankee neighbors, make that solution equally unlikely.

The result of this unresolved problem, according to both Oster and Riding, is a deep and abiding cultural self-hate. This feeling has been oddly translated into a cultural preference for a pure Anglo physical type—the pale-skinned, blue-eyed blonde—as the idealized standard of beauty.

Four hundred years after racial amalgamation supposedly made such physical taxonomies impossible, modern Mexicans still establish hierarchies of preference, and refer to themselves on the basis of variations in skin color. Common terms include *negro* (very dark-skinned), *moreno* (medium dark), *medio-moreno* (light to medium dark), and *guero* or *blanco* (white). The desirability of being *guero* is indicated by the widespread use of blue-eyed, blond models in commercial advertising and by the fact that, for many Mexican men, the height of informal status is to be seen in public with *una guera* ("a blond woman") (Riding, 1989). For women who happen not to have been born blond, there is always hair coloring. In Mexico, the advertising slogan that "blondes have more fun" may be more accurate than its original creators ever could have dreamed.

It is not clear just how or if this problem ultimately will be resolved. The official position taken by the government has been that of attempting to promote a feeling of *Mexicanidad* ("Mexicanness") that emphasizes the superiority and desirability of the physical and cultural amalgam that is the mestizo. This official position so far has not been taken seriously by the Mexican upper and upper middle-classes. Perhaps these classes see their own standing in the international First World stratification system as contingent on their ability to dissociate themselves from their past. Until such time as some sort of Bronze Power movement is able to generate a genuine sense of pride in the special blend that is Mexico, an entire population must continue in its collective search for a viable identity and will continue to live in the shadow of its own imagined inferiority.

DISCUSSION QUESTIONS

1. In what sense is modern Mexico a "nation of bronze"?

2. What lessons do you think Mexican people who are interested in creating a sense of na-

tional pride (*Mexicanidad*) might be able to learn from the 1960s and 1970s Black Pride movement in the United States?
3. The three countries that make up North America—Mexico, the United States, and Canada—each have sizeable Native Indian population groups. Go to the library and read about Indians in Canada. How does their situation compare to those of native groups in Mexico and the United States? Are they better off, worse off, or about the same in terms of social and economic living conditions?

FOCUS ON
JAPAN

A Growing Yen for Diversity?

Modern Japan represents one of the most homogeneous societal populations in the contemporary world. Most other mature industrial societies are characterized by a large variety of culturally and racially distinct population subgroups. However, 99 percent of Japan's population is of Japanese origin. This is the result of geographic accident, as well as deliberate social and political policy.

As an island nation, Japan is geographically separated and isolated from the Asian mainland. Other Asian societies are in close proximity to one another, and historically, their common borders have allowed for the relatively easy interchange of different racial and ethnic groups. But Japan is protected from the mainland by a watery buffer that is 120 miles wide at its narrowest point. It is further protected by strong winds (*kamikaze* or "divine winds"), which saved Japan from Mongol invasions during the thirteenth century and which, for centuries, were an effective barrier to seagoing attempts to breach its border. This geographic isolation from Asia proper not only protected Japan from outside intrusion by other ethnic groups, but also helped foster a sense of common identity and unity among its people (Hendry, 1987).

Ethnocentrism

A strongly developed sense of ethnocentrism has been an important part of this identity, as it was extended to embrace the belief in the racial superiority of the people as well. It became the basis for a pattern of avoidance and exclusion of foreign (i.e., not Japanese) things and people, a pattern known as **xenophobia**. For years, it has been immigration policy to restrict severely or to cut off completely the flow of foreigners into the country.

The largest foreign minority group in Japan today is Koreans, some 700,000 strong, making up approximately 80 percent of Japan's foreign population. They represent the remnants and descendants of guest workers from the Second World War era. For them, life in Japan is far from pleasant (*Economist*, 1989b).

They occupy a social status roughly equivalent to that of many racial and ethnic minorities in the contemporary United States, forming a distinct subgroup, defined by popular prejudices as profoundly inferior to the majority group. They are consigned by widespread discriminatory acts to restricted social, economic, and political opportunities, which guarantee Koreans' actual social inferiority to most Japanese. This, in turn, confirms the initial Japanese belief in Korean racial and cultural inferiority, the often observed vicious circle characteristic of many situations of dominant-minority group relations (Myrdal, 1964).

In the face of the overwhelming numerical, political, and economic superiority of their hosts, the Koreans responded in much the same way as other minority groups in other societies and in other times (e.g., Chinese Americans in the United States in the last century and in this one).

They closed ranks and formed mutual benefit associations to meet their daily needs. Tensions between Japanese and Koreans remain high, however, and recent changes in Japanese foreign immigration policy may make the delicate situation even more touchy. These changes involve a growing, although reluctant, opening of existing restrictions on foreign immigrants, including those from Korea. They have been necessitated by important economic and demographic changes in Japanese society.

Minority Labor

As a result of an exploding economy and a general rising standard of living in the country, Japan has begun to experience a real shortage of labor in what Japanese call "three-K" jobs: occupations that are *kitanai* ("dirty"), *kitsui* ("hard"), or *kiken* ("dangerous"). They typically include unskilled labor and service jobs such as those in restaurants and in construction. Positions available in these areas greatly exceed the number of workers seeking full-time or part-time employment, so that companies have had to cut back on their hours of operation for lack of help (Jameson, 1989). With Japanese workers unwilling to take on such jobs, employers have begun to look outside the country, tapping Malaysia, the Philippines, Pakistan, and South Korea for laborers. Despite strong sanctions by the Japanese government and widespread exploitation by labor gang leaders who arrange for passage and employment, the number of illegal foreign workers has risen dramatically in the past few years. It promises to continue to do so, as economic expansion generates a real need for unskilled labor that cannot or will not be met by domestic workers.

More women and older people are being recruited to fill these lower-echelon positions. But demographic changes taking place within the Japanese population make it extraordinarily unlikely that the problem can be solved without the importation of large numbers of unskilled foreign laborers in the near future.

Japan is a rapidly aging society. Beginning in 1995, the number of people between fifteen and sixty-four years of age is expected to decrease by some 4.4 million by the year 2005. In that same year, the number from fifteen to twenty-nine years will have decreased by approximately 2.3 million (Jameson, 1989). The latter group is critical for the unskilled labor and service market. With such a domestic labor shortage, Japan is going to have to rethink either its past and current exclusionary immigration policies or its economic expansionist policies. Since the second alternative could likely result in a leveling or even a decline in current living standards, the first is much more likely. Recognizing this prospect, some government leaders already have begun to call for the development of new, enlightened immigration policies.

Suppose that such new policies were enacted. Unskilled foreign workers from other Asian and Pacific rim societies would be permitted to enter the country to fill jobs and perform services necessary for its modern lifestyle but rejected by its workers. One might predict that this infusion of foreign cultures and the beneficial economic contributions being made by such individuals would lessen ethnocentric feelings against outsiders. In the general context of widespread economic well-being, the Japanese people should be able to afford to be less prejudiced and less discriminatory against foreigners. This would especially be true when they could readily perceive that the labor of such foreigners was partially responsible for that well-being. However, historical evidence from other societies and from Japan itself might argue against such a prediction.

The *Burakumin*

For many years, the most severely disadvantaged minority group in Japan has been one that is not really foreign in any normal sense of that term. The *burakumin*, as this group is called, consist of between two to three million people (over 2 percent of the total Japanese population). They are culturally, nationally, and racially identical to the Japanese but are nonetheless treated with extreme prejudice and discrimination by that larger population.

The basis for this societywide reaction to the *burakumin* is the perception and definition of this group as being ritually polluted. In this sense, they represent an outcaste group, much in the manner of outcastes in the Indian caste system (Yoshino and Murakoshi, 1983). Like other outcaste groups in other caste-stratified societies, the *burakumin* remain effectively excluded from mainstream society. This is accomplished by a host of legal, social, and cultural institutions that keep them ritually isolated and thus neutralize their symbolic threat to the larger society (it is believed that their pollution is contagious).

The source of the Japanese belief that the *burakumin* are *eta* ("pollution abundant") or even *hinin* ("nonhuman") was the types of occupations traditionally held by that group. These occupations were associated with death (gravedigging, butchering) or with objects connected with death (tanning, leather work), and were considered so degrading that they would forever contaminate those who engaged in them. It made no difference in what ways *burakumin* and Japanese were alike, the association with contaminated work made *burakumin* distinct and inferior.

Once this initial distinction was established, it led to the development of beliefs about other differences that also supposedly existed between the two groups. The fact that these beliefs happened to be erroneous was of little consequence. The fact that they were believed to be true became the basis for systematic discrimination against the *burakumin* that continues to this day.

In a similar way, Jews once were defined by European Christians as ritually impure, polluted people. After all, they were believed to be responsible for the death of Christ, and thus were damned forever. As the European continent began to modernize, however, the need for skilled financiers and other money occupations created a major dilemma. These occupations were defined as usury by traditional Christian beliefs. As such, they were inherently damning activities that consigned those who practiced them to everlasting hell. The dilemma was solved by having Jews, who were already an outcaste pariah people, assume the jobs that no decent Christian could or would do. The needs of the evolving economic order thus were solved without any real moral cost. Those who occupied damning financial positions were already damned anyway.

The fact that Jews would perform such work became further "proof" of their intrinstic inferiority and their deserved outcaste status. (The fact that they had no real choice in the matter, since they had been systematically excluded from other occupational opportunities, was overlooked or ignored.) It also later became the source of additional stereotyping, predjudice, and discrimination against this group in Europe and in the New World ("they're always involved with money"). In the case of what may be good people performing dirty work, the people themselves become dirty. As sources of possible contamination for good people, the dirty group then must be removed from normal society.

In the case of the *burakumin* in Japan, the types of jobs that were defined as being fit only for subhuman or nonhuman outcastes were those that were thought to be dirty, demanding, or undesirable (Yoshino and Murakoshi, 1983). These are exactly the kinds of jobs now being proposed for unskilled foreign workers, since no Japanese who had any other options would willingly choose to perform them. A traditional feeling already exists among the Japanese that foreigners in general and specific foreigners in particular (Koreans, in this case) are culturally and racially inferior. Having such peoples imported to perform jobs defined as polluting will not likely change beliefs about them. If anything, it will only increase such ethnocentric patterns.

Cheap foreign labor may be an economic necessity in the Japan of the near future, but it is also likely to be a major source of intergroup conflict. Short of a basic change in Japanese ideologies, increasing cultural diversity may well translate into social turmoil.

DISCUSSION QUESTIONS

1. What physical factors have contributed to the strong tradition of ethnocentrism in Japan?
2. You are the prime minister of Japan and are concerned about the possibility of increasing racial and ethnic conflict because of the entry of large numbers of foreign workers into your country. What kinds of practical steps can you take to minimize such intergroup hostilities?
3. Go to the library and find materials about the untouchables, or outcaste group, in India. How have changing economic conditions in that country affected this particular minority group?

CHAPTER SUMMARY

1. Minority groups are composed of people who possess traits that make them distinctively different from dominant majority societal groups and that are negatively valued in the larger population. These minorities often are relegated to subordinate positions at the bottom of the stratification hierarchies of their societies.

2. Race and ethnicity are concepts that give rise to a great deal of confusion and misunderstanding. Racial minorities consist of people who are (or who are thought to be) genetically and physically different from the majority group. Ethnic minorities are composed of people culturally different from the dominant societal group. Both racial and ethnic minority groups face stereotyping, prejudice, and discrimination by the majority.

3. Stereotyping is the tendency to ignore individual differences among members of a given group and to define all its members as alike. Prejudice is an irrational, negative feeling or belief about members of some particular group. Discrimination is unfair, unequal treatment of members of a particular group.

4. In different times and different societies, members of majority and minority groups have interacted in a variety of ways. Assimilation refers to the incorporation of various minorities into the mainstream of their surrounding society culturally, socially, or biologically. Although the United States has often been described as a melting pot of diverse racial and ethnic groups, the actual pattern more often was one of Anglo conformity, in which immigrants were expected to become Americanized in the prevailing Anglo-Saxon cultural pattern. Functionalists regard assimilation as the most desirable form of racial and ethnic intergroup relations.

5. Pluralism refers to the retention of individual racial and ethnic group differences in a given society, and the mutual adjustment of these groups to one another. In some societies, the rights of minorities are maintained through legal protection. In others, population transfers may keep minorities separated from majority group members.

6. Economic, political, and social subjugation of minorities is a fact of life in many societies. Conflict theorists in the Marxist tradition claim that it is based on economic exploitation by powerful social classes.

7. Extermination or genocide is the attempt to destroy physically a given racial or ethnic group. Hitler's treatment of the Jews during the Second World War is the best-known modern example.

8. African Americans constitute the largest racial or ethnic minority in the United States, and are the only group in this society to have been held in slavery. Although legal segregation and other racist forms have been abolished, institutionalized racist practices continue to restrict income, and educational and occupational opportunities, for this group. African Americans remain significantly below whites in most quality-of-life indicators.

9. Native Americans preceded white European settlers in the United States, but they lacked the newcomers' military technology, and were overwhelmed by the colonists. Both physically and culturally distinct from the Anglos, Native Americans have been relegated to reservations managed by the Bureau of Indian Affairs. They remain the most severely disadvantaged minority group in terms of income, education, occupation, and other quality-of-life indicators.

10. Hispanic Americans are people from Spanish or Latin American origins, including Mexican Americans, Cubans, and Puerto Ricans. Their economic and social circumstances differ by subgroup, and many experience economic, educational, and occupational deprivation. A rising tide of illegal immigrants, especially in the Southwest, has led to growing resentment of many Anglos against this group.

11. Because of their educational and economic successes, Asian Americans have been portrayed as a superminority. However, many recently arrived immigrants from southeast Asia have not been able to share in these successes; nor have all Chinese Americans or Japanese Americans done well. Old stereotypes, prejudices, and discrimination against Asian Americans may be on the rise as a result of their rapid population growth in this society as well as strained economic relations between the United States and Japan. Racial slurs and hate crimes against this group currently seem to be on the rise.

12. Poverty is the experience of economic deprivation. Relative poverty refers to the deprived condition of a specific group relative to that of other groups; absolute poverty means the inability to

meet minimum requirements for physical survival. Racial and ethnic minorities are overrepresented among those living in poverty in the United States; however, the specific factors responsible for this observed pattern remain the subject of much dispute.

13. Although many racial and ethnic minority groups in the United States have made substantial gains in the past few decades, deteriorating economic conditions seem to have generated a resurgence of negative feelings and behaviors against many of them.

7

GENDER AND GENDER ISSUES

T wo infants lie side by side in a hospital nursery. Born within a few seconds of one another, they are physically and mentally intact and in overall good health. Both are members of the same race, and both come from families of identical and secure socioeconomic background. In nearly all other respects they appear to have been cast from the same mold; they even share the same body weight and length.

Looking at these two peacefully sleeping infants, one might think that nearly all things are possible for them at this point in their lives. To borrow a classic statement from sports commentator Curt Gowdy, "Their futures are still ahead of them." Those futures have not yet been influenced or clouded by any contact with the outside world. What these children can and will become some day is to a large extent a function of their individual strengths and weaknesses, their individual hopes, dreams, and fears.

Yet in a real sense the futures of these two infants are not entirely "still ahead of them." Rather, they already have been defined and molded significantly by social and cultural forces unknown to them and beyond their control. For these two brand-new members of society are not identical, as the color-coded name cards on their respective bassinets now make clear. One infant happens to be a female and the other a male.

This particular accident of birth, as we will see, is sufficient to create separate and unequal futures for these new human beings. Quite apart from considerations of individual abilities and disabilities, their likely social paths have been shaped in different directions by virtue of their sex and gender. In nearly all human societies, anatomical and biological differences among individuals have become the basis for a host of social, political, economic, and other differences that drastically affect the quality of people's lives. U.S. society is no exception.

QUESTIONS TO CONSIDER

1. What is the difference between sex and gender as social categories for classifying human beings?
2. What does existing research from the biological and social sciences' tell us about natural physical, intellectual, and emotional differences between women and men?
3. What is gender assignment, and why is this phenomenon such an important factor in individuals' lives?
4. How do chronological aging and movement into late adulthood affect people's gender identities and behaviors?
5. According to classical functionalist theorists like Talcott Parsons, in what ways are traditional gender roles and a sex-based division of labor functional or beneficial for society?
6. From the standpoint of conflict theory, what is the major function of a sex-based division of labor and traditional gender roles in a society like the United States?
7. What is "the pink-collar ghetto"?
8. How do human capital interpretations explain observed female-male occupational salary differences in modern societies?
9. What is the feminization of poverty, and what factors have contributed to its development?
10. What difference does it make that relatively few women hold political office at the federal or state level of government in U.S. society?
11. How do rape laws in the United States show a double standard of morality when it comes to men and women?
12. What is *Roe* v. *Wade*? Why was this such an important event for proponents of greater gender equality?

UNDERSTANDING SEX AND GENDER

Like race, sex and gender are concepts subject to confusion and misunderstanding in popular usage. They often have been thought of as alternative names for the same phenomenon, and frequently have been employed interchangeably. They certainly are related in the sense that both are ways of classifying people on physical grounds; however, they are by no means equivalent.

Biological Considerations

From a purely scientific standpoint, **sex** represents a classification system based on anatomical differences among individuals. In addition, sex differences include chromosomal and hormonal factors that distinguish females from males. Thus, members of the female sex have different physical organs from males (ovaries and a vagina, rather than testicles and a penis). They display a particular chromosomal pattern (XX) that differs from that of males (XY), and their bodies produce hormones in different proportions from males (primarily estrogen rather than androgens).

Psychological and Sociocultural Considerations

In contrast to sex, which classifies people based entirely on anatomical and biological features, **gender** classifies people based on physiological, psychological, and sociocultural characteristics. A given individual's gender is a function of his or her identification with a given sex and adoption of a lifestyle deemed appropriate for that sex. If I define myself as a man, think and feel like a man, and behave in a masculine way, my gender is that of man.

One's identification as either female or male is based on anatomical characteristics that supposedly are obvious and objective, but the whole process is infused with nonphysical and nonobjective elements from the very beginning. In most societies, cultural beliefs have established the basic "truth" that differences in human physical anatomy are linked inherently to important differences in intellect, emotions, and other dimensions. By virtue of their physiology and its connection to the childbearing process, for example, women are known (i.e., believed) to be "naturally" gentle and nurturing. Lacking such a basic and intimate connection to childbearing, men are "naturally" less gentle and less nurturing. By virtue of their hormonal cycles, women are considered to be more emotional and more subject to mood swings than men. Lacking these monthly cycles and the hormonal changes that accompany pregnancy and childbirth, men are believed to be emotionally stable, more rational and logical. By virtue of their smaller physical size, women are thought to be weaker and more frail than men and thus dependent on men for continued survival. Being physically larger and temperamentally more aggressive, men are believed to be best suited and responsible for the continued survival of "their" women.

With only minor variations, these **gender stereotypes** or categorical portrayals of women and men are common to many nations of the First, Second, and Third Worlds. In all societies where they have been found, stereotyped beliefs and assumptions about the basic natures of women and of men have served as the bases for the formation of gender roles. **Gender roles** assign individuals to particular and different tasks specifically because of their sex and its assumed characteristics. Typically, they involve assignment to positions that categorically lead to unequal rewards for women and men. The result is that **gender stratification**—the formation of inequality hierarchies based on sex—has been an enduring feature of most human societies (Crompton and Mann, 1986).

Thus our gender identity represents much more than simply a realization that we are anatomically female or male. It involves recognizing what it means to be a woman or a man, as those meanings have been established within a specific social and cultural context. Gender also involves an acceptance and internalization of this cultural definition, and an attempt to structure our lives by it. Sex—being female or male—is thus a matter of biology. Gender—being woman or man—is a matter of cultural orientation and social practices as well as biology. Gender is our individual interpretation of our society's interpretation of anatomical differences among its population members.

TRADITIONAL GENDER STEREOTYPING AND GENDER ROLES

Sexual Morphology and Gender Differences

The widespread and continuing belief in basic intellectual, emotional, and other dissimilarities between women and men is premised on one fundamental idea. *Differences in sexual morphology* (i.e., anatomical features) *generate differences in rationality and temperament.* For centuries, many people throughout the world have believed that women and men think and behave differently from one another because they are anatomically different. Women are the way they are because they are females; men are the way they are because they are males (Basow, 1986).

Empirical evidence from a growing inventory of biological, psychological, and anthropological research has begun to challenge these long-standing beliefs. This research has involved detailed examinations of female-male differences within given societies, as well as comparisons of women and men across societies. Although the final word on this subject has yet to be written, existing evidence strongly suggests that many traditional beliefs concerning "natural" differences between the sexes lack empirical support.

Biological Findings

One common element of gender stereotyping is related to physical size. Because men generally are larger and stronger, they are assumed to be physically superior.

The fact that most men in a given society may be physically larger than most women in that same society does not necessarily imply that they are physically superior. Cultural values notwithstanding, bigger does not always mean better. The larger frame and heavier musculature of men do give them an advantage in terms of sheer physical strength. However, women have the advantage in terms of long-term physical endurance. The question of which of these two traits, immediate strength or long-term endurance, is superior is typically answered by cultural preferences rather than purely biological considerations.

Evidence that women are not biologically inferior to men can be found in birth and death patterns. Male embryos are more likely to abort spontaneously than female embryos, and males are more likely than females to die during infancy (Baker et al., 1980). Furthermore, females tend to outlive males in most societies of the world. In the United States, for example, the average life expectancy for females born in 1988 was 78.3 years. For males, the comparable figure was 71.4, a difference of almost seven years (U.S. Bureau of the Census, 1990). In Japan, where overall longevity rates are the highest in the world, female life expectancy is 81.8 years compared to 75.9 years for males (*Japan Times,* 1990). In Mexico the overall life expectancy rates (70 years in

1989) are lower than in Japan or in the United States, but the same differences in longevity can be found. Mexican females outlive Mexican males by slightly more than four years (Wilkie and Ochoa, 1989). Biological evidence thus fails to support the assumption of male physical superiority.

Psychological Findings

A second component of gender stereotyping relates to intellectual and emotional traits. According to common belief, women and men view the world and respond to what they see in ways that are inherently different. Women are thought to be more emotional and artistic, whereas men are seen as much more rational and pragmatic. These presumed differences in thought and temperament, it is believed, will continue as long as women and men remain physically different. They represent the effects of the different ratios of estrogen and androgen hormones that distinguish the two sexes and that play such a major role in shaping their respective personality structures and behavioral patterns.

These are the widespread beliefs about the psyches of women and men, but what are the facts? The existence of female hormonal changes associated with menstruation, childbirth, and menopause is a matter of established record. However, the exact consequences of such changes insofar as female psychology and temperament are concerned are matters of continuing dispute. So, too, are questions concerning the relation between sex-linked hormones and intellectual, emotional, and behavioral patterns of women and men.

What do we know about such patterns? Several reviews of the existing research literature (Jacklin, 1989; Maccoby and Jacklin, 1974, 1980; Shapiro, 1990) suggest that the actual range of female-male differences is much smaller than commonly believed. Evidence indicates that females and males demonstrate consistent differences in only four major areas: verbal ability, mathematical ability, visual-spatial ability, and aggression. However, these differences are not always large or significant (Jacklin, 1989). Collectively, research findings do not support the conclusion that women and men are significantly different in temperament or in intellect (Shapiro, 1990; Tavris and Wade, 1984).

Anthropological Findings

For many years, anthropologists have made the study of cross-cultural differences in sex and gender an important part of their ethnological research. As a result of their efforts, we now possess a great deal of information about how people in different parts of the world conceptualize and treat anatomical differences among their respective population members. Collectively, these ethnological data point to the variability and elasticity of what we otherwise might take to be natural biological differences.

The most famous work in this tradition is Margaret Mead's classic study of three tribal groups in New Guinea (Mead, 1963, original 1935). In two of these groups, Mead found very few differences between women and men in terms of psychological patterns or social behaviors. Among the Arapesh, both women and men displayed what we might think of as essentially feminine traits: sensitivity, cooperation, and overall absence of aggression. In contrast, among the Mundugumor, both women and men typically were insensitive, uncooperative, and very aggressive, traits our culture might define as essentially masculine.

The third group studied by Mead, the Tchambuli, made clear and significant distinctions between women and men. Surprisingly (at least from the standpoint of our culture), these distinctions were quite the opposite of what we might have expected. The Tchambuli defined women as the aggressive, rational, capable sex, and men as the emotional, flighty sex. Women were socially dominant, assuming primary economic and political roles in the group. Men were socially passive, assuming artistic and leisure roles.

The lesson to be drawn from the work of Mead and other anthropologists is clear. Like race and age, sex may be a biological phenomenon, but it is not merely that. Sex may provide certain resources and impose certain limitations on members of specific groups, but these resources and limitations form only broad outlines of what may or may not be possible for people. The specific detailing of these outlines, what people actually will do and what actually will be done to them, is more likely to be the result of social and cultural factors than of biological determinism (Gould, 1976).

A growing number of researchers have argued that we may never be able to resolve fully the question of innate differences between women and men. Biological differences are surrounded and confounded by cultural beliefs and social practices that especially manifest themselves in the ways that the two sexes are socialized. As one researcher (Deckard, 1983) observed, "So long as boys and girls are brought up to behave very differently, it will be impossible to disentangle the innate from the learned" (p. 26).

 ## Becoming Women and Men: Gender Socialization

As we saw in chapter 4, human beings are not born with any preexisting knowledge of, or orientation to, their world. What we come to know and think and feel about life (and about ourselves) we learn through socialization. So it is with gender identity and behaviors. We are born female or male; we become girl or boy, then woman or man. The social mechanism through which this transformation occurs is that of **gender socialization.** Like other aspects of socialization, it is a lifelong process, beginning at birth and continuing to death.

Infancy and Childhood

The presentation of the newborn infant to its parents as girl or boy represents the first in a long line of social classifications to which the typical person will be subjected throughout life. This **gender assignment,** or categorization of the individual as female or as male, is of enormous significance in structuring the infant's relationships to its immediate world, both inside and outside of the family (Fagot et al., 1985; Rossi, 1984).

The use of gender assignment and stereotyping to define appropriate relationships toward and by children is widespread and effective. By the time children are three to four years old they already have formed an image of themselves as girl or boy, and a growing knowledge of what being girl or boy means in terms of their own behavior (LaFreniere et al., 1984). With relatively little actual social experience behind them, they are well on their way to absorbing and accepting society's definition of what they as individuals should be like by virtue of their anatomy. "She" and "he" are becoming important considerations in the development of "me."

Adolescence and Early Adulthood

Adolescence represents a critical period for gender socialization. It is precisely during these difficult years of transition between childhood and adulthood that gender identities and roles are consolidated and solidified (Eccles, 1987). For the majority of adolescents, this means accepting the patterns to which they were exposed during childhood. A good deal of the socialization efforts of parents, teachers, counselors, and others during this period seems to be directed to this end. Preparation for future adult roles often entails learning about activities deemed appropriate for members of one's sex. Learning to be an adult thus translates into learning to be a proper adult woman or adult man.

By the time most individuals cross the threshold from adolescence into adulthood, they have accepted the gender information offered them by the major agents of socialization in their society. Young adult females leave the world of formal schooling and step into the occupational, marital, and parental roles that await them. In many instances, these roles embody prevailing cultural definitions of what is natural and normal for women. Their primary emphasis is on nurturing activities, whether for one's own family or for others.

Young adult males also complete their formal education and begin to assume adult occupational, marital, and familial roles. These, too, often reflect stereotyped assumptions and beliefs about the nature of men. Successful careers and occupational achievements come first. Successful family life, that is, earning a good living for one's family, represents the fruits of one's labors.

Middle and Late Adulthood

For the average person, advancing age brings increasing participation in traditional adult social roles. Careers must be constructed, daily living needs attended to, and children looked after. Prevailing beliefs in most societies typically define certain of these activities as being the primary responsibility of one sex rather than the other. The time and energy commitments required by these stereotyped roles lock individuals into a set of structured behaviors and relationships that reiterate and reaffirm their sense of femininity or masculinity.

Movement into later adulthood precipitates a number of gender role changes. For women who have defined themselves primarily as mother and wife, the loss of children through their own passage into adulthood or the loss of husband through death represents a potential crisis of self-identity and self-worth (Williamson et al., 1980). For many other women and most men, significant role changes associated with advancing age arrive in the form of retirement from an occupational career.

In this culture and many others, the adult role is defined as one involving active mastery of some occupational task and productive contribution to society. Jobs provide people with positive social identities and (as we saw in chapter 5) also serve as a major indicator of their position in the socioeconomic hierarchy. Perhaps even more fundamentally, occupation is the primary vehicle for acquiring the material resources that make life possible and comfortable. Retirement therefore may symbolically tell the world—and the retirees—that their days of productive contribution to society have come to an end. This realization, coupled with the financial decline that often accompanies retirement, may generate a severe identity crisis for some individuals (Chown, 1977).

Another major role change for many people occurs with the decline of health and physical abilities that is associated with advancing chronological age. Such physical decline may be forestalled for a time, but it cannot be held in check forever. In a culture where adult status is defined in significant part by physical vigor, the loss of such capacities may be read by the individual and by others as loss of adulthood.

Thus, with advanced age both women and men face the prospect of having to redefine their conceptions of who and what they are. This process of unlearning an old social identity and learning a new one necessarily involves a reassessment of one's femininity or masculinity. This may consist of the realization that one can no longer measure up to existing cultural ideals of gender appearance and activities. In a society where youth is valued and old people are subject to negative stereotyping, the new self-identity of many older people may be that of someone who is a lesser person than before.

Alternatively, the changes experienced with age could lead people to reassess the nature of gender roles and stereotypes themselves. Conceivably, they could recognize that these cultural portraits no longer apply to them or to many of their contemporaries. They could begin to challenge the validity of gender ideals that appeared so far removed from the real world. This second alternative, however, is likely to remain more of a theoretical possibility than an actual occurrence.

THEORETICAL INTERPRETATIONS AND EXPLANATIONS OF GENDER ROLES

The presence of distinctive gender roles in virtually every human society has been subjected to a number of differing theoretical explanations. This sexual division of labor has been interpreted as a mechanism for creating and preserving a successful social system. It also has been seen as a deliberate mechanism for the systematic exploitation of half of the world's population.

Gender Roles as Salvation: Classical Functionalism

Structural-functional theorists have attempted to explain gender roles in terms of their contributions to societal survival. They argue that there must be some good and compelling reason for the fact that separate social roles for the sexes have been found throughout human history. The classic statement of this position was offered by the foremost functionalist theorist of the twentieth century, Talcott Parsons (1954), and his associate Robert Bales (Parsons and Bales, 1955).

Parsons and Bales assumed the critical importance of the family as a basic unit of human social organization. It is the family, after all, that has ultimate responsibility for producing and raising new members of society. In addition, it is an important unit of consumption in the modern economy. Consequently, its continued viability and good health is a matter of great significance for the survival of the society itself.

Like other units, the family must deal with two kinds of relationship problems if it is to persist over time. The first involves **instrumental tasks**—goal-directed activities that link the family to the surrounding society in order to acquire necessary material resources. A family member must take on a full-time occupation as a source of income, and must assume responsibility for deciding how this income will be spent on different types of needed goods, such as food, housing, and medical care.

The second problem involves **expressive tasks**—the creation and maintenance of a set of positive, supportive, emotional relationships within the family unit. Family members have to feel loved and cared for so that they can develop their full potentials as individuals. Therefore, someone within the family must take on the responsibility for these expressive tasks. The expressive role creates the kind of atmosphere that will nurture the growth of all family members, allowing them to deal successfully with the challenges and disappointments they will face in the larger society.

Parsons and Bales maintained that these two different but complementary roles could be performed most efficiently if they were undertaken by different individuals. Traditional patterns of socialization that prepared women and men for separate roles also created different personality profiles in the two sexes. According to Parsons and Bales (recall that they wrote in the generally conservative atmosphere of the 1950s), women were better suited to perform tasks that were people and relationship oriented. Compared to men, they were more emotional and empathetic. Most men were more interested and skilled in performing activities that were task and production oriented. Compared to women, they were more competent and more confident in these areas.

Classical functionalists viewed traditional gender-based divisions of labor as contributing to societal well-being. According to this interpretation, this Tibetan woman is promoting her society's best interests by devoting her expressive skills to the nurturing of children, while leaving political and other instrumental-oriented activities to men.

The net result is that a division of labor by gender is functional for the continued survival of the family. The assignment of the expressive role to the wife/mother and of the instrumental role to the husband/father ensures that both types of tasks will be performed at the highest level of effectiveness. The family thus will prosper and, with it, the larger society. By implication, any significant change in this beneficial arrangement will lead only to decreasing efficiency in the performance of these vital roles. The family then will suffer and, with it, the larger society.

Critique of the Functionalist Perspective   Like other functionalist interpretations of social phenomena in the contemporary world, this explanation for the existence and persistence of sex-based divisions of labor has been criticized severely. For one thing, it failed to take into account the fact that throughout history, women in many societies frequently played important roles in economic and other productive activities (Collins, 1988a; Layng, 1990). In point of fact, their instrumental actions often have been critical for maintaining the viability of the overall society (Layng, 1990).

Second, in their efforts to describe the beneficial aspects of the sexual division of labor, the classical functionalists ignored its dysfunctional consequences. Gender identities and roles are based on assumptions about differences in female-male abilities and interests that often simply aren't true. Prevailing arrangements define certain types of behaviors as natural for one sex or the other, and other types of behaviors as unnatural. In so doing, they may misallocate and waste a great deal of potential individual talent.

For example, women who otherwise might make world-class engineers or corporate chief executive officers are prevented from even considering these career options by cultural beliefs and prohibitions that limit their role to the domestic sphere. Men who otherwise might make superb child-care providers are kept from pursuing this possibility by prevailing beliefs that emphasize the association of members of their sex with economic, political, and other instrumental roles. In both cases, the larger society suffers when well-qualified people are removed from serious consideration for important social roles. The potential loss and misapplication of talent is enormous, and represents decreased capacity of society to deal successfully with survival problems.

Finally, the functionalist interpretation fails to explain why social roles differentiated on the basis of gender should be *stratified*. If both instrumental and expressive tasks are equally important for societal survival, they should receive equal rewards for successful performance. However, expressive roles seldom command the levels of property and prestige awarded to instrumental activities. For example, in the United States, the services of mothers and of elementary school teachers (most of whom are women) receive a great deal of verbal praise and support. Their yearly incomes, however— nothing in the case of mothers; slightly more than nothing in the case of most elementary teachers— do not at all reflect the importance of their work with children. Some critics (Collins, 1988a) argue that these unequal rewards reflect significant power differences built into the structure of society. By ignoring the power differentials that exist between instrumental and expressive roles (and between the people who perform them), classical functionalists have missed a critical element in the gender work arrangements of most societies.

Gender Roles as Suppression: The Conflict Model

The portrait of gender roles offered by conflict theorists stands in stark contrast to that of the functionalists. Conflict theorists view traditional gender definitions and gender roles as instruments of oppression in society. Their only real function is to preserve patriarchal systems in which cultural patterns and social practices are structured to ensure the individual and collective advantages of males over females in most aspects of social life (Basow, 1986; Collins, 1971, 1975).

According to this interpretation, gender role differences in human societies never have been based solely on biological considerations. Rather, they are a consequence of advances in productive technologies that created economic surpluses, inheritable private property, social class hierarchies, and a structure of patriarchy (Engels, 1902, original 1884). Women were defined as a form of property and came under the possession and control of men, who were able to dominate women by virtue of their superior physical strength. Males increasingly became involved in economic, political, and military roles, and females increasingly were restricted to domestic, nurturing roles (Collins, 1975).

As male dominance and the role separation of the sexes increased, cultural ideologies were established to explain and to justify this arrangement. Typically, these ideologies stressed the supposed natural physical and intellectual superiority of males over females, and the natural mothering/nurturing instincts of females. However, these arguments were merely a convenient fabrication. The real basis for sex stratification was that patriarchal systems clearly were beneficial for males, who had the physical power to impose their will on females. Economic, political, and social dominance allowed men a disproportionate share of all the good things that life had to offer, and they were not about to let such a system slip through their hands (Layng, 1990).

Conflict theorists agree that significant changes in this long-standing patriarchal pattern are not likely to occur unless women make them happen. Just as an aggressive, politically active civil rights movement was necessary before conditions for racial minorities in the United States improved, a comparable gender rights movement is necessary if the case for women is to advance. As the oppressed class, women must come to recognize their own collective exploitation and organize collectively to end it.

Critique of the Conflict Perspective   Like functionalism, the conflict explanation of gender roles and gender inequality represents a selective, simplified view of a more complex reality. It can be criticized for its overemphasis on the inherent conflicts between women and men, and on the destructive consequences of all existing gender relations. If at least some radical feminist versions of the conflict model (Barry, 1979) were taken at face value, we would have to rule out entirely the possibility that women and men *ever* do things together in a cooperative spirit of sharing or love. We would have to conclude that the appearance of such harmony is always just an appearance—a hidden agenda maintaining the oppression of the one sex by the other lies somewhere under the surface.

A second criticism of some (Marxist) versions of conflict theory relates to the assertion that gender oppression is associated exclusively with capitalism. Both Marx and Engels viewed the social position of women in modern industrial societies as an extension of the system of class exploitation and conflict. Women's oppressed condition could be improved only as the oppressed conditions of all laboring people could be improved, by the destruction and elimination of the private property systems on which class distinctions were founded. From this perspective, economic stratification is the spring from which all other forms of social inequality flow. An examination of gender relations in noncapitalist societies, however, shows that this argument is empirically without merit.

The Soviet Union is a society founded on a revolution driven by socialist ideas and structured on socialist principles. It is also a society in which occupational, economic, and other forms of gender inequalities are widespread and significant (Daniloff, 1982; Rossides, 1990; Treiman and Roos, 1983). Like many women in such capitalist societies as Japan, Mexico, and the United States, women in the USSR are concentrated in lower-paying occupations and largely excluded from important political leadership roles.

Spanning a broad range of societal types, then, gender stratification is not a consequence of any one particular economic or political system. Gender inequalities may be similar to class inequalities in some important respects, but they are not identical to them. Modern stratified societies, as Max Weber pointed out, are multidimensional systems whose individual hierarchies are at least partially independent of one another. An understanding of socioeconomic class arrangements in a given society may promote a better understanding of gender dynamics and arrangements in that society, but it cannot be a substitute for an examination of gender inequality phenomena (Crompton and Mann, 1986). It is to an examination of such phenomena that we now turn.

PATTERNS OF GENDER STRATIFICATION

In our daily lives all of us at one time or another encounter firsthand evidence of social inequalities. This evidence may come in the form of a sleek new BMW convertible racing past our Ford sedan on the freeway, or of a homeless person scouring the dumpster behind our favorite restaurant for leftover food. It may even present itself as the college degree that allows us to escape from a life of manual labor in the local factory.

For the most part, our experiences with these inequalities are likely to be personal. We encounter and deal with them as individuals. But as we have attempted to show in this chapter and the two preceding ones, social inequalities are more often categorical than individual, more often patterned than random. The inequities faced by women and men are no exception.

Although they may be encountered individually by women or men, different kinds of inequalities confront individuals exactly because they happen to be women or men. Many of the most important experiences that we are likely to have in our lives—occupational, economic, political, and legal—are shaped by sex and gender considerations. In the majority of such cases, the pattern is the same: men dominate and women are subordinate. These widespread institutionalized inequities are indicative of the fact that the United States, like almost every other society in the modern world, is a gender-stratified system.

Gender and Work

Whereas some women in our society have always worked outside the home, female participation in the U.S. labor force increased steadily and dramatically in the last half of this century. A large number of women who otherwise would have remained out of the workforce were pressed into service by the acute shortage of men during the Second World War. Most of them returned to their households and their families after the war, but many remained gainfully employed.

Between 1960 and 1988 the number of working women in the United States more than doubled, to nearly 38 million (see Table 7.1). In 1960, 34.8 percent of all women who were eligible by age to work were in the civilian labor force; by 1988, that figure

TABLE 7.1   U.S. Female Labor Force as Percentage of U.S. Female Population,
1960–1988

Year	Total	Single*	Married
1960	34.8	44.1	30.5
1965	36.7	40.5	34.7
1970	42.6	53.0	40.8
1975	46.0	57.0	44.4
1980	51.1	61.5	50.1
1985	54.5	65.2	54.2
1988	55.9	65.2	56.5

*As used here, "single" does not include women who are divorced or widowed.
Source: U.S. Bureau of the Census, *Statistical Abstract of the United States, 1990.*

had increased to 55.6 percent. Many of these women were married and living with their husbands. Although fewer than one-third of all married women (30.5 percent) were working in 1960, more than half of all married women (56.5 percent) were in the labor force by 1988. Many women may work because they want to, but most do so because they have to. Frequently, they help provide their families with basic resources such as housing and education. Far from being a luxury or an indulgence, their contribution has become a necessity for family survival. This is especially true for divorced or separated women with children and for single mothers.

Many women entering the workforce find their employment prospects limited in ways that those of men are not. Depending on their educational backgrounds, both women and men might opt for a variety of blue-collar, white-collar, or professional and managerial occupations. Within these categories, however, women often are steered into a much narrower range of choices that largely are segregated by sex. Thus they come to occupy what have been called "pink-collar" jobs (Bernard, 1981).

The kinds of occupations that make up the pink-collar ghetto tend to be in some way or other extensions of the traditional female nurturing role. They include such positions as prekindergarten and kindergarten teachers, nurses, dental hygienists, and secretaries. In each case, well over 90 percent of all persons employed in these occupations are women (see Table 7.2). Even outside of their own households many women end up performing what amount to domestic roles. More than 95 percent of all people employed in child care or as servants in private households in the United States are women.

These patterns are by no means unique to the United States. In a cross-cultural study of work and gender in a dozen modern industrial societies including the United States and Japan, Roos (1985) found striking similarities in employment segregated by sex. In all twelve societies, women are concentrated in clerical, sales, and service occupations. In contrast, men predominate in administrative and managerial positions, as well as in high- and medium-prestige production jobs (Roos, 1985). These patterns may be interpreted as evidence of continuing gender stereotypes that cut across individual cultures and societies. Such stereotypes "encourage" women and men to seek employment in keeping with their presumed natures.

But things have begun to change. As Table 7.3 demonstrates, the number of women completing specialized postgraduate training in the United States has increased dramatically since 1960. Once only a negligible minority in law, medicine, and dentistry,

TABLE 7.2 Pink-Collar Jobs in the United States, 1988

Occupation	Total Employed	Women as Percentage of Total Employed
Licensed practical nurses	423,000	96.0
Registered nurses	1,559,000	94.6
Teachers, prekindergarten and kindergarten	393,000	98.2
Teachers' aides	423,000	95.9
Secretaries	4,030,000	99.1
Receptionists	848,000	97.1
Dental assistants	165,000	98.7
Child-care workers	378,000	97.3
Cleaners and servants	476,000	95.6

Source: U.S. Bureau of the Census, *Statistical Abstract of the United States, 1990.*

women now constitute a significant and growing proportion of these prestigious occupations. Thus, for some, formal education has become a ticket out of the pink-collar ghetto.

Gender and Income

The U.S. Bureau of the Census figures reveal that in 1988, women working full-time in the United States had a median income of $18,545. In comparison, men working full-time had a median income of $27,342, or 147 percent of women's salaries for that year. These figures reflect a pattern that has continued throughout this century. Women now may be full participants in the labor market, but many have yet to receive a full share of the income rewards.

These salary discrepancies have been interpreted by economists and sociologists in a number of ways. One explanation centers on what are called **human capital factors,** the resources that individuals bring with them to the labor market. Such resources include interests and aptitudes, formal education, occupational training, and previous work experience. They represent "investments" made by job seekers to enhance their

TABLE 7.3 Females as Percentage of Degrees Conferred in Selected Professions, 1960–1987

Year	Medicine (M.D.)	Law (L.L.B. or J.D.)	Dentistry (D.D.S. or D.M.D.)	Theological (B.D., M.Div., M.H.L.)
1960	5.5%	2.5%	0.8%	(NA)
1970	8.4	5.4	0.9	2.3%
1975	13.1	15.1	3.1	6.8
1980	23.4	30.2	13.3	13.8
1985	30.4	38.5	20.7	18.5
1987	32.4	40.2	24.0	19.3

Source: U.S. Bureau of the Census, *Statistical Abstract of the United States, 1990.*

employment prospects, making some individuals more attractive and desirable to employers, who will pay a premium for their services. These higher-paying jobs represent the occupational "return" on the human capital investments made by successful applicants.

According to the human capital argument, the salary discrepancies reflect the fact that men typically possess more resources than women. They generally have more interest, training, and previous work experience in occupations (e.g., law, medicine, business, science, engineering) that command the highest salaries. Because men have more human capital to offer, they are able to negotiate better positions and higher salaries for their services.

On the other hand, some women have chosen to invest their time and energy in having and raising children rather than in pursuing a career. The demands of child rearing keep them out of the labor force for an extended period of time, during which years their male counterparts gain job experience and seniority. Child raising might also require women to take jobs that are close to home or that offer flexible hours so they can be with their children when necessary. Because the obligations associated with their role as mothers put these women at a human capital disadvantage in the job market, they must settle for whatever positions and salaries they are offered. They are no longer in a position to bargain with employers as effectively as men who are not encumbered by domestic considerations.

Several studies of female-male salary differentials in the United States and other modern societies found some support for the human capital interpretation (England and Farkas, 1986; Roos, 1985). However, these same studies observed that human capital resources are not the only, or even the most significant, contributing elements in the income gender gap; two additional factors may be of equal or greater importance.

First, this and many other industrial societies have a **dual-labor** or **segmented-labor market** structure (Bielby and Baron, 1984; Roos, 1985; Treiman and Roos, 1983). As we saw in chapter 6 in connection with racial and ethnic minority groups, such a system contains two distinct tiers of jobs. At the top tier are professional, administrative, and technical occupations offering high income and prestige rewards but requiring high levels of skills and training. At the bottom tier are service, domestic, and other unskilled jobs that do not require much education or training and do not offer many salary or prestige rewards.

According to some analysts (Bielby and Baron, 1986; Roos, 1985; Roos and Reskin, 1984) the sex-segregated jobs filled primarily by women are, not coincidentally, those at the lower tier of the dual-market structure. A good deal of "women's work" is largely supportive, nurturing, and at least symbolically domestic. This type of work is neither desirable nor financially rewarding in modern economic systems. Because far more salary and prestige rewards are to be found among the occupations that make up the top tier, lower-level jobs will be relegated to less powerful, less valued groups. In this respect, women may be considered a minority group within the larger, patriarchal society (Hacker, 1951, 1974) who must compete against other minorities for low-echelon, low paying jobs.

The second factor that must be considered in understanding female-male income differentials is gender discrimination. Simply stated, the large and wholesale gaps between women's and men's salaries can be explained by the fact that women continue to be treated unequally and unfairly in the labor market (England et al., 1988; Gold, 1983; Reskin and Hartmann, 1985). This is true even when their educational qualifications match or exceed those of men (see Table 7.4).

TABLE 7.4 Average Earnings by Education Attainment and Gender, 1987*

Education Level	Male	Female
Less than 8 years	$16,863	$10,163
8 years	18,946	12,655
9–11 years	21,327	13,136
12 years	24,745	16,223
1–3 years college	29,253	19,336
4 years college	38,117	23,506
5 or more years college	47,903	30,255

*Figures are for year-round, full-time workers eighteen years old and older.
Source: U.S. Bureau of the Census, *Current Population Reports,* series P-60, no. 162.

Gender discrimination occurs in any number of different forms. Women may be excluded systematically from certain types of occupations on direct ("this is no job for a woman") grounds. That is, they are denied the right to hold the position just because they are female. In the U.S. armed forces, for example, women currently are prohibited from serving in direct combat roles. Presumably, their nurturing instincts would make it very difficult or impossible for them to take the lives of other human beings. Not being burdened by such instincts, men supposedly are able to meet the requirements of the job without undue stress.

Women also face systematic exclusion from certain occupations on indirect grounds. Here, job requirements are structured to eliminate all (or most) women from

In some societies, women continue to be thought of as biologically or psychologically unfit for certain "demanding" social roles. These Indian police officers, however, do not give the appearance of being unable to reconcile their biological sex with their occupational roles. Once relegated to auxiliary and minor political roles, women are beginning to ascend into central and powerful political offices, though not without controversy and opposition.

consideration, even though sex itself may not be a formal criterion for the position. For example, police and fire departments in many U.S. cities may impose minimum height and weight standards that effectively eliminate virtually all women candidates. Even after court rulings that these physical standards often have little or nothing to do with intrinsic requirements of the job, they continue to be employed until they are challenged on a case-by-case basis.

Discrimination is reflected, too, in promotions. Even when women are hired in substantial numbers for a given occupation, men are much more likely to be on the "fast track," receiving larger and more rapid promotions than women. This may be especially true in organizations and work settings that traditionally have been dominated by men (Blum and Smith, 1988). Women executives at middle and higher levels in some of this country's largest corporations, for example, recently testified to the federal government about a "glass ceiling" of entrenched male discrimination that keeps them from successfully moving into the highest positions. Even though no formal or visible barriers keep women out of these elite positions, the beliefs and values that make up the male subculture of the corporate upper class effectively exclude them from real consideration. Women can see the promised land, but they can't reach it (*San Diego Union,* 1990h). However, growing government attention and response to these glass ceilings may help lessen this particular form of discrimination.

The Feminization of Poverty   A further indication of women's subordinate economic status relative to men is an alarming trend that has been termed the **feminization of poverty** (Pearce, 1978, 1990; Peterson, 1987). Throughout the last thirty years, growing numbers of women of all ages have been descending into the ranks of the "official" poor. By the end of the 1980s, close to two-thirds of all the adult poor in the United States were women, many of them members of racial and ethnic minority groups.

As we saw in chapter 6, the official poor in the United States are individuals and families whose yearly incomes fall below the minimum poverty line established by the federal government. This poverty line represents the number of dollars needed to meet basic requirements for food, housing, clothing, and other material necessities of life. In the battle for long-term physical survival, members of the official poor are losing the war.

Much of the growth in female poverty since the 1960s is related to major changes taking place in the composition of the family. The most significant of these has been the dramatic increase in single-parent families, especially in the number headed by women. Between 1970 and 1989, according to the Bureau of the Census (1989b), married-couple families decreased from 71 to 56 percent of all family units in the United States. During this period, the proportion of white families maintained by women alone rose from 9 percent to 13 percent. For African American families the increase was from 28 to 44 percent; for Hispanic families, from 21 percent (in 1976) to 23 percent.

Whereas female-headed families made up about one-sixth of all households in the United States in 1989, they accounted for *over one-half* of all poor households in the country. A great deal of this poverty is related to the presence of dependent children: the number of children under the age of eighteen living with one parent doubled since 1970, and nearly 90 percent live with their mothers rather than with their fathers. Their average family income is less than one-third of that for children living with both parents, and only one-half the comparable figure for those children living with their fathers (U.S. Bureau of the Census, 1989c). Nationally, about one out of every six families with children under eighteen years of age lives in poverty, and nearly half of

OURSELVES AND OTHERS

Growing Up Female in Bangladesh—
"This Is Not Discrimination But a Way of Life"

Kulsum is serving eggs to her small son Shoukat. Standing by her side are her two young daughters, crying. Kulsum shouts at them not to bother her while she is preparing their brother for school.

Five-year-old Seema protests: "You give him an egg every day, but never to us."

A sharp slap lands on Seema's right cheek. "How many times do I have to tell you that there are no eggs for you girls. Don't ask again."

The mother's explanation for her favoritism is the conventional one. "Believe me," she says, "they are all my children and I love each one of them dearly. But I have no means to buy eggs for them all. The son has to be fed properly so that he grows up strong enough to bear the family responsibilities."

In strongly patriarchal societies, where women's unpaid work goes totally unrecognized and tradition does not allow them to do paid work outside the home, boys are seen as potential bread-winners—girls as bread-losers.

Millions of women like Kulsum will find themselves discriminating every day against their own female children for reasons that are primarily economic.

The result: in Bangladesh girls get fed 16 percent less than their brothers. They get less nutritious food which often results in protein deficiency and stunted growth.

And, not surprisingly in a country where 85 percent of the population suffers from some degree of malnutrition, they grow to be small, slight women who give birth to vulnerable, underweight babies more likely to die within their first year—especially if they are girls.

"This is not discrimination but a way of life," says the mother. "My son gets preferential treatment for financial reasons, but also because that is what I have learned. My mother used to do the same and I never regretted it."

Land laws are often blamed for the particularly marked form of discrimination against girls that occurs in rural Bangladesh. The land laws dictate that family property can only remain intact if passed down through the male line. A daughter's inheritance will automatically go to her husband when she marries. The family with many sons may therefore accumulate a lot of land—at the expense of the family with many daughters.

The traditional dowry system further reinforces the need for sons. "Daughters are a liability," says Ratan Kumar. "For the past decade I have not lived a full life because I am saving for my four daughters who are all of marriageable age.

"When my first son was born we celebrated for days. But then my second, third, fourth and fifth children were all daughters. This has only added to the family burden and brought embarrassment to me.

"I wanted a big family with many sons. If we had many sons we would be one of the happiest families now. Instead, when we meet in the evenings we spend most of the time worrying about the future of our daughters."

The need for sons has a powerful influence over how many children parents bear. It is estimated that son-preference adds an average of two to three children to the size of families worldwide.

Holding his new baby boy, engineer Mansoor Ahmad explains: "This little one will keep the name of my family. I will be known through him even when I am dead."

Mansoor's five-year-old daughter does not feel quite so positive about it all. "These days people come to see my brother and play with him," she says. "They ignore me."

Source: "Discrimination Against Girls" [original title] was an extract from the United Nations Population Fund's State of the World Population Report, 1989, by Dr. Nafis Sadik, Executive Director. Reprinted with permission.

all such families that are headed by females are poverty stricken. Over two-thirds of African American and Hispanic children live in such conditions (U.S. Bureau of the Census, 1989a).

A number of factors have made if difficult for single mothers to avoid falling into poverty or, once in poverty, to escape it (Kneisner et al., 1988). As we have seen, women face the likelihood of lower-paying, less-prestigious jobs in a labor market that is segmented on the basis of gender. Many are unable to find adequate child-care arrangements and must restrict their employment to meet the needs of their dependent children. Still others receive little or no child support under a legal system that often seems unable or unwilling to ensure adequate financial assistance from absentee fathers.

Women also are at a decided disadvantage in terms of social and political power. They are likely to remain in that position until the time they can mobilize effectively to gain a measure of control more in proportion to their population numbers and their many contributions to society.

Gender and Politics

In a democratic political system, election to government office represents one major avenue for individuals or groups to improve their social situations. The state (i.e., political structure) serves as the primary mechanism for distributing the various rewards that society has to offer its members. Those who control the offices of the state can shape this distribution system to meet their own specific needs and interests. It is not surprising that those who control the offices of the state throughout most of the world are males.

The domination of formal politics by men has been one of the hallmarks of most societies in the past and in the present. It was accomplished in any number of ways. In the United States, for example, women were denied any measure of real involvement in the political process during the eighteenth and nineteenth centuries by the fact that they were prohibited from voting. It was not until 1920, and the ratification of the Nineteenth Amendment, that women's constitutional rights to full participation in national, state, and local elections were formally guaranteed. The passage of this constitutional amendment came only after intense and sustained efforts by members of the Women's Suffragette Movement. At the time, it was bitterly opposed by many men (and some women), who felt that giving women the right to vote would destroy an effective and orderly way of life. After all, voting requires a certain degree of rationality and calculation, and women were believed to be deficient in this department. The prevailing sentiment was that women might be able to vote with their hearts, but not with their heads.

Predictions of doom notwithstanding, the voting rights of women in the United States have been in place for over seventy years, but women still lag far behind men in terms of political strength. For example, even though they register to vote in slightly larger numbers than men, and even though their voting turnout is virtually identical to that of men, they remain grossly underrepresented in political offices held at the higher levels of government.

No woman has ever been elected to the presidency or the vice presidency of this country. It was not until 1984 that a woman, Geraldine Ferraro, even received a major political party's endorsement as nominee for vice president. Women also are conspicuous by their absence in the U.S. Congress. In 1989 there were only 27 women in the 101st Congress: 25 representatives out of a total of 433 and 2 senators out of a total

Because of her outspoken views, French Premier Edith Cresson has been the object of much criticism and the source of some embarrassment for French President François Mitterrand.

of 100 (U.S. Bureau of the Census, 1990). These figures represent the largest number of female members of the U.S. Congress in the history of that body.

At the state government level, women fare only slightly better. In 1989 only forty-five women held statewide elective executive office (three of them governorships) throughout the fifty states. Women constituted slightly under 17 percent of all state legislators in the country in that same year (U.S. Bureau of the Census, 1990). These figures clearly are well below women's actual representation in the general societal population and in the population of registered, active voters. The critical question is precisely what this numerical and proportional underrepresentation means in terms of women's societal position.

The presence of some specific number or proportion of women in federal, state, and local governmental offices by itself does not guarantee that "the women's view" automatically will be considered and promoted. However, it would be a mistake to assume that the presence of female political office holders makes no difference at all. An absence of women from important decision-making positions promotes the likelihood that their perspectives and interests will not be taken into account in the creation and implementation of social and political policies.

The fate of the Equal Rights Amendment may provide a case in point. Designed to eliminate discrimination and inequities on the basis of sex, the ERA was approved by both houses of Congress in 1972. Although it enjoyed widespread support among the U.S. public, it expired in June of 1982, lacking ratification by just three state legislatures. Had there been more women in governors' offices and in state assemblies to lobby for the ERA and to urge its passage, it might now be part of the Constitution. If organized politics represents the voice of the people, the fact remains that women in this society have spoken most often in a whisper.

Things are improving, however. Women have begun to move more heavily into political offices at the local (municipal and county) levels. They also have established and sharpened important leadership skills through significant involvement in grass-roots political movements. As they become increasingly experienced, their political voice has grown louder and has been heard more often than in the past.

Gender and Law

In contemporary societies like the United States, individuals are likely to interact with the legal system in a variety of ways. At the most general level, we all experience the law on a daily basis as a set of rules to be followed for the common good. At a more specific level, some individuals may experience the legal system in a more immediate way. They may interact with the criminal justice system either as accused perpetrators of some crime or as wronged victims seeking justice. In such dealings, women are quite likely to be treated significantly differently from men.

Historically, the law has been dominated by males, who overwhelmingly make up legislative, judicial, and police bodies in this society and most others. From the perspective of conflict theory, this might illustrate the use of societal superstructures by one group to develop and employ power over other groups. In this interpretation, as advanced by a number of socialist feminists (Jaggar, 1983), men recognize law as a critical power resource and have deliberately seized control over the legal structure to further their own ends. They have created, interpreted, applied, and enforced the law to maintain their own advantaged position in the economic hierarchy. Law is employed as an instrument of patriarchy.

But one does not have to be a conflict theorist to recognize the potential for social domination that exists when most members of a given institution as powerful and important as law are drawn from a single social group. In such an instance, no deliberate conspiracy really is required to achieve this end. From a symbolic interactionist perspective, for example, such effective domination is a consequence of a unified world view. The law reflects men's belief in the natural physical and intellectual inferiority of women. It defines women as helpless and in need of protection by and from men. That is, women are logically impaired and therefore not capable of such intellectually demanding activities as property ownership and voting. The overall effect has been to preserve gender inequalities already in place and to create new ones (Kirp et al., 1986).

Laws concerning rape and abortion illustrate this phenomenon. These laws typify what has been called a "double standard of morality based on biological deterministic thought" that is built into the legal process (Richardson, 1988, p. 104).

Rape   Historically, rape was regarded legally as a crime that could be committed only against women. Laws were designed specifically to protect the chastity of women, especially girls (Richardson, 1988). Girls who were under a specified legal age (typically sixteen or eighteen, depending on the individual state) were defined as being incapable of consenting to sexual intercourse, although no similar assumption was made regarding boys of the same age. On the other hand, women over the specified legal age often were implicitly perceived as inciting or tempting men to commit rape. They were regarded as somehow being responsible for the crime in ways that victims of other crimes were not. Whereas past sexual histories of rape perpetrators, including previous rape accusations or convictions, were not admissible as evidence in trial, past sexual histories of the victims were examined in detail. For many women, the trials were often as much of an ordeal as the crime itself (Holmstrom and Burgess, 1978). In effect, they were being raped twice—once by the perpetrator and once by the criminal justice system. For this reason, a high percentage of rapes are never reported to authorities, even though the number of these and other sexual assaults on women continues to skyrocket (Salholz et al., 1990).

Feminists argue that rape is an act of power and violence, not of sex (Brownmiller, 1975; Richardson, 1988). From their perspective, it is an act of terrorism, a tangible and a symbolic method for men to keep women in their supposed proper place. At the same time, it is an act of symbolic violence against another male, a husband or boyfriend who possesses exclusive sexual access to the woman. According to this interpretation, rape is a form of property crime, with the property in question a woman. Thus the "owner" (husband or boyfriend) is as much a victim as the woman herself (Griffin, 1973).

Regardless of how one wishes to interpret it, the fact remains that the high frequency of this crime in the United States (where the rate is more than twenty times higher than in Japan) and the fear of it restrict the lives of women in ways foreign to men (Salholz et al., 1990). Prudence requires that women limit their choices of jobs, travel, education, recreation, and residence to safe areas and safe times. However, even these precautions may not be enough. In many instances, rape is committed by an acquaintance or friend of the victim, what is sometimes termed "date rape." Women who are victims of date rape on college campuses or in other ordinary settings often find it impossible to convince authorities that a crime actually occurred. They often are viewed as being at least partially to blame for a situation that simply got out of hand (Sweet, 1985). After all, as one midwestern political official put it, "the only difference between rape and seduction is salesmanship" (*Newsweek,* 1990, p. 17).

Abortion A second significant and controversial area of sex-related law concerns abortion, which many observers regard as *the* critical gender issue of the past (and perhaps next) several decades. Abortion is a complex and explosive question that has divided the public as few other issues have in recent years. For many people it has come to symbolize the continued viability of gender equality and the feminist movement.

In 1973 the U.S. Supreme Court issued its landmark *Roe* v. *Wade* decision affirming the constitutional right of women to decide for themselves whether or not to terminate a pregnancy during the first trimester. This decision was hailed by various feminist and other change-oriented groups as a major step in granting women control over their own bodies and freedom from male domination of their reproductive activities. It was also blasted by many conservative and antifeminist groups as legalized murder of unborn human beings. These two interpretations of abortion, reproductive rights versus homicide, defined the boundaries of the dispute and made any sort of real compromise impossible.

Supporters of the *Roe* ruling describe themselves as pro-choice. Individually, they may or may not be advocates of abortion itself. Collectively, however, they affirm a woman's right to choose the course of action for her pregnancy that she deems appropriate. In addition, pro-choice advocates hold the belief (at least implicitly) that, in its earliest stages of development, the fetus cannot be considered a human being. Thus, abortion cannot legally or morally be construed as the taking of a human life.

Opponents of the Supreme Court's ruling describe themselves as pro-life. Both individually and collectively, they affirm the humanity of the fetus from the moment of conception. For them, therefore, the termination of a fetus at any stage of development represents the unjust taking of a human life, and as such is legally and morally wrong under any circumstances. Their efforts are geared toward establishing the right of the states to intervene in the lives of individual women in the name of the higher common good by regulating (i.e., virtually eliminating) abortion.

In the nearly twenty years since *Roe* v. *Wade,* pro-life groups have mounted a series of challenges to the principle of individual decision making established by that ruling. Perhaps reflecting the growing political and religious conservatism of the 1980s, individual state legislatures (e.g., Louisiana, Pennsylvania, Utah) passed bills that significantly restrict women's autonomy in the question of abortion. Pro-choice groups responded by appealing these legislative actions to state and federal courts, or by lobbying sympathetic state governors to veto the bills.

As each side continues to redefine and enlarge the scope of the question, abortion promises to become perhaps the watershed issue for both proponents and opponents of gender equality. Pro-choice groups like NOW (the National Organization for Women) argue that an overturning of the *Roe* decision would be the first step in sustained attempts to limit or ban contraceptive freedom for women altogether. Women's reproduction would once again be in the hands of men, who would use this power and control for their own collective advantage. Pro-life groups argue that any continuation of the *Roe* decision would be the first step in a societywide attempt to enlarge the population of expendable human beings. They believe that if the lives of unborn infants are sacrificed in the name of greater freedom for women, perhaps in the near future the lives of the aged and the severely disabled also might be jeopardized for the sake of social convenience.

Gender Equality and Social Theory

As might be anticipated, functionalist, conflict, and symbolic interactionist analyses of the gender equality movement differ substantially in their reading of this phenomenon. For functionalists, the greatest challenge may be the one posed to society if that movement succeeds. Functionalists, it may be recalled, maintain that traditional gender roles promote societal survival and stability. These definitions maximize effective social relations within families, as well as those between family units and the larger society. The performance of expressive roles by women and instrumental roles by men complement one another on behalf of greater social productivity. Deeply embedded in cultural definitions of the nature of reality, these gender-based role assignments also serve as anchors for a host of other social relationships and social structures. Any challenge to their basic premises represents a genuine threat to crucial social and cultural patterns that have made human survival and comfort possible.

Functionalists believe that, because the feminist movement raises just this type of fundamental challenge, it will encounter strong natural resistance, and this resistance is in the best interest of the social system. If the movement succeeded too well and too quickly, it could generate catastrophic changes that might destroy society. Certainly, not all functionalists would oppose all the goals of the movement, but most might be opposed to a rapid and wholesale implementation of those that would shatter the equilibrium of the established order so completely that it could not be restored. As in the case of other movements seeking radical social transformations, the pace of gender equality must be maintained at a tolerable level if the system is to avoid being fatally shaken.

For conflict theorists, on the other hand, the greatest challenges of the gender equality movement lie in the area of generating enough effective power to overcome the massive resources and deliberate resistance of entrenched ruling groups. Such power will be created only if the differences that presently divide gender and other minority groups can be overcome.

Subgroup Differences   Women as a group may have in common their sex and the gender stereotypes that have developed around that sex, but they nonetheless are characterized by a number of important subgroup differences. Their membership includes individuals of various racial and ethnic backgrounds, class levels, religions, and sexual orientations, differences that are likely to generate different kinds of social realities. For example, African American women may find that in many important ways they have less in common with white women than they do with African American men. Upper-class women may find they have less in common with lower-class women than they do with upper-class men. Lesbians may find they have less in common with heterosexual women than they do with gay men.

These subgroup differences create what political sociologists call "cross-cutting cleavages." Their net effect is to make it difficult for the larger group to achieve a high level of overall unity and cohesion. Women speak with many different voices reflecting their diversity, rather than in a single voice. Being divided in social objectives and political agendas, they find themselves politically weakened.

To have any reasonable chance of success, feminist leaders must convince members of racial, ethnic, age, and sexual orientation minorities that their interests and goals are identical to those of all women. Such a "pan-minority" movement, as this might be termed, is not an easy or likely prospect. Moving beyond the real differences in social experiences and subcultural perspectives that separate these minorities has been problematic in the past and will continue to be in the future. It is in the best interests of established dominant groups to keep potential coalitions of minority groups from forming. They will pursue this strategy by using available social resources to play minorities off against one another. For example, in the dual- or segmented-labor market, minorities are put into direct competition for low-paying, low-prestige jobs that are becoming increasingly scarce. Elite-controlled media may emphasize the divisive aspects of affirmative action directives that again place various minority group members in direct competition for established quotas of more desirable jobs. The effect in both cases is that minority gains are portrayed as a zero-sum game in which one group's advancement comes at the expense of others. Under such perceived conditions, it may be nearly impossible to develop cohesive coalitions of the socially disadvantaged. As long as such coalitions can be blocked, real equality for any minority group will remain only a dream.

The focal points of conflict analyses of the gender equality movement, then, are the strategies and resources employed by movement leaders, by leaders of the status quo, and perhaps even by counter-movement leaders (Richardson, 1988) to generate power. Like money, power talks, and ultimately, the loudest voice will have the final word on the topic of full equality for women and for men.

Symbolic Interactionism   For symbolic interactionists, the gender equality movement is essentially a question of the meanings attached to "men" and "women," and the significance of these cultural meanings for societal relations. Existing gender stereotypes and roles are embedded deeply within a web of cultural beliefs and social patterns. They are supported by a host of daily individual and institutional practices that have the very real—if not always intended—effect of perpetuating them over time. These gender conceptions form an intrinsic part of the social definition of reality into which members of a given population are born, and often are accepted as a given element of the natural world by that population. Any serious attempt to question their validity thus would require a symbolic deconstruction and reconstruction of the world that people have come to take for granted as real and natural. Such an action could pose a serious threat of culture shock to those attempting it.

Seen in this light, for symbolic interactionists the real objective of and challenge to the gender equality movement is the reconceptualization of sex and gender, an acceptance of the premise that anatomy is not destiny. The success of the movement ultimately will hinge on its ability to promote this new portrait of women and men as fundamental equals, distinguished but not determined by physiological differences. For these theorists, socialization practices of such important agents as parents, schools, the mass media, and peers are of critical importance. It is through their efforts that individuals first come to form an impression of the world, and it will be through their efforts that this world-taken-for-granted will be changed. Until and unless the symbolic significance attached to sex and gender is altered, social roles and opportunities will continue to be based on the assumption of the intrinsic inequalities of males and females. In this particular struggle, the first battle must be waged and won inside people's minds.

FOCUS ON
MEXICO

A Man's Life, A Woman's Place

In 1519 Spanish conquistadors under the command of Hernan Cortes landed on the Mexican shore near what is now the city of Vera Cruz. They brought with them horses, cannons, muskets, armor, and other sophisticated instruments of war—but no women. To correct this deficiency, they acquired women from local Indian groups, most often through kidnap and rape. What was to be the conquest of the Aztec Empire thus began with the conquest of the empire's women. In the process, the conquistadors unwittingly created a complex of psychological, cultural, and social forces that still haunt and shape gender definitions and female-male relations in modern Mexico. Nearly 500 years after the Spanish Conquest, an entire segment of the society continues to show evidence of what has been described as a collective post-rape trauma syndrome (Goldwert, 1983).

If a single word could capture the essence of the gender relations in contemporary Mexican society, that word would be *machismo*. Inherited from Old World Spain and found throughout New World Latin America, *machismo* (as we saw in chapter 2) is a cult of male virility that emphasizes honor, courage, and bravado as essential and desirable characteristics of "real" men (Mathews, 1987). At its core, *machismo* includes a deep-seated belief in the natural biological, intellectual, and social superiority of men over women. According to this belief, it is the essential nature of men to be aggressive and conquering, and the essential nature of women to be passive and submissive. The ideal male is brave, courageous, and bold. The true *macho* shows no signs of weakness or fear; rather, he is supremely confident in his own abilities, dominating others by the sheer force of his personality and his inner strength.

At the same time, *machismo* beliefs define the ideal woman, depicting her in what has been called the *marianismo* image (Collier, 1986; Stevens, 1973). Modeled after the character of the Virgin Mary as manifested in the figure of the Virgin of Guadalupe (who first appeared to Indian peasants in the year 1531 and who has since become the *madre* or mother of all Mexicans), the "perfect" woman is innocent and pure, gentle and obedient. Long-suffering and self-denying, she places her concern for the welfare of her family ahead of her own personal interests or worldly needs (Escobar et al., 1987). Her quiet devotion and strength form the foundation on which the family and the society are built. Whereas she may assume actual control of the daily running of the household, she nonetheless defers to her husband's greater formal authority within the family structure. She is also content to leave the conduct of social affairs in the more capable hands of men.

In the particular case of Mexico, according to some observers (Goldwert, 1983; Oster, 1989; Riding, 1989) the cult of *machismo* has been given an additional component that compounds and confounds the complexities of relations between women and men. Historically, the conquest of the Aztecs by the Spanish involved not only the rape of Indian women by Cortes and his relatively small army, but also the active and voluntary participation of at least some Indian women in the forced taking of Aztec culture. According to historians, Cortes would not have been able to subdue the Aztecs without the aid of his Indian mistress, Dona Marina (Goldwert, 1983; Miller, 1985). An Indian princess who had been sold into slavery and later given to Cortes, Dona Marina, or *La Malinche* ("The Tongue") as she is known to contemporary Mexicans, paved the way for Cortes' success by serving as his translator as well as his advisor on Indian customs and psychology. Her knowledge and insights proved invaluable, saving the Spaniards on more than one occasion. Many modern Mexicans believe that without her traitorous help the overthrow and destruction of what had been a sophisticated, thriving Indian civilization could not have taken place.

Theory of Cultural Neurosis
According to this analysis, part of the continuing legacy of both the rape of Indian women by Spanish conquistadors and the complicity of *La Malinche* in the subsequent rape of Indian culture is a profound mistrust of women and a deep-seated fear of betrayal by women on the part of Mexican men (Goldwert, 1983; Riding, 1989). In turn, these feelings are symptomatic of more basic underlying feelings of insecurity and denial.

In this interpretation, men feel profoundly insecure about their own masculinity and ability to hold onto their women. The historical experience of the Spanish Conquest serves as a constant reminder to them that their Indian ancestors were not men enough to protect women from the foreign conquerors. At the same time, men have a need to deny their own psychological feelings of passivity and dependency, which are rooted in their Indian ancestry but which also are identified as culturally devalued feminine traits. The mechanism through which these feelings of insecurity and feminine weaknesses are suppressed is *machismo*.

From this perspective, "fear of femininity and of female betrayal are the twin psychohistorical insecurities at the core of Mexican machismo" (Goldwert, 1983, p. 35). *Machismo* is "a cruel bravado that masks a fragile masculinity" (Oster, 1989, p. 266). In this largely Freudian interpretation of gender relations, men act so aggressively and so callously toward women exactly because they need to demonstrate to themselves that they truly are men (Cubitt, 1988). Thus, the cult of *machismo* represents perhaps a classic illustration of the psychological defense mechanism known as reaction formation. In reaction formation, individuals (or, in this case, an entire population subgroup) attempt to avoid acknowledging an inferior trait by engaging in behaviors that appear to reflect an opposite and superior trait. People who in fact are painfully shy may become the life of the party; cowardly individuals may engage in dangerous and even foolhardy acts of presumed courage like parachuting or mountain climbing. Men who inwardly are troubled by fundamental doubts about their own masculinity may make an outward display of toughness, sexual exploits, and other actions believed to be indicative of true masculinity. The unconscious objective here is to hide one's true self from oneself by masking personal flaws and deficiencies under a covering cloak of public actions and accomplishments.

Whether or not this psychological cultural neurosis interpretation of *machismo* is valid, the fact remains that in modern Mexican society the structure of most male-female interactions mirrors the basic premises of this cult of male superiority. Economic, political, familial, and other social relationships are essentially hierarchical, and women form the bottom of the hierarchy. In virtually all aspects of life, men dominate and women are subordinate, and this pattern shows little sign of changing in the near future (Hall, 1987). The pattern is sustained by a pronounced double standard in gender relations that persists despite changes in the educational and occupational status of a growing number of women.

Sexual Double Standard

Prevailing Mexican cultural beliefs define men as inherently sexual by nature. It is both a man's need and a man's right to have as many sexual experiences as possible; indeed, such exploits are a hallmark of the true *macho* and a matter to be proud of. Simultaneously, the same complex of beliefs defines women as inherently asexual. According to the *marianismo* image, sex is meant for reproductive rather than recreational purposes. It is not an activity that women are supposed to find pleasurable or fulfilling; rather, it is the end product of sexual activity— children—that forms the true source of their pleasure and fulfillment (Mathews, 1987; Riding, 1989).

Under this set of beliefs, women are separated into two distinct groups: "good" women who submit to sex as a means for having children, and "bad" women who in fact enjoy sex and seek it out for their own carnal pleasure. Good women, as epitomized by one's own mother, are family homemakers and procreators. Bad women, as epitomized by one's mistresses, function to bring pleasure to men. But even bad women are in a sense good, since they validate the *machismo* of the man who possesses them and thus bring him social honor in a culture that values virility so highly. For this reason, most men, married or otherwise, seek as many sexual adventures as possible. These episodes typically are defined as conquests, since they ordinarily do not involve emotional attachment or long-term commitment. As one Mexican woman described it, "You know, men are like children. They always want to eat the meal [have sex], but they never want to pay the check" (quoted in Mathews, 1987, p. 228). Adultery is technically a violation of the law in Mexico, but male adultery is so widespread as to be considered normal, and is even institutionalized in the form of the *casa chica* ("mistress") of upper-class and middle-class husbands (Hall, 1987). On the other hand, female adultery still is regarded as a

serious offense, and women who stray can expect serious informal if not formal punishment for their sins (Oster, 1989; Riding, 1989).

This sexual double standard is also evident in the high rates of sexual harassment and rape in most Mexican cities (Hall, 1987; Oster, 1989). The cult of *machismo* almost gives men a sexual hunting license as part of their gender birthright, and most women are considered fair game in this "sport." As is also the case in the United States, most rapes and sexual assaults go unreported, since victims can expect to be brutalized by medical and judicial authorities as much as by the actual rapist (Oster, 1989). Unless he is a habitual offender with a history of attacks on children, the rapist typically is released with only a warning (Hall, 1987). To an extent even greater than in the United States, it is the Mexican victim who is stigmatized by the crime. In the worst tradition of blaming the victim, she is now viewed as "damaged goods" and subject to reclassification as a "bad" woman.

In the simplistic good woman–bad woman dichotomy held by the Mexican *macho,* wives occupy a rather ambiguous place. Since they bear a man's children and provide for his household, wives could be defined as good by their husbands. Since they also serve as receptacles for men's sexual pleasure, they could be defined as bad. As Riding (1989) observed, in the male's world view, the feminine roles of devoted mother, dutiful housewife, and available sex partner are not supposed to be performed by the same woman.

Observed patterns of husbands' behaviors toward their wives seem to indicate that many men define their wives as bad and therefore deserving of harsh treatment. In lower-class households many wives remain virtual prisoners, kept continuously pregnant by husbands who refuse any thought of birth control or abortions to limit the number of "their" children (Hall, 1987). Many husbands refuse to allow wives to go out of the house alone, apparently fearing that they will "go crazy" sexually and betray them with other men (Mathews, 1987; Oster, 1989; Riding, 1989). Physical beatings of wives are common, and the law is reluctant to prosecute abusive husbands (Hall, 1987). Although laws also require absentee fathers to provide financial support for their families, they seldom are enforced. As a result, most of the nearly 50 percent of all nuclear families headed by women live in great poverty (Oster, 1989). Within intact Mexican families, the husband/father reigns supreme, the final formal authority in the household. With or without their wives, men are given great freedom in their daily lives; with or without their husbands, women are not. Men may structure their lives as they see fit; women's defined place in society largely remains confined to the home and the family.

An Uncertain Future

Although Mexican society as a whole has made a number of significant strides in the modernization process, the *machismo* view of gender is changing very slowly. A number of intertwined cultural, social, and perhaps psychological factors seemingly contribute to its persistence and continued impact.

The *machismo* complex, it must be remembered, has a nearly 500-year tenure. The sheer longevity of its basic gender assumptions and definitions has led to unquestioned acceptance by the overwhelming majority of the population, men and women alike. Like other aspects of long-standing cultural frameworks, they form part of the established environment into which a given society's members are born and which they come to see, over a period of time, as natural.

These traditional beliefs about the intrinsic natures of men and of women also have been objects of deliberate socialization efforts by a host of important social agents, including families, schools, the Catholic Church, and the government. More recently, they have been the objects of perhaps unintended socialization efforts of popular culture media such as comic books (Hinds and Tatum, 1984) and television advertising (Gilly, 1988). As a result of the combined efforts of these agents, the message that men and women are inherently and irrevocably different is continuously reinforced.

The daily experiences of most Mexicans also reinforce the belief that men and women are not only different but fundamentally unequal. Despite the rise of a highly educated middle class of urban bureaucrats and professionals over the past few decades, the stratified structure remains "bottom-heavy" with a large lower-class population. The members of this class generally lack both a high level of formal education and the types of occupations that put them in contact with modern cultural ideas or social practices. Historically, the rise of gender equality ideologies and movements has been associated with the development of a large, urban-based, educated, middle class. The experiences and interests of this class generally are conducive to the development of nontraditional beliefs and behaviors. Mexican society currently lacks such a broad population group, and with the continuing socioeconomic problems confronting its people, it remains to be seen just when or if such a modern stratification structure will develop.

In the meantime, the work, family, and other daily situations of the large majority revolve around a world where men lead their lives and women know their place. Although stirrings of feminism are felt within the small upper and middle classes, feminists remain, in the eyes of many, "*macho* women with no hearts" (Hall, 1987, p. 53). Until the country as a whole develops a heart, and until the men learn to forget the past and to start living the present, the cult of *machismo* will continue to constrain and demean millions of Mexican women.

DISCUSSION QUESTIONS

1. What is *marianismo,* and how has this phenomenon influenced the lives of modern Mexican women?
2. You are a Mexican woman who happens to be a college graduate and a division manager in the business firm that employs you. Your work entails supervising the activities of a dozen men, some of whom are traditional in their attitudes about women. What do you think will be the most likely sources of tension and friction between you and your employees? Can you think of any strategies to help resolve these difficulties?
3. *Machismo* is a cultural pattern that presumably pervades all Latin societies. Go to the library and read about female-male relations in contemporary Spain. Does the evidence indicate any widespread presence of the *machismo-marianismo* complex in modern Spanish society?

JAPANESE WOMEN: CHANGING BUTTERFLIES IN A CHANGING SOCIETY

Set in early twentieth-century Japan, Puccini's classic opera *Madama Butterfly* tells the tragic tale of a young Japanese *geisha* who falls in love with a U.S. Navy lieutenant. Cio-Cio-San, the heroine, has been raised in the Japanese tradition of living to serve men. She renounces her religion, her friends, and even her family for Pinkerton, her handsome but callous American lover. The two are married, even though Pinkerton has plans to return to the United States to find "a real American wife." He does just that, leaving Cio-Cio-San behind with their son. She refuses to believe that he has left her for another woman, and lives with the hope that one day he will return to her. When Pinkerton finally does return (bringing his American wife with him) to claim his son, Cio-Cio-San can no longer escape the awful truth. Having rejected all that was important in her life for her love of Pinkerton, she now has been rejected and abandoned by him. Knowing that she cannot live under such shame, she makes the ultimate sacrifice, taking her own life in the opera's dramatic and moving finale.

For many Western observers, the character of Madame Butterfly, who lived and died for an uncaring man, seems to capture the essence of Japanese women, who, according to this portrait, are defined and treated as complete inferiors to men. They are socialized from birth to live in the shadow of men, sacrificing their own identities and dreams in service to the important males in their lives. Quiet and docile, they walk—symbolically, if not literally—three steps behind their men in the social world.

Although this portrayal once may have been true, it would no longer seem to apply to a very large number of women in contemporary Japan. Japanese society has undergone remarkable changes during the past forty-five years, and the structure of female-male relationships has been part of those larger societal transformations. Japanese women, like their counterparts in the United States, still are far from being the social equals of men, but their position has improved dramatically from what it was as recently as a quarter-century ago.

Women in Premodern Times

In ancient times, according to some scholars (Bingham and Gross, 1987; Reischauer, 1988; Warshaw, 1988b), Japanese society was a matriarchal system in which women exercised a great degree of social and political influence. The Japanese believe that their land originally had been settled by the descendants of *Amaterasu Omikami* ("Great Heaven-Shining Mother") the sun goddess. The heirs of the goddess became the first Japanese emperors, and to this day emperors trace their lineage to this supreme deity in the Shinto religion (Cherry, 1987).

However, this matriarchal social structure did not last long. In the sixth century A.D., the Japanese emperor began to embrace the teachings of Buddhism and Confucianism that had been introduced from Korea and China. The rise of Confucianism, in particular, marked the beginning of a patriarchal system that was to last in Japan for over a thousand years.

A basic tenet of Confucianism holds that, in the natural hierarchical order of the world, women are inferior to men. They are thought to be given to the "five weaknesses—disobedience, anger, slanderousness, jealousy, and the lack of intelligence" (Warshaw, 1988b, p. 105). Women's primary purpose in life became defined as providing for the comfort of the males who were the important elements in the family, and producing male heirs to carry on the family lineage. During the medieval feudal period of the Kamakura and the Ashikaga shogunates (A.D. 1185–1603), this life mission was summed up for women under what became known as "the three obediences." Women were to show obedience to their fathers before marriage, to their husbands after marriage, and to their sons (especially their eldest son) after their husband's death (Fewster and Gorton, 1988).

In the pyramidal structure that characterized the extended family from the eighth to the mid twentieth centuries, women constituted the base of the pyramid. In a hierarchical society in which the family household, or *ie,* was the single most important structural unit, their general social status mirrored their position within the *ie.* For all practical purposes, women in premodern Japan, especially during the Tokugawa Period (A.D. 1603–1867), had little or no formal social standing. In custom and in law, their lives were characterized by the absence of any appreciable rights. The conditions of those lives were defined and controlled effectively by the men who dominated what had become a patriarchal system. Dutiful daughters remained in their father's household until their arranged marriages. As dutiful wives, they then moved into their husband's *ie,* where they were expected "to become dyed in the family ways" (*kafu ni somaru*) of their husband's home. Here they remained subject to their husband's mother until the time that control over the running of the household was passed to them in the symbolic form of the household rice paddle by their aging mother-in-law (Cherry, 1987; Hendry, 1987).

Modernization

The opening of Japan to the West and to the forces of modernization during the period of Meiji Restoration (1868–1913) brought significant changes in the social situation of many women (Bando, 1986). The needs of the developing industrial economy, especially those of the early textile industry, required the employment of large numbers of women outside the family household. During this same period, women started to receive a formal education. For the most part, however, the purpose of such education was to foster the traditional objective of producing *ryosai kenbo* ("good wives and wise mothers") (Cherry, 1987). Even women employed full time in the mills and factories were expected to work only until they married and had children. At that point, their primary obligations as wife and mother were to become the guiding principle in their lives.

Many women submitted to these long-standing cultural expectations, but others, exposed to the ideas and practices of the Western world, did not. In the 1880s and again in 1911, groups of feminists began calling for increased legal, political, economic, and social rights for women (Bando, 1986; Bingham and Gross, 1987). Their efforts largely were unsuccessful, however, as civil codes passed during this period effectively barred them from political activities and reinforced their subservient legal status. These codes confirmed the primacy of men's authority in the *ie* and the primacy of the *ie* itself as the basic unit of Japanese social organization.

Japanese women's status as socially inferior to men remained in effect throughout the 1920s and the following decades of imperialism and war, although the war years mobilized the work efforts of many women in industry. It was only with the defeat of Japan and the postwar Allied Occupation that a series of basic changes establishing women's legal rights in educational, employment, and political sectors was begun. Coupled with the dynamics of the economic miracle that swept the nation in the postwar era, these forced changes altered both the status of women and the relations between women and men significantly and, perhaps, irrevocably.

Passed in 1947, the Fundamental Law of Education mandated equal educational opportunities for both sexes. It lengthened compulsory education from six to nine years, established coeducation from the level of secondary school on, and gave women equal access to university education for the first time in the country's history. As a result of this law, the percentage of women completing a high school or other secondary education after their compulsory schooling rose from 13 percent in 1930 to 95 percent by the mid-1980s. At the same time, the percentage of women completing a junior college or university education rose to within seven points of men: 34.5 compared to 40.6 for men (Bando, 1986).

Education and Employment Today

Despite these legal changes and the increasing entry of Japanese women into higher levels of education, the educational system remains highly gender stratified. The bulk of women who pursue an education beyond senior high school do so in a junior college rather than in a four-year university. In these junior colleges, which are filled almost exclusively by women, the curriculum remains traditional and "feminine," with emphasis on preparing women for a lifelong career in marriage. Women are trained in useful household skills and the social graces (Reischauer, 1988). For those who do enroll in a four-year university, the humanities and social sciences remain the most frequent choices of academic major. Like their counterparts in the United States, Japanese women are underrepresented in the sciences, in engineering, and in other traditionally male academic fields (Cherry, 1987). These separate educational background paths become a major influence shaping the different employment patterns that women and men experience when they enter the labor market (Brinton, 1988, 1989).

Like higher education, employment shows a clear pattern of differences based on gender. About half of all Japanese women are employed, and they make up a significant proportion of the entire labor force—over 40 percent as of 1988 (Solo, 1989). But both the structure and the meaning of outside employment are quite different for women than for men. In many respects, the traditional view that women should be concerned with "inside" (i.e., inside the house) matters and men should be concerned with "outside" (i.e., outside the house) matters remains alive and well in the workplace (Makihara, 1990).

Among women working full-time, the largest single grouping, about one-third of the entire female labor force, is made up of o-eru ("office ladies") who provide secretarial and clerical services throughout the Japanese industrial complex (Cherry, 1987). Typically, the so-called OLs are young junior college graduates living at home before getting married who are depicted as leading a relatively carefree lifestyle given largely to shopping and travel (Solo, 1989). For this group, full-time employment represents an interlude between school and marriage. Consequently, the low pay and lack of advancement generally associated with their jobs are not especially troublesome (Christopher, 1983).

However, for other Japanese women working full-time, the lack of salaries and of viable career advancement possibilities comparable to those of men are problematic. On average, the salaries of full-time female employees are only half those of full-time working males, one of the lowest female/male wage ratios among the industrialized nations of the world (Roos, 1985). For example, in 1989, the average salary of working men was $37,692; for women that same year, the comparable figure was $17,692 (Parade, 1991). Japan is also one of the few modern societies in which the female-male wage gap actually increased during the 1970s and early 1980s (Cherry, 1987). Although the number of women managers increased 50 percent between 1982 and 1987 (Solo, 1989), men still are ten times more likely than women to be promoted to managerial ranks in most companies (Brinton, 1988). In the dual-track business system, most men enter into the high-prestige managerial track, and the majority of women still are relegated to the low-prestige, dead-end "office lady" track.

Demographic and Economic Shifts

Most observers of the Japanese occupational structure agree that the situation is coming rapidly to a head. Significant demographic and economic changes are bringing more women into the full-time labor force in dramatic numbers, as well as challenging established patterns of male dominance and female subordination in the workplace. On the demographic side, three important changes are contributing to the influx of women into the labor force: declining birth rates among women of childbearing age, increasing longevity, and the rapid aging of the existing population.

In prewar Japan, the average adult woman gave birth to five children over a twelve-year span; now, the average woman will give birth to two children over a two- to three-year span (Bando, 1986). Many women will complete their childbearing activities and have their children enrolled in school while they still are relatively young. Freed from the restrictive obligations of motherhood, they can participate in outside employment in ways that their mothers could not.

At the same time, the projected life span of women has increased to nearly eighty-two years, including some thirty-five years after their last child has completed compulsory education and over twenty years after their husband's retirement. These empty nest years allow women the opportunity to fulfill their dreams of material goods in a society increasingly geared to conspicuous consumption. Through outside employment, they now can also escape from their retired husbands, whose full-time presence often disrupts established household routines. In popular female slang, retired husbands are referred to as *sodai gomi* ("giant garbage") because women don't know what to do with them (Cherry, 1987).

Finally, the fact that so many Japanese women are living well into old age creates problems of financial security. Many of these women have been housewives for the majority of their lives, and have had to depend on a husband's income for survival and comfort. As more and more of them outlive their husbands, they may find a real need for employment to provide for their own economic well-being. This problem is becoming especially acute as a result of changes in family structure that have led to replacement of the traditional extended family by the nuclear family as the modal type (Bando, 1986).

The net effect of these demographic and economic factors is that Japanese women now form a large pool of individuals who want to enter the full-time labor market and who constitute a potentially huge supply of workers. On the demand side of the equation, the increasing number of positions generated by a rapidly expanding economy and the decreasing number of traditional (young male) employees created as a result of falling birth rates has resulted in a serious and growing labor shortage in almost all sectors of the economy (Solo, 1989). For the first time, employers are actively recruiting young women for career-track, full-time employment, and older women for full-time employment. They also are discovering that the "new" Japanese woman worker will not submit to inferior treatment as her mother once did.

Political Participation

Given their higher levels of education, exposure to Western ideas of equality, and increasing involvement in the political process, a growing number of Japanese women are asserting their rights to better pay, higher prestige, and equitable treatment in the workplace. Under the provision of the Equal Employment Opportunity Law, they have successfully sued employers who denied them promotion on the basis of gender (*San Diego Union,* 1990e). They also have filed sexual harassment suits to put an end to traditional male sexist practices that treat office ladies and other women employees as decorative sex objects or toys (*Economist,* 1989c; Graven, 1990). These actions in part reflect a growing awareness among women of their own potential political power.

Since being granted the right to vote in 1945 as a result of legislation mandated by the Allied Occupational Force, women have increased their electoral participation to the point that they now show slightly higher voting rates than men (Smith, 1990). Until very recently, however, like women in the United States, they were conspicuously absent from higher public office. The Liberal Democratic Party (LDP) that has ruled Japan for the past three decades has nominated very few women for office, and does not seem inclined to do so in the near future. It took a series of financial and sexual scandals involving LDP politicians to propel a woman, Takako Doi, to the leadership of the Japan Socialist Party (JSP) in

No longer content to remain shy butterflies, Japanese women are taking increasingly important and active parts in traditionally male social roles. Ms. Takako Doi, former chairwoman of the Japan Socialist Party, has emerged as one of the leading and best-known figures in contemporary Japanese politics.

1986, and to convince newly elected LDP prime minister Toshiki Kaifu to appoint two women to cabinet minister posts (Jensen and Sullivan, 1989). However, what had been signs of a growing "Madonna factor" (Impoco and Sullivan, 1989) galvanizing Japanese women to vote and to seek political office in 1989 seems to have lost momentum in the early 1990s.

Some observers (Makihara, 1990; Reischauer, 1988; White, 1987) are not at all surprised that Japanese women have yet to be mobilized into the potent political force that their numbers and increasing role in the economy could make them. Unlike women in the United States, Japanese women do not see their housewife position as oppressing or degrading. Their role is defined chiefly in terms of motherhood and, in a society where children are viewed as the country's greatest treasure, those who create and oversee that treasure are also highly valued. Japanese cultural beliefs place a high premium on successful mothering and offer significant if intangible emotional rewards to those who pursue that calling (White, 1987). On a more tangible level, many women who control the financial and other daily activities of their households

in the absence of their husbands find that power to be a satisfying reward. The important point is that the culture supports and emphasizes the importance of both female expressive and male instrumental social roles. In this sense, modern Japanese society may come closer to approximating the functionalist model of complementary gender roles than the United States or other modern industrial societies.

But as more and more Japanese women choose to enter full-time careers in lieu of motherhood, or to return to full-time employment after motherhood, they will encounter the reality of an economic and occupational structure that remains essentially paternalistic and discriminatory. As that occurs, what is now a quiet gender equality revolution may become far less quiet. According to one traditional proverb, *Onna sannin yoreba kashimashii* ("Put three women together and you get noise") (Cherry, 1987). Japanese women have the potential to make a great deal of noise, and may yet be heard from. Barring any real change in entrenched gender relation patterns, a more militant and confrontative brand of feminism remains a distinct possibility.

DISCUSSION QUESTIONS

1. With respect to Japanese women's lives, what are "the three obediences"?
2. Imagine that you are a modern Japanese woman who has recently married. Your new in-laws, you discover, are very traditional in their views about the proper roles of men and women in a successful marriage. What do you think will be the largest and most serious disagreements you will have with your new husband's parents?

3. Whereas some societies such as Japan have a tradition of female subordination, others have been more liberal in their gender policies. Go to the library and read about gender relations and the role of women in one of the contemporary Scandinavian countries —Denmark, Sweden, Norway, or Finland. How do women's lives in these societies compare to those in Japan and in the United States?

CHAPTER SUMMARY

1. All human societies distinguish among their members on the basis of sex or differences in physical anatomy, chromosomes, and hormones. In most societies, sex also is believed to be responsible for important differences in physical and intellectual abilities, as well as psychological temperament.

2. Gender is the sense of being either woman or man, and of possessing the attributes characteristic of one's sex. In a large number of societies,

gender stereotypes categorically portray the two sexes as possessing different essential attributes. This has led to the creation of gender roles that assign individuals to social positions based on their sex, and to gender-stratification systems in which sex differences become the basis for social inequality hierarchies.

3. A large body of biological, psychological, and anthropological research findings indicates a general absence of significant and consistent intellectual or emotional differences between females and males. These same data suggest that assumptions about what is natural for the sexes depend more on cultural beliefs and values than on empirical realities.

4. People acquire their gender identities and behaviors through the lifelong process of socialization. From the time they are first introduced to their society as girls or boys, individuals are subjected to powerful influences of parents, teachers, peers, the mass media, and other important agents of socialization. Throughout childhood and adolescence, they learn and practice attitudes and behaviors deemed appropriate for someone of their particular sex, establishing a self-image based on sexual identity in the process.

5. As adults involved in a web of occupational, parental, and marital roles that often reflect traditional gender beliefs, individuals have their sense of femininity or masculinity reinforced. However, these identities later may be threatened by retirement from occupational careers, declining health and physical abilities, and other age-related changes.

6. Classical functionalist theorist Talcott Parsons attempted to explain the nearly universal existence of gender roles in terms of their contribution to societal survival. According to this argument, it was much more efficient and productive for men to specialize in the instrumental family tasks, and for women to perform the expressive family tasks, for which they were best suited based on their sex. This sex-based division of labor thus promoted the well-being of the larger society.

7. Conflict theorists interpret gender roles as mechanisms for the exploitation of women. Building on the work of Marx and Engels, they view traditional cultural beliefs and social practices as devices for preserving power structures that clearly favor the interests of men over those of women. These patriarchal arrangements will end only when women and other suppressed minorities can acquire enough power to force basic social changes.

8. Like many other modern societies, the United States perpetuates significant inequalities between the sexes in the areas of work, income, politics, and law, among others. Despite the fact that most women now work full-time, many remain in low-paying, sex-segregated, pink-collar jobs. Whereas female-male occupational and income differences have been treated to a number of explanations including differences in human capital resources, gender discrimination seems to be a significant contributing factor. Women whose educational credentials are equivalent to men's nonetheless are paid less, and often encounter obstacles to promotion to the highest ranks of corporations or other organizations. Within the past thirty years, the feminization of poverty has become a significant problem in the United States. Increasing numbers of females and female-headed families are experiencing severe economic deprivation.

9. Women register and vote in numbers equal to those of men, but they remain underrepresented in political office at federal and state levels. This lack of representation may be at least partially responsible for the absence or slowness of government policies that might promote gender equality. At the local level, women have gained numbers in city and county offices, and also have gained important political leadership experiences through involvement in grass-roots movements.

10. Laws concerning rape, abortion, and other sex-related issues also contribute to gender inequality. Both the frequency and the fear of rape restrict women's lives in many ways. The handling of this crime by the criminal justice system often puts the victim on trial and suggests that women somehow are at least partially responsible for their own attack. As both pro-life and pro-choice forces mobilize for action, abortion promises to become the major gender issue of the decade. The Supreme Court's 1973 *Roe* v. *Wade* decision is being challenged by state laws that limit or deny women's access to abortion. Both sides view abortion laws in terms of larger ideological issues.

11. The three major sociological theoretical perspectives view the gender equality movement in very different ways. For functionalists, a major question revolves around the scope and speed of social and cultural changes brought about by the movement. Changes that are too rapid and too far-reaching could threaten the foundations of the social order and thus the survival of society. For conflict theorists, the key issue concerns strategies for acquiring effective power to overcome the re-

sistence of established elites and bring about necessary fundamental social changes. In this view, gender equality essentially is a political question whose answer will be based on power considerations rather than on moral or philosophical merit. For symbolic interactionists, the main considerations are the meanings attached to "male" and "female," and the social significance of prevailing cultural views of gender. From this perspective, socialization agents and the socialization process itself are critical variables, since the most important battle to be won lies inside the heads of the population members.

8

CRIME, DEVIANCE, AND SOCIAL CONTROL

The blaring sound of a police siren pierces the night air as officers pursue three men high on drugs who have just robbed a convenience store. The spectacular high-speed chase almost kills several bystanders and is followed by a shootout that leaves one policeman dead and two suspects wounded. A month later the district attorney and a public defender match wits in a dramatic jury trial. Two of the suspects are convicted, and the third is set free because the police neglected to read him his Miranda rights. The outraged partner of the dead officer stalks the killer of his friend, and is instrumental in the man's arrest and conviction for another capital offense.

Is this crime and justice in the United States? It is, according to forty years of television programs such as "Kojak," "Miami Vice," and "Hill Street Blues." Bank robberies, daring burglaries, and drug deals can make for high drama and entertainment, but these offenses project a view of criminal activity (as well as the cost of crime) in the United States that is only partially accurate. A more realistic picture reveals something quite different from the "cops and robbers" scenario portrayed in the media. The staggering cost of illegal activity in terms of dollars (and possibly lives) is a direct result of crimes that take place "in the suites" rather than "in the streets."

In the early 1970s the Senate Judiciary Subcommittee on Antitrust and Monopoly estimated that the cost of corporate crime to the American public was between $174 and $231 billion annually. The Joint Economic Committee of the U.S. Congress put the yearly losses from street crimes at approximately $4 billion in the 1970s, "less than 5 percent of the estimated losses from corporate crime" (Coleman, 1989, p. 7). But the cost of corporate crime to date may be nothing compared to the current savings and loan disaster. One observer thinks the collapse of these fraud-ridden institutions will cost taxpayers between $500 billion and $1 trillion, or approximately $2,000 to $4,000 for every man, woman, and child in the United States (Reeves, 1990).

Although the cost of street crimes such as robbery, assault, and rape in terms of misery and pain is extremely high, so-called nonviolent crimes also take their toll in human suffering and death. In the 1970s, tens of thousands of women were injured by the Dalkon Shield, a faulty intrauterine birth control device. Data from Wisconsin indicate that as many as 45 percent of all industrial accidents in that state are the result of safety code violations (Coleman, 1985). The B.F. Goodrich Company plotted to sell defective air brakes to the air force by faking test results and falsifying laboratory reports. As Hagan (1986) noted, "National security and the lives of fighter pilots appeared to be of little concern" (p. 136). Corporate irresponsibility (if not technically illegal) can also cost lives. The General Dynamics Corporation allegedly ignored an engineer's warnings concerning defects in DC-10 cargo doors. Two years later a DC-10 crashed in France, killing 346 people when the plane's cargo doors blew open in flight.

This chapter examines street and corporate crime, as well as a variety of other deviant and criminal acts. Attention also is given to some of the techniques and strategies used to control nonconforming and criminal behavior. Before launching into a survey of such behaviors and the various theories attempting to explain them, we must take a closer look at the phenomenon of deviance.

Questions to Consider

1. What is deviance? Do all societies have deviant behavior? Why?
2. What are the differences among the absolutist, normative, and reactive perspectives of deviance?
3. What is the difference between deviant behavior and criminal behavior?
4. According to Emile Durkheim, in what sense is criminal behavior "normal"?
5. How is crime "functional," or good for society?
6. According to Robert Merton, what is anomie? What types of deviant behaviors does anomie produce?
7. Is differential association simply a "bad apple" theory?
8. According to Marxist theorists, why are prisons in the United States filled with poor people?
9. How do social control theorists explain deviance?
10. Why is date rape prevalent in American society?
11. What is the difference between white-collar crime and occupational crime?
12. What are some of the arguments for decriminalizing drugs?

Deviance: A Sociological View

All societies, from the most primitive to the most advanced, have a system of norms designating acceptable and unacceptable types of behavior. These norms regulate all facets of human conduct such as sexual activity, marriage, the ownership of property, and the division of labor. **Deviance** is behavior contrary to norms of conduct and social expectations. Some rules of conduct thought to be especially important to a society's well-being are codified, or put into a legal code. Violation of this code (criminal laws) constitutes a crime and is subject to formal punishment by the state.

Just as rules of conduct are found in all human societies, so too are people who violate these rules (Edgerton, 1976). Erich Goode (1990) theorized that deviance exists because human beings are "evaluative creatures" who continually make judgments about their own behavior and that of others. In other words, people in every society divide much of the social world into two broad categories: the good and desirable, and the bad and undesirable. Behavior falling into the latter category is considered deviant and is usually subject to some form of social control.

One can define deviance from the absolutist, normative, and reactive perspectives. From the **absolutist perspective** "deviance resides in the very nature of an act itself" (Goode, 1990, p. 13), and is wrong at all times (past, present, and future) and in all places. A deviant act may be thought of as an "offense against the order of the universe" (p. 13) or transgression against the laws of God. The absolutist perspective is characteristic of people who have strong (and often unyielding) religious views. For

The relativeness of deviance is evident in this photo of Soviet leaders kissing. A similar expression of friendship and affection in the United States most likely would be viewed as deviant, unacceptable behavior.

example, some right-to-life adherents believe that abortion is "absolutely" wrong un-der any and all circumstances. They argue that abortion can never be justified, regard-less of the circumstances surrounding the pregnancy, including rape and incest. From this perspective, even if the laws of society permit abortion, the laws of God are supreme and the act of terminating a pregnancy is murder.

The **normative perspective** sees deviance as the violation of a specific group's or society's rules at a particular time in history. Deviance, therefore, is a relative phe-nomenon, not inherent in the act or behavior itself. As stated by Goode (1990), "We can tell when an action is deviant by consulting the customs of society" (p. 14). Throughout most of human history, abortion has been an acceptable and widely prac-ticed form of birth control. It was so common in post–World War II Japan that by 1950 the number of terminated pregnancies exceeded that of live births (Warshaw, 1988b). In the United States, the 1973 *Roe* v. *Wade* Supreme Court decision ruled that states do not have the right to restrict women from having abortions. Nevertheless, millions of Americans oppose the practice (some violently) for religious and moral reasons. Although the laws of the country as well as the norms of some people condone a woman's right to terminate a pregnancy, the values and norms of other people strongly condemn such action. If the laws are eventually overturned, antiabortionists will have the law on their side, so to speak.

To take another example, opium was used in virtually all segments and classes of American society before and during the Civil War (Edgerton, 1976). Rambunctious children were routinely calmed with opium derivatives, and the drug was a principal ingredient in many patent medicines. After the war, however, opium was redefined as troublesome and dangerous, with laws eventually being passed prohibiting its distri-bution and use. In both of these illustrations, the prevailing normative order of different groups at different moments in history determined to what extent the behavior in question was considered deviant.

From the **reactive perspective,** behavior is not deviant until it has been recognized and condemned. In other words, deviance lies in the sanction or disapproval of be-havior, not in the behavior itself. Keeping with the abortion example, the practice would be considered deviant *only* when it was discovered and prosecuted by the criminal justice system. If an abortion did not come to the attention of the authorities, it would not be considered deviant. From the reactive perspective, then, it is the *negative sanction* and not the behavior that constitutes deviance. Pollner (1974, in Goode, 1990) summarized it in a simple, straightforward manner: "No reactions, no deviance" (p. 15). Those who adhere to this position would argue that the tens of thousands of people who commit crimes in the United States each year, but are not caught and punished, are not deviant.

Figure 8.1 shows the relationship between deviant behavior and criminal behavior. When a person is following group standards, and by so doing is also obeying the law, he or she is engaging in conforming behavior. Virtually everyone engages in conforming behavior most of the time. **Deviant behavior** is a violation of reference group or subcultural group norms, but is not in violation of the legal code of the larger society. It may include the violation of religious laws and customs, severe ideological differences between group members, homosexuality where not illegal, divorce, alcoholism, mental illness, and spouse swapping. **Criminal behavior** occurs when the laws of the larger society are not supported by the norms of an individual's subculture. A good deal of criminal behavior is not considered deviant according to the values and norms of the subculture. Examples include gambling, prostitution, incest, fighting, taking drugs, stealing, and cheating on one's income tax. **Deviant and criminal behavior** violates

FIGURE 8.1   Deviant and Criminal Behavior

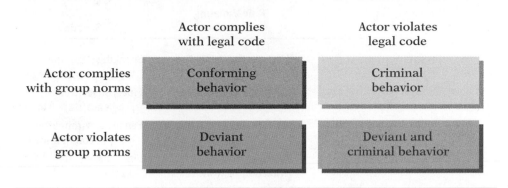

both subcultural norms and society's laws. Examples are murder, rape, treason, arson, and child molestation.

As we saw in chapter 4, individuals become committed to the values and norms of their group and the larger society to such an extent that they engage in conforming behavior most of the time. (Even criminals marry and have families, buy presents for their children, etc.). If this were not the case, societies would crumble under the weight of widespread deviance and crime, or turn into totalitarian states that ruthlessly control every aspect of human conduct. Socialization is never completely effective, however, and rule violation does occur. When people violate rules and laws and their transgressions are discovered, they typically are subject to the disciplinary action of some agent of social control. As Table 8.1 indicates, this control can take place within a formal or an informal setting. Young children caught smoking generally are punished by their parents (informal social control). If they are discovered smoking at school, they will also be disciplined by teachers and administrators in an organizational setting (formal social control). The state, through the criminal justice system, is the one agent of social control empowered to place people on probation, imprison them, and even take their lives by execution.

Approaches to both explaining and controlling deviance have varied and "competed for ascendancy throughout Western history" (Little, 1989, p. 337). Under the influence of Christianity in medieval Europe, deviance was thought of as sinful and evil—a fall from grace. Mechanisms of social control emphasized atoning for one's sins through penance or corporal punishment. Over the past hundred years and with the rise of modern medicine, however, more and more deviance is being explained and "cured" from a medical perspective. The deviant is typically thought of as physically or psychologically sick and in need of treatment. The disease model of deviance took a significant step forward with the formation of Alcoholics Anonymous (AA) in 1935. Since the mid-1960s this perspective has become increasingly popular in the United States and has resulted in the creation of groups such as Narcotics Anonymous, Cocaine Anonymous, Overeaters Anonymous, Sex and Love Addicts, Fundamentalists Anonymous (for those who join fundamentalist religions), Gamblers Anonymous, Workaholics Anonymous, and Swearers Anonymous.

In his book *Diseasing of America* (1989), psychologist Stanton Peele argued the "disease theory" of addiction is based on the following assumptions: (1) the addiction exists *independent* of the rest of a person's life and *drives* all of his or her choices; (2)

TABLE 8.1 Institutions, Rule-Violating Behaviors, and Sanctions

Institution	Agent	Rule-Violating Behavior	Sanction
Family	Parents	Youth disobedience	Spanking, "grounding," withholding privileges
Clubs, social organizations	Officers	Violations of club rules	Fines, suspension of privileges, expulsion
Religion	Minister, priest, rabbi	Sin	Penance, withholding rites, excommunication
Business	Employer	Absence, laziness, violation of work rules	Fine, suspension, dismissal
Professional group	Officer	Ethical violations	Fine, license revocation, expulsion from group
Political state	Police, prosecutor, judge	Violation of civil and criminal laws	Fine, probation, imprisonment, damage suit, execution
Military	Superiors	Disobeying orders	Fine, imprisonment, loss of rank and privileges
Schools	Teachers, administrators	Disobeying rules, failure to maintain appropriate grade point average	Probation, expulsion

Source: Adapted from Marshall B. Clinard, 1979, *Sociology of Deviant Behavior,* 5th edition. New York: Holt, Rinehart and Winston. Copyright © 1979 by Holt, Rinehart and Winston. Reprinted by permission.

it is progressive and irreversible, so that the addiction *inevitably worsens* unless the person seeks medical treatment or joins an AA-type support group; (3) addiction means the person is incapable of controlling his or her behavior. The person engaging in deviant behavior is considered a victim rather than an abuser, as in the phrase "alcohol abuse victim." The exercise of free will has been removed to a great extent regarding the behavior in question, and people are pushed or driven into deviance by physiological or psychological factors beyond their control.

At least one form of behavior considered by many to be deviant is moving beyond the category of disease. Homosexuality has gone from being a "sin to crime to sickness and, most recently, demedicalization" (Little, 1989). After an intense political struggle, in 1974 the American Psychiatric Association voted to abolish the classification of homosexuality as a form of mental illness. This illustrates the obvious (although often overlooked) political component of deviance. The winners of a given political struggle may have a good deal to say in determining what deviant behavior is or is not and how it should be treated.

The study of deviance not only tells us a great deal about a society's ethical standards and system of justice, but also helps us understand how, and in what direction, a society is being transformed as people continually redefine rules of conduct. Sociologists are especially interested in how certain types of behavior come to be defined as deviant, how norms and rules that define acceptable and unacceptable behavior change over time, and why certain groups of people are more likely than others to be sanctioned for rule-violating behavior.

THEORIES OF CRIME AND DEVIANCE

Biological Explanations

Biologically grounded explanations of behavior in general, and criminal behavior in particular, go back hundreds if not thousands of years, and are all based on the same fundamental assumption: structure determines function. In other words, human behavior is directly related to, and somehow a result of, an individual's physical makeup. It logically follows, therefore, that if our actions are a function of our physiology, those who are structurally different should engage in different forms of behavior. Criminals, according to this argument, should be physiologically distinct from the noncriminal population and similar to one another.

In the aftermath of Charles Darwin's groundbreaking work in biology, some researchers attempted to ascertain anatomical differences between criminals and noncriminals. One of the pioneers in this area was the Italian physician and criminologist Cesare Lombroso (1835–1909). According to Lombroso, some people are born criminals and destined to a life of crime. These individuals are atavistic, or biological throwbacks to a "past race" of mankind. The born criminal is physiologically distinct from noncriminals, and these differences are measurable and predictable (Savitz, 1972). It is important to understand that these physical distinctions do not cause criminal behavior, but are indicators of biological deficiency; they are outward manifestations of underlying physiological and mental inferiority (Bryjak and Soroka, 1985).

Lombroso and his disciples found numerous similarities between the anatomy of criminals and that of animals, especially primates. Criminals, for example, often have a "chin receding or excessively long, or short and flat, as in apes" (Lombroso-Ferrero, 1972, p. 16) and "ears of unusual size, or occasionally very small, or standing out from the head as those of chimpanzees (p. 19). Implicit in Lombroso's criminology is a belief in the stratification or inequality of the human races. This racial hierarchy is the result of various courses and speeds of human evolution. Working in a period of European expansion and colonialism, Lombroso put Caucasians at the top of his hierarchy, followed by the numerous "other races" and peoples to which he often referred. Although he made a valuable contribution in attempting to find the root causes of crime, his work was not very scientific. For example, his physical measurement of criminals was limited to those individuals incarcerated for crimes, hardly a representative sample of the criminal population. Although he claimed that criminal tendencies were inherited, Lombroso never gathered evidence to support this assertion (Sanders, 1983).

A more recent attempt to find the link between biology and crime focused on one of the twenty-three pairs of human chromosomes that determine gender characteristics. Whereas males normally have an XY pair (females XX), some have an extra Y chromosome, making for an XYY configuration. This additional chromosome was thought to produce a kind of "supermale," generally taller and more violent than XY males, and ten to twenty times more likely to break the law (Herrnstein, 1986). Even with such high rates of criminal activity, however, XYY males comprise less than one-tenth of 1 percent of the entire male population and could account for only a small percentage of the total crime picture.

The latest and most promising area of biological research into criminal activity focused on identical twins who share identical genes. Bartollas and Dinitz (1989) noted that the results of a number of studies in Europe and the United States indicated that the criminality of adopted twins is more likely to follow the pattern of behavior of their biological parents than of their adoptive parents. A Danish study of 4,000 adopted boys found that "the more serious an offender a biological parent was, the greater the risk of criminality for his or her child, particularly for property crimes" (Herrnstein, 1986, p. 3).

Criminologist Deborah Denno (1986) cautioned that, although promising, twin studies must be viewed with caution because they explain only property crimes and not violent crime. In addition, any biological characteristics associated with criminal behavior may be the result of prenatal influences, and not heritable, genetic factors. This means that biological variables related to criminality could be the result of poor nutrition or inadequate health care when a woman was pregnant (Denno, 1986). Since these conditions are most likely to affect poor women, prenatal factors may well be class linked and rooted in socioeconomic conditions.

Sociological Perspectives

Functionalist Theory   The first ten minutes of the local television newscast in any big city is usually a chronicle of the day's criminal events. We see tearful individuals recount stories of assault, robbery, and rape, and police officers working around the clock to fight the rising tide of crime. At election time, politicians routinely tell us they will get tough with criminals and make the streets safe for law-abiding citizens. Is it possible to rid society of crime once and for all, or is the loss of life and property, as well as the incalculable human suffering that results from criminal behavior, something we have to accept?

According to the great French sociologist Emile Durkheim (1938, original 1895), crime is "normal" because it is impossible to imagine (or find) a society that does not have criminal behavior. Durkheim did not mean crime is normal in the sense that it is good. Rather, he used the term in the sense of statistical normalcy; crime is everywhere. Therefore, Durkheim reasoned, if it is present in all societies at all times, it cannot be abnormal. He gave three reasons for the normalcy of criminal behavior.

First, crime and deviance persist because it is impossible to reach complete agreement on what the rules and norms of society are or should be. Without absolute agreement and acceptance of the rules, the behavior of one group of people will be considered deviant by the standards of another group.

Second, crime is normal because no society can enforce total conformity to its rules and laws (Coser, 1971). Even under the most repressive regimes and totalitarian governments, officials find it impossible to gain complete obedience to the laws of the land. For example, robbery, murder, prostitution, and black market activity existed even in the darkest days of the Stalinist era in the Soviet Union.

Third, crime is inevitable because "man is a normative creature" (Nisbet, 1974, p. 216), continually dividing the social world into what is acceptable and unacceptable. That which is deemed unacceptable becomes criminal.

Although Durkheim believed that crime was normal and inevitable, he did not mean that all societies would have identical rates of crime, nor would the same acts be considered criminal in every social group. Depending on the forces in society contributing to criminal behavior and the mechanisms of social control, rates could be high or low. Also, behavior considered criminal will vary across social groups. In one of his most famous passages, Durkheim (1938, original 1895) asked us to "Imagine a society of saints, a perfect cloister of exemplary individuals. Crimes, properly so-called will be there unknown; but faults which appear venial to the layman will create the same scandal that the ordinary offense does in ordinary consciousness" (p. 53). He was saying that even in a society of perfect human beings there will be deviance; although not the types of deviance we are used to seeing in the modern world. Rather, it will consist of rule-violating behavior of that specific group. In Durkheim's society of saints, it might be praying six hours a day instead of eight, and failing to meditate in a strict, erect posture.

Durkheim argued further that if crime is present in all societies, it must be functional, or necessary. In other words, the continuous violation of rules and laws must result in some social good. Remember that functionalist sociologists consider the consequences of behavior at the group, institutional, and societal levels of analysis. Therefore, the impact of crime may be harmful (dysfunctional) for individual victims and their families, while this same behavior is functional (desirable and necessary) for the larger society. According to Durkheim, crime is functional for society in four ways (Martin et al., 1990).

There is a "vital relation between deviance and progress" in society (Nisbet, 1974, p. 219). The same tolerance that permits for the healthy flow of originality, resulting in positive social change in society, also opens the door for a good deal of undesirable deviant behavior. One seemingly obvious solution to this problem would be to permit and encourage positive deviance, and discourage negative deviance. In hindsight, this is relatively simple, but at the moment of occurrence it is not always easy to tell what forms of behavior will transform society for the better. Labor leaders, suffragettes, abolitionists (those who opposed slavery), Jesus Christ, Mohandas Gandhi, and Martin Luther King, Jr., were all treated as radicals and/or criminals whose ideas would contribute to the destruction of the established social order.

The second function of deviance is that of a warning light, or a visible signal that something is wrong in society and in need of immediate attention. The high rate of drug use in this country should result in probing questions on the part of citizens and politicians as to why this behavior is so widespread. What is happening (or not happening) politically, socially, and economically in the United States at this moment in history, that so many people from every social stratum are using and dealing drugs? In this warning-light function, Durkheim compared crime to physical pain: it is normal and necessary, as it tells us something is wrong with the body social (Martin et al., 1990).

Crime also helps clarify boundaries. Every time a rule or law is violated and society reacts to it, it sends a message stating this sanction is important and the law must be obeyed. Conversely, if the violation of a norm is ignored or results in only a minor sanction, the message is that this norm at this particular time is not considered as important as others. For example, with few exceptions, prostitution is illegal throughout the United States; however, prostitutes can be seen walking the streets and working out of bars with little if any fear of being arrested. They know police are using their limited resources to fight the "war on drugs." They also realize that neither the police nor society in general considers prostitution as dangerous (and "dysfunctional") as the drug problem.

Finally, criminal behavior facilitates social solidarity. Violation of the law can draw members of a community together in their revulsion toward the criminal act and the criminal. Speaking of a murder in his district, a Wyoming police chief stated, "It was a crime against everyone. It's drawn the whole community together" (Magnuson, 1981, p. 18). Functionalist sociologists do not advocate mass murders to enhance social cohesion. Nevertheless, crimes can bind a community together like few other events.

Anomie Theory   Durkheim used the word **anomie** to describe the breakdown of societal rules and norms that regulate human behavior. Examining France and other European countries in the years after the Industrial Revolution, he argued that the rapid economic, political, and social transformation of these societies produced anomie, or normlessness. This condition resulted in disruptive patterns of social interaction and high rates of suicide (Williams and McShane, 1988).

In 1938 Robert Merton used the concept of anomie to characterize a feature more firmly rooted in the social structure of society and responsible for a variety of criminal and deviant behaviors. For Merton all societies socialize their members to aspire to a number of culturally defined and acceptable goals, and teach people to attain these goals by a variety of available and legitimate means of behavior. In other words, societies provide a set of culturally acceptable goals, as well as the means for achieving them. However, in societies of the "American type" the emphasis is much more on being successful (goals) than on how success is attained (means). This overemphasis on achieving one's goals, and corresponding underemphasis on how they are realized, is at the heart of Merton's theory and is responsible for a significant amount of deviant behavior in American society.

Merton (1968) used monetary success as an example of a goal actively pursued by individuals in every stratum of society in the United States. The "goal-means dysjunction" (or gap) results in five different types of behavior, or adaptations, depending on whether individuals accept or reject both the goals and the means of achieving them. Note that these adaptations do not represent personality types. People can move from one adaptation to another at different points in their lives.

1. *Conformity*   This adaptation is followed by most of the people most of the time. Individuals accept both the culturally prescribed goals and means, which include working in an automobile factory, striving for a professional career by way of a college degree, and starting one's own business.

2. *Innovation*   This adaptation is the most common of the four deviant types and usually takes one of two forms. In the first instance an individual accepts the societal goal of financial success. However, the "opportunity structure," or means of achieving this goal, is blocked. Merton argued that this lack of opportunity is most evident in the lower classes and places tremendous pressure on these people to engage in deviant behavior. Because of high rates of unemployment, inadequate school systems, and racial and ethnic discrimination, people in the lower classes resort to "innovative" or criminal means of attaining financial success. In the second instance the legitimate means for achieving one's goals are available, but rejected because they are not expedient or take too much effort. Students who cheat on examinations are innovators inasmuch as they have accepted the goal of doing well in school, but reject the legitimate means of studying and working hard for grades. Many white-collar and corporate criminals are also innovators. Although they may be quite wealthy, they want even more money and material possessions, and are willing to circumvent the law to satisfy their desires.

3. *Ritualism*   A strong desire for financial gain may result in a life of luxury, but for everyone who becomes a multimillionaire, tens of thousands fail. Because it is often associated with a significant loss of self-esteem, failure can be difficult for people to accept. One way to avoid personal defeat is to scale down or reject ambitious goals, while continuing to work hard and to meet one's economic and social obligations. Although this adaptation is not deviant behavior of the same magnitude as crime, Merton considered it deviance because ritualists reject a fundamental value in the United States of continually striving for monetary success and upward mobility.

4. *Retreatism*   Retreatists take ritualism one step farther and reject culturally pre-scribed means as well as goals. Some homeless people, chronic alcoholics, and drug addicts are retreatists. Merton (1968) noted these individuals have turned their backs on the social world and are, strictly speaking, "*in* the society but not *of* it" (p. 207). Retreatists are a twofold social liability. Not only are they nonproductive members of society, but many use social services in the form of the criminal justice system, mental institutions, and rehabilitation programs. William Sanders (1983) described some re-treatists as "double losers," as they fail both to achieve their goals by legitimate means and to become successful criminals or innovators.

5. *Rebellion*   This revolutionary adaptation comes about when people reject both the culturally prescribed goals and means, and substitute an alternative set grounded in different values. Rebels want to change society in fundamental ways, not reform it. Many of those involved in the radical and abrupt transformation of Eastern European nations in 1989 and 1990 were rebels.

Merton's perspective of deviance is important for at least two reasons. Written when biological and psychological theories of deviant behavior were popular and readily accepted, his view of deviance offered a purely sociological interpretation of rule-violating behavior. Instead of innate biological impulses or psychological maladies, the social structure exerted "a definite pressure upon certain persons in the society to engage in nonconforming rather than conforming conduct" (Merton, 1968, p. 186). Second, the same pressure in society that produces conformity (striving for success) also produces nonconformity: "a cardinal American virtue, 'ambition,' underlies a cardinal American vice, 'deviant behavior' " (Merton, 1957, p. 146).

Differential Association   According to Edwin Sutherland, a noted U.S. criminologist, criminal behavior is not the product of inborn biological abnormality or the result of low intelligence or personality defects. People are not predisposed to commit crimes, and criminal behavior does not occur spontaneously; instead, such behavior is learned. Sutherland advanced these ideas as part of his **differential association** theory. He argued that criminal behavior is not learned from the mass media, but "is learned in interaction with other persons in a process of communication" (Sutherland and Cres-sey, 1970, p. 75). People learn techniques for committing crimes as well as "the specific direction of motives, drives, rationalizations, and attitudes" (p. 75). In other words, people learn much more than the mechanics of how to commit a crime. They also internalize a series of attitudes that permit them to rationalize this behavior to themselves and others.

Sutherland stated, "A person becomes delinquent because of an excess of definitions favorable to violation of law over definitions unfavorable to violation of law. This is the principle of differential association" (in Sutherland and Cressey, 1970, p. 75). Crimi-nologist William Sanders (1983) offered a simple formula to illustrate this crucial aspect of the theory:

Definitions favorable to violations of the law   (DFVL)

Definitions unfavorable to violations of the law   (DUVL)

If DFVL is greater than DUVL, an individual will engage in criminal behavior, but if DUVL is greater than DFVL, he or she will not. Sutherland (in Sutherland and Cressey, 1970) stressed the "duration," "priority," and "intensity" of relationships in determining whether or not a person would perform criminal acts. Duration refers to the length of time we have known people. Individuals we have just met will not have as much influence on our behavior as those we have known for many years. Priority refers to how early in life we have been exposed to DFVL or DUVL. Patterns of criminality observed or learned early in life will have a greater impact on our behavior than those learned later in life. Intensity is a measure of the strength of the relationship. People with whom we have a strong emotional bond ("primary relations") will influence us more than those with whom we have a more "secondary" relationship. Putting these three components together, if an individual learns DFVL starting early in life, from influential people, over a long period of time, he or she is very likely to engage in criminal conduct.

Differential association has been dismissed as nothing more than a "bad apple" theory; someone who hangs around with criminals will naturally become a criminal. However, the theory does not focus on the person making DFVL or DUVL, but on the definitions themselves. For example, if children see their parents steal ("borrow") things from work on a regular basis, and hear them brag about these activities, they are receiving powerful DFVL even though the parents are not criminals (i.e., they have never been caught and punished) and do not think of themselves as criminals. Similarly, a new insurance agent may learn from co-workers the best ways to cheat customers

Although cocaine is illegal in the United States, many people do not consider drug use to be deviant. Some groups may demand that their members use one or more drugs if they are to be fully accepted.

("aggressive sales techniques") and how to rationalize this behavior ("everybody does it"). Even though DFVL are not coming from "criminals," they have the effect of facilitating criminal behavior. Differential association goes beyond the commonsense notion that law-violating behavior is learned only from juvenile delinquents, gang members, and hardened criminals.

Labeling Theory Most theories of deviant and criminal behavior attempt to explain why people engage in rule-violating acts by identifying factors that cause people to transgress social norms or to break the law. The **labeling theory** shifted the focus, concentrating instead on the social creation of, and reaction to, deviant behavior. Howard Becker (1963) noted that "*social groups create deviance by making the rules whose infraction constitutes deviance,* and by applying those rules to particular people and labeling them deviant" (p. 9). From this perspective, "deviant behavior is behavior that people so label" (p. 9).

Labeling theorists argue that since so many laws and rules govern human conduct, almost everyone engages in deviant or criminal behavior. The important question, therefore, is not why they do so, but rather why only certain people are labeled deviants and criminals. But do most people routinely violate rules and laws? According to the results of one study, an estimated 90 percent of all youths commit delinquent and criminal acts. Other research suggested that little difference exists between the behavior of incarcerated youths and that of typical high school students (Siegel, 1989).

The labeling perspective of deviance can be divided into two parts: (1) an explanation of how and why some people are labeled, and (2) what effect the label has on a person's future behavior (Orcutt, 1973). Regarding the first aspect, people with low social status and little power are most likely to have the acts they engage in defined as deviant, and are also more likely to be labeled as deviants by formal agents of social control—the criminal justice system and mental health professionals. For example, tens of thousands of people have been convicted and sentenced to prison by criminal courts for committing burglary, whereas the relatively few individuals and corporations convicted of cheating the public (often out of enormous sums of money) typically serve little if any jail time. Inasmuch as labeling theorists view laws whose infraction constitutes deviance as created by the powerful to control the lower classes, the labeling perspective of deviance is quite compatible with conflict theory.

Individuals and organizations who actively campaign to discredit an activity or lifestyle of another group of people are called *moral entrepreneurs* (Becker, 1963). In the 1970s, a number of Christian fundamentalist groups and their spokespersons attempted to stigmatize further (and, if possible, to criminalize) homosexual behavior in the United States. These individuals tried to convince the nation their views of sexuality were correct and should be regarded as the standard for evaluating everyone's sexual orientation. Politically active antiabortionists who vociferously denounce pro-choice supporters as "murderers" and "baby killers" would also be considered moral entrepreneurs.

The process by which people become labeled and recognized as deviants is called a *status degradation ceremony* (Garfinkel, 1956). When an individual is convicted and sentenced in criminal court, the state is making a public declaration that this person has violated the public trust (laws) and is "not one of us." The problem with this aspect of social control is there is no "status reintegration ceremony" (Garfinkel, 1956, p. 423) whereby a person can be given back his or her status as a citizen in good standing upon completing a prison term. As a result of degradation ceremonies, individuals may be forced to live with a master status for an extended period of time (if not the rest of their lives). A *master status* is a central identifying characteristic of an individual and takes precedence over any other role the person plays. For example, an individual who has served time in prison may be viewed by others first and foremost as an "ex-con." It is as if this person were walking around with a neon sign proclaiming, "I spent time in prison," in much the same way as Hester Prynne was forced to wear a crimson A for her adulterous behavior in Nathaniel Hawthorne's *The Scarlet Letter.*

The concept of master status is also an important component of the social control aspect of labeling theory. According to this argument, people labeled criminals in degradation ceremonies often end up committing additional crimes because they have so much trouble finding a job. Once the label becomes a master status, individuals may find that criminal activity is the only way they can survive in a society where people think in terms of "once a deviant, always a deviant" (Goode, 1990, p. 66).

A person can also internalize the given label until he "becomes the thing he is described as being" (Tannenbaum, 1938, pp. 19–20). In other words, the label may become an important part of the self-concept. It makes little difference if the label is applied by those who are trying to punish, or by those who are trying to help, the individual. For example, some drug treatment programs believe the first step to recovery is admission that one has a serious illness in the form of a drug problem, to admit that one is an addict. From the labeling perspective, individuals can easily become trapped in this negative definition of self. If they accept the label of drug addict (internalization of a master status) they may also accept the corresponding idea that addicts are never really cured.

Speaking of labels applied by the "addiction treatment industry" and internalized by their members, Peele (1989) noted, "The person is now convinced that a single slip will mean a complete return to the addiction or to alcoholism—a fate that befalls many 'successful' graduates" (p. 112). In other words, the label of alcoholic may become a self-fulfilling prophecy, helping to ensure that a person continues to drink and is dependent on alcohol for the remainder of his or her life. Deviant behavior that occurs as a result of being labeled is called **secondary deviance** (Lemert, 1951). The initial act, or first few episodes of nonconforming behavior, is **primary deviance.** Labeling theorists are much more concerned with secondary deviance, the deviant behavior an individual engages in after he or she has been labeled by control agents.

Although sociologists have been critical of self-help organizations that encourage members to label themselves and others, they generally agree that many one-time alcoholics have abstained from drinking for considerable periods of time thanks to the AA program. Shur (1979) commented that "contrary to the central labeling thesis, the application of 'negative labels' in this context appears to have predominantly deviance-reducing effects rather than deviance-amplifying ones" (p. 388). Similarly, members of a weight-reducing self-help organization were continually reminded they were fat, and that the word fat was an essential and permanent component of their identity, no matter how much weight they lost. According to this program, a change in identity would remove the best safeguard a person has against future weight gains. Researchers concluded that the internalization of a negative label—fat—helped bring about the desired nondeviant behavior—reduction in food intake and slimness (Laslett and Warren, 1975). However, a successful behavior change may require a lifetime commitment to the organization.

Marxist Theory Power, profit, and class struggle are concepts at the heart of **Marxist** conflict **theory.** In a capitalist society the bourgeoisie (capitalist class) own and control the "modes of production" (factories, machinery, technology), and in so doing, systematically exploit the working class (proletariat). Their superior political power and

OURSELVES AND OTHERS
Fighting Crime Just Doesn't Pay. Ask a Policeman.

Warsaw, September 9 — A few weeks ago, the police here went to war against one of the roving gangs of pickpockets that prowl the cavernous main train station.

It was a rout. Within minutes, the officers were repulsed by thieves wielding guns armed with paralyzing gas and wooden planks ripped from the station's seats. Only 2 people in a crowd of about 20 combatants were arrested; a policeman was hospitalized after a pitched battle that began on the train platforms and continued in front of the train station.

The Polish police were once a hated and feared extension of this country's security apparatus. But these days, the combined effect of low starting salaries, retirements and the dismissal of thousands of former Communists has left the local police demoralized and undermanned.

Across the country the police forces are looking for a few good men, and so far, they haven't found many.

"It's not so simple to get people to work for us," said Jan Tarasiewicz, a spokesman for the Warsaw Police. "We know that the salaries are not competitive—it's $110 to $120 a month. Would anyone in the United States want to put his life in danger for that kind of money?"

The Butt of Jokes

Mr. Tarasiewicz said there were 9,500 policemen in Warsaw, about 4,000 below what is considered a full complement.

Police officers say the problems of recruitment stem from more than just the low salary. Under the Communists, the police were frequently used for political purposes, including, beating street demonstrators. In retaliation, popular culture made the police the butt of dozens of subversive jokes that variously depicted them as stupid and corrupt.

This summer, in an effort to burnish the image of the police, the Government changed the name of the police from "milicja," or militia, to "policja." Shortly afterward, the Warsaw police opened a recruitment office for two weeks on a downtown thoroughfare.

With jobs scarce in Poland, more than 2,000 filled out applications, but only about 150 met the age, education and health requirements, and the recruiters said they encountered a lot of skepticism.

Crime Is on the Rise

"It's going to take years to rebuild the authority of the police," said Anna Napieraj-Zolunek of the Warsaw police. "The criminals are brave right now because they're not afraid of the police. The usual behavior of hooligans when they are caught is to yell, 'I'm being beaten by the police.' People come to his side immediately."

The recruitment center was reopened this month with an added inducement: young people facing military service can volunteer instead for jobs with the police.

Government statistics suggest that the shortage of police officers is having an effect.

In the first six months of this year, crime was up 69 percent, with theft the most frequently reported offense. Handguns and gas guns are now routinely available in shops in the major cities, but the levels of violent crime remain well below those of the major American cities.

From January to July, this nation of 38 million people had 236 murders, up 12 percent from the same period last year.

For many years, crime in Poland was as much a political issue as a problem of law enforcement. One often-repeated criticism of the Western countries, as churned out by the propaganda machine, was that the rapacious capitalist system forced millions to become criminals.

Westerners, so the propaganda went, might live a bit better, but they faced constant fear that a thief would take away their precious money or their life.

Many Crimes Ignored

Crime was rare in this workers' paradise, it was argued, because everyone's material needs were taken care of by the state. On those rare occasions when someone did lose their head and break the law, they were inevitably rounded up by a police force that was said to combine the brains of Sherlock Holmes with the brawn of Dirty Harry.

Consider the crime statistics for 1989, the last year of Communist rule. According to the Warsaw newspaper Gazeta Wyborcza, the police said that 100 percent of reported crimes were solved nationwide.

People who lived here always knew that this was nonsense, and these days police veterans acknowledge the obvious: For years, they routinely ignored many crimes because they were ordered to concentrate on political investigations, like the surveillance of Solidarity members or the clandestine press.

"For them, it was more important to catch a few leaflets than protect the citizen in the street," said Mr. Tarasiewicz, the police spokesman.

The central train station, across the street from Warsaw's towering new Marriott Hotel, is one of the more dangerous spots in the city. Last month, the husband of an American Peace Corps volunteer in Poland was attacked by several thieves, sprayed with mace, and beaten so severely that his leg was broken.

The problems at the train station appear to stem from the manpower shortage. A total of 37 people are assigned to the station; a police officer said 75 is the minimum required.

Most of those assigned there are actually young high-school graduates who are doing the work as an alternative to military service. Such temporary policemen receive only four months' training. They carry nightsticks and Polish-made gas grenades that, in the words of one policeman, "are likely to harm only ourselves." The pickpockets are armed with French gas pistols that can be fired from long distance.

One policeman who declined to give his name said the professional police officers responsible for the station stay in their offices and seldom visit the train platforms where the thieves ply their trade.

"We just walk up and down the platform," he said. "There are too few of us and the pickpockets don't give a damn about us."

Source: Stephen Engelberg, *The New York Times,* International, September 10, 1990. Copyright © 1990 by The New York Times Company. Reprinted by permission.

economic holdings permit the bourgeoisie to accumulate vast amounts of wealth at the expense of the proletariat who lead lives of poverty and despair. Because their economic interests are different and incompatible, these two groups are locked in a continuing, antagonistic relationship, or class struggle. This struggle between the capitalist and proletariat classes produces crime.

Marxist criminologist Richard Quinney (1977) asserted that class conflict even determines what types of crimes the two groups will commit. Members of the capitalist class commit crimes of "domination and repression." These are motivated by the desire (1) to extract as much money as possible from the lower classes, and (2) to prevent the proletariat from disrupting society, and challenging the position and power of the bourgeoisie. The proletariat, meanwhile, engage in crimes of "accommodation and resistance." These are primarily motivated by a desire to survive in a repressive society, and the frustration, rage, and anguish resulting from this repression.

For Quinney (1977) and other Marxist criminologists, crime in a capitalist society like the United States is not a disease, but a symptom. The real disease is the unequal distribution of wealth and power that results in poverty, unemployment, and the economic crisis of the capitalist state. The economic crisis inherent in capitalism is the real cause of crime. This is why Marxist sociologists do not focus on criminal behavior per se, but rather on how criminal laws come into being, whose interest they serve, and how they are applied. Quinney (1970) called crime a "social reality" in that it is created by people in society. That is, criminal definitions (laws) are made by the capitalist class and enforced by their agents (police, judges, prison personnel).

It follows from Quinney's analysis that the behavior of rich and powerful people (those who directly or indirectly make the laws) is less likely to be defined as criminal than the behavior of relatively powerless numbers of the lower classes. That is why prisons are disproportionately filled with African Americans and Hispanics who commit street crimes, as opposed to affluent Caucasian males who engage in various forms of corporate and white-collar crime.

For Marxist sociologists, there is only one solution to the crime problem: the end of capitalism. Since the unequal distribution of wealth and the resulting class struggle are inherent in capitalism, the system cannot be salvaged. Capitalism generates racism, sexism, and myriad social injustices, all of which directly or indirectly cause crime. The answer to the crime problem is a society established along socialist principles of criminal justice, a system that satisfies the needs of all members of society.

Social Control Theories Social control theorists approach the phenomenon of deviance from yet another perspective, asking, "Why *don't* people engage in deviant behavior?" From this point of view the deviant motivation leading to rule-violating behavior that other theories (anomie theory, differential association) see as problematic, or try to explain, is taken as a given. In his containment theory, Walter Reckless (1967) observed that individuals are under pressure to engage in deviant behavior by factors such as poverty, unemployment and economic insecurity, and minority group status. They are also pulled or drawn into nonconforming activity by delinquent and criminal subcultures, deviant groups, and the portrayal (glorification?) of deviant activity by the mass media. A final impetus is internal psychological pushes such as feelings of hostility, aggressiveness, rebellion, need for immediate gratification, and inferiority "which batter the self" (Reckless, 1967, p. 480).

People avoid rule-violating activity to the extent that these pressures and pulls to deviate are held in check or contained. For Reckless, a barrier of *outer containment* consisting of supportive family and friends, responsible supervision, and reasonable expectations can prevent people from engaging in deviant behavior. Factors such as ego strength, a positive self-image, and high frustration tolerance are part of a barrier of *inner containment.* Psychological pushes are often "too strong for the self to handle or for nuclear groups such as the family to contain" (Reckless, 1967, p. 480). The result is deviant behavior.

Sociologist Travis Hirschi (1969) maintained that delinquent behavior is minimized or avoided in those youths who are bonded strongly to society. Social bonding consists of four elements. Strong *attachment* to family, teachers, and law-abiding friends is especially important. It is through these relations that children accept the values and norms of society as well as develop a social conscience. *Commitment* means embracing conventional activities such as studying, working hard, and saving money for the future. The more that youths are committed to mainstream values and goals in society, the less likely they are to engage in deviant behavior. *Involvement* refers to the expenditure of time and energy in conventional behavior. The more time and energy expended on nondeviant activities, the less likely an individual will be to engage in rule-violating behavior. *Belief* in commonly held values, such as respect for the police and for the law, bonds individuals to the rules of the larger society and reinforces the legitimacy of that society. These four bonds are analytically distinct, although they are interrelated in the real world.

Control theories of deviance focus on the clash between deviant motivation and the extent to which this motivation is held in check by an individual's commitment to societal values and norms, and integration into various nondeviant groups. From this perspective, the maximization of internal (psychological) and external (social) controls will be more effective in reducing deviant (especially criminal) behavior than any attempt to decrease deviant motivation, which is much less amenable to our control.

DEVIANT AND CRIMINAL BEHAVIOR

How Much Deviance?

Published annually by the Federal Bureau of Investigation, the *Uniform Crime Report* (UCR) is the best known and most widely used source of criminal statistics. Approximately 15,000 law enforcement agencies throughout the United States voluntarily send the FBI crime reports on a quarterly basis. These statistics are not a measure of all the crime that occurs in the United States annually, but rather those crimes known to police. The UCR gives detailed information on four violent crimes—murder, robbery, rape, and aggravated assault—and three property crimes—burglary, larceny-theft, and motor vehicle theft. Usually referred to as the *index crimes,* these seven offenses are expressed in terms of the total number of crimes committed in a particular area (city, state, region, nation) and a crime rate. For example, in 1989, 14,251,400 index crimes in the United States were known to police. The *crime rate* is the number of crimes committed per 100,000 population. Table 8.2 indicates that in 1989 5,741 index crimes were committed for every 100,000 people.

Crime rates allow us to compare rates of criminal activity in cities and states of various sizes. For example, common sense would tell us that Los Angeles had more index crimes than a city one-tenth its size. However, by computing a rate of criminal activity, we might find that the smaller city had a much higher crime rate (number of crimes per 100,000 population) than Los Angeles did. Using crime rates we can also compare rates of criminal activity across time as the population of cities, states, and the nation changes. Table 8.2 shows that the rate of violent crime in the United States went up from 556.6 in 1985 to 663.1 in 1989, an increase of 19 percent in five years.

The UCR has been criticized (especially by Marxist sociologists) because it is primarily a count of street crimes committed by the lower classes and excludes white-collar offenses more likely to be committed by middle- and upper-class individuals. As a result, the crime problem in the United States is typically reported and viewed by the public as a series of offenses committed by the poor. The UCR also undercounts the frequency of crime. Hundreds of thousands of people do not call the police when they are victimized, for a variety of reasons, including fear and hatred of the police, fear of reprisal from the offender, and a belief that the police can do little if anything to rectify the problem (apprehend the offender, retrieve their stolen property).

To learn more about crime victims (who they are, what happened to them, why they do not always contact the police, etc.), the National Crime Survey (NCS) was begun in 1972. Also known as a *victimization survey,* it is a survey of 60,000 households containing about 136,000 people. Household members over twelve years of age are interviewed twice a year and asked how many times in the past six months they have been victims of specific crimes. On the basis of these findings, projections are made regarding the total number of victimizations for a select number of crimes every year. Data from a recent NCS indicate that approximately thirty-four million crimes and attempted crimes occurred in 1986, or 2.57 times as many as reported by the UCR. The NCS data reveal that blacks are more likely to be victimized than whites, and the unemployed and poor more than working individuals. Males are much more likely to

252   Chapter 8 Crime, Deviance, and Social Control

TABLE 8.2   Index of Crimes, United States, 1980–1989

Population	Crime Index Total	Violent Crime	Property Crime
TOTAL NUMBER OF REPORTED CRIMES, 1980–1988			
Population by year			
1980 – 225,349,264	13,408,300	1,344,520	12,063,700
1981 – 229,146,000	13,423,800	1,361,820	12,061,900
1982 – 231,534,000	12,947,400	1,322,390	11,652,000
1983 – 233,981,000	12,108,600	1,258,090	10,850,500
1984 – 236,158,000	11,881,800	1,273,280	10,608,500
1985 – 238,740,000	12,431,400	1,328,800	11,102,600
1986 – 241,077,000	13,211,900	1,489,170	11,722,700
1987 – 243,400,000	13,508,700	1,484,000	12,024,700
1988 – 245,807,000	13,923,100	1,566,220	12,356,900
1989 – 248,239,000	14,251,400	1,646,040	12,605,400
Percentage change:			
Number of offenses			
1989/1988	+ 2.4	+ 5.1	+ 2.0
1989/1985	+14.6	+23.9	+ 13.5
1989/1980	+ 6.3	+22.4	+ 4.5
NUMBER OF CRIMES PER 100,000 INHABITANTS, 1980–1989			
Year			
1980	5,950.0	596.6	5,353.3
1981	5,858.2	594.3	5,263.9
1982	5,603.6	571.1	5,032.5
1983	5,175.0	537.7	4,637.4
1984	5,031.3	539.2	4,492.1
1985	5,207.1	556.6	4,650.5
1986	5,480.4	617.7	4,862.6
1987	5,550.0	609.7	4,940.3
1988	5,664.2	637.2	5,027.1
1989	5,741.0	633.1	5,077.9
Percentage change: Rate			
per 100,000 inhabitants			
1989/1988	+ 1.4	+ 4.1	+1.0
1989/1985	+10.3	+19.1	+9.2
1989/1980	− 3.5	+11.1	−5.1

Source: Federal Bureau of Investigation, U.S. Department of Justice, 1989, *Uniform Crime Report,* Washington, D.C.: U.S. Government Printing Office.

be the victims of violent crimes than women, and the elderly are *less* likely to be victimized than people of any other age group (Bartollas and Dinitz, 1989).

The final mechanism for gathering information about crime in society is the *self-report study.* People are asked to reveal their involvement in certain types of criminal and deviant activities; for example, the number of times they used illegal drugs, cheated on their income tax, were engaged in domestic violence, and were driving while intoxicated. Self-report studies are especially important in addressing questions concerning the relationship between social status and crime. Do people in the lower classes really commit more crimes (as indicated by arrest rates and the prison population) than individuals in the middle and upper classes? What offenses do people in the middle and upper classes commit? What types of offenses are class linked and which are not? The linkages between social class and crime are discussed in the following section.

The Offenders

Information regarding the composition of the criminal population in the United States is incomplete and limited primarily to street criminals who are arrested or incarcerated for index crimes. Since the criminal justice system (police, courts, prisons) spends such a small portion of its time and resources investigating and prosecuting white-collar crime, we know relatively little about the individuals who commit these offenses. The following is a profile of criminal offenders in the United States. Keep in mind that these observations are based primarily on street criminals, and then only on a fraction of that population. Approximately one of every five index crimes known to police results in an arrest.

Gender   Men commit more crimes than women. This is true not only in the United States but in "all nations, all communities within a nation, all age groups, all periods of history for which data are available" (Sutherland and Cressey, 1970, p. 126). In 1988, 82 percent of the people arrested were males. Men also are much more likely to be arrested for serious crimes such as murder, robbery, assault, and burglary. Arrest records as well as data from jails and prisons suggest that women who commit crimes are typically involved in property offenses such as larceny, forgery, and drug offenses. After reviewing forty-four self-report studies, researchers concluded that males were engaged in significantly more street crimes (especially those of a serious nature) than women (Smith and Visher, 1980). Males also have a "virtual monopoly" on the commission of organized, corporate, and political crime in the United States (Beirne and Messerschmidt, 1991).

Age   Crime is overwhelmingly a youthful activity. In 1988 approximately 60 percent of all those arrested in connection with the seven index crimes were under twenty-five year of age, and 31 percent were under age eighteen. However, victimization studies indicate that youths under eighteen commit fewer serious crimes than adults. After age twenty-four arrest rates drop sharply and continue to fall until they are negligible for people sixty-five and over.

This decline in the crime rate as people age is called *aging out* (Siegel, 1989). Wilson and Herrnstein (1985) noted that after the transition from adolescence to adulthood "one would expect crime to subside" (p. 147). Whereas young people often commit crimes for money, sex, alcohol, and status, they have access to these things as adults. At the same time, social and psychological reinforcers for not committing crime increase as people marry, have a family, and are integrated into the larger community. Sociologists Hirshi and Gottfredson (1983) rejected the "life-course" explanation, however, stating that as plausible as this interpretation may sound, rates of crime decrease as people grow older regardless of whether or not these events occur. Wilson and Herrnstein (1985) also believed that as people age and mature they become much better at delaying gratification; that is, the need to have one's desires and wants satisfied immediately diminishes. Older people are less hedonistic than younger individuals and "their time horizons extend further into the future" (p. 147).

Race and Ethnicity   Of the people arrested in 1988 for all crimes, 69 percent were white and 30 percent were black. In 1984 blacks made up 40 percent of all jail inmates and 46 percent of the state and federal prison population. Hispanic Americans (who may be either black or white) comprised approximately 13 percent of all those arrested in 1988. The percentages of blacks arrested and incarcerated are disproportionately high since blacks account for only 13 percent of the U.S. population.

According to Samuel Walker (1989), blacks have such high rates of arrest and imprisonment "because of a bias against crimes committed by lower class people" (p. 250). This bias comes about for the simple reason that individuals generally commit the types of crimes available to them. White business executives commit corporate crimes, and unemployed black youths commit index offenses like burglary and robbery. It is highly unlikely that a Fortune 500 business executive is going to sell crack in an urban ghetto, or that a nineteen-year-old from the inner city will be involved in an antitrust conspiracy to fix the price of airline tickets. However, the criminal justice system does not measure crime (the UCR) in terms of corporate offenses, nor does it vigorously seek out and prosecute white-collar criminals. Inasmuch as the police and courts are primarily interested in controlling street crime, it is hardly surprising that such disproportionate numbers of black Americans are in prison.

Social Class   One of the oldest and most controversial topics in criminology concerns the relation between social class and crime. Official statistics (UCR) have reported consistently that rates of crime and arrest are higher in urban ghettos and lower-class neighborhoods. But do these statistics accurately reflect the true picture? Is there really more crime in lower-class America?

Charles Tittle et al. (1978) reviewed thirty-five studies that examined the relation between social class and crime. They found a very weak association between the two variables and concluded that it was time for researchers to "shift away from class-based theories" (p. 654) of crime. John Braithwaite (1981) examined over 200 studies of social class and crime and concluded that lower-class youths did have higher rates of criminal activity. He also noted that whereas a criminal justice system biased against the lower classes may be a problem in some jurisdictions, "for many courts and police departments this bias may be minimal or nonexistent" (p. 40). Therefore, it would be a mistake for sociologists to move away from class-based theories of criminality. The contradictory findings of these two studies can be at least partially explained by methodological problems of social research, including the measurement of social class and some types of crime, but they do indicate that the class-crime question has yet to be resolved.

Sexual Deviance

In the time of Christ there were 36,000 *registered* prostitutes in Rome. By the late Middle Ages, the profession was firmly entrenched in European society and attempts to eliminate it were abandoned (Little, 1989). Today, it abounds in both the developed and developing nations of the world. Economist Helen Reynolds (1986) examined the economic stratification of prostitutes in the United States. The approximate costs of a prostitute's services in 1983 dollars could easily be doubled in the 1990s. Large cities generally have most, if not all, of the following categories of prostitutes.

- *Streetwalkers* These women make contact with customers (Johns, tricks, dates) by walking back and forth over a given territory ("stroll") and soliciting pedestrians or men in cars. A high proportion of these prostitutes are poor, black women. The sexual act takes place in the customer's car, an alley, doorway, or cheap motel. Prices range from $10 to $50.

- *Masseuses* Working out of massage parlors, these prostitutes typically offer manual and oral stimulation, services that cost between $20 and $50 as set by management. Individuals can make extra money by providing other sexual acts.

- *Escorts* These women are assigned to a customer through an escort service. The sex act usually takes place in the customer's home or a hotel. Prices may be negotiated between the escort and the man ($50 to $100 plus).

- *Bar girls* These women solicit their own customers in bars. With experience, they become adept at avoiding men who may harm them, as well as undercover vice officers ($20 to $100 plus).

- *Call girls* At the top of the prostitution hierarchy, these women are usually well educated and very attractive. Contacts are made by telephone. Customers usually are successful professionals who can afford to pay the minimum $100 fee for services.

Prostitutes live in a dangerous world. Most are at constant risk of being physically abused by customers, arrested by the police, and infected with sexually transmitted diseases, particularly acquired immunodeficiency syndrome (AIDS). Streetwalkers are especially vulnerable when they get into a car with an unknown "John." For example, between 1977 and 1989, forty-five black, drug-using prostitutes were stabbed and strangled in Kansas City. In San Diego, dozens of prostitutes have been killed in the past few years. The number of women turning to this occupation in order to support a crack cocaine habit has increased so dramatically that in some areas of Kansas City they are turning tricks for as little as $3.50 (Turque and Hammill, 1989).

In many developing nations, prostitution is a major growth industry. For example, the tourist city of Bangkok, Thailand, is estimated to have 100,000 prostitutes. With high rates of unemployment, young women and girls with few if any skills may have little choice but to enter this field. With half the world's women predicted to be living in urban areas by the year 2000, the number of prostitutes in developing nations will only increase (Shaw, 1987).

Working for as little as the cost of a bottle of soft drink, these women and girls in developing nations are both victims and major transmitters of AIDS. "It is estimated that some 25–60 percent of Nairobi's 10,000 prostitutes are infected, and in one slum where prostitutes average 1,000 partners a year, the estimated figure is as high as 80 percent" (Shaw, 1987). The prevalence of AIDS among prostitutes in other African cities, as well as some urban areas in Brazil, is also high.

In the United States, the percentage of prostitutes infected with the virus that causes AIDS is much lower, especially among those who are not intravenous drug users. Two facts explain why AIDS is only rarely spread from prostitutes to their customers: almost all prostitutes use condoms, and the disease is not easily transmitted through vaginal and oral heterosexual intercourse (Goode, 1990).

Social scientists have tried to discover why women become prostitutes, and engage in an activity that is considered so deviant. *Psychological approaches* typically examine the personality and life histories of these women (Perry and Perry, 1976). A number of studies have found that prostitutes come from dysfunctional families. As children many of them were sexually abused and battered. Of 153 New York City prostitutes interviewed, 139 "were seriously abused in one way or another" (Zausner, 1986, p. 5). *Sociological approaches* seek to discover the motivation for, as well as the process involved in, becoming a prostitute. Davis (1971) offered a three-stage model whereby women drift from promiscuity, to exchanging sex for money occasionally, to the final stage of full-fledged prostitution. An additional economic explanation is survival, which appears to be a major reason for adopting this lifestyle for tens of thousands of women in developing nations.

Homosexuality also has existed in the majority of cultures throughout history (Little, 1989). In some societies this behavior is tolerated, but in others it has been repressed, sometimes violently. Homosexuality is considered deviant behavior in the United States because most people do not approve of it, and their disapproval takes the form of condemnation, stigmatization, and punishment (Goode, 1990).

People typically consider (and react to) an individual's sexual orientation as either heterosexual or homosexual, but this is not always the case. In their famous report on sexuality in the United States, Kinsey and his associates (1948) revealed that almost one-half of American men fell between the group who were exclusively heterosexual and those who were exclusively homosexual. Approximately 37 percent of white American males had at least one homosexual experience between their teenage years and old age.

The prevalence of homosexuality can be especially high in institutions like the military and prisons where individuals are segregated by sex for extended periods of time. Sometimes referred to as *situational homosexuality,* this behavior is more a function of available alternatives than of sexual preference. In prison one has only three choices regarding sexuality: abstinence, masturbation, and homosexuality (Little, 1989). One study found prison homosexuality especially prevalent for females, with over 50 percent of inmates sexually active with other women (Ward and Kassebaum, 1965). Only 5 percent were homosexually active before entering prison.

Efforts to discover the cause(s) of homosexuality, especially one specific reason, have not been successful. *Biological explanations* have focused on chemical or hormonal imbalances; however, results of studies comparing hormone levels of heterosexuals and homosexuals have been inconclusive, contradictory, and methodologically suspect (Nass and Fisher, 1988). *Environmental explanations* concentrate on patterns of childrearing, early sexual experiences, and a variety of other factors that suggest homosexuality is learned behavior. In one large study, researchers conducted in-depth interviews (three to five hours) with 979 homosexual men and women and 477 heterosexual men and women (Bell et al., 1981). Two hundred questions on numerous aspects of these individuals' childhood and adolescent lives and experiences failed to uncover an adequate explanation for sexual preference. Masters et al. (1988) described homosexuality as possibly the result of some complex combination of biological and social factors. Researchers may eventually learn that there are various types of homosexuality, each with a distinct cause.

Since the first AIDS-related death in the United States in 1981, the homosexual community has been hit especially hard by this disease. During the 1980s approximately two-thirds of the people with AIDS were homosexual or bisexual men. The disease is more easily spread through the anal intercourse practiced by many homosexual males than by heterosexual intercourse. In the early years of the disease, the promiscuity of some gay men was partially responsible for its reaching epidemic proportions in some homosexual communities (McKusick et al., 1985). In recent years, however, more homosexual men have been engaging in "safe sex." As a result, the rate of infection with the human immunovirus (which leads to AIDS) has been slowed. Currently, the people among whom the disease is spreading most rapidly are intravenous drug users.

Because of the relatively sparse research in the area and the fact that lesbians often maintain a front of heterosexuality, it is difficult to determine the number of female homosexuals in the United States (Clinard, 1974). According to Kinsey, 13 percent of American women had a homosexual experience to the point of orgasm. Lesbians are tolerated in the United States more than their male counterparts for a number of reasons. Like women in general, they have fewer but longer lasting sexual relationships. They are not as promiscuous as male homosexuals, nor are they generally perceived as unabashedly flaunting their lifestyle. In addition, society is more likely to think of lesbians as being in a state of sexual limbo, "unawakened heterosexually, merely waiting for the right man to appear" (Gagnon and Simon, 1973, p. 177). In other words, these women are considered salvageable, whereas male homosexuals are more apt to be considered a lost cause. Finally, lesbians are not associated in the public mind with the spread of AIDS, sometimes referred to as the "gay plague."

This association of male homosexuality with AIDS is partially responsible for the violent practice called gay bashing. The homosexual population is subjected to more criminal violence in the United States than is the population as a whole (Goode, 1990). One explanation for this is the more conservative social and political mood in the nation beginning in the 1980s. Informal social control in the form of harassment, beatings, and sometimes murder has been investigated and prosecuted with something less than full vigor by formal agents of control, the criminal justice system.

Violence

Of the 14,251,400 index crimes known to police in 1989, approximately 12 percent (1,646,040) were crimes of violence (murder, robbery, rape, aggravated assault). Over 21,000 people were killed, with black Americans hit especially hard. On average, forty-eight of every one hundred victims were white, and forty-nine were African Americans. Homicide was the leading cause of death for black males between fifteen and twenty-four years of age. The southern states have the highest homicide rate in the nation, and large cities have about twice the number of murders than smaller cities and rural America.

Sociologists Luckenbill and Doyle (1989) asked, "What is there about residing in an urban or southern area that generates a high rate of violence?" They noted that a significant number of people in these areas (young, male, lower-income) have a lifestyle characterized by "disputatiousness." These individuals share a culturally transmitted willingness to settle disputes (especially ones perceived as a threat to their masculinity or status) by using physical force. In an earlier, related work, Luckenbill (1977) stated that homicide is the product of a "character contest." During the course of an argument, insults and threats are traded until escalating tension brings the matter to a point of no return, with participants and bystanders agreeing that the "contest" can be resolved only by violence. Obviously, the more often people settle their disputes by physical force, the greater the likelihood that someone will be killed, even if the intent to do so is absent. Many homicides take this form and can be characterized as overly successful aggravated assaults: A wants to hurt B (not kill him), but in the heat of battle and with the use of weapons, B ends up dead.

Rape Rape is a major crime of violence in the United States. Between 1979 and 1985 572,470 rapes were known to police. During that same period, the National Crime Survey estimated that 1,164,560 rapes, or approximately twice the number known to police, had actually occurred. A 1985 report issued by the Bureau of Justice and based on more than 2.6 million interviews yielded the following:

- In 1983, 1 of every 600 women and girls over twelve years of age was a rape victim.
- Eighty-one percent of all victims were white, although black women were significantly more likely to be raped.
- Two of every three rapes involved women between ages sixteen and twenty-four years.
- More than 90 percent of the victims reported incomes below $25,000; half reported family incomes under $10,000.

Date rape is a form of the crime that is prevalent in the United States. Muehlenhard and Linton (1987) interviewed 600 college students and found that almost 15 percent of the women reported having had intercourse against their will. Seven percent of males reported having had intercourse when their dates did not want to have sex. Thirteen percent of female respondents in *Ms.* magazine's 1985 poll of 7,000 students on thirty-five campuses reported that they had been raped. Alex Thio (1988) considered date rape to be so prevalent in our society because it is an extension of a traditional cultural value that "males are expected to be aggressive rather than shy in dealing with females . . ." (p. 140). This value, coupled with the attitude held by a significant number of men *and* women that date rape is not really rape, can only exacerbate the problem.

Gang Violence Long-time student of organized gangs, sociologist Walter Miller (1976, in Wilson and Herrnstein, 1985) argued that these groups account for a significant amount of all violent crime in the United States. After a period of decreased activity in the 1960s (when many leaders were involved in the civil rights and antiwar movements), gang membership and related crimes began to rise in the early 1970s (Siegel, 1989). By the end of the decade gangs were especially numerous in Los Angeles, Chicago, Philadelphia, and New York. In Los Angeles, the two largest ones (Crips and Bloods) have a combined membership of 15,000 youths. Although some street gang members in Los Angeles as in other parts of the country are white, the great majority come from other racial and ethnic groups, such as blacks, Mexicans, Vietnamese, Filipinos, Samoans, Koreans, Jamaicans, Guatemalans, and other recent immigrants to the United States (Vigil, 1988).

Some gangs have become involved in the highly lucrative and dangerous drug trade. Sophisticated distributors in large cities can take in hundreds of millions of dollars a year (Taylor, 1990, in Gwynne, 1990). With incredible amounts of money at stake, heavily armed gang members fight for territory and dominance on city streets. The results of these battles are deaths and injuries equal to those of a small war. In 1990 Los Angeles averaged one gang-related homicide a day, with as many as ten people (often innocent bystanders) killed in a single weekend. Less affluent gang members have robbed and occasionally killed people for high-priced, high-status athletic shoes and jackets. One researcher argued that these individuals have a distorted version of the American success dream (Taylor, 1990, in Gwynne, 1990). Like Merton's innovators, they accept societal goals but reject the means for achieving them. Gang members want immediate recognition and financial rewards, and are willing to kill to attain them.

Family Violence   Although most people may equate violence with street crime and fear the knife-wielding mugger, rapist, and gang member, evidence indicates "a person is more likely to be assaulted by a family member than by a stranger" (Goode, 1990, p. 215). The 1990 U.S. Advisory Board on Child Abuse and Neglect stated that the number of *reported* cases of child abuse reached 2.4 million in 1989. "Each year, hundreds of thousands of children are being starved and abandoned, burned and severely beaten, raped and sodomized, berated and belittled" (in Cimons, 1990). These findings are indicative of an additional problem in that abused children often grow up to be violent adults. Gelles (1980) reported, "One of the most consistent conclusions of domestic violence research is that individuals who have experienced violent and abusive childhoods are more likely to grow up and become child abusers than individuals who have experienced little or no violence in their childhood" (p. 878).

Family violence often follows domestic power relations: the husband beats the wife who in turn abuses the children, the older children learn to hit their younger siblings, and the family pet ends up as the ultimate victim (Gelles, in Anderson, 1983). Animal-protection groups in some cities disclosed an increase in cruelty to animals, and interpreted this behavior in terms of family violence and child abuse, according to a 1990 report on National Public Radio. Violence in the family also can run contrary to traditional power relations, with husbands being abused by wives, and parents and grandparents victimized by their children.

White-Collar Crime

The two forms of *white-collar crime* are occupational and organizational (Clinard, 1983). **Occupational crime** is committed by individuals or small groups of people in connection with their work. These offenses are not limited to businessmen and high-status professionals (physicians, attorneys, politicians, etc.), and can be committed in one form or another by almost anyone who is employed. Gerald Mars (1983, and in Barlow, 1990) devised an interesting and useful typology of occupational crime based on a number of factors in the workplace. Most people who commit work-related crimes ("fiddles") can be placed into one of four categories.

1. *Hawk jobs*   Hawks have a good deal of freedom concerning how and when they do their jobs, and are not constantly under the supervision of bosses, owners, and regulatory agencies. Occupations in this category include owner-operator cab drivers, independent salespeople, owners of small businesses, lawyers, doctors, and university professors. The favorite fiddles or crimes of hawks are padding expense accounts and charging for work never performed.

2. *Donkey jobs*   Assembly-line workers, supermarket clerks, and retail salespeople all have occupations in this category. Donkeys take advantage of the fact that they are not continually watched by management and perform repetitive tasks. A typical donkey crime is committed by the cashier who sells a $10 item, rings up $5 on the register, and pockets the difference.

3. *Wolfpack jobs*   Wolves operate in packs and are found in occupations where people work in teams or crews such as longshoremen, miners, garbage collectors,

fishermen, and prison guards. The wolfpack has access to property (longshoremen) or a situation that can be used to their financial benefit. Prison guards who sell contraband to inmates would be an example of the latter.

4. *Vultures* Truck and taxi-cab drivers, postal delivery people, and many service and sales jobs are in this category. In their jobs "competition hinges around good routes and bad routes; good territories and less good; preferred 'stations' or tables and those waiters despise" (Mars, 1983, p. 163). Because the jobs are unstable and competitive, and paychecks can vary significantly from week to week, vultures supplement their incomes by fiddling. One driver in Mars's study used the company truck to sell black-market clothing as well as make his regular deliveries.

Like other law violators, people who commit occupational crimes engage in a form of mental gymnastics or rationalization whereby they convince themselves (and others) that their behavior is "noncriminal" and "necessary" (Clinard, 1974; Cressey, 1953). These individuals "neutralize" the laws they violate by using a number of rationalizations (Sykes and Matza, 1957). Justifications in the form of "the company can afford it," "they owe me that much and more," and "everybody does it" allow them to maintain a positive self-image in spite of their criminal activity.

Organizational crimes are offenses committed by individuals or groups to further the goals of a particular organization. **Corporate crime** is a type of organizational crime committed by officials for their corporations, and also includes the crimes of the corporation itself (Clinard and Quinney, 1973). According to Clinard and Yeager (1983), two of the foremost authorities in the area of corporate crime, three industries seem to violate government regulations and laws more than any others. The oil industry has been involved in the restriction of independent dealers, excessive profits, contrived shortages, misleading advertising, and interlocking directorates. The auto industry has engaged in deceptive advertising, unreliable warranties, unfair dealer relations, and violations of safety standards. The pharmaceutical industry has been guilty of false advertising, inferior product quality, improper research and inspection, and excessive markups.

Corporate crime not only costs consumers hundreds of billions of dollars each year, but also threatens the public's health and safety. For example, between 1942 and 1953 the Hooker Chemical Company dumped 20,000 tons of toxic chemical waste into the Love Canal in Niagara Falls, New York. After the company sold it to the city for one dollar, a playground, grammar school, and apartment complex were built on the dump site. When poisonous material seeped to the surface in 1977, tests revealed the presence of twelve carcinogenic chemicals, including one of the deadliest toxins ever made — dioxin (Simon and Eitzen, 1986).

Drug Abuse

Historian and physician David Musto (in Kagan, 1989) stated that the current crack cocaine epidemic is but the latest drug crisis to occur in the United States. These epidemics follow a cycle of predictable events that play themselves out over a number of years. The drug crisis of the 1980s and 1990s, therefore, is similar to the cocaine era that began in the 1880s, and the marijuana-hallucinogen years of the 1960s.

In the initial phase of the cycle, one or more drugs are "discovered" and considered harmless (if not beneficial) by responsible people. In the absence of proof to the contrary from medical experts, the drugs are generally accepted and used by a significant portion of the population. As a result of deaths and a rising crime rate, health

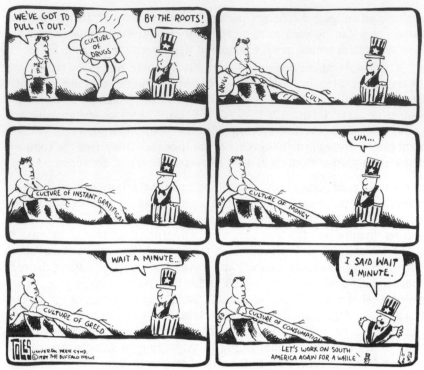

The production, distribution, and consumption of drugs is related to some fundamental American values. Therefore, any significant, long-term reduction in drug use will be difficult to accomplish. (Toles © 1990. The Buffalo News. Reprinted with permission of Universal Press Syndicate. All rights reserved.)

officials reevaluate the harmful effects of drugs. The weight of changing public opinion and accumulated scientific evidence begins to stem the use of drugs. At this point in the cycle people start to associate drug use with the lower classes as well as racial and ethnic minorities, regardless of the truth of this association. Drug use becomes a powerful symbol of evil, and increasingly differentiates middle-class America from the hated and feared lower-class minorities (in Kagan, 1989).

Some have argued that drug use is an inevitable consequence of human nature. Psychopharmacologist Ronald K. Siegel stated, "I have come to the view that humans have a need—perhaps even a drive—to alter their state of consciousness from time to time" (in Beaty, 1989, p. 58). Donald X. Freeman, an expert on substance abuse policy, thinks that drugs have such a powerful allure simply because they make people feel so good (Parachini, 1986). Even if this practice does have a biological basis, it does not negate the fact that people learn how to use and abuse drugs; they do not instinctively smoke crack or know how to free-base cocaine. In addition, a biological explanation in and of itself does not tell us why the rate of drug use varies so dramatically both between and within cultures, and from one historical period to the next. Any biological drive toward mind-altering substances would have to be extremely malleable and susceptible to social pressures, values, and norms to account for the fundamental observation that tens of millions of peoples do not use drugs.

The long use and transitory acceptance of drugs as outlined by Musto (in Kagan, 1989) has led to hundreds of studies conducted in an effort to discover why people use and abuse mind-altering substances. Although the results have been varied and at times contradictory one general and important finding has emerged: drug use, at least initially, is learned behavior. Even if there is such a thing as an addictive personality, individuals must learn where to buy drugs and how to use them, as well as how to rationalize such use to themselves and others. We know that some of these attitudes and patterns of behavior are learned in ghettos, in middle-class neighborhoods, and in corporate boardrooms. With users from all social classes, and every racial and ethnic background and occupation, it is evident that people use and deal drugs for a number of reasons: because they do not have enough money or have too much; because they are attempting to escape painful situations or seek adventure; because they are depressed or overjoyed, bored or have too much to do. Regardless of whether people are pushed by emotional problems or pulled by the allure of money and excitement, drug use is learned and reinforced in a social context (Bryjak, 1990).

Statistics reveal that the number of people who admit to having used an illegal drug in the past thirty days decreased from 23 million in 1985 to 14.5 million in 1988. Unfortunately, frequent users of cocaine (once a week or more) went from 647,000 to 862,000 — a 33 percent increase — during this same period, and daily users increased 18.6 percent — 246,000 to 292,000. Habitual users are of concern because they are thought to engage in a disproportionate amount of antisocial and criminal behavior. Although the causal link is as yet uncertain (Siegel, 1989), the number of people who test positive for drugs at the time of their arrest is high. A 1988 study by the National Institute of Justice of sixteen of the largest cities in the United States found that the number of males who had traces of drugs in their system at the time of arrest ranged

The United States has attempted a number of strategies to stop the flow of drugs coming into the country. None of them have been very successful. (Toles © 1990. The Buffalo News. Reprinted with permission of Universal Press Syndicate. All rights reserved.)

from 56 percent in Phoenix to 84 percent in Philadelphia. A 1988 survey of inmates of state correctional facilities discovered that in the month before their current offense, 43 percent of the prisoners were using drugs on a daily or near daily basis (Innes, 1988).

Discussions about solutions to the country's drug problem usually end up in a debate over *decriminalization*—the reduction or elimination of penalties for using drugs. For example, decriminalization might involve the imposition of fines or medical treatment for using drugs instead of arrest and criminal prosecution (Galliher, 1989). Advocates of decriminalization such as political scientist Ethan Nadelmann (1990) believe their strategy would result in "substantial reductions in drug-related crime and violence; diminished opportunities for organized and unorganized criminals; substantial savings in criminal justice costs; reduced risks of overdoses, hepatitis, AIDS and other illnesses that result from adulterated and dangerous means of drug consumption . . . substantial opportunities for tax revenue from legal sales of psychoactive drugs and so on" (p. 135).

Opponents argue that the fundamental problem with drugs is not their legality or illegality, but that they destroy people (Decter, 1990). Decriminalization is an illogical, unworkable, and monumental mistake that would only result in more drug use, misery, and death. Drug laws not only specify a range of punishments for their violation, but partially define and declare a society's values. Decriminalization would send the wrong message to people, especially adolescents, that drug use was not only permissable, but morally acceptable. James Jacobs (1990) wondered what would happen if the federal government got into the drug business: "Deciding which drugs to sell might pose problems. For example, would the government sell a drug whose addictive properties are as strong as crack? If it didn't would a black market for such a drug be created?" (p. 137).

Crime in the Third World

Ample evidence supports the contention that crime trends in nations throughout the world over the past 200 years reveal a "generally consistent response to the process of development" (Shelley, 1981, p. 137). Global-historical patterns of crime indicate that both the *process* and *achievement* of development are highly conducive to criminality. Not only will rates of crime in emerging countries increase and begin to approach those of industrialized nations, but the patterns of criminality in the former will begin to resemble the latter. For example, between 1970 and 1975, crime rates in developing nations were approximately 40 percent of those in developed countries and increasing at a faster rate. Rates of criminal activity are escalating in modernizing nations for all offenses, especially drug-related crimes and property crimes involving violence (Shelley, 1981).

Most of this criminal activity is located in metropolitan areas. There are a number of reasons for this upsurge in crime. Rural-to-urban migration has brought about the relocation of tens of millions of high-crime-risk young males from the countryside to the city. Urban centers, especially the largest cities, become focal points of a nation's foreign investment and industrial expansion. They are centers of wealth and offer the greatest opportunity for committing a wide range of offenses, most notably property crimes. "Consequently, such huge cities as Bombay, Calcutta, Bangkok, Seoul, Manila, Caracas, Bogota, Mexico City, Cairo, Lagos, Abidjan, and Nairobi experience far higher—and more sharply rising—crime rates than their respective countries national averages" (Clinard, 1983, p. 597). In addition, because there is so much poverty in cities of the developing nations, virtually anything and everything is of value to somebody. Clinard (1983) noted, "Even the simplest object—a used shirt, an iron pipe, a light bulb—can mean money to its possessor because the potential market for any stolen goods is far greater than in most developed countries" (p. 598). Finally, the increasing demand for prestige articles leads people to steal items that enhance their status and "sense of modernization" (Clinard and Abbott, 1977).

The explanation that patterns and rates of criminality in modernizing countries follow a universal pattern of development was sharply criticized by Marxist criminologists John Horton and Tony Platt (1986). For example, they maintained that Brazil's exceptionally high rate of crime has more to do with multinational corporations keeping labor costs low in a repressive political state than that country passing through a "dangerous transition period" of development. They questioned whether Cuba's seemingly low rate of criminality (lower than the United States') was a function of a rural, relatively underdeveloped population, or the result of "socialist construction." For Horton and Platt, just as there are numerous roads to modernization, there are different patterns of criminality at the state level. According to these authors, most comparative criminologists are committed to the idea of a global pattern of crime and development because of their capitalist political ties and biases.

Conflict sociologists also note that Third World nations are increasingly victimized by illegal and unethical behavior on the part of large corporations in the developed world. Through a process called **corporate dumping,** hazardous products that have been banned, not yet approved for sale, or strictly regulated in developed nations, are sold (dumped) in emerging nations. The following are examples of corporate dumping.

- After the Dalkon Shield intrauterine device killed at least seventeen women in the United States, the manufacturer withdrew the product from domestic markets and sold it overseas (Simon and Eitzen, 1986).
- Winstrol, a synthetic male hormone that retards growth in children, is widely available in Brazil where it is sold as an appetite stimulant (Simon and Eitzen, 1986).
- Depo-Provera, an injectionable contraceptive that was banned in the United States because it caused malignant tumors in beagles and monkeys, is sold by Upjohn Company in seventy countries (Simon and Eitzen, 1986).
- In an effort to circumvent safety regulations and save high disposal costs, companies in the industrialized world have been illegally dumping hazardous waste material in developing nations. An Italian waste-disposal firm unloaded 8,000 barrels of highly toxic waste, and 150 tons of polychlorinated byphenyls (PCBs) on the shores of a fishing village in Nigeria. "Visitors to the site described conditions worse than anyone's imagination" (French, 1990, p. 12).
- Two British researchers estimated that, in 1988, Western corporations dumped more than twenty-four million tons of hazardous waste in West Africa alone (French, 1990).

Not only does corporate dumping endanger the health and safety of poor, uninformed people in developing nations, but when these practices are eventually uncovered, they contribute to anti-American sentiment (Simon and Eitzen, 1986). In the long run this can only be detrimental to our foreign policy and trade relations with developing countries. In the short run some corporate dumping has a dangerous boomerang effect. According to the U.S. General Accounting Office, about 25 percent of the 400 to 600 million pounds of pesticides exported annually by the United States are either banned or severely restricted for domestic use (French, 1990). These agents are sprayed on fruits and vegetables later exported to the United States and available in supermarkets across the country. This phenomenon is often referred to as "the circle of poison."

FOCUS ON
MEXICO

CRIME AND DEVIANCE IN MEXICO: THE CURE IS WORSE THAN THE DISEASE

The pre-Spanish Aztec culture had an unusually severe set of punishments for those who violated societal laws. Robbery, the theft of corn (the staple of life in Aztec society), stealing in the market place, and murder were all capital offenses. Sex crimes were also serious violations and were dealt with harshly. Those found guilty of incest were hung, and adulterers usually had their heads crushed by a stone. In deference to their gender, female adulterers were strangled before being stoned (Johns, 1978). Although justice in Aztec society was severe, it tended to be egalitarian. If anything, perpetrators in the upper classes received harsher punishment than the peasants. Once the Indians were subjugated by the conquistadors, however, their lives came under the strict control of Spanish friars. Idleness, drunkenness, and other forms of moral apathy were punished by whippings, various forms of religious penance, and temporary incarceration.

With independence in 1810, and the end of almost 300 years of Spanish rule, Mexico was still a vast and vicious frontier country. Cumberland (1968, in Johns, 1978) noted that "highwaymen and robbers were everywhere and people felt they were never safe" (p. 57). A hundred years later, the Revolution of 1910 claimed approximately one million lives and was marked by "wholesale murder, pillage, theft, and rape" (p. 59). The nation's political struggle often served as a pretext for several types of banditry and the settling of old scores. By 1929 and the end of almost twenty years of fighting and political intrigue, power was firmly in the hands of the National Revolutionary Party (PRI). The new government hammered out a "confused and convoluted" system of federal courts, state courts, and civil laws that was heavily influenced by the Spanish tradition of civil law and the thinking of French legal scholars (Johns, 1978).

Complete crime statistics for Mexico are not available, and even the International Police Association (INTERPOL) has almost no information on crime in that country. However, a study by a Mexican sociologist of all the accessible data over a forty-year period ending in the late 1960s found that assault and battery (32 percent), robbery (25 percent), and homicide (15 percent) were the three leading crimes reported to police during that period (Wen, 1975). Professional thieves were generally found in urban areas and tended to specialize in burglary and picking pockets. In rural Mexico violent crimes are typically related to "land disputes, water rights, family feuds, disputes between rival villages, and insults to women" (Wen, 1975, p. 346). In the early 1970s the relatively low rate of drug use by Mexicans was beginning to increase. Trafficking in narcotics (especially smuggling to the United States) was also on the rise.

Narcotics

International trafficking in narcotics means that drug problems in Mexico and the United States are intertwined in a profitable and deadly game of supply and demand. The voracious appetite for heroin and marijuana north of the Rio Grande is partially satisfied by producers and distributors of these drugs south of the border. Approximately one-third of the heroin and marijuana consumed in the United States originates in Mexico, and as of the mid-1980s our southern neighbor has been a major conduit for South American cocaine that eventually enters the United States. Oddly enough, the so-called Mexican heroin problem can be traced back to a U.S. request during World War II that Mexico increase its cultivation of heroin-generating poppy and marijuana. The poppies were to produce the pain-killing drug morphine and, to a lesser extent, marijuana for hemp to make rope (Pastor and Castaneda, 1988). When the war ended, Mexico took steps to eradicate the fields, but the state of Sinaloa (where most of the poppies and marijuana were grown) resisted the government's efforts and continues to raise the prohibited plants.

With the demise of the notorious French connection in 1972 (and the interruption of the flow of heroin originating in the Middle and Far East), Mexico became a major source of "black tar" and "brown" heroin entering the United States. The President's 1986 Commission on Organized Crime stated that Mexico was a logical choice for supplying the American heroin market, as it contains extensive regions suitable for both cultivating and refining opium, and shares a lightly guarded 2,000-mile border with the United States. Some of the regions are virtually controlled by drug lords, and peasants have little choice but to grow and do what they are told. Sociologist Howard Abadinsky (1989) contended that much of the heroin coming into the United States is supplied by "extended familial organizations" (p. 195), most notably the Herrera family, a cartel of six interrelated networks headed by former police officer Jaime ("Don Jaime") Herrera-Nevarez. Inasmuch as these organizations are bound together by blood, marriage, and fictional ties, they have been difficult to infiltrate.

The sheer volume of drugs entering the United States from Mexico has led many Americans to believe that the Mexican government is doing little if anything to halt the cultivation and distribution of heroin and marijuana. One U.S. senator went so far as to say that the source of the drug problem was the same as that of Mexico's other problems, "a government dominated by corruption and fraud" (Pastor and Castaneda, 1988, p. 270). However, Mexican officials are quick to point out that in the past few years over 300 soldiers and security men have been killed in the war against drugs, and that at any given time, approximately 20 percent of the Mexican army is involved in efforts to stop both cultivation and trafficking.

From Mexico's perspective, the United States has a very skewed and unrealistic view of the drug problem. Lest we forget, Mexicans are apt to remind us that all the heroin, cocaine, and marijuana in the world is worthless if there is no demand for these substances. This demand comes from north of the border, not their country. One American narcotics official noted, "Mexico is the only country in the hemisphere that produces significant amounts of opium-heroin with little internal abuse" (Pastor and Castaneda, 1988, p. 250). The Mexican economy does not even realize much of the profit from this billion-dollar industry. "According to all reliable accounts," the majority of money earned by Mexican drug lords is invested "in the medium-sized and small banks of the U.S. Southwest, which have received billions of dollars in Mexican deposits since the mid 1970s" (Pastor and Castaneda, 1988, p. 253). Why, ask Mexican officials, are American authorities far less diligent and enthusiastic about policing this part of the drug problem?

Urban Gangs

To date, Mexico appears to have escaped much of the tragedy and violence associated with drug abuse, but the country may be on the verge of a prolonged confrontation with urban gangs. By one estimate, Mexico City has as many as 700,000 gang members (Oster, 1989). Fortunately, these *chavos bandas* ("boys' gangs") have not been engaged in criminal activity on the same scale as and with the same viciousness characteristic of so many gangs in the United States. However, with extremely high rates of unemployment in cities throughout Mexico, and the increasing desire for material possessions and success in a modernizing society, this situation could change quickly. American journalist Patrick Oster (1989) pointed out that some Mexico City gangs have patterned themselves after Britain's punk rockers. With names like *Los* Sex Pistols and *Los Mierdas* Punk ("The Punk Shits"), gang members represent a growing number of desperate, alienated, and hostile young men. According to Mexico City police, 70 percent of robberies and thefts are committed by Mexican males between fifteen and eighteen years of age, the majority of whom belong to gangs.

Homosexuality

In chapter 2 we saw the impact a nation's core values have on a people's world view and behavior. In his book *The Labyrinth of Solitude,* Nobel prize-winning writer Octavio Paz (1985) commented on the relationship between machismo and homosexuality. He stated that "masculine homosexuality is regarded with a certain indulgence insofar as the active agent is concerned. The passive agent is an abject, degraded being" (p. 39). In other words, the dominant, macho partner in a homosexual encounter or relationship may be tolerated by the larger society, whereas the weak, "passive" partner (associated with feminine characteristics) is scorned. Homosexuality can be accepted in Mexico as long as it is engaged in from a position of power and strength. The *pasivo* individual may so completely adopt the role of a woman that he wears dresses and acts in an extremely effeminate manner (Oster, 1989).

From a labeling theory perspective, the dominant partner may be able to escape the negative label and master status resulting from his actions, should his deviant behavior be discovered. However, the passive individual will undoubtedly be stigmatized. In a society that "worships at the altar of machismo" (Oster, 1989, p. 226), such a person is totally discredited.

If Paz is correct, much homosexual behavior in Mexico resembles the *situational homosexuality* commonly found in prisons. "Wolves" or "jockers," the aggressive, often older males who take the inserter role in homosexual encounters, do not see themselves as homosexuals. However, "queens" or "fags"—individuals who engage in homosexual acts as a result of sexual preference—are stigmatized inside prison just as they would be branded and disgraced in the larger society (Little, 1989).

Homosexuals in Mexico are subject to verbal ridicule and physical abuse just as they are in the United States. Occasionally, they are even killed. In a society where image and status are so important, prominent homosexuals are subject to blackmail. A researcher from the United States noted, "If you are rich and you get caught, you pay and pay and pay" (Oster, 1989, p. 230).

Homosexuality is linked to the AIDS virus in Mexico, although the malady has not spread as rapidly as it has in the United States. Some cases of the disease were apparently brought into the country by affluent citizens who had homosexual relationships in the United States and Europe. It also entered as a result of poor, undocumented Mexican workers who acted as male prostitutes in the United States. Desperately in need of money, these men caught the disease from gays while working in this country and then returned home. Once there, they could pass AIDS on to their wives (Oster, 1989).

Law Enforcement

In most societies, people view the police with a combination of respect, fear, and anger, depending on the local crime rate and whether or not they received a speeding ticket in the past few months. In Mexico, the citizenry have rather strong feelings about their police. "To say that Mexicans hate their police doesn't quite capture the feeling. Abhor? Loathe? Revile? Well, yes, those are closer, but still not quite it. Abominate! Yes, that's the feeling I encountered when talking with Mexicans about the police. Mexicans abominate their police" (Oster, 1989, p. 166). In addition, the people are fearful of extortion, robbery, torture, and even murder: "That's what happens *after* the police arrive" (Oster, 1989, p. 166). A national joke is that any kid in Mexico can play cops and robbers—by himself.

The most visible and ubiquitous form of police corruption is *la mordida*—"the bite" of the traffic cop (Riding, 1989). Police in Mexico will stop any moving vehicle and take a bribe in lieu of writing a ticket. This procedure is simple and straightforward because most drivers would rather pay off the police than go to the time and trouble of paying a more expensive fine. In some areas of the country, *mordida* is so common and institutionalized that truck drivers simply stop when they see a parked Federal Highway Patrol car and hand over money much the same as if they had encountered a toll booth. There were even reports that after the devastating 1985 Mexico City earthquake police looted the homes and apartments of victims (Riding, 1989). Police and customs officials are infamous for "shaking down" illegal aliens from Central America who come to work in Mexico or are traveling to the United States. Rather than deport these individuals, the police simply take most of their money and let them go (Conover, 1987). Police corruption is ubiquitous in Mexico and was so widespread in the state of Morelos in 1985 that the governor fired the entire state police force and started all over again.

Riding (1989) commented that corruption can be explained in part by the fact that police are paid so poorly. Not only are the wages low, but the typical officer has to buy his job, uniform, pistol, and even his bullets. Police officers do not "have" jobs as much as they "rent" them. This rent has to be paid on a daily basis to supervisors, who in turn must pay off their superiors. This pyramid of tribute and corruption permitted a recent Mexico City chief of police to amass a fortune estimated at between $7 million and $200 million on an annual salary of less than $10,000.

From a Marxist perspective, the police in Mexico are hired guns used to maintain order and make sure the working class remains weak and submissive. They are recruited from the ranks of the poor, and routinely exploit members of their own class. Some of this illegally obtained money they keep, with the rest going to the ruling elite. As a result of police power and corruption, the bourgeoisie not only manage to control the proletariat, but make a nice profit at the same time.

While such abuses in Mexico's police departments are serious, they are not uncommon in developing countries. In India, for example, criminal suspects have been systematically blinded by police who are sometimes hired by wealthy farmers to repress peasant-led reform movements. Indeed, police brutality and corruption are not unknown in the United States. The 1972 Knapp Commission reported that more than half of New York City's almost 30,000 police officers had been involved in some form of corruption. Los Angeles police gained national attention in 1991 when a video recording showed members of the department brutally beating a suspect while other officers stood by and watched. And between 1963 and 1967, three patrol officers reported seeing over a hundred incidents of police brutality in one Brooklyn, New York, precinct (Inciardi, 1984, p. 284).

The problem with Mexican police is not only the abuse of authority and power, but the fact that this behavior is deep seated and institutionalized. When corruption is not only blatant, but accepted as an inevitable and unalterable part of the system by victims and perpetrators alike, it becomes extremely difficult to root out. Inasmuch as the criminal justice system is society's foremost mechanism of formal social control, and more often than not supports the ruling party, the task of reform becomes even more complex and politically delicate. If Mexico is to become a modern *democratic* state as well as an economic power, the criminal justice system will have to enforce and administer the law impartially in accord with the nation's constitution.

DISCUSSION QUESTIONS

1. In what sense are drug problems in the United States and Mexico intertwined?
2. Although Mexico produces a significant portion of the drugs consumed in the United States, Mexicans have a relatively low rate of drug use. Speculate on the reasons for Mexico's apparent rejection of an activity that is so popular in the United States.
3. Why do some police officers and judges rely on *la mordida* for a substantial portion of their income?
4. Speculate on the impact you think modernization (especially economic advancement) will have on crime in Mexico.
5. Who will have a more difficult life as a result of being labeled a sexual deviant (prostitute or homosexual)—someone in the United States or someone in Mexico? Explain your answer.
6. Go to the library and gather information about some form of sexual deviance in a Third World country. Compare and contrast this behavior with a similar form of deviance in the United States.

CRIME AND DEVIANCE IN JAPAN: YOUTHFUL REBELLION
IN A PEACEFUL SOCIETY

The transition from a traditional to a modern society has resulted in a longer and healthier life, as well as an abundance of material goods and services, for tens of millions of people around the world. Unfortunately, modernization has also been associated with a significant increase in criminal and deviant behavior. The two notable exceptions to this phenomenon are Japan and Switzerland. The case of Japan is especially intriguing, inasmuch as the rate of industrialization and urbanization in that country (especially in the years after World War II) has been much faster than in many other modern states (Shelley, 1981).

In the first few months of the post–World War II era, it was not surprising that the Japanese crime rate went up. With the destruction of the nation's major cities, and the economy in ruins, people survived by any legal or illegal (especially theft, prostitution, and the black market) means possible. For the next forty years, however, the number of penal code offenses in Japan decreased, while the population increased. Then, in 1985, Japanese officials noticed that the crime rate was beginning to rise. On closer examination of the data, they discovered that this increase was attributable to one specific group of people — those under twenty years of age. It was especially prominent in fourteen- and fifteen-year-olds, with offenders coming from all social classes. For individuals over age twenty, crime continued to decline at the same postwar pace (Becker, 1988).

Carl Becker (1988) of Japan's Tsukuba University identified two major causes for this increase in teenage crime. First, young people in Japan are under enormous pressure to succeed in school, and instructors are evaluated on the percentage of their students accepted at leading universities. As a result, Japan's brightest young people receive most of the attention in school, and the poorer students are all but ignored by teachers and administrators. Along with top-notch university candidates, the Japanese educational system is now producing a growing number of *ochikobore* ("in-school dropouts") who have little idea of what is going on in the classroom, and who are becoming increasingly alienated from society. To make matters worse, extracurricular activities are also dominated by the best students, leaving those with lesser ability no place to excel. Shunned by school officials and their successful peers, *ochikobore* have looked to each other for recognition and camaraderie. They form gangs, hang out in the streets, and engage in a variety of criminal and deviant activity such as petty theft and sniffing glue.

Second, gangs of another and more dangerous type called *bosozoku* ("violent running tribes"), made up of men and women in their twenties who refuse to live in accord with the rules of a conforming, disciplined society, have been increasing at an alarming rate over the past few years. With names like "Black Emperor," "Killer Alliance," and "Death Lovers," gang members travel in packs of fifty to one hundred people, annoying, intimidating, and beating up passersby. Capable of explosive fits of violence, *bosozoku* beat a prominent journalist to death in front of his wife and dozens of witnesses after the man chastised them for being too noisy (Yates, 1990). In 1989, police received approximately 115,000 calls for assistance from people who were threatened or attacked by *bosozoku,* a 34.7 percent increase over the previous year. A Tokyo psychologist views this proliferation of *bosozoku* as a manifestation of his country's strict rules of conduct. "I think bosozoku are a direct result of Japan's failure to allow young people to express themselves openly and honestly" (Yates, 1990).

The other major source of criminal activity in Japan is the *yakuza,* or criminal gangs. *Yakuza* (literally, "gangster," "gambler," "good-for-nothing") can be traced back to the Tokugawa shogunate (1603–1867) when they engaged in a wide variety of criminal activity including gambling, organized vice, extortion, and blackmail. In 1980 police estimated that Japan had almost 2,500 criminal gangs (with over 100,000 members). *Yakuza* represented a sizeable portion of all offenders arrested for serious crimes in 1980, including 26 percent of the suspected murderers and 50 percent of narcotics traffickers.

An Emerging Drug Problem?

Although the use and distribution of drugs is a problem in most industrial countries, Japanese authorities have been quite successful in keeping drugs originating in other nations out of their society. However, there is some indication that the war against cocaine is just beginning. Criminal justice officials believe that tougher laws and a more active drug campaign in both the United States and Europe mean that Colombia's cocaine cartels have targeted Japan as their next major market (*San Diego Union,* 1990d). Prior to 1990 police never confiscated more than a pound of cocaine in Japan during an entire year. The country's appetite for mind-altering substances seems to be growing, however, and in one drug bust in February of that year authorities seized over fifty pounds of cocaine. An administrator of a drug rehabilitation center believes his countrymen are going to love cocaine because, "It's fashionable overseas, it gives you a quick high, and you don't have to punch holes in your arm to take it" (in *San Diego Union,* 1990d). *Yakuza* will no doubt be an integral part of Colombia-Japan drug connection and prove to be increasingly troublesome to the police. Wars between rival *yakuza* for control of the lucrative drug trade could erupt on Tokyo's streets just as they have in cities of United States and Europe.

The other drug problem authorities are concerned about was, ironically, started by their

Many Japanese believe young people are losing the work ethic and respect for traditional values that helped make Japan an economic superpower. From a functionalist perspective, some of this youthful rebelliousness could be viewed as an important safety valve, helping to reduce the tension and fatigue of long hours at school and work.

own government. During World War II the militarist regime freely distributed methamphetamines ("speed") to soldiers and factory workers to enhance stamina and productivity. Outlawed in the postwar era, these drugs were effectively controlled by a nationwide police crackdown. However, the long hours of hard work largely responsible for Japan's economic success in the past ten years have resurrected the desire and market for "awakening medicine," one of the street names for methamphetamines. Japanese police estimate there are between 200,000 and 600,000 speed addicts in the country.

Even with this recent upsurge in criminal and deviant activity, Japan has an incredibly low rate of crime and may be one of the world's safest societies. For example, in 1980, New York had 10 times as many murders as Tokyo, and 225 times as many robberies (Fenwick, 1982). These amazing differences are hardly the result of taking liberty with, or juggling, crime statistics. Sociologist David Bayley (1976) noted that Japanese statistics are more accurate than those in the United States, where crime is less likely to be reported to police.

The reasons why Japan's crime rate is so much lower than that of other comparable capitalist, democratic societies have been discussed widely (Bayley, 1976; Fenwick, 1982; Yoshio, 1983; Parker, 1984; Becker, 1988). Most experts point to a number of cultural and social-structural explanations. After each of these explanations, where applicable, we list one or more of the theories previously examined that account for this phenomenon.

1. As we saw in chapter 6, Japan is a homogeneous nation. This means there are relatively few diverse groups with different ethnic and racial origins, languages, religions, and cultures. As societal homogeneity goes up, the potential for intergroup conflict, hostility, and crime goes down. (Conflict theory: a relatively homogeneous population translates into little culture conflict.)

2. Informal groups working through traditional institutions like the family, school, and, more recently, the company instill a strong sense of loyalty in their members. The Japanese have "a collective consciousness, that stresses that a person should not bring shame on his family, friends, work associates, or nation" (Fenwick, 1982, p. 64). (Containment and control theories; also Sutherland's theory of differential association: children learn definitions *unfavorable* to violations of the law.)

3. Although the Japanese school system seems responsible for some deviance (*ochikobore*), it curtails deviant behavior in the majority of Japanese youth. Teachers have much more authority and exert greater control over the lives of students in Japan than they do in many countries, especially the United States. Aggressive behavior in school is not tolerated, and students are likely to be suspended from classes for two or three days for misbehaving in even a minor way.

4. There appears to be general satisfaction with economic conditions in Japanese society, where 90 percent of the populace consider themselves members of the middle class. Unemployment is low, and the undesirable, low-paying jobs that exist in any society are increasingly being performed by workers from poor neighboring Asian nations who are only too glad to have employment and who do what they are told. (Marxist theory: exploiting guest workers who perform low-paying undesirable jobs. Merton's theory of anomie: a relatively small number of innovators.)

5. Japan's major religions seem to converge at a point where they are antagonistic to nonconforming behavior. The Citizens Crime Commission of 1973 noted, "The religions of Japanese Shintoism, Buddhism, and Confucianism are all meditative at their base and tend to stress proper conduct more than theological variations of heavenly reward. The old-time religion is undoubtedly in decline in Japan, but its influence toward passivity rather than violence is still greater than any counterpart in the U.S." (in Fenwick, 1982, p. 65). (Marxist theory: religion is the opiate of the people. Containment and control theories.)

6. Guns and other lethal weapons are strictly controlled by the government. In 1979 there were fewer than 900,000 rifles and pistols of all types in the hands of properly authorized individuals. In that same year in excess of sixty million such weapons were privately owned by American citizens.

The role and behavior of the police have also been credited with keeping the crime rate low. In his 1976 study of Japanese police, Bayley (1976) noted that Japan is "heaven for a cop," and "with respect to law enforcement it is a different world" (p. 1). This different world view begins in training or police boot camp. Whereas a recruit in the United States gets from a few weeks to a maximum of six months of training, his or her Japanese counterpart receives six to thirteen months of initial training, and receives additional instruction for a few weeks every year. However, the major dissimilarity between police in these two societies is that they operate in very different moral climates. Whereas American officers must often rely on the threat or use of force to maintain order and make arrests, Japanese police are much more likely to rely on the authority of their position, which is recognized and accepted by the majority of people. Bayley (1976) captured the essence of this difference in the following: "An American accused by a policeman is very likely to respond 'Why me?' A Japanese more often says 'I'm sorry.' The American shows anger, the Japanese shame" (p. 150). This combination of greater moral authority and significantly more respect from citizens also means that Japanese police are relatively safe in their work. In 1979, for example, five police officers were killed while on duty; the corresponding number for police in the United States was one hundred (Fenwick, 1982). The fact that the United States has twice the population of Japan hardly accounts for the difference.

As a result of a low crime rate and an excellent record of solving criminal offenses, Japanese police generally have the trust and admiration of the populace. They are also much freer than police in the United States and Europe to pick up suspects as well as detain people who appear to be on the verge of engaging in some form of criminal activity (Becker, 1988). In recent years, however, the image of the Japanese police as supercops has begun to tarnish due to their practice of extracting confessions from suspects in interrogating sessions that go on for ten or twelve hours and last up to twenty-three days (Jameson, 1984). There are also reports of physical abuse during these sessions. Suspects are handcuffed and tied to chairs in a small interrogation cubicle where they are shouted at by police all day long. They are often kept under twenty-four-hour surveillance "deprived of sleep, fed meager rations of food and denied the toilet for long periods" (Schoenberger, 1989).

The obvious question that arises from this brief survey of crime, deviance, and the police in Japan is, what can we learn and incorporate from Japanese culture, society, and system of policing that would effectively reduce crime rates in the United States? The best place to start is to establish what we as Americans cannot do. First, we cannot become Japanese in our fundamental values and patterns or behavior. A society that has a historically rooted, strong individual ethos will not easily embrace the Japanese style of group orientation and loyalty even if it could be demonstrated irrefutably that such an orientation would result in a much lower crime rate. Second, we are not likely to become Buddhists or Confucianists simply because those religions preach nonviolence and self-discipline. However, there are a number of things we can learn and adapt from the Japanese police system.

Whenever and wherever possible, police can abandon their patrol cars in favor of walking the streets, interacting with, and gaining the trust of people in local neighborhoods. Some modified system of Japanese *kobans* and *chuzaisho* could be introduced in American cities. *Kobans* are small neighborhood police stations staffed by from four to twelve officers. A *chuzaisho* is a small residential post with one or two officers on duty around the clock. Japan has over 16,000 *kobans* and *chuzaishos,* and people are encouraged to seek out officers for assistance in both criminal and noncrime-related matters. The idea is that if family and neighborhood problems can be nipped in the bud, they are less likely to erupt into criminal behavior. Senior police officials can be rotated from precinct to precinct on a regular and frequent basis. This policy not only gives them greater experience and familiarity in police matters, but is a safeguard against long-standing, institutionalized corruption.

Perhaps in the final analysis, the real question concerns our desire and political will to experiment with ideas and techniques concerning crime and justice from a very different society— ideas and techniques that certainly seem to work.

1. Why has the rate of crime for teenagers and those in their twenties increased in Japan in recent years?
2. Why is drug use increasing in Japan? Will authorities be more or less successful than American officials in controlling their country's drug problem?
3. Which sociological theories best explain the low rates of criminal behavior in Japan? Speculate on other reasons for this phenomenon.
4. As police chief of a large American city, what advice would you give a Japanese policeman who will be working in your department for the next two years? Assume this officer has little if any knowledge of American society and culture.
5. Go to the library and gather information on drug abuse in the Soviet Union or one of the Eastern European countries (Poland, Czechoslovakia, Hungary, Romania, or Bulgaria). Is drug abuse a serious problem in that country? How has the government attempted to control this behavior? Have they been successful?

CHAPTER SUMMARY

1. There are three basic perspectives of deviance. From the absolutist perspective, deviance resides in the nature of the act itself and is wrong at all times and in all places. The normative position sees deviance as a violation of a group's or society's rules at a particular moment in history. According to the reactive position, behavior is not deviant until it has been recognized and condemned.

2. Over the past one hundred years an increasing amount of deviance has been explained and "cured" from a medical perspective. Deviants are thought of as sick and in need of treatment.

3. Biological explanations go back hundreds of years. The basic logic of all these theories is that "structure determines function"; that is, human action is in some manner the result of an individual's physical makeup.

4. According to functionalist sociologists like Emile Durkheim, crime is "normal" because all societies have criminal behavior. Crime and deviance persist in human societies because it is impossible for all members of society to agree on what the rules and norms should be. Crime is also inevitable because human beings are moral animals who continually divide the social world into the good and the bad. Behavior that is bad or undesirable is deviant.

5. Functionalists also believe that a certain amount of crime is functional or "good" for society for a number of reasons: (a) tolerance permitting the existence of crime and deviance results in tolerance for the creativity and originality that produce social change; (b) crime serves as a warning light that something is wrong in society and requires remedial action; (c) crime clarifies the social boundaries of society; and (d) crime facilitates group solidarity.

6. In his theory of anomie, Robert Merton noted that a significant amount of crime and deviance in societies of "the American type" is caused by the pressure put on people as a result of the gap between the institutionalized goal of monetary success and the means available for achieving this goal. Deviant adaptations to this pressure are innovation, ritualism, retreatism, and rebellion.

7. Criminologist Edwin Sutherland stated that criminal behavior is learned in interaction with other people. If individuals have an excess of definitions favorable to the violation of the law over definitions favorable to obeying the law, they are likely to be involved in criminal activities.

8. Labeling theorists argue that social groups create deviance by making laws whose infraction results in deviance. They are interested in how these laws are applied to particular people who are then labeled as deviants. "Moral entrepreneurs" campaign to have their values translated into laws designating some behavior as criminal. Primary

deviance is the initial act, or first few episodes of deviant behavior, and secondary deviance is the behavior that results from being labeled.

9. According to Marxist criminologists, the struggle between the capitalist class and the proletariat produces crime. Members of the capitalist class commit crimes of domination and repression, and the working class engages in crimes of accommodation and resistance. Crime is symptomatic of the real problem in a capitalist society—the unequal distribution of wealth and power.

10. For control theorists deviant motivation is present to some extent in all people. Therefore, the most important question is, why doesn't everybody engage in deviant behavior? Control theorists focus on the individual's commitment to societal values and norms. For most people most of the time, this commitment controls or contains their deviant motivation and produces conforming behavior.

11. Crime is measured by the *Uniform Crime Report* (UCR), victimization surveys, and self-report studies. The UCR is primarily a measure of street crimes (murder, robbery, rape, aggravated assault, burglary, auto theft, larceny, arson). Victimization surveys indicate significantly more crime is committed than reported by the UCR.

12. Data on offenders indicate that (a) men commit more crimes than women, (b) crime is primarily a youthful activity, and (c) a disproportionate number of people arrested for street crimes are minority group members. A controversy exists among sociologists regarding the class origin of offenders in the United States. Some researchers maintain that criminals come disproportionately from the lower classes. Others argue against any class-linked explanations.

13. Approximately 11 percent of crimes known to police are violent. Victimization studies indicate over 1,100,000 rapes took place in the United States between 1979 and 1985. Gangs are prevalent in large cities throughout the country, with heavily armed members responsible for a sig-

nificant number of deaths and injuries. There were approximately 2.4 million cases of child abuse nationwide in 1989. If abused children become child abusers as adults, this form of family violence will perpetuate itself and remain a serious problem.

14. Occupational crime is committed by people in connection with their work. Corporate crime is committed by officials for their organizations, and includes crimes of the organization itself. Corporate crime costs the American public much more than street crime, and can also be violent.

15. Drug epidemics occur in the United States in predictable cycles. Drugs are "discovered," widely used, and finally condemned. In this final stage they are typically associated with racial-ethnic minorities, whether this association is true or not.

16. Drug use (at least initially) is learned behavior. People may eventually become addicted to drugs, but they had to learn where to buy and how to use them. They also had to learn how to rationalize this behavior to themselves and others.

16. Prostitution flourishes in both the developed and developing worlds. In the United States, streetwalkers are at the bottom of the prostitution hierarchy and call girls are at the top. Prostitutes are major transmitters of AIDS in some developing nations.

17. Kinsey and his colleagues found that almost half of American males fell between those who were exclusively heterosexual and those who were exclusively homosexual. The homosexual community has been hit hard by the AIDS epidemic. This has resulted in an increase of violence against homosexuals.

18. As nations modernize, their rates of crime begin to increase, eventually approaching those of developed nations. Rates of drug-related crime and property crime in urban areas are especially prone to increase. Developing nations are being victimized by developed nations who dump their hazardous products and toxic waste material on these countries.

9

SOCIAL INSTITUTIONS

Beginning in the early 1960s, thousands of Americans became members of **cults**—new and different religious bodies that exist in a state of relatively high tension with other more established religions in a society (Stark and Bainbridge, 1979). One of the cults that flourished during this period was the Unification Church (UC) of Reverend Sun Myung Moon. Commonly known as "Moonies," converts to this religion typically are white, working-class and middle-class individuals, under age thirty, and with at least some college education (Robbins et al., 1976). Research indicates that people who join cults are lonely and detached from society to some extent (Marciano, 1988). This suggests some aspect(s) of their family life may have been less than satisfying, and the cult represents a place where they find fulfillment and psychological security.

When a person joins the UC he or she is said to join the family. Although the Church does not require members to sever ties with their biological family, it becomes quite clear that Reverend Moon and his wife are one's "true parents." Perhaps the strongest appeal of the UC is a ready-made, sincere, and caring surrogate family. As one member told sociologist Thomas Robbins (1975), "It completely amazed me, the cleanliness of the people, the warmheartedness of the people, and togetherness of heart, and not just in the geographical sense and actually in heart, really like a family!" (p. 116). For people who never have had a satisfying home life, or who currently are having severe difficulties with their parents and siblings, finding a group of same-age persons who shower them with attention and affection can be a powerful incentive to become a member of the Church.

The UC also has a sociopolitical agenda that many people find appealing. For those who want to bring about far-reaching, religiously grounded social change in the world, and who see little hope of realizing this goal through traditional religions, Reverend Moon provides a comprehensive plan for world transformation. The UC is an example of what John Lofland (1977) called a "world-saving" religion. That is, unlike Eastern cults that emphasize turning inward through meditative techniques in one's search for meaning, followers of Reverend Moon want to change the external world and make it as close to a heaven on earth as possible. Fervently anticommunist with a conservative agenda, the UC has been politically active since it enthusiastically supported Richard Nixon in the darkest days of his presidency. In the 1980s the UC was reported to have sent money to the Contras fighting in Nicaragua.

This brief look at the Unification Church illustrates the interplay of three of society's most important institutions: the family, religion, and government. From a sociological perspective, **social institutions** are orderly, enduring, and established ways of arranging behavior and doing things. Social relationships in institutions are structured

Cults often serve as "families," providing members with primary group relations and a sense of belonging. Here, the Rev. Sun Myung Moon, leader of the Unification Church, performs a mass wedding ceremony for a number of his devoted "children." The Unification Church is a controversial religious organization with operations in the United States and worldwide.

for the purpose of performing some task(s) or accomplishing specific goals. Obviously, all three of the aforementioned institutions have a significant impact on our world view and behavior, beginning with childhood socialization, if and how we believe in a future life, and how much freedom we have in this one. Although each of these institutions will be discussed in turn, keep in mind that they are interdependent and continually affect each other in society.

The family is the primary source of an individual's world view, including religious beliefs. Parents determine what religion (if any) children will be taught, and how important these beliefs will be compared to other aspects of their lives. However, as they grow older, many people reject the religious tradition of their youth in favor of a new belief system. Some survey research indicates that 40 percent of Protestants belonged to denominations different from the ones in which they originally had been socialized (Marciano, 1988). Because of changing needs resulting from a variety of personal and collective experiences, many people become members of religions like the UC that are not only different from, but completely at odds with, their original belief system.

Cults are not the only religious groups in the United States to become involved in politics. The Catholic Church and, lately, the new religious right, or conservative Protestants, have been politically active, with much of this activity directed at the family. For example, between 1939 and 1967 Francis Cardinal Spellman, the archbishop of New York, "imposed a distinctly conservative tilt to the church's effort to influence the public realm" (Wald, 1987, p. 221). Sometimes referred to as the "American Pope," he was suspicious of the civil rights movement and labor unions and staunchly anticommunist. By the 1980s, however, Catholic bishops in the United States had become decidedly more liberal in their foreign policy views. In 1983 they issued a letter stating that nuclear weapons could almost never be used in accord with the Church's standards for a "just" war, and called on governments throughout the world to disarm as soon as possible. Today more and more Catholics oppose Church doctrine concerning birth control, abortion, homosexuality, and divorce. They regard personal and family morality as a private matter not subject to the authority of Rome. The abortion issue increasingly pits Catholics against one another in the political arena, with each side attempting to elect legislators sympathetic to their position.

In the 1980 presidential election, the recently formed New Christian Right enthusiastically supported the candidacy of Ronald Reagan. Other conservative Christian organizations raised funds for the former California governor and provided him with speaking engagements. The 1984 Republican convention came to a close with a prayer by Moral Majority leader Jerry Falwell, who referred to Ronald Reagan and George Bush as "God's instruments for rebuilding America." Believing in a traditional, male-dominated family, the New Right derided the Democratic Party for "assaulting our basic values. . . . They attacked the integrity of the family and parental rights. They ignored traditional morality" (in Wald, 1987, p. 194). The now-defunct Moral Majority was convinced that it had the right to influence political decisions as well as impose its system of values on nonbelievers. Amendment VII of the Christian Bill of Rights stated, "We believe in the right to influence secular professions, including the fields of politics, business, legal, medical, in establishing and maintaining principles of Scripture" (in Wald, 1987, p. 191).

Conservative Christians of all denominations are of the belief that only a return to basic religious values will save the American family from disintegration in an increasingly immoral and secular world. To preserve the family, these groups are increasingly politically involved, battling their enemies in voting booths, state legislatures, and the halls of Congress.

QUESTIONS TO CONSIDER

1. What are social institutions?
2. How do functionalist sociologists see the role of the family in society?
3. How do conflict sociologists view the family in society?
4. What factors are associated with a successful marriage in the United States?
5. What factors are associated with divorce in the United States?
6. What effects does divorce have on children?
7. What is the relationship between modernization and the family?
8. From a functionalist standpoint, what is the function of the state in modern human societies?
9. How do conflict theorists like Karl Marx interpret the role of the state as the major political institution in modern societies?
10. Who (or what) is the "power elite"?
11. What is the relationship between socioeconomic status and political participation in the United States?
12. What is the difference between power and authority as forms of political rule?
13. Why is some form of religion found in every human society?
14. According to functionalists like Emile Durkheim, how does religion benefit society?
15. For conflict theorists like Marx, what is the primary role or consequence of religion in modern societies?
16. What is the Protestant ethic?
17. What is the electronic church?
18. What is the relationship between modernization and religion?

MARRIAGE AND THE FAMILY

Theoretical Perspectives

Because the family is such a basic and important social institution, sociologists have attempted to explain not only how it works, but also how it relates to other institutions from different perspectives.

Functionalist Theory   Functionalists are concerned primarily with how the family contributes to the overall functioning of and, therefore, the good of society. From this perspective, the family performs six major functions in all societies to one degree or another, although the way they are performed varies significantly (Queen et al., 1985, pp. 5–6).

1. The family meets its members' biological and economic needs for food, clothing, and shelter, as well as providing for other material necessities.

2. The family legitimizes some sexual relationships while at the same time prohibiting others. For example, in Western societies it is believed that the exclusive sexual bond between husband and wife strengthens their commitment to each other, which in turn helps them meet familial duties and responsibilities. In every known society incest taboos regulate the sexual behavior of people related within certain degrees of kinship.

3. Every society must reproduce to survive and ensure the continuity of the group. Reproduction typically occurs within the family unit.

4. A significant portion of childhood socialization takes place in the family. Children learn standards of behavior appropriate to their age and gender, as well as internalize ever increasing aspects of their material and nonmaterial cultural heritage.

5. As a social hierarchy, the family provides membership within a societal structure that gives individuals an ascribed status.

6. Finally, the family provides members with emotional support and companionship. It also acts as a buffer between the individual and other institutions such as the workplace that can be competitive, tiring, stressful, and even degrading. It is this final function that makes the family an especially important institution in modern, industrial states.

Conflict Theory   Conflict theorists who view the family as an institution of "power, dominance, and conflict" have been highly critical of the hidden conservative view they see built into the functionalist interpretation (Collins, 1985a, p. 18). Friedrich Engels wrote about the link between exploitation in the larger society and the exploitation of women and children in the family. According to Engels, men who are paid subsistence wages by powerful, corporate owners in a capitalist society that cares nothing about their well-being soon become demoralized, frustrated, and callous. Misery breeds misery as workers beaten down by the capitalist system in turn exploit and brutalize their families. It is not as if men enjoy terrifying loved ones; rather they take their frustrations and hostilities out on the most readily available individuals.

From a Marxist perspective, women are victimized twice in a capitalist society. Fulfilling their roles as wives and mothers, they are unpaid for their work in the home, and they toil for less than what men earn if they do enter the workforce. Having women work at home without pay allows men to leave their families and be turned into what Marxists call "wage slaves" by the capitalist class. In other words, exploitation of women at home is necessary for capitalism to exist. Joan Landes (1979) described how the family socializes children to be obedient wage slaves as they are prepared for a life of dutiful exploitation: "Within the family, patterns of hierarchy (of men over women and parents over children) serve to introduce workers to the hierarchical labor patterns of the workplace. The ideology of the workplace helps to teach workers that these patterns are 'natural' as well as legitimate" (p. 224).

From a conflict perspective the family is hardly a sanctuary full of love, companionship, and emotional support. Instead, in a capitalist society it is a microcosm of the tension, conflict, and exploitation existing in the larger society. Marxist sociologists use the family as an example of how the evils of capitalism pervade our most "sacred institution" and negatively affect the lives of men, women, and children at the most personal and intimate level.

Sociologist Randall Collins (1975) observed that conflict within the family goes well beyond capitalist societies. Stable family organization is the result of sexual conquest and dominance. Males who are on the average bigger and stronger than females physically overpower women who become "sexual prizes." The men who take permanent possession of particular females create biological families. Collins notes that men now own these women and the children they bear. The fundamental motive for subordinating women is the sexual gratification of men, but females (and later their children) can be used for their labor value as well.

Another conflict interpretation was offered by sociologist Jetse Sprey (1966, 1969), who contended that the impartiality of the world of work, casual associations, and friendships may counteract the conflict and hostilities that are built into the family bond. In a complete reversal of the functionalist position, Sprey saw conflict anchored in the family as members compete with each other for real and symbolic resources such as money, attention, and power. Marital problems leading to separation and divorce are not due to personality differences between partners (these are natural and inevitable), but occur because husbands and wives have not learned to live with and successfully negotiate each other's differences.

Love, Marriage, and Divorce American Style

Anthropologist Serena Nanda (1980) maintained that every society must solve three basic problems: the regulation of sexual behavior between males and females, the division of labor between males and females, and the assignment of responsibility for the care and socialization of children. The universal practice of marriage is the way societies typically regulate the exchange of products and services between men and women and solve these fundamental problems. Marriage is the socially approved sexual union between a man and a woman that is presumed to be permanent, and is recognized as such both by the couple and by others. Although marriage and the family are common to all human societies, family structure, customs of mate selection and residence, marriage forms, and patterns of authority and descent vary considerably across cultures. In the United States most people live in nuclear families, practice endogamy in the selection of a spouse, have a neolocal residence, are monogamous, are moving toward or are in an egalitarian marriage, and have a bilineal descent system. (See Table 9.1 for a definition of these terms.)

One of the most significant changes in the structure of the American family has been the reduction in the size and importance of kinship networks. Extended families and large kinship groups, once common among New England upper classes, Southern plantations, and *haciendas* (ranches or farms) in the Southwest, have given way to smaller nuclear families. Personal ties and patterns of interaction that once united three or four generations and a host of cousins are much less evident today than in the past (Queen et al., 1985). Today Americans live in nuclear families that have significantly diminished in size since the first census was taken in 1790. Almost 99 percent of married couples maintain a household of their own, and approximately 60 percent of married women have jobs outside the home. The number of working married women will continue to increase because women are becoming better educated, having fewer children, and living longer (Queen et al., 1985). Women have demonstrated they can work as well as men in hundreds of occupations, and currently have the protection of laws (albeit incomplete) against gender discrimination in the workplace that did not previously exist. With women bringing home a paycheck in over half of the marriages, power relationships in the family are shifting to a more equal or egalitarian form.

In the majority of American families children are preceded by marriage, which in turn is preceded by dating and romantic love. Although there are no laws in the United

TABLE 9.1   Marriage and Family Terminology

Term	Definition
FAMILY STRUCTURE	
Nuclear family	Family group consisting of a mother, a father, and their children. This is the family of procreation.
Extended family	A family group that extends beyond the immediate relationship of husband, wife, and their children, and includes several generations.
Blended family	The family created by remarriage. It includes step-children and half-brothers and -sisters.
MATE SELECTION	
Endogamy	Custom that requires individuals to choose marriage mates from within their own tribe, community, social class, nationality, or other grouping.
Exogamy	Custom that requires individuals to choose marriage mates from outside certain groups.
RESIDENCE	
Matrilocal residence	Residence of married partners near or in the wife's family's home.
Patrilocal residence	Residence of a married couple near or with the husband's family.
Neolocal residence	System in which both marriage partners reside apart from their family of orientation.
FORMS OF MARRIAGE	
Monogamy	Marriage form permitting each person to have only one spouse.
Polygamy	Marital system that permits the taking of several spouses. It includes both polygyny and polyandry.
Polygyny	Marital system that permits the taking of several wives.
Polyandry	Marital system that permits the taking of several husbands.
AUTHORITY	
Matriarchy	A system in which power and authority are vested in females.
Patriarchy	A system in which power and authority are vested in males.
Egalitarian	A system in which power and authority are shared equally by husbands and wives.
DESCENT AND INHERITANCE	
Matrilineal descent	Family membership and inheritance traced through the female line, from mother to her children.
Patrilineal descent	Family membership and inheritance traced through the male line, from father to his children.
Bilineal descent	Family membership and inheritance traced through the lines of both parents to their children.

Source: Adapted from Randall Collins, 1985, *Sociology of Marriage and the Family—Gender, Love, and Property,* Chicago: Nelson-Hall, pp. 477–483; and Gerald R. Leslie and Sheila K. Korman, 1989, *The Family in Social Context,* New York: Oxford University Press, pp. 581–592.

States requiring people to date and marry within a specific group (endogamy), most people select mates with backgrounds much like their own. The tendency to marry individuals whom one resembles physically, psychologically, and/or socially is called **homogamy.** In the United States most marriages occur between two people of the same social class, within the same racial group, of the same religious faith, with similar levels of education, with the same physical and psychological characteristics, and who live within a few miles of each other (Collins, 1985a).

Homogamy occurs because people are attracted to one another in a system of exchange that could be characterized as a marriage market. Just as goods and services are exchanged in the economic marketplace, human resources are negotiated and traded in the social world. According to Collins (1985a, pp. 121–124), everybody has a market value and typically dates and marries someone of approximately the same worth: "Your own resources include your social status (class, race, ethnicity; your family background; your current occupation), your wealth and your prospect for making more in the future, your personal attractiveness and health, your culture. Even personality traits such as your 'magnetism' or charisma are social resources. . . . The people in your 'opportunity pool' of course have their own degrees of attractiveness depending on their resources." Although people may not be consciously making comparisons in the dating-marriage marketplace, we have all been socialized to play "Let's Make a Deal" on the basis of our current and potential value.

Marriage After people sort themselves out in the dating marketplace, they eventually marry. The success or failure of their marriage is linked to a number of social, psychological, and economic factors. Jeanette and Robert Lauer (1985) interviewed 351 couples who had been married for at least fifteen years in an effort to discover why these marriages lasted. In Table 9.2, notice that the first two reasons have to do with compatibility ("My spouse is my best friend"; "I like my spouse as a person"). However, reasons three and four given by both spouses reveal their commitment to the institution of marriage, and belief that marriage is something sacred. Also, reasons number eight for males and eleven for females indicate that the individuals in this sample who have been married for a long time believe that "An enduring marriage is important to social stability." Lauer and Lauer's research indicates an important social component to successful marriages, that is, the belief that marriage is a sacred, long-term commitment. We tend to think of marriage and divorce almost exclusively in terms of psychological variables (love, compatibility, trust, etc.) and interpersonal dynamics. However, we should not overlook factors that bind people to the institution of marriage itself.

The quality of long-lasting marital relationships can vary enormously as couples adjust to each other, particular situations, and different conceptions of marriage. Cuber and Harroff (1983, pp. 319–329) interviewed 107 men and 104 women who had been married for ten or more years and constructed the following typology of these enduring marital relationships (not personalities).

1. *The conflict habituated* This marriage has a good deal of tension and conflict, although these are largely controlled and confined to the home, away from relatives and friends as much as possible. Husband and wife acknowledge that their "incompatibility is pervasive," accept this fact, and stay together for the sake of children, their careers, etc.

2. *The devitalized* During the early years of their marriage these people were deeply in love, enjoyed each other's company, and had a good sex life. Currently their time together is "duty time," spent entertaining friends and associates, being with their children, and engaging in community activities. These marriages are devoid of tension and conflict, as well as the original zest that made the relationship alive and enjoyable in the first place.

TABLE 9.2   What Keeps a Marriage Going?

Men	Women
1. My spouse is my best friend.	My spouse is my best friend.
2. I like my spouse as a person.	I like my spouse as a person.
3. Marriage is a long-term commitment.	Marriage is a long-term commitment.
4. Marriage is sacred.	Marriage is sacred.
5. We agree on aims and goals.	We agree on aims and goals.
6. My spouse has grown more interesting.	My spouse has grown more interesting.
7. I want the relationship to succeed.	I want the relationship to succeed.
8. An enduring marriage is important to social stability.	We laugh together.
9. We laugh together.	We agree on a philosophy of life.
10. I am proud of my spouse's achievements.	We agree on how and how often to show affection.
11. We agree on a philosophy of life.	An enduring marriage is important to social stability.
12. We agree about our sex life.	We have a stimulating exchange of ideas.
13. We agree on how and how often to show affection.	We discuss things calmly.
14. I confide in my spouse.	We agree about our sex life.
15. We share outside hobbies and interests.	I am proud of my spouse's achievements.

Note: These are the top reasons respondents gave, listed in order of frequency.

Source: From Jeanette Lauer and Robert Lauer, June 1985, "Marriages Made to Last," *Psychology Today,* pp. 22–26.

3. *The passive-congenial* Whereas devitalized couples have memories of happier days, people in this type of a marriage have been in a lifeless relationship from the beginning. Individuals in the passive-congenial mode arrive at this point by default or intention. Since their emotional commitment to each other was so weak to begin with, some couples simply drift apart. Others deliberately pursue interests and careers that are incompatible with those of their mates.

4. *The vital* These people derive enormous satisfaction from participating together in shared activities (hobbies, community service, etc.) and important life segments involving children and careers. "Their sharing and their togetherness is genuine. It provides the life essence for both man and woman" (p. 324).

5. *The total* This is the type of relationship found in Broadway musicals and romantic novels. Similar to the vital marriage, total relationships are more multifaceted. These people are completely intertwined and lovingly do everything as a couple. "It is as if neither spouse has, or has had, a truly private existence" (p. 326). Such relationships are rare.

Divorce Divorce has become a common, accepted fact of life in the United States as well as other modern nations (Figure 9.1). In the 1800s, marriages typically endured until one of the partners died, with only 3 percent ending through divorce. According

FIGURE 9.1   The Changing American Family

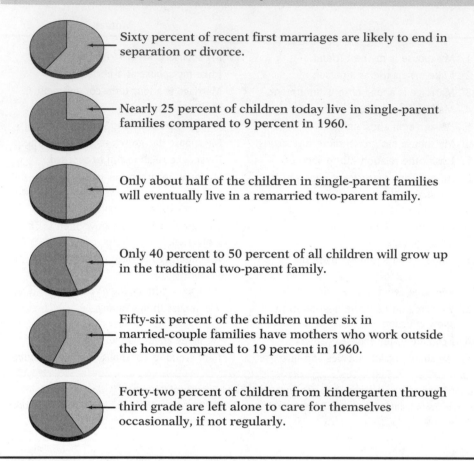

Sixty percent of recent first marriages are likely to end in separation or divorce.

Nearly 25 percent of children today live in single-parent families compared to 9 percent in 1960.

Only about half of the children in single-parent families will eventually live in a remarried two-parent family.

Only 40 percent to 50 percent of all children will grow up in the traditional two-parent family.

Fifty-six percent of the children under six in married-couple families have mothers who work outside the home compared to 19 percent in 1960.

Forty-two percent of children from kindergarten through third grade are left alone to care for themselves occasionally, if not regularly.

Source: Center for Demography and Ecology, University of Wisconsin-Madison, Child Welfare League: U.S. Bureau of Labor Statistics. Compiled by Patricia Mitchell, *Los Angeles Times.* Copyright © 1990 by the Los Angeles Times Syndicate. Reprinted by permission.

to Martin and Bumpass (1989), at current rates, over 60 percent of marriages will end in separation or divorce. The probability of a marital breakup is not randomly distributed throughout the population; rather, it is associated with a number of factors (Collins, 1985a; Eshleman, 1985; Leslie and Korman, 1989; Thornton, 1985; Raschke, 1988).

1. *Age*   Divorce rates are highest in marriages involving young people.
2. *Duration of marriage*   Divorce generally occurs within the first seven years of marriage, with rates in the first three years especially high.
3. *Social class*   Although divorce has been increasing at all socioeconomic levels, it has an inverse relationship with social class; that is, rates are highest in the lower class.
4. *Race*   The divorce rate for blacks tends to be higher than for whites.

5. *Religion* Although the evidence is sketchy, Catholics tend to have lower divorce rates than Protestants. One study found unusually high rates among Fundamentalists and Baptists.

6. *Intergenerational* Children of divorced parents are slightly more likely to divorce.

Why Marriages Fail Just as psychological variables and interpersonal dynamics do not completely explain why some marriages endure, these same factors give an incomplete picture of why other marriages fail. Divorce in the United States is associated with general economic trends, something that affects everyone in the country to a certain extent, depending on one's socioeconomic status. For example, the divorce rate in the United States rose slightly during the prosperous Roaring Twenties, and began to decline with the stock market crash of 1929, reaching a low in the depths of the Great Depression in 1933. With the sluggish economy of the mid-1970s, the rate peaked at 5.2 per 1,000 population in 1980 and then declined to 4.8 per 1,000 in 1988. Higher rates of unemployment during these periods and an uncertain economic future tend to keep families together even if internal factors are pulling them apart.

Gallaway and Vedder (1986) observed that increases in the rate of inflation (especially when unanticipated) lead to financial problems and interpersonal tensions, and contribute to a high divorce rate. Traditionally in our society, marriage has been a contractual agreement, a trade-off of services between husbands and wives. Husbands "provided income, affection, and some household maintenance services to the wife in exchange for other household maintenance services, domestic services, affection, and sexual favors" (Gallaway and Vedder, 1986, p. 286). Divorce occurs when one or both of the partners do not comply with this contractual trade-off. During periods of unemployment and inflation it is the husband who does not fill contractual obligations. However, if the wife begins working and cuts down on housework, she no longer depends solely on her husband for income. He in turn no longer has as many household services to buy from her. From this perspective a key component of an enduring marriage is economic harmony between husbands and wives. Unfortunately, economic factors like high unemployment cannot be controlled at the family level. This is another example of the link between institutional variables and individual behavior. Economic slow-downs and inflation, which hit people in the lower classes the hardest (including the disproportionate number of blacks in this category), partially explain why divorce is inversely related to social class and is higher among blacks than whites.

Divorce and Children Divorce affects not only the men and women who terminate their marriages, but hundreds of thousands of children as well (see Figure 9.2). Since 1900, approximately 25 to 30 percent of all children in the United States have experienced divorce, and in the 1980s 40 to 50 percent of children were so affected. Although divorce is typically a traumatic, painful experience for children, there is conflicting evidence on both its short- and long-term consequences on their emotional well-being and behavior. Some researchers maintain that children adjust to the divorce and a new family situation within two years of the breakup, whereas others indicate negative effects of a divorce can last well into adulthood (Price and McKenry, 1988). Raschke and Raschke (1979) found that children living in single-parent families (usually as a result of separation or divorce) had the same self-concept scores as children from intact and reconstituted families (one biological parent, one step-parent). Collins (1985a, p. 256) stated, "Divorce does not seem to produce any lasting psychological damage or unusual social behavior among children."

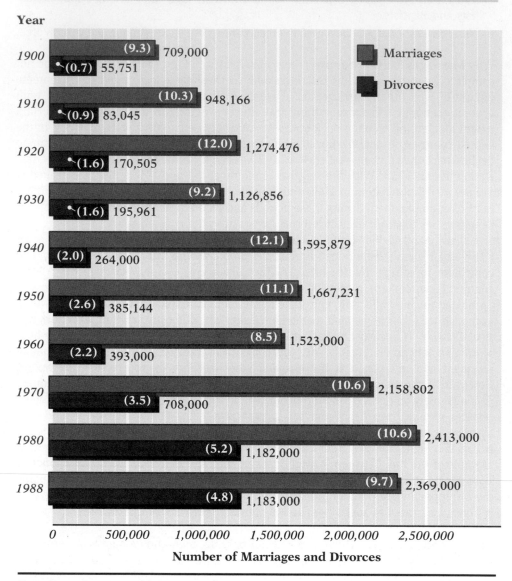

FIGURE 9.2   Marriages, Divorces, and Rates in the United States, 1900–1988

Year

Year		
1900	(9.3)	709,000
	(0.7)	55,751
1910	(10.3)	948,166
	(0.9)	83,045
1920	(12.0)	1,274,476
	(1.6)	170,505
1930	(9.2)	1,126,856
	(1.6)	195,961
1940	(12.1)	1,595,879
	(2.0)	264,000
1950	(11.1)	1,667,231
	(2.6)	385,144
1960	(8.5)	1,523,000
	(2.2)	393,000
1970	(10.6)	2,158,802
	(3.5)	708,000
1980	(10.6)	2,413,000
	(5.2)	1,182,000
1988	(9.7)	2,369,000
	(4.8)	1,183,000

Marriages

Divorces

0   500,000   1,000,000   1,500,000   2,000,000   2,500,000

Number of Marriages and Divorces

Note: Data refer only to events occurring within the United States, including Alaska and Hawaii, beginning with 1960. Numbers to the right of the bars indicate actual numbers of marriages and divorces. Rates per 1,000 population are given within the bars, in parentheses.

Source: National Center for Health Statistics, U.S. Department of Health and Human Services. Adapted from *The World Almanac and Book of Facts,* 1990. New York: Pharos Books.

On the other hand, Ann Goetting (1983) commented on a number of studies showing that marital disruption adversely affects children's cognitive ability in the classroom and success in school. Peterson and Zill (1986) also found that it results in a wide range of problems for children. However, living in a household with biological parents is no guarantee of happiness and well-being; persistent long-term conflict in homes is just as harmful to children as divorce.

Longitudinal research by Wallerstein and Kelly (1980) showed both the positive and negative effects of divorce on children. These investigators periodically interviewed all of the members of sixty divorced families in California during a five-year period beginning with the dissolution of the marriage. Eighteen months after the breakup they found a significant difference in the attitudes and behaviors of boys and girls. Boys were more opposed to the divorce, were preoccupied with fantasies of reconciling the family, and were generally more depressed. Girls were happier and more likely to see their present circumstance as an improvement over predivorce days. Five years later one-third of the children were happy and well adjusted in their new life; another one-third were angry with one or both parents and quite unhappy; and the remaining one-third were doing reasonably well in their new home environment and in school.

These often contradictory findings and interpretations are not necessarily the result of sloppy scholarship and/or poor research designs. The impact of divorce on children is obviously complicated. Among the many factors to be considered are the circumstances surrounding the divorce, the degree of hostility between parents, the ages of the children, the emotional attachment of parents and children, custody arrangements, and the families' financial status after the divorce. Typically, the populations of children studied are not identical on all of these dimensions.

The Family and Modernization

In countries like the United States the family has changed significantly in the past 200 years. Since these changes paralleled the industrialization of society, it is not difficult to reach the conclusion that industrialization has been the principal, if not sole, factor responsible for them. Sociologist William J. Goode (1963) argued persuasively, however, that the relation between Western industrialization and the family is much more complex than simply cause (industrialization) and effect (family). To begin with, families in Europe were already changing from an extended to a nuclear structure in the seventeenth century, long before the Industrial Revolution (approximately 1800) began to spread. This certainly calls into question the commonly held assumption that the nuclear family "emerges when a culture is invaded by industrialization and urbanization . . . " (Goode, 1963, p. 10).

According to Goode the link between the nuclear family and industrialization is one in which the former met the "demands" of the latter. For example, an achievement-based, open-class, industrial society requires both geographical and social mobility. Neolocal nuclear families facilitate this mobility, allowing people to break kinship ties and sell their labor in the open market. Freed from the intense social control of nearby relatives, individuals can more easily change their speech, dress, and overall lifestyle while conforming to the demands of new jobs in an urban environment. Goode contended that Western industrialization would have been much more difficult (and certainly slower) if "family systems had perhaps been patriarchal and polygamous, with a full development of arranged marriages and a harem system" (p. 22).

The fit between the nuclear family and "certain industrial demands" was enhanced by the ideologies of economic progress and upward mobility, and of the conjugal family itself. These are powerful assertions that destroy hundreds of years of tradition. They emphasize the worth of the individual as opposed to the inherited aspects of wealth and social position. In other words, individuals are to be evaluated not on the basis of lineage (an ascribed status), but on ability (an achieved status). Goode noted that a "strong theme of democracy runs through this ideology" (p. 19), and encouraged

Although the relationship between modernization and family structure is far from a simple cause-and-effect sequence, industrial development and a nuclear family system tend to be closely associated. With the planned modernization of many contemporary societies already well underway, extended families such as this Indian group may become a thing of the past, replaced by a more streamlined nuclear structure.

people not to submit to the tyranny of the group, including the family. If an individual is not satisfied with family life, then he or she has the right to change it.

Inasmuch as the nuclear family is bilineal and does not pass on its wealth to the eldest son (or give it exclusively to males), the difference in life chances for sons and daughters is much less unequal than in other inheritance systems. Therefore, significantly more young people are able to develop their talents and take their place in an industrializing society. The nuclear family ideology enters society before industrialization has begun and prepares individuals for the demands of the new economic order that is to follow (Goode, 1963).

The Impact of Industrialization

William Goode saw the parallel development or harmonious fit between the conjugal family and the modern industrial system. Christopher Lasch (1979) was more interested in how industrialization affected the family in the United States once that process was under way. According to Lasch (1979), the family did not simply evolve in response to industrialization; rather "it was deliberately transformed by the intervention of planners and policy makers" (p. 13). Nineteenth-century educators and social reformers viewed newly arriving immigrant families as so many foreign obstacles in the path of the homogenization of America. The family was the haven of foreign religions, languages, and alien cultures that retarded the growth of an integrated community and state. With the aim of eliminating the influence of these unwanted cultures, reformers sought to minimize the impact that parents had on their children by maximizing the influence of the state and school.

Early twentieth-century reformers were also of the opinion that the family no longer provided for the needs of children, a philosophy that justified the expansion of school and social welfare services. Families began to lose control of their offspring as schools were charged with the task of education plus "the physical, mental, and social training of the child as well" (Lasch, 1979, p. 14). However, the family did not gradually "lose" childrearing duties as societies industrialized; on the contrary, these duties and other aspects of parental influence were taken away by the state in a rather short period of time.

The Developing World

The work of Goode and Lasch sheds light on the relation between industrialization and the family in developed countries like the United States, but how can we apply these insights to the relation between the family and modernization now occurring in the developing world? To begin with, the ideologies of economic progress and the nuclear family are known in the developing world, at least among the educated classes. We can also assume that, with the spread of information by movies, radio, and television in the so-called global village, these ideologies are common knowledge to tens of millions of less-educated people as well. Given that knowledge, any further movement from traditional family structures to nuclear families is likely to depend on economic conditions and political philosophies. As a country industrializes, the demands of progress will affect family structures as people change their patterns of behavior, including the organization of the family to meet those demands. One does not have to be a Marxist to see how the economic and material conditions of a society affect its patterns of behavior.

Families in Third World countries can be changed in large measure as a result of governmental policy in much the same way that American families were changed by social reformers beginning in the nineteenth century. For example, in an attempt to slow down population growth, China introduced a policy of one child per family in the 1970s. The ramifications of such a program are staggering for the family. Because children do not have brothers and sisters, their children will not have aunts and uncles. A tradition of extended families and kinship networks that existed for thousands of years can be drastically altered in the space of two generations. To the extent that the one-child policy has been successful, the Chinese people have had a three-person nuclear family structure imposed on them by their government.

The way in which a society treats women also affects the family. Where discrimination by custom or law exists, women are less likely to get an education and, therefore, less likely to be employed outside of the home. In such a society a more egalitarian family may exist as an ideology, but the structure and everyday working of the family will continue to be patriarchal and patrilineal with the tacit approval of the government.

Although it is impossible to predict how family structures in the more than one hundred developing nations will change as a result of modernization, we can be certain of at least two things: change will come much faster than it did in the past, as many Third World nations attempt to industrialize as soon as possible, and governments, both democratic and totalitarian, will have a growing impact on the family as they attempt to control population growth, limit migration from rural to urban areas, and maintain control over specific segments of the population (e.g., women).

Politics as a Social Institution

From ancient times to the present, people have had to make important decisions about how to spend their time and resources. These decisions often have had critical consequences for the survival and well-being of the society. Do we walk toward the sun or away from it to find the buffalo herds that feed our people? Do we welcome immigrants seeking refuge in our land, or do we keep that land for ourselves? Do we employ economic boycotts to change the unwelcome behaviors of people in neighboring societies, or do we threaten them with military invasion?

When people show significant differences in their beliefs about the desirability or correctness of one choice compared to another, they must come to some agreement about how final decisions will be made in their society. The alternative, as the philosopher Thomas Hobbes concluded centuries ago, would be chaos and anarchy: a war "of every man, against every man" (1881, p. 93). Individuals and groups would be locked in open and constant conflicts as they tried to exercise **power** — the ability to carry out their own will despite resistance from others (Weber, 1947).

Regardless of which particular form they happen to assume in a given society, these agreements to regulate the exercise of power and decision making represent the creation of some sort of political institution. Such institutions are an ancient and enduring fact of human societal life whose importance has grown with the increasing complexity of social organization.

In modern or developed societies like the United States and Japan, and in many developing societies like Mexico, final decision making and other political activities rest

MAP 4 Political Freedom in the Modern World (1988)

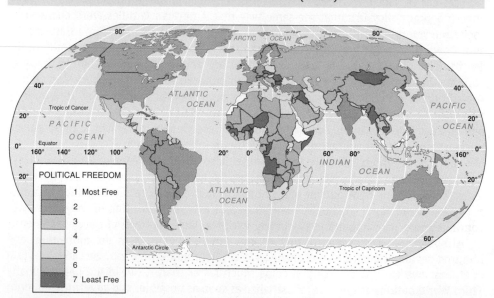

Criteria for a high rating include recent free and fair elections and an effective parliament. Military or foreign control and the denial of self-determination are factors that contribute to a lower rating.

with the **state,** the institution that holds a monopoly over the legitimate use of force and exercises governing power. Sociologists of all theoretical persuasions are in agreement about the pervasive and critical impact of the state in most contemporary societies. However, they are in sharp disagreement about how the state's activities affect those societies and their citizens.

Theoretical Interpretations of Political Institutions

The Functionalist Perspective   Sociologists in the structural-functional tradition have tried to understand and explain the growth of modern political institutions in terms of their contributions to societal survival. Functionalist theorists claim that the state (or **polity,** as they call it) plays a critical societal role in what Talcott Parsons (1971) referred to as "goal-attainment" activities.

According to this argument, every society possessing a surplus of economic resources must decide how that surplus will be used. Societal goals (e.g., a strong national defense) must be established and communicated to population members. Specific groups (branches of military service, joint chiefs of staff, etc.) must be assigned responsibility for particular objectives, and provided with the resources (weapons, support hardware, troops) necessary for their successful attainment. Individuals must be mobilized to join the specific goal-oriented groups and carry out assigned group responsibilities (e.g., salary levels and other benefits for both enlisted and commissioned personnel may be increased dramatically to retain existing troops and recruit new ones). Finally, people's behaviors and beliefs must be controlled and directed toward the fulfillment of these goals (e.g., the state may institute compulsory military service for all citizens in a specific age group; employers may be required by law to give time off to workers participating in reserve military training activities).

This cluster of activities, according to functionalists, constitutes the essence of institutionalized political behavior in any society. The polity decides what, when, where, how, and by whom important societal actions will be carried out. In so doing, it helps to ensure that activities necessary for developing and maintaining society will be performed efficiently.

The Conflict Perspective   Whereas functionalists emphasize the role of political institutions in establishing and coordinating societal goals for collective well-being, conflict theorists focus on the coercive and divisive aspects of the polity. For sociologists in this perspective, the state, as the ultimate source of power in society, is an important resource employed by some groups to gain and maintain control over other groups. As with so many other aspects of conflict theory, the classic statement was made by Marx.

As you may recall from earlier discussions, Marx regarded the political apparatus in capitalist societies — the state — as the ultimate instrument of class oppression. Like other superstructural elements, political institutions reflect the underlying economic substructure on which they are founded. More than most other derived social or cultural elements, however, the state plays a direct and active role in maintaining bourgeoisie dominance and proletarian subordination. The state generates legislation (e.g., tax and inheritance laws) that keeps both owners and workers in their respective places. It makes daily decisions and establishes societal policies (e.g., the taxpayer-funded bailouts of failed savings and loan organizations in the late 1980s and early 1990s) that favor the advantaged and add to the burdens of the disadvantaged. When necessary, the state supplies the physical force to reassert the rule of the ownership class and squash proletarian attempts to gain justice (e.g., the criminal justice system's tendency to punish lower-class crimes severely and to give white-collar or corporate criminals slaps on the wrist).

Avoiding some of Marx's rhetoric, modern conflict theorists maintain the assertion that the polity and the economy are intertwined in a symbiotic (mutually supportive) relationship (Collins, 1988b). They speak of a "political economy" that supports and furthers existing social inequality arrangements. As Turner (1972) commented, "Whether intended or not, a major consequence of political allocation [of valued economic resources] is to establish and reinforce the stratification system in a society" (p. 266). More often than not this effect is very much intended. Control of the polity is recognized as a prize with enormous consequences for economic and social advancement by those both in and out of power. It is hardly an accident that the history of various minority group movements in the United States has been one of growing political activism and attempted political takeover. For conflict theorists, the cynical version of the Golden Rule—he who has the gold makes the rules—has an equally cynical (but accurate) converse: he who has the rule makes the gold.

The U.S. Political System

Freedom and the Constitution   The promise of freedom has been a large part of the historic appeal of the United States to the millions of immigrants who have swollen our ranks over the last two centuries. Our culture's strong emphasis on *individual liberty* is a reminder of the fact that this society was created as a political experiment, a truly New World where people could escape the tyranny of Old World monarchies and shape the conditions of their own lives. A government "of the people, for the people, and by the people" is what the framers of our Constitution had in mind. They attempted to embody that concept in a democratic political system that disbursed power evenly among the many different segments of the population. The extent to which they succeeded has been a matter of continuing debate among political sociologists and other observers of the U.S. political scene for many years.

The major issue in this debate centers on how closely the reality of the U.S. political structure fits the model outlined in the Constitution and in other official documents. Attempts to address the issue focus on two related aspects of political life: the distribution of power within and among population segments, and the extent and depth of people's involvement in political activities.

The Structure of Political Power   In his farewell address to the nation before stepping down from office in 1961, President Dwight D. Eisenhower warned the American public of a growing "military-industrial complex" that threatened to take control of government and subvert the democratic process. Although hardly what one would call a conflict theorist or a radical social critic, the outgoing chief executive was echoing the words of someone who was both.

Five years earlier, the radical conflict sociologist C. Wright Mills argued that the takeover of the U.S. political system by what he termed a **power elite** was already an accomplished fact (Mills, 1956). A coalition of high-ranking officials from the largest corporations ("corporate chieftains"), the branches of military service ("warlords"), and the executive branch of the federal government ("political directorate") formed a "higher circle of power" that effectively controlled the running of the political system and was instrumental in all aspects of important societal decision making (pp. 3–4).

Their ascension to the highest levels of political influence reflected the enormous power of the large formal organizations that now structured and controlled most societal activities in the United States. It also signified the growing loss of control over most daily activities by individuals. This power elite, Mills claimed, formed the apex or top level of a pyramid of political power in our society. Despite the magnitude of its impact on societal and political affairs, however, this group's existence remained unknown to the general population.

Directly below the power elite lay the group that, according to Mills, was *believed* by the people to have control: the elected officials who make up the Congress and the other offices of government. Referring to this group as the "middle level of power" (p. 4), Mills claimed that their actual influence was restricted to relatively unimportant issues, and was further weakened by their lack of overall coordination and consensus. Their primary role was to serve as a front for the power elite by providing the illusion of democracy for the benefit of the larger population.

Mills argued that this larger population was fragmented and alienated into a societal **mass** consisting of millions of individuals who, for the most part, were uninterested and uninvolved in political affairs. Through a combination of this apathy and the manipulations of the power elite, the people were virtually powerless. In the vacuum created by their withdrawal from the political sphere and the limited activities of the middle levels of power, members of the corporate, military, and political elite could and did exercise a stranglehold over the U.S. political system. This was scarcely the democracy envisioned by the founding fathers or described in high school civics textbooks.

The Pluralist Model   Mills' portrayal of an American political system run by and for a small group that was accountable neither to the public nor to the formal system of government checks and balances generated an immediate and heated response. Some Marxists criticized Mills for failing to recognize the social class basis of the composition and operation of the U.S. political structure, and most critics blasted him for his assertion that democracy of any sort in this society was a myth (Domhoff and Ballard, 1968, assembled a number of these critiques). On the contrary, they asserted that democratic political rule was alive and well in this society, although in a different form from that commonly imagined.

Proponents of this so-called **pluralist** perspective concede the fact that political power in the United States is in the hands of large organized groups rather than individuals. But the number of such groups and the different interests they represent prevent any single group or coalition of groups from acquiring controlling power over the system. Instead, these groups act as "veto groups" (Riesman, 1961) that shift according to the issues at hand, restraining one another's power and limiting each other's influence to specific situations. In this model, individuals retain final political power by joining and becoming involved in various organized interest groups.

For example, in a large city, individual residents exercise very little power or control over the governing of the metropolis. But the organized groups to which these individuals belong—community planning groups, taxpayers' associations, and business or service clubs—may possess some clout in shaping the course of urban affairs. At times, the interests of these groups may coincide, and so they can form a coalition that will have an even louder voice in political decision making. Both citizens' and business groups, for example, may rally around plans to improve a community park in their neighborhood, believing that safe, attractive recreational facilities will stimulate people to live and shop in the area. However, at other times, their interests may diverge, and so each group finds itself speaking out against the others. Plans to rezone single-family neighborhoods to allow for the development of apartment and condominium complexes often generate heated disputes between neighborhood groups and business interests. In this case, the effective power of each group may be weakened considerably by opposition from the other.

U.S. Society—A Power Elite System? Recent studies of the U.S. power structure provide evidence that the power elite interpretation may have greater validity than the pluralist model, although neither provides a completely accurate picture of power in this society. In a continuing series of analyses conducted over the past fifteen years, for example, Thomas Dye (1976, 1979, 1983, 1986, 1990) examined the institutionalized centers of power in this country (political bodies, corporations, the mass media, major universities, top legal firms, civic and cultural organizations) and the social origins of the people who occupy key positions in these institutions. His findings indicate a strong concentration of power in the hands of a relatively small number of highly influential organizations, and a pattern of common socioeconomic class backgrounds for key office holders across the different institutional sectors.

At the same time, data also show that the social origins and political interests of elites in the various sectors are not identical. Although corporate leaders, top political officials, and directors of large research foundations (among other elites) at times may see the world in similar terms, they often display significant disagreements among themselves on particular issues. These internal divisions keep these powerful groups from forming the kind of completely unified power elite described by Mills. Overall, however, their shared world view makes them more like one another than like the nonelites who make up the bulk of the population. The paths of entry into their positions also make it very difficult for individuals from lower-, working-, and (in many cases) middle-class backgrounds to add new and different views to the top rungs of power. The result is a power structure, as well as social and political policies, that generally reflects compatible (although not necessarily identical) definitions of social and political reality. Recent events in this society would seem to lend support to this conclusion.

Perhaps more than in other presidential administrations, the years of Ronald Reagan's tenure in the White House were marked by a close, friendly working relationship between the federal government and big business. During this time President Reagan made good on his promise to get government off people's backs. Federal regulatory agencies were disbanded entirely or had their operations curtailed so that corporations could do what they did best—make profits. These profits, in turn, were to be plowed back into the economy. Eventually they would trickle down and throughout the various social layers, fostering growth and prosperity as they trickled. In the end, all segments of the society would benefit. Seldom during the past half-century have the visions of the political and economic sectors seemed so closely aligned. It was a time of unrestrained capitalism and exuberant affluence—for some.

As the Reagan era came to a close, mounting evidence began to indicate that the shared vision of federal government and corporate leaders had worked to the best advantage of a much smaller population group than originally projected (Phillips, 1990a). During the decade of the 1980s, the economic position of the wealthiest segment of the U.S. population improved, while that of virtually all other groups either dropped or remained stagnant (*San Diego Union,* 1990a). Racial and ethnic minority group members, in particular, lost economic ground (*San Diego Union,* 1990l). Tax reforms passed during this period seemed to increase top income-receiving groups' share of after-tax revenues and fall most heavily on lower- and middle-income groups

(Phillips, 1990b; *San Diego Union,* 1990c). Snowballing savings and loan association collapses and a deepening federal deficit dug deeply into middle- and lower-income taxpayers' pockets, seemingly leaving upper-income groups untouched. The gap between the haves and the have nots widened, with many more individuals sinking into the latter category. If we assume that the outcomes of social and political policies reflect *someone's* interests, these patterns are more indicative of a special-interest rather than public-interest political structure, a power elite rather than a pluralist system.

Patterns of Political Participation   The evidence regarding the distribution of political power in this society is ambiguous enough to permit a number of different conclusions about the true shape of power in the United States. In contrast, data concerning the involvement of the American people in their political system are clear and consistent. Among the political democracies in the contemporary world, this country ranks close to the bottom in terms of its citizens' participation in electoral politics (Marger, 1987). For most people, most of the time, politics remains a matter of only passing and passive interest.

Voting   Of all the different ways that people living in a democratic society might express involvement in political affairs, voting in national, state, and local elections would seem to be the most obvious and most important. After all, it is precisely the legal right to vote that distinguishes democracies from other types of political systems. The people who founded this society fought a revolutionary war to establish the right to elect their leaders. Over the years, their successors, including many members of this generation, fought other wars to preserve that right. In our system of cultural beliefs, voting is as much a moral obligation as a civil right. Failure to exercise it is often regarded as failure to meet the minimum requirements of citizenship.

If there is any truth to this belief, a significant number of people in this society are not very "good" citizens. Their involvement in the political life of society does not extend as far as the simple act of casting a ballot in the elections through which government leaders formally enter and leave office. This pattern of widespread non-voting is true even in the case of presidential elections.

According to U.S. Bureau of the Census figures (1990), voter turnout in presidential elections since 1932 has failed to exceed 63 percent of the registered, voting-age population. Most often, the figures have averaged in the low to mid-50 percent range. In the 1988 election, for example, the George Bush–Michael Dukakis race brought only about half (50.2 percent) of the eligible public to the polls. Voting percentages for off-year (i.e., nonpresidential) congressional elections for the same time period are even smaller, as low as 33 percent.

For state and local elections the figures are lower yet. In a recent statewide California primary election to decide, among other things, candidates for the governor's race, only 25 percent of eligible voters actually cast votes. In some instances, more Californians play the state lottery than vote in local elections, even when those elections have state- and national-level implications (O'Connell, 1990).

Studies of voting patterns and the social correlates of voting are consistent in their findings of who votes and who doesn't (Conway, 1991). The likelihood of voting increases with age, with people between the ages of thirty and sixty-five more likely to vote than younger and older groups. For example, well over 60 percent of people over age thirty-five contacted by the U.S. Bureau of the Census reported that they had voted in the 1988 presidential election. In contrast, fewer than 40 percent of those under age twenty-five claimed to have done so (U.S. Bureau of the Census, 1990).

Class, Race, Gender, and Voting As Table 9.3 indicates, members of higher socioeconomic status (SES) groups vote with much greater frequency than members of
lower SES groups. Formal educational level, in particular, appears to be the critical
class-related factor influencing participation in the electoral process. In the 1988 elections, 37 percent of people with an eighth-grade education or below, and 55 percent
of high school graduates reported voting, compared to nearly 78 percent of college
graduates (U.S. Bureau of the Census, 1990).

Race and ethnicity are important factors in voting, with whites having higher levels
of participation than either African Americans or Hispanics. Again, in the 1988 presidential elections, 59 percent of white respondents to the Census Bureau reported
voting, compared to 51.5 percent of African Americans and only 29 percent of Hispanics.

Gender differences are reflected somewhat in voting patterns, with females typically not as likely to vote as males. However, that particular gap appears to be closing,
as so-called gender politics have become more evident in the past decade (recall our
discussion of gender and politics in chapter 7). In fact, a slightly higher percentage of

TABLE 9.3 Self-Reported Voting in Presidential Elections by Sex, Race, Age, and
Education (in percentages)

Characteristic	Election Year			
	1976	1980	1984	1988
Sex				
Male	59.6	59.1	59.0	56.4
Female	58.8	59.4	60.8	58.3
Race/ethnicity				
White	60.9	60.9	61.4	59.1
Black	48.7	50.5	55.8	51.5
Hispanic	31.8	29.9	32.6	28.8
Age (years)				
18–20	38.0	35.7	36.7	33.2
21–24	45.6	43.1	43.5	38.3
25–34	55.4	54.6	54.5	48.0
35–44	63.3	64.4	63.5	61.3
45–64	68.7	69.3	69.8	67.9
65 and over	62.2	65.1	67.7	68.8
Education				
8 years or less	44.1	42.6	42.9	36.7
High school				
1–3 years	47.2	45.6	44.4	41.3
4 years	59.4	58.9	58.7	54.7
College				
1–3 years	68.1	67.2	67.5	64.5
4 years or more	79.8	79.9	79.1	77.6

Source: Adapted from U.S. Bureau of the Census, *Statistical Abstracts of the United States, 1990,* p. 262, Table 439.

women (58 percent compared to 56 percent for men) reported voting in the 1988 presidential election (U.S. Bureau of the Census, 1990). Summarizing these patterns, voters, as one pollster put it, "tend to be older, more educated, whiter and more upscale in income than non-voters" (Field, quoted in O'Connell, 1990, p. A11).

   A Passive Electorate   Other forms of political involvement such as following campaigns and campaign issues, discussing politics with other people, becoming active in a campaign (working for a candidate, making telephone calls, wearing campaign pins, etc.), and contributing money to a candidate or campaign show similar social and demographic patterning. Although perhaps difficult to imagine, the levels of participation in these political activities are substantially lower than voting levels (Conway, 1991). Most citizens of the United States just do not appear appreciably involved in the political life of their country.

   This disengagement from the political process has been subject to a number of interpretations, ranging from contentment with the system ("things are working just fine; I don't need to get involved") to disgust ("things are rigged; why waste time getting involved?"). The definitive explanation has yet to be written, but evidence points to a growing cynicism in people's perceptions of how politics works, and a sense that individuals make little or no real difference in a mass-based polity (Conway, 1991; Shogan, 1990).

   These feelings may or may not be an accurate reflection of the reality. The danger is that, with so many people holding these feelings and acting—or, rather, not acting—on them, what they believe to be true may become true. If those who believe in the existence of some kind of controlling elite structure let that belief remove them from active political participation of any sort, they very well may have a hand in confirming their own worst fears.

Politics in a Changing World

If human social patterns are at all subject to general laws, the one law that would seem to apply in the case of politics is that anything and all things can happen. Modern nation-states and their complex political structures arose from the widespread technological and economic changes that swept through traditional societies, turning their worlds upside down. As the center of planning and decision making for these developing (and now developed) societies, the state attempted to gain control over the forces of social and cultural change so that stability could be regained. In the process, what had been political rule by physical force—the king's army—became transformed into what Max Weber (1978, original 1921) called **rule by authority.** Raw power was replaced by a sense of moral obligation as the basis for the orders and decisions of political leaders being followed by members of the population. As both the rationalization and the secularization of societies grew, **charismatic authority** (rule based on some extraordinary personal quality of the political leader) and **traditional authority** (rule based on long-standing social customs) were replaced by what Weber called **rational-legal authority** (rule based on the reasonableness of laws and the acceptability of law-making procedures). The growth of these large-scale, legitimate political systems promoted and reflected continuing economic and societal development, ushering in the modern era.

   However, significant political change did not end with the emergence of the modern state; nor do political changes in the modern world follow any singe route. Events taking place during the past few decades and in the current one point out the weaknesses of assuming, as some sociologists once did, that either social or political development unfolds according to some natural, inevitable sequence.

The Collapse of Communism? In a 1960 visit to the United States, Soviet Premier Nikita Khrushchev predicted that, in the near future, communism would bury capitalist societies like the United States. At the time, the Soviet style of government appeared to be on the move. Both Eastern Europe and the People's Republic of China were in its camp, and portions of Latin America were leaning in its direction. Today, it is Soviet communism that is sinking into the ground. Capitalism is replacing socialism throughout Eastern Europe, and some of the republics that make up the Soviet Union (e.g., Lithuania, Latvia, and Estonia) have already established their independence from Soviet government. This disintegration of communism appears to be linked to the failure of the governments of these societies to provide citizens with the kinds and levels of economic goods they need and want. As sociologist Seymour Martin Lipset (1963) once observed, successful political rule depends as much on government being perceived by citizens as effective as it does on granting legitimacy to political leaders.

The fact that communism is declining does not necessarily mean that U.S.-style democracy will triumph in the Soviet Union's front yard, however. The governments that may emerge throughout Eastern Europe will have to demonstrate quickly that they are able to solve pressing economic problems, and to create and maintain higher living standards for their populations. If they are unable to meet the rising expectations of their people in a relatively short period of time, they may find themselves facing the same type of revolutionary mood that brought them into power in the first place (Davies, 1962). For example, in the years since the 1986 overthrow of Ferdinand Marcos and the establishment of a popular democracy in the Philippines, the Aquino government has not been able to bring about significant improvements in that country's depressed economic conditions. Despite its initial popularity with the people, the new government has been subjected to half a dozen overthrow attempts from disenchanted population groups. People may be more loyal to concrete economic and social improvements than to abstract political ideologies.

An End to U.S. Supremacy? As we have seen, the reality of the U.S. political system bears little resemblance to ideological conceptions of a government of, for, and by the people. With the inability of the United States to win a long military war in Vietnam and its possible loss of an economic war to Japan, this society's days as the premier world superpower may be drawing to a close (although the rapid U.S.-led military action in the Persian Gulf War may forestall people's recognition of that fact). Tensions with a large number of societies throughout the world, including Canada and Mexico, also point to what may be a growing disillusionment with U.S. political policies and practices. "We're number one" may be a phrase that soon will no longer be heard in this country outside of sporting events. For example, in a recent series of magazine ads, a certain U.S. car manufacturer boasted that one of its vehicles had ranked within the top ten list of quality-made automobiles, the only U.S. entrant in an otherwise all-Japanese and German grouping. "We're number five!" became a cause for corporate celebration and an extensive advertising campaign.

Whether or not people in this society can adjust to not being number one remains an interesting and significant question. Given the fact that Americans have always assumed the superiority of our way of life, it is not likely that people will adapt to the new reality rapidly or easily. As we saw in chapter 6, the growing number of hate crimes directed against Asians and Asian Americans in the United States during the past several years may be linked to the growing sense of frustration felt by many Americans. They can see their nation's power and prestige in the world declining, but don't know how that slide might be stopped. This is the kind of uncertainty that often leads to the destabilization of political systems, as the ineffectiveness of political leaders generates challenges to their legitimacy. In a real sense, perhaps the rise of the new Christian right in this society is symptomatic of things to come in U.S. politics.

The Rise of Third World Nationalism   As both First World societies such as the United States and Second World societies such as the Soviet Union experience decline, some Third World societies such as Mexico may be on the rise. With control over supplies of petroleum and other resources vital to the industrial and postindustrial economies of the current superpowers, they are in a position to exert considerable influence and leverage over international political and economic markets. First and Second World powers competing for the export products and political allegiance of developing nations must grant these societies concessions that increase their power and prestige in the world sphere.

In some cases, developing societies have rejected modern social and cultural forms altogether, overthrowing established leaders in an attempt to return to a simpler and purer traditional way of life. The successful Shiite-led revolution against the Shah of Iran in 1979 and the establishment of a postrevolutionary fundamentalist government

Although nationalistic political movements most often have been associated with developing Third World countries, people in developed societies recently have begun to express similar actions. Like their counterparts in other Eastern European countries, these citizens of the Baltic Republic of Lithuania are demonstrating for their independence from the Soviet Union.

OURSELVES AND OTHERS

Beyond Plain Vanilla: Immigration Has Accentuated Canada's Diversity

As the historical story goes, when Jacques Cartier, the French explorer, stepped ashore in 1535 at the rapids near what was to become Quebec City, he confronted a band of curious natives. Looking around at the pristine countryside, he asked them in French and sign language what they called that place. The Indians, looking about their humble village, replied "kanata." It is the Huron-Iroquois word for "settlement."

Thus conceived in bilingual misunderstanding did the world's second-largest country get its name, Canada. There have been many such "kanatas" in Canada's history. The French-English split, highlighted by the failure last month of the Meech Lake accord, an attempt to draw Quebec into accepting the country's eight-year-old constitution by acknowledging the French province as a "distinct society," is but the most dramatic.

Although from the outside its image is that of a vat of vanilla yogurt, Canada in fact has always consisted of many disparate pieces sprawling over a country so immense that its southernmost tip in Ontario is actually closer to the Equator than to the top of Canada.

This geography, harsh climate, different languages and divergent cultures often make that land seem less like a single nation and more like a conservative collection of feuding fiefdoms. Quebec has its own vibrant culture and celebrities who are virtually unknown next door in Ontario and vice versa. Canada's politically under-represented West resents the economic dominance of central Canada, which is jealous of the West's oil and gas. Every region tells ethnic jokes about the residents of Newfoundland, Canada's newest province, where they refer to people from other provinces disparagingly as C.F.A.'s (Come From Aways).

Recruited Immigrants

Centrifugal forces are always at work in Canada, which was settled not by waves of immigrants moving inexorably from sea to sea, but by many ethnic groups recruited overseas to settle in particular places where the young country needed more people. Though efficient, this method did not create a population with a broad sense of the land. Canada's immigration laws help perpetuate these ethnic pop-ulation pockets and identities by creating a special status called Landed Immigrant, which allows newcomers to become Canadian while keeping their old nationality.

Even native Canadians work to isolate themselves; the Indians and Inuit of the vast Northwest Territories plan to divide that 40 percent of Canada's geographic mass along racial lines into two pieces.

From the beginning, each segment looked out for its own. In 1867, under the threat of expansion by the United States, Britain finally persuaded Canada's disparate regions to become a single country. As the price of its assent, British Columbia insisted on a rail line to connect it with the rest of the vast new nation.

Even now, each group is striving to be heard. The required ratification of the Meech Lake accord by the 10 provincial legislatures was blocked not by an English- or French-speaker but by the filibuster of Elijah Harper, a Cree Indian in the Manitoba Legislative Assembly who wanted distinct recognition for native peoples.

Recognizing Everyone

Also awaiting special recognition were Canada's feminists, not to mention groups representing the mushrooming ranks of Canada's newer immigrants from Commonwealth lands in Africa, the Caribbean, Hong Kong and East Asia. Today, nearly half the children in Vancouver's school system have English as a second language. The city of Toronto, Canada's largest, routinely sends out property tax notices in six languages—English, French, Chinese, Italian, Greek and Portuguese.

But many Canadians now see a fraying of traditional civility into the kind of outspoken divisiveness that has characterized the mixed records of other bilingual countries. There has been vocal resentment in some areas over the impact of rich Chinese fleeing Hong Kong, bidding up Canadian real estate prices, replacing traditional bungalows with mansions seen as ostentatious by neighbors. Shouting matches and racial slurs erupted in Calgary recently over a school board decision to allow teen-age Sikh boys to wear their ceremonial daggers in school when other youths were not allowed even pocket knives. Earlier, the Federal Government decided that Sikhs who become Mounties can wear their turbans instead of the traditional trooper hat. Even though the number of such Sikhs may one day be counted on one hand, it was the kind of "foreign" symbol that now arouses some Canadians to raise their voice.

Quebec has always taken the lead in separatist actions. The province's move in late 1988, in open defiance of a Supreme Court decision, to outlaw any outdoor English signs while continuing to demand special protections for French-speakers offended even many liberal Canadians elsewhere. It seemed to violate the unwritten agreement that Quebec's minority English community would be protected. As one result, nearly 100 communities outside the province passed resolutions declaring themselves English only, a meaningless move since few had many French residents anyway.

Then there are the political divisions. Newfoundland, the other stumbling block to Meech Lake's ratification, is governed by Premier Clyde Wells, a close confidant of Pierre Elliott Trudeau, the former Liberal prime minister who has long opposed the accord.

Jean Chrétien, the newly elected leader of the opposition Liberals, calls Canada's current mood "a growing distemper."

"The world," he warns, "has known other serene communities that have come apart from internal tensions."

There is evidence, too, that while the specter of Quebec's separation struck terror into the hearts of most Canadians before the defeat of a provincial referendum on the issue 10 years ago, the prospect of Canada and Quebec falling out of love now draws fatalistic shrugs.

"It is," Peter C. Newman, an author and nationalist, said sadly, "as if Quebec is growing out of Canada and the rest of the country says, 'Enough already with your constant demands for special this and special that.' "

The political price of all this unrest is likely to be steep for Prime Minister Brian Mulroney. He treated the high-pressure, high-stakes Meech Lake talks like the former labor negotiator he is, relying on last-minute concessions that did not come. And the three-year Meech Lake process allowed too much time for an initial consensus to erode. Mr. Newman likened it to 10 co-workers who agree to lunch together and then schedule an hour's debate on where to go.

"Nothing in life is unanimous," he said, "especially in Canada."

Source: Andrew H. Malcolm, *The New York Times*, July 8, 1990. Copyright © 1990 by the New York Times Company. Reprinted by permission.

in that country illustrates the fact that not all societal populations accept the view that Western-style modernization necessarily represents human progress. The disenchantment of Christian fundamentalist groups with societal trends and the rise of the new conservative religious-political movement in the United States during the 1980s may indicate that not all members of our own society equate modernization with progress.

At other times, resistance to modernization has reflected a growing nationalistic spirit (an ideology that emphasizes self-governance and the importance of the nation-state) that rejects any form of social or political structure, whether democratic or socialist, imposed from the outside. Nationalism has been and is a significant force in many Third World societies. In the Persian Gulf War of 1991, for example, the situation remained volatile as the Allied coalition against Iraq was constantly tested by strong Arab nationalistic feelings against both Israel and the Western nations. At any given moment, the internal dissensions that divided the Arab states and permitted some of them to align with the United States–led forces could have been overshadowed by bonds of cultural unity.

Nationalism has been an especially powerful unifying political force in countries that once had been colonial territories (Lenski and Lenski, 1987). As we will see in chapter

12, many contemporary African states resulted from the "devolution" or internally forced breakup of what had been established political entities in the Third World. Ethnic groups that had been arbitrarily split and grouped through decisions made by outside powers fought bitterly to establish their own political self-determination and national boundaries.

These nationalistic movements, however, are not confined to developing countries trying to resist forced modernization. The declarations of independence that sent Russian tanks and troops into the Baltic republics in January 1991 were based as much on a resurging ethnic political consciousness as on deteriorating economic conditions. Somewhat closer to home, the separatist movement that periodically threatens to split French-speaking Quebec from the other provinces making up the Canadian federation also shows obvious nationalistic overtones.

Contemporary populations show tremendous social, cultural, economic, religious, historical, and geographical diversity. Given these vast differences, continuing political diversity and change is about as close to a certainty as one is likely to encounter. The assumption that any specific system represents a final, highest stage of political or societal evolution reflects ethnocentrism, or at least a mistaken belief in stability, far more than social science observation. In the world of human politics, any thing and all things are possible.

 ## RELIGION AS A SOCIAL INSTITUTION

Throughout our history we humans have attempted to understand and explain the world in which we live. During all that time, religion has been an important part of social life. In some form or other, organized religious beliefs and practices have been present in all societies, from the earliest hunting and gathering bands to the most modern industrial and postindustrial systems. Such activity reflects our need to deal with what the French sociologist Emile Durkheim (1965, original 1915) called the **sacred**—those extraordinary elements of life that inspire a sense of reverence, awe, and fear in people.

Our attempts to make sense out of the world invariably have fallen short of perfection, and it seems that some areas of existence will always remain outside the limits of science or other rational mechanisms of knowledge. It is exactly these areas, according to Durkheim, that make up the essence of human religion. Religious beliefs are matters of faith, which, unlike the **profane** (commonplace or ordinary elements of everyday life), cannot be proved or disproved through empirical means.

Religious statuses and roles were among the first noneconomic positions to be defined and differentiated in those early societies in which a surplus of resources existed (Lenski, 1966; Lenski and Lenski, 1987). As the economic surplus grew and these societies became further differentiated and increasingly complex, religious activities became more elaborate. They were entrusted to a group of full-time specialists who exercised a great deal of influence over all or most group behaviors. Durkheim (1965, original 1915) claimed that religion was such an important and integral part of these early societies because it involved a symbolic recognition of the power of the society itself over its individual members. In worshipping supernatural deities, humans in effect were celebrating their own collective existence.

As societies developed and understanding became more sophisticated, philosophical and then scientific explanations of the world replaced supernatural interpretations, and the actual need for a body of sacred beliefs perhaps decreased. By that time, however, religion as an institutionalized social structure had become intertwined with other major institutions. It was a fundamental part of the world-taken-for-granted. Even in highly rational, highly secular societies like the contemporary United States that rely heavily on science, religion continues to exert considerable effects in many areas of life.

Theoretical Perspectives on Religion

Functionalist Interpretations   Durkheim's analysis of religion, which was one of the first attempts to understand this phenomenon in sociological terms, was also cast squarely in the functionalist theoretical mold. He attempted to explain the universal presence of religion throughout human history in terms of its contributions to societal survival. In this regard, he was led to conclude that religion served several important functions, all related to the establishment and furthering of social solidarity.

It provides a basis for *social cohesion* by uniting the members of the population in shared beliefs and values, as well as a common set of rituals (formalized expressions of religious beliefs, such as the Roman Catholic Mass). Religion not only unites people spiritually, but brings them together socially. In addition, it promotes *social stability* by infusing cultural norms and political rules with sacred authority (remember, for example, Christ's message to "render unto Caesar the things that are Caesar's"), thus increasing the likelihood that people will follow them. Peter Berger (1967) viewed this legitimizing effect as providing a "sacred canopy" that shields and protects political regimes. The postrevolutionary rule of the Ayatollah Khomeini in Iran is probably the best recent example of this hand-in-glove relationship between religion and politics. In this case, the same person was both political and religious leader to millions of devout followers.

Finally, Durkheim maintained that religion helps maintain people's allegiance to societal goals and participation in social affairs by giving them a sense of *meaning and purpose*. It tells people why sometimes, in the words of one best-selling book, "bad things happen to good people" (and why good things sometimes happen to bad people). In providing people a larger context—a divine plan—in which to understand specific events, religion keeps them from falling into despair and withdrawing from society. As we saw in chapter 1, Durkheim also thought that religion often prevented people from withdrawing from life altogether through suicide.

Conflict Interpretations   Conflict interpretations view religious beliefs and practices in an entirely different vein. For these theorists, religion is a means of exploitation rather than integration, of social damnation rather than heavenly salvation. As Karl Marx so eloquently put it, "Religion is the sigh of the oppressed creature, the heart of a heartless world and the soul of soulless conditions. It is the opium of the people" (1970, original 1844, p. 131).

Marx claimed that organized religion, like other social and cultural patterns, is a reflection of the underlying mode of economic production whose basic structure is responsible for shaping all other facets of human social life. Like those other super-structural elements, religion's purpose is to preserve the economic substructure and the relations of production that allow one class to enslave all others. By focusing workers' attention on the sweet by-and-by of the afterlife with its promises of eternal bliss, religion deflects their attention from the not-so-sweet here and now and thus perpetuates their misery in the present life. It is a smokescreen, blinding the workers from recognizing the ruling class as the true source of that misery. As long as the proletariat remain focused on the afterlife, they never will be a revolutionary threat to the ruling class in this life. For this reason, religion, like the productive system it serves, is inherently dysfunctional for the survival of everyone but the ruling class. It is a powerful weapon used by capitalists in the class struggle.

Conflict theorists since Marx also emphasized the dysfunctional elements of religion, especially in large heterogeneous societies like the United States. Differences in beliefs and values often serve as the basis for the formation of subcultural groups with radically different moral views and policy agendas. The attempts by particular groups within the society to impose their own religious views and practices on all other groups results in conflicts and power struggles that divide these groups and the society at large. One need only think of the current religion-based controversy over abortion that has polarized the population of the United States to understand the dynamics at work.

The Protestant Ethic and the Rise of Capitalism   These divisions, however, point to a significant role of religion overlooked by Marx—that of a catalyst for social change. Just as (according to Marx) changes in the organization of the proletariat would lead to class conflict and the eventual overthrow of the capitalist system, changes in the organization of religious systems could lead to fundamental and sweeping changes in the larger societal system. This argument, in fact, was the basis for one of the most famous sociological analyses of religion to date: Max Weber's examination of the role of the **Protestant ethic,** the world view and values associated with the new Protestant religions, in the rise of modern capitalism (1958, original 1904).

In this well-known controversial thesis, Weber argued that the European system of capitalism that triggered Marx's critique of religion represents an outcome of the Protestant Reformation that swept through Western Europe during the sixteenth and seventeenth centuries. Prior to this time, the Roman Catholic Church had dominated the European continent and supported the existing feudal system. Catholicism discouraged economic expansion or change through its doctrine that making money through lending money (what was called usury) was sinful. However, Martin Luther's break from the Catholic Church led to the development of several new religious systems that created an ideological climate supportive of rational economic activity and the accumulation of wealth.

One significant component of this climate was the concept of **predestination**—the belief that one's fate in the afterlife was decided before (or at) one's birth, and that no amount of prayer or good works could change that outcome. According to Weber, this belief created an uncertainty in people's minds as to their own particular fate. Although the question never could be answered fully, one likely indicator of success or failure in the afterlife was success or failure in this life. Economic prosperity, therefore, became a fundamental goal and a driving force in people's lives. Although not a cause of spiritual salvation, such prosperity was a sign that one was among the elect.

A second critical element of this new religious ideology was the doctrine of **worldly asceticism,** or denial of material self-indulgence. According to this belief, the simple, frugal life was morally superior to foolish concern for the things of this world. Like prosperity, thrift became a sign of virtue.

Weber concluded that, in combination, these two beliefs encouraged people to try to succeed in their work efforts, and directed them to apply and reapply the proceeds of past efforts to future efforts. The Protestant ethic led them, in short, to activities that translated into capital formation and capital expansion. The result was a revolutionary change in the structure of European social systems.

Weber recognized that the change from feudalism to capitalism was not the direct result of the Protestant ethic alone, and a reciprocal or two-way relationship existed between the new belief system and the new economic system. His point was that religion can serve and has served as an important medium for significant social change. It is a point well taken.

Religion in the United States: From Puritans to Televangelists

Since the first days of its existence as New World colonies, what is now the United States has been singular in terms of religious expression. Unlike the European societies from which the largest numbers of its population have come, this society has been one of religious pluralism and tolerance. Many of the early settlers were religious dissenters fleeing persecution in their homelands. They came seeking a new land in which they would be free to worship as they saw fit. This cultural value of freedom of religious expression and the rejection of a state-supported or state-imposed religion was incorporated into the Constitution. It has been the guideline for the social organization of religion in the country since that time.

From its founding, the United States has been a society whose members at least claim a set of religious beliefs and practices. Many of the original thirteen states were the successors of colonies (e.g., Puritan settlements in Massachusetts Bay) that had been conceived as religious "experiments." Their founders viewed these colonies as attempts to establish the heavenly society in an otherwise unheavenly world (Erikson, 1966). The social patterns of the communities were grounded in the religious beliefs of the people, who attempted to construct all aspects of daily life according to their particular reading of the Word of God. They were joined later by millions of ethnic immigrants from traditional societies for whom religion also was an important organizing social force. These immigrants brought their old religions with them, adding to the growing number of faiths in American society.

The number of specific religious groupings that have appeared in the United States at one time or another has been very large, but most people have affiliated historically with one of three "great traditions" (Williams, 1989): Protestantism, Catholicism, or Judaism (see Figure 9.3). They form what sociologists refer to as **denominations,** or formal religious organizations that are well integrated into their society and recognize religious pluralism. Such denominations coexist with the larger society and with one another. As of 1988, for example, 56 percent of the U.S. population age eighteen or over expressed a preference for or affiliation with Protestantism, 28 percent with Catholicism, and 2 percent with Judaism (U.S. Bureau of the Census, 1990).

Although these three great traditions have defined the general shape of the religious landscape in the United States, they do not account for all its specific details. Peter Williams (1989) chronicled the development of what he calls "little traditions" of folk and popular religions throughout U.S. social history. **Folk religions** represent particular interpretations and modifications of more formalized religious traditions to meet the needs of specific population groups; for example, the set of beliefs and practices of Italian Catholic or Polish Catholic immigrants. These little traditions can be thought of as translations or adaptations of mainstream denominational religions.

In contrast, what Williams terms **popular religions** represent sets of beliefs and practices that lie outside of or perhaps span the boundaries of recognized denominations. Their appeal is not to a specific group or groups but, rather, to large-scale or mass audiences drawn from a variety of backgrounds. These popular religions are generated

FIGURE 9.3 Religious Affiliation in the United States

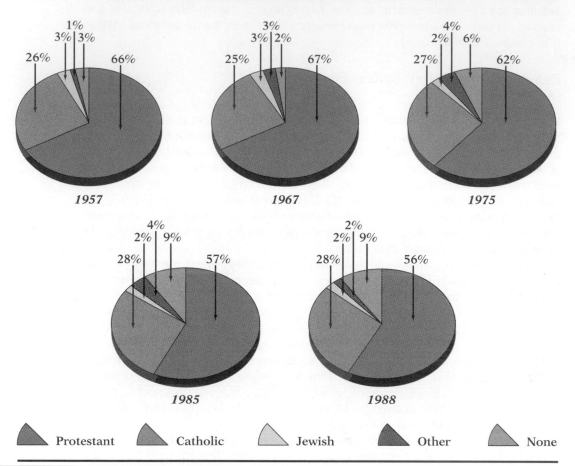

FIGURE 9.3 Religious Affiliation in the United States

Protestant   Catholic   Jewish   Other   None

Note: Because of rounding, percentages do not always add to 100%.
Source: Adapted from U.S. Bureau of the Census, *Statistical Abstract of the United States, 1990*, p. 55, Table 75.

by people's experiences of cultural and social disorganization, and the inability of established denominations to resolve this confusion and chaos. As such, they generally stand in opposition to the established sociocultural order. They offer their members a different vision of what societal life could and should be like, and a different path to achieve that vision. In this respect, they resemble what sociologists refer to as religious **sects.** The recent proliferation of Christian evangelical and pentecostal movements, and the various "televangelistic" ministries, illustrate the growth of these popular religions in the contemporary United States.

Religion in the Counterculture Movement   During the 1960s and the decade of the counterculture movement, observers in this country were announcing the death of God and of religion. The increasing rational planning and organization of nearly all societal activities, coupled with the increasing concern of people with material comfort and affluence, presumably had led to the **secularization** of society (the transformation from a religious to a civil and worldly basis) and a significant decline of religion in everyday life. Attacks on "the establishment" by the so-called hippies that occurred during the decade also seemed to involve a defection from established religious traditions as well as a rejection of the secular social order.

The members of the counterculture may have been seeking mystical experiences in their struggle against what they saw as a depersonalized, militaristic society, but they were not finding those experiences through traditional American religions. In their eyes, established denominations had themselves become bureaucratic and depersonalized, out of touch with the real world and its many social injustices. Traditional religious groups (especially Roman Catholicism and mainline Protestant denominations like Presbyterians, Methodists, and Episcopalians) began to experience significant declines in membership and attendance.

While some members of the counterculture in fact did reject religion altogether, many others began to experiment with new, nontraditional systems of religious expression. These new forms ranged from simple beliefs and rituals last practiced in hunting and gathering or horticultural societies to Hinduism, Buddhism, and other Eastern religions dating back thousands of years. Their common denominator seemed to be the strong sense of community that had been lost from the churches and synagogues of the established denominations. Religion itself was not dead in the United States, although some conventional religions were looking a little unhealthy.

To combat declining memberships, some of the traditional denominations began to become more involved with the surrounding world, addressing themselves to pressing social issues such as poverty and racial discrimination. At the same time, they developed a new ecumenical spirit that emphasized the underlying continuities among various established religious groups rather than doctrinal differences. Within the Catholic Church, the Second Vatican Council, held in Rome from 1962 to 1965, eased many of its traditional authoritarian rules. It also introduced a number of liberal and local elements into U.S. Catholicism. Masses now were conducted in English rather than Latin, and folk songs replaced conventional organ music and church choirs. Many Catholic nuns gave up their old habits as their regimented convent life was replaced by more egalitarian communal living arrangements and a more active role in societal affairs.

The Rise of Fundamentalism Ironically, the changes introduced by these established denominations to keep and attract members during the 1960s seem to have helped spark the fundamentalist revival that began in the 1970s and gained such prominence during the 1980s. The groups that made up "the resurgence of conservative Christianity" (Dobson et al., 1986, p. xiv) were appalled by what they saw as the triumph of the secular over the sacred in everyday life, as well as the steady rise of **humanism**— the belief that humans, rather than God, are the center of their own destiny.

Fundamentalists see evidence of creeping secular humanism, as they call it, in changing public attitudes and political policies toward abortion, women's proper roles in society, and homosexuality, among other things. They are convinced that this trend is one of the most dangerous threats of the modern age to decent Christians throughout the country. They also are convinced that many, if not all, of the established Catholic and Protestant denominations are not much better than secular institutions. In becoming connected to the world of secular affairs, these churches have become too much like that world. The war against liberal Protestantism that had spawned fundamentalism earlier in the twentieth century now has intensified into a war against the secular humanism that is poisoning government, education, the family, and mainstream religious denominations in the United States. These contemporary fundamentalists also are militantly opposed to a number of other "isms"—liberalism, communism, and left-wing evangelicalism (Dobson et al., 1986, p. 2)—that they see as antithetical to the goals of true Christianity.

In the 1980s this militant opposition and anger took a decidedly political turn as fundamentalist minister Rev. Jerry Falwell announced the formation of the Moral Majority. This conservative Christian action group would spearhead a movement to change the course of political elections in the United States and restore the country to the path of righteousness. It claimed a decisive role in the outcomes of both the 1980 and 1984 presidential elections, as well as many state and local campaigns. However, in 1986, Falwell "killed" the Moral Majority and replaced it with a new coalition group, the Liberty Federation, which remains active in promoting the political activism of its "new right" Christian members.

Like the "old" fundamentalism, the groups that make up this new movement stress a back-to-basics, doctrinal approach that distinguishes them sharply from mainline Protestantism. Five main beliefs make up what their adherents call the essential fundamentals of fundamentalism (Dobson et al., 1986, pp. 7–11):

1. The inspiration and infallibility of Scripture (the Bible is the Word of God and is literally true).
2. The deity of Christ, including His virgin birth (Christ is the Son of God). This is "the most essential fundamental of all" (p. 8).
3. The substitutionary atonement of Christ's death (in dying on the cross, Christ atoned for mankind's sins).
4. The literal resurrection of Christ from the dead (Christ rose bodily, not just spiritually, from the dead).
5. The literal return of Christ in the Second Advent (Christ will return in bodily form to bring all of history to its ultimate conclusion).

The new fundamentalism, however, differs from the old in several important respects. It is not identified with specific and well-defined denominations. Rather, it represents what Williams (1989, p. 3) called "extra-ecclesiastical" religion. The people who make up the new Christian right come from a variety of established religious groups, or from none at all. They do not refer to themselves in terms of a specific denominational affiliation (e.g., Methodist or Lutheran), preferring instead the more diffuse term Christian or, for those who have had a life-altering conversion experience, born-again Christian.

Second, whereas the old fundamentalism was almost exclusively a lower-class, rural, and regional (southern) phenomenon, the new fundamentalism appeals to a much wider variety of socioeconomic class, residential, and geographical backgrounds. At least one recent U.S. president (Ronald Reagan) espoused what certainly appeared to be fundamentalist Christian beliefs.

Finally, a good deal of the new fundamentalism is conveyed through the medium of television, appealing to a dispersed mass audience that numbers in the millions (Elvy, 1987). Conservative Christian ministers such as Jerry Falwell and Jimmy Swaggart have become nationally known (and controversial) figures. However, the message of this "electronic church," as it has been called, has been transformed by its preaching medium.

The Electronic Church Television is a visual medium that relies on the pictorial image rather than the spoken word to make its primary impact. It also requires large sums of money to purchase broadcasting time or maintain broadcasting facilities. The wholesale and, in some cases, exclusive use of television to convey religious beliefs has led to programming that often is more in the nature of entertainment than doctrinal presentations. A large portion of this "entertainment" often is devoted to appeals for financial offerings from the faithful. These appeals have been successful enough that the electronic church has taken in hundreds of millions of dollars to further its work and carry on its ministries (Packard, 1988).

Fundamentalists, of course, are not the only prime-time preachers. A large number of evangelical Christian ministers who do not hold a conservative, back-to-basics, doctrinal view (e.g., the Rev. Robert Schuller) also carry on much of their work over the television airwaves. Their broadcasts differ considerably from those of the fundamentalists and from each other. What they all seem to have in common, however, is their largely visual appeal and simple doctrinal message, and the devotion of a substantial amount of their air time to appeals for financial contributions. Although they sometimes have been accused (and, in the case of Jim Bakker, convicted) of financial wrongdoing, their ministries appear to be thriving. Even a series of sex scandals that brought down two of their most famous brethren and led to an intense, highly publicized "holy war" among themselves has failed to unplug the electronic church. Obviously, these programs must be appealing to someone and something in the living rooms of America.

The "someone," according to observers of the phenomenon, are generally older people of lower income and educational levels who already are involved in religion through church membership and participation in religious activities like Bible reading. Women and nonwhites are more likely to be regular viewers of televangelists than men and whites. For these people, the electronic church is an extension of, rather than a substitution for, more conventional religious expression (Hoover, 1988).

The "something" that religious television broadcasting appeals to can and does vary from viewer to viewer. According to Hoover (1988), personal crises of some sort (e.g., the sudden and tragic death of a loved one, serious illness, or financial misfortune) initially attract many viewers. Other analysts (Williams, 1989) claim that these programs appeal to those segments of the population most likely to feel a sense of social and cultural dislocation. These people, in a sense, are part of the human wreckage of the modernization process, and are looking for some means to make sense out of a world that is puzzling and increasingly hostile to them. If this is the case, the future of the electronic church may be assured for some time to come.

Religion Today Several recent studies (Greeley, 1989; Wuthnow, 1988) suggest that, although significant changes have occurred over the past forty years and are occurring now, the place of religion itself in the American fabric seems secure. A high proportion of the U.S. population— 65 percent in 1988, according to figures presented by the U.S. Bureau of the Census— claim membership in a church or synagogue. A smaller but still substantial proportion (42 percent) report actually attending religious services during that time. These figures are not appreciably different from those over the last several decades. Overall, the data suggest a restructuring of existing religious groupings rather than a decline of religious expression per se. The losers in this restructuring have been traditional, mainline Protestant denominations, and the winners have been the rapidly growing branchline evangelical, pentecostal, and charismatic Christian groups (Perrin, 1989).

Religion in this society is not likely to become extinct in the foreseeable future. In fact, according to recent estimates, the United States may be experiencing something of a return to religion as the now middle-aged baby boomers who jettisoned organized religion in the 1960s are returning to reclaim it in the 1990s (Roof and Roozen, cited in Woodward et al., 1990). Although no "official" religion is promoted or required by our government, we nonetheless are a recognizably religious society. Our daily public lives are infused with the symbols of being a population steeped in a belief in a supreme being and dedicated to a moral course of action. Both U.S. presidents and witnesses in criminal trials are sworn into office with their hand resting on a Bible. "In God We Trust" is engraved onto our paper currency, and we pledge allegiance to one nation under God. This civil religion, as Robert Bellah (1988) called it, reflects the fact that this country was founded, and still operates, on a Judeo-Christian moral and religious framework. The Bible-spouting fundamentalist may be an object of people's ridicule and sometimes even anger, but the avowed atheist has an equally poor reputation. Most Americans may be only sporadic church or synagogue attenders, but many claim to be religious in their own way, and acknowledge that faith is an important part of their lives.

In the final analysis, the same force that has led us to a greater understanding and appreciation of our surrounding physical world — the rational development and application of the scientific perspective — may be responsible for the persistence of religious sentiments and practices. As one old saying puts it: the more we learn, the more we find we don't know. For many people in this society, religion will continue to help provide an understanding of what we don't yet know.

Religion and Modernization

According to the United Nations, approximately 80 percent of the world's population profess some religious belief, with two-thirds stating that they are active in their faith (see Table 9.4). Like other institutions in society, religion is not a static entity. Some faiths are gaining adherents while others are losing members. For example, Islam continues to attract converts as it exerts an ever increasing impact on international economic and political affairs. On the other hand, Buddhism has declined in China since 1900, although it has become more popular in Western nations (Bush, 1988). Christianity is the fastest growing religion in Africa, but appears to be at a standstill in the rest of the world, the exception being "independent, evangelical groups that are growing in number" (Bush, 1988, p. 7).

As students of sociology we are concerned with more than the number of people who believe and worship in a particular manner. Rather, we are interested in how religion affects the way people behave politically, economically, and socially, and how belief systems are related to social change, especially modernization. The relationship between religion and modernization is complex inasmuch as religion can affect the development process or, in turn, be changed by the forces of modernization. Concerning the former, there are numerous examples of how religion has acted both to help and hinder development in the now rich countries as well as the less developed nations of the world. Keep in mind that sociologists are concerned with how the content, practice, and organization of a given religion affects people's behavior as individuals, and as members of groups and institutions.

TABLE 9.4   Religious Adherents in the World, 1989

Religion	Percentage of Total World Population
Roman Catholics	18.7
Protestants	6.7
All other Christians	7.5
Muslims	17.8
Hindus	13.2
Buddhists	6.0
Chinese folk religionists	3.3
Sikhs	0.3
Jews	0.3
Confucians	0.1
Shintoists	0.1
Other religionists	4.8
Nonreligious	16.7
Atheists	4.5
Total	100

Source: Adapted from David B. Barrett, 1990, Adherents of All Religions by Seven Continental Areas, Mid-1989, *Encyclopaedia Britannica Book of the Year 1990,* Chicago: Encyclopaedia Britannica, p. 316.

As a nation develops, it requires the services of an educated, literate group of people that can fill the growing number of management, leadership, and technical positions in business, industry, and government. At the time of the Industrial Revolution in Europe, it was the Catholic Church together with numerous Protestant denominations that provided a system of formal learning from the primary to the university level. The system of free, universal, compulsory, state-sponsored education typically associated with modern industrial nations did not begin to appear until much later in the nineteenth century. Similarly, in the United States, the first and most prestigious institutions of higher education such as Harvard, Yale, and Princeton were church affiliated. In fact, all three Ivy League schools were originally seminaries. We already reviewed Max Weber's thesis that the Protestant ethic in the form of Calvinism provided the moral climate that helped give rise to capitalism.

The Umbanda religion of Brazil, which began as a small cult in the 1920s, now has over thirty million members and is a powerful religious and political force in society. It accompanied the economic and industrial expansion of Brazil as a whole and, more specifically, the development of the nation's two largest cities (São Paulo and Rio de Janeiro) where it is most deeply rooted. The earliest adherents of Umbanda were former slaves and newly arrived immigrants anxious for economic success and upward mobility. According to Maria de Queiroz (1989), Umbanda promised that individuals who were good in this life would see their social and economic positions improve in a future incarnation. This view of the world was commensurate with the goals of the lower and middle classes in a growing urban, consumer-oriented society. Umbanda kept people who were certain their dreams would be fulfilled in the next life working

Many people throughout Latin America, such as the Nicaraguans pictured here, traditionally have been followers of Roman Catholicism. However, that church's stance with respect to questions of population control and other aspects of modernization have begun to erode popular support for Catholicism as these countries develop.

hard in this one. By integrating people of different races and classes in an extremely heterogeneous society, it contributed to the political stability of Brazil, an important component of the development process.

A Force Opposing Modernization   Religion has also been a powerful force against modernization. In a papal decree issued in 1863, Pope Pius IX stated that it was heresy for anyone to believe "that the Roman Pontiff can, and ought to, reconcile himself to, and agree with, progress, liberalism, and modern civilization" (in Bettenson, 1974, p. 273). In 1907 Pope Pius X produced an encyclical thoroughly condemning "modernism." He noted that the basic error of this process was "twisting unalterable truth to suit modern thought" (Wilson and Clark, 1989, p. 171). Religious opposition to stabilizing population growth by various methods of birth control makes it more difficult for developing nations to modernize. Most, if not all, of their economic progress is consumed by a larger and younger population. In 1968 Pope Paul VI issued an encyclical that reaffirmed the Catholic position prohibiting all artificial forms of contraception. In the Muslim world, some conservative religious leaders (especially in Pakistan) have denounced birth control as un-Islamic (Smith, 1971).

In India, liberal Hindus argue that the beliefs of more strict, orthodox Hindus have contributed to their nation's poverty, disease, hunger, and overpopulation (Converse, 1988). For example, orthodox Hindus who believe in karma, the notion that whatever one's present condition in life, one has earned it by his own past deeds, adhere to a fatalistic world view whereby people passively accept their lot in life as unalterable. Orthodox Hindus are also likely to believe that the world is currently passing through a cycle whereby conditions are naturally and progressively growing worse (Converse, 1988). These beliefs are contrary to the view held by most people in modern societies that human beings control their own destiny and, within limits, can change the world to suit their needs and desires. Hinduism is a religion with hundreds of holidays at the individual, regional, and national levels that result in an annual loss of tens of millions of man-hours of work and other productive activity. Millions more hours are lost to sometimes daily rituals concerning purity and pollution, as well as pilgrimages to hundreds of holy cities and shrines. In addition, the many ascetic holy men who wander through the streets and countryside represent a double loss to society, as they must be supported by others while making no contribution to the economic well-being of the nation (Converse, 1988).

When Reza Khan became the Shah (Persian title for emperor) of Iran in 1921 he embarked on a policy to modernize and Westernize his nation. This policy left little room for the Islamic scholars, or mullahs, who had always played an important role in Iranian political and social affairs (Nangi, 1988). The drive toward modernization was continued by the Shah's son, Mohammed Reza, who was forced to abdicate in 1979 as a result of widespread dissatisfaction with his oppressive and ruthless regime. With the birth of the Islamic Republic of Iran under the leadership of the Ayatollah Khomeini, the process of modernization, and especially Westernization, was halted and in some instances reversed.

Buddhism appears to be the major world religion that has had the least effect (positive or negative) on the modernization process that began with the Industrial Revolution. In some nations Buddhism is attempting to adapt to the changes brought about by economic development. Maraldo (1976) noted that present-day Buddhism is "prepared to encounter and learn from the secular world . . ." (p. vi). As stated by one Zen scholar, "The Buddhism of the future . . . will be grounded in the natural sciences, and in a humanism which liberates and cultivates human nature; and it will be open to all the world" (in Maraldo, 1976, p. 224). In Singapore, Buddhism is currently undergoing major changes as a result of economic development and the pressures of competing religions. Other faiths (especially Christianity) are typically viewed as more adaptive to the modern world. Hoping to reverse the decline in the number of people professing Buddhism from 56 percent in 1980 to 42 percent in 1986, leaders are taking their religion "out of the temple and into . . . the realities of everyday life" (Clammer, 1988, p. 27).

These examples indicate that religion and modernization are involved in a complex web of cause and effect relationships that have both helped and hindered the development process. When we consider how important religious beliefs and behavior are to so many people, this intricate relationship is hardly surprising, especially that between religion and politics. Henri St. Simon, one of the founding fathers of sociology, noted that "the religious institution—under whatever spirit envisages it—is the principal political institution" (in Robertson, 1989, p. 20). Although St. Simon may have overstated the political significance of religion, there can be little doubt that religious beliefs and institutions will be a major factor in the modernization of Third World nations.

MEXICO

THE MEXICAN POLITICAL SYSTEM: A STATE OF SIEGE

Like its Yankee neighbor to the north, the modern Mexican state was born of violence. From 1910 to 1920 the country was torn by revolution and civil war, its population decimated by the struggle to break the hold of upper-class aristocracy and return the land to the peasants who had worked it so long for so little.

The Mexican Constitution of 1917 contained articles guaranteeing fundamental land and labor reforms. However, its passage did not end the country's political violence, which continued into the 1930s. Nor did it really alter the highly unequal distribution of social resources that had sparked the revolution against the long (1884–1910) dictatorship of Porfirio Diaz. What ultimately did emerge from the aftermath of Revolution and Constitution was the single most important and continuing force in Mexican political affairs for the past sixty years— the *Partido Revolucionario Institucional* (Institutional Revolutionary Party), or PRI.

What eventually would become the modern PRI was founded in 1929 by then-President Plutarco Elias Calles as the National Revolutionary Party. The PRI was not and is not a political party in the sense that we might think of political parties in the United States, that is, organized groups competing for public support in order to elect their members to government office. Rather, the PRI is a mechanism for minimizing political conflict and strengthening government power in Mexico (Cornelius and Craig, 1988).

In practice, the PRI is an arm of the federal government. It is a mechanism for identifying and appointing people to office throughout the ranks of government without risking the possibly disrupting effects of wide open political campaigns and elections. It has served remarkably well in this capacity. Until losing the race for governor in Baja California in 1989, it had successfully won every presidential election and virtually every other important state and municipal election in Mexico since 1929, usually by an overwhelming margin. In so doing, the PRI introduced continuity into a system where stability of any sort otherwise might be sorely lacking. But this political stability has come at a price. Wealth and power in contemporary Mexican society remain as highly stratified as they did before the overthrow of Porfirio Diaz in 1910. However, events surrounding the most recent presidential election (July 1988) suggest that it may now be the PRI's turn to pay the price for its policies of the past six decades.

In a fiercely contested election that drew worldwide attention, Carlos Salinas de Gortari, the chosen candidate of the PRI, was officially elected president by the slimmest margin of victory in modern Mexican political history. According to the official count, Salinas received 50.36 percent of the popular vote, a bare majority of the nineteen million votes cast in the election. The PRI itself lost ground in the Mexican Chamber of Deputies (the equivalent of the U.S. House of Representatives), falling below the two-thirds control necessary to make changes in the Constitution. For the first time also, the PRI failed to capture all the seats in the Senate (*Time,* 1988). The closeness of the election was unprecedented, and the widespread public outrage and accusations of fraud that followed the election were even more so (McGuire, 1988).

The PRI's primary opposition in the 1988 presidential election came from Cuauhtemoc Cardenas, a former member of the PRI. At one time the PRI-backed governor of the state of Michoacan, Cardenas later broke from the party to join the *Partido Autentico de la Revolucion Mexicana* (Authentic Party of the Mexican Revolution). Like a number of other leftist Mexican parties, members of PARM believe that the PRI has lost the vision and ideologies of the Revolution. They charge that as it became more entrenched over the decades, the PRI also became more of a conservative, counterrevolutionary group. It consistently sides with the affluent upper and middle classes at the expense of the urban lower classes and the rural peasants who make up the majority of the country's population. Leftist groups claim that the PRI is more interested in preserving its own rule than in furthering either the original democratic spirit or the social and economic goals of the Revolution.

The Iron Law of Oligarchy

If this in fact is what has happened to the PRI, and there is ample evidence to suggest that it has, it would not be the first time (or the last) that a broad-based democratic movement became transformed into an antidemocratic establishment. At about the same time the Mexican Revolution was unfolding, sociologist Robert Michels was analyzing socialist parties in Germany and formulating his famous iron law of oligarchy (Michels, 1966, original 1915). According to this argument, the need for organization, leadership, and administration in mass movements like political parties inevitably leads to a widening gulf between leaders and rank-and-file members of the movement. As time passes, more of the leaders' activities and the movement's resources become deflected from the original purposes of the movement toward establishing and maintaining a permanent structure, as well as a permanent leadership group. Initial zeal for change increasingly becomes a reluctance to change. Government by the many becomes rule by the few. In Michel's words, "Who says organization says oligarchy" (p. 365).

In 1988 Cuauthemoc Cardenas was able to forge a coalition of leftist parties and dissatisfied moderates into the first real challenge to PRI power in decades. Part of his success had to do with his personal identity. Cardenas is the son of Lazaro Cardenas, the legendary president of Mexico (1934–1940) who nationalized the petroleum industry and effected wide-ranging labor and land reforms on behalf of the lower classes.

The continuing charisma of the Cardenas name with the Mexican people put him in a good position to be listened to and believed when he spoke against the PRI as the party of elite interests. In the minds of the people, Cardenas knew what he was talking about.

The real boost to Cardenas' challenge, and to the challenge mounted against the PRI by the late Manuel Clouthier, the candidate of the conservative, business-oriented *Partido Accion Nacional* (National Action Party), was structural rather than personal. By the mid-1980s the economy had deteriorated to the point that the tens of millions of people who constitute the peasant and urban lower classes were facing conditions that were life-threatening, with no relief in sight. They were able to make a direct connection between these intolerable conditions and the ruling PRI, and an even more direct linkage between the economic disaster and the PRI's candidate for president in 1988.

An Uncertain Future

Carlos Salinas had served for six years as Minister of Planning and Federal Budget for President Miguel de la Madrid. As chief economist for the most recent presidential administration, he was officially responsible for the country's economic development policies; in this case, failed policies that added to the burden of ordinary Mexicans' lives while enhancing the lives of the wealthy. Faced with inescapable evidence of government ineffectiveness, people began to lose faith in the PRI and challenged political structures and practices that had always been taken for granted in the past.

As the PRI responded to these challenges and accusations with a combination of indifference and violence, the broad-base class of workers and peasants who had been a major source of support took their support elsewhere. Large numbers of peasants, especially, moved toward Cardenas, who, like many of them, is of Indian heritage and had demonstrated his concern for their concerns (*Economist*, 1988a). Perhaps as a result of their exposure to formal education and other modern institutions, members of the urban working and lower middle classes also began to defect. The ruling PRI's claim to traditional authority no longer could disguise the fact that they were not playing by the at least formal rules of the political game shared by the people as part of the Revolutionary ideology. As the modernization of the country was changing the world view of many citizens, the PRI's decades-old approach of loyalty to powerful individual political figures, patronage, and corruption became perceived as out of step with the needs of the times. In an age of international trade markets, world economies, and instantaneous communications, the PRI is seen increasingly as a political dinosaur whose day in the sun should come to an end (*Economist,* 1988b).

Since his inauguration, President Salinas has promised to make sweeping changes within the PRI that would bring Mexican politics into the twentieth century. Among other things, these reforms would involve the elimination of "backroom" practices and the establishment of genuinely open elections with candidates honestly picked by the Mexican people. However, his efforts have been resisted by many old-guard PRI members who enjoyed decades of benefits under the existing structure. President Salinas also encountered increasing opposition from outside his party, generated by public beliefs that the 1988 elections were tainted by PRI fraud, and by widespread reports of PRI-directed violence against political dissenters after the elections. For example, Cuauhtemoc Cardenas' new leftist coalition, the Democratic Revolutionary Party, claimed that fifty-six of its members were killed by or on behalf of the PRI since the 1988 elections (Miller, 1990a). These allegations have done little to dispel the perception that Salinas' presidency is simply the latest incarnation of PRI business as usual.

The largest barrier to political reform continues to be the country's faltering economic climate. Recognizing that economic uncertainties create political turmoil, Salinas moved for immediate economic reform measures as a necessary precondition for political reform. In what has come to be referred to as "Salinastroika" (Robinson, 1990; Silver, 1990), the president introduced measures to open the Mexican economy to free market forces. These measures include "privatizing" banks and telephone services by turning them over (or, in the case of banks, back) to private enterprise, encouraging the growth of *maquiladoras* (plants in which imported parts are assembled into finished products for export) in the northern border states, and granting permission for foreign companies to conduct operations in Mexico without surrendering ownership control to Mexican nationals. In the first two years of his term, President Salinas gained growing support as his policies restored some hope to the Mexican people.

The acid test for both Salinastroika and the PRI is likely to be the president's push for a free-trade alliance with the United States and Canada that would create a North American common economic community similar to that in Europe. Given long-standing feelings of distrust by Mexicans toward the United States and equally long-standing Mexican pride in going it alone, it is not clear when (or if) Salinas will be able to sell the free-trade idea to the Mexican Congress or the people. His ability to do so may pave the way for some measure of economic recovery and true political reform. His failure to do so could well signal the breaking point for the grass-roots Mexican population and the last hurrah for the PRI.

DISCUSSION QUESTIONS

1. How is Mexico's Institutional Revolutionary Party (PRI) different from the major political parties in the United States?
2. Imagine that you are the leader of one of the opposition parties in Mexico and are involved in a critical campaign for the governorship of your state. What techniques do you think might be most effective in convincing voters to support your party rather than the ruling PRI? What major obstacles will you have to overcome to win this election?
3. Mexico is not the only society in which the long-standing rule of a single political party is being challenged by popular-based opposition groups. Go to the library and read about the current political turmoil in the Soviet Union. What conditions in the USSR have fostered these attacks on the Communist Party rule? Are these similar to conditions found in modern Mexico?

Religion in Japan: Many Gods but Little Faith

Japan has a long and varied spiritual legacy as a result of numerous religious invasions, and a history of governments that either embraced or rejected these belief systems for political reasons. Over the past 2,000 years five religious traditions have had a significant impact on the Japanese people: Shinto, Confucianism, Buddhism, Christianity, and *shinko shukyo* ("new religions").

Shinto

The nation's only major indigenous religion, Shinto ("the origin of the gods") predates the introduction of Chinese writing in the fifth century. Ancient Shinto focused on the worship of natural phenomena, mythological ancestors, and a large number of kindly, supernatural beings called *kami*. A primitive faith with no ethical system or meaningful concept of an afterlife, Shinto was eventually superseded in Japan by Buddhism (Christopher, 1983). With the Meiji ("enlightened rule") Restoration of 1868, however, and the reemergence of the emperor as the supreme ruler, Shinto became a significant force in the modernization of Japan. The government used it to support both the emperor and an emerging national identity as the nation began making the transition from a rural, agricultural society to an urban, industrial state (Earhart, 1983).

With the fusion of church and state Shinto quickly became the official religion of industrializing Japan. The government supported shrines throughout the country, and Shinto beliefs were taught to virtually all school-age children. Strictly speaking, state Shinto was not a religion but a this-worldly set of beliefs revolving around nationalism, loyalty, and obedience to the emperor. Japanese leaders realized that Shinto was a powerful mechanism for fashioning a disciplined, hard-working population and creating a strong sense of nationalism (Cooper, 1983). The leaders of the Meiji period were determined to catch up to the West and bring Japan into the modern

world as soon as possible. Shinto was to be a major factor in realizing this goal.

State Shinto reached its peak of nationalism and hatred of foreigners in the years preceding World War II. In the aftermath of Japan's defeat and occupation by American forces, Shinto was stripped of its imperial status as a state religion. With the separation of church and state a part of the new Japanese constitution, teaching Shinto in schools was prohibited. A multifaceted sectarian Shinto exists today, with some sects preaching world brotherhood and peace. Most Westerners are surprised to learn that the religion plays an important role in Japanese business, science, and technology. Many leading corporations, including Toyota and Hitachi, have Shinto shrines at their headquarters, and Shinto priests routinely take part in ground-breaking ceremonies of new factories (Rubenstein, 1987).

Confucianism

Confucianism made its way into Japan from China between the sixth and ninth centuries. Although it never existed in Japan as an organized religion of any consequence, it did have an impact on the nation's social philosophy and cosmic outlook (Grapard, 1983). More of a guide for ordering social relationships and living a virtuous life than a religion, Confucian schools of philosophy had a significant influence on Japan until the nineteenth century. Thereafter, its effect waned quickly. The Confucian view of the cosmos was shown to be woefully inaccurate compared to the rapid and numerous advances being made by Western science. Reischauer (1988) pointed out that while the Japanese are not Confucianist in the sense that their ancestors were, the ethical values of that system, including an emphasis on interpersonal relationships, faith in education, and hard work, are alive and well. Few people consider themselves to be Confucianists, but in a practical sense almost all Japanese are (Reischauer, 1988). This is a good example of how religious values, even in the

Although Japan has a long history of religious traditions that include Shintoism, Confucianism, and Buddhism, the nation itself cannot be said to be religious in an "other-world oriented" sense. More often, Japanese religions have served an ethical and/or political role, providing people with a set of principles for daily living and furthering the cause of a nationalistic spirit.

absence of a formal organization, can affect the social and economic history of a nation long after that religion has, for all practical purposes, ceased to exist.

Buddhism

Buddhism came to Japan from India by way of China (and later Korea) beginning in the sixth century. According to Reischauer (1988), it played the same role in Japan that Christianity did in northern Europe, being a "vehicle for the transmission of a whole higher culture" (p. 206). It highly influenced intellectual thought as well as the arts and architecture. For hundreds of years Shinto and Buddhism were Japan's ma-

jor religions, and had a significant impact on the day-to-day lives of the people. With the ascendancy of state Shinto during the Meiji Restoration, Buddhism was attacked by a government that would not permit anything to stand in the way of an emperor-centered political system. Although it has left its mark on Japan, it survives in that country principally in the form of tradition.

Christianity

Christianity was introduced to Japan by Portuguese missionaries in 1549. The hard-working Jesuits met with early success, and by 1579 there were as many as 100,000 converts to Catholicism. By the first decades of the seventeenth century this number was approximately one million, including some feudal lords. However, this brief but fruitful period of conversions came to an abrupt halt beginning in 1623 with the ruthless and violent oppression of the country's Christian community. Missionaries were kicked out of Japan and thousands of Japanese Christians were tortured (even crucified) and banished from their homelands (van Wolferen, 1990). By 1638 the spread of Christianity had come to an end, and the religions of Europe were all but eradicated.

Cooper (1983) stated that some Japanese rulers believed the missionaries were an advance guard preparing their country for European colonialism. Always watchful for trouble, the ruling shoguns considered the growing number of Christians a potential threat to their power and dominance. A new religion advocating that one's love, loyalty, and obedience ultimately belonged to some "alien Lord above shogun and emperor, even if this Lord was only in heaven, must have been very frightening to those who ruled" (van Wolferen, 1990, p. 280).

In the years following the opening of Japan by Commodore Perry in 1854, Westerners were permitted to enter the country and Christianity was reintroduced. With the destruction of state Shinto after World War II, the Christian influence was felt in Japan on yet a third occasion. Cooper (1983) believed that Christianity made inroads in Japan during times of sudden and significant social change. Perhaps during these periods of transformation and anomie it presented people with a much needed, all-encompassing set of values and rules, as well as a view of the afterlife that they found reassuring.

Japan Today

Today in Japan less than 1 percent of the population is Christian, with that number almost evenly split between Catholics and Protestants. However, the impact of the Christian community is disproportionate to their small number. Some of the best educated, most influential people in the country are Christians, and many of the ethical values common to the Japanese mind today are associated with that faith.

The *shinku shukyo* began approximately 150 years ago, although the real proliferation of these groups started after World War II and the intro-

duction of religious freedom. These new religions range from utter simplicity in both belief and custom to the bizarre. For example, members of the *Denshinkyo* ("the electricity religion") worshipped Thomas Edison. According to van Wolferen (1990), these new religions meet a definite social and psychological need of hundreds of thousands of people. They are havens of mutual support in a group-oriented society where many people are not members of that all-important organization, the corporation. Devotees of *shinko shukyo* are typically lonely housewives, bar hostesses, and workers in marginal occupations.

In a fundamental sense, religion has never really taken root in Japan (van Wolferen, 1990). Historically, any belief system oriented toward other-worldly, supernatural concerns was simply not tolerated by the nation's ruling elite. Only nonthreatening belief systems concerned with everyday matters of the here and now were acceptable. Anything else was viewed as an affront to the established political order and crushed. Regardless of whether this relatively low regard for the supernatural is a function of centuries-old political coercion, or is an inevitable by-product of the trend toward secularization in modern society, the fact that only 33 percent of the population has religious convictions may prove troublesome.

Recall that Durkheim thought of religion as a kind of glue that held together. It fosters social cohesion or solidarity by providing for collective worship, deference to the same god(s), and a common world view, including a system of morality. Van Wolferen (1990) maintained that if Japan's secular religion built on values of hard work, self-discipline, submission to authority, and loyalty to the corporation were to wear off, little if anything would be left to hold the nation together. To the extent they are currently practiced, neither Shinto nor Buddhism provides a comprehensive view of life and moral standards.

The deterioration of secular values combined with a lack of religious beliefs and standards of behavior could leave the Japanese without a coherent system of morality on which to orient and evaluate their own behavior. The ensuing state of anomie or normlessness at the societal level, as well as on the part of individuals, could result in high rates of deviant behavior and social change in an unknown direction.

1. What impact did the Shinto religion have on the modernization of Japan?
2. In what sense was Buddhism in feudal Japan a "functional equivalent" of Christianity in northern Europe?
3. Will the number of new religions (*shinku shukyo*) and followers of these religions in-

crease or decrease in Japan in the coming years? Explain.
4. Go to the library and gather information on the role of religion in a European country such as Spain, Germany, or Norway. What impact (if any) did religion have on the modernization of this nation?

CHAPTER SUMMARY

1. From the functionalist perspective, the family performs six major functions in all societies to one degree or another. It meets the biological and economic needs of its members; it legitimizes some sexual relationships and prohibits others; biological reproduction within the family ensures the group's continuity over time; it is where a major portion of childhood socialization takes place; it provides individuals membership within a larger social structure; and it provides people with emotional support and companionship.

2. Conflict theorists are more likely to see the family as an institution of domination and exploitation. According to this perspective, males exploited by the bourgeoisie in a capitalist society become frustrated and abuse their wives and children. The family is considered a microcosm of the tension, conflict, and oppression that exist in the larger society.

3. In the United States, most marriages occur between two people (1) of the same social class, (2) within the same racial group, (3) of the same religion, (4) with similar levels of education, (5) with the same physical and psychological characteristics, and (6) who live within a few miles of each other.

4. In the United States, the chances that a marriage will end in divorce are associated with the following: age at marriage, length of marriage, social class of the couple, race, religion, and whether their parents have been divorced.

5. Research on the effect of divorce on children is inconclusive and sometimes contradictory. Some investigators report that children adjust to a

divorce and their new family set-up within two years of the breakup. Others have found that the negative consequences of divorce can affect children for many years, even after they have become adults.

6. According to William J. Goode, families in Europe were changing from an extended to a nuclear structure before the beginning of the Industrial Revolution. The nuclear family met the needs of an achievement-based, open-class industrializing society that also required both geographical and social mobility. Freed from traditional patterns of behavior and the intense social control of nearby relatives, individuals could adapt to the demands of an emerging industrial, urban society.

7. Christopher Lasch argued that reformers in the United States attempted to rid society of the influence of the foreign languages and cultures they believed impeded the development of an integrated community and nation. By the early twentieth century, families started to lose childrearing duties as the state began to take a more active role in socializing and controlling children through education and social welfare services.

8. In all human societies, political institutions regulate the exercise of power by various social groups. Of the various political structures in modern societies, the most significant is the state, the institution having a monopoly over the use of coercive force.

9. For functionalists, the state or polity plays a critical role in "goal attainment," the process by which important societal objectives are defined, resources are allocated and mobilized toward the

realization of these goals, and social control is exercised over individual actions. From this perspective, without the state, society would remain directionless and foundering, torn by widespread conflicts.

10. For conflict theorists like Karl Marx, the state and other political institutions are powerful weapons used by ruling classes to preserve their own advantaged positions in the economic and social order. Laws passed and enforced by the state are seldom neutral; rather, they reflect the power and the interests of the owning classes. The net effect of the political apparatus is the protection of the societal status quo and the preservation of vested class interests.

11. Sociologists have disagreed sharply on the question of how political power is structured in the United States. Radical conflict theorist C. Wright Mills saw evidence of a power elite composed of corporate, political, and military chieftains who effectively controlled decision making and dominated higher-level government. Pluralists like David Riesman viewed political power in the United States as being dispersed among a number of groups and organizations that act as veto groups, preventing any single group or coalition from becoming dominant. Although empirical evidence often is far from conclusive, data do seem to point to a significant concentration of national and local political power in the hands of a relatively small segment of the population, drawn primarily from upper-SES (socioeconomic status) ranks.

12. With respect to political participation in the United States, existing data indicate a clear pattern of widespread disinterest and noninvolvement in voting, campaign activities, and other forms of political expression, especially among minorities, the young, and members of lower-socioeconomic status groups. This massive apathy might be interpreted as cynicism and distrust of politics, and it creates the kind of climate in which nondemocratic, self-interested power can be exercised.

13. Modernization and societal development brought with them the replacement of political rule based on force and power by rule based on charismatic, traditional, or rational-legal moral authority. Recent events throughout the contemporary world point to the potential instability of any political system. Communism is crumbling throughout the Soviet bloc, U.S. world supremacy is being challenged by the emergence of Japan and other countries as economic superpowers, and

some Third World societies are rising under the twin impulses of strategic resources and nationalistic movements.

14. As a long-standing social institution, religion reflects humans' need to deal with sacred aspects of life—those elements that inspire a sense of reverence, awe, and fear. Religious statuses and roles were among the first specialized positions to be differentiated in early human societies.

15. Functionalists like Durkheim contend that religion promotes societal solidarity, strengthens social control, and gives societal members a sense of meaning and purpose in life. As a conflict theorist, Marx claimed that religion was a powerful tool employed by ruling classes in capitalist societies to maintain their position by deflecting the attention of oppressed classes from real world concerns to those of an afterlife. For Marx, religion was the "opiate of the masses."

16. Max Weber disagreed with Marx, maintaining that religion could be an important factor in social change. His analysis of the Protestant beliefs in predestination and worldly asceticism indicated that this Protestant ethic created a climate that encouraged the development of capitalism in European societies.

17. For most of its history the United States has been both a religious and a religiously tolerant society. Most Americans may identify as Protestant, Catholic, or Jewish, but many folk religions and popular religions cut across traditional religious denominational lines. In recent years, Christian fundamentalism, stressing a back-to-basics religious approach and a rejection of secularism and humanism, has become an important and growing social and political force. This fundamentalist revival has used television and other mass media as effective channels for reaching millions of people.

18. The relationship between religion and modernization is complex, with religious beliefs both helping and hindering the development process. As noted, Protestant and Catholic churches in Europe and in the United States established systems of formal education long before any schools were funded and controlled by the state. On the other hand, religious opposition to artificial birth control as a method for slowing rapid population growth has made modernization increasingly difficult for some poor nations. Large-scale, violent clashes between Muslims and Hindus in India, as well as recent events in the Middle East, clearly indicate that religion will be a major factor in the economic and political development of many nations.

10

POPULATION

Suppose that after graduation you decide to go into business for yourself. Your experience, aptitude, and preferences lead you to the retail clothing business—specifically, fashions for professional women between twenty-five and forty-five years of age. Before going to the bank to secure a loan, however, you will have to ask yourself (and answer) some important questions. How many potential customers live or work within reasonable driving distance of your establishment? Will this number increase or decrease in the coming years? By what percentage? How much money do these women earn annually? How much is disposable income that can be spent for the type of clothing you sell? What you need (and the bank will want to see) are the characteristics of your target population, including size, short- and long-term growth projections, geographical distribution, and income and earning potential.

Population characteristics such as these are included in the area of study known as demography, a word from the Greek *demos* ("people") and *graphein* ("to describe"). **Demography** is the scientific study of population. Demographers are especially interested in population growth and how this growth is affected by birth, death, and migration rates. Accurate demographic statistics are important for individuals and institutions for a variety of reasons. Businesses, as we have seen, require such information to determine what range of products can be sold to a given population and how the items can be marketed most successfully. For example, a demographic profile of the United States reveals that hundreds of thousands of people in the huge baby boom generation born between 1946 and 1964 have already turned forty. The graying of these individuals, together with an increased life expectancy and decline in the birth rate after 1960, has raised the median age of the population to thirty-three. Any business targeting a particular age group will have to take this factor into consideration.

Governments also must have demographic information to determine the needs of a given segment of the population and the proper allocation of tax dollars—for example, the number of schools and retirement homes that must be built, and the size and distribution of a population infected with a communicable disease. In a world that is replete with social, economic, and environmental problems, accurate up-to-date data are of the utmost necessity.

Demography is an interdisciplinary subject with ties to sociology, economics, geography, business, biology, and medicine. It is used in all of these disciplines to address different sets of questions and issues. As students of sociology, we are primarily interested in (1) population processes (fertility, mortality, migration), (2) the size and distribution of a population, and (3) the structure and characteristics of a population. Demography is crucial to our understanding of some of the most significant global trends of the past 250 years, such as unprecedented population growth, urbanization, and the modernization of societies across all major institutions. A knowledge of demographic trends also provides some insight as to how population variables will affect societies around the world in the years to come.

Questions to Consider

1. Why is demography so important to social scientists, business people, and governments?
2. What is the crude birth rate and why is it a "crude" measure of fertility?
3. What are the major communicable diseases in the Third World that kill tens of thousands of people each year?
4. Why do people in Japan live twice as long as people in the African country of Chad?
5. Historically, what are the most important push and pull factors that account for rural-to-urban migration?
6. What is the Malthusian theory of population growth? Was Malthus correct?
7. What is the theory of the demographic transition? Why and in what stage of the transition are most Third World countries "stuck"?
8. What are some of the major problems resulting from overpopulation in less developed countries? Can these problems be solved?
9. Why is the fertility rate declining in some developed nations?
10. What is the link between fertility and religious beliefs?

FERTILITY

Fertility refers to the number of children born to women in a given population. The fertility rate is a function of two factors, one biological and the other social. The biological component is called **fecundity,** that is, the physical ability to conceive and bear children. For most women, this period lasts approximately thirty-three years, between the ages of twelve and forty-five. Fecundity may be thought of as a necessary, but not sufficient, condition of fertility. In other words, the fact that a woman is able to give birth does not mean that she will, nor does it determine how many children she will bear.

The number of children to whom a woman will give birth is related to a series of psychological and, especially, social factors in her environment. Kingsley Davis and Judith Blake (1956) cited social factors such as race, religion, and education that are powerful yet indirect influences on fertility. Their effects are filtered through a group of intermediate variables such as age at first intercourse, the use of contraception, and induced abortion. William Pratt and colleagues (1984) modified the Davis and Blake schema and devised three sets of intermediate variables. **Intercourse variables** refer to the commencement of and frequency of sexual activity over a given period of time. For example, the more time spent in marriage the more likely a woman will become

Fertility rates will partially determine if some developing nations sink or swim economically in the coming years. (Reprinted by permission of UFS, Inc.)

"I'm only gonna say this one more time: Our only chance is self-control."

pregnant. Data for the United States indicate that if a marriage is broken, a woman's fertility will be lower than if the union had remained intact (Weeks, 1986).

Similarly, the longer marriage is postponed, the fewer children a woman is likely to have. Beginning in the 1960s and 1970s, large numbers of women pursued a college education (and advanced degrees) and had high occupational goals, resulting in both delayed marriage and a lower rate of fertility. Because they postponed starting a family in favor of having a career, many women in their late thirties and forties are now worried that their "biological clock" is rapidly winding down and they will never have children. The term **biological clock** refers to the ages between which women are physically able to conceive; it is said to wind down when women reach upper limits of fecundity, approximately forty-five years of age.

Fertility is also influenced by a number of **conception variables,** especially contraception. It is common knowledge that the widespread use of contraceptive devices (artificial infertility) reduces the number of live births in a given population. The oral contraceptive pill, intrauterine device, condom, and diaphragm are all considered highly effective methods of birth control and have been used by tens of millions of people (especially in modern, industrial societies). The presence (and duration) or absence of breast-feeding can also have a significant impact on fertility. The average woman will not become pregnant for about two months (a period of infecundity) after the birth of a child; however, a woman who is breast-feeding her children may not conceive for between ten and eighteen months (Konner and Worthman, 1980). Fertility rates in many areas of the less developed world would be significantly higher were it not for this innate yet socially determined method of birth control. In other words, the length of time a woman breast-feeds her child (if she does at all) is largely a function of the customs of her social group. Bongaarts (1982) found that in societies with generally high birth rates, fertility tends to be lower where breast-feeding is common and higher in countries where it is not as widely practiced.

Pregnancy or **gestation variables** (miscarriage, stillbirth, induced abortion) determine if a fetus will come to term, resulting in a live birth. Induced abortion is undoubtedly humanity's oldest and most frequently used form of birth control. It was a significant factor in the reduction of births in both Japan and Mexico and is a major reason why the birth rate in the United States is low. The number of legally induced abortions in the United States increased from 750,000 in 1973 (the year of the *Roe* v. *Wade* decision) to 1.5 million in 1985. Supreme Court decisions beginning in 1989 reducing public funding for abortions and giving states more of a say in determining policy could substantially decrease the number of *legal* abortions in future years.

Fertility Measures

Now that we have seen how birth rates can be affected by numerous social factors and intermediate variables, it is time to examine how demographers measure fertility. The most commonly used statistic is the **crude birth rate (CBR)** — the number of births per year for every 1,000 members of the population. This statistic is aptly called crude because it does not take into consideration a society's age structure or, more specifically, the number of people in a given population who are actually at risk of having children. For example, a typical industrial nation may have 15 percent of its population in the peak childbearing years (fifteen to forty-five), whereas in a poor, underdeveloped country the figure may be 30 percent. An actual CBR of twenty would be high for the developed nation, in which only 15 percent of the population were in their reproductive years, while the same figure would be low for the developing country in which twice the percentage were at risk of reproducing. The poor countries of the world have much younger populations (37 percent under age fifteen) and therefore a larger percentage of women of childbearing age. The CBRs of these countries as a group is thirty-one (births per 1,000 people), with some nations having a rate as high as fifty-one (Benin, Niger, Malawi) and fifty-four (Kenya). On the other hand, some wealthy industrial countries with much older populations have CBRs as low as ten (Italy) and eleven (Japan, Denmark, West Germany [prior to reunification], Spain).

Another important fertility statistic is the **total fertility rate (TFR),** which is a measure of completed fertility, or total number of children born to women of a particular cohort (group). For example, in 1982 the projected TFR in the United States was 1,829 per 1,000 women, or 1.8 children per woman. In 1955 that figure was twice as high, or 3.6 children per woman (Weeks, 1986). An increase in the TFR can make a significant difference in population growth in a relatively short period of time. As of 1988, the TFR per 1,000 African women was approximately 6,000, or 6 children per woman. At that rate, one woman could have 36 grandchildren and 216 great grandchildren, for a total of 258 people in four generations. Comparable multigenerational numbers for the United States and West Germany are fourteen and six, respectively (Matthews, 1989).

 MORTALITY

The size and structure of a population is also affected by the number of people who die. The three major reasons why people die in any society are that they degenerate, they are killed by communicable diseases, or they are killed by products of the social and economic environment (Weeks, 1986). Degeneration refers to the biological deterioration of the body. In modern societies like the United States, the primary degenerative conditions are cardiovascular or heart disease, cancer, and stroke. These three maladies accounted for 68 percent of all deaths in 1982. Physical degeneration leading to death can be facilitated by an individual's lifestyle and personal habits. For example, the American Lung Association estimates that 350,000 people die prematurely each year in the United Sates from cigarette smoking–related diseases. "Smoking kills more Americans each year than died in battle in World War II and Vietnam put together" ("Tobacco's Toll on America," 1987, p. 4).

Communicable Diseases

Communicable diseases are conditions contracted from another human being. Smallpox, which has ravaged human populations throughout history, was effectively eliminated by the World Health Organization in the late 1970s. An outbreak of the disease occurred on the island nation of Madagascar in 1989, however, and it may yet recur in other areas. Communicable diseases are especially deadly where medical facilities and treatment are poor and population density is high. These conditions exist in numerous Third World countries where chicken pox, cholera, diphtheria, and malaria still claim thousands of lives annually. People, especially children, weakened by lack of food and inadequate diets are particularly vulnerable.

Acquired immunodeficiency syndrome (AIDS) is a communicable disease contracted directly from another person through sexual activity and by contact with infected blood (usually a transfusion or intravenous drug use). It is caused by the human

The AIDS epidemic will slow, but not stop, rapid population growth in many African nations. Scarce resources used to care for AIDS victims means less money is available for economic development and other aspects of modernization, such as education and primary health care.

immunodeficiency virus (HIV), new strains of which are continually being discovered. Pregnant women infected with the virus can also transmit the disease to their babies. As of August 1988, 72,024 cases of AIDS had been reported in the United States. The Public Health Service estimates that a total of 365,000 patients will be diagnosed by the end of 1992, with 263,000 cumulative deaths. The disease has also been spreading rapidly in many developing countries, especially Uganda. In 1988 the World Health Organization described the AIDS epidemic in African and other Third World nations (where the disease is spread primarily through heterosexual intercourse) as "potentially devastating." By late 1990 an estimated eight to ten million people worldwide had been infected with the HIV virus.

Social and Environmentally Related Diseases

Deaths related to the social and economic environment include those resulting from unsafe products, hazardous working conditions, and pollution. According to Ashford (1974), occupationally caused diseases account for as many of 100,000 deaths annually in the United States, a figure approximately five times greater than the number of murders in this country each year. American industry produces eighty-eight billion pounds of toxic waste a year, and the Environmental Protection Agency estimates that only 10 percent of it is disposed of properly (Coleman, 1989). Simon and Eitzen (1986) observed that between 75 and 90 percent of all cancers in the United States are environmentally related. The relationship between toxic by-products and numerous forms of illness (especially cancer) is hotly debated in a number of industrialized nations.

Deaths related to industrial pollution are not limited to the rich nations of the world, however. In their attempt to modernize as quickly as possible and make optimum use of limited capital, developing nations have spent relatively little money on environmental safeguards. As a result, they are polluting the environment at an alarming rate and jeopardizing the health of their people. For example, breathing the air in Calcutta, India, is the equivalent of smoking one pack of cigarettes a day, and fish put in some stretches of the Ganges River die in less than twenty-four hours as a result of toxic industrial waste.

Mortality Measures

Demographers also have a series of statistics for measuring mortality. The most frequently cited is the **crude death rate (CDR)** — the number of deaths per year for every 1,000 members of the population. Like the crude birth rate, the CDR does not take into account the age composition of the population. The rates in developed countries like the United States, Japan, and France are relatively low, even though these nations have older populations. They are the result of quality medical care, few deaths resulting from nutritional deficiencies, and the ability to control communicable diseases. The CDR of the world's developed nations in 1989 was ten (per 1,000 people).

In developing nations, the CDR ranges from a low of three in Brunei to a high of twenty-three in Guinea and Afghanistan. In other words, the poor nations of the world have CDRs both lower and higher than the rich nations. Low rates are the result of two factors. First, because they are growing so rapidly, developing nations have very young populations, with up to 50 percent of their citizens under fifteen years of age. Young people die at a much lower rate than older individuals. Second, communicable diseases have been controlled effectively in much of the Third World. The ability to minimize death from epidemics is a function of modernization and the work of agencies like the World Health Organization — for example, the immunization of millions of people from infectious diseases in the years after World War II. Mortality, however, did not fall at the same rate in all Third World countries. For a variety of reasons (political, economic, environmental) the CDR of countries like Afghanistan and Guinea are still high. But on the whole, the death rate in these nations has declined significantly in a short period of time. Between the early 1960s and 1970s (excluding China), it fell from seventeen to twelve, and by 1989 it was down to eleven.

Another often-cited mortality statistic is the **infant mortality rate:** the number of deaths during the first year of life per 1,000 live births. This statistic clearly and tragically indicates the differences in income, education, health care, and nutrition that exist between rich and poor nations. For example, the infant mortality rate for developed countries is fifteen, being very low in nations like Japan (4.9) and Iceland (3.4). In the United States it is 9.9 (the eighteenth lowest in the world), a figure that varies significantly by social class. Children of poor women in the United States are 50 percent more likely to die in their first year than children of more affluent women (Gortmaker, 1979). Although infant mortality has continued to drop in developed nations, children in Third World countries are twenty-five times more likely to die in the first year of life than those born in rich countries. In 1988, developing nations had an infant mortality rate of 84 per 1,000 births, with twenty African nations having rates over 120. It is estimated that fifteen million Third World children, approximately 41,000 every day, die every year before their first birthday.

Women are susceptible to health complications and death at childbirth. The **maternal mortality rate** is a measure of the number of women who die per 10,000 live births. Because these figures are relatively low, this summary statistic is calculated per 10,000 births, and not 1,000. Deaths while giving birth in the United States have declined from 58 per 10,000 in 1935 to a point at which they have now been virtually eliminated. In developing countries, however, approximately 500,000 women lose their lives annually due to complications during pregnancy and childbirth.

Social Correlates of Mortality

In our discussion of mortality we have examined some of the major causes of death in the United States, as well as various statistics and how they differ in the developed and developing worlds. By way of conclusion, we will look at a number of social correlates of death in the United States. Although death may appear to be a random phenomenon, data indicate that mortality rates differ significantly from one segment of the population to another. Studies from which these summary statements are drawn were compiled by Weeks (1986, pp. 154–158).

1. As a group's occupational prestige goes up, death rates go down. A study of white males found that laborers had a higher mortality rate and professionals a lower rate than the population of males as a whole.
2. As income and education go up, mortality goes down. "For virtually every major cause of death, white males with at least one year of college had lower risks of death than those with less education."
3. Nonwhite mortality is higher than white mortality by at least 10 percent in every group up to age eighty years.
4. People who are married (especially men) have lower rates of mortality than single people.
5. As a group, women live approximately seven years longer than men in the United States.

This final statement has to do with life expectancy—the statistical average length of time a person in a given population can expect to live. In the developed world, life expectancy is seventy-three years; in the developing nations it is sixty years. A person born in Japan in 1990 can expect to live seventy-nine years (the highest in the world), compared to forty-one years for someone born in Ethiopia (the lowest in the world). Of course, many people in Ethiopia are over forty-one years of age; however, the average life span in that country is drastically reduced when all of the children who die in the first year of life are entered into the equation. Once an individual makes it through that first dangerous year, his or her chances of living past age forty-one increase dramatically. Those who reach their fifth birthday (another significant milestone) will live even longer.

Inasmuch as the life expectancy of an individual is affected by both biological and social variables, the fact that the Japanese as a group can expect to live almost twice as long as people in Ethiopia is best explained by a number of socioeconomic factors. Levels of income, technology, nutrition, education, and health care are vastly superior in a country like Japan. Another important reason for longevity differences between developed and developing nations is the high rate of infant mortality in the latter.

Research indicates that even in developed countries people may be reaching the upper limits of average life expectancy, about eighty-five years. Even if cures were found for leading causes of death such as cancer, heart disease, and diabetes, people in the United States would live, on average, only a few years more. According to Jay Olshansky of the University of Chicago, "Once you go beyond the age of 85, people die from multiple-organ failure. . . . Basically they die of old age" (*Los Angeles Times,* 1990a). Olshansky notes that, barring the reversal of aging at the molecular level, the rapid increases in life expectancy are over. However, other researchers maintain that if factors such as smoking, obesity, and blood pressure can be controlled, the average life expectancy could be as high as ninety-nine years (*Los Angeles Times,* 1990a).

 MIGRATION

We tend to think of population growth solely in terms of the relation between fertility and mortality. However, the movement of people from one location to another affects not only the rate of growth, but the distribution of the population. The study of geographic mobility or migration is one of the major subareas of demography. **Migration** is defined as the relatively permanent movement of people from one place to another.

As students of society, sociologists are concerned with the reasons people move, as well as the number of individuals who change their place of residence. Migration is usually the result of social, political, or economic conditions. One or more of these conditions may push or pull individuals and groups, resulting in streams of migrants moving within or across national boundaries. **Push factors** serve to drive off or send a stream of migrants from a particular locale. **Pull factors** are socioeconomic magnets and draw migrants to a given geographical area. Historically, some of the more important push factors have been the decline of natural resources in an area, loss of employment, persecution (racial, religious, political), and natural disasters (flood, fire, drought, famine). When people decide to leave an area, they search for a location that will enhance life chances for themselves and their children. The most important pull factors are increased opportunity for employment and income, better living conditions (climate, housing, schools, health), and the possibility of new and different activities (Bogue, 1969).

Internal versus International Migration

Demographers make a distinction between internal and international migration. **Internal migration** refers to the movement of people within a political state. The United States has always been a nation of movers, and migration has significantly altered the distribution of its population. The U.S. Bureau of the Census estimates that ninety-one million Americans five years of age or older in 1980 lived in a different residence from where they lived in 1975. A major shift has been movement from rural to urban locales. Between 1800 and 1980, the urban population increased from 5 percent to 77 percent as a result of both natural increase in the cities and migration. In addition, in the last twenty-five years the most significant movement has been from the northeastern and midwestern "frost belt" to the "sun belt" stretching from Florida to California. Ninety-one percent of the population growth between 1980 and 1984 occurred in ten western states (including Alaska) and the South. In the 1970s, nonmetropolitan areas began growing faster than cities as tens of thousands of people left urban America for the countryside.

Large-scale **international migration**—the movement of people across political states—is a relatively recent phenomenon in human history, occurring for the most part over the past 400 years (Bouvier and Gardner, 1986). Although most of it has been voluntary, some of the largest movements were either forced or were the result of fear and political pressure. For example, with the independence and partition of India in 1947, approximately seven to eight million Hindus and Sikhs found themselves residents of a country that was predominantly Muslim (Pakistan), and an estimated equal number of Muslims were then residents of a state that was overwhelmingly Hindu (India). In a desperate attempt to become citizens of societies made up of members of their own religion, millions of people moving to India and Pakistan embarked on one of the largest migrations in history (Bryjak, 1986).

FIGURE 10.1   Legal Immigrants Admitted to the United States, by Region of Last Residence for Selected Years

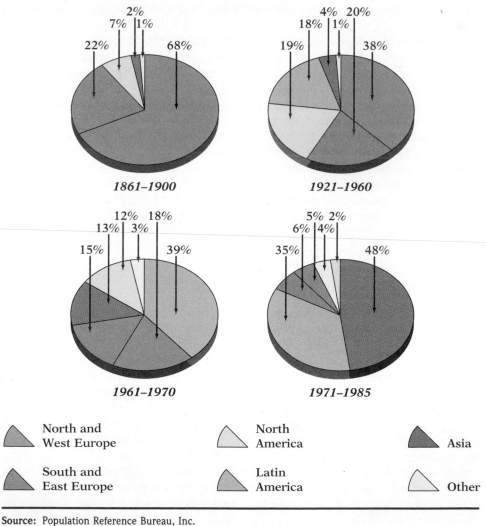

1861–1900

1921–1960

1961–1970

1971–1985

North and West Europe

North America

Asia

South and East Europe

Latin America

Other

Source: Population Reference Bureau, Inc.

Prior to 1800 an estimated ten to twenty million Africans were transported forcibly to the New World. With this notable exception, migration to the United States has been voluntary. Between 1820 and 1979 approximately forty-nine million people migrated (legally) to the United States. The peak years of this influx were between 1881 and 1920. The tremendous number of people who came to the United States during this period, coupled with the depression of the 1930s, resulted in the passage of restrictive immigration laws and a significantly lower number of immigrants. However, after World War II and the liberalization of quotas, relatively large numbers (many of them political refugees) entered the country. As Figure 10.1 indicates, the composition of migrants has changed drastically. Between 1861 and 1900, 68 percent were from northern and western Europe. By 1981–1985 that number was reduced to 5 percent, with the majority coming from Asia (48 percent) and Latin America (35 percent).

Illegal Immigration

Illegal immigration is a highly controversial topic. Estimates of the number of people residing illegally in the United States in the late 1970s and early 1980s range from 1.5 to 6 million. Approximately 95 percent of those apprehended entering the country illegally attempt to cross the U.S.-Mexican border, and 50 to 60 percent of these "illegal aliens" are from Mexico. The Bureau of the Census recognizes three groups of illegal immigrants. *Settlers* come to the United States on a more or less permanent basis; *sojourners* such as farm laborers do seasonal work and then return to Mexico; and *commuters* cross the border daily (Bouvier and Gardner, 1986). Almost half of all illegal immigrants born in Latin America live in California, and another 31 percent reside in New York, Texas, Illinois, and Florida.

These illegal immigrants crossing the Rio Grande into the United States are pulled by opportunities for a better life in El Norte *and pushed by high unemployment and rapid population growth in Mexico and other Latin American countries.*

The impact illegal aliens have on the U.S. economy is not clear. Muller and Espenshade (1985) noted that these workers take the lowest-paid jobs, displacing American-born laborers who then move up the economic ladder. According to McCarthy and Valdez (1985), illegal Mexican labor helped California's economy by "enabling many low-wage industries to continue to expand at a time when their counterparts were contracting in the face of foreign competition" (p. 26). Others argue that illegal aliens take thousands of jobs from American citizens, as well as depress their wages (Briggs, 1985; Marshall, 1986).

POPULATION COMPOSITION

Sex Ratio

Demographers are interested in the composition of a population as well as its size and rate of growth. A simple summary statistic that tells us a great deal about a given society is the **sex ratio**—the number of males per 100 females in the population. A sex ratio of 100 (balanced) means that there are equal numbers of males and females. In 1910 the sex ratio of the United States was 106, indicating a surplus of males (106 males for every 100 females). This unbalance was due in large part to the disproportionate number of males who immigrated to America around the turn of the century (Broom and Selznick, 1970). By 1986 the sex ratio had declined to 95.2, revealing a surplus of females and indicating the fact that women live longer than men in the United States, as they do in most societies.

The Extra Man Is the Man of the 90's

The plight of older women in search of available, interested men became a cultural cliché of the 1980's. Now it seems that the lament of the 90's might come from younger men. Demography dictates that they will have to fight over a smaller pool of potential mates.

According to the Census Bureau, for every six single men in their 20's there are only five women in the same age group. Altogether, this leaves 2.3 million young men without a match. Actually, there might be even more of a discrepancy since some sociologists believe that the Census Bureau misses many young men, who tend to move more frequently than women.

To make matters worse, young men often find themselves competing with older men for the same women.

Though this has always been true, the deceleration of the baby boom is making the rivalry more intense. From 1957 to 1975 the number of births in the United States fell by an average of 1.7 percent a year. For men in their 20's this means fewer and fewer younger women to meet.

"Men in their 20's simply may not have many women available who are younger," said William Beer, deputy chairman of the sociology department at Brooklyn College. "Older men are poaching."

The ideal solution would be for more men to marry older women. While this is becoming more common, a 1985 survey by the National Center for Health Statistics found that the man was older than the woman in two-thirds of all marriages, with an average age difference of 5.3 years.

Source: *The New York Times*, January 21, 1990. Copyright © 1990 by The New York Times Company. Reprinted by permission.

The sex ratio and growth rate can also tell us something about people's chances of getting married in a given population. More males are born than females; but because males also have a higher mortality rate, by the age of twenty to twenty-four years, the sex ratio is balanced (100). From age twenty-five and up there is a surplus of females; and, because American women marry men two or three years older than themselves, there are not enough men to go around. During the baby boom years (1946–1964), each year's crop of babies was bigger than the year before, meaning that still fewer males two or three years older were available for American women to choose from when they were of marriageable age. The so-called marriage squeeze received a good deal of publicity, and one magazine even reported that by age thirty-five never-married baby boom females were more likely to be killed by terrorists than to find a husband. Research by Neil Bennet (1989), however, indicated that, with the end of the boom, the sex ratio favoring men (more females than males) began to change, and females born between 1960 and 1975 would find a surplus of husbands. He said, "For women who indeed want to marry, they will see an upswing in available men" (Bennet, 1989).

Age/Sex or Population Pyramid

Another important device for understanding the composition of a population is an **age/sex** or **population pyramid,** which summarizes the age and sex characteristics of a given society. Figure 10.2 presents age/sex pyramids for the United States, Mexico, and Japan. The Mexican pyramid is called a true pyramid and indicates a rapidly growing population with each age cohort (group) larger than the preceding one. Societies with age/sex pyramids like Mexico will continue to grow for the foreseeable future. In fifteen years, all of the females under age fourteen at the present time will be between fifteen and twenty-nine, their peak reproductive period. There are so many young people in a country like Mexico that if each couple were to have only two children (replacement level), the population would continue to grow for many years. The narrowing near the top of the Mexican pyramid indicates that the death rate in developing countries for middle-age and older people is much higher than in rich societies.

The age/sex pyramids of Japan and the United States tell a much different story. They illustrate populations that are aging and have a slow rate of growth. The narrow bases (typical of developed countries) reflect a low birth rate. With a relatively small percentage of females (potential mothers) under age nineteen, fertility rates will remain low for the coming generation. The large cohorts in the United States pyramid between twenty and thirty-nine are the baby boomers. The aging of this large group combined with a low fertility rate indicates that America is growing old. The median age of the population in 1970 was twenty-eight, meaning that half of the people were younger and half were older than this number. By 1990, increased longevity and the aging of boomers raised the median age to thirty-three.

The U.S. Bureau of the Census predicts that the number of elderly individuals will continue to increase until at least the year 2050, when the median age of the population will be between 35.2 and 48.5 years. Beginning in 2010 the baby boom generation will trigger a "senior boom," with over fifty million Americans over age sixty-five by the year 2020. The estimate of the number of elderly people in the first half of the next century is probably accurate because these people are alive today, and only mortality rates have to be considered (Soldo and Agree, 1988). Predicting the median age of the population in the next century is much more difficult because (unknown) fertility rates must be estimated and factored into the equation.

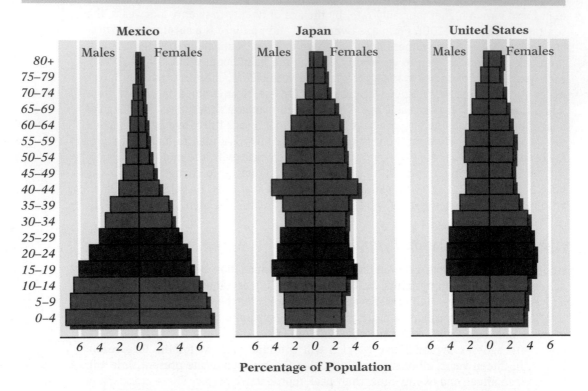

Mexico's population pyramid is typical of rapidly growing developing nations. Sometimes called a true pyramid, it has a broad base and narrow peak, indicating high fertility and relatively high (although declining) mortality. The population pyramids of Japan and the United States no longer resemble true pyramids. Having completed the demographic transition, developed countries have low birth and death rates, slow growth, and an aging population.

Source: The Population Reference Bureau, Inc., and the Population Crisis Committee.

The Bureau of the Census also records the changing racial and ethnic composition of the country. In 1985 blacks were the largest minority group in the United States, making up 12.1 percent of the population (28.9 million), up from 11.8 percent in 1980. New York has the most black residents, and California has the fastest growing black population. As of 1985 California had approximately one-third of the 17.5 million Hispanics in the United States, followed by Texas, New York, and Florida. The Hispanic population is growing rapidly because of high birth rates and international migration.

POPULATION OF THE UNITED STATES

Preliminary statistics from the 1990 census reveal at least three population trends in the United States: (1) the continuing movement of people to the southern and western regions of the country; (2) a population shift from the cities to surrounding suburbs; and (3) in some areas of the country, a rapidly increasing minority population.

With a 1990 population of approximately 250 million, hundreds of thousands of Americans moved south and west in the 1980s, continuing a pattern of migration that began in the late 1700s. The population of the western region increased by 22.5 percent in the 1980s, and the South remained the most populous of the four principal census regions (Fulwood, 1990). Table 10.1 reveals that nine of the ten states with the largest population increase in the 1980s were in the southern and western regions. The last census also revealed a "hollowing out" of the nation's midsection. Seven of the ten states that gained the fewest people or actually declined in population are in the Midwest.

The majority of people who migrated in the last decade relocated for economic reasons (Haub, in Fulwood, 1990). People were pushed from the Northeast or Midwest as a result of a perceived or real downturn in the economy, and pulled to the West and South because of perceived or real economic opportunity in those regions. The migration of people in the 1980s will have significant political ramifications in the 1990s. With the beginning of the 103rd Congress in 1993, California will have seven additional congressional seats and Florida will add four. Texas will pick up three seats, and five other western and southern states will gain one congressperson apiece. New York

TABLE 10.1   State Populations Ranked by Growth 1980–1990

State	1990 Population	Percentage Growth 1980–1990	State	1990 Population	Percentage Growth 1980–1990
1. Nevada	1,206,152	50.7	26. Connecticut	3,295,669	6.1
2. Alaska	551,947	37.4	27. New Jersey	7,748,634	5.2
3. Arizona	3,677,985	35.3	28. Kansas	2,485,600	5.2
4. Florida	13,003,362	33.4	29. Massachusetts	6,029,051	5.1
5. California	29,839,250	26.1	30. Missouri	5,137,804	4.5
6. New Hampshire	1,113,915	21.0	31. Oklahoma	3,157,604	4.4
7. Texas	17,059,805	20.0	32. Wisconsin	4,906,745	4.3
8. Georgia	6,508,419	19.1	33. Alabama	4,062,608	4.3
9. Utah	1,727,784	18.3	34. Arkansas	2,362,239	3.3
10. Washington	4,887,941	18.3	35. New York	18,044,505	2.8
11. New Mexico	1,521,779	16.8	36. Mississippi	2,586,443	2.6
12. Virginia	6,216,568	16.3	37. Montana	803,655	2.2
13. Hawaii	1,115,274	15.6	38. South Dakota	699,999	1.3
14. Colorado	3,307,912	14.5	39. Indiana	5,564,228	1.3
15. Maryland	4,798,622	13.8	40. Kentucky	3,698,969	1.0
16. North Carolina	6,657,630	13.2	41. Nebraska	1,584,617	0.9
17. Delaware	668,696	12.5	42. Ohio	10,887,325	0.8
18. South Carolina	3,505,707	12.3	43. Louisiana	4,238,216	0.8
19. Vermont	564,964	10.5	44. Michigan	9,328,784	0.7
20. Maine	1,233,223	9.7	45. Pennsylvania	11,924,710	0.5
21. Oregon	2,853,733	8.4	46. Illinois	11,466,682	0.4
22. Minnesota	4,387,029	7.6	47. North Dakota	641,364	−1.7
23. Idaho	1,011,986	7.2	48. Wyoming	455,975	−2.9
24. Tennessee	4,896,641	6.7	49. Iowa	2,787,424	−4.3
25. Rhode Island	1,005,984	6.2	50. West Virginia	1,801,625	−7.6

Source: U.S. Bureau of the Census.

will lose three representatives to the House, and twelve other states will lose one or two seats each.

The 1990 census also revealed that while half the nation's population lives within the thirty-nine largest metropolitan areas, the composition of these areas is changing. Metropolitan expansion in the 1980s was predominantly a function of suburban growth. Demographer William Frey notes that the United States is a "suburban nation," with the central cities losing both economic and political importance (in Clifford and Roark, 1991). No longer the exclusive haven of the more affluent members of society, many suburbs are part slum and part suburb. Edwin Bailey (in Clifford, 1991) refers to this new residential pattern as a **sluburb.** A partial explanation for this phenomenon is that suburbs are becoming ports of entry for new immigrants. In other words, the path of residential mobility from central cities to suburbs typical of movement in years past is no longer the only road to the outer environs. This rapid influx to the suburbs is putting a tremendous strain on social services, especially schools (Estrada, in Clifford, Roark, and Horstman, 1991).

Finally, some areas of the country recorded a significant increase in minority group members in the 1980s. This is especially true of California, the new home to nearly one of three newcomers to the United States in that decade. In 1980 approximately one-third of the total population of the state was made up of minority groups. That figure had increased to 43 percent in 1990. With at least three minority-majority counties in 1990, over 50 percent of California's population will consist of minority group members in the not too distant future.

WORLD POPULATION

The history of world population growth can be divided into three periods. The first encompasses almost all of human existence and lasted until the eighteenth century. High birth rates were matched by almost equally high death rates, and world population grew slowly. Any regional spurts in fertility were nullified by plagues and famines (Merrick, 1986). The second period began in the 1800s with the Industrial Revolution. Population grew rapidly in Europe and America during this period, not as a result of increased fertility, but because of a rapid and unprecedented decline in mortality that was directly related to industrialization. Mechanization brought about a substantial increase in food supplies, reduced the dangers of famine, and resulted in a healthier population. When nutritional needs are met, people are more resistant to disease. Parallel advances in medical knowledge and technology helped prolong life, and infant mortality was also sharply reduced. Merrick (1986) noted that this European-based population increase lasted until the end of World War II and the beginning of the third stage of world population growth.

This third phase is usually referred to as the population explosion and is currently taking place in the developing world. Whereas substantial growth in Europe and those areas of the world populated by Europeans took almost 200 years, an enormous surge of growth occurred in the developing nations in only a few decades. Unfortunately, the poor nations of the world benefited selectively from the developed countries. Their economies grew at a meager rate, and the infusion of medicine and public health systems from the West resulted in a substantial reduction in mortality. Antibiotics, sanitation, immunization, and insecticides checked the heretofore widespread misery

OURSELVES AND OTHERS
Overpopulation Called Threat to Human Race

LONDON—According to the U.N. Population Fund, 50 percent more couples worldwide must practice family planning to meet growth limitation targets and avoid overpopulation that could endanger human survival.

In its 1991 annual report, "The State of World Population," the agency predicted that 44 billion condoms, 8.76 billion cycles of oral pills and 310 million intrauterine devices will be needed annually to meet U.N. targets for lowering fertility from 3.8 children per woman to 3.3.

Dr. Nafis Sadik, the fund's executive director, said the number of couples practicing voluntary contraception in developing countries must grow from 381 million to 567 million by 2000, an increase of about 50 percent.

Sadik warned that without control of population growth, the world faces increased food shortages, unchecked urban growth, environmental damage and unwanted migration.

"The consequences of missing targets are dire, and we can already see the warning signs in today's world if we look closely," she said. "These warning signs represent trends that, unless checked, portend an ominous future for human survival."

Under the U.N. projections aimed at stabilizing the number of people on the planet, world population, now 5.4 billion people, would reach 6.4 billion in 2001 and 10.2 billion by 2075.

"While these figures may sound daunting, I believe these targets are realistic and can be achieved," Sadik said. "Strong, well-managed family planning programs, using purely voluntarily means, have achieved smaller family size, healthier mothers and children, and more balanced rates of population growth."

Over the past two decades, Thailand, Indonesia, China, Colombia and Mexico are among developing countries that have dramatically reduced their birth rate, the U.N. official said.

Thailand cut its fertility rate of 6.5 births per woman to 3.5 in eight years, and Indonesia lowered its rate from 2.4 to 1.8 in two decades, Sadik said.

"The seedbed for future family planning success has been prepared," she said. "Today more women than in any previous generation say they want fewer children."

Sadik emphasized that education for women and girls and raising their status in society was an essential part of creating an "environment of freedom" that allowed men and women to make their own choices.

"Higher status for women brings with it the increased ability to choose," she said. "When choice is available to them, women will always exercise it."

Family planning programs worldwide will cost $9 billion annually by 2000, twice what is spent now. Of the total, international organizations will contribute $4.5 billion, the U.N. agency $1 billion, developing countries $3.5 billion, and the remainder will come from the users themselves.

Source: William B. Ries, *San Diego Union,* May 14, 1991. Reprinted with the permission of United Press International, Inc.

and death brought about by malaria, smallpox, and a host of other diseases (Murphy, 1985). While mortality was dropping rapidly, fertility rates that had been high for hundreds of years declined only slightly.

An overarching view of world population history is shown in Table 10.2. It took from two to five million years for the population of the world to reach one billion, but only 187 years more to hit five billion. A person born in 1930 and living until 1998 will see the population of the earth triple, from two to six billion. Table 10.3 shows the evolution of the world's most populous countries based on projections for the year 2000. Notice that all but four of these nations are in the developing world.

TABLE 10.2 World Population Growth

Population Level	Time Taken to Reach New Population Level (years)	Year Attained
First billion	2–5 million	About A.D. 1800
Second billion	Approximately 130	1930
Third billion	30	1960
Fourth billion	15	1975
Fifth billion	12	1987
Sixth billion (projected)	11	1998

Note: It took two to five million years for world population to reach one billion. The second billion took approximately thirty years, and the last four billion people were added in the span of one lifetime—sixty-eight years.

Source: Population Reference Bureau, Inc.

TABLE 10.3 Evolution of the Most Populous Nations from 1930 to 2000 (estimate)*

Country	Population (in millions)			
	1930	1950	1990	2000
China	430	540	1,120	1,240
India	335	370	844	975
USSR	160	180	291	315
USA	120	155	251	260
Indonesia	60	77	189	220
Brazil	40	53	150	177
Bangladesh		40	114	148
Pakistan		35	114	141
Nigeria	19	28	119	161
Japan	64	84	123	130
Mexico	16	26	88	110
Vietnam	22	25	70	88
Philippines	12	20	66	75
Thailand	11	19	56	68
Turkey	11	21	57	70
Iran	14	20	56	64
Egypt	14	21	55	61
Italy	41	47	58	61

*Germany is not included. The combined East and West German population in 1990 was estimated at 79.5 million. In the year 2000 that figure is estimated to be 81.2 million.

Source: Adapted from *A Strategic Atlas: Comparative Geopolitics of the World's Powers* (1983) by Gerard Chaliand and Jean-Pierre Rageau. English translation by Tony Berret (1985). New York: Harper and Collins. Reprinted by permission of Harper Collins Publishers.

TABLE 10.4   Rate of Population Growth

	Country		
	A	B	C
Crude birth rate	50	40	30
Crude death rate	30	20	10
Difference	20	20	20
Rate of growth (%)	2.0	2.0	2.0

Note: Although all of the countries here have the same rate of growth—2.0% per annum—they have different rates of birth and death. Population growth is not the result of either a high birth rate or a low death rate, but the difference between the two.

Discounting migration for the moment, keep in mind that population growth is a function of the relation between fertility and mortality. Neither high fertility nor low mortality alone will result in rapid population growth. Table 10.4 shows three hypothetical countries with different crude birth and death rates. All of these countries, however, have the same growth rate, 2.0 percent per annum.

Malthus and Marx

The first major attempt to explain and project population growth and its consequences was undertaken by the English economist and clergyman Thomas Malthus (1766–1834). In "An Essay on the Principle of Population," published in 1798, Malthus predicted that mankind was in for big trouble, to say the least. He reasoned that food supply increased arithmetically (one-two-three-four, etc.), whereas population increased geometrically (two-four-eight-sixteen, etc.). It was only a matter of time before humans outstripped what contemporary biologists call "carrying capacity," the point at which the environment can no longer sustain the population. When this point is reached, the result will be widespread misery, famine, and death. Malthus realized that before people starved to death, however, they would be killed off by disease, war, and vice. He referred to these growth limits as *positive checks.* This horrible scenario could be avoided if people used *preventive checks* (delayed marriage or moral restraint, i.e., celibacy) to control their fertility. A conservative clergyman, Malthus rejected any form of contraception, abortion, or infanticide.

Malthus' theory attracted much attention and was roundly criticized. Weeks (1986) described three of its major shortcomings. First, the idea that food production could not keep up with the population was wrong. The Industrial Revolution brought about dramatic increases in food production and agricultural knowledge. Today, enough food is available in the world to provide every human being with 3,600 calories per day. The problem is not one of production but one of distribution. Second, the belief that preventive checks (moral restraint) are the only way to reduce fertility is a moral position and not a scientific one. Effective mechanisms of birth control using various methods of contraception and abortion are practiced in many nations of the world. Finally, the conclusion that poverty is the inevitable result of population growth is false. Recall that population increases in Europe and North America brought about by the Industrial Revolution resulted in a higher, not lower, standard of living.

One of the harshest critics of Malthus was Karl Marx, who argued that the work of the "Parson of Doom" (as Malthus was often called) was superficial, unimaginative, and just plain wrong. Marx thought that problems like poverty due to overpopulation were not the result of any natural laws (arithmetic and geometric progressions of food and people), but of an oppressive exploitive capitalist system. The solution was not moral restraint but socialism, an economic system that would outproduce capitalism and ensure an equitable distribution of food, material goods, and services. Under socialism, birth rates would also decline because of a rising standard of living and a reduction of child labor. The Marxist position, in turn, has been criticized for being long on faith and short on scientific research.

The Demographic Transition

The inability of Malthus, Marx, and others to adequately explain population dynamics in the modern world led to the **demographic transition theory.** This perspective was developed by Warren Thompson in 1929, and later expanded by Frank Notesien in 1945. According to the theory, birth and death rates of a country will change as they pass through three stages (Figure 10.3).

Stage one lasted for tens of thousands of years and was characterized by high birth and death rates. Birth rates were high because human labor was a necessary and valued

FIGURE 10.3   Stages of the Demographic Transition

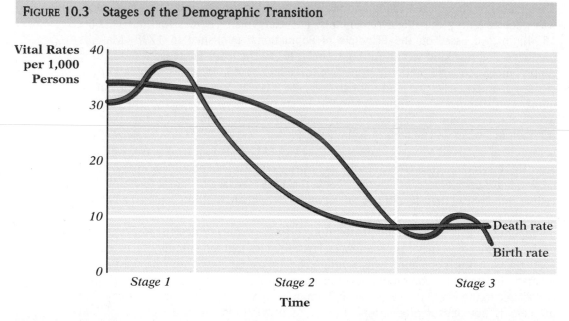

Stage 1 of the demographic transition is characterized by high birth and death rates. Although population growth is slow, high birth rates provide the potential for rapid growth. During stage 2, death rates drop significantly, resulting in rapid population growth; in the latter part of this stage, birth rates "catch down" with death rates. In stage 3, both birth and death rates are low, resulting in a slow rate of growth.

Source: Adapted from *Population: An Introduction to Concepts and Issues,* Third Edition, by John R. Weeks. Copyright © 1986 by Wadsworth, Inc. Reprinted by permission of the publisher.

commodity. Death rates (including infant mortality) were high because of an overall low standard of living and lack of medical knowledge. Population growth during this period was modest and slow. Because of high birth rates, Notesien referred to this stage as one of *high growth potential.*

Stage two was a period of *transitional growth* made up of parts A and B. Part A began with the Industrial Revolution and had high birth and rapidly declining death rates. With advances in medicine and better nutrition, mortality rates (especially infant mortality) fell dramatically. This was a period of explosive population growth.

In part B, fertility began to "catch down" with mortality as people gained both the desire and ability (contraception) to control fertility. Up to this point in the evolution of human societies, children were almost always regarded as economic assets to the family. As Caldwell (1980) noted, "The flow of wealth is upward from children to parents and even grandparents, and high fertility is profitable, at least in the long run to parents" (p. 225). Children supported elderly parents financially, and also treated them with considerable respect—two significant reasons for having large families. As nations began to modernize, however, children became an economic liability and fertility began to decline.

Caldwell (1980) stated that in societies where fertility is declining (or just about to fall), education plays a significant role, and it brings about lower rates of fertility in a number of ways. First, children attending school are less likely to work either inside or outside the home, thereby reducing their economic benefit to the family. Second, education is expensive, especially for peasants, as parents have to pay for tuition, uniforms, books, supplies, and outside spending money. Finally, education tends to alter traditional family relationships. "With schooling, it becomes clear that the society regards the child as a future rather than a present producer, and that it expects the family to protect the society's investment in the child for that future" (Caldwell, 1980, p. 226). All of these changes make the child less productive, less responsible for the family's present survival, and more costly to the family. Together they result in declining fertility.

Stage three is that of *incipient decline,* with low fertility and mortality, and therefore low population growth. Contraceptive use is extensive and socially acceptable. Women have gained economic and political rights and work outside of the home, and children are increasingly viewed as an economic liability. The developed nations of the world have completed the demographic transition and are in this final stage.

Societies may differ somewhat in the time it takes to complete the transition, but once the process has begun it is irreversible. Developing nations are in stage two of the transition, accounting for approximately 90 percent of world population growth. Death rates dropped much faster in stage two for the developing nations in the years after World War II than they did for the developing countries after the Industrial Revolution. Because of this time factor and lack of economic development, the birth rate in poor countries has not declined as fast; hence the population explosion in nations least able to cope with it.

The demographic transition theory has been criticized for not being able to predict when fertility will decline (stage two), and for its ethnocentrism (Weeks, 1986). Concerning the first, demographers were of the opinion that fertility decline was dependent on the spread of industrialization or the rate of economic development. However, in an important restatement of demographic transition theory, John C. Caldwell (1976) stated, "Fertility decline is more likely to precede industrialization and to help bring it about than to follow it" (p. 358). Regarding the criticism of ethnocentrism, the assumption was that since the developed nations completed the transition in a particular manner and time frame, the developing countries would do the same. To date they have not. It is easy to fall into the trap of believing that what transpired and benefited the industrialized nations will also take place in and be good for the rest of the world.

Underpopulation

Population problems are usually thought of in terms of rapid growth and its social, economic, and environmental consequences. Although the ramifications of rapid population increase in developing countries are grave, demographers are also investigating the population *decrease* that may occur in many industrialized countries before the end of this century. The average family size in most of these nations is less than the 2.1 children per couple necessary for a population to remain stable over the long run. For example, as of 1985, Western European nations had a mean family size of approximately 1.61 children per couple, with comparable numbers in Japan of 1.71, the United States of 1.85, and West Germany 1.42. Demographer Nathan Keyfitz (1986) noted that the number of births in Austria is less than the number of deaths, and if the current rate of reproduction continues, the country's population will decline by 25 percent in each successive generation. Explanations for the declining fertility rate in developed nations have been advanced by a number of researchers.

In a study of Australia, New Zealand, Canada, the United States, and Japan, Preston (1986) reported that data from all of these countries indicate "a rise in the proportion of married couples practicing contraception and a switch by the contracepting population toward more efficient methods" (p. 41). Not only have more people in these nations decided to limit the size of their families, but they are better able to do so with increasingly effective birth control devices. Abortion has also contributed to reduced fertility in these countries. For example, the ratio of legal abortions to live births in the United States increased from 0.24 in 1973 to 0.43 in 1981.

According to Davis (1986), high divorce rates are also related to declining fertility. In a study of twenty-four industrial nations "not one showed a decline in divorce during the thirteen years between 1970 and 1983" (p. 57). Thus divorce lowers fertility in at least two ways. First, it simply reduces the time men and women spend in marriage. Second, a high divorce rate is indicative of marital instability, and people with marital problems often postpone having children.

Among other things, the twentieth century will be remembered as the time when women entered the labor force in increasing numbers. As of 1910 only 9 percent of married women in the United States were gainfully employed; by 1985 that figure had climbed to 54.2 percent. Davis (1986) stated that wives' participation in the labor force "has a chilling effect on fertility in several ways" (p. 58). For example, to get better-paying, more prestigious jobs, single women often postpone marriage in favor of continuing their education. Facing more competition from increasingly better educated women, men also opt to delay marriage and stay in school. When two working people marry, the husband is in no position to demand that his wife quit her job.

The employment of married women also contributes to marital instability. "By giving the wife an income of her own, it lessens her need for a husband; by providing social contacts at the workplace, it enables her to meet other men; and by focusing her attention on an occupation, it gives her a role—a personal identity—apart from that of childcare and household responsibility" (Davis, 1986, p. 58). Working wives who desire children and a career may be forced to play "superwoman" in their attempt to meet the duties and responsibilities of being a wife, mother, and full-time employee. One way out of these conflicting and time-consuming role demands is to have a single child or, perhaps, forgo a family altogether in favor of the rewards of a successful career.

Keyfitz (1986) believed that the "pleasures of modern life" could not be overlooked in accounting for the drop in fertility. The more time people spend raising children, the less time they can devote to pursuing a wide range of increasingly affordable activities. For example, most people have the money to buy a car, occasionally travel by air, purchase electronic equipment, attend sporting events, and so on. These things were not available in the high-fertility years that ended in the 1930s, or were just beginning to appear in the high-fertility period of the 1950s. The current desire to lead the "good life," plus the financial ability to do so when both husband and wife work, has contributed to the growing number of DINKs (double income, no kids) in the developed world. If Keyfitz is correct, these egoistic tendencies in consumer-oriented, affluent societies could help keep the fertility rate low for an indefinite period of time.

Although the explanations for a reduced rate of fertility over the past twenty-five years have been clearly spelled out, the social, economic, and political implications of below-replacement-level fertility are less certain. When a population stops growing (or declines in number), the median age of that group of people will increase; that is, the society in question will grow older. An older society will have less crime and, therefore, less need for criminal justice personnel and facilities. It also will result in a more experienced workforce, less job turnover, and lower unemployment (Moore, 1986). Homes can be smaller, use less energy, and reduce the amount of pollution in the environment. On the negative side, an older population will tend to be more conservative and less innovative. Its medical costs will increase as a higher proportion of people live into their seventies and eighties, with these costs falling heavily on a dwindling number of people in their productive (working) years.

Jean Bourgeois-Pichat (1986) posited that below-replacement-level fertility and the impending population "implosion" threatening numerous industrialized nations would soon replace the population explosion as our main area of concern. For demographer Davis (1986), however, low levels of fertility in these countries "is a blessing, not a calamity. It is a solution to a major problem, not the problem itself" (p. 62). Aging societies in the developed world help (if only slightly) reduce the high rate of global population growth.

Problems of Overpopulation

With so many developing countries stuck in stage two of the demographic transition, the world's population is increasing at an alarming rate. At current rates of growth, in developing nations it will increase from four billion to eight billion in thirty-two years, with some countries and regions expanding at an even faster pace. For example, Africa, the poorest region of the world, has a **doubling time**—the number of years it takes a given population to double in size—of only twenty-four years. Population pressure triggers a range of economic, social, political, and environmental problems that affect people in rich and, especially, poor nations. Werner Fornos (1987) of the Population Institute listed the major problems associated with overpopulation. We will incorporate his outline into our own and examine the impact of rapid population growth in developing nations.

Pressure on Cities Third World cities are growing three times as fast as urban areas in the developed world, and most African cities will double in less than ten years. These urban areas are growing rapidly because of *natural increase* (births over deaths) and *rural-to-urban* migration. As we will see in more detail in the next chapter, millions of people around the world are attempting to escape the grinding poverty and hopelessness of the countryside by moving to Third World cities. As a result, problems of congestion, housing, and pollution in many urban areas are almost incomprehensible. Most cities in developing nations have slums and squatter settlements containing from one-fourth to two-thirds of the population. Of Calcutta's one hundred municipal wards, ninety-seven have slums, and tens of thousands of so-called pavement dwellers are born, live, and die in the streets. Power and water shortages are everyday occurrences, and the streets are choked with people, animals, and cars. It can take hours to travel from one side of the city to the other.

Pressure on Societies   In Latin America and Asia almost 40 percent of the population is under fifteen years of age, and Africa is an even younger continent, with 45 percent of the people under age fifteen. The coming generation will witness three billion people entering their reproductive years in the Third World. With doubling times of thirty-two years or less, the entire infrastructure (health, education, transportation, communication, etc.) of developing nations will have to double as well just to maintain the low standard of living that now exists in these countries.

Between 1987 and the year 2000, approximately 800 million new jobs will have to be created if the next generation of Third World residents are to lead self-sufficient, productive lives. The old adage that "with every mouth God sends two pair of hands" begs some very important questions ("Labour and Population," 1977). What will these hands do? Where will people work? Willingness and the ability to work do not necessarily translate into the availability of jobs. Many developing nations currently have unemployment rates of between 30 and 50 percent.

If people are going to find employment in a modernizing world, they must be educated, if only at minimal levels. Usually considered a right in the developed countries, a basic education is a privilege for millions of people in the Third World. For example, in Kenya, 70 percent of the students are jammed into classrooms, with "children sitting in the windows, children carrying their chairs to school" (Morah, in Fornos, 1987, p. 10). Lacking the education necessary for a growing number of jobs in modernizing societies, people are more likely to remain or retreat to the agricultural sector. Already small plots of land are continually subdivided to a point at which they are "hopelessly inefficient" (Lenski and Lenski, 1987, p. 365).

Pressure on Human Health   Life chances of people in poor, overcrowded nations, already more limited than those of individuals in rich countries, are initially diminished while they are still in the womb. A study of forty-one developing nations found that children born less than two years apart are about two and one-half times more likely to die in their first year than children born more than two years apart. The cycle of rapid pregnancies is not only debilitating to women's bodies, it also results in the low birth weight of their children. Low birth weight, in turn, is a major cause of death in the first twenty-eight days of life, and because it is associated with brain damage, survivors have a one-in-three chance of being mentally retarded. Life can be difficult in even the best of circumstances. What kind of life will mentally impaired individuals in poor Third World countries lead?

At the other end of the life cycle, longevity is increasing in developing nations. Currently 55 percent of the world's population age fifty-five and over live in developing countries, a figure that will rise to 72 percent in the next thirty years. A country that lacks the resources to reduce high rates of infant mortality will have little money to spend on the needs of the aged. Overpopulation means that basic health care, which is already a scarce commodity in poor countries, will become even more difficult, if not impossible, for the masses to attain.

Pressure on Ecologies   Overpopulation makes enormous demands on both renewable and nonrenewable resources. The industrialized nations grew wealthy in part because they developed when oil and natural gas were cheap and plentiful, but those days are gone forever. As more nations modernize and struggle to keep up with the demands of burgeoning populations, the finite reserve of fossil fuels will be further diminished. Renewable resources are also being depleted often at a rate much faster than needed to replenish themselves. The World Bank estimates that in Tanzania, for example, an average family spends between 250 and 300 working days each year looking for and gathering wood for fuel. This labor, although necessary for survival, does not result in the production of food, products, or services. In Africa, twenty-nine trees are cut for every one that is planted. The search for firewood and farmland has resulted in the destruction of twenty-seven million acres of rain forests annually, an area approximately the size of Pennsylvania. These rain forests contain about one-half of all of the plant and animal species in the world.

Ecologists have noted that deforestation leads to a reduction of rainfall, which, in turn, facilitates soil erosion. Called the "quiet crisis" because it is not as readily observable as other environmental problems, twenty-six billion tons of topsoil are lost each year. Once the land loses the ability to sustain vegetation, it becomes desert. Ecologists estimate that the Sahara Desert is expanding at the rate of six miles per year. Agricultural productivity is obviously affected by this tragedy, and people are forced to use higher slopes for farmland.

Pressure on Economies   Overpopulation is a major factor retarding economic growth in the developing world. Demand for products and services is low in societies where the majority of people are poor or unemployed. Manufacturers can produce only what the domestic population can afford to buy, the alternative being to compete in an international marketplace dominated by developed countries. A study by Russett et al. (1964) found a moderately strong association between a society's birth rate and the annual growth of per capita productivity; as fertility goes up, economic growth goes down. High rates of population growth mean that any increase in economic prosperity is likely to be nullified by the addition of new members to society. For example, a country whose gross national product and population are growing at the rate of 3 percent a year is not making economic progress.

Many Third World economies cannot keep up with rapid population growth and are losing ground. Instead of moving forward, the modernization process in these nations may be stopped, or even reversed. Fornos (1987, p. 16) noted that, "in virtually every African nation, per capita agricultural productivity and per capita income have fallen consistently over the past ten years." African countries whose economies are based on agriculture used to be exporters of grain to the rest of the world. Today they cannot even feed themselves.

One of the most debilitating consequences of grinding poverty in rural areas of the Third World is that millions of people have lost hope of ever improving their economic lot in life. John Kenneth Galbraith (1979, p. 60) described the rural poor as having "accommodated" to the "equilibrium of poverty"; that is, they have come to terms with and accepted the poverty they have known for generations. He noted this accommodation is not a sign of weakness of character, but a rational response to a dismal situation: "Poverty is cruel. A continuous struggle to escape that is continually frustrated is more cruel. It is more civilized, more intelligent, as well as more plausible, that people, out of the experience of centuries, should reconcile themselves to what has so long been the inevitable" (p. 60). If Galbraith is correct, overpopulation exacerbates this vicious cycle of misery and despair: more people, more poverty, more accommodation, more people, and on and on.

Pressure on International Security   According to Robert L. Heilbroner (1980), Third World countries could engage in "wars of distribution" against the developing world. The proliferation of nuclear weapons and the possibility that they could fall into the hands of determined, desperate terrorists makes this idea all the more horrific. Political extremists in an overpopulated, perhaps starving nation could engage in a form of nuclear blackmail, demanding, "Give us food and money or one of your major cities will be destroyed." In an age of "backpack" nuclear weapons that can be carried by one person, the possibility of such an event cannot be ignored.

Of more immediate concern, however, are regional conflicts erupting in the Third World as poor nations compete with one another for raw materials, markets, and political dominance. In 1980 the U.S. National Security Council wrote, "The example of warfare in recent memory involving India, Bangladesh, El Salvador, Honduras, and Ethiopia and the growing potential for instability in such places as Turkey, the Philippines, Central America, Iran, and Pakistan, surely justify the question of population pressures being raised" (Fornos, 1987, p. 21).

Although the threat of nuclear war is an ever present danger, the "aspiration bomb" and not nuclear weapons may prove to be the biggest threat facing the developed world. This bomb is made up of young, Third World people living in poverty with little or no hope of prosperity in their homeland. Residing close to affluent nations, these individuals are cognizant of the riches that are available there, and cross the frontier in search of a better life. For example, Mexico and the nations of Central America have a combined population of 110 million people. By the year 2015 this number will swell to 220 million. In no more than a generation, millions of individuals may be attempting to enter the United States illegally, some chasing a dream of wealth and the good life, others just hoping to survive.

Pressure on Political Institutions   A study by the Population Crisis Committee (1989) ranked 120 countries on two scales, with every country receiving a composite score based on the five dimensions that made up each scale. The first scale was demographic indicators, and consisted of population growth, percentage of population under age fifteen years, rate of urbanization, growth of labor force, and heterogeneity of the population. The second scale, problems of governance indicators, was made up of changes of government, political rights, civil rights, communal violence, and dissatisfied youth. The researchers compared the magnitude of demographic pressures (first scale) with the performance of national political institutions (second scale). "Of the countries studied, 101 fit the expected patterns; that is, their demographic performance corresponded generally to their past political performance and potential instability" (p. 1). Only a small number of countries with serious demographic problems had democratic governments that safeguarded political and civil rights.

Overpopulation can be related to problems of food, water, power, and housing shortages, as well as high levels of communal violence among rival ethnic groups competing for scarce resources. The threat of political unrest and revolution often leads to totalitarian regimes intent on preserving order and maintaining power. Heilbroner (1980) saw the eventual rise of "iron" governments of the military socialist type as a consequence of overpopulation in the developing world. However, the threat to democratic institutions can come from the right as well. Although Indian economist Raj Krishna (1982–1983) did not foresee a revolution in his country in the near future, he believed that if one does come about, it will bring to power a "noncommunist dictatorial junta" (p. 90). Under such a regime, population growth would probably be controlled at the price of fundamental human rights.

Pressure on the International Banking System   In the early 1970s the price of raw materials (especially petroleum) and agricultural goods produced by Third World countries increased. Riding a wave of prosperity, poor nations eager to modernize and diversify their economies began to borrow heavily from banks in developed countries. Believing that the price of Third World exports would remain high, these banks were only too eager to loan substantial amounts of money. For a short while everybody was happy; poor countries were earning the money they needed, and the banks were making a handsome profit. In many cases, loans to developing countries were the banks' most profitable venture. By 1981, however, the good times were over. The world economy slid into the worst recession since the 1930s, and the price of raw materials produced by these nations dropped. To make matters worse for the borrowers, the value of the U.S. dollar increased, making it even more difficult to make loan payments. For example, in August 1982, Mexico announced that it was unable to meet its $75 billion foreign debt. The international debt crisis had begun. By 1988 Latin American countries owed world banks $413 billion, and the total Third World debt was approaching $1 trillion.

The banking community had little choice but to restructure the loans. To write them off as a loss, or a default, by some of the largest borrowers (Mexico and Brazil) would throw the International Banking System and the developed world into financial chaos. Even the wealthy nations could not afford to lose $1 trillion. Austerity measures imposed on developing nations by agencies like the International Monetary Fund reduced some of the financial pressure, but left these countries in a difficult position. Every dollar that went to pay the debt was one dollar less that could be used to modernize their societies and meet the demands of rapidly growing populations. In an effort to comply with the terms of restructured loans, governments began to cut back services and raise prices on basic foodstuffs and transportation; overnight the price of subway tickets in Mexico City increased from one to twenty pesos. Unable to cope with these severe economic measures, people took to the streets in demonstrations and riots in Mexico and Peru. Rioting as a result of austerity measures was also widespread in Colombia in 1989.

CRISIS IN AFRICA

The population-associated problems discussed are ubiquitous in the Third World, but nowhere are they more severe than in Africa. A harsh environment, never-ending wars, the legacy of colonial exploitation, corrupt and incompetent political systems, massive foreign debts, and bankrupt economies compounded the problems of overpopulation and created human suffering that only portends to become worse.

With 661 million people in 1990, Africa is the fastest-growing region in the world. At present rates of growth, the population will triple in forty years. Over half of Africa's fifty-one countries have a doubling time of less than twenty-five years, including Ethiopia, the poorest nation in the world. Sub-Saharan women help keep Africa's growth rate at 3.1 percent per annum by giving birth to an average of 6.9 children. Africa is also a very young continent, with half of the population under fourteen and 70 percent of the people under twenty-five years of age. Because so many individuals will come of reproductive age in the next generation, the population will continue to increase even if fertility were to drop to replacement level. Lenski and Lenski (1987) observed that the developed nations are partially responsible for Africa's population explosion by promoting the idea that economic development could solve all of the continent's problems. Although Western medical missionaries have worked to reduce mortality, they have done little to encourage controlling high rates of fertility.

Along with the problem of runaway population growth, most African economies are in shambles. During the 1960s when much of the continent became independent, some economic growth took place. However, by the late 1970s and early 1980s, there was a sharp economic decline, and massive quantities of food were sent to Africa to avert a famine in 1983. Nevertheless, hundreds of thousands of people died (Matthews, 1989; Population Reference Bureau, 1986). In 1987 per capita income was stagnant or declining in twenty-four of Africa's nations. With populations increasing at over 3 percent per annum, food production is up only 1 percent a year.

The tragic consequence of these man-made and natural disasters is that Africa has a near monopoly of those countries with low rankings on measures of social well-being. For example, nine of the ten countries with the lowest life expectancies in the world are in Africa, as are nine of the ten countries with the highest infant mortality rate. "Six of the ten countries with the lowest literacy rates and eight of the ten countries with the lowest rate of access to safe water are also in sub-Saharan Africa" (Hiltzik, 1990). A recent U.N. report on economic conditions in Africa stated, "It is a measure of the socio-economic decay and retrogression of our continent that the number of (African) countries officially classified as least developed countries — the wretched of the earth as they have been categorized — rose to 29 in 1990 . . . and many more, I regret to say, are still knocking at the door to join" (Hiltzik, 1991).

Climatic conditions in Africa have also contributed to the present crisis. Approximately 30 percent of the continent is covered by desert or too sandy for agriculture, and some of the least developed countries have been victimized by fluctuating weather conditions. Matthews (1989) noted that "rainfall in Africa can vary by as much as 40 percent from year to year, and droughts can persist for several years" (p. 33). Even when weather conditions are relatively constant, countries may show a 5 percent variation in their gross national product depending on the rainfall. For poor nations attempting to feed rapidly growing populations, a 5 percent decrease in food production can mean the difference between life or death for thousands.

The solution to Africa's many problems are complex, requiring a combination of both internal and external solutions. In 1986 Africa received $10 billion from developed nations (the United States gave $1.01 billion), a paltry sum when compared to the $1 trillion these countries spend annually for weapons. A Population Institute (1988) report to the 101st Congress stated, "Nothing less than a massive commitment of international economic assistance will be required to rewrite Africa's bleak future" (p. 23). Africans will also have to do a better job of helping themselves, as well as making the most of the aid they receive. Failure rates of agricultural projects recently funded by the World Bank were much higher there than in any other region. Resources cannot be squandered, and economic reconstruction must begin immediately. Still, there is no guarantee that untold human suffering can be averted. The world may witness the sort of misery and death in Africa that Malthus foretold almost 200 years ago.

CONTROLLING FERTILITY

As we have seen, population growth in developing nations is the result of rapidly declining mortality in the years after World War II. The three ways this growth can be slowed are to decrease fertility, increase mortality, or employ some combination of these. Since increasing mortality is not realistic for a number of moral, religious, and practical reasons, the second and third alternatives can be dismissed. This leaves us with controlling fertility as the only acceptable way of reducing the rate of population increases. Unfortunately, population growth was not even viewed as a problem until the 1950s, and then by only a few countries. On the contrary, large populations were seen as a source of strength (more labor power) and, therefore, a boon to modernization. Socialist countries like China were loath to admit they had population difficulties, viewing such an admission as tantamount to saying their economic system (communism) was less than perfect, unable to meet the needs of an expanding society.

In 1952 the Indian government implemented the Third World's first major program to limit birth rates. By the late 1970s U.N. surveys indicated that 81 percent of Third World people lived in countries whose governments wanted to curb rates of growth (Loup, 1980). Undoubtedly, the most ambitious and controversial population policy was introduced by China in 1979. Using a system of rewards and punishments, and a nationwide propaganda campaign, the government hoped to limit families to only one child. Although highly criticized in the West, this program has reduced the Chinese birth rate. Less controversial strategies have met with some success in other nations, and between 1975 and 1985 the average family size in the developing world fell by more than 20 percent.

According to the theory of the demographic transition, birth rates should drop as a nation industrializes. Loup (1980) noted that, "although causality cannot be proved" (p. 70), a link does seem to exist, with birth rate decreasing as development increases. To the end of reducing birth rate, an egalitarian distribution of the profits of economic development may be just as important as development itself. Loup stated that in the Indian state of Kerala, as well as the nation of Sri Lanka, birth rates fell despite low levels of economic growth. "In both cases, however, income distribution within the country is relatively egalitarian; moreover, infant mortality is low, and the literacy level is high" (p. 70).

Demographer John Weeks (1986) observed that the desire to have children is rarely an end in itself, but a means to some other goal(s). A major reason people in developing countries want children is for financial security—someone to take care of them in their old age. This is especially true in rural areas where health care services are sparse or nonexistent. Needless to say, poor people in these countries do not have retirement funds or old-age pensions. People also want children (especially sons) for a variety of social and religious reasons. Therefore, if the birth rate is to be reduced voluntarily, the motivation to have a large family must also be lowered. This may be accomplished in whole or part through economic changes (e.g., the implementation of old-age pensions) and education (alerting people to the dangers of overpopulation). Reducing the motivation to have children, however, is a necessary but not a sufficient condition for decreasing birth rates. Short of total abstinence of sexual activity (which has never been very popular), readily available contraceptives are also necessary.

Fornos (1987) believes that government-sponsored contraceptive research has resulted in some "promising products." For example, Norplant is a small capsule implanted in a woman's upper arm that releases trace amounts of hormonal contraceptives over time. Good for up to five years, it is quite effective and starts working within twenty-four hours of insertion. Capronor functions in much the same way but lasts for only two years. Unlike Norplant, however, it biodegrades and does not have to be removed surgically. Extensive research is also being done on postcoital or "morning after" contraceptives. Injectable contraceptives for men are being tested and may be available sometime in the 1990s. The widespread distribution of these products, together with sound educational programs, could go a long way toward reducing fertility and stabilizing world population in the twenty-first century.

Although the link between contraception and reduced fertility is clear, the United States withdrew its entire proposed $25 million contribution to the United Nations Fund for Population Activities (UNFPA) in 1986 because of the Fund's involvement with the People's Republic of China's family planning program. Opponents of this program argued that it involves compulsory abortions and involuntary sterilization. However, advocates of the Fund contended that the withdrawal of economic assistance also denied family planning assistance (including contraceptives) to 130 developing nations. Representative James Moody of Wisconsin, chairman of the Congressional Coalition of Population and Development, stated, "Bangladesh, Haiti and other similar countries will be the ones to suffer in order to satisfy a purely domestic American dispute" over abortion (*Popline,* 1986). Supporters of the UNFPA in both the First and Third Worlds are likely to view the withdrawal of U.S. economic assistance as a callous disregard for the welfare of people in developing nations. However, opponents of financial aid for contraception counter that artificial birth control is nothing more than "genocide in the bedroom." Any public policy that regulates such an important aspect of human activity as sexual behavior and reproduction is going to be politically volatile; and a policy that deals with life and death issues embedded in the domain of religion will be especially controversial.

At first glance, the link between fertility and religion seems quite obvious. Rates of fertility vary widely from one group to another, and often these groups subscribe to different faiths and patterns of religious behavior. However, religion is usually associated with a host of other variables such as race, income, and education; and it may be these factors in addition to, or in lieu of, religion that affect fertility. For example, in most of the world, Muslims have a higher fertility rate than people who practice any other major religion, including Hinduism. But a study in India showed that after income and education were taken into account, Hindus and Muslims are almost equally as likely to practice family planning (Weeks, 1986). The strength of one religious belief may be more important than the content of the belief system as far as fertility is concerned. Weeks noted that in general, the more religious a group is, the higher its fertility is likely to be, regardless of the religious content. In the last hundred years the fertility of Catholics in the United States has been higher than that of Protestants. As of late, however, the rates of these two groups in America are approximately the same.

THE POLITICS OF FOOD

Flipping through cable television channels, one often sees the emaciated bodies of people (usually children) in some far-off land as an announcer appeals for money. Although the organization making the appeal may or may not be legitimate, the problem is very real. Although as many as 2 percent of the world's people may be starving at one time, the real problem is chronic malnutrition (Harper, 1989). At least 25 percent of the Third World population does not have a daily minimal intake of protein or calories. This is especially tragic for children, who fall victim to a variety of malnutrition-related diseases.

The reasons people do not get enough to eat are twofold. Ecologically related causes of food shortages include weather conditions, poor soil and soil erosion, and pests. These variables determine to a large extent how much food can be produced. *Political* and *economic variables,* on the other hand, are not only related to how much food is produced, but how it is distributed. The consensus among experts in the field is that the world food shortage is primarily a function of political and economic conditions. India, for example, exports food, and yet 40 percent of the population lives below a very minimal poverty line, and millions more are malnourished. Chronic unemployment and underemployment, coupled with a highly unequal distribution of wealth, means that people cannot afford to feed themselves. The same problem exists in the United States with the hungry and homeless, albeit on a much smaller scale.

Political and economic decisions made by leaders of developing countries significantly affect both the production and the distribution of food. As of 1988, twelve of the fifty-one African countries were involved in civil wars and border disputes; and the sub-Saharan countries collectively spent $1 billion on defense. One of the poorest countries in the world, Ethiopia, allocates 42 percent of its annual budget for military purposes. In an attempt to modernize as soon as possible, developing nations typically assign a disproportionate amount of revenue to urban projects and industrialization. Almost 40 percent of the gross national product of African countries comes from farming, yet governments typically put only 10 percent of their budget back into the agricultural sector (Matthews, 1989). Speaking of Africa, Thayer Scudder of Cal Tech

Famine is the result of both an inability to produce enough food and the unequal distribution of available nourishment. People without land to farm or jobs cannot afford to buy enough food, even when supplies are plentiful. In Africa, severe weather conditions and the loss of topsoil and forests have produced hundreds of thousands of "environmental refugees"— people in search of food and work in neighboring countries.

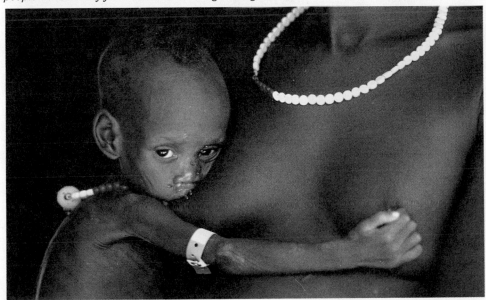

noted, "Food shortages are often the result of national policies that favor the urban, industrial sector of the economy" (Todaro and Stilkind, 1981, p. 1). Such "city bias and rural neglect" acts as a disincentive to farmers, resulting in agricultural yields that are significantly below maximum potential output. To keep peace in rapidly growing cities, Third World governments too often buy food from farmers at artificially low prices so that they can sell it in urban areas for equally low prices.

Even the much-praised and highly acclaimed Green Revolution could not end the problem of world hunger. Designed to boost production, these programs placed little if any emphasis on the distribution of food. Begun in Mexico in the 1940s and India in the 1960s, results of the Green Revolution were nothing short of spectacular. Using new hybrid seeds, faster-growing and more resistant to insects, India's wheat production tripled in a few years and rice production increased by one-third (Bryjak, 1985). However, the financial benefits of the Green Revolution were not shared equally. Because new seeds required large amounts of fertilizer and a sure supply of water (irrigation), the advantages of this procedure were confined to already-prosperous farmers. Although food production increased substantially and the well-to-do farmers became wealthier, real farm incomes have stagnated for thirty years. The impact of the Green Revolution on millions of landless peasants is best expressed by a poor Indian farm worker: "If you don't own the land, you don't get enough to eat, no matter how much it is producing" ("Hunger Myths and Facts," 1989).

The United Nations Food and Agriculture Organization estimates that with only subsistence farming methods, 64 of 117 Third World countries will be unable to feed their projected populations in the year 2000; 36 would not be self-sufficient with intermediate levels of farming (fertilizers, chemicals, improved seed); but only 19 would face food shortages with advanced farming technologies (like those used in the United States). Political and economic decisions made by world leaders in the next ten years will determine how many people welcome the new century with hope and optimism, and how many millions will face starvation, disease, and death.

FOCUS ON
MEXICO

POPULATION GROWTH IN A DEVELOPING NATION

Pregnant by Juan Carlos, a forlorn Maria learns that her lover has fathered children with another woman. At a neighborhood clinic she tells her troubles to a sympathetic doctor (in Alinsky, 1977, p. 106):

Maria: Why does Juan flaunt the children of that other woman? Why does he play with my feelings?

Doctor: Maria, that's how we are *"macho"* . . . virile males. *Macho* is not the same thing as "man." For a Mexican male the more women he has sexually, the more *macho* he feels when these women have children.

Maria: But why? Is Juan Carlos emotionally sick?

Doctor: Not just as an individual. It's society that is sick, with values that corrode men's souls. This spiritual sickness can't be seen when a man looks in a mirror.

Maria: How do Mexican men get this spiritual sickness?

Doctor: By treating a woman as an object and by fathering many children, because deep inside themselves men feel insecure . . . .

Beginning in 1973 this scene was viewed and heard by millions of Mexican women. It was part of a sixty-episode series designed and sponsored by the government in the hope of reducing the birth rate. Alarmed by a rapidly growing population, Mexican officials decided to attack the deeply ingrained values of *machismo.*

Mexico's population explosion is a recent phenomenon, however. Indians first migrated to central Mexico more than 10,000 years ago, and by 1500 B.C. numerous population centers had developed (Kaleidoscope, 1988). When Cortes arrived in 1518 the population was in the millions, with some estimates as high as twenty-five million (Ross, 1982). By the end of the sixteenth century the indigenous population had been reduced to approximately one million. Cortes' small army of conquistadors killed thousands, and tens of thousands more fell victim to diseases brought to the new world by the white man (small pox, influenza, measles). During the nineteenth century the population grew steadily, and on the eve of the revolution in 1910, there were 15.2 million Mexicans. The violence of the revolution claimed almost a million lives, and an influenza epidemic killed thousands more. From 1940 to 1964 the population grew from twenty million to forty million; and in the next twenty-three years it doubled again, reaching approximately eighty-five million in 1990, making Mexico the eleventh most populous country in the world.

There are three reasons for this tremendous growth (Alba and Potter, 1986). The first was the need to populate the northern regions as well as make up for the losses suffered during the revolution. Second was the unexpected jump in population as a result of declining mortality. The final reason was a function of Mexico's economic success: an expanding economy in a period of optimism made it possible for the country to cope with a burgeoning population. The second and third reasons are closely related. Economic growth and political stability coupled with modern medicine and better living conditions contributed to a sharp decrease in the mortality rate. For example, between the 1930s and 1990 the infant mortality rate was reduced from 135 to 50 per 1,000 live births.

Until the mid-1960s both the government and the church agreed that population growth was acceptable and desirable (Ross, 1982). By 1970, however, the government began to realize the magnitude and complexity of problems that lay ahead if population growth was not controlled. Therefore, in 1973 the Ministry of Health and Welfare and the Mexican Institute of Social Security began a nationwide program of family planning. The government launched a campaign (television, radio, posters, T-shirts, popular music) with the goal of persuading young Mexicans to postpone sexual activity. Although the Catholic Church was not enthusiastic about family planning, it did not challenge the government's programs in any significant way (Vasquez, 1984).

To date these programs have had a significant impact. From 1975–1976 to 1981, the crude birth rate (number of live births per 1,000) dropped from 41 to 33. The number of women practicing birth control rose from 1.8 million in 1976 to 7 million in 1989, representing 53 percent of "women in union" (Miller, 1989; Gill, 1990). By 1982 the goal of a 2.5 percent annual growth rate had been achieved, although the long-term goal of 1 percent growth by the year 2000 seems doubtful. Abortion (as controversial in Mexico as it is in the United States) is another effective mechanism of birth control. According to Miller (1989), one family specialist estimated that a million illegal abortions are performed annually, resulting in the deaths of 50,000 women. The federal government claims the number is only 250,000. In December 1990 the southern state of Chiapas legalized abortions for family planning as well as for life-threatening conditions during the first three months of pregnancy. Abortion opponents including the *pro-vida* (pro-life) group called for an immediate repeal of the law (Cleeland, 1990). Whether or not legislation permitting abortion is limited to or overturned in Chiapas, or spreads to other states, remains to be seen. One thing is certain, however. The Chiapas situation will only intensify an already furious clash between pro- and anti-abortion factions. Those in favor of legalizing abortion know that the Catholic Church and cult of *machismo* are formidable, although apparently not unbeatable, opponents.

Characteristic of developing nations, the young population (42 percent under fifteen years of age) has stretched the capacity of the country's institutions to the breaking point. With a labor force projected to double in the next twenty years, the Mexican economy would have to create one million jobs annually for the coming two decades to provide work for all its citizens (Fornos, 1987). Currently 100,000 to 200,000 jobs are created each year in a society with a 28 percent unemployment rate and 20 percent underemployment (Alinsky, 1983). This employment shortage functions as a powerful push factor sending young Mexicans to the United States in search of jobs. Those who work in the United States (legally and illegally) send back some $6 billion annually to their families, a figure that represents a substantial amount of the nation's gross annual earnings.

Because they are willing to work for low wages at jobs most Americans will not even consider, Mexican migrants usually find employment. According to one estimate, 3 to 6 percent of the entire U.S. labor force is made up of illegal aliens from Mexico. With so many people coming of working age each year, the search for employment will intensify; and with a population doubling time of twenty-nine years, the migration of young Mexicans to *El Norte* has just begun.

DISCUSSION QUESTIONS

1. Why did Mexico's population grow so rapidly beginning in 1940?
2. What role has the Catholic Church played in Mexico's population growth?
3. What push factors are responsible for the migration of young Mexicans to *El Norte?*
4. Make a list of programs or strategies the Mexican government could implement to reach its goal of 1 percent population growth by the year 2000.

5. What factors besides the value of *machismo* contribute to Mexico's high fertility rate?
6. What is the relationship between religion and fertility in countries like India, Iran, Nigeria, and Israel? Go to the library and gather information concerning the impact (if any) of Islam, Hinduism, and Judaism on rates of fertility on these or other nations.

FOCUS ON
JAPAN

GROWING SLOW, GROWING OLD

In 400 B.C. Japan was populated by approximately 30,000 hunters and fishermen. Fostered by the introduction of wet rice cultivation at the beginning of the modern era (A.D. 1), the emergence of the formal state in A.D. 650 started a 1,000-year period of slow, steady growth, bringing the population to thirty million in 1700 (McEvedy and Jones, 1985). From 1853, and the opening of Japan by Commodore Perry, to 1950, the nation's population increased from 32 million to 84 million. Most of this growth occurred in the final thirty years (1920–1950) as Japan was transformed from a developing to a developed nation (Muramatsu, 1982).

Japan became the first (and to date only) Asian country to complete the demographic transition. At the end of World War II the Japanese realized that if their severely diminished standard of living was not to decrease even further, the birth rate would have to be reduced. In 1948 the Eugenic Protection Law was passed containing the following provisions (Muramatsu, 1982): (1) the government would train and deploy family planning workers; (2) induced abortion was legal for certain health reasons (the next year economic reasons were included); and (3) sterilization was permissible for health reasons.

The abortion provision ended the brief (1947–1949) baby boom, and by 1950 the number of abortions exceeded live births (Warshaw, 1988b). By 1960, however, contraception was the preferred method of birth control, and the proportion of abortions in Japan declined. From 1973 to 1989 the crude birth rate (number of live births per 1,000 people) declined from 9.4 to 1.1, one of the lowest in the world. Population projections to the year 2000 estimate an annual increase of approximately 620,000 people; and, even with this low rate of growth, Japan has significant population-related problems.

Approximately the size of California (142,811 square miles), Japan has over four times as many people. Because of its rugged, mountainous terrain, the entire population is squeezed onto 16 percent of the land. Agricultural production is near maximum yield per acre, and the country currently imports 15 percent of its food requirements (Warshaw, 1988b).

One of Japan's most serious problems is the changing composition of its population. A low fertility rate coupled with increased longevity is rapidly transforming Japan into a low-growth, aged society. As of 1989 women of childbearing age had on average 1.57 children, the lowest fertility rate in the world. The government is quite concerned about the low rate of population growth, and in one rural prefecture officials are running a television spot showing a little boy playing with a puppy. The caption in the ad reads, "For the child's sake, one more" (Impoco, 1990).

Whereas the birth rate has dropped sharply in Japan, the number of people reaching old age is increasing. In 1980, 9 percent of the population was age sixty-five and over, in 1989 that figure was 11 percent, and in 2010 it is projected to be 18 percent. This leaves a smaller percentage of people in the productive ages (sixteen to sixty-four) to take care of the needs of senior citizens. In 1987 there were seven persons working for every retiree; in 2025 that ratio will be cut to three to one (Jones, 1988). The relatively small number of people fifteen years old and under means that Japan faces the prospect of a tremendous labor shortage. A Japanese research institute estimates that the country's workforce could be reduced by 10 million in the next thirty years, and by as many as 50 million over the coming century (Impoco, 1990).

Japan, therefore, finds itself in a demographic dilemma. If the birth rate goes up, additional food will have to be imported; urban areas will become increasingly populated, polluted, and congested; and the quality of life will diminish. Even though Japan has a slow rate of growth (doubling time of 141 years) this projects to a population of 246 million in the twenty-second

Japan's high rate of employment and economic prosperity has come at a steep price for millions of people in densely populated cities. These workers are lined up for one portion of a round-trip journey to the central business district that can take up to four hours. Subway employees literally push individuals into subway cars, helping pack as many people as possible on each train.

century—all living in an area the size of West Virginia. On the other hand, if population growth remains low, the elderly will consume a greater proportion of the gross domestic product and economic growth will be slowed. The International Monetary Fund estimates that government pension and medical care spending will jump from 9 percent of the gross national product in 1980 to 21.5 percent in 2025.

Regardless of their financial position, senior citizens in Japan will have trouble finding a place to live. Smith (1987) noted that, by tradition, elderly people live with the oldest son. In reality this means that while the son is off working, the daughter-in-law bears the responsibility of taking care of her aged in-laws. As of late, however, women have been less inclined to take on this traditional duty, especially since more of them are employed outside the home. One solution to this problem is the construction and staffing of thousands of nursing homes throughout the country (Smith, 1987). This would be an additional expense for a government that will already be spending a significant amount of its budget for elderly health care and social services.

Japan will also have to find a way to meet its labor needs. With an unemployment rate of only 2.2 percent in 1989, an average of 132 jobs were available for every 100 workers seeking work. To make matters worse, young Japanese refuse to work at jobs they associate with the nation's minority and Korean and *barakumin* population. As a result of these factors, the shortage of individuals in the low and semiskilled labor market is severe. For example, so few people are willing to work as waiters and waitresses that restaurants often have to close early because of a lack of help. This already acute labor deficit is only going to become worse. Between 1995 and 2005 the number of people age fifteen to sixty-four (the peak productive years) will be drastically reduced. In an effort to alleviate this condition Japan admitted approximately three million immigrants (mostly from the Philippines, Pakistan, Malaysia, and South Korea) in 1988 and 1989. In such a homogeneous and race-conscious country this has created problems. Extreme right-wing political groups argue that this influx of unskilled workers will destroy Japan's identity as well as contribute to a host of social problems such as urban slums and crime.

The aging of Japan combined with the growing labor shortage illustrates how the composition of a population can affect a society's major institutions. A nation's demographic profile does not determine its destiny; but the size, age, and distribution of the population delimit what is reasonably possible. Japan's remarkable economic success since World War II will be increasingly affected by demographic variables.

DISCUSSION QUESTIONS

1. What is the major population problem in Japan today?
2. Japan finds itself on the horns of a demographic dilemma. Explain.
3. What steps has the government taken to solve the nation's population problem? What else could be done?
4. Which nation has the more serious population problem, Japan or Mexico? Explain.
5. Will other nations eventually have the same population problem as Japan? Identify some of these countries. Is underpopulation an inevitable consequence of modernization? Explain.

CHAPTER SUMMARY

1. Demographers in the field of sociology are interested in (1) fundamental population processes such as fertility, mortality, and migration; (2) the size and spatial distribution of a population; and (3) the structure and characteristics of a population.

2. The number of children a woman will give birth to is a function of three sets of intermediate variables. Intercourse variables refer to the commencement of and frequency of sexual activity over a period of time. Conception variables concern the use of items and strategies that may inhibit conception, such as birth control devices and breast-feeding. Pregnancy or gestation variables (miscarriage, stillbirth, induced abortion) determine if a fetus will come to term and be born.

3. There are three major reasons that people die in any society: (1) they degenerate, (2) they are killed by communicable diseases, and (3) they are killed by products of the social and economic environment.

4. In Third World nations the crude death rate (CDR) is both lower and higher than the CDR in developed nations. Low CDRs in the developing world are a result of two factors. These nations have very young populations, with as many as 50 percent of their citizens under fifteen years of age; young people die at a much lower rate than older individuals. For a variety of political, economic, and social reasons some nations continue to have a high death rate.

5. Although death may appear to be a random phenomenon, mortality rates differ significantly from one segment of a population to another. In the United States mortality rates are related to variables such as occupation, gender, race, and marital status.

6. The Bureau of the Census has three categories of illegal immigrants to the United States: (1) *settlers* arrive on a more or less permanent basis, (2) *sojourners* do seasonal work and then return to their country of origin, and (3) *commuters* cross the border on a daily basis. Some people argue illegal aliens help the U.S. economy by taking the lowest-paid jobs no one else will do. Others believe illegals take jobs from U.S. citizens as well as depress the wage scale in this country.

7. Population pyramids of nations like Mexico are true pyramids and reflect a young population with high rates of growth. Population pyramids of Japan and the United States are indicative of slow growth, aging populations.

8. Thomas Malthus reasoned that it was only a matter of time before population growth (geometric increase), outstripped the earth's food supply (arithmetic increase). *Positive checks* such as war, disease, and vice would eventually halt the rate of growth. *Preventive checks* of delayed marriage and celibacy would reduce population growth without the tremendous suffering that accompanies the positive checks.

9. According to the theory of the demographic transition, every country will eventually pass through three demographic stages: (1) *high potential growth* characterized by high birth rates and high death rates; (2) *transitional growth* of high birth rates and declining birth rates (currently most less developed nations are stuck in this phase), and (3) *incipient decline* with low birth and death rates. Developed countries are in this final stage of the transition.

10. Some modern nations are facing a population decrease as they move toward the end of the century. A problem of underpopulation comes about when people are having fewer than the 2.1 children per couple necessary to maintain a stable population over time.

11. Rapidly growing Third World nations face serious economic, social, political, and environmental problems due to population pressures. If these pressures are not reduced (at least in part) these societies will have little chance to become economically successful, politically stable, modern nations.

12. Population-related problems exist throughout the Third World, but they are at their most dangerous level in Africa. With 661 million people and a crude birth rate of thirty-one per 1,000, Africa has a population doubling time of twenty-four years. Many of the economies on this continent are in shambles, and environmental and political problems are making the situation in these countries even worse. Some African nations also have to deal with the nightmare of AIDS, which has the potential to decimate entire societies.

13. Attempts to limit fertility in Third World nations have met with some success. These strategies range from China's policy of one child per family to forced sterilization. Government sponsored contraceptive programs and new birth control devices like Norplant and Capronor may prove effective in lowering fertility in poor nations.

14. The world's food shortage is related to the following factors: (1) *ecological*-related causes of food shortage include bad weather conditions, poor soil, soil erosion, and pests; and (2) *political and economic variables* determine how food is distributed.

11

URBANIZATION

I t was the best of times it was the worst of times, it was the age of wisdom, it was the age of foolishness . . ." So begins Charles Dickens' classic novel *A Tale of Two Cities*. Dickens was referring to the political and social climates of London and Paris in the years just prior to the French Revolution of 1789, but his words aptly describe current conditions in hundreds of cities throughout the world. Cities represent mankind's most notable and grandiose achievements, showcasing our greatest accomplishments and ingenuity in architecture, construction, and the arts. As centers of political, military, and economic power, they have played a major role in the rise and fall of civilizations since ancient times.

Cities are also testaments to centuries of human failure and folly. Currently the world's great urban centers are breeding grounds for a long and growing list of social and environmental problems. Nowhere is the unequal distribution of wealth and life chances more evident than in the cities. The urban landscape is a visible barometer of a nation's prosperity as well as its social conscience. The ratio of fashionable town-houses to street people living in cardboard boxes reveals more about a nation's commitment to social and economic justice than the rhetoric of countless politicians and the lofty pronouncements of elegantly worded political treatises.

Herein lies the crux of the love-hate relationship that so many people have with cities. Individuals are attracted and excited by the diversity of activities to be encountered in urban areas and at the same time repelled by things like violent crime, traffic jams, and air pollution. Problems in urban America express large patterns of gender and racial inequality, poverty, and political dominance and corruption that we addressed in earlier chapters. Inasmuch as we are an urban nation, the manner in which we choose to address or ignore these problems will in large measure determine the future quality of life of 200 million Americans.

Because of extremely high rates of population growth, cities in the developing world face even greater challenges than those in wealthy, industrial nations. To make matters worse, Third World countries do not have the economic resources necessary to solve the tremendous problems associated with burgeoning urban populations. The outlook for these cities is ominous at best; at worst, a series of disasters of monumental proportions could be anticipated in the near future.

In this chapter we trace the birth and development of cities from ancient times, through the Industrial Revolution (especially in the United States), to the giant urban centers that exist in both rich and poor nations. Because urbanization is highly correlated with industrialization and modernization, we will examine the process by which developing nations are struggling to transform their economic, political, and social institutions in order to survive and, one day, prosper in a highly productive, technologically sophisticated world.

QUESTIONS TO CONSIDER

1. When and under what circumstances did human beings first live in permanent settlements?
2. What is the relationship between urbanization and industrialization?
3. What are the major theories of the human ecology school?
4. When and why did suburbanization begin in the United States?
5. Do people who live in cities lead more stressful lives than those who reside in rural areas?
6. What accounted for the rapid growth of sunbelt cities?
7. Why have the populations of so many winter cities declined over the past twenty-five years?
8. What are the major problems facing cities in the United States?
9. Who are "the truly disadvantaged" inhabitants of the city?
10. Why are so many people leaving American cities and moving to rural areas and semirural towns?
11. Why are Third World cities growing at an unprecedented rate?
12. What are the major problems facing cities in developing nations?
13. What can be done to solve the myriad social, economic, and environmental problems confronting cities throughout the world?

EARLY CITIES

For three million years our ancestors survived by gathering eatable vegetation and hunting wildlife. With the emergence of modern humans (*Homo sapiens*) some 50,000 years ago, this pattern of wandering and living off of the land continued. However, sometime about 8000 B.C. the first permanent settlements began to appear. Cohen (1978) speculated that successful hunters and gatherers began to deplete the heretofore inexhaustible supply of food. Contemporary biologists and geographers would say these wandering tribes had surpassed the land's "carrying capacity," that is, the number of individuals a particular geographic area can support at a given time. The food shortage was solved by domesticating animals and turning to agricultural production (Spates and Macionis, 1987). As these permanent farming settlements grew in size and number, they slowly evolved into villages, and by 4000 B.C. they became cities.

There are three principal theories on how these early cities actually emerged (Parker, 1982). The first and most popular is the **agricultural surplus theory**. According to this perspective, cities came into being as a result of a surplus of basic foodstuffs. Agricultural surplus freed some people from having to produce their own food and permitted them to develop new occupations. This clustering of emerging economic, political, and religious roles formed the basis of city life. This interpretation is in accord with **central place theory**. Cities emerged because farmers needed a central market to exchange and distribute their produce. Jane Jacobs (in Parker, 1982) advanced a **trading theory** of city growth that rejects the notion that a surplus is necessary to produce occupational specialties. Jacobs reversed the logic and suggested that specialists were responsible for producing the food surplus vital for the growth of cities. Traders introduced new seeds and livestock, resulting in improved crops that launched a successful agricultural revolution.

The importance of cities in the evolution of human societies cannot be overstated. Spates and Macionis (1987) noted that as cities began to grow, the fundamental structure of societies was dramatically transformed. Regardless of which of the three theories is correct, as cities developed the division of labor became more complex. Specialists in war, religion, politics, trade, art, and an assortment of crafts emerged, greatly increasing the types and forms of human interactions. Existence no longer revolved around hunting and gathering, and specialization led to a hierarchical power structure. Because not all jobs are equally important to the group, and not all people have the same ability, individuals began to accumulate vastly different amounts of wealth, prestige, and power. Cities are thus inextricably linked to the stratification of society. It is within their confines that people first began to interact with each other as less than equals in any systematic, prolonged manner.

PREINDUSTRIAL CITIES

By the beginning of the modern era and the birth of Christ, cities were common in the Near East, India, China, and the Americas. Most had populations of about 10,000, with some as large as a quarter-million people (Spates and Macionis, 1987). Many were located in strategic areas such as trade routes and important waterways. They were inhabited by priests, government officials, craftsmen, merchants, laborers, and, sometimes, slaves, and supported by agriculturalists who lived outside the urban area. They were not only trade centers but places of refuge and shelter, their high walls protecting the inhabitants from wandering nomads and attacking barbarians.

As societies grew and empires flourished, so did their cities; and none was grander than Rome. By the second century A.D. the capital of the Holy Roman Empire had a metropolitan population of approximately one million. Rome was an engineering marvel, with over 50,000 miles of well-constructed roads, and an aqueduct system that provided the city with fresh water for homes, public baths, fountains, and hydrants along its main streets (Spates and Macionis, 1987). Forerunners of modern apartment buildings, called *insulae,* were six to ten stories high. As the center of an empire built on military conquest, Rome was more heterogeneous than most ancient cities. Its marvels that still attract countless tourists today are indicative of the tremendous disparity of wealth and power that existed. Monuments, roads, and spillways were built by the poor and vanquished for the well-being of the rich.

When the Roman Empire fell in A.D. 476 the organization, stability, and commerce that sustained Rome and other European cities collapsed as well. The threat of barbarian invasions increased, and once prosperous cities rapidly dwindled in size, some disappearing completely (Spates and Macionis, 1987). People were more concerned with survival than prosperity as Europe entered a 600-year period of stagnation commonly referred to as the Dark Ages. The Norman conquest (1066) brought a degree of political stability to the region as a number of capitalist enclaves emerged in feudal Europe between 1150 and 1450 (Light, 1983). By 1600 the feudal order was in decline, and capitalism was beginning to flourish in Europe. In the midst of this renaissance, cities prospered and bustled with activity. Sociologist Ivan Light (1983) commented on the importance of cities and interplay of forces that culminated in the "industrial urbanization" of Europe: "Without medieval towns, there would have been no capitalist societies; without capitalist societies, no Scientific Revolution; without science, no industrial technology; without capitalism, science, and technology, no Industrial Revolution; without Industrial Revolution, no industrial urbanization of Europe" (p. 65).

CITIES IN THE MODERN WORLD

From ancient times until the beginning of the Industrial Revolution cities remained essentially the same. Peasants provided the agricultural surplus, which made specialization and a more complex division of labor possible, and the entire community was integrated into an urban social system characteristic of Emile Durkheim's "mechanical solidarity" (see chapter 1) (Berger, 1978). However, the Industrial Revolution significantly changed the size, structure, and composition of European and American cities. On the eve of this revolution in 1800, England had 106 towns with 5,000 or more inhabitants. By 1891 this figure had increased to 622 with nearly twenty million people (Hosken, 1985). With a concentration of workers and potential workers (nearby agriculturalists), as well as being situated on trade routes and waterways, these towns were the perfect places to build factories. Labor shortages were quickly alleviated by the influx of peasants who left their farms in the hope of finding a better life in the city. Unfortunately, most simply traded rural for urban poverty. Jammed into hastily built, overcrowded apartments, they lived in squalor and despair. Sanitary conditions were abysmal, and untold thousands died during typhoid, cholera, and dysentery epidemics (Hosken, 1985).

As noted earlier, urban life significantly changed the way people related to one another. Traditional patterns of interaction with family, friends, and organizations such as the church were altered. Informal mechanisms of social control effective in keeping people from engaging in deviant behavior were disrupted and, for some, permanently severed. As a result, many of the social problems now associated with cities (especially crime) began to rise dramatically. In the United States these problems were exacerbated by the arrival of large numbers of immigrants from Poland, Germany, Italy, and Ireland beginning in the middle of the nineteenth century. The values and behavior of these people clashed (often literally), as they were crowded together in one area of the city: the slum. Big cities also brought big government. Political corruption and incompetence were rampant. In many cases public officials were part of a long list of problems rather than their solutions. Zastrow and Bowker (1984) noted that although "machine politics" and corruption were not invented in the middle of the nineteenth century, the latter was "brought to a higher level of development" (p. 420).

In spite of increasing social problems and the wretchedness of urban life for the masses, many people prospered as cities in the United States, Europe, and other parts of the world grew rapidly. Between 1800 and 1970 the world's urban population

Toronto is considered one of the most livable cities in North America. Although the quality of life in this Canadian metropolis is high, residents still must cope with typical urban problems such as crime, traffic congestion, and pollution.

increased 4,570 percent, twelve times faster than its population increased (Light, 1983). This was a period of rapid **urbanization**—growth in the proportion of people living in urban areas. Societies differ as to the *number* of people and the *proportion* of citizens residing in urban areas. For example, approximately 26 percent, or 222 million, of India's 853 million people reside in cities. In the United States the figures are roughly 74 percent, or 185 million of the country's 250 million people. Even though both nations have approximately the same number of people living in cities, the United States with a higher proportion (74 percent compared to 26 percent) is a much more urban society.

Over the past one hundred years the world has become increasingly urban. In 1900 an estimated 10 percent of the population lived in cities. That figure reached 41 percent in 1989. By the year 2010 the figure could be as high as 50 percent. As you may have guessed, the proportion of people living in cities in developed nations (73 percent) is greater than that in less developed nations (32 percent). However, cities in developed countries have been growing relatively slowly at 0.8 percent per year, a rate that is expected to decline by the end of the century. On the other hand, cities in developing nations have been growing at an incredible rate of 3.6 percent per annum, which represents a doubling time of less than twenty years.

HUMAN ECOLOGY AND THE CITY

In their 1921 book, *An Introduction to the Science of Sociology,* Robert Park and E. W. Burgess first used the term human ecology. Broadly speaking, ecology is the study of the relationship between organisms (plant, animal, and human) and their environment. Following Darwin, ecologists focus on the manner in which organisms relate to each other as they struggle to survive. Recognizing the "fundamental unity of animal nature," **human ecology** concentrates on the "form and development of the community in human populations" (Hawley, 1950, p. 8).

Human beings have much in common with other living creatures, but are capable of behavior that other life forms are not. For example, unlike any other animal, we have the ability to construct and modify our physical and social environment. Once altered, the environment may result in new ideas, values, and patterns of behavior. Just as we change the environment, our behavior is altered as we respond to these changes. To test their theories and observe the relation between humans and the world they constructed, ecologists used the city as a vast, natural laboratory. They posed (and attempted to answer) two fundamental questions: (1) do cities tend to develop a common, general physical form? and (2) what accounts for this form? (Shannon, 1989).

The Concentric Zone Model

One of the first and most important contributions of human ecology was the **concentric zone model** (see Figure 11.1). This model views the city as a series of zones emanating from the center, with each one characterized by a different group of people (or institutions) and activity. It assumes that cities have one center, and have a heterogeneous population (Berger, 1978) competing for livable space as well as jobs. According to Burgess's (1925) version of the concentric zone model, the city has five distinct zones.

FIGURE 11.1   The Nature of Cities

**Three Generalizations of the
Internal Structure of Cities**

Districts

1. Central business district
2. Wholesale light manufacturing
3. Low-class residential
4. Medium-class residential
5. High-class residential
6. Heavy manufacturing
7. Outlying business district
8. Residential suburb
9. Industrial suburb
10. Commuters' zone

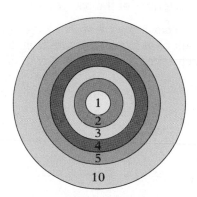

Concentric Zone Theory

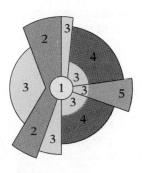

Sector Theory

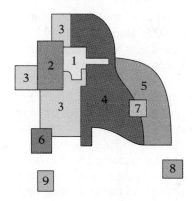

Multiple Nuclei

For Harris and Ullman (1945), the concentric zone model is a generalization for all cities. The arrangement of the sectors in the sector model varies from city to city. The diagram for multiple nuclei represents one possible pattern among innumerable variations.

Source: Reprinted from "The Nature of Cities" by Chauncy D. Harris and Edward L. Ullman, 1945, in volume no. 242 of *The Annals* of The American Academy of Political and Social Sciences.

Zone 1   The central business district consists of stores, offices, light industry, and commercial establishments.

Zone 2   The zone of transition has some business and commerce as a result of growth and expansion in zone 1. It is also home to unskilled laborers (often first-generation immigrants) who live in poorly maintained tenements.

Zone 3   The zone of workingmen is made up of simple one- and two-family dwellings of semiskilled workers (often second-generation immigrants) who have managed to escape from zone 2. This is the area of ethnic enclaves, Deutschland and Little Italy, for example.

Zones 4 and 5 The apartment house and commuter zones are inhabited by middle- and upper-middle-class people, the city's more successful and permanent residents. These neighborhoods are relatively free of the crime and deviance characteristic of the poorer areas of the city.

Ecologists were studying the city when rates of population growth (primarily as a result of in-migration) were high. Steady growth pushed city limits outward as zone 1 encroached on zone 2, which in turn moved into zone 3, and so forth. This dynamic process of expansion was caused by a phenomenon called invasion and succession. Newly arrived immigrants would settle in the zone of transition (invasion) and take the place (succession) of those more upwardly mobile residents who were moving to the next zone. Over the years the concentric zone model has been criticized for being simplistic, overgeneralized, and inaccurate (zones do not really exist). Nevertheless it has maintained its popularity and importance, and appears in virtually all urban geography texts (Larkin and Peters, 1983).

The Sector Model

As a result of studying the composition and configuration of 142 cities in 1900, 1915, and 1936, Homer Hoyt (1939) rejected the notion that cities were arranged in concentric zones and advanced his own spatial interpretation of urban America known as the **sector model** (see Figure 11.1). Rather than a bull's-eye layout, Hoyt argued that urban zones were pie- or wedge-shaped sectors radiating outward from the **central business district** or CBD (the major shopping and commercial area of a city). More exclusive neighborhoods were usually found along transportation lines or high ground near lakes and rivers, forming a sector that ran from the center city to the suburbs. Similarly, industries developed in sectors with rivers and railroads passing through the CBD. The sector model has the advantage of taking into account the existence of hills, mountain ridges, and rivers that exist in many cities, as well as the significance of shipping and transportation lines.

Although it was an important step in the development of urban ecology, the sector model is not without shortcomings. Larkin and Peters (1983) maintained that it places too much emphasis on the role of the upper classes in determining spatial organization and neglects the part played by other socioeconomic groups in understanding the distribution of space.

The Multiple Nuclei Model

Rejecting the notion of a single CBD in any given city, Harris and Ullman introduced the **multiple nuclei model** of urban spatial organization in 1945 (see Figure 11.1). They described cities as having "several discrete nuclei," in some cases existing from the start of the city (London), and in others increasing as the city grew and diversified (Chicago). Nuclei may develop around a number of activities, including manufacturing, retailing, wholesaling, and education. The type and number of these nuclei differ for two reasons: certain areas of the city are more suitable for some activities than others because of terrain and transportation, and, as in Los Angeles and Chicago, multiple nuclei are a function of growth; they simply incorporate a host of smaller cities. The major criticism of the multiple nuclei model is that most cities really have only one center, and the other nuclei are merely subcenters (Parker, 1982).

FROM JAMESTOWN TO MANHATTAN AND BACK

With the settlement of Jamestown, Virginia, by the British in 1607, the initial step leading to the eventual urbanization of America was taken. By the end of the seventeenth century, New York, Boston, and Philadelphia were relatively small, although prosperous, colonial cities. Located on rivers and sea coasts, many of these early cities were centers for the export of raw materials to Europe (Spates and Macionis, 1987). Until the early 1800s, most were free of congested areas and serious social problems, although in the coming years slums emerged in New York and Boston (Butler, 1976). Even though the number of Americans living in urban areas was increasing, not everybody viewed cities in a positive light. Some were of the opinion that cities were a potential threat to political stability. Thomas Jefferson believed that they were "ulcers on the body politic," places where "mobs" could undermine good government (Jones and Van Zandt, 1974, p. 112).

Cities played an important role in the country's westward expansion. Completed in 1825, the Erie Canal, running from New York City to Buffalo, opened the Great Lakes and much of Canada for trade. Between 1820 and the start of the Civil War in 1860, the U.S. population doubled, and city growth increased 500 percent. A significant portion of this increase can be attributed to European immigrants, who made up 19 percent of the northeastern population. The Civil War era was a landmark period in the evolution of American cities. Prior to the war, most cities were commercial centers; however, with the completion of hostilities and shift toward manufacturing, America was catapulted into the Industrial Age. The economic and social transformation of the United States, especially urban America, was under way. Between 1860 and 1910 the nation's population increased from thirty-one million to ninety-two million, with the urban population rising from six million to almost forty-five million.

Suburbanization

The industrial cities of the late nineteenth and early twentieth centuries were concentrations of large numbers of people in small places. In the 1920s, however, a process of decentralization began. During the ten-year period ending in 1930, suburban population growth outstripped that of the central cities for the first time in U.S. history. This initial period of suburbanization was a direct result of the prosperity and technological advancements of the Roaring Twenties. Automobile ownership during these ten years jumped from nine million to twenty-six million, and access to outlying areas coupled with affordable tract homes made this early exodus possible.

With the Great Depression in the 1930s, the good times and the spurt in suburban growth came to a halt. When World War II ended and the U.S. economy was converted from a wartime to peacetime posture, the suburbanization of the country resumed, and at an accelerated pace. Figures from the U.S. Bureau of the Census show that by 1986, 33 percent of Americans lived in central cities and 44 percent resided in suburbs. Figure 11.2 illustrates how suburbanization transformed America's largest urban areas. By the 1970s many cities resembled the multiple nuclei model.

In an effort to avoid city taxes and social problems, sidestep centrally located unions, and find pools of skilled labor, a growing number of businesses and industries joined the flight to the suburbs (Shannon, 1989). The construction of large areas of

FIGURE 11.2   The Changing Composition of U.S. Cities

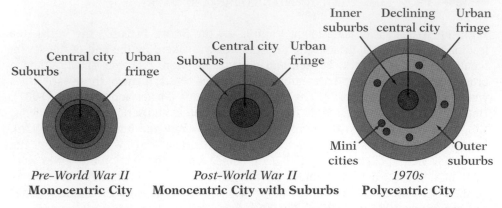

Central city   Urban
Suburbs   fringe

Pre–World War II
Monocentric City

Central city   Urban
Suburbs   fringe

Post–World War II
Monocentric City with Suburbs

Inner   Declining   Urban
suburbs   central city   fringe

Mini   Outer
cities   suburbs

1970s
Polycentric City

Prior to World War I the American metropolis was dominated by a monocentric (one center) city. At the end of World War II spatial configurations changed rapidly as people and some industries moved to the suburbs. By the 1970s, urban areas were increasingly characterized by a declining core and a double layer of suburbs, as well as being surrounded by a number of mini- or satellite cities.

Source: From Peter O. Muller, *Contemporary Suburban America,* copyright © 1981, p. 7. Reprinted by permission of Prentice-Hall, Englewood Cliffs, New Jersey.

relatively low-cost housing made available through federally insured loans opened the suburbs to working-class families—that is, white working-class families. Discrimination and a lack of buying power kept blacks out of those areas in any substantial number until the 1970s. However, during this decade the number of blacks in suburban America grew faster than the number in central cities (Shepard, 1987). More recently, Chinese, Filipino, and Japanese Americans have experienced barriers in their effort to find employment and housing in the suburbs (Chow, in Muller, 1981).

The suburbanization of America since 1945 is a good example of the process of invasion and succession as outlined in the concentric zone model. Figure 11.3 shows that in the 1950s and 1960s the elderly, poor, and minority groups were left behind, and out-migrants (working- and middle-class individuals) were replaced by poor blacks and whites from the South. During the 1970s and 1980s central cities in some parts of the country, especially the Southwest and some mountain states, became home to an increasing number of illegal immigrants from Mexico and Central America. By the 1970s, this massive flow of people in and out of the cities resulted in the economic stagnation of the nation's older metropolitan areas in the northeastern and north central states, and split many metropolitan areas in two: one part affluent and predominantly white (suburbs), the other extremely poor and disproportionately made up of minority groups (urban) (Figure 11.4).

Gentrification and Exurbanization

Although not as significant as those previously mentioned, other population movements are beginning to affect the composition of the nation's metropolitan areas. The first is **gentrification**—the return of middle- and upper-class people to deteriorated central city neighborhoods. These young, white, married but often childless, well-educated professionals (yuppies) buy run-down apartments and homes and convert them into expensive, fashionable dwellings. On the positive side, these "gilded ghettos, affluent islands in a sea of poverty" (Larkin and Peters, 1983, p. 104) raise the urban tax base and help preserve buildings that would otherwise be vandalized or torn down. Unfortunately, the demand for goods and services by these new, well-to-do residents often comes at the expense of the poor, who are displaced by upscale specialty shops and boutiques. As a result, parts of many inner cities are being taken over by the "croissant culture" (Butler, 1976). Speaking of gentrification, Spates and Macionis (1987) declared that "virtually every major city in the country has seen this process begin and quickly spread" (p. 379).

With some affluent suburbanites moving to central cities, others searched for a more rustic environment. This "suburbanization of the suburban elite" is called **exurbanization** (Weeks, 1986, p. 338). The "exurbs" want and can afford to have it all.

FIGURE 11.3 Net Population Movements in Northern Metropolitan Areas During the 1950s and 1960s

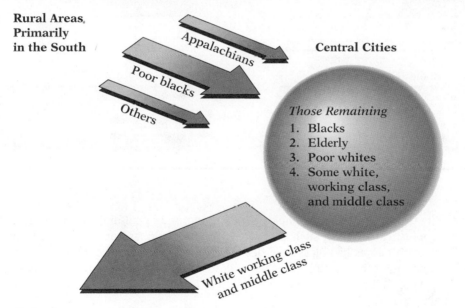

The age, race, and ethnic composition of northern cities was significantly changed in the 1950s and 1960s by the process of invasion and succession. Poor blacks and whites migrated to the cities, and more affluent whites moved to the suburbs. The poor, elderly, and people of various minority groups were left behind to struggle with the numerous social problems afflicting urban America.

Note: Width of arrows indicates relative size of the population movements.

Source: From Thomas R. Shannon, *Urban Problems in Sociological Perspective,* p. 33 (Copyright © 1983), reissued 1989 by Waveland Press, Inc., Prospect Heights, Illinois. Reprinted with permission of the publisher.

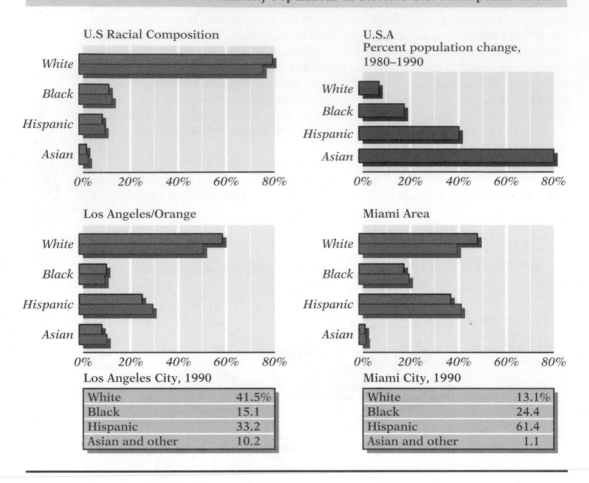

FIGURE 11.4 Concentration of Minority Populations in Selected U.S. Metropolitan Areas

U.S Racial Composition

U.S.A
Percent population change, 1980–1990

Los Angeles/Orange

Miami Area

Los Angeles City, 1990

White	41.5%
Black	15.1
Hispanic	33.2
Asian and other	10.2

Miami City, 1990

White	13.1%
Black	24.4
Hispanic	61.4
Asian and other	1.1

The city provides them with employment and serves as a cultural shopping center for their sophisticated tastes, such as theaters, the arts, and fashionable shops. Living in villages with names like Blossom Valley and East Aurora takes them back to a romanticized notion of the simpler times and a lifestyle free of big-city problems. The exurbs are trying to find a new, peaceful Jamestown in the midst of a high-technology, rapidly changing society.

SUNBELT CITIES

In a 1969 book analyzing national political trends, Kevin Phillips coined the term "sunbelt." Although not in vogue until the mid-1970s, this loosely defined word has come to represent the vast southern region of America stretching from the Carolinas to California. The 1970s witnessed a significant shift in population as millions of Amer-

FIGURE 11.4   Continued

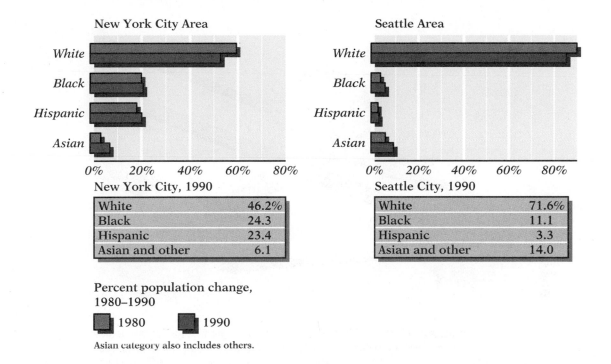

New York City Area

White

Black

Hispanic

Asian

0%   20%   40%   60%   80%

Seattle Area

White

Black

Hispanic

Asian

0%   20%   40%   60%   80%

New York City, 1990

White	46.2%
Black	24.3
Hispanic	23.4
Asian and other	6.1

Seattle City, 1990

White	71.6%
Black	11.1
Hispanic	3.3
Asian and other	14.0

Percent population change,
1980–1990

■ 1980   ■ 1990

Asian category also includes others.

This figure illustrates the growing concentration of minority populations in some of the nation's largest metropolitan areas and cities. Note that with the exception of Seattle, all of these cities are composed primarily of minority groups. Except for Miami, however, the metropolitan areas are predominantly white.

Source: Copyright © 1990 *Los Angeles Times.* Reprinted by permission.

icans left northeastern and north central states (Figure 11.5) and moved south and west. States with the most significant population increase between 1970 and 1980 were California (3.7 million), Texas (3 million), Florida (3 million), Arizona (1 million), and Georgia (875,000). The population of most eastern and central states increased only slightly during this period; two states, New York and Rhode Island, even lost population. As of 1984, four of the ten largest cities in the nation were "winter" cities; by the early 1990s only New York and Chicago are likely to remain on that list. Houston, Dallas, San Antonio, Phoenix, and San Diego are growing at a phenomenal rate as well as becoming important economic centers.

Explanations for the rapid growth of sunbelt cities, and the concomitant decline of frostbelt cities, are numerous and often complex. Thomas Shannon (1989) outlined five general theories for this population shift.

1. *Wage rates* Because of a more conservative political environment, sunbelt states have always had lower wage rates than eastern states. The large number of illegal workers in this region from Mexico and Central America also tends to depress

FIGURE 11.5   Approximate Migration Flows in the 1970s Among Regions

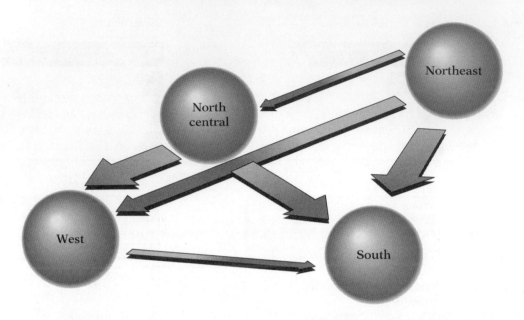

Growth in the sunbelt took off in the 1970s (especially the first half of the decade) as people left the winter cities and states and headed for the southern and western regions of the country.

Note: Width of arrows indicates approximate relative size of net migration flows.

Source: From Thomas R. Shannon, *Urban Problems in Sociological Perspective,* p. 44 (Copyright © 1983), reissued 1989 by Waveland Press, Inc., Prospect Heights, Illinois. Reprinted with permission of the publisher.

---

wages. Inasmuch as labor costs are a significant part of overall production expenses, industries began closing up shop in snowbelt cities and relocating to a warmer (and less expensive) part of the country. This runaway plant phenomenon resulted in the loss of 1.4 million jobs between 1966 and 1975.

2. *Avoiding unionization*   The major reason labor costs are relatively low in sunbelt states is because unions have had little success organizing workers. Right-to-work laws have effectively locked unions out, and conservative law enforcement officials are more likely to view labor disputes from management's perspective. These observations have not been lost on foreign-based, multinational corporations that are more likely to build their American-based plants in the sunbelt than in the frostbelt.

3. *Tax incentives*   Because they pay their employees higher wages and have more extensive social service and welfare programs, northern cities have the highest tax rates in the country. Lower rates of taxation can be a powerful incentive to move, for both individuals and, especially, industry. In fact lower corporate tax rates act as a kind of government subsidy, partially offsetting the cost of relocating a company to the sunbelt.

4. *Federal expenditure patterns* A significant number of senior congressmen come from the sunbelt. As a result of their influence and position, a large share of pork-barrel projects such as power dams, harbor improvements, and river transportation systems have found their way to those states. Many of these projects not only create jobs, but encourage industry and commerce. Military spending has also been important in this increasingly high-technology aerospace region. Between 1951 and 1976 the share of military contracts awarded to southern-based businesses increased from 11 percent to 25 percent (Abbot, 1987).

5. *Changing structure of the economy* In a very real sense the sunbelt was in the right place at the right time. The South, Southwest, and Mountain regions benefited as the nation began a gradual (and often painful) transition from a heavy-industry, manufacturing economy, to a postindustrial economy based on high technology, information processing, and light manufacturing. Anchored in the old economic order, winter cities had a much more difficult time making the transition to new economic activities.

The growth of sunbelt cities is not limited to matters of dollars and cents, however. Warm weather is important to people who have more leisure time and are increasingly concerned with health and physical fitness. Retirees and tourists flock to the region in pursuit of mild winters and endless summers. Arizona and California are invaded annually by a small army of people in recreation vehicles escaping the cold and snow of frostbelt states (Huth, 1989). For some the warm weather is merely a pleasant bonus. These individuals come to the sunbelt with thoughts of leaving behind the crime, pollution, and congestion of old industrial cities.

Like other sunbelt cities, Tucson, Arizona, experienced rapid economic and population growth in the 1970s and 1980s. The future growth of many communities in this region will depend on economic recovery in frostbelt cities and on the availability of water.

But paradise found could all too soon become paradise lost. Heavyweight boxing champion Joe Louis said of one of his opponents before a fight, "He can run but he can't hide." The same may be true of urban problems, which appear endemic to big cities. These problems are no longer hidden in the South and Southwest, and they certainly won't go away. Crime is on the rise in many sunbelt cities as economic prosperity often translates into increased opportunities for both street criminals and white-collar offenders. For example, in 1988 rates of violent crime in Atlanta, Dallas, Houston, Las Vegas, and New Orleans were higher than the rates in the winter cities of Boston, Buffalo, Cleveland, Pittsburgh, and Philadelphia.

Levels of pollution and traffic congestion are also on the rise. Already a serious problem, gridlock on the streets and freeways of Los Angeles is expected to increase 500 percent by the year 2010. Economic prosperity has been a hallmark of the sunbelt, but not everybody has shared the wealth. Low wages in the region have fostered what Chudacoff (1981) called "sunbelt poverty," a large group of workers who are so underpaid that they lack adequate incomes. Oil revenues that partially fueled growth in the 1960s and 1970s and helped keep taxes low began drying up in the mid-1980s. Aftershocks from the decline in oil production hit Oklahoma, Texas, and Louisiana especially hard.

The most serious issue threatening the continued prosperity of some sunbelt cities and states is the lack of water, a resource found in almost inexhaustible supply in the northeastern and north central states. During the oil crisis of the early 1970s, an expression often heard in the sunbelt regarding the shortage and price of heating oil in the frostbelt was, "Let the bastards freeze in the dark." One day soon a taunting cry aimed at sunbelt residents may come from the likes of Philadelphia and New York, "Let'em die of thirst in the heat."

WINTER CITIES

In the 1960s and 1970s urban economic growth in the United States appeared to resemble a zero-sum game, with the prosperity for sunbelt cities coming at the expense of frostbelt cities. One explanation for this phenomenon is that sunbelt cities are finally catching up to northeastern and north central urban areas. Domination of certain economic activities by sunbelt cities represents a temporary shift in the overall American economy, however, and is not a permanent regional transformation. According to this perspective, an eventual "convergence" or evening out of urban economies will take place across the country (Shannon, 1989). A contrasting point of view is that the nation's economic growth is uneven, with each section developing in a specific manner and time. Specializing in heavy industry and manufacturing, winter cities were dominant during the heyday of the Industrial Revolution. They erected "development barriers," successfully preventing other areas of the country from competing with them in their areas of specialization. However, when the United States moved into the postindustrial era emphasizing high technology and light industry, the major sphere of economic activity shifted to the sunbelt. Rather than convergence at some future date, the theory of uneven development suggests that if winter cities are to be prosperous again they will have to cultivate new economic activities.

With the ascendancy of Japan, Germany, and a number of rapidly developing Third World nations, winter cities must revitalize their economies if they expect to compete successfully in the domestic and international marketplace. Sunbelt cities have thrived as a result of economic growth in agriculture, oil and gas, tourism and leisure, defense, high technology, and real estate and construction (Sachs, Palumbo, and Ross, 1987). Winter cities can compete in the last three areas (as some are already doing) with more success than in the others. Boston and other New England cities are leaders in the microcomputer industry, and Pittsburgh has made a major transformation from steel and manufacturing to the service sector and trade. Recent free-trade agreements with Canada could make Buffalo, on the U.S.-Canadian border and Lake Erie, a major port city again. Once known for its rubber industry, Akron is home to a growing number of Fortune 500 companies. Even the textile industry, which many have conceded to Third World low-wage competitors, could flourish under the right circumstances. Economist Lester Thurow (in Mann, 1990) maintained that the high-labor-cost West German textile industry has been so successful in the international market because it produces high-quality goods. If American workers can do the same, garment districts in New York and other winter cities could flourish and capture a greater share of the world market.

To the extent that people have deserted northern cities because they are tired of freezing temperatures and snow, the effects of bad weather can be partially alleviated by technology and innovative architectural designs. For example, bus stops can be enclosed, heated, and made more accessible. Stretches of roads, streets, and sidewalks could be electrically heated to melt snow and reduce hazardous driving (this is already being done in Sweden, especially downtown Stockholm). Montreal has an eye-appealing underground city with hundreds of stores that is kept at a constant, comfortable temperature year around. With today's technology, the creation of large, enclosed winter gardens and indoor parks for recreational and leisure activities could be no more than a few years away (Gappert, 1987). Swedish architect Paul Brobert (in Gappert, 1987) envisioned the possibility of a "continuous and connected city where buildings are joined together by an enclosed urban room and where optimal climatic zoning creates a whole new energy situation" (p. 11).

The future of American cities was succinctly summarized by Hanson (1987): "It is increasingly clear that the critical factor in urban development in an advanced economy is not whether a city is located in the Sun Belt or Frost Belt, but the functions that it has performed in the past and those that it is capable of performing in the future" (p. 266). A city's capability and potential, however, are not enough to ensure its economic viability. Difficult decisions in both the private and public sectors will have to be made if urban America is to prosper in an increasingly interdependent and competitive global economy.

 THE METROPOLITAN TRANSITION

As noted in the preceding sections, beginning in the 1970s the metropolitan areas of the United States witnessed significant shifts in population. Tens of thousands of people left cities and moved to rural and semirural towns. As a result, the long-term population growth of cities slowed, and in many cases was reversed. Sociologist William Frey (1990) offered three significantly different explanations for this phenomenon.

According to the **period explanation,** the slowdown and reversal of urban growth was unique and therefore a temporary distortion of continuing expansion resulting from the convergence of economic and demographic factors. The 1973–1975 recession (and oil shortage) led to disinvestment in the heavily industrialized winter cities.

At the same time, smaller cities and towns gained population as less oil-dependent light industries and services emerged. Meanwhile, a growing number of elderly Americans was adding to the population of nonmetropolitan areas.

The **regional restructuring** position viewed the deindustrialization that hit the winter cities so hard as a component of "a new geography of metropolitan growth" (Frey, 1990, p. 10). According to this argument, urban populations will increase in different geographical regions of the country for reasons unrelated to past growth. Areas that successfully make the transition to a postindustrial, high-technology, more service-oriented economy will prosper; those unable to make this transition will continue to decline.

The **deconcentration explanation** sees the slow increase and reversal of population growth in many of the country's largest cities as a fundamental break with the past. Proponents of this interpretation argue that Americans have long preferred to live in smaller cities and semirural areas but were unable to do so because of the lack of jobs and economic opportunities. The recent shift away from an industrially based economy, however, coupled with advanced technology in communications and production, freed tens of thousands of people from working and living in large cities. High technology means that increasing numbers of Americans can live wherever they choose, and they are choosing to live outside metropolitan areas. The deconcentration perspective differs from the period and regional restructuring explanations in that it views the population gains of small cities and towns that started in the 1970s as "the beginning of a long-term shift away from urbanization" (Frey, 1990, p. 10).

The health and direction of the nation's economy in the next thirty to fifty years will be a crucial factor in determining which of these explanations (if any) is most correct. Economic prosperity typically results in an expanded number of life chances and choices that people have, including where they want to reside. On the other hand, slow, uneven economic growth or stagnation reduces these chances and, demographically speaking, pulls people to specific areas where they are most likely to find employment. Social problems such as crime and environmental pollution also affect where people want to and can live.

URBAN COMPOSITION AND LIFESTYLES

Cities not only are larger than towns and villages but differ in their makeup or composition on at least three dimensions (Fischer, 1976). First, urban residents are on the average younger than nonurban persons. They are also less likely to be married, and if married, they are less likely to have children. Second, as city size increases, the number of racial, ethnic, and religious minorities increases. In other words, minority group members are attracted to, and usually concentrated in, cities. Finally, on the average, the larger the community the higher the mean educational, occupational, and income levels of the population.

Early Theorists

Early to middle twentieth-century sociologists believed that to the extent the composition and structure of urban America differed from small-town and rural areas, so too would the values and patterns of behavior of urban residents. Georg Simmel (1858–

1918) examined the influence urban structures had on individuals, and Louis Wirth (1857–1952) was interested in everyday, observable patterns of interaction in cities (Berger, 1978). For Simmel, life in the city forced people to respond selectively to the almost overwhelming amount of stimuli they are bombarded with in a rapidly changing, culturally diverse environment. Because of such overstimulation, people interact with one another more superficially, that is, as members of a particular social class or category rather than as individuals. The result is a nation of detached, self-serving urban residents living in what Davis (1949) called "the world of physically close but socially distant strangers" (p. 331). For Wirth (1938) the greater size, heterogeneity, and density of city life led to numerous, impersonal, "secondary" type relations, as opposed to the warm, intimate, personal contacts or "primary" relations characteristic of rural life. Fewer primary relations (the exception being close friends and family) lead to a variety of individual maladies, including anomie, alienation, and psychological stress. These, in turn, are responsible for a long list of problems including crime, alcoholism, drug abuse, broken families, mental illness, and the extremes of apathy and aggression.

The view of the city as a major source of evil in the modern world may tell us more about the researchers' bias than the phenomenon they were trying to understand. This antiurban sentiment, coupled with a nostalgic longing for a wholesome, unspoiled rural life, has a long tradition in American thought. Disdain for cities is a common theme in both our history and fiction dating back to the days of Thomas Jefferson. However, attempts to show that urban life is a singularly stressful, anomic, or alienating condition, or that urbanites are more unhappy than rural people, have been ambiguous or unsuccessful (Shannon, 1989). For example, Fischer (1976) found that people have approximately the same levels of mental health regardless of where they live. Rates of deviance may be higher in urban areas because these types of behavior are more visible and accurately recorded. It is also probable that rural people with problems (e.g., alcoholism) or less socially acceptable lifestyles move to the city to be with others like themselves (Fischer, 1976). Even the commonly held notion that small cities are friendlier than large ones is in doubt. Whyte (1988) found that as far as the frequency of interchange is concerned, "the streets of the big city are notably more sociable than those of smaller ones" (p. 6).

It appears that the rural-urban (gemeinschaft-gessellschaft) dichotomy of Tonnies (see chapter 1) and others is at best only partially true. To the extent that urban residents live in "ethnic enclaves" or are bound together by some common trait or interest, they can create a "quasi-gemeinschaft" community with personal relations much closer and warmer than either Simmel or Wirth would have predicted (Berger, 1978, p. 170). In effect, urban neighborhoods can be so many small towns loosely bound together by the same political and economic entity—the city.

Contemporary Theorists

In the tradition of Wirth and Simmel, contemporary urban investigators have observed patterns of interaction on city streets. For example, Dabbs and Stokes (1975) discovered that the amount of room pedestrians gave each other as they passed was related to, among other things, beauty. During the course of an experiment, a woman wearing tight clothes and attractive makeup was given more room as she passed, by both males and females, than the same woman wearing baggy clothes and no makeup. The researchers interpreted their findings in terms of social power, with people deferring to those farther up on the scale of beauty. Longtime urban researcher William Whyte (1988) observed that pedestrians in great metropolitan centers from different countries act more like one another than like people from smaller cities in their own cultures. They walk fast and aggressively and tend to cluster in the middle of the sidewalk. For Whyte this is not surprising, because people in giant cities are "responding to high-density situations and to a range of stimuli not found in smaller cities" (pp. 23–24). Because of their size, structure, and relatively fast-paced lifestyle, large cities may have a homogenizing or leveling effect on certain aspects of people's lives.

Herbert Gans As a result of its cultural diversity, rapid turnover of residents (invasion and succession), and high rates of deviance and crime, the inner city has been well researched by sociologists since the early days of human ecology in the 1920s at the University of Chicago. In a 1962 article, Herbert Gans constructed a typology of inner-city residents that is still useful. *Cosmopolites* are intellectuals and professionals as well as students, writers, and artists who live in the inner city to be near special cultural facilities. In the 1980s and early 1990s people contributing to the gentrification of inner cities made up a sizeable portion of cosmopolites. The *unmarried or childless* consist of two subgroups, those who move to the outer city when they can afford to, and those permanent, low-income individuals who live in this zone of transition for the rest of their lives. *Ethnic villagers* are those residing in quasi-gemeinschaft neighborhoods who successfully isolate themselves from the anonymity of big-city life, and find a good deal of satisfaction in intraethnic, primary group relations. The *deprived* and the *trapped and downwardly mobile* are the very poor, emotionally disturbed, and handicapped residents. This primarily nonwhite population makes up the growing underclass in urban America—those who are unemployed and unemployable. Some times called America's Third World population, these individuals are only marginally integrated into the larger society and lead difficult, unfulfilling lives.

William Whyte Urbanologist Whyte (1988) examined one group of trapped and downwardly mobile city dwellers—street people. He discovered that the toughest, hardiest individuals in this category are shopping-bag ladies. Dirty and disheveled with all of their possessions in two or three bags, most of these women in New York City come from middle-class backgrounds, and some are well educated. Whyte stated that they have no ties to social service agencies and are "totally outside the system" (p. 47). They typically resist efforts to reintegrate them into the more normal pattern of life, and become confused and frightened when institutionalized.

Beggars range from professional blind persons who work six hours a day and average upwards of $18 an hour, to the "Bowery bums" who lack the skills to be gainfully employed. Whyte estimated that the number of beggars on the streets of midtown New York doubled between 1980 and 1988.

From a conflict perspective, street people are victims of a capitalist society that cannot provide employment for those who want to work, and refuses to finance social support systems to care for individuals who are unable to work. New York State released 50,000 people from mental hospitals who were conditioned (sometimes for years) to a highly structured, institutional setting (Whyte, 1988). Lacking basic interaction skills and having few possibilities for employment, these individuals often roam the streets in a frightened and confused state of mind. Although free to come and go as they please, they are often victimized in a hostile and dangerous urban environment.

URBAN PROBLEMS

Urban Poverty

A drive through any big city in the United States will reveal a host of increasingly dismal social, economic, and environmental problems. The human by-products of these problems in the form of beggars, bag ladies, and the homeless are a constant reminder of what we have permitted our cities to become. To be sure, twentieth-century Americans didn't invent these problems; however, they appear to be more serious here than in comparable highly industrialized, capitalist societies, and strangely out of place in the world's wealthiest nation. The most serious affliction, and one no doubt related to other urban problems, is poverty.

Although there is more rural than urban poverty, people living in urban ghettos make up the largest concentration of poor in the United States. This is especially true of winter cities (Zastrow and Bowker, 1984). In 1987, thirty-two million people in the United States lived in poverty. Approximately one-third were elderly or disabled, one-third were temporarily poor because of personal misfortune, and one-third were chronically poor although able-bodied. This last group includes at least 2.5 million people who make up the nation's underclass. Residing almost exclusively in urban areas, these individuals have a high frequency of being school dropouts, from female-headed families with children, dependent on welfare, and without jobs or with only irregular employment (Sawhill, 1989). In the past twenty years the number of desperately poor people, especially African Americans, living in cities has increased tremendously. By 1980 approximately 38 percent of all poor blacks in the ten largest cities lived in census tracts classified as extreme-poverty areas. A decade earlier this figure was 22 percent (Wacquant and Wilson, 1989).

John DiIulio (1989, p. 35) reasoned that "the truly disadvantaged" (urban underclass) exist mainly because they are consistently victimized by "the truly deviant"—predatory street criminals. These criminals victimize the underclass both directly (muggings, rapes, murders, creating a general climate of fear) and indirectly (discouraging neighborhood economic development, providing bad role models for children, loss of local male population to prisons and jail). Research indicates that inner-city residents are much more likely to be robbed than people who reside in suburbs or outside the metropolitan area. Victimization studies conducted between 1973 and 1984 discovered that 67 percent of robbery victims had family incomes of less than $15,000.

Crime, however, is not the only cause of chronic poverty. Between 1947 and 1972 American cities lost more than one million manufacturing jobs. In 1954, Chicago had over 10,000 manufacturing plants that employed almost 500,000 blue-collar workers. By 1982 the 5,000 remaining plants employed fewer than 162,000, a loss of 63 percent (Wacquant and Wilson, 1989). In the 1940s two of every three employees in Cleveland worked in manufacturing; by 1987 that number was down to one of three. Whereas median family income rose for suburbanites by 5 percent between 1969 and 1978, it fell by 4 percent for city dwellers during that same period.

Bernard Friedan (1989) argued that even when office and service jobs are available in central cities, poor people have difficulty finding employment. Many positions are filled by word of mouth (friends of friends), but as few of their friends or relatives are employed, poor people miss out on jobs for which they are qualified. In addition, inner-city residents often lack the education necessary for even relatively low-paying entry-level work. According to Kasarda (in Sawhill, 1989) in New York City during the 1970s the number of jobs available for people who had not finished high school declined by 40 percent, while the number of jobs for college graduates increased by 61 percent. With the amount of money school districts spend per pupil per year ranging from $200 to $10,000, many inner-city schools cannot compete for the best teachers and purchase the necessary equipment to train people in a computer-literate society. Finally, many poor people (especially single women with children) are not looking for work. Unable to find or afford day care, these young to middle-age women are depressed and eventually lose hope of finding employment.

The Homeless Poverty and the deinstitutionalization policies of psychiatric facilities since the mid-1960s and 1970s produced large numbers of homeless people. A multicity study revealed that 29 percent of the homeless are mentally ill, and that a significant number are Vietnam veterans (Finn, 1988). Numerous studies indicate that between 25 and 45 percent of these individuals are alcoholics (although it is not entirely clear if alcoholism causes homelessness, or homelessness causes alcoholism). Another fourteen million Americans are considered near homeless—one paycheck away from losing the roof over their heads.

As the number of people living on the streets increased in the 1980s, they became a more diverse population. At the beginning of the decade these individuals were mostly single men and women; by 1989, however, a significant number were intact families and women with children (Figure 11.6). In Minneapolis in 1989, 65 percent of the people without a place to live were single, divorced, or abandoned women and their children. The relatively high cost of renting an apartment in many cities now means that being employed is no guarantee of a place to live. The 1989 Minneapolis survey found that 25 percent of the homeless were working (many full-time), and 27 percent were graduates of a vocational school or university.

What Causes Urban Poverty?

Because poverty is an important component of urban problems, many researchers and policy makers have attempted to explain why this condition is so pervasive in American cities. In his 1974 book *The Unheavenly City Revisited,* Edward Banfield stated that the poor have no one to blame for their sorry plight in life but themselves. According to Banfield, they are a lazy, dirty, apathetic, impulsive, aggressive, and suspicious group of people whose only interests in life are sex and good times. Possessing a distinct set of values, attitudes, and patterns of behavior that makes economic success next to impossible, the poor live in a self-perpetuating "culture of poverty."

A completely different explanation was offered by Savitch (1978), who considered inner-city poverty to be a result of "domestic colonialism." According to this primarily Marxist view, inner cities were systematically exploited by the bourgeoisie in the same way that African and Asian countries were exploited by colonial powers beginning in the nineteenth century. Savitch claimed that suburbanites drive to work each day, use the city's resources (water, power, streets, police, etc.), and drive back home in the evening leaving the poor to foot the bill. Moreover, the rich continue to take advantage of the inner city's politically impotent, minority workforce by paying them low wages.

FIGURE 11.6   Profile of U.S. Homeless

Who They Are

U.S. Conference of Mayors looks at urban homelessness in 1990

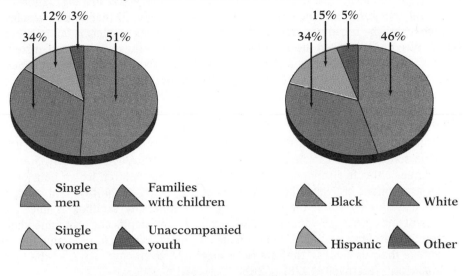

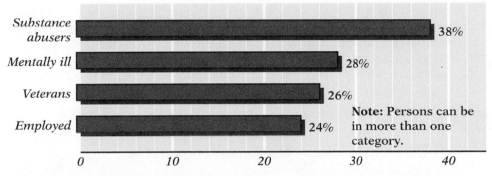

Note: Persons can be in more than one category.

The majority of homeless people in the United States are males. A disproportion of individuals who live on the streets are from minority groups, especially African Americans.

Source: Knight-Ridder Tribune News Graphics Network. Reprinted with permission.

For those who manage to break the cycle of poverty and leave the ghetto, new migrants take their place (invasion and succession). When labor forces in winter cities demanded and won higher wages as a result of union activities, the capitalist class moved their factories to the sunbelt and found a new class of workers to exploit. Sternlieb (1978) rejected this interpretation, arguing that it is not exploitation, but indifference and abandonment that brought bad economic times to inner cities: *"The major problem of the core areas of our cities is simply their lack of economic value"* (p. 26). As you may have guessed, Marxists are likely to see "indifference and abandonment" as the final stage of exploitation.

The deplorable conditions in which millions of inner-city residents live will not improve until those in power begin looking at this underclass from a different perspective. Wacquant and Wilson (1989) noted that conservative political ideology in the United States has defined the problems of ghetto dwellers in "individualistic and moral terms. . . . The poor are presented as a mere aggregation of personal cases, each with its own logic and self-contained causes" (p. 9). This conservative ideology ignores the "structural changes in the society, economy, and polity" (p. 9) that caused wholesale urban poverty. The urban underclass will increase as long as politicians fail to exercise what C. Wright Mills called the *sociological imagination*—the ability to recognize that maladies like poverty afflicting a significant number of people cannot be explained at the individual level of analysis (the unemployed are sick, lame, lazy, stupid, etc.), but are rooted in the structure of society. Only changes in that structure (economy, polity, education) will resolve them.

Failure to implement the sociological imagination will result in moving from one failed solution to another in a halfhearted effort to solve the problems of the urban poor. One solution (if it can be so called) is the muddle-through approach. Sternlieb likened inner cities to a sandbox where adults park their children for an hour or two with an assortment of toys to keep them busy. Engrossed in the toys and sand, the children play quietly while the adults relax. The inner-city sandbox is filled with government-sponsored programs that don't result in any significant economic change but keep the residents busy and, more important, quiet. When old programs (like old toys) outlive their usefulness, they are repackaged and given new names—"the height of sandboxism" (Sternlieb, 1978, p. 28).

A partial solution for many cities is to annex the suburbs. This could significantly increase the urban tax base and take some of the burden off poor people who are currently paying a disproportionate share of expenses for city maintenance. However, this strategy usually requires a referendum by the suburbs, which are not inclined to view such action favorably. This is so despite the apparent success of Miami and Dade County, and of Nashville and Davidson City (Zastrow and Bowker, 1984).

URBAN EXPLOSION IN DEVELOPING NATIONS

The Industrial Revolution was responsible for the initial and continued growth of scores of cities in Europe and North America. The growth of cities, as Hoselitz (1954–1955) pointed out, "is a necessary condition of economic development" (p. 278). It is of no surprise, therefore, that modernization in the Third World would be accompanied by high rates of urban growth. What is astonishing is the incredible and unparalleled rate of population increase in these cities. In 1950 only thirty-one had over one million inhabitants. By 1985 that number had increased to 146 urban areas, and is expected to reach 279 in the year 2000. At current rates of growth, almost 500 Third World cities will have more than one million residents in the year 2025 (Dogan and Kasarda, 1988).

In the twentieth century the population of cities in the developing world will increase seventy times—nine times faster than the cities of developed nations when they were expanding rapidly in the nineteenth century (Light, 1983). In 1960 three of the ten largest urban areas in the world were in developing nations; by 1985 that number had increased to seven; in the year 2025, demographers estimate that it will be nine of ten. Figure 11.7 shows that of the world's one hundred largest cities in the late 1980s, only thirty-seven were in the developed nations.

Many Third World nations such as Mexico, Bangladesh, and Egypt have primate cities, that is, one giant metropolitan area at least twice as big as the nation's second-largest city, which serves as the country's economic, political, and cultural center. Some observers argue that primate cities are good for a nation's urban development due to the trickle-down effect of advanced technology and economic momentum from these giants to smaller cities. Others insist that the concentration of resources in primate cities effectively slows down the development of middle-size urban areas. Primate cities can become so overpopulated and congested that vital economic and political functions are severely impeded (Spates and Macionis, 1987).

FIGURE 11.7 Distribution of the World's One Hundred Largest Metropolitan Areas, by Population

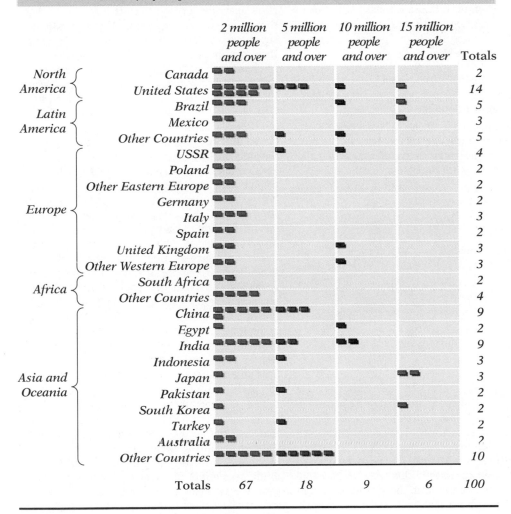

		2 million people and over	5 million people and over	10 million people and over	15 million people and over	Totals
North America	Canada	■■				2
	United States	■■■■■■	■■■	■	■	14
Latin America	Brazil	■■		■	■	5
	Mexico	■■			■	3
	Other Countries	■■■	■	■		5
Europe	USSR	■■	■	■		4
	Poland	■■				2
	Other Eastern Europe	■■				2
	Germany	■■				2
	Italy	■■■				3
	Spain	■■				2
	United Kingdom	■■		■		3
	Other Western Europe	■■		■		3
Africa	South Africa	■■				2
	Other Countries	■■■■				4
Asia and Oceania	China	■■■■■	■■■			9
	Egypt	■		■		2
	India	■■■■■	■■	■■		9
	Indonesia	■■	■			3
	Japan	■			■■	3
	Pakistan	■	■			2
	South Korea	■			■	2
	Turkey	■	■			2
	Australia	■■				2
	Other Countries	■■■■■	■■■■■			10
Totals		**67**	**18**	**9**	**6**	**100**

Source: Reprinted by permission of the Population Crisis Committee.

OURSELVES AND OTHERS
Surviving in the Streets of a Third World City

Imagine you are a rural-to-urban migrant in some Third World nation who has just arrived in one of your country's largest cities. You are poor, probably illiterate, and have no job skills outside of farming, and carry only enough money to eat for a few days, a week or two at most. The unemployment rate is over 25 percent and you don't know a soul. What would you do? How would you live? To survive you would no doubt work in the streets like tens of millions of other people in cities around the world. For three years beginning in 1978, geographer and economist Ray Bromley studied how poor people worked and survived in the streets of Cali, Colombia. The street occupations investigated in that country's third-largest city are grouped under the following major headings:

Retail distribution   The selling and trading of foodstuffs and manufactured goods, including newspaper distribution.

Small-scale public transport   The operation of *motocarros,* three-wheeled motorcycles used to carry passengers and cargo, horse-drawn carts, handcarts, and the work of porters.

Personal services   Shoe shining, shoe repair, watch repair, document typing, etc.

Security services   Night watchman, car parking attendant, etc.

Scavenging   Door-to-door collection of old newspapers, bottles, etc., searching for similar products in dustbins, garbage heaps, and the municipal dump.

Prostitution   Or, to be more specific, soliciting for clients.

Theft   Including robbery with violence.

Begging

Of the above groups, retail distribution was the largest, accounting for approximately 32 percent of the street workforce. Bromley discovered that working in the streets was highly competitive even though the pay on average was only $3 (1977 U.S. equivalent) per day. The law of supply and demand tended to keep earnings in this sector of the economy low, just as it would in the international marketplace. As an occupation became increasingly successful, it attracted more practitioners who, in turn, forced incomes down to their previous level.

Most street occupations are characterized by the relatively small amount of capital required for equipment and merchandise. Vendors, for example, typically have no more than $100 tied up in their inventory of food, clothes, religious items, toys, or books and magazines. Bromley noted that street vendors play a particularly important role in the economy of developing nations by providing a variety of goods that poor people can afford. A price survey conducted in Cali revealed that they sell small quantities of food at costs much lower than those offered in supermarkets. However, whereas street merchants help keep the cost of living down, they may unwittingly depress the wage scale for unskilled and semiskilled workers. If factory owners realize that individuals can survive on a small salary in an intensely competitive job market, they have little incentive to pay a more livable wage.

Bromley maintained that with the exceptions of scavenging, begging, and theft, street occupations are functional for the entire socioeconomic system. For example, unemployment goes down while the amount of affordable goods and services goes up. We would add that people getting by in the streets are also less likely to engage in criminal behavior or potentially revolutionary political activity. Marxists, however, would tend to view the latter as a negative consequence of street work, arguing that the institutions responsible for a society's poverty must be eliminated. From this point of view, a latent function of working in the streets is the perpetuation of a system that must be dismantled (by revolution if necessary) if a more equitable distribution of wealth is to occur. Whereas a street vendor may well go along with this argument in principle, it does little to alter the fact that survival on a day-to-day basis is more important for most people than distant, probably unrealistic political goals.

Bromley discovered that although 70 percent of those working in the streets were males between eighteen and fifty-five years of age, women and children also contributed a significant amount of labor to this segment of the economy. Inasmuch as they earn so little money, have no guaranteed income, and may be victims of theft, arbitrary arrest, or the loss of job opportunities, the more people in a family who worked, the better their chances for survival. Unfortunately, just as stratification based on ascription exists in virtually every other area of the marketplace, women and children are generally employed in the least rewarding and lowest-paid jobs. Lacking even the meager amount of capital required to be street merchants, these individuals usually find that the only sources of income open to them are scavenging and prostitution.

This fascinating research reveals that street workers are part of an economy within an economy, employing and servicing a significant part of the population in a Third World city. People in these occupations work just as hard as (in many cases much harder than) other individuals, routinely putting in long hours seven days a week. This work not only helps them survive in a harsh economic environment, but also provides a measure of self-esteem and social stability in an otherwise desperate and potentially volatile political situation. As residents of a developed nation, we tend to think of economic success more often than not in terms of giant corporations and six figure salaries. But economic "smarts" and toughness aren't limited to grandiosity. No doubt some of the shrewdest and most dedicated business people in the world (for their lives depend on it) are to be found on the streets of Bombay, Cairo, and Mexico City, as well as hundreds of other urban areas in developing nations.

Source: Adapted from Ray Bromley. 1982. "Working in the Streets: Survival Strategy, Necessity, or Unavoidable Evil?", in A. Gilbert, J. E. Hardoy, and R. Ramirez, eds. *Urbanization in Contemporary Latin America*. New York: John Wiley and Sons, pp. 59–77.

As noted in the preceding chapter, rapid population growth in Third World cities is the result of two factors: *natural increase* (births over deaths) and *rural-to-urban* migration. Newland (1980) estimated that the latter accounts for up to 75 percent of urban growth in poor countries. Another way of viewing explosive growth as a consequence of high rates of in-migration is that "overurbanization" (more urban residents than the economies of cities can sustain) is caused in large measure by "overruralization" (more rural residents than the economies of rural areas can sustain) (Dogan and Kasarda, 1988). Recall our discussion of push and pull factors from chapter 10. As a result of government programs that favor urban development at the expense of agricultural development, poor farmers are pushed off of the land and drawn or pulled to the city in search of a better life (Todaro and Stilkind, 1981).

Sachs (1988) compared a Third World city to a giant Las Vegas, with the bulk of the population made up of gamblers; but these gamblers are playing very different games. "Instead of roulette and blackjack, their games are job security, individual social mobility, better access to education for their children, and hospitals for the sick" (p. 338). As miserable as life can be in horribly crowded cities of the developing world, migrants have a glimmer of hope for a higher standard of living. On the other hand, tens of millions of rural peasants (many of them landless) have virtually no hope for a more prosperous life if they remain in the countryside, and they know it.

In cities the poor suffer and starve on an individual basis, whereas in rural areas starvation is often a mass phenomenon. The city also attracts people because it is a never-ending spectacle, with "pageants, carnivals, military parades, public executions, soccer championships, and, increasingly, television" (Sachs, 1988, p. 338). Continuing the gambling analogy, regardless of the economic climate in developing nations, cities will continue to grow. During periods of economic prosperity people will flock to urban areas in search of newly created jobs, while in hard times (which usually affect rural

These garbage pickers' shacks in Manila are typical of slums in Third World cities. Tens of millions of people live in deplorable conditions such as these, lacking an adequate supply of water and proper waste disposal. The continued migration of individuals to these cities is indicative of the lack of economic opportunities in rural areas.

areas hardest), the rural poor will take a chance and move to cities "as a solution of last resort" (Sachs, 1988, p. 340). This as yet unabated rural-to-urban migration in the developing world has brought about a series of social, economic, and environmental problems of catastrophic proportions.

Hell Is a City

In his book *Inside the Third World*, Paul Harrison (1984) said that "hell is a city." This is an obvious exaggeration, but urban slums in developing nations are densely packed areas of human misery and suffering, quite unimaginable to most people living in the developed world. Harrison described his first impressions of Calcutta as follows:

> I had seen a good deal of India and of the Third World before I visited Calcutta. But it was still a culture shock to arrive there, in a hot and damp rush hour, as dusk fell. It is the nearest human thing to an ant heap, a dense sea of people washing over roads hopelessly jammed as taxis swerve round hand pulled rickshaws, buses run into hand-carts, pony stagecoaches and private cars and even flocks of goats fight it out for the limited space. . . . A young woman in a sari, her head leaning on her hand with a sleepy air of melancholia, reached for breath out the window, though the air outside was almost as dank and malodorous as inside. (pp. 165–166)

The Population Crisis Committee conducted a study in 1991 to determine the living conditions in the world's one hundred largest metropolitan areas. On the basis of data received from ninety-eight cities, the committee ranked their livability as very good, good, fair, and poor. Of the fifty-four cities in the fair and poor categories, fifty-three are in developing nations. Singapore was the only Third World city to be ranked very good.

Housing   The list of problems facing Third World cities is long: high rates of unemployment and underemployment; water, air, and noise pollution; water, food, and power shortages; lack of transportation and communication; not enough schools and hospitals; and, quite often, massive corruption at every level of public and private bureaucracies. However, the most serious and debilitating of these shortcomings is the lack of housing. For example, in India's four largest metropolitan areas (Calcutta, Bombay, Delhi, and Madras) approximately one-fourth to one-third of the population live in dwellings considered unfit for human habitation. Over 400,000 migrants come to Mexico City each year and typically end up in central-city slums or squatter settlements on the periphery appropriately called *los villas miserias,* or "cities of the miserable" (Spates and Macionis, 1987, p. 222). As of 1990, 42 percent of Mexico City's residents lived in slums.

In the developing world, urban slums are increasing at twice the rate of these rapidly growing cities as a whole. The housing shortage is so acute in many poor countries that in all likelihood it will never be resolved. In Kenya, three million new housing units would have to be built each year to accommodate that country's urban growth—the equivalent of building fifteen new Nairobis. The availability of housing in the Third World is not the only problem. According to World Bank estimates, the poorest 25 percent of the population in most African and low-income Asian countries cannot afford the least expensive permanent housing. Even relative prosperity is no guarantee of securing adequate housing in some Third World cities. For example, the acquisition of an apartment in Bombay may require a "deposit" of up to 50 percent of the selling price. This deposit does not count toward the eventual purchase of the dwelling, and both parties realize this down payment is little more than a bribe (Bryjak, 1982–1983).

As is so often the case, children seem to suffer disproportionately wherever there is large-scale human misery. Abandoned by parents who are too poor to house, feed, and clothe them, children roam the streets of cities throughout the Third World. With little hope for the future, they often travel in packs, doing anything they can to survive. Armed with knives and razors, young thugs in Bogota, Colombia, live in *gallads,* gangs of ten to twenty-five. They steal what they can, and fight with each other as well as the police (Harrison, 1984). According to one estimate, Brazil alone has as many as two million abandoned children (National Public Radio, 1991). In India tens of thousands of children beg in the streets, some deliberately mutilated to make them more pitiful and increase their earning power.

Violence   If inadequate housing is the most serious social and economic problem in Third World cities, the potential for collective violence is the greatest political threat. Newly arrived rural-to-urban migrants are relatively content with their lot in the city no matter how poor they may be. Compared to the intractable poverty and despair of those left behind in the country, they are better off. Feelings of relative prosperity do not last forever, however—seldom more than a generation or two. Thus it is only a matter of time before the masses begin comparing themselves to their more affluent urban neighbors and demand a share of the wealth. Speaking of the urban poor, the late Indira Gandhi (in Szulc, 1982) said, "What is happening is that they see their poverty—even though it is an improved situation—with much sharper eyes. Before they tolerated it; today they say, 'Why shall I tolerate it?' " (p. 5).

The potential for wide-scale violence (or revolution) becomes evident when one considers the composition of migrants to the city. A disproportionate number in Africa and Asia are young (between fifteen and thirty), single males with a higher than average education than nonmigrants. It is this group of people, young and ambitious, cut off from the stabilizing influence of family and friends in villages, who are most likely to engage in violence. In India, urban riots (controlled only by the military in some cases) over the past ten years have left thousands dead. Clashes between rioters and the police, and between groups of people of various religious, ethnic, and racial backgrounds, occur on a daily basis in overcrowded cities around the world.

In an environment where shortages of food, water, power, housing, and employment are facts of life, a growing number of Third World cities are powder kegs just waiting to explode. When their collective rage turns to rebellious behavior, the urban masses will not have to look very far for leaders. These cities (especially primate cities) are filled with unemployed university graduates who cannot find work commensurate with their education. Living in a society with a very limited opportunity structure, some are willing to tear that society down and start all over again. An educated, frustrated intelligentsia, no longer content to wait for their just reward, will no doubt find many sympathetic ears among the urban poor. As cities continue to grow and living conditions deteriorate, the number of people looking for some way out of their misery can only increase.

FOCUS ON
MEXICO

MEXICO CITY: *NUMERO UNO EN EL MUNDO*

When Spanish explorer Hernan Cortes and his army of 500 men entered the Aztec capital of Tenochtitlan in 1519, it had a population of between 80,000 and 300,000, rivaling the great cities of Europe and Asia (Vasquez, 1983). The heart of the Aztec empire, Tenochtitlan was destined to become the site of a great city because of its historical significance and location. Situated at the southern end of the Mexican plateau between the Sierra Madre Oriental and Sierra Madre Occidental mountains at an altitude of 7,800 feet, the ancient capital had an ideal climate and fertile soil. Like the Indians who came to the region centuries before them, the conquistadors soon learned that living on the plateau was superior to life on the coastal lowlands where they had to battle ubiquitous insects and parasites (Dogan, 1988).

With the destruction of the Aztec empire, Tenochtitlan gave way to Mexico City, which was built on the ruins of the old Indian city. Population growth over the ensuing 300 years was slow, and Mexico's largest city had approximately 350,000 people at the time of independence from Spain in 1821. In the years after the bloody and protracted Revolution of 1910, the population increased rapidly, and Mexico City had approximately one million residents in 1930. Land reform in the 1930s slowed rural-to-urban migration somewhat, although the population reached 1.5 million in 1940. World War II brought about a significant era for the economic and demographic history of Mexico. A sharp reduction in the supply of goods previously imported from the United States and Europe stimulated the growth and development of local industry. Meanwhile, deteriorating conditions in the countryside forced tens of thousands of peasants off of the land and into the cities (Riding, 1989). This combination of urban pull and rural push factors was responsible for an influx of peasants from the countryside that has continued unabated to this day.

Increased by approximately 6.2 million people streaming into the city between 1940 and 1970 (over 550 a day), the population of Mexico's capital almost doubled each decade for thirty years. The mostly young migrants also contributed to the city's incredible rate of growth with high rates of fertility. By 1980 its population was in excess of fourteen million people, with projections for the year 2000 running as high as thirty-two million—the largest city in the world. Migrants from rural areas currently stream into the capital at the rate of 1,000 a day; and the millions of people of childbearing age now residing there mean that the population will continue to increase for years even if the rate of fertility declines. This combination of youthful residents and extensive rural-to-urban migration is transforming Mexico into an urban giant.

In 1983, fifty-five million of seventy-nine million Mexicans lived in cities. In the year 2025 it is estimated that 131 million out of 154 million people will reside in urban areas, the equivalent of thirteen cities of ten million each (Dogan and Kasarda, 1988). However, at the present rate of increase, Mexico City alone

Air pollution in Mexico City is among the worst in the world, and the Mexican capital's future is threatened by these toxic fumes. Unable and/or unwilling to invest in environmental clean-ups, Third World cities often are far more polluted than metropolitan areas in developed countries.

would have a population well over fifty million by the year 2025.

Problems facing the capital are mind boggling, and thirty years from now it could well be unfit for human habitation. Former president Miguel de la Madrid was not being an alarmist when he warned, "If we become careless, Mexico City can become uninhabitable. Catastrophe is not out of the range of possibility" (Vasquez, 1983). The present situation is at a crisis level, and daily life in Mexico City is a struggle to survive for hundreds of thousands and a series of major inconvenience for everyone. To make matters worse, virtually every resident of the metropolitan area faces potentially life-threatening health hazards. Commuting to and from work can take as long as four to five hours a day, up to 30 percent of the time an individual is awake. A housing shortage of over 800,000 units in 1985 means that tens of thousands of people live in the streets. Summoned by irritated residents, police routinely and forcibly remove squatters from their makeshift homes. With little money and no place to go, the homeless make their way from one *barrio* ("neighborhood") to another, only to have the cycle of relocation and resettlement repeat itself.

The reality of an overcrowded city with millions of poor people presents a formidable (some would say hopeless) difficulty for authorities. Intractable poverty and high unemployment means that even with more housing units, hospitals, and a better system of transportation, the lives of millions of people would not be significantly improved. People mired in poverty do not have the wherewithal to take advantage of expanded services, no matter how inexpensive they may be. In 1974, 70 percent of Mexico City's economically active population earned the minimum wage or less (Gilbert and Ward, 1982). A 1982 government report estimated that 10.3 percent of the metropolitan population lived in extreme poverty, and another 22.6 percent did not earn enough money to satisfy their basic needs (Riding, 1989).

The unequal distribution of wealth in Mexico City has produced a standard of living for some that is as luxurious and extravagant as any place in the world, whereas others are forced to burn garbage to keep disease-carrying fleas and rats away. What is quite possibly the most polluted air in the world affects rich and poor alike as they move about the valley of the Aztec gods. The almost three million cars and roughly 60,000 factories fill the atmosphere with 11,000 tons of pollutants every day. Trapped by surrounding mountains, the fouled air cannot escape, forming a second or inversion layer over the city and compounding an already formidable problem. A recent United Nations study concluded that air pollution in Mexico City was three to six times above recommended safety levels; by anotherestimate, just breathing the air in the Mexican capital is the equivalent of smoking two packs of cigarettes a day. Fifty percent of newborn infants tested in 1987 and 1988 had toxic levels of lead in their blood. A recent World Health Organization study found blood toxicity in 70 percent of the fetuses examined (Gardels and Snell, 1989). Lead levels of this magnitude could reduce intelligence quotient (IQ) levels as much as 10 percent. This means that the number of mentally retarded individuals in Mexico City (IQ below 80) could be as high as 20 percent of the population, or four million people.

Everyone is affected by the polluted air, although the wealthiest residents can buy a good deal of protection from these poisons. They have air filtered through their hermetically sealed homes, order bottles of oxygen from delivery services, and purchase it in tanks from drugstores that cater to the rich. In 1991 a private company began installing oxygens kiosks in some areas of the city. Approximately $2 buys a twenty-second hit of clean air (Cleeland, 1991). For many people that price is the equivalent of two or more hours of work.

If people are not dissuaded from living in or moving to the capital because of air pollution, the shortage of fresh water may well be the ultimate check on how large the city eventually becomes. In the years prior to rapid population growth, Mexico City obtained its water from subsoil and wells. But the use of water from underground sources in such enormous quantities resulted in entire city blocks sinking as much as nine inches a year (Riding, 1989). Water now has to be diverted to the city from rivers hundreds of miles away at an enormous cost. As any student of stratification would predict, the use of a commodity as precious as water is closely related to social class. Residents of one high-income neighborhood consume nine times as much water as those in a lower-income section of the city, and Schteingart (1988) reported that 9 percent of the city's population uses 75 percent of available water.

Mexico's urban problems could have been mitigated in years past by an aggressive federal government passing and strictly enforcing tough pollution laws, as well as funding badly needed public works projects. Unfortunately, it did neither, being content to sit by and watch the city and its difficulties grow. Only in recent years has the government taken any steps to reduce pollution, and this may well turn out to be a classic case of doing too little too late. Nor were federal authorities as involved as they should have been with urban planning and construction. The government did not take over and improve a badly out of date public transportation system (particularly buses) until 1981, and the capital city's mass system that should have been started after World War II at the latest is barely twenty years old. The enormous cost of implementing a subway in an area the size of Mexico City at this time is probably beyond the capability of any Third World country (Schteingart, 1988).

In November 1989 the government instituted a four-month (the worst air pollution months) program in Mexico City requiring motorists to leave their cars immobile one day each week between 5 A.M. and 10:00 A.M. Vehicles are color coded with registration stickers, and violators are fined $115 and have their cars impounded for twenty-four hours (McDonnell, 1989). This strategy has obvious merit, but it will remove only 2,000 of the 11,000 tons of pollutants spewed into the atmosphere each day for a mere sixteen weeks each year. Ecologists also note the positive effects of this program were quickly neutralized by an estimated 275,000 automobiles newly registered in Mexico City during 1990 (Miller, 1990b).

Mexico City is a tragic example of what can go wrong in a developing nation with a high rate of population growth and prolonged rural-to-urban migration to a primate city. In his surrealistic novel *Christopher Unborn,* about Mexico in 1992, Carlos Fuentes (in Gardels and Snell, 1989) painted a grim picture of his country's capital city: "That jammed city of toxic air and leafless trees may be the first to know the asphyxiation of progress. . . . One of the world's oldest civilizations suffers mankind's newest affliction. Mexico City warns the rest of the species of all that has gone wrong with modernity's promised millennium of happiness" (p. 15).

DISCUSSION QUESTIONS

1. What are the principal push and pull factors that resulted in the rapid growth of Mexico City and other Third World cities? Are these factors likely to continue fueling the growth rate in urban areas of developing nations as we approach the twenty-first century? Explain.
2. Why will the population of Mexico City continue to increase even if the fertility rate declines and the number of rural-to-urban migrants is sharply reduced?
3. Imagine that you are a senior advisor to the president of Mexico. What advice would you give him concerning the many social and environmental problems confronting Mexico City? Make a list of five problems and solutions in order of seriousness and the urgency with which they must be solved. Be prepared to defend your statements should the president disagree with you. Keep in mind that Mexico is still a relatively poor country that owes world banks tens of billions of dollars.
4. Would you suggest the government of Mexico consider legislation that would limit the number of people who can move to the capital each year? What might be some of the latent (unintended) consequences of such a law?
5. Go to the library and gather information on one of the Third World's largest metropolitan areas other than Mexico City. How have the officials in that city dealt with explosive urban growth? What strategies dealing with problems of overcrowding and pollution have been successful? What strategies have been ineffective? Why have they failed?

TOKYO: NO LONGER A ROSE

Attaining the highest level of urbanization in the preindustrial world, 10 percent of Japan's residents lived in cities of 10,000 or more by the end of the eighteenth century (Light, 1983). The urban population continued to grow as Japan was transformed from a feudal to an industrial state in the latter half of the century. By 1950 almost 40 percent of the populace resided in cities, increasing to 70 percent in 1965. By 1988, as in the United States, slightly over three-fourths of Japanese citizens lived in urban areas.

Although cities throughout Japan increased in size as a result of industrialization, the focal point of urban growth has been in Greater Tokyo and the east coast of the island of Honshu. Founded in the twelfth century as the city of Edo, it was the capital of feudal Japan from 1603 to 1868. In 1721 Edo was already one of the world's great cities, with approximately one million inhabitants; by 1900 Tokyo had one and one-half million population. Today, Greater Tokyo has twenty-eight million residents, and the Tokaido ("east coast road") megalopolis, consisting of Tokyo, Kawasaki, Yokohama, Osaka, Kyoto, and Nagoya, has sixty million residents. This concentration of almost 50 percent of the nation's population on 1.25 percent of the total land is an inevitable consequence of topography. Japan is a mountainous country (70 percent) about the size of Montana, and its heavily populated east coast road is built on the nation's only significant, flat, coastal area.

Like Mexico City, Tokyo is the nation's cultural, economic, and political hub. Both cities have grown as a result of in-migration, and both attract approximately 1,000 new residents a day. Unlike the Mexican capital, however, Tokyo continues to grow as a result of prosperity, not poverty. Attempting to escape a life of hardship and limited opportunity, rural peasants arrive in Mexico City only to find an overcrowded metropolis with a high rate of unemployment and little opportunity. On the other side of the world, newcomers to Tokyo also encounter a crowded city, but one in which they are almost certain to find work. However, obtaining a place to live is becoming more difficult and certainly more expensive. With the decline of smokestack industries in small-town Japan, the influx of migrants to Tokyo is unlikely to subside in the near future (Smith, 1987).

Pressures on Prosperity

Japan's post–World War II economic miracle produced an affluent, Tokyo-dominated, urban society that is beginning to buckle under the weight of its own success. Unable to expand geographically, the city has experienced some of its most significant growth in recent years vertically. With the expansion and construction of 135 high-rise buildings between the economic boom years of 1960 and 1980, office space increased 450 percent. At the same time, subway lines were expanded from 43 to 197 kilometers, transforming Tokyo to what the local planning commission proudly calls a "three-dimensional city."

Unfortunately, for all of the planning, construction, technological innovation, and money, the city has not been able to overcome a number of serious growth-related problems. As noted in chapter 10, Japan has an old and increasingly aging population. In 1983, 7 percent of Tokyo's population, or 900,000 people, were over age sixty-five, with those figures estimated to be to be 12 percent and 1.5 million by the year 2000. Not only will an enormous amount of money be needed for geriatric health care, but all of Tokyo's public facilities will have to be remodeled to accommodate an elderly, more physically impaired population greater than the size of all but the world's largest cities.

Tokyo is the nerve center of an economic giant; more than four million people commute from the suburbs and peripheral areas to downtown Tokyo every day. Between 7:00 A.M. and 10:00 A.M., buses, trains, and subways are filled to three times their designed capacity as people jammed into public transportation by "pushers" uncomfortably make their way to work (Allinson, 1984). The daily round-trip commute takes two to three hours and results in the loss of well over a billion hours of productivity each year. Never-ending traffic jams paralyze the downtown area even though 46 percent of the labor force take some form of public transportation to work each day (in the United States that figure is 22 percent).

With the steady expansion of urban activities, the physical environment has taken a severe beating, and recently enacted pollution control standards have met with only limited success. For example, although the pollution of rivers has been reduced by 50 percent and the amount of carbon monoxide in the atmosphere was slashed some 80 percent between 1965 and 1980, the accumulation of nitrogen dioxide in the air doubled during that same period. As of 1979, the number of officially confirmed cripples resulting from all forms of pollution was 76,340, with unofficial estimates running as high as 200,000 (Light, 1983). Given more pollution and environmental destruction than any other capitalist country, the price of rapid economic and urban growth has been very high. Thanks to the Liberal Party's (which is really quite conservative) victory in February 1990, the pro-big-business policy of lax enforcement of pollution laws is likely to continue.

The combination of prosperity, population growth, and land shortage has produced real estate prices in Tokyo like nowhere else in the world. In one recent twelve-month period housing and land prices increased 95 percent as opposed to 7 percent in the rest of the country. As of 1987, a 720-square-foot house located an hour by train from downtown Tokyo cost $275,000; mortgages (typically fifteen and thirty years in the United States) have been extended up to sixty years. In 1989 city officials sponsored a lottery with the winners getting a chance to buy the "last affordable homes" in Tokyo. Over 34,000 people participated in a drawing for houses that sold for between $380,000 and $530,000. Apartments don't come cheap either, with three-bedroom luxury units in central Tokyo renting for $9,000 a month. Ever-increasing real estate prices also make for windfall profits. In December 1989 the Myanmar government sold 7,500 square meters of land around its downtown Tokyo embassy for $237.5 million—a sum greater than the nation's annual export revenue. A fifty-three-acre, government-owned former railroad yard in Tokyo's Ginza district is estimated to be worth up to $47 *billion*.

Although the number of housing units in metropolitan Tokyo is greater than the number of households, estimates are that three of four homes are below average standards as set by the national government. They are small and poorly built, many don't have private toilets, and virtually every house in the city is a firetrap. Nakamura and White (1988) asserted that the relatively small size of these homes is partially responsible for the fact that Japan exports more than it imports. A 750-square-foot home (in the United States the median home size in 1987 was 1,755 square feet) does not leave much room for accumulating the vast amount of material possessions we have come to consider normal. One look at an apartment complex in Tokyo with rows of washers and dryers permanently situated on an outside balcony, with long hoses extending to the kitchen, lends credibility to this perspective.

Residents of metropolitan Tokyo have one more (potential) problem that they share with people in southern California and San Francisco: they are waiting for the big earthquake that experts say is sure to come. In 1923 the great Kanto earthquake killed 100,000 people in Japan (the San Francisco quake of 1906 claimed 700 lives). As staggering as the death toll was from that disaster, the number of casualties resulting from a quake of similar magnitude in modern Tokyo would be much worse. With over a hundred high-rise buildings, land reclaimed from the sea that would sink back into the water, and tens of thousands of highly flammable wooden structures, a major earthquake in Tokyo could well be the most destructive natural disaster in the modern era. Not only would the megalopolis be devastated physically, but Japan's high-powered economy would be crippled for years.

Tokyo may well be the best example of what the world's giant cities can expect (or hope) to be like even under the most favorable economic and social conditions. The fact that almost everyone has a roof over their heads, employment is high, and crime rates are low indicate that even in a metropolitan area with a population of almost thirty million, humans can live in comfort and safety even if they must cope with an overcrowded, polluted environment. However, the list of urban problems also indicates that rapid modernization and affluence are no guarantee that these problems can be sidestepped or fixed with money alone. If the wealth of Japan is no remedy for the ills of Tokyo, what can we expect in the way of solutions to urban problems in hundreds of overcrowded, desperately poor Third World cities?

CHAPTER SUMMARY

1. The first permanent human settlements appeared about 8,000 years ago. According to the agricultural surplus theory, cities came into being as a result of a surplus of basic foodstuffs that freed people from growing their own food and allowed them to do other types of work. Central place theory argues that cities emerged because farmers needed a place to distribute their produce. Trading theory states that traders introduced new seeds and livestock that led to a successful agricultural revolution, food surplus and eventually cities.

2. By the beginning of the modern era and the birth of Christ, cities located on trade routes and important waterways were thriving in many parts of the world. Some of them had large populations even by today's standards. In the second century A.D. Rome had approximately one million people. After a long period of decline known as the Dark Ages, cities began to prosper in Europe during the Renaissance. Cities and the Industrial Revolution had a positive effect on each other, with both thriving in a period called the industrial urbanization of Europe.

3. With the Industrial Revolution, both the number and size of cities in the United States and Europe grew rapidly. People flowed into urban areas from the countryside and typically lived in hastily built, overcrowded, unsanitary apartments. Tens of thousands of immigrants from Europe also relocated to American cities in the middle of the nineteenth century.

4. Human ecologists constructed theories explaining the relationship between humans and the social/physical world they constructed, especially cities. Concentric zone theory views the city as a series of zones emanating from the center, with each one characterized by a different group of people and activity. Sector theory envisions urban areas as pie- or wedge-shaped sectors radiating outward from the central business district. According

to multiple nuclei theory, cities do not have one major center, but several nuclei or centers scattered throughout the urban area.

5. In the 1920s American cities began to decentralize as the growth of the suburbs exceeded that of the central cities. Suburbanization slowed considerably during the Great Depression and resumed with the end of World War II in 1945. White, working-class families followed many businesses and industries to the suburbs, while minority groups were left behind.

6. In the early 1970s the sunbelt began to grow for at least five reason: (1) conservative legislation and illegal workers from Mexico and Central America kept the cost of labor down making the region attractive to business; (2) industries began leaving the Northeast to escape the relatively high cost of union labor in that region; (3) local governments started subsidizing new industries by giving them generous tax breaks; (4) influential sunbelt politicians were successful in winning big military contracts and physical improvements such as highway projects from the federal government; and (5) the region benefited as the economy changed from heavy industry and manufacturing to one based on high technology and information processing.

7. According to one interpretation the success of sunbelt cities and the corresponding decline of winter cities is a temporary rather than permanent shift in the American economy. Eventually the economic fortunes of these areas will converge and even out. Another view is that economic development is always uneven, with each region of the country developing in a different manner. We are now in a period of growth that favors the sunbelt. There are signs that some winter cities are on the road back to economic recovery.

8. American cities are beset with a wide range of serious problems. Urban ghettos have the largest concentration of poor people in the country. The flight of business and industry to the suburbs and sunbelt have contributed to high rates of unemployment and poverty in many of the nation's largest cities. When jobs are available inner-city residents often lack the education and technical skills necessary to fill them. The deinstitutionalization of mental hospitals has contributed to the growing problem of homelessness.

9. Cities in Third World nations are growing much faster than urban areas in the developed world when the latter were modernizing. This tremendous growth is a product of two factors: a substantial, natural increase in urban populations (births over deaths), and unprecedented rural-to-urban migration as people leave the countryside in the hopes of finding employment and leading a better life in the cities. What they typically encounter is overcrowding, unemployment, pollution, and violence.

10. Many American cities have serious problems, and there is little hope for significant improvement in the near future. If they are to be saved and prosper once again, concerted action will have to be taken at both the individual and collective levels. The prospect of solving monumental problems in desperately poor Third World cities with unprecedented rates of population growth is not encouraging.

12

MODERNIZATION

In his book *The City of Joy,* Dominique Lapierre (1985) tells the poignant story of a poor Bengali family in India. Caught in a downward spiral of poverty and despair, sharecropper Hasari Pal loses his land, becomes an agricultural laborer, and eventually migrates to Calcutta when he can no longer find work in the village of his birth. The Pal family settles in a section of Calcutta named *Anand Nagar,* "the city of joy," by a jute factory owner who housed his workers there at the turn of the century. Home to the poorest of the city's poor, this minuscule patch of Calcutta (the size of three football fields) has approximately 70,000 residents, the densest concentration of people anywhere on earth. In the span of a few short days and less than a hundred miles, Hasari Pal, his wife, and their children have moved from the world of the old to that of the new India. They are but five of the tens of thousands who move to urban areas each year in search of food, work, and prosperity. Behind them lies a desperately poor, although stable, village existence with a pattern of social relations and values that have remained relatively unchanged for centuries. Before them looms Calcutta, a giant, overcrowded city filled with people, places, and things about which illiterate peasants know little if anything. So begins the process of modernization for five people, a process that is not slow, smooth, and uniform, but rapid, gut wrenching, and unforgiving—adapt and survive, or die.

As we saw in chapter 1, the word **modernization** describes the transformation from a traditional, usually agrarian society to a contemporary, industrially based state. Inasmuch as modern societies like the United States and Japan are wealthy, modernization research has focused more on economic growth than on the development of other institutions and patterns of behavior in society. The economic development of today's now rich countries (NRCs), as well as that of less developed countries (LDCs), is related to four primary aspects of industrialization (Harper, 1989): (1) economic growth through transformations in energy (from human and animal power to machines), (2) a shift from primary production (agricultural and mining) to secondary production (manufacturing), (3) growth in per capita income, and (4) an increase in the division of labor (diversification of occupations).

Industrialization is a powerful mechanism of change affecting the intellectual, political, social, and psychological aspects of society. In turn, industrialization is itself affected by these same dimensions. Once the process of change and development is accelerated by a momentous incident (e.g., war) or a continuing factor (e.g., industrial revolution), the major institutions, values, and patterns of behavior become both independent and dependent variables, causing and being affected by change. Modernization, therefore, is a very uneven process of development, with some institutions changing faster and more than other institutions, social values, and modes of interaction to which they are related.

Social scientists became interested in modernization in the aftermath of World War II. The new world order dominated by American economic and military power, coupled with the crumbling of European colonialism, prompted researchers to take a closer look at the Third World. They wanted to understand the modernization process that was beginning to unfold in many poor, primarily agricultural nations. Interest in Third World development is also linked to a rediscovery of classical nineteenth-century sociological theories dealing with widescale social transformation (Evans and Stephens, 1988). In this chapter we examine both classical and contemporary theories of modernization, and discuss the most significant problems that developing nations must overcome if they are to make the change from traditional to industrial states.

QUESTIONS TO CONSIDER

1. What are the personal qualities and characteristics of modern humans?
2. How did the biological sciences influence nineteenth-century theories of social change?
3. What do evolutionary and modernization theories have in common?
4. What are "mechanical solidarity" and "organic solidarity"?
5. What are the major criticisms of modernization theories?
6. What assumptions does world system theory make about the modern world?
7. What is neocolonialism and how does it affect economic development in Third World nations?

8. What is the difference between fast and slow economies?
9. What is devolution and how is it related to violence in Third World nations?
10. What are some of the major problems confronting developing nations today?

 Modern Man

Discussions of modernization are usually focused at the institutional level, that is, the transformation of a society's political, cultural, and, especially, economic organizations. However, the fundamental unit of change in any group or social system is the individual. So before launching into an investigation of how and why modernization occurs, we have to determine in what respects modern people differ from their traditional counterparts, and under what circumstances this change from the old to the new takes place.

Alex Inkles (1973) identified a set of personal qualities he believed accurately characterize modern individuals. The most important of these are (1) openness to new experience both with others and with ways of doing things, (2) increasing independence from traditional authority figures such as parents and priests, (3) belief in the power and effectiveness of science and medicine, with a corresponding disregard of a fatalistic view of life, (4) ambition for oneself and one's children to be upwardly mobile and successful, and (5) a strong interest in community activities as well as local, national, and international affairs (see Figure 12.1).

To see if the process of modernization had an effect on the values and behaviors of people in developing nations, Inkles and his research assistants (1973) interviewed

---

FIGURE 12.1 Selected Abbreviated Questions from Scales Measuring Individual Modernity (italic alternative indicates modernity)

1. What is the ideal amount of schooling for children like yours?   low to *high years*
2. If a boy suggests a new idea for farming, should father *approve*/disapprove?
3. Which should most qualify a man for higher office?   *education*/popularity/family/tradition
4. One's position in life depends on fate always to *own effort always.*
5. Do you prefer a job with *many*/few/no responsibilities?
6. Will we someday understand nature?   *fully*/never can
7. Limiting the size of families is *necessary*/wrong.
8. Do you consider yourself primarily a citizen of a *nation*/region/state/city?
9. How often do you get news from newspapers?   *daily*/often/rarely/never
10. Would you prefer a rural life/*urban life*?
11. Can a person be good without religion?   *yes*/no
12. Would you choose a spouse to suit your parents always/*yourself always*?

Source: Adapted from Alex Inkles, 1983, *Exploring Individual Modernity.* New York: Columbia University Press, pp. 78–82.

The parents of these school children in Peru hope that a good education will lead to a higher standard of living for their sons and daughters. However, if jobs are not available when these children become young adults, their frustration could turn to anger and violent revolutionary behavior.

6,000 people in Argentina, Chile, India, Israel, Nigeria, and East Pakistan (now Bangladesh). They concluded that people in these countries did in fact take on the above characteristics, and the term "'modern man' is not just a construct in the mind of social theorists" (p. 345). Indeed, the personality and behavioral characteristics of modern individuals were the same in all six societies. On the basis of this finding Inkles speculated on a psychic "unity of mankind." "There is evidently a system of inner, or what might be called structural, constraints on the organization of the human personality which increase the probability that those individuals—whatever their culture—who have certain personality traits will also more likely have others which 'go with' some basic personality system" (p. 347). Data also indicated that formal education was the most powerful variable in determining how an individual scored on the modernization scale. School, therefore, is not only a place where individuals learn a set of facts and skills, it is also an institution that changes the way people think of themselves, others, and the society in which they live.

The factory was the second most important organization in changing a person's personality or character, "serving as a general school in attitudes, values, and ways of behaving which are more adaptive for life in a modern society" (Inkles, 1973, p. 348). Significant changes arising in the workplace even occurred when individuals were adults. Commenting on the findings of Inkles et al., Robert Lauer (1982) noted that no claim is made that modern societies make modern individuals or vice versa. "Rather, there is interaction with individual modernity facilitating societal modernity and, in turn, societal modernization generating greater numbers of modern individuals" (p. 103).

Modernization and Religion

Another important area of individual and societal change in the transformation from a traditional to modern world view is the role of religion. Sociologists have long known that as societies modernize they become increasingly secular. **Secularization**, as discussed in chapter 9, is the process whereby worldly institutions and values become more important than religious institutions and values. In a secular society where rational thought is paramount, people believe they not only can understand their world in terms of the biological, physical, and social sciences, but that they can (within limits) change and control that world. Although religion does not disappear in secular societies, people are less likely to resign themselves to fatalistic attitudes often associated with religious views, that the world and everything in it is a result of God's will and cannot be changed.

Theologian Harvey Cox (1965) viewed secularization as an inexorable "historical process, almost certainly irreversible . . ." (p. 20). Peter Berger (1977), however, flatly rejected this notion, arguing that a secularized "modern consciousness" is not superior to a traditional religious orientation, nor is the process of secularization associated with modernization irreversible. In a similar vein, Joseph Gusfield (1967) did not believe that modernity necessarily weakens tradition. In fact, the technological consequences of increased transportation and communication can facilitate the spread of ideas and influence of great religious traditions. In India, for example, movies have made Hindu teachings more accessible to millions of illiterate and semiliterate peasants, and railroads have facilitated pilgrimages to distant shrines and holy cities.

Inkles presented convincing evidence that an individual's world view can be transformed from a primarily traditional to a modern perspective. Gusfield, however, maintained that some traditions (e.g., religious beliefs and practices) are not easily eradicated by the forces of modernization. On the contrary, development may even strengthen some aspects of long-established customs. Thus it is a mistake to view societies as either traditional or modern; rather, all societies, even the most technologically advanced, are a blend of the old and the new. The question for developing countries is which traditions will fall by the wayside and which will endure and, perhaps, be made stronger by the modernization process.

 MODERNIZATION THEORIES

Evolutionary Models

Theories of modernization that attempted to explain the industrialization and development of Africa, Asia, and Latin America were directly related to nineteenth-century evolutionary explanations (Applebaum, 1970). These, in turn, were influenced by Darwin's monumental works, *On the Origin of Species* and *The Descent of Man*. The founding fathers of sociology reasoned that if biological laws could explain the evolution of animals (including humans), an identifiable set of social laws must be responsible for the development and progress of human societies. Much of the work of this period was an attempt to discover and articulate these "social laws." Not only did nineteenth-century sociologists incorporate much of the philosophy of the biological sciences (the search for laws, emphasis on experimentation and observation), but they also began to think of society as a living organism. Using an organic analogy, they viewed society as an organism that continually develops and matures as it passes or grows through a number of stages. Cyclical theorists eventually added stages of decay, decline, and death to their grand schemes of social change (Applebaum, 1970).

Auguste Comte and Herbert Spencer   Auguste Comte believed that societies evolved as they passed through three stages, and that their development was "natural and unavoidable." Societies invariably change because of the human being's instinctive quest for self-perfection. This evolutionary movement toward a final state of perfection was smooth and uniform. Comte viewed society as "the Great Being" that became increasingly complex, interdependent, and subject to central authority (Applebaum, 1970, p. 210).

English sociologist Herbert Spencer depicted societies as passing through a series of stages as they became increasingly complex and interdependent. Depending on the presence or absence of external conflict, they were either militant or industrial, in response to their social and natural environments (Coser, 1971).

Ferdinand Tonnies   For Ferdinand Tonnies, the two societal types were gemeinschaft and gessellschaft. Gemeinschaft, or community, denotes societies that are informal, traditional, and based on primary as opposed to secondary relations. Family and kinship relations are paramount, and social control is a function of shared values, norms (folkways and mores), and religious beliefs (Martindale, 1981). Gessellschaft means association or society and refers to relations that are, "contractual, impersonal, voluntary and limited" (p. 98). These large, urban societies are dominated by economic institutions and the quest for material success. The principal forms of social control are public opinion and the law. Tonnies predicted the rapid demise of gemeinschaft societies and the corresponding ascendancy of gessellschaft ones. This troubled him, as it could lead to the death of culture itself if some gemeinschaft traditions were not kept alive.

Emile Durkheim   Durkheim, as you will recall, was concerned with the social and psychological factors that bonded individuals and groups together to form a common entity, or society. In societies characterized by "mechanical solidarity" with a minimal division of labor and little role specialization, people share a common world view or "collective conscience" (Durkheim, 1933, originally 1895). Lacking an opportunity for individual experiences, members of society are bound together by their sameness and devotion to common values. The polar opposite "organic solidarity" is found in large, complex societies with a significant division of labor. Specialization in the workplace means that people have different experiences and are less likely to view and interpret events in the same manner. In societies of the organic type (the modern world), the "individual conscience" is well developed, resulting in fewer shared values. Social solidarity, therefore, is a function of mutual dependence: people need the skills and services that others provide in their daily lives. For Durkheim, a growing population and the corresponding increase in interaction ("moral density") were major factors in the transition from mechanical to organic solidarity.

Impact of Classical Theorists

Nineteenth-century evolutionary thinkers like Durkheim and Spencer had a significant impact on contemporary modernization theorists. According to most of these **unilinear theories of change,** societies would undergo a similar (if not identical) set of transformations, resulting in the same end product: the modern industrial state. Modernization was also considered a universal and highly predictable event (Applebaum, 1970). Writing in the evolutionary tradition, contemporary sociologist Neil Smelser (1973) saw modernization primarily in terms of economic development. Notice the dual-stage model implicit in his view of the "technical, economic, and ecological processes frequently accompanying development" (p. 269). In other words, development is the transition from traditional societies (stage 1) to modern societies (stage 2) on four dimensions. Concerning technology, a change occurs from the simple and traditional toward the use of scientific knowledge. In agriculture the transformation is from subsistence farming to specialization in cash crops and the use of wage labor for agricultural work. In industry the transition is from human and animal power to machines for the purpose of mass production and making a profit. Demographically, the movement is of people from farms and villages to urban centers.

These processes have a significant impact on the entire society, and one of their results is that human groups become increasingly differentiated; that is, there are more specialized and "autonomous social units." For example, education is no longer carried out informally by the family but is conducted in schools by trained professionals. With modernization and the expanding division of labor, a highly specialized system of education is necessary to train doctors, lawyers, and engineers, as well as workers in the hundreds of other occupations that make up the industrial workforce. This increased specialization and differentiation renders the "old social order" or patterns of integration obsolete.

In Durkheim's terms, integration has changed from "mechanical" to "organic" solidarity. Social cohesion is now more a matter of mutual need than of shared values.

Smelser cautioned that the transformation from a traditional to modern society does not occur without paying a price. Social disturbances such as "mass hysteria, outbursts of violence, and religious and political movements" (1973, p. 279) reflect the unevenness of large-scale social change. These disturbances also occur because people are fearful of new social arrangements or have a vested interest in maintaining the existing system of stratification.

Rostow's Take-Off Model

One of the more influential theories of modernization was economist W. W. Rostow's (1962) multistage take-off model. He compared economic development to an airplane moving down the runway building up speed and momentum as it prepares to take off, or, in the case of a developing nation, reaches a point of self-sustaining growth (Harper, 1989). Rostow delineated five stages of economic development culminating in a successful take-off.

1. *Traditional setting*　Using traditional technology the economy has a limited potential for production; there are large subsistence sectors and few developed markets.
2. *Preconditions for growth*　There is widespread desire for growth, a degree of mass literacy, and a central government. Of crucial importance is the development of an infrastructure that will support economic expansion (communications, transportation, banking, investment, credit systems).
3. *The take-off*　In this stage, industrial technology develops rapidly in a few economic sectors (typically agriculture or mining), and between 5 and 10 percent of the gross national product is reinvested in economic growth.

4. *The drive to maturity* High technology is applied across many sectors of the economy.

5. *The mature industrial economy* A diverse mass consumption economy develops.

Figure 12.2 shows stages 3 through 5 of Rostow's model of economic growth for twenty countries. The gap between stages 4 and 5 for Great Britain, France, Germany, and Russia indicates that economic development was halted during World War I. Sim-

FIGURE 12.2   The Final Three Stages of Rostow's Model for Economic Development from Twenty Selected Countries

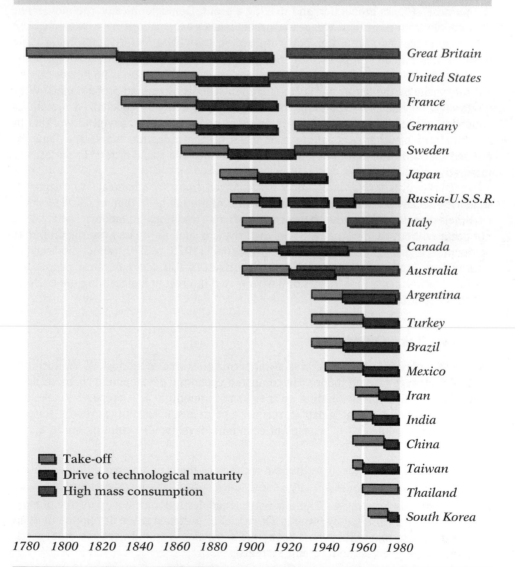

Take-off
Drive to technological maturity
High mass consumption

1780 1800 1820 1840 1860 1880 1900 1920 1940 1960 1980

Source: From *The World Economy: History and Prospect,* by W. W. Rostow, p. 51, Austin: The University of Texas Press, 1978. By permission of the author and the publisher.

ilarly, the gap between these same periods in Japan, Russia, and Italy shows that development stopped during World War II. The time lost by Japan (roughly twelve years) during and after the war make that country's economic ascendancy over the past thirty-five years even more remarkable. Note that the take-off period for Iran, India, and the other developing nations in the postwar era is relatively short compared to the same period for Great Britain and other now rich countries. This is partially due to the fact that industrial technology did not have to be developed anew. Rather, existing industrial hardware and technological know-how could be incorporated and readily used.

Criticisms of Evolutionary Models

Evolutionary models (including Rostow's multistage explanation) have expanded our knowledge and understanding of the modernization process, but they are not without shortcomings. The most damaging criticism is that they are long on description and short on explanation. In other words, they do a good job telling us *how* the process of modernization takes place and unfolds, but not *why* it occurs in the first place. Sociologist Alejandro Portes (1976) suggested that these theories "beg the entire question" (p. 64) of large-scale (macro) social change. For example, they do not tell us why social transformation happens in some societies and not others, why differentiation takes place at various rates, and if and when the process can be reversed. Another fundamental criticism is that change is generally viewed as smooth and gradual. However, a cursory view of development in many (if not most) Third World nations reveals that modernization is anything but slow and even; rather it is a process fraught with strife, conflict, and, too often, the loss of life. These evolutionary/modernization theories also ignored the possibility that patterns of development in the twentieth century were distinctly different from those experienced by NRCs when they began industrializing over 150 years ago (Evans and Stephens, 1988).

Yet another shortcoming of these theories is that their explanations often seem "actorless." The processes of "urbanization, bureaucratization, and the other components of modernization appeared driven by inexorable forces rather than by the interests and actions of states, classes and other social actors" (Evans and Stephens, 1988, p. 739). Just as evolutionary/modernization theories tend to ignore the actions of human beings as causal agents of change, they also remove societies from the international context within which they exist. That is, they focus almost exclusively on the *internal* mechanisms of social change and neglect the "interrelationships among nations and the impact of such factors on the internal structures of each" (Portes, 1976, p. 66).

This leads to a final criticism, that evolutionary/modernization theory is ahistorical. Social change, especially something as far-reaching as modernization, does not happen in a sociohistorical vacuum. Although many similarities across nations exist regarding their social development, each country has a unique history that must be taken into account in explaining and predicting the country's developmental path. Whereas sociology attempts to make general statements about a particular category of events (e.g., modernization), and some things may be said about all of the countries in this category (energy changes from muscle to machine power), we cannot ignore the fact that a given country's cumulative experience will affect its path and speed of modernization. For example, we need consider only India, Iran, and Nicaragua to see how each nation's individual historical record has affected its development process.

In spite of these many criticisms, evolutionary/modernization theories cannot be dismissed en masse. As we have seen, they were an integral part of the development of sociology. Pioneering sociologists were spectators during the first wave of industrialization that began in the nineteenth century and sought a general, theoretical explanation for the changes they were witnessing. Flawed as they were, these early theories demonstrated that systemic social change could be explained only from a scientific perspective that considered the interplay of all the major institutions in society. Such a discipline was sociology. In the post–World War II era, modernization theorists challenged social scientists and historians to explain development that was occurring in the so-called Third World. This helped broaden the base of inquiry as researchers focused their attention on the developing as well as the developed nations of the world. A renewed interest in the process of development partially set in motion work by sociologists with a completely different view of modernization: world system theory.

 ## WORLD SYSTEM THEORY

At the end of World War II, most African and Southeast Asian countries were members of European-dominated colonial empires. In the aftermath of a war that took such a heavy toll in lives and money, even victorious nations like England and France were unable and/or unwilling to put down movements for independence sweeping across their colonies. The eventual success of these movements resulted in a heightened awareness and concern in the United States regarding the future of Third World nations. A major worry was that these newly independent states would turn communist. The Cold War of the 1950s saw the world divided into two hostile camps: East and West, communist and capitalist. To keep former colonized nations political allies of the West and ensure that economic development followed a capitalist as opposed to socialist path, a substantial amount of foreign aid was pumped into Third World countries. According to Chirot (1977, p. 3), this aid was to accomplish four goals:

1. Outdated traditional values in Third World countries that inhibited savings, investment, and a rational organization of the economy had to be changed.
2. Antiquated, insufficiently democratic political structures had to be modernized, to encourage progress and effectively undermine leftist revolutions.
3. People had to be trained in order to provide an adequate supply of skilled labor and managerial personnel.
4. Money in the form of loans and gifts had to be made available to speed up the development process.

These goals were based on a fundamental assumption of evolutionary theory; that is, modernization occurs gradually and uniformly along a relatively smooth path. Post–World War II theorists and policy makers assumed that the realization of these goals would accelerate the development process. They believed that money and technical assistance from the United States would prime the modernization pump, and economic development would quickly come pouring out.

But the water never did flow, and the plight of many Third World countries did not improve; on the contrary, in some the conditions deteriorated. So what went wrong? A new generation of scholars called world system theorists argued that the fundamental assumptions of modernization theory were wrong, and that the theory totally ignored

According to world system theory, U.S. foreign policy (including military deployment and intervention) is designed to help American based multinational corporations maximize profits in Third World countries. (Gary Huck. Reprinted with permission.)

the destructive side of capitalism (Apter, 1986). They offered an alternative view of the development process based on a new interpretation of history. This particular view of modernization, therefore, is as much an interpretation of history as it is a sociological theory.

Immanuel Wallerstein and His Followers

Foremost world system theorist Immanuel Wallerstein made three assumptions about the modern world (Harper, 1989). First, since approximately 1500, the modernizing countries of Europe had contact with most of the nations of the world, with contact after 1800 taking the form of colonial empires and colonized nations. Second, after 1900 these empires gradually dissolved, although they maintained control as a result of their domination of world trade. Third, in the contemporary world, global economics are dominated by an interdependent, capitalist *world economic system* of trade and investment.

The colonial periods outlined in the first two assumptions are of crucial importance to an understanding of **world system theory** (WST) and require additional explanation. Before proceeding with this explanation, however, we must examine the international stratification system from the WST perspective. A central component is the Marxist notion of classes and class conflict; that is, capitalist societies consist of two antagonistic groups or classes, the bourgeoisie and the proletariat. WST extended this notion to a global level and, in a sense, viewed the world as one large, interrelated, interdependent society with upper, middle, and lower classes. On the global level, however, classes are not made up of groups of people, but of countries. The international upper class is called the **core,** the lower class the **periphery,** and the international middle class is known as the **semiperiphery** (see Figure 12.3). The result of this stratification is an international division of labor where lower-class countries work at the least desirable jobs for low wages and enrich upper-class societies.

FIGURE 12.3   The Capitalist World System

THE CAPITALIST WORLD SYSTEM IN THE EARLY 1900s

Core societies were industrial, economically diversified, rich, powerful nations relatively independent of outside control. They were the United Kingdom, Germany, United States, and France.

Lesser core societies were not as powerful or as influential as the major core nations, including Belgium, Sweden, The Netherlands, Denmark, and Switzerland.

Semiperipheral societies were midway between the core and the periphery. These nations were trying to industrialize and diversify their economies, and were not as subject to outside manipulation as peripheral societies. They were Spain, Russia, Austria-Hungary, Japan, and Italy.

Peripheral societies were economically overspecialized, relatively poor, and weak societies subject to the manipulation or direct control by the core. The rest of the world made up these societies.

THE CAPITALIST WORLD SYSTEM TODAY

Core societies are the United States, Western Europe, Japan, Canada, Australia, and New Zealand.

Semiperipheral and peripheral states make up the rest of the world. These categories are not as sharply defined today as they were at the beginning of the century. They include some oil-rich countries and newly industrializing states, as well as nations that are poor but increasingly important regional powers because of their large populations. These countries are relatively independent of the core. Examples are Saudi Arabia, India, Iran, Turkey, Israel, Indonesia, Mexico, Argentina, Egypt, Taiwan, South Korea, Singapore, and Hong Kong.

Truly peripheral societies are peripheral in the old (1900) sense of the world. Today they include communist as well as capitalist countries. Most of sub-Saharan Africa, smaller countries of Latin America and the Caribbean, and some south and Southeast Asian nations are in the group.

Source: Adapted from Daniel Chirot, 1977, *Social Change in the Twentieth Century.* New York: Harcourt Brace Jovanovich, pp. 24–25; Daniel Chirot, 1986, *Social Change in the Modern Era.* San Diego: Harcourt Brace and Jovanovich, pp. 232–233.

But how did this international system of stratification come about? According to WST, the answer is colonization. Bergesen (1980) posited that "formal" core domination of the periphery occurred in two waves. The first wave was centered in North and South America and lasted from the sixteenth to the early nineteenth century. The European powers (France, England, Spain, Portugal) destroyed or forcibly moved indigenous Indian populations to make way for settlers and institutions from the core, and the transplanting of slaves from Africa. The second period of colonization was centered in the Americas once again, as well as in India and Asia, and lasted from the late nineteenth century to the mid-twentieth century. This wave was less a matter of conquering and displacing local populations "and more a question of domination and control through political occupation" (Bergeson, 1980, p. 122). A third wave (beginning in the early 1970s) that *does not* involve formal colonial rule, but economic and arms dependence of peripheral countries, is less severe (for the peripheral nations) than the first two periods.

In 1980, developing nations spent $81 billion for armaments (18 percent of world expenditure), with much of this money flowing to arms dealers in the developed world. Countries like India and Pakistan have formidable, well-equipped armies as a result of these purchases. In 1991 a U.N. coalition of over 500,000 troops was required to drive Iraq out of Kuwait. Iraq is a relatively poor nation that used its oil money to assemble the world's fourth-largest army. That army was built through arms purchases from numerous industrial countries, especially the Soviet Union and France.

The second period of formal colonization (1870 – 1945) is the most important for our understanding of development currently taking place in Third World nations. Chirot (1977) maintained that in the 1870s, the "French, the Germans, and the British set out on a hysterical race to divide up what was left of the world (and there was still quite a lot left at that time)" (p. 49). This mad scramble for territory was a result of the mistaken belief that the world was running short of raw materials and agricultural products. However, capitalism is predicated on a profit motive requiring continual growth and expansion, so that even if the world was not running out of natural resources, colonies became lucrative areas where capital could be invested at a high rate of return. According to V. I. Lenin, the core's imperialistic ventures signaled the final, or most mature, phase of capitalism. Lenin wrote that profits in "backward countries are usually high, for capital is scarce, the price of land is relatively low, wages are low, raw materials are cheap . . ." (in Szymanski, 1981, p. 37).

The years of colonial expansion and high profits came to an end in 1910 when the world was essentially "filled up"; that is, there were no new, easy countries left to conquer and dominate. The demand for raw materials and new markets, coupled with an arms buildup that had been taking place for decades, led to a giant explosion — World War I (Chirot, 1977). After a brief postwar economic recovery, the world capitalist system was on the verge of collapse in the 1930s. The international economic system was in shambles as a result of a terrible depression that ravaged the United States and other core nations. Germany, Italy, and Japan had turned fascist, with Germany attempting to regain core status after its defeat. In World War I, Japan and the Soviet Union (semiperipheral states at the time) were also trying to get into the core. It follows from Chirot's perspective that World War II was not an ideological struggle, but an attempt to control and alter the world system. In its aftermath and the destruction of the Japanese and German empires, the United States emerged as the undisputed leader of the capitalist world system. However, revolutions in the periphery (the colonies), beginning with the independence of India in 1947, signaled that the age of imperialism was coming to an end.

As this discussion indicates, Third World nations (especially former colonies) did not benefit from contact with the West as modernization theory assumes, but took a significant economic step backward. Thus "underdevelopment in the less-developed countries arose at the same time and by the same process as did development in the richer industrial nations" (Harper, 1989, p. 212). In other words, underdevelopment and development are not two separate stages or phases as some modernization theorists believe, but two sides of the same coin. Andre Gunder Frank (in Harper, 1989) claimed, "The rich countries could not have become that way without exploiting the poor ones, so that underdevelopment is simply the reverse side of development" (p. 212). Speaking of WST, Portes (1976) stated that underdevelopment is not a backward, more primitive state prior to capitalism, but is a variant of capitalism and "a necessary consequence of its evolution" (p. 74). It is important to keep in mind, however, that in spite of the exploitative relationship between the core and periphery, the core did not cause the *initial* poverty in these countries; it existed prior to their arrival. The core did, however, "create peculiarly lopsided economies and a slow pace in economic diversification" (Chirot, 1977, p. 36).

Colonialism and Modernization

The importance of the colonial period in understanding modernization today cannot be overemphasized. According to one variation of WST, the world modernized in the latter half of the nineteenth century and the first half of the twentieth century. At the end of this period, there were economic winners and losers. The core countries obviously won, and the losing peripheral nations would never successfully transform their economies to core level no matter how long and hard they worked. One reason for this inability to modernize fully is that exploitation did not end with the demise of colonialism in the post–World War II era. Even though 100 of the world's 175 nations gained political independence between 1946 and 1987, the majority (if not all) of them

MAP 5   The Colonial World in 1914

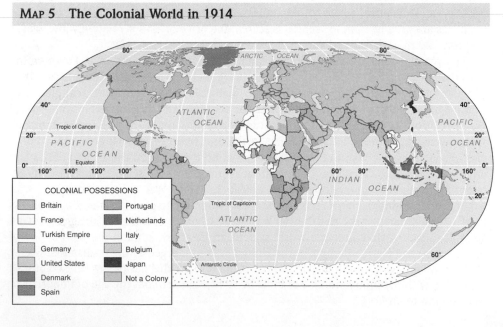

COLONIAL POSSESSIONS

Britain		Portugal	
France		Netherlands	
Turkish Empire		Italy	
Germany		Belgium	
United States		Japan	
Denmark		Not a Colony	
Spain			

remain economically dependent on industrialized states to a significant degree. For example, coffee produced in the African nations of Kenya, Tanzania, and Ethiopia, as well as most Latin American countries, is sold to a handful of multinational corporations. Inasmuch as these corporations control the price of coffee in a buyer's market, the producers have little choice but to sell their crops for whatever they are offered (Harper, 1989).

This neocolonialism in the form of economic domination by multinational corporations ensures that modernization in the Third World can never be more than moderately successful. For example, between 1970 and 1980 the flow of investment capital from the United States to the Third World was approximately $8 billion. During those same years, the return flow from the Third World to the United States "in the form of dividends, interest, branch profits, management fees, and royalties was $63.7 billion" (Parenti, 1989, p. 21). Chase-Dunn (1975) cited the slow rates of economic growth in peripheral nations penetrated by foreign capital, and concluded that countries subject to external control in the form of multinational corporations "cannot appropriate their own surplus capital for investment in balanced development" (p. 735). Based on data gathered from eighty-six peripheral and semiperipheral countries, researchers found that as the economic penetration of these countries by multinational corporations increased, their (the poor nations') "domestic well-being" (measured by caloric intake, life expectancy, infant mortality, etc.) decreased (London and Williams, 1988).

Core countries operate to further their own growth and profits, and have little interest in the economic or social development of their host nations. The presence of multinational corporations in Third World countries perpetuates a system in which the rich get richer and the poor get poorer. Parenti even rejected the label *developing countries*, stating that the term is false and misleading. Most Third World countries are neither underdeveloped nor developing. Instead, they are more impoverished than ever, and should be labeled overexploited and maldeveloped.

Overspecialization

As a result of having been developed in a lopsided manner that would benefit the needs of the core, many former colonies are economically overspecialized. Their economies are centered around the production of a few cash crops or raw materials that they trade and sell in the international marketplace. When the price of coffee, cocoa, sugar, rubber, tin, and cotton begins to fall, countries that are economically dependent on these products can experience a rapid and severe decline in revenue. For example, farmers who attempt to make up for monetary losses by growing more coffee the following year may be rewarded by even lower prices if supplies increase (other growers doing the same thing) and demand remains steady. Jacques Delacroix (1977) claimed that developed countries help keep underdeveloped nations in the position of raw material exporters by controlling their access to technology and capital from the outside world. Acting as "gatekeepers," developed nations block the importation of money, goods, and the technological know-how necessary for industrialization, and prevent poor countries from "becoming either self-sufficient or exporters of processed goods" (p. 96).

Another problem with agricultural overspecialization is that many primary food-producing countries cannot hope to see their markets expand significantly, no matter how healthy the economy of the developed world. For example, someone in the United States who sees his or her income double in the course of a year may buy twice as much stereo equipment, thereby helping the economy of some industrial nation. However, this person is highly unlikely to start eating twice as many bananas and significantly boost the earnings of a Honduran farmer. There is also the danger that an increasing number of natural commodities like rubber and hemp will be partially if not totally replaced by synthetic products (Harper, 1989). Economic overspecialization at the hands of the core during the colonial period will no doubt limit developmental possibilities for some Third World countries for many years to come.

Internal System of Stratification

One reason for high rates of poverty and misery in Third World nations is their internal system of stratification. Typical of these countries is a class structure dominated by a small economic elite whose political and financial interests are tied to the core. As described by Rubinson (1976), this class structure, "ultimately generates a very unequal income distribution when compared to the dominant countries, which have experienced just the opposite process of class formation" (p. 643). In the United States, the income ratio between the richest and poorest fifths of the population is approximately thirteen to one, and in some Third World countries the income disparity is as high as thirty to one (MacDougal, 1984). In explaining these wide (and growing) income gaps, Rubinson (1976) indicated that the lower the degree of "state strength" (the more dependent a Third World nation is on the core economically), the greater the degree of internal income inequality. From a WST perspective, the economic dependence of Third World nations not only accounts for their lack of economic development, but also explains their very unequal distribution of income and wealth.

Criticism of World System Theory

A theory as all-encompassing and ruthless in its assessment of capitalism as WST is not without critics. Carlos Rangel (1989) maintained that even the poorest and most backward countries in the world have progressed as a result of international capitalism. They are better off "in measurable indexes of economic growth, public health, education, consumption, and better off in something not measurable but essential: spiritual tone, the condition of being awake, alert and demanding" (p. 31). Rangel cited the four "little dragons" (Japan is the big one) of the Far East—South Korea, Singapore, Taiwan, and Hong Kong—as benefiting significantly from contact with capitalist countries.

Thomas Sowell (1983) claimed that explanations of colonial and neocolonial exploitation for underdevelopment beg the central question of why these countries were poor in the first place, long before the arrival of the European powers. Even if colonialism is a major factor in underdevelopment, how long can this explanation (excuse?) be used? South and Central American countries have been free of their colonial masters for over 150 years, yet remain relatively poor. Sowell and others reasoned that the sad state of affairs in so many Third World nations is more a factor of internal problems (e.g., inefficient, corrupt governments) than of external exploitation. Whereas WST is correct in its criticism of modernization theory for neglecting a country's ties to the outside world, it errs in the opposite direction by not taking into consideration numerous internal mechanisms of change. Finally, WST is criticized from a scientific perspective. Because it is not made up of interrelated propositions, it cannot be tested easily. Rather, it is a grand historical vision, a sociohistorical model meant to apply to a plurality of situations. It is a catchall explanation for everything that is wrong with the Third World.

Regardless of the validity of these criticisms, WST has made valuable contributions to our understanding of the modernization process, especially the relationship between developing and developed nations. It rejected the assumption of modernization theorists that increased contact between the core and periphery would further development in the periphery. Although the idea that contact between rich and poor nations is *always* to the detriment of poor nations may be equally false, WST was correct in calling for a careful examination of this relationship. Unlike modernization theories that view internal class struggles as minor aberrations in need of "adjustment" (Evans and Stephens, 1988), WST correctly points out that these antagonistic relationships are *long-term* affairs with major political, economic, and social consequences for all concerned. The theory examines the modernization process in the real world of continuing competition, conflict, and violence, both domestically and in the international political-economic arena.

THE NEW GLOBAL ECONOMY?

Two observers of economic and political change at the international level predicted a potentially bleak future for many developing nations in a new global economy. With the demise of communism in Eastern Europe (and quite possibly in the Soviet Union), Alvin Toffler (1990) believes the post–World War II division between capitalism and

These young Chinese women work for a large toy manufacturer based in a developed nation. World systems theorists would view this arrangement as economic exploitation—poor people working for low wages because of high rates of unemployment, underemployment, and population growth in their country.

OURSELVES AND OTHERS
The Trials of a Poor Peasant Family

Abu and Sharifa live with their six children in a one-room bamboo house with broken walls and a leaky straw roof. They are poor peasants, and year by year they are becoming poorer.

"I wasn't born this way," says Abu. "When I was a boy I never went hungry. My father had to sell some land during the '43 famine, but still we had enough. We moved to Katni when he died—my mother, myself, and my three brothers. We bought an acre and a half of land. As long as none of us brothers married that was enough, but one by one we married and divided the land."

"I was young," recalls Sharifa, "and I worked very hard. I husked rice in other women's houses to earn money, and finally I saved enough for us to buy another half acre of land. But my husband's mother was old and dying, and he wanted to spend my money to buy medicines for her. He threatened to divorce me if I didn't give him the money, so I gave in. The money was wasted—she died anyway—and we were left with less than half an acre. Then the children came. Our situation grew worse and worse, and we often had to borrow to eat. Sometimes our neighbors lent us a few *taka*, but many times we had to sell our rice to moneylenders before the harvest. They paid us in advance and then took the rice at half its value."

"People get rich in this country by taking interest," Abu interjects bitterly. "They have no fear of Allah—they care only for this life. When they buy our rice they say they aren't taking interest but really they are."

"No matter how hard we worked," continues Sharifa, "we never had enough money. We started selling things—our wooden bed, our cattle, our plow, our wedding gifts. Finally we began to sell the land."

Today Abu and Sharifa own less than one-fifth of an acre of land. Most of this is mortgaged to Mahmud Hazi, a local landlord. Until Abu repays his debt, he must work his own land as a sharecropper, giving Mahmud Hazi half the crop. "I can't even earn enough to feed my family," he says, "let alone enough to pay off the mortgage."

Sharecropping is difficult. "When I work for wages," he explains, "at least we have rice, even if it's not enough to fill our stomachs. But I don't eat from my sharecropping until the harvest. To plow the land I have to rent oxen from a neighbor, plowing his land for two days in exchange for one day's use of his animals. In this country a man's labor is worth half as much as the labor of a pair of cows!"

When Sharifa can find work husking rice, she usually receives only a pound of rice for a day's labor. Often she cannot find employment. "If we had land I would always be busy," she says. "Husking rice, grinding lentils, cooking three times a day. Instead I have nothing to do, so I just watch the children and worry. What kind of life is that?" She unwraps a piece of betel nut from the corner of her *sari*. "Without this we poor people would never survive. Whenever I feel hungry I chew betel nut and it helps the pain in my stomach. I can go for days without food. It's only worrying about the children that makes me thin."

Soon after our arrival in Katni, Abu fell ill with a raging fever. For a month he was unable to work. Sharifa husked rice in other households and their children collected wild greens, but finally hunger and the need to buy medicine forced the family to sell another bit of land: three-hundredths of an acre. They slipped a little further towards total landlessness.

Six months later, in the lean season before the autumn harvest, Abu and Sharifa could not find any work. Again the family faced a crisis. "Sharifa will tell you she lost her gold nose pin," a neighbor whispered to Betsy. "It's a lie. If she had really lost it, her husband would be beating her. He sold it in the bazaar. How else would they be eating rice tonight?"

The money from the nose pin was soon gone, so one sunny afternoon Abu cut down the jackfruit tree beside his house. He had planted it four years earlier, and in another year it might have borne its first fruit. By selling it as firewood in town he hoped to get 25 *taka*. Sharifa and a young son watched as he dug up the roots, which he could also sell as fuel. "Do you know what it is like when your children are hungry?" asked Sharifa. "They cry because you can't feed them. I tell you, it's not easy to be a mother."

She brushed a strand of hair from her forehead and unconsciously fingered the small twig stuck in socialism will be replaced by a split between *fast* and *slow* economies. In fast economies, advanced technology speeds the entire business cycle from the rapid movement of investment capital to the delivery of the final product to distributors and customers. However, in the slow economies of less developed countries, "tradition, ritual, and ignorance" (p. 34) (not to mention a lack of investment capital) can reduce the production process to a snail's pace. With outdated communication and antiquated transportation systems these nations are no match for the speed and efficiency of fast economies.

Toffler used the clothing industry as an example of a changing fast-economy industry. Because fashions can change as often as six times a year, retailers do not want to risk being stuck with big inventories. This means that manufacturers have to be able to respond quickly with new styles, colors, and sizes if they are going to fill the orders of merchants who want to meet the demands of their customers. The problem is that Asian suppliers 10,000 miles away require as much as three months' notice to make these changes and deliver their products to the United States. To reduce this increasingly unacceptable time lag, one major U.S. shirt maker recently transferred 20 percent of its production back to the United States after fifteen years overseas. Toffler (1990) stated that the new economic imperative is straightforward: "Overseas suppliers from developing countries will either advance their own technologies to meet the world speed standards, or they will be brutally cut off from their markets—casualties of the acceleration effect" (p. 38).

If Toffler is correct, fast economies of NRCs will severely undercut the LDCs' major asset in the world marketplace—cheap labor. Whereas South Korea, Hong Kong, Taiwan, and Singapore were able to launch economic development successfully on the backs of their citizens working for low wages, countries like Mexico that are currently using this same strategy are less likely to see it produce big dividends in the future. (Mexico should be less affected because of its proximity to the United States.) Another long-standing source of foreign capital for LDCs, natural resources, may also be dwindling in an era of high oil prices (which can make the price of shipping very expensive), the use of synthetic materials, and resource conservation. A report from the International Monetary Fund revealed that Japan consumed only 60 percent of the resources in 1984 that it did in 1973 to produce the same volume of industrial output.

One partial solution to these growing and potentially disastrous problems is for LDCs to invest in weather satellites, genetics, and new technology in an effort to develop their neglected, backward agricultural sectors (Toffler, 1990). Besides being able to feed growing populations, money now leaving these poor nations to buy foodstuffs could be used for indigenous economic development. Emphasizing agricultural development would also slow rural-to-urban migration and help alleviate some of the horrendous problems afflicting Third World cities.

Electronic Imperialism

David Lyon (1988) concluded that as NRCs become "information societies" in the postindustrial era, the wealth gap between the rich and poor nations of the world will increase. To use Toffler's terminology, fast societies will increasingly dominate the slow societies as we enter a stage of *electronic imperialism.* Just as Third World countries lagged behind the developed nations for approximately 200 years in the industrial era, they will fall even farther behind as a result of the information revolution ushered in by high technology and extremely sophisticated computers.

According to Juan Rada (in Lyon, 1988), inasmuch as an information society (fast-economy) is "the *consequence* of development, not its *cause*" (p. 109), many LDCs are in a no-win situation. In other words, some sort of a quick technological fix in the form of an infusion of high technology will not work. Rada argued that information technology can be successfully applied only to already existing manufacturing plants, offices, and services. Where these plants do not exist, or exist in some rudimentary form, space-age technology is useless. The idea that LDCs can use information technology to "leapfrog industrial development is thus mistaken" (Rada, in Lyon, 1988, p. 109).

Electronic imperialism will also have significant cultural affects. As of 1988 about eighty corporations controlled 75 percent of the international communications market (Lyon, 1988). This means that the Western world view in the form of movies, television programs, and commercials "dominates the world." People clustered around the communal television set in poor Asian villages are already watching programs like "I Love Lucy" and "Miami Vice" sponsored by Pepsi Cola. Prolonged exposure to a Western consumer-oriented culture will no doubt alter their values to some extent. Millions of Third World people will be like children looking at toys through the showroom window, filled with desire for things they cannot afford to buy. This cultural imperialism could significantly devalue local traditions, especially in the eyes of impressionistic young people, and feelings of relative deprivation may eventually lead to political instability.

These pessimistic outlooks regarding the new global economy should not be surprising. The NRCs were relatively fast economies and certainly more powerful than LDCs long before the invention of computers. Sophisticated technology only makes them that much more rapid and powerful. Rather than some space-age solution to the problems of underdevelopment and the unequal distribution of wealth in the world community, fast information societies could well place many LDCs at such a significant disadvantage in the world marketplace that they will never catch up. If Toffler's global economic outlook proves to be correct, his next book may divide the world into societies that are thriving and those that are dying.

Women in the Third World

In the early 1970s a tobacco advertisement featured a fashionably dressed young woman smoking a cigarette with the caption reading, "You've come a long way, baby." The distance women (babies?) in the United States have traveled in their struggle for equality is debatable, but the journey for Third World women is just beginning. Consider the following summary statements and situations regarding females in developing nations (Sivard, 1985; Heise, 1989):

- Rural women account for more than half the food produced in developing nations, and as much as 80 percent of the food production in Africa.
- In developing countries, two-thirds of the women over age twenty-five (and about half the men) have never been to school.
- Nutritional anemia afflicts half of the women of childbearing age in developing countries, compared with less than 7 percent of women that age in developed nations.
- Maternal mortality rates are five to ten times higher in Latin American and Caribbean nations than in more developed countries.
- In Bangkok, Thailand, a reported 50 percent of married women are beaten regularly by their husbands. In Peru a woman must have the permission of her husband to act in any commercial affairs.
- In Sudan, girls' genitals are mutilated to ensure virginity until marriage.

Although women in developed nations are also exploited and physically abused by males, the rate and intensity of degradation at the hands of men is significantly greater in the Third World. For example, consider the grotesque and needless tragedy of dowry deaths or bride burning in India. At the time of marriage the bride's family pays a dowry of money or goods to the groom as part of the nuptial agreement. This practice is increasingly viewed as a get-rich scheme on the part of husbands, with young brides meeting tragic deaths if the agreed-upon dowry is not delivered (Heise, 1989). One of the most common ways of killing these women is burning them alive, later claiming the fiery death was an unavoidable "kitchen accident." The bereaved widower is now free to try for another marriage and another dowry. In 1987, Indian police recorded 1,786 dowry deaths, although a women's action group estimated that approximately 1,000 bride burnings occurred in the state of Gujurat alone.

Females are even discriminated against before they are born. Until forced to stop as a result of political pressure, an Indian sex-detection clinic (using amniocentesis) advertised that it was better to spend $38 for aborting a female pregnancy now than spend $3,800 later on the young woman's dowry. One study examined 8,000 fetuses in six Bombay abortion clinics: 7,999 were female (Heise, 1989).

Education

Although not as obvious and vicious as bride burning, discrimination in other spheres of life adversely affects millions of women in the world's poorest nations. In rural areas a young girl's labor is viewed as more important than her education. As a result, in many countries nine out of ten women over age twenty-five have no schooling whatsoever (Sivard, 1985). When Third World women are allowed to pursue an education, they are overwhelmingly channeled into traditional female majors in the humanities, education, and fine arts. Such educational deprivation not only affects each woman as an individual, but also has significant consequences for population growth and other aspects of development.

Numerous studies have shown that education is the most effective way to reduce child mortality, "not because it imparts new knowledge or skills related to health, but because it erodes fatalism, improves self-confidence, and changes the power balance within the family" (Heise, 1989, p. 41). It also follows that as child mortality goes down, the birth rate drops. In other words, as the number of children dying in the first five years of life decreases, so does the need for additional pregnancies. Educated women also want (and many have) smaller families than those with little or no schooling. For example, in Brazil, women with no education give birth to 6.5 children, whereas those with a secondary education give birth to only 2.5. Educated women are also more likely to have jobs, another variable associated with family size. A World Fertility Survey of twenty countries between 1972 and 1984 found that working women had, on average, almost three fewer children than women without jobs (*Christian Science Monitor,* 1984). Education can help break deeply rooted cultural expectations of pregnancy at an early age (under sixteen), as well as the pattern of repeated childbearing at short birth intervals.

Reproductive Capacity and Control

That women give birth is an obvious fact of life. Not so obvious, however, is the way their reproductive capacity is socially defined and controlled. In developed countries the number of children a woman has is most likely the result of a decision made jointly with her husband. In addition, although having a family may still be the most socially acceptable lifestyle in rich nations, little if any stigma is attached to being childless. Gender relations are significantly different in more traditional societies. Tens of millions of women are under enormous economic and cultural pressure to have large families. In many Asian countries, for example, a woman gains security and respect by bearing sons who will take care of her when she is old. Having daughters is preferable only to having no children at all; in Muslim societies, however, the failure to bear sons is cause for a man to consider finding a new wife.

Pregnant women in the United States are usually given special attention and thought to be particularly "cute" and feminine when they are "with child." In developing countries, however, having a baby is more likely to be a physically draining, possibly life-threatening ordeal than a time of excitement and anticipation. A pregnant woman living in a developed nation is surrounded by friends who shower her with attention. In the Third World, she is surrounded by other pregnant women who share her poverty. Numerous pregnancies over a short period of time, coupled with an inadequate diet, pose serious health problems for these women. Every pregnancy is a tremendous drain on a woman's body, requiring approximately 100,000 calories of nourishment (Sivard, 1985). Whereas it might be assumed that these women would be given nutritional priority because of their biologically demanding condition, the exact opposite is often true. In many societies it is customary for men to eat first, boys next, then girls, and finally, women. A pregnant woman residing in a protein-deficient environment is a prime candidate for malnutrition and anemia (a poverty-related disease that saps people's strength and increases their chances of becoming ill). Inasmuch as 50 percent of pregnant women in developing nations have anemia, it is not surprising that maternal mortality rates (deaths per 100,000 live births) are 370 in India, 700 in Afghanistan, and over 1,000 in parts of Africa. In Scandinavian countries, by comparison, maternal deaths range from between 2 and 8 per 100,000 births (Sivard, 1985).

Political Sphere

Politically, females have been the last major population group given the right to vote. Although they can now cast their ballot in most countries of the world, they have been effectively locked out of political office, especially at the highest levels of government, in all but a handful of nations. Where they have made progress securing fundamental political rights, they are still discriminated against on a daily basis as a result of religious and customary laws. For example, segregation based on gender is part of Saudi Arabia's legal system. Zimbabwe's constitution of 1979 outlawed discrimination on the basis of race, tribe, place of origin, political opinion, color, or creed; gender discrimination was not included. In many developing nations, women are legally denied access to land and any other income-producing property (Sivard, 1985).

Effects of Modernization

Modernization has undoubtedly been a positive force in the lives of millions of Third World women, especially in terms of education and general health care. Although they still lag behind men on most indicators of well-being, the gap is not as wide as it was just a generation ago. Development is a double-edged sword, however, with its effect on females cutting both ways. For example, in Bangladesh rural males who migrate to cities in search of employment often abandon women and children who must fend for themselves in economically depressed rural areas. Faced with the task of surviving alone in a poor village, women are often victimized yet a second time by the forces of modernization. In recent years traditional markets for domestic handicrafts have been severely undercut by mass-produced factory items. In those factories where women work beside men, they often do so for significantly less money. On returning home, these second-class citizens face another full day's work taking care of their families. Needless to say, millions of women in developed nations also work two full-time jobs, although most have the luxuries of running water, electricity, and indoor plumbing. Paul Harrison (1984) called this "double day . . . the most long-lasting of all women's oppressions" (p. 442).

In many developing nations, women are equated with beasts of burden and treated as sex objects. Some now have to contend with an additional element of sexism that emphasizes physical beauty as well as trying to meet myriad culturally defined requisites of femaleness. In Bangladesh women are being deserted by husbands in search of younger, more attractive mates (Alam, in Macionis, 1989).

Even the modernization of agriculture has left women increasingly dependent on males (Sivard, 1985). Because mechanization and training are aimed almost exclusively at men, "women and their economic functions have been by-passed by the new labor saving technology" (p. 17). Although agricultural innovations and policies are certainly not the only (or even the principal) causes of female poverty in developing nations, they have helped make women the largest group of landless laborers in the world. Even the activities of international agencies can be skewed in favor of men. In 1982 the U.S. Agency for International Development spent only 4 percent of its $1.3 billion budget for "women in development" activities.

Modernization has the capacity for doing a great disservice to already severely oppressed women. The development process not only may increase the existing disparity of wealth, status, and power between the sexes, but can function to legitimate these inequalities as well. The amount, pace, and direction of change associated with modernization can be very difficult for Third World people (as it was in the United States when we were modernizing) and for women in particular, who toil in centuries-old, male-dominated societies. If males extend and consolidate their power over females as a by-product of the development process, a significant number of women may find themselves living in societies with the material trappings of modernization, and the social, political, and economic reality of an even stronger patriarchal system.

DEVOLUTION AND THE RISE OF NATIONALISM

According to Bernard Nietschmann (1988), World War III has been fought on a continuing basis since 1948 and has already claimed the lives of millions of people. The antagonists in these "dirty little wars" are not fighting over competing political ideologies or territory, but over issues of autonomy and independence. These conflicts are centered around a process that political scientists call **devolution**—the surrender of powers to local authorities by the central government—and are often rooted in specific historical events. For example, at the Congress of Berlin in 1884–1885, a number of European powers created many of the still existing political boundaries in Africa. Unfortunately, the map makers paid more attention to natural boundaries (rivers, mountains, valleys) than they did to the sociohistorical realities of the people who inhabit the African continent. As a result of the Congress of Berlin (and colonization), more than 2,000 tribes and ethnic groups became members of political states arbitrarily created by their European masters. The consequences of this partition were felt in the years after World War II and in the demise of imperialism.

Vanquished colonial governments were often replaced by bureaucrats who showed little concern for the diverse ethnic, linguistic, religious, and overall sociocultural composition of their newly independent populations. When local officials decided that existing political boundaries should be redrawn to reflect these cultural divisions more accurately, the fighting began.

Another way of viewing this situation is that World War III is now a forty-plus-year-long second or advanced colonial revolution. The initial colonial wars led to the overthrow of foreign masters who not only dominated indigenous populations, but refused to recognize and respect their individuality. The second part of this war of independence is the continuing struggle on the part of millions of people to win their freedom from homegrown leaders who also refuse to recognize these differences and grant minority populations more autonomy or complete self-determination. Nietschmann (1988) wrote that in the years after World War II, people throughout Africa sought decolonization but were forced to settle for recolonization "with brown and black colonial rulers instead of white" (p. 88). World War III, therefore, is a struggle between nations and states.

A **state** is a political entity occupying a designated territory, with a government that has the authority and ability to use physical violence against citizens who resist its laws. A **nation** is a group of people with a common history and culture. In the Third World today, a significant number of nations are attempting to withdraw from existing states and create their own independent political entities. Of the 120 conflicts in the world in 1988, 98 percent (118) were being fought by Third World nations, and 75 percent (90) were between nations and states.

One of the most bitter nation-state confrontations was the battle between Nigeria (a former British colony) and the indigenous Biafran nation. In a three-year period (1967–1970), over one million people were killed and the Nigerian economy was reduced to a shambles from which it has yet to recover fully. That figure represents more than twice the number of fatalities suffered by American troops in World War II and Vietnam combined. In Zaire (formerly the Belgian Congo), the province of Katanga has been fighting to become a separate state since 1960. With independence in 1947, the Indian subcontinent was partitioned and the newly independent state of Pakistan created. As a result of this division, millions of Sikhs and Hindus were trapped in predominantly Muslim Pakistan, while an almost equal number of Muslims were trapped in primarily Hindu India. Almost one million people were killed in especially brutal fighting as the two groups attempted to leave India and Pakistan and join their religious brethren. Although the death toll was high, how many more people would have died in a protracted civil war if partition had not occurred? In 1971, residents of East Pakistan (whose only link with citizens of West Pakistan was their common Islamic faith) staged a successful revolt that resulted in the formation of Bangladesh. Since 1980 the Indian government has had a series of bloody confrontations with Sikh separatists who want to secede and create the independent state of Khalistan.

Nietschmann (1988) pointed out that nations fighting for independence are rarely known or identified by their real names; "instead they are referred to as rebels, separatists, extremists, dissidents, terrorists, tribals, minorities, or ethnic groups" (p. 88). For example, the Oromo in Ethiopia are called Ethiopian rebels and the five million Karen people of Myanmar are known as terrorists. Nietschmann claimed that

This rebel soldier of the Karen people of Myanmar (formerly known as Burma) has taken up arms against his government. In 1991, the Bush administration moved to impose economic sanctions on Myanmar, a nation one U.S. senator referred to as "a hell for human rights." Economic development may come at the expense of some ethnic, tribal, and religious groups in Third World countries—especially countries like Myanmar lacking democratic institutions.

in their effort to maintain and cultivate political allies, superpowers like the United States and the Soviet Union almost always side with the state in its attempt to suppress nationalist movements.

Although World War III is well under way in developing countries, industrial states are hardly immune from these conflicts. Canada was faced with demands for an independent Quebec until the *Parti Quebecois* was defeated in the 1985 provincial elections. However, the separatist movement is far from dead in Quebec, and a strong drive for independence may yet prevail. Northern Ireland has long sought sovereignty from the British Empire. The Basques of northern Spain were crushed by Franco's army in the 1930s, but some Spanish and French Basques are still fighting a sporadic guerrilla war with their respective nations. Movements for more autonomy or independence in the Soviet republics of Estonia, Latvia, Lithuania, Armenia, and Azerbaijan erupted in 1989. In Yugoslavia, Croatian and Macedonian nationalists have agitated for independence since that country was created in the aftermath of World War I. Military clashes involving Serbs, Croatians, and the Yugoslavian army in 1991 resulted in widespread violence and the destruction of property. With the changing of political and economic systems in Eastern Europe, nationalist movements are likely to emerge and gain momentum in some (if not all) of these countries as well.

We live in an era when the spirit of freedom and the drive for self-determination are especially strong. Enough nationalist movements have been successful in recent history to serve as examples for all those with dreams and visions of independence. Although the rightness or wrongness of these movements can be debated on an individual or collective basis, one thing seems remarkably clear and certain: in the short term, millions of desperately poor people on both sides of the struggle will suffer as developing countries spend badly needed funds to defeat separatist movements. At this moment in history, it is difficult to ascertain if a larger (more political states) and more fragmented Third World would facilitate or undermine modernization.

 ## PROBLEMS AND SOLUTIONS

Some of the most serious and pressing problems facing Third World countries are related to high rates of population growth and were discussed in an earlier chapter. In this final section on modernization, we will examine numerous internal and external obstacles confronting developing countries and evaluate some proposed solutions.

Corruption

Probably no government in the world is completely free of corruption, although in some societies conditions are much worse than in others. Unfortunately, residents of Third World countries who are least able to afford the monetary and psychological costs of rampant bureaucratic corruption are victimized by dishonest officials and practices on a daily basis. People are beaten down mentally if not physically, and have little faith in their leaders and institutions. As a result, modernization is severely hampered. For example, during his tenure as president of Zaire in the 1960s, Mobutu Sese Seku amassed a personal fortune conservatively estimated at $3 billion. During this same period, government officials stifled economic development by taking 20 percent of every dollar that entered the country in the form of foreign aid. As a consequence of widespread smuggling and underinvoicing, Zaire's $400 million 1977 coffee crop yielded only $120 million of revenue for the national treasury (Lamb, 1984).

Corruption is so widespread and entrenched in Mexico that ordinary citizens often refer to public officials as *bola de rateros*—"a gang of thieves." Alan Riding (1989) claimed that conflicts of interest, nepotism, and influence peddling are no longer considered wrong, and "honesty itself is seemingly negotiable" (p. 116). One politician stated that "corruption itself has been corrupted" (in Riding, 1989, p. 116), and everything from overcharging by industrialists to overcharging by shoe-shine boys is considered normal. Former president Lopez Portillo bought a $2 million villa for his mistress and constructed a mansion for himself complete with tennis courts, swimming pools, and stables (Riding, 1989).

Sixty percent of respondents to a survey conducted in Delhi, India, believed approximately half of all government officials were corrupt (Hardgrave and Kochanek, 1986). The *Hindustan Times* reported that corrupt policemen in one Delhi neighborhood collect money from shopkeepers every Saturday afternoon. No extra services are provided, and vendors who refuse to pay are harassed. Officers can make as much as 15,000 rupees (about $1,250) a month in this illegal activity (Hiro, 1976). That is very good money in a country where the per capita annual income is about $300. Two months after the assassination of Indira Gandhi in October 1985, her son Rajiv won a landslide election and became India's new prime minister. The young Gandhi (who was assassinated in 1991) promised Indians he would rid the government of corruption once and for all. However, in late 1989, V. P. Singh and the Janata Party defeated Gandhi by convincing voters that the government was more corrupt than ever. Gandhi and his Congress Party were linked to a $40 million bribe paid by Swedish businessmen in exchange for a huge weapons contract. Whether the charges were true or false, Gandhi no doubt learned that to maintain or increase his political power he had to engage in or turn a blind eye to widespread corruption. This is not to condone or excuse dishonesty; rather it is a realization that corruption is so tightly woven into the fabric of political, economic, and social life in much of the Third World that these practices will be difficult if not impossible to eradicate.

Widespread poverty does not inevitably lead to corruption, but people who live from day to day in an unstable and uncertain economic climate are much more likely to do what is necessary to survive, even if that means engaging in rule violating behavior. In societies where the majority of the population are desperately poor, many affluent people realize they are never far away from a life of poverty and misery. In societies that cannot provide people with health and unemployment insurance, welfare payments, food stamps, and so on, the temptation to get what you can when you can is no doubt hard to resist.

Economic Strategies

Evolutionary theorists argued that poor nations will follow the same path of development as the now rich societies did when they began modernizing in the nineteenth century. However, the world of the 1990s is significantly different from the world of the mid-1800s. For example, when the United States was modernizing, industry was *labor intensive* (in need of unskilled and semiskilled workers) and could soak up the millions of people who came to this country in search of employment and prosperity. Machines in giant factories were operated by skilled and semiskilled workers, and tens of thousands of rapidly trained laborers performed repetitive tasks on a labyrinth of assembly lines. Today, manufacturing is very different. Industry has become *capital intensive* (requiring enormous amounts of money), and needs fewer but more highly skilled and trained workers. Most Third World countries cannot afford to build modern, technologically sophisticated factories, however. Meanwhile their young, rapidly growing, undereducated populations are streaming into cities looking for work. This all too common demographic profile of a developing nation, coupled with the realities of a high-cost, high-technology, economic world, means that Third World countries face conditions entirely different from those encountered by a modernizing United States in the 1800s.

Another economic problem facing developing nations is the enormous amount of investment capital necessary to compete successfully in a global economy. Whereas there will always be room for the relatively small investor in the international marketplace, modernization will proceed at a snail's pace if a country's industrial output is limited to low-priced goods. The success of Japan, Hong Kong, Singapore, Taiwan, and South Korea was the result of their ability to penetrate the world market for big-ticket items such as steel, automobiles, and sophisticated electronic equipment. However, the capital required to begin producing these goods is well beyond the means of wealthy individuals, or even a group of investors. Consider how much investment capital it would require to build an automobile factory and compete successfully with General Motors and Toyota. Even governments in developed countries have a difficult time generating that amount of money. For Third World countries, it's next to impossible.

Developing nations have to compete against the economic superpowers of North America, Europe, and Asia, as well as each other. When the United States was modernizing, such formidable, experienced, and well-financed competition did not exist. According to the "infant-industry" argument (Waud, 1980), the difficulties inherent in competing with well-established economic nations can be partially alleviated. Fledgling companies in developing nations can be protected at home as well as given a degree of preferential treatment in the international marketplace until they can successfully compete on their own. Problems with this strategy include identifying companies that are most likely to succeed, and being able to tell when "maturity" has arrived and protectionism can be removed. Critics also question whether developed countries would support such programs, especially if their own industries are struggling or attempting to expand.

Regardless of what economic strategies are adapted, it is hard to believe that countries like Bangladesh or Chad will someday be as economically developed and successful as the United States and Japan. On the other hand, it is not a foregone conclusion that even the poorest countries will remain in a state of chronic poverty. The future of most of these nations is likely to be one of modest, intermittent economic growth, contingent on a host of variables including population increase, the state of the world economy, and internal political stability.

Distribution of Wealth

In the chapter on population we noted that even though India exports food, millions of people in that country suffer the chronic and debilitating effects of malnutrition. Unfortunately, the ample production of wheat and rice does not translate into an equitable distribution of foodstuffs in much of the Third World. In a similar vein, Simon Kuznets (1955) maintained that a country's economic growth does not automatically translate into a uniform, improved standard of living for all concerned. He claimed that economic development initially leads to a more *inequitable* distribution of income before this trend is subsequently reversed and begins to improve. Although a number of statistical studies have supported his hypothesis, contrary findings indicate that "Kuznets' law represents more of a tendency than a deterministic relationship" (Loup, 1983, p. 117). For example, in countries like Brazil and Mexico economic growth (as Kuznets predicted) led to a more inequitable distribution of income, whereas in other nations such as Taiwan and the Ivory Coast income distribution improved.

Jacques Loup (1983) concluded that it is not rapid growth per se that leads to more inequality, but the form that growth takes, as well as the economic history of a given country. Even before Brazil and Mexico began modernizing by way of "export-oriented industrialization," they had an inegalitarian distribution of wealth. In the absence of any mechanisms to redistribute economic growth (land reform, income transfers, taxation), the existing system of inequality was simply perpetuated, if not made significantly worse.

According to Loup at least four major factors affect a country's distribution of wealth: population growth, education, agricultural mechanization, and land distribution. Rapid population growth means that agricultural land will be subdivided generation after generation, making it increasingly difficult for farmers to maintain an adequate standard of living, as well as reducing their share of the nation's growing wealth. Education (especially primary) and literacy appear to have a favorable impact on a country's distribution of income. Schooling presumably leads to increased productivity (and income) in the industrial, service, or agricultural sector of the economy. However, while the increased mechanization of agriculture may lead to higher yields of food, it displaces workers and contributes to a nation's unemployment. Mechanized agriculture also has the adverse consequence of pushing unskilled peasants off of the land into already overcrowded cities.

Land ownership is another important factor in the distribution of wealth in developing nations that are, by definition, still dependent to a large extent on the agrarian sector of their economies. For example, in the years after World War II, South Korea, Taiwan, and China redistributed land to peasants to create more egalitarian societies. On the other hand, most Latin American countries have never engaged in such policies, and have, as a result, an extremely inegalitarian system of land ownership and income distribution.

The Political Sphere

Lenski and Lenski (1987) cited numerous political roads to successful development, and called modernizers "a heterogeneous lot" (p. 373). Consider the following examples. Under the leadership of Jawaharlal Nehru, India attempted a form of democratic socialism that has evolved into a mixed economy—a combination of socialism and capitalism. Until the elections of 1988 and the ascendancy of the National Action Party (PAN), Mexico had a less than democratic, one-party system. Ferdinand Marcos had dictatorial powers in the Philippines from 1973 until he was toppled in 1986 by a movement that represented a cross section of the Filipino people. Marxists such as Fidel Castro and Mao Zedong attempted to modernize their countries with varying degrees of success, and Myanmar became a one-party socialist republic in 1974.

A democratic form of government as opposed to a totalitarian system certainly makes a difference in terms of individual freedoms and liberty in a given society, but neither political orientation is a guarantee of developmental success or failure. Marxist China has made significant strides since the revolution of 1948, but Marxist Cuba has been an economic failure requiring the financial support of the Soviet Union in the amount of almost $2 million a day. Democratic India has progressed at a much slower pace than democratic Costa Rica. To be sure, a host of other variables (e.g., population growth) have to be taken into account in any explanation of relative developmental success or failure, but these countries underscore the notion that a political system in and of itself is not the crucial factor in the modernization process.

One cannot say, however, that political variables are unimportant in a country's social and economic development. According to Harper (1989), four such factors are absolutely essential if modernization is to occur. The first is *political stability.* A climate of civil wars, revolutions, and palace coups can only undermine the modernization process. Not only does conflict drain a country's treasury and resources, but people preoccupied with their own safety and well-being are less likely to invest sizable amounts of time and energy to any aspect of development. In addition, countries involved in internal or external conflict are not likely to attract foreign investment or multinational corporations. Modernization was stalled in Bangladesh between 1975 and 1982 by four coups and countercoups. Little in the way of progress can be accomplished in a climate of political intrigue and uncertainty.

A second factor is that *modernization must be the government's top priority.* The main thrust of its time, energy, and resources has to be development if a nation is to make any meaningful progress. The third political necessity is the *commitment of a strong central government to intervene in virtually every aspect of the modernization process.* Economist John Kenneth Galbraith (1979) stated, "No country that has industrialized in modern times, not Japan, Taiwan, Brazil, Mexico, or Iran, has done so without intensive intervention and support by the state" (p. 115). This intervention must include (1) adequate security for people against physical threat to their property; (2) protection against excessive taxation; (3) a reliable system of roads, ports, electric power, and communications; (4) a supply of investment capital; and (5) some publicly sponsored industries that "have the peculiar merit of bringing others in their wake" (p. 115). If a country is large enough, these industries should be steel and chemicals or petrochemicals, including the production of fertilizer. The state can also shield local industries from much stronger multinational corporations, promote an aggressive export policy, and organize the usually scarce managerial and technological help so necessary for development.

Finally, only the government can ensure that economic development is directed at the many and not the few; that modernization is not a continuation of centuries-old policies by which the rich grow more prosperous and the poor become increasingly miserable and destitute. The economic miracle in Brazil did little if anything to advance the plight of that country's impoverished classes. As former Brazilian president Emilio Medici stated, "Brazil is doing well, but its people are not" (in Harper, 1989, p. 219). No government can guarantee that all members of society will prosper, but any stable regime should be able to ensure that if economic gains are made, they are shared in some equitable manner by everyone who made them possible.

The International Context

World systems theorists emphasize how vulnerable developing nations are to external events over which they have little if any control. Like all countries, these societies are part of an international economic system characterized by periods of prosperity and periods of slow growth and stagnation. Even WST's sharpest critics have to agree that the 175 nations of the world make up a global economic order of interdependent players. However, the industrially weak, economically overspecialized Third World countries are more likely to be affected (both positively and negatively) by changes in the international marketplace than are those economically diverse and industrially powerful developed nations.

During the 1960s the world economy was flourishing and many Third World nations made significant economic strides. By the late 1970s and early 1980s, however, this period of expansion was over and economic growth sharply declined. As a result of this slowdown, development was adversely affected, regardless of how well the nations' economies were structured and performing internally. For example, if the price of sugar and copper drop on the world market and developing nation X exports sugar and/or copper, that nation's economy (and people) are going to suffer. This means that whereas internal factors such as political stability and a disciplined work force may be *necessary* conditions for sustained economic growth, they are not in and of themselves *sufficient* conditions for prosperity. An international market that is buying what country X is producing at a price high enough to meet expenses, make a profit, and expand is a requisite for successful modernization.

Price of Oil   Another extremely important factor is the price of oil on the world market. In the late 1960s in southern California (at the height of the gas wars), gasoline sold for as little as 20¢ a gallon. This is indicative of the frequent observation that developed nations became economically rich and powerful on a sea of cheap oil. We all know how expensive it is to keep our automobiles running when gasoline costs $1 or more a gallon. Imagine how difficult it is for a small businessman in India, El Salvador, or Zambia to maintain his fleet of trucks when fuel is $3 a gallon. Oil is often used to fuel the large turbines that provide energy for industries in countries with few if any

These captured Iraqi soldiers in Kuwait are prisoners of war. Was the Persian Gulf War waged over democratic principles, or was it fought to keep oil flowing from the Middle East to the world's industrialized nations?

fossil fuels or hydroelectric power. A poor country that produces only a small fraction of its own fuel must spend hard-earned cash to import what it needs to survive and compete in the global marketplace. The huge price increase for a barrel of oil in 1973 as a result of OPEC's (oil producing and exporting countries) policies was a major setback for Third World nations. The same thing occurred as a result of the Persian Gulf crisis in 1990–1991.

Economic Assistance   Over the past thirty years it has become increasingly clear that some developing nations will not modernize (indeed may not even survive) without the sustained economic assistance of developed nations. In the 1960s, bankers from rich countries were rushing to see who could loan Third World nations the most money. The world economy was expanding rapidly and developing nations were making both their loan payments and economic progress. Now, after almost two decades of sluggish growth, many of these nations are unable to make good on the money they borrowed. Collectively they owe world banks over $1 trillion. Payment on the interest alone is well beyond the financial capacity of many of them, and money paid to foreign banks cannot be used for development. Third World countries find they now have to compete with newly democratic Eastern European countries and the deeply troubled Soviet economy for financial assistance. For example, Africa's problems grow more serious, but developed nations are contributing less money to its relief efforts. Some officials refer to this phenomenon as "donor fatigue" (Hiltzik, 1991).

Developing nations have also been victims of a forty-five-year superpower arms race. In a world that spends approximately $1 trillion annually for military expenditures, the amount of money allocated to foreign aid is paltry in even the best of years. In 1987 the world's military budget was equal to the combined income of 2.6 billion people (over half the population of the world) in the forty-four poorest nations (Sivard, 1987). Perhaps the much-talked-about peace dividend associated with the easing of tensions between Soviet bloc countries and Western democratic nations will mean that more funds can be diverted to Third World development. The thawing of the Cold War and redefinition of Moscow as something other than world headquarters for the "evil empire" could mark the beginning of an era when our attention and resources are directed toward alleviating some of the enormous problems facing over 80 percent of the world's population.

Sustainable Development

Since 1900, the number of people on earth has more than tripled and the world economy has expanded twenty times. This incredible growth (both economic and population) has been fueled by a thirtyfold increase in the consumption of oil and natural gas, almost all of which has been used by the developed nations (MacNeill, 1989). With approximately 20 percent of the population, rich countries consume about 80 percent of the world's total industrial productivity and natural resources. The overall environmental pollution and degradation spawned by this growth is evident in every corner of the planet.

Inasmuch as most developing nations and large sectors of primarily industrial states have resource-based economies (economies whose productivity is dependent on the use of the soil, forests, fisheries, water, and parks, and the use and export of raw materials), can all 175 nations of the world modernize without seriously (if not totally) depleting these resources? Is "sustainable development" possible? That is, can we continue to make economic and social progress and "meet the needs of the present without compromising the ability of future generations to meet their own needs"? (MacNeill, 1989, p. 157).

The problem of resource-based economies is especially serious for Third World nations (see Figure 12.4). Not only are these countries vulnerable to the vagaries of the international market because their economies are heavily dependent on a few crops and minerals, but their basic economic capital (resources) is being consumed much faster than it can be replaced. For example, twenty years ago forests covered 30 percent

FIGURE 12.4   Resource Dependence of Selected Developing Countries

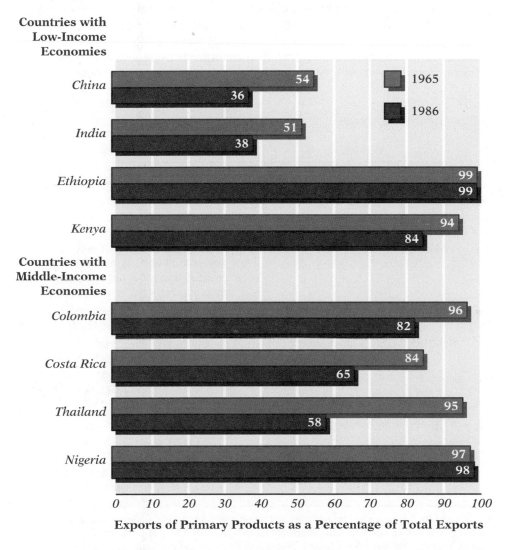

Exports of Primary Products as a Percentage of Total Exports

Resource dependence of selected developing countries is apparent in the percentage of their total exports that are "primary products" fuels, minerals, metals, and agricultural products.

Source: Adaptation of figure "Resource Dependence of Selected Developing Countries" from "Toward a Sustainable World" by William Ruckelhaus, *Scientific American*, September 1989, pp 166–175. Reprinted by permission.

of Ethiopia; today, that figure is down to between 1 and 4 percent (MacNeill, 1989). The fivefold to tenfold increase in economic activity necessary to meet the demands of a rapidly growing world population over the next fifty years will put an incredible strain on the earth's natural resources. Not only will Third World countries use these resources to meet the needs of their own people, but they will become increasingly dependent on exporting primary products to generate capital for economic development. Figure 12.4 shows how vitally important fuels, metals, minerals, and agricultural products are to these nations.

If nothing else, almost 200 years of economic development in the West clearly indicate that modernization requires an enormous amount of resources, regardless of whether a country is capitalist or socialist, democratic, or totalitarian. Even if fossil fuels could be abandoned for safe, efficient nuclear energy, the cost involved in such a transition would be well beyond the reach of Third World nations. William Catton (in Rossides, 1990) commented that developed countries became wealthy by relying on resources from "elsewhere"; today, both rich and poor nations are borrowing more and

TABLE 12.1   The Economy of Death

Amount	Paid for	Could Have Paid for
$20 million	20 Patriot missiles	Vaccines to protect all the women in Africa from tetanus
$65 million	1 E-2C Hawkeye aircraft	The estimated total amount of external funds spent on AIDS in Africa in 1990
$450	1 M-16 rifle	The training of a primary health care worker to respond to such community needs as immunization, oral rehydration, antibiotics, safe births, and postnatal care
$350 million	Two days of air combat	UNICEF's 1990–1991 budgeted expenditures (*plus* $48 million)
$12.3 billion	Noncombat costs, January–March	The total current annual amount of investment in water supply in the developing world
$500 million	One day of air and ground combat	Oxfam's operating budget—forty-six times over—for 1989–1990
$6.9 million	1 CH-47D army transport helicopter	All of Save the Children's refugee programs in Indonesia and Thailand, 1989–1990 (providing services for 25,000 people)
$20,000	1 Stinger missile	Basic medical equipment and building materials for a maternity center in Mali

Note: If you were to spend $1.2 million a day for ten years you would spend $44 billion, the estimated amount spent on the Gulf War alone (not including long-term costs of operating a base in Saudi Arabia or reconstructing Kuwait). Although the threat of a superpower war appears to have diminished, the nations of the world (including Third World countries) still have a combined annual military expenditure of approximately $1 trillion. Every dollar that is spent for arms is one dollar less that could be allocated for desperately needed projects in developing countries. This table notes just how expensive operations Desert Shield and Desert Storm were in terms of current and potential aid and programs for the developing world.

Sources: Center for Defense Information, PATH (Program for Appropriate Technology in Health), Oxfam, UNICEF, and Save the Children. Reprinted with permission from Ms. Magazine © 1991. Compiled by Julie Felner.

more resources from "elsewhen." According to one estimate, by the year 2030, 90 percent of the world's known petroleum reserves will be depleted. The modernization of Third World countries (as well as the continued development of now rich nations) not only raises questions of what *can* be done, but also of what *should* be done. For example, do we have the right to jeopardize the well-being of future generations so that we may prosper and live comfortably during our lifetime? Do the developed nations of the world have the right to ask or tell developing countries that they must conserve and not pollute, when they themselves became wealthy and powerful by freely using any and all available resources, polluting the planet with little regard for anybody or anything?

Lester Brown (in Pacher, 1987) stated that we are moving into an "extraordinarily difficult, complex period" (p. 91). The world is just beginning to wake up to the fact that economic and ecological threats to human security are even greater than the threat of full-scale military confrontation, although the costs of preparing for and wagering even limited wars are staggering (see Table 12.1). Since the economy and environment are interdependent components of the developmental process, sustainable modernization in its beginning, intermediate, and advanced stages must be the central focus of our attention as we approach the twenty-first century.

MODERNIZATION AND *MAQUILADORAS*

With the country plagued by political instability, the fifty-year period after Mexico's independence from Spain in 1821 was one of economic stagnation. Under the dictatorial regime of President Porfirio Diaz from 1876 to 1910, however, Mexico began to develop rapidly. Foreign trade increased substantially, as did foreign investments in oil and agriculture. Railroads and seaports were built, and the peso was a valued currency of trade in much of Southeast Asia. Unfortunately, this prosperity was enjoyed by only a small fraction of the population, however. By the turn of the century, 3,000 families owned half of the country while most of the remaining thirteen million people lived in dire poverty (Riding, 1989). This unequal distribution of wealth led to the Revolution of 1910.

General economic advancement was minimal until the 1930s and the administration of President Lazaro Cardenas. The popular Cardenas instituted land reforms and incorporated the country's strongest unions into the revolutionary party. His most enduring accomplishment was the expropriation of foreign-owned railroads and oil companies. In all, seventeen oil companies were nationalized, and the Mexican petroleum industry (PEMEX) was created.

After World War II, Mexico ended its inward-looking isolationist policy and began to change its economy from agriculture to industry. Between 1940 and 1970, industry's share of the gross national product increased from 25 to 40 percent. However, during this same period the population was growing at 3.6 percent per annum, forcing the government to increase spending on education and health drastically. In the 1960s the textile industry (along with others) was booming, and the country was hailed as an international model of modernization. It was a period of rapid economic growth in a prospering world economy with much talk and admiration for Mexico's development.

But once again, economic prosperity was not evenly distributed. The cities grew richer in the 1970s under President Louis Alvarez Echeverria while rural peasants languished in poverty.

Pushed by despair and pulled by the dream of monetary success, rural peasants moved to the cities, especially to Mexico City. In an effort to keep these individuals content, the government began paying farmers a higher price for food than they were selling it to the urban poor. Between Echeverria's subsidized food program, lavish spending on public works projects, and widescale corruption, the economy was in shambles in 1976 when Lopez Portillo became president.

In 1977 the government announced that vast reserves of oil had been discovered, and it appeared that Mexico's economic troubles were finally over. To get the oil out of the ground, Portillo began borrowing money from financial institutions around the world; seeing an opportunity to make a lucrative profit, bankers loaned him hundreds of millions of dollars. The oil began to flow; and, between 1978 and 1982, the country's petroleum revenue increased nearly 900 percent (*Economist,* 1989a). On the negative side, the oil boom made the economy thrice dependent (Dominguez, in Stoddard, 1987): (1) a *market dependency,* with most of the country's exports and two-thirds of its oil shipped to the United States; (2) a *regional dependency,* with a reliance on the Chiapas area for economic development; and (3) a *product dependency* (overspecialization), with most of Mexico's economic eggs stuffed in one oil-filled basket. Unfortunately, the bottom dropped out of the basket when the price of oil on the world market collapsed in 1980. This unexpected drop, combined with bad investments and mismanagement, plunged the country into an economic abyss. Loans couldn't be paid and the national debt soared. By 1989, Mexico owed the world's banks over $100 billion.

Babbit (1989) warned that if Mexico is to extricate itself from this economic crisis and continue to modernize it must restructure and pay its foreign debt, increase international trade, and encourage foreign investment. In an effort to attract outside investment, Mexico embarked on the *maquiladora* or *maquilas* program in 1965. Also known as the twin plant program, components manufactured in the United States (first plant) are shipped duty-free to a factory in Mexico (second plant), assembled or turned into a finished product (e.g., running shoes, televisions, clothing), and sent back to the United States. Customs duty is assessed *only* on the value added in Mexico, that is, the cost of the finished product minus the cost of the components. With Mexican labor costs as low as one-seventeenth of that in the United States, manufacturers can increase their profit substantially. The number of *maquiladoras* has increased from fewer than 100 in 1970 to almost 1,500 in 1990, and they are increasing at the rate of 20 percent per year. At this rate of growth, there would be over 3,700 *maquiladoras* by 1995 (Lindquist, 1989). These plants represent the fastest-growing sector of the Mexican economy. Only the petroleum industry generates more foreign capital.

Approximately 90 percent of the *maquiladoras* are American owned, although Japanese, French, Israelis, and South Koreans have invested in this industry. In 1989 the Japanese (the second largest investor) had fifty factories in Mexico. President Salinas de Gortari (elected in 1988) openly expressed his admiration for the Japanese work ethic and seems eager to attract investment capital from the Far East. For their part, the Japanese, like businessmen from other developed nations, seem eager to take advantage of Mexico's cheap labor and favorable business climate.

The *maquiladora* program has been a highly controversial issue on both sides of the border. Some see this industry as a partial solution to Mexico's unemployment problem and a major step toward modernization. Others view it as another example of multinational corporations exploiting impoverished people in the Third World. Supporters cite the following advantages:

1. In a country that must add almost one million jobs annually, these plants employed approximately 500,000 people in 1990. *Maquiladoras* created between 50,000 and 60,000 jobs a year in the late 1980s.

2. *Maquiladora* industry comprises 17 percent of the Mexican economy and was expected to generate about $2.5 billion in foreign capital in 1990 (Lowery, 1990–1991). Since 1984 it has been the second-largest source of foreign exchange after oil. As such, it is now an integral part of the economy.

3. Employees at these plants typically have high self-esteem, are generally happy with their jobs, and are more likely than millions of less fortunate Mexicans to enter Mexico's emerging middle class.

4. As employment in Mexico goes up, the number of people illegally entering the United States goes down.

5. Political stability is enhanced. People with jobs are less likely to engage in rebellious and revolutionary activities, and a stable political climate will attract even more foreign investment.

6. *Maquiladoras* allow American firms to be competitive with companies in the Far East (Singapore, Taiwan, Hong Kong, South Korea), where labor is much cheaper than in the United States.

7. American consumers are rewarded with lower-priced goods.

Opponents of the *maquiladora* industry make the following arguments:

1. For every U.S. company that builds an assembly plant in Mexico, hundreds if not thousands of Americans lose their jobs. As Middleton (1990) pointed out, however, *maquiladoras* "create jobs in the United States for custom brokers, transportation companies, accountants, lawyers, and others" (p. 6). This may be true, but it is of little comfort to blue-collar workers who see their jobs heading south of the border.

2. Mexican employees typically work for $47 a week in a border economy where food and other basic goods are often as expensive as in the United States (Satchell, 1991). Tens of thousands of people can barely get by, subsisting on a diet of tortillas and beans. Meat is a luxury consumed once or twice a month, and necessities such as eggs are often purchased by the unit. The notion that *maquila* workers are on the threshold of a middle-class life is a myth.

3. Although many plants are clean and efficient, others are hot and dirty, with temperatures sometimes reaching 110 degrees. Workers are not always protected from strenuous, potentially debilitating conditions (e.g., looking through a microscope all day) and are exposed to hazardous chemicals. Those who can no longer perform their duties because of overwork, job-related illness, or disability are simply fired.

4. Approximately 65 percent of the workers are women. Management prefers to hire women because they are easier to control than men. This is especially true in a male-dominated *machismo* society. Women are also paid less than

men, representing an even greater savings on labor costs. Jobs going to women who have not traditionally been part of the economically active population have contributed to already high rates of male unemployment.

5. Only 25 percent of *maquiladoras* are unionized. Management claims this is by choice, although many workers say they have been threatened or beaten for attempting to unionize.

6. Rural-to-urban migrants streaming into border towns like Tijuana and Ciudad Juarez have pushed those cities beyond their limits to provide adequate water, sewage, electricity, and communications services. Housing is either unavailable or too expensive for people working for low wages in *maquiladora* plants.

7. Poorly regulated plants are polluting the environment, with some of this pollution drifting over the border to the United States. In Texas more than one hundred million gallons of raw sewage combined with solvents, heavy metals, and pesticides are dumped into the Rio Grande each day from Ciudad Juarez and other Mexican border cities. One physician in Laredo, Texas, believes the Rio Grande is a "public-health disaster waiting to happen" (in Satchell, 1991). He notes the incidence of hepatitis between Brownsville and El Paso, Texas, is six times the national average. A report published by the American Medical Association in June 1990 stated the border region is a "virtual cesspool and breeding ground for disease." The AMA concluded, "Uncontrolled air and water pollution is rapidly deteriorating and seriously affecting the health and future economy on both sides of the border" (in Satchell, 1991, p. 34).

8. *Maquiladoras* are nothing more than offshore assembly plants and do little to strengthen Mexico's industrial capacity. Less than 1 percent of the components assembled in *maquilas* originate in Mexico, and less than 1 percent of the products are sold in Mexican markets (Babbit, 1989). Critics also contend that *maquiladoras* are helping create two separate and poorly integrated Mexican economies, one in the south and one in the north.

Sociologist Ellwyn R. Stoddard (1987), who studied the *maquiladora* industry extensively, concluded that it has been partially beneficial and partially destructive to Mexico and the borderlands. He notes how difficult it is to evaluate this industry inasmuch as plants, products, and working conditions have changed over the past twenty years. "Thus *what is true of the* maquila *industry in one era may not be as accurate in subsequent periods, what is true of* maquiladoras *in one product or service sector may not be representative of another . . .*" (Stoddard, 1987, p. 26, emphasis in the original).

The diversity of *maquiladoras,* coupled with lack of critical research and stories in the popular press, has given rise to views of multinationals operating in Mexico that may not be accurate. Stoddard maintained that multinational corporations in the industry have generally provided more extra-wage benefits and better worker relationships than Mexican factories. He also noted that males earn more than females because they have more technical training and work in higher-paying positions. When statistical analyses are made within occupational categories, men and women are paid identical wages. Income inequality, therefore, is rooted in the structure of Mexican society (e.g., accessibility to formal education and technical training by gender) and was not created by multinational corporations. Compared to other wages and working conditions available to women in the same locale, those in *maquiladoras* are usually better. "Only distortions induced by dubious comparisons of American working women with Mexican female *maquiladora* workers minimize these as work opportunities for women who *must* find work" (Stoddard, 1987, p. 63).

Of course, for world system theorists, providing "work opportunities for women who *must* find work" means that people have little choice but to toil for the going wage no matter how low it is. The fact that multinational corporations are "giving" Mexicans (men and women) jobs certainly doesn't justify the low wages they are being paid, even if it is more than the average individual earns. Outside the *maquiladoras,* surveys reporting that people are satisfied with their jobs may indicate only that they are relatively content compared to those who have little if anything in terms of job security, food, and shelter. Although it is certainly true that multinational corporations did not create the poverty and tremendous disparity in wealth and life chances that exist in Mexico, world system theorists would argue that they are definitely taking advantage of this situation. From a modernization perspective, the *maquila* industry is an important aspect of Mexico's industrial development. It might even be considered part of the take-off phase.

Economists Mirowski and Helper (1989) indicated that in the *maquiladoras* "Mexico has a tiger by the tail"—afraid to hold on, but equally afraid to let go. Owing the international banking community approximately $100 billion, the country must generate as much capital as possible. On the other hand, the longer it relies on multinational capital, the more difficult it will be to develop its own industrial base.

Regardless of where the truth lies in the *maquiladoras* controversy, one thing is certain: the number of factories and employees will increase in the foreseeable future. They are an integral component of Mexico's struggle toward modernization, neatly summarized by Alan Riding (1989): "The issue is not whether Mexico should develop—it must develop—but rather whether it grows, changes and modernizes in harmony with the majority of the population" (p. 371).

DISCUSSION QUESTIONS

1. What contributions did President Cardenas make to economic development in pre–World War II Mexico?
2. How has the discovery of petroleum affected the Mexican economy?
3. What are *maquiladoras* and what part have they played in the modernization of Mexico?
4. What are the advantages and disadvantages of *maquilas* for Mexican workers as well as for the Mexican and American economies?
5. What advice would you give the president of Mexico regarding *maquilas* and economic development? (Review the section "The New Global Economy?" before answering this question.)
6. Choose a developing nation in Asia, Africa, or Latin America. Go to the library and investigate what impact multinational corporations have had on that nation over the past ten to twenty years. Have these corporations helped or hurt economic development in that country? Have they helped or hurt the overall well-being of the people who work for these companies?

THE BIRTH OF AN ECONOMIC SUPERPOWER

In 1868 a fourteen-year-old boy became imperial ruler of all of Japan. Emperor Mutsuhito's reign signaled the end of the Tokugawa shogunate (1603–1867) and marked the beginning of his country's drive toward modernization. During the Tokugawa period, 250 *daimyo* ("barons") pledged their allegiance to the shogun but were allowed to rule their own domains. In the latter days of this era, cities and merchants thrived, while the fortunes of *daimyo,* the samurai, and rural peasants were in a state of flux.

In 1853 Commodore Perry opened Japan to the West, and the once powerful shogunate was unable to resist foreign intrusion. Other nations followed, and within five years Japan was forced to sign treaties with five Western powers. The decline of a warrior government and improved trade agreements, coupled with the Meiji Restoration (1868–1912), started Japan on a road to modernization that was to make it a world power in less than seventy-five years.

The Japanese were humiliated for having to acquiesce to the West. They realized how their nation lagged behind the industrial world and were determined to catch up as soon as possible (Fukutake, 1982). The Meiji Restoration was a revolution from the top as opposed to a broad-based peasant revolution from below. It was not motivated by democratic ideas of equality, fraternity, and liberty, nor was there any pretense of class struggle and a redistribution of wealth (Warshaw, 1988b). Economic development was of paramount importance as Japan's leaders understood that success in the modern world was contingent on a strong economy and a powerful military. The spirit of the time is contained in a popular phrase *fokoku kyohei* ("rich country, strong arms"). Wealth and strength were to be attained by changing Japan from an agricultural to an industrial society.

Toward this end Japan's leaders Westernized the country's system of education. By 1872 six years of school were mandatory for boys and girls. Japan sent observers to study the major institutions of the industrial powers and eventually adopted France's Napoleonic code of criminal law and Prussia's civil and commercial framework. Although many Western ideas and technology were liberally incorporated into Japanese institutions, the paramount notions of independence and individualism were rejected. On the contrary, neo-Confucionist beliefs stressing loyalty, dedication, and, above all, obedience to one's superiors and the emperor were resurrected and made into a state religion under the banner of Shintoism.

The restructuring of Japanese society began to pay dividends almost immediately. From 1859 to 1880, exports rose from $0.6 million to $25 million. World War I turned out to be an unexpected (if short-lived) windfall. While the European powers were busy fighting among themselves, their Asian customers were cut off from the normal supply of manufactured goods. The Japanese stepped in and quickly filled the void, their textile industry doing especially well, primarily at the expense of Great Britain. Between 1914 and 1918 industrial production and trade grew 400 percent; and although a country of predominantly light industry, Japan was now in the middle stage of industrialization (Masao, 1968).

This economic expansion came to an abrupt halt in the aftermath of World War I when international trade normalized and lucrative foreign markets began to contract. In 1929 a world depression began and the Japanese economy (almost entirely dependent on foreign trade) collapsed. It was during this period that the *zaibatsu* ("money cliques") began to exert significant economic and political influence. Emerging in the Meiji period, the *zaibatsu* were a group of families owning large holding companies, with close ties to the government, industry, and banking. With no middle class to speak of and most of the wealth in the hands of the *zaibatsu,* there was no one to stop the tide of militarism sweeping across the country (Warshaw, 1988b). Japan invaded Manchuria in 1931 and China in 1937. Four years later the *zaibatsu* and military reached an agreement, and the military-industrial complex that helped propel Japan into World War II was created.

The war devastated Japan. Three million people were killed, 25 percent of the buildings in major cities were destroyed, tens of thousands of people wandered the streets, and the economy was in shambles. The gross national product was half the prewar level, and industrial production was down 70 percent. During the American occupation and subsequent economic postwar recovery, the power of the *zaibatsu* was broken, trade unionism encouraged, and some farm land redistributed. Japanese leaders targeted five basic industries (iron and steel, shipbuilding, coal, power, and fertilizer) to be the foundation of the new economy; and by the end of the Korean War (1950–1953) economic conditions began to improve significantly (Frank and Hirono, 1974). Between 1953 and 1965 the nation's gross national product had an average annual gain of 9.4 percent, while the comparable growth rate for fourteen other countries was 4.6 percent. With the end of the American occupation in 1951, the *zaibatsu* once again became a dominant and controlling force in the economy.

A resource-poor country, Japan has become successful by importing raw materials, turning them into high-quality goods, and selling these products all over the world. Factories are located near seaports, reducing time and expenditure in the importation-exportation process. Between 1965 and 1980 the average annual growth rate of Japan's exports was 11.4 percent, second only to Spain's on a list of industrial market economies. Japan, however, exports approximately eight times the monetary value of products of Spain. Between 1980 and 1985 these exports increased 6.4 percent annually. In 1980 Japan had a trade deficit of $11 billion; by 1988 the trade *surplus* was $78 billion, the largest in the world. In 1986, 38 percent of all exports went to the United States, approximately the same amount that was sold to Australia, Canada, China, West Germany, Latin America, and South Asia combined (World Development Report, 1988, Table 11, p. 243). With half the population of the United States, Japan has two-thirds the gross national product of America. Although they account for only 2.3 percent of the world's population, the Japanese are responsible for 14 percent of global economic activities.

Chalmers Johnson (in Fallows, 1989, p. 47) described Japan as being in a "capitalist development state" where the government has attempted to suppress domestic consumption, channel personal savings to industrial investment, and hold onto the lead it has in industries such as automobiles and electronics. In areas where it is not dominant, imports are restricted until fledgling companies can grow and compete successfully (Fallows, 1989). From this perspective Japan's economic ambitions are one-sided. "By continuing to launch new industrial assaults rather than simply buying better, cheaper products from abroad, Japan suggests that it does not accept the basic reciprocal logic of world trade" (Fallows, 1989, p. 45). However, under the administration of Prime Minister Nakasone (1982–1988), personal savings were taxed (a policy designed to encourage spending and consumption) and a media campaign was launched urging people to buy foreign products.

In 1989 Japan announced a $43 billion assistance program to developing countries, the third in three years. Responding to this tremendous outlay of funds a Western diplomat remarked, "One can be cynical about it, but Japan has been using its resources generously and effectively" (*San Diego Union,* July 12, 1989). The motivation for this endeavor is probably some combination of a sincere effort to share its economic success with less fortunate nations, and a desire to cultivate a more favorable world image. The Japanese are increasingly portrayed as greedy, having built an economic empire with a self-serving trade policy. Money given to poor countries today may speed up the process of modernization and generate tomorrow's trading partners.

Reasons for Success

Regardless of the validity of the unfair trade advantage argument, this explanation alone hardly accounts for Japan's spectacular economic success. It has been attributed to many factors. The following are some of the more salient reasons.

1. If they were to be prevented from once again becoming a world power, the Japanese were going to become an economic giant. Throughout their history they have thought of themselves as a "chosen people" in one endeavor or another. The belief that Japanese mo-

rality coupled with Western technology was a formula for success is captured in a slogan from the Meiji period: *toyo dotoku sieyo gakugei* ("Western technology, Eastern ethics").

2. As noted in previous chapters, people in Japan work very hard. The average American works 225 days a year, whereas the average Japanese toils an average of 40 more days and is often reluctant to take time off from work or go on vacation. The typical student in Japan attends classes 240 days a year, whereas American students are in class an average of 180 days. As a result of this intense training, Japanese high school graduates have an education roughly equivalent to college graduates in the United States.

3. The Japanese are more tightly bound to their jobs and careers than are Westerners. Their place of employment is likely to be viewed as an extension of the family. Foremen are addressed as "brother," and the chief executive officer of a company is a father figure. This blending of family and work strengthens primary relations and facilitates dedication, loyalty, and obedience, characteristics that result in increased efficiency and productivity.

4. A substantial amount of the money necessary for initial business ventures and expansion comes from banks, and the Japanese save approximately four times more of their annual income than Americans (18 to 20 percent versus 5 percent). The Japanese save so much money, that they generate $100 billion more a year than the economy can absorb in the form of investment capital (Holstein, 1990). In 1989 Japan invested three times more in factories and industrial equipment than the United States.

5. Japan has highly advanced industrial technology. For example, by 1991 the United States had 37,000 industrial robots; the Japanese had 176,000. In the early 1970s, 450,000 Japanese auto workers produced 2.5 million cars; by the 1980s the same number of workers produced 11 million automobiles. Japan's high level of technological sophistication is the result of a vigorous, organized program of research and development. The Economic Research Center estimated that 45 percent of the country's growth is a result of technological progress (Bank of Switzerland, 1972).

6. One of the most significant differences between the United States and Japan is the relation between government and business. The U.S. business community has tended to see government as a meddler in economic affairs, often resulting in an adversarial relationship between the two. The laissez-faire attitude that government should not interfere with any aspect of the economy has been paramount in the history of American business. Japanese government, however, has been working with business since the Meiji Restoration (Frank and Hirono, 1974), providing "administrative guidance" in the form of a "whole range of aids and incentives, including finance, research and development grants, and other forms of support" (p. 20). The powerful Ministry of International Trade and Industry "coordinates the efforts of industries and other public agencies for the national welfare" (Warshaw, 1988b, p. 113). This gives Japan the advantage of being able to react quickly to both economic adversity and opportunity. It also permits long-range planning, something the United States has been sorely lacking.

The Down Side of Success

The government does not have the legal power to compel businesspeople to follow a particular plan of action, but it does have a great deal of moral authority. Even though the "acquisitive heart," as economist J. K. Galbraith called it, beats as strongly in Japan as it does in the West, it is more likely to beat in harmony with others for the economic well-being of the country.

For all of its success, Japan's economic miracle has a down side, and life in that country is less desirable than many would imagine. Salarymen are locked into jobs, making it difficult if not impossible to change employers after the first two years of work. Karel van Wolferen (1990) claimed that, by design, Japanese corporations either will not accept white-collar employees from other companies, or place them in a considerably lower position if they are hired at all. From this perspective the much-talked-about loyalty of Japanese workers is not so much given to corporations by dedicated employees, but demanded by companies as a condition of employment. Expected routinely to put in long hours and demonstrate allegiance to one's company, the typical Japanese businessman has little time and energy for family life. In 1990 Japanese salarymen spent on average one minute a day in child-care activities.

If van Wolferen is correct, Japan is hardly a society held together by harmony and consensus, as functionalist sociologists would argue. Rather, the ruling class systematically controls and exploits a well-socialized and docile proletariat. From a Marxist perspective, the workers are worse off than their counterparts in other capitalist countries. Because the Japanese have an ancient culture that stresses obedience and loyalty, they are not even close to challenging the power and supremacy of the ruling capitalist class.

Even though they work extremely hard the Japanese do not live nearly as well as Americans. They have to work five times as long to buy a pound of fish or rice, nine times as long to purchase a pound of beef, and three times as long for a gallon of gasoline (Tsurumi, in van Wolferen, 1990). The tremendous cost of small, cramped, housing has even been linked to Japan's low fertility rate. According to this argument, people are reluctant to have larger families and raise children in rabbit-hutch-size homes in polluted cities. One Japanese physician believes the nation's low birth rate "is a kind of birth strike. . . . It's a form of reprisal against a society for putting priority on economic growth at the expense of a humane way of life" (in Impoco, 1990, p. 56).

Leisure facilities are incredibly expensive as well as lacking in quality and quantity. Peter Tasker (1987) commented on the average individual having a good time in Japan: "Golf? Fine, if he can afford a membership fee high enough to fund the construction of an entire British golf course. A trip to the beach? Hundred-mile tailbacks (stop-and-go traffic) and mud-colored sand layered with trash. . . . A weekend skiing? All-night train journeys spent sprawled on the floor outside an ill-functioning toilet; two-hour waits at the ski lifts . . ." (p. 65).

Regardless of many shortcomings in Japanese society, the combination of hard work, advanced technology, the availability of investment capital, and a productive government-business relation means that Japan will be economically successful for years to come. William J. Holstein (1990) argued that Japan's economic success has allowed them to change the rules of competition for the entire industrial world. The new rules are, "Match our work ethic, our productivity, and our long-term drive, or we win. If you blink, you lose" (p. 171).

Discussion Questions

1. When and under what circumstances did the economic development of Japan begin?
2. How did the Japanese go about rebuilding their economy in the years following World War II?
3. What are some of the more important factors responsible for the Japanese economic miracle? Can any of these factors be applied to the U.S. economy?
4. Compare and contrast the relationship between government and business in the United States and Japan.
5. Using both your sociological imagination and knowledge of Japanese society, make a list of factors most likely to help and hurt Japan's economy in the next ten years.
6. The Japanese became successful by importing raw materials, turning them into high-quality goods, and selling these products all over the world. Can poor countries like Bangladesh and Ethiopia do the same? Do the Japanese have or know something that these countries do not? Explain.

Chapter Summary

1. People in modern societies are different from those individuals in more traditional nations. They are open to new experiences; increasingly independent of traditional authority figures; less fatalistic and more inclined to accept science and modern medicine; ambitious, seeking to improve their

standing in society; and interested in community, national, and international affairs.

2. The founders of sociology reasoned that if biological laws explained the physical evolution of animals and human beings, social laws could be identified that explained development and progress in human societies. These early theorists believed that societies evolved or passed through recognizable stages.

3. Ferdinand Tonnies and Emile Durkheim advanced dual-stage theories of social change. For Tonnies, gemeinschaft societies were traditional societies based on primary relations. Gessellschaft societies were contractual, impersonal, and characterized by secondary relations. For Durkheim, societies based on "mechanical solidarity" had a minimal division of labor. People in these nations had a common world view or collective conscience. Modern societies held together by organic solidarity have a complex division of labor. The individual conscience in these nations is well developed and people have fewer values in common.

4. World system theory focuses on the political and especially economic interdependence of the world's nations. From a WST perspective, the developed societies of the world became rich and powerful by systematically exploiting poor and militarily weak countries. In the nineteenth and first half of the twentieth centuries this was accomplished through colonization or imperialism. In the post–World War II era, economic domination of the periphery by the core continued through multinational corporations (neocolonialism). This long-lasting and continued economic domination of poor nations by rich states means the modernization of Third World countries will never be more than moderately successful.

5. Some observers believe that fast economies of the developed world will increase the economic gap between these nations and slow economies of the developing world. The technological and information-processing superiority of fast economies will increasingly dominate slow economies as we enter a phase of electronic imperialism.

6. In most Third World nations, the political, economic, social, and physical well-being of women is significantly below that of men. As a result of their inferior status, women are often denied an education or have significantly less formal schooling than men.

7. The modernization process has helped close the education gap and also resulted in improved health care for millions of Third World women. However, technological and economic assistance programs have generally targeted males and made it even more difficult for women to succeed economically. Modernization, therefore, has both helped and hurt Third World women.

8. In the developing world today, many nations are attempting to withdraw from existing political states. Violent clashes between groups seeking more autonomy or independence and governments blocking any such move have claimed the lives of millions of people over the past forty years. These confrontations are likely to continue as the spirit of freedom and self-determination spreads throughout the world.

9. Third World nations face a number of internal and external obstacles in their drive toward modernization. Some of the more serious problems are government corruption, lack of investment capital, unequal distribution of wealth, and political instability.

10. Both rich and poor nations have resource-based economies. If Third World countries follow the modernization path of now rich states, collectively the nations of the world will seriously deplete if not completely exhaust resources such as oil and forests. Sustainable development will be humankind's most formidable challenge as we approach the twenty-first century.

Glossary

absolute poverty The inability to maintain physical survival on a long-term basis.

absolutist perspective The view that deviance resides in the act itself and is wrong at all times (past, present, and future), and in all places.

age/sex or **population pyramid** Summarizes the age and sex characteristics of a given population by five-year cohorts or groups. For example, a population pyramid of the United States would indicate the number of males and females ages five to nine, ten to fourteen, and so on.

aggregate Social collectivity whose members occupy the same physical space at the same time.

agricultural surplus theory Theory stating that cities came into being as a result of a surplus of basic foodstuffs that allowed some people to develop occupations outside of agriculture.

altruistic suicide The self-destructive act resulting from overinvolvement in a group. The individual takes his or her life for the good of the group.

amalgamation Biological reproduction across different racial group lines.

Anglo conformity The philosophy and policy that immigrants to the United States must abandon their old ways and conform to prevailing Anglo-Saxon cultural patterns.

anomic suicide The self-destructive act that results from unregulated desires and ambition. It occurs in periods of rapid social change.

anomie A word used by Durkheim to describe the breakdown of societal rules and norms that regulate human behavior. According to Merton, the gap between culturally acceptable goals and the culturally acceptable means of achieving them leads to deviant behavior. Overemphasis on goals in societies like the United States also contributes to deviance.

anticipatory socialization The early learning of appropriate behaviors and attitudes that will be required for some future social role.

apartheid The legal system of racial segregation in South Africa.

ascription The principle of filling social positions on the basis of personal qualities or characteristics.

assimilation The process in which minority groups become absorbed or incorporated into the majority group's sociocultural system.

biological clock Term referring to the ages between which women are physically able to con-

ceive. The upper limits of fecundity occur at approximately forty-five years of age.

biological drives Drives experienced as a bodily imbalance or tension leading to activity that restores balance and reduces tension.

bourgeoisie Marx's term for people who own and control the means of production in a capitalist society.

burakumin Minority group in Japan whose members, although culturally and racially identical to the Japanese majority group, are regarded as ritually polluted and treated as outcasts.

bureaucracy In Weber's formulation, an administrative device for maximizing human efficiency through the logical, orderly structuring of individual behaviors within a particular setting. Bureaucracies are characterized by well-defined spheres of responsibility and authority; standardized, impersonal procedures; recruitment and promotion on the basis of technical expertise; and a distinction between organizational and personal life.

category Social collectivity whose members are clustered statistically on the basis of common or shared characteristics.

Caucasoid Ethnological term for Indo-European or "white" race.

causal relationship An empirical association between two or more variables in which change in one factor (the independent variable) is assumed to be responsible for changes occurring in the other factor(s) (the dependent variable[s]).

central business district The major shopping and commercial area of a city.

central place theory Theory stating that cities emerged because farmers needed a central market to exchange and distribute their produce.

charismatic authority Weber's term for political rule based on some extraordinary personal quality of the political leader.

class In Weber's model, the position of individuals within the larger society characterized by a common level of life chances in the economic hierarchy.

class conflicts Power struggles between unequal groups that, according to Marx, occurred in all stratified societies.

closed-caste structure A society characterized by maximum inequalities of condition and of opportunity.

coercive organizations In Etzioni's typology, organizations such as prisons or asylums that people join involuntarily and that restrain their members from normal contact with the larger society.

concentric zone model View of the city as a series of zones emanating from the center, with each zone characterized by a different group of people (or institution) and activity.

conception variables Factors that determine if a woman will become pregnant or not. The use of contraceptives and the presence or absence of breast-feeding have a significant impact on conception and, therefore, a society's fertility rate.

constructs Components or elements of the human world that do not have a direct empirical or physical existence.

continued subjugation Intergroup pattern in which minority groups are kept in a subordinate social and economic position.

control group In experimental research, the subject group whose members will not be exposed to the effects of the experimental condition (changes in the independent variable).

control theories of deviance Theories that take deviant motivation as a given, and attempt to explain why people do not engage in deviant behavior. According to this perspective, deviant motivation is contained by internal factors like a positive self-image and external factors such as a supportive family and friends.

core In world system theory, term describing industrial, economically diversified, rich, powerful nations relatively independent of outside control.

core values Values especially promoted by a particular culture, and often important identifying characteristics of that culture.

corporate crime A form of organizational crime committed by officials for their corporations, and crimes committed by the organization itself to maximize profits and enhance its position in the marketplace.

corporate dumping The sale to less developed nations of hazardous products that have been banned or are strictly regulated in the developed world.

countercultures Groups whose members share values, norms, and a way of life that contradict the fundamental beliefs and lifestyle of the larger, more dominant culture.

criminal behavior Behavior in violation of society's laws that is not condemned by the norms of an individual's subculture.

cross-cultural research The gathering of comparable data from different societies.

crude birth rate (CBR) The number of births per year for every 1,000 members of the population. This statistic is crude because the age

structure or distribution of the population is not considered.

crude death rate (CDR) The number of deaths per year for every 1,000 members of the population. This is a crude measure of mortality inasmuch as it does not take into account the age distribution of a population.

cult A new and distinctive religious organization that exists in a state of high tension with the established religions in society.

cultural anthropologists Researchers who study the social organization and patterns of behavior primarily of premodern people throughout the world.

cultural assimilation The giving up of established cultural patterns by a minority group and the acceptance of the majority group's cultural pattern.

cultural lag The process whereby one aspect of culture changes faster than another aspect of culture to which it is related. In modern societies, material culture (especially technology) typically changes faster than associated values, norms, and laws (nonmaterial culture).

cultural relativism The belief that there is no universal standard of good or bad, right or wrong; and that an aspect of any given culture can be judged only within the context of that culture.

culture A people's way of life or social heritage that includes values, norms, institutions, and artifacts that are passed from generation to generation by learning alone.

culture shock The experience of encountering people who do not share one's world view that leads to disorientation, frustration, and, on some occasions, revulsion.

Davis-Moore theory A functionalist interpretation of social stratification that attempted to explain social inequality in terms of its contribution to social survival.

debunking Looking for levels of reality other than those given in the everyday and official interpretations of society.

deconcentration explanation View of the slowdown and reversal of population growth in many of the country's largest cities as a fundamental break with past trends. More people are deciding to live in smaller cities and semirural areas.

decriminalization The reduction or elimination of penalties for a specific offense. For example, some individuals think the use of currently illegal drugs in the United States should be decriminalized.

de facto racism Discriminatory actions that exist in practice, but are not supported or required by law.

definition of the situation Concept developed by symbolic interaction theorist W. I. Thomas

(1928) stating that "situations defined as real are real in their consequences" (p. 572).

de jure racism Discriminatory practices that are required or supported by law.

demographic transition theory The perspective that explains population changes in the modern world. The theory divides this change into three stages: stage one (high growth potential) has high rates of birth and death, and slow growth; stage two (transitional growth) has a high birth rate and a low death rate, resulting in explosive population growth; stage three (incipient decline) has both low fertility and mortality, and therefore slow population growth.

demography The scientific study of population. Demographers are especially interested in population growth and how that growth is affected by birth, death, and migration rates.

denominations Formal religious organizations that are well integrated into their society and recognize religious pluralism.

deviance Behavior contrary to a group's or society's norms of conduct or social expectations.

deviant and criminal behavior Behavior that violates both subcultural norms and society's laws.

deviant behavior Behavior that is a violation of reference group and/or subcultural norms, but not of the legal code of the larger society.

devolution The surrender of powers to local authorities by the central government.

differential association Sutherland's theory stating that if definitions favorable to violations of the law are in excess of definitions unfavorable to violations of the law, the individual will engage in criminal behavior.

discrimination Unequal, unfair treatment toward members of some specific group.

doubling time The number of years it takes a given population to double in size.

dual-labor/segmented-labor market The division of an economy into an upper tier of high-paying, high-prestige jobs and a bottom tier of low-paying, low-prestige jobs.

dyad A social group consisting of two members.

ego In Freudian theory, that conscious part of the human personality that negotiates and mediates between the opposing forces of id and superego.

egoistic suicide Suicide that results from a lack of group integration and commitment to other people.

endogamy Social interaction system in which individuals are limited to forming relationships only with others in their own membership group.

ethnic group People who possess a distinctive, shared culture and a sense of common identification based on that culture.

ethnocentrism The tendency to believe that the norms and values of one's own culture are superior to those of others, and to use these norms as a standard when evaluating all other cultures.

exogamy Social interaction system in which individuals are required to form relationships with others outside their own membership groups.

experimental group In experimental research, the subject group whose members will be exposed to the effects of the experimental condition (changes in the independent variable).

experimental research Causal research designed to explain observed social patterns or predict future ones.

expressive tasks Activities carried out on behalf of establishing or maintaining satisfying emotional relationships within a group.

extended family Family arrangement characterized by several generations of blood-related individuals (and their spouses and offspring) occupying a single household under the authority of a household head.

extermination/genocide The attempted physical annihilation of a particular minority group.

external migration The movement of people from a given society to another society.

exurbanization The movement of people to towns beyond the ring of big-city suburbs. This process has been referred to as the suburbanization of the suburbs.

fatalistic suicide The result of overregulation and lack of control over one's life. It is the self-destructive act committed by slaves.

fecundity Term referring to the physical ability of women to conceive and bear children.

feminization of poverty The increasing association between being female and being economically deprived.

fertility Term referring to the number of children born to women in a given population.

folk religions Interpretations and modifications of more formalized religious traditions to meet the needs of specific population groups.

folkways The customary, habitual way a group does things; "the ways of the folks."

formal organizations Large, deliberately planned groups with established personnel, procedures, and rules for carrying out some objective or set of objectives.

game In G. H. Mead's theory, any organized group behavior that requires the child to interact with other people.

gemeinschaft According to Tonnies, a traditional type of communal relationship based on personal emotions and long-standing customs among the members of a population.

gender A system for classifying people as girl or boy, woman or man, based on physiological, psychological, and sociocultural characteristics.

gender assignment The process by which individuals are defined, typically at birth, as being either female or male.

gender roles Specific social roles assigned to individuals on the basis of sex.

gender socialization Social learning process through which individuals acquire and internalize the proper role of female or male as defined by their culture.

gender stereotypes Categorical portrayals of all members of a given sex as being alike in terms of basic nature and specific attributes.

gender stratification Social inequality hierarchies based on sex.

generalized other In G. H. Mead's theory, the surrounding social and cultural community of which the child is a member, that ultimately provides the frame of reference from which the child views the world and him- or herself.

gentrification The return of middle- and upper-class people to deteriorating central city neighborhoods.

gesellschaft According to Tonnies, a modern type of associational relationship based on impersonal, rational, secondary group relations among the members of a population.

gestation variables Factors (e.g., miscarriage, stillbirth, induced abortion) that determine if a fetus will come to term, resulting in a live birth.

goal displacement/bureaucratic ritualism Phenomenon often found within bureaucracies, in which adherence to organizational rules becomes more important than fulfilling the original objectives for which the organization was created.

grand theory A theory that deals with the universal aspects of social life and is usually grounded in basic assumptions (as opposed to data) concerning the nature of humans and society.

group Social collectivity whose members possess a feeling of common identity and interact in a regular, patterned way.

Hawthorne effect The effect that knowledge of being part of a research study has on the subjects. People who know they are being studied often will attempt to be "good" subjects, behaving according to their perceptions of the researcher's expectations.

Hispanization The forced adoption of Spanish cultural patterns by Indian and African population groups in colonial Mexico (similar to Anglo conformity policy in the United States).

homogamy The tendency for people to marry individuals like themselves physically, psychologically, and/or socially.

horizontal mobility Social movement within a given level in the stratification hierarchy.

human capital factors Resources such as education, interest, and aptitude that give individuals a better bargaining position to sell their labor in the occupational or job market.

human ecology The area of sociology concerned with the study of the spatial distribution and aspects of human life.

humanism The belief that humans, rather than God, are the center of their own destiny.

I In G. H. Mead's terminology, the subjective, creative, individual part of the social self.

id In Freudian theory, that unconscious part of the human personality representing inherited aggressive and sexual impulses.

ideal types Logical constructions that present, in exaggerated and idealized form, the distinguishing features of some phenomenon.

imitation perspective According to this point of view, children learn to speak by repeating the spoken word of others.

infant mortality rate The number of deaths during the first year of life per 1,000 live births. It is often used as a measure of a country's economic well-being. Developed nations typically have low infant mortality rates, and poor nations have much higher rates.

informal organization The actual set of relationships developed by the members of formal organizations as they carry out the activities defined by organizational objectives and procedures.

innateness hypothesis According to this perspective of language acquisition, human beings learn to speak because our brains are biologically constructed or prewired to acquire language.

instincts Biologically inherited predispositions that impel most members of a species to react to a given stimulus in a specific way.

institutionalized racism A discriminatory pattern that has become embedded in prevailing societal structures.

Institutional Revolutionary Party (PRI) The political party that has dominated Mexican government for the past sixty years.

instrumental tasks Activities carried out in pursuit of some specific group objective or goal.

intercourse variables Commencement and frequency of sexual activity over a given period of time.

intergenerational mobility Social movement from one generation to another; for example, the social position of sons compared to fathers.

internal migration The movement of people from one area to another area within the same society.

international migration The movement of people across political states.

interview Survey research procedure in which the researcher gains information through verbal interaction with the respondents.

intragenerational mobility Social movement of individuals within their own lifetimes.

labeling theory A theory stating that societies create deviance by making rules and laws whose infraction constitutes deviance, and then applying these rules and laws to certain individuals. Labeling theorists are interested in how and why some people are labeled, and how this label affects their future behavior.

laws Norms that have been codified or formally written into a legal code.

legal protection of minorities Legislative actions and policies designed to safeguard the rights of minority groups.

liberation theology Interpretation of Christian faith and practice that focuses on the obligation of Christians to help free oppressed peoples from poverty and suffering. It is primarily a Third World Catholic theological stance.

life chances In Weber's model, the levels of access to basic opportunities and resources in the marketplace that defined individuals' positions in the economic inequality hierarchy.

lifestyle In Weber's model, a distinctive orientation or relationship to the social world that formed the basis for prestige or honor.

looking-glass self In Cooley's theory, the sense of personal identity individuals acquire through interactions with other people.

machismo The cult of masculinity in Spanish America that dates back to the days of the conquistadors.

macrolevel Dealing with large-scale social phenomena such as societies.

majority group A recognizable group of people who occupy the dominant position in a given society.

marital/physical assimilation Intermarriage and reproduction across majority-minority group lines leading to the gradual blurring of distinctive group differences.

Marxist theory of crime Theory stating that in a capitalist society, crime is the product of the struggle between the bourgeoisie and the proletariat. The ruling class commits crimes as a result of its effort to exploit and control the working class. Workers commit crimes as a result of their brutal treatment at the hands of the bourgeoisie and their effort to survive economically.

mass (society) Societal population consisting of millions of fragmented, alienated individuals who are uninterested and uninvolved in political affairs.

material culture That aspect of culture comprising things people make and use in society.

maternal mortality rate The number of women who die in childbirth per 10,000 live births. In developed nations, maternal mortality rates are extremely low (two or three), whereas in poor countries complications and death during childbirth are still common.

me In G. H. Mead's terminology, the objective, predictable part of the social self that corresponds to one's social statuses and roles.

mechanical solidarity Social cohesion in preindustrial societies resulting from a minimum division of labor, common experiences, and a strong collective conscience.

melting pot Name for an image of racial and ethnic group relations in the United States in which individual immigrant groups each contribute to the creation of a new "American" cultural and physical end product through the process of amalgamation.

membership group Social group to which an individual belongs and participates in.

mestizoization The physical amalgamation of Spanish, Indian, and African populations in Mexico, resulting in a new physical type.

microlevel Dealing with small-scale social phenomena such as families and committees.

middle-range theories Theories that focus on relatively specific phenomena or problems in the social world. A theory of white-collar crime would be a middle-range theory.

migration The relatively permanent movement of people from one place to another.

minority group A recognizable group of people who occupy a subordinate position in a given society.

mode of production In Marxian theory, the mechanism by which wealth was produced in a given society.

modernization The transformation from a traditional, usually agrarian society to a contemporary, industrially based state.

Mongoloid Ethnological term for Asian or "yellow" race.

mores Types of norms in any given society that must be obeyed. Members of society believe that obeying mores is essential to the well-being of the group.

multidimensional model An interpretation of stratification developed by Weber that argued that modern societies are characterized by several hierarchies of inequality.

multiple nuclei model Model in which the city is seen as comprising multiple centers or nuclei. In some cases these nuclei have existed since the origin of the city, while in other instances they increased as the city grew and diversified.

nation A group of people with a common history and culture; a nation may or may not be a political state.

Negroid Ethnological term for African or "black" race.

neutral observation Research technique in which the researcher is identified to the subject group and remains removed or detached from the group while observations are being made.

nonexperimental or descriptive research Noncausal research aimed most often at providing valid, reliable information about some aspect of social reality.

nonmaterial culture That component of culture lacking a physical substance, although created by human beings. Ideas, religions, beliefs, customs, laws, and economic systems are examples.

normative organizations Also called voluntary associations, in Etzioni's typology, public interest organizations such as Scouts or PTA groups that people join for nonmaterial reasons.

normative perspective The view that deviance is the violation of a specific group's or society's rules at a particular time in history.

norms Rules stating what human beings should or should not think, say, or do under given circumstances.

nuclear family In modern societies, the typical family unit consisting of two spouses and their immediate offspring.

objective class analysis A technique for defining and measuring social class based on objective factors such as income, education, and occupation.

objective classes In Marx's theory, groups defined on the basis of relationship to the economic system. In modern society, the two major classes are bourgeoisie (owners) and proletariat (workers).

objectivistic Arguing that the tangible, objective facts of social reality are of primary importance in shaping people's lives and events.

observation study Research technique in which the sociologist observes subjects' behaviors directly in order to form conclusions or make inferences about attitudes and values.

occupational crime Law-violating behavior committed by individuals or small groups of people in connection with their work.

open-class society A social system in which inequalities of condition and of opportunities are minimized.

operational definitions Procedures that specify how phenomena having no direct empirical existence (constructs) are to be measured empirically.

organic solidarity The social bond found in large industrial societies where people are dependent on one another because of a special-

ized, complex, highly developed division of labor.

oversocialized conception of human beings The mistaken view that all aspects of human lives are controlled by society through the socialization process.

pan-Indian movement An intertribal political coalition united to promote the common interests of Native Americans in the United States.

participant observation Research technique in which the researcher participates in the actions of the subject group while observations are being made. The researcher may be identified to the group (overt study) or the researcher's identity may be kept hidden from the group (covert study).

parties In Weber's model, groups composed of individuals sharing a given level of power.

patriarchal family Family structure in which males dominate females, and married couples usually reside with the husband's parents. In patriarchal families, family descent is typically traced through the male lineage.

peer group/peers People of approximately the same social position and same age as oneself.

period explanation View of the slowdown and reversal of urban growth that began in the 1970s as a singular and therefore temporary distortion of metropolitan expansion resulting from the convergence of economic and demographic factors.

periphery In world system theory, term describing economically overspecialized, relatively poor, weak societies subject to the manipulation and direct control of core nations.

play In G. H. Mead's theory, behavior in which children pretend to be parents or other specific people.

pluralism The retention of minority group diversities and identities in a given society.

pluralist Holding the view that political power in modern societies is dispersed among a variety of competing groups and organizations, with no single unit or combination of units dominating the system.

political hierarchy In Weber's model, an inequality hierarchy defined on the basis of power differences.

polity In Parsonian functionalist terminology, another name for the state.

popular culture The culture of everyday life as expressed through sport, music, hobbies, television, movies, books, magazines, comic books, and so on.

popular religions Sets of beliefs that lie outside of or span the boundaries of recognized denominations and appeal to mass audiences drawn from a variety of backgrounds.

population Name given collectively to all the members of a specific group being studied in a survey research design.

population transfer The voluntary or involuntary movement of minority groups to separate them from the dominant majority group in a given society.

positivism The belief that knowledge can be gained only through people's sensory experience.

poverty The condition or situation of economic deprivation.

poverty line As measured by the U.S. federal government, the yearly income needed to provide a nutritionally adequate diet for a typical non-farm family of four.

power The ability of an individual or group to accomplish desired objectives even in the face of opposition from others.

power elite Term used by radical conflict sociologist C. Wright Mills to describe a coalition of corporate, political, and military elites who, according to Mills, secretly control the state in the United States.

predestination As part of the Protestant ethic, the belief that one's fate in the afterlife had been decided before or at one's birth, and could not be changed through prayer or good works.

prejudice An irrational, negative feeling or belief about members of a certain group based on presumed characteristics of that group.

prescriptive laws Laws that spell out what must be done. Income tax laws, traffic laws, and draft laws require people to do things at specific times and places, and under given circumstances.

prestige Reputation or social honor.

primary deviance The initial act, or first few incidents, of deviant behavior.

primary groups As described by Cooley, social groups such as one's family or close friends that are essential in the formation of individual self-identity.

primary socialization The first social learning experienced by individuals, typically in the setting of the family.

profane The commonplace, ordinary elements of everyday life.

proletariat Marx's term for the working class in a capitalist society. These people survive by selling their labor power to the bourgeoisie.

property Income, wealth, and other material resources.

proscriptive laws Laws that state what behavior is prohibited or forbidden. For example, laws against robbing people or harming them physically are proscriptive and carry some form of punishment administered by the state.

Protestant ethic Weber's term for the world view and values associated with the Protestant Christian religions that developed in Western Europe during the sixteenth and seventeenth centuries.

pull factors Socioeconomic magnets that draw migrants to a given geographical location. They include increased opportunity for employment and better living conditions.

push factors Factors that drive off or send a stream of migrants from a particular locale. These include little economic opportunity, and racial, religious, and political persecution.

questionnaire Survey research instrument in which questions are posed to respondents in writing for them to answer in writing.

race A classification of human beings that is based on genetic characteristics.

rational-legal authority Weber's term for political rule based on the reasonableness of laws and the acceptability of law-making procedures.

reactive perspective The view that behavior is not deviant until it has been recognized and condemned.

reference group Social group whose perspective is adopted by an individual as a frame of reference for personal behaviors and attitudes.

regional restructuring From this perspective the deindustrialization of many winter cities in the 1970s is a component of a new geography of urban growth. Cities will expand in different geographic regions of the country for reasons unrelated to past growth.

reinforcement theory The language acquisition theory stating that children are positively reinforced when they say something correctly, and negatively reinforced when they say something incorrectly.

relative poverty The condition of economic deprivation relative or compared to some other individual or group.

representative sample A smaller segment or subgroup of a particular population that reflects the attributes of that larger group. For the sample to be representative, each member of the population must have an equal chance of being included in the sample.

resocialization Rapid and dramatic secondary socialization experiences in which established behaviors and attitudes are removed and new patterns are created.

role conflict Contradictory role expectations arising from two or more statuses occupied by an individual at the same time.

role/formal role The set of expected behaviors and attitudes associated with a particular status in a group or society.

role performance An individual's actual behaviors and attitudes in response to role expectations.

role playing The process in which, during play, children begin to duplicate the behaviors and attitudes of the specific people being imitated.

role strain The inability to meet all the expectations attached to a particular social role.

role taking During play activities, the process in which children begin to view and evaluate the world from the perspective of the people being imitated.

rule by authority Political rule based on a sense of moral obligation, rather than raw power and force.

sacred Those extraordinary elements of life that inspire a sense of reverence, awe, and fear in people.

scapegoat An innocent, powerless target for a more powerful individual's or group's frustration and aggression.

secondary deviance Nonconforming behavior that occurs as a result of being labeled deviant.

secondary groups Social groups such as customers and clerks that are more formal, less inclusive, less emotional than primary groups, and typically organized for some specific purpose.

secondary socialization Social learning experienced during adolescence and, in particular, during adulthood.

sector model Model of the city in which urban zones are wedge-shaped sectors radiating out from the center, or central business district.

sects Religious subcultural or countercultural groups that offer their members a different vision of the social and the spiritual life.

secularization Societal transformation from a religious to a civil and worldly basis, with a significant decline of religion in people's everyday lives.

self An individual's awareness and concept of personal identity.

semiperiphery In world system theory, term describing nations midway between the core and the periphery that are attempting to industrialize and diversify their economies.

sex A system for classifying people as female or male based on anatomical, chromosomal, and hormonal differences.

sex ratio The number of males per hundred females in a given population.

significant others People who are important in creating an individual's self-concept.

significant symbols Physical stimuli that have been assigned meaning and value by a social group. People respond to these symbols in terms of their meanings and values, rather than their actual physical properties.

sluburb A residential area part slum and part suburb.

social collectivity Any collection or situation involving more than one person.

Social Darwinism A social and political philosophy, the proponents of which believed in the existence of natural laws of social evolution and argued for a hands-off approach to human social affairs.

social hierarchy In Weber's model, an inequality hierarchy based on prestige or social honor accorded to individuals by others.

social institutions Orderly, enduring, and established ways of arranging behavior and doing things.

socialization The social learning process through which individuals develop their human potentials and also acquire the established patterns of their culture.

socialization agents Parents, teachers, and other important groups involved in the socialization of individual societal members.

social marginality The condition of being caught or poised between two recognized societal groups without being fully a member of either.

social mobility The movement of individuals and groups within and between social levels in a stratified society.

social self In G. H. Mead's theory, the human personality structure that results from the individual's interaction with others through play and game activities.

social stratification The systematic division of a societal population into categories in which people are defined and treated as social unequals.

social structure The organization of a societal population into various groups, and the patterned relationships that exist within and among these groups.

societies Self-perpetuating groups of people who occupy a given territory and interact with one another on the basis of a shared culture.

sociology The study of the social organization and patterns of behavior of people in primarily large, complex, modern, industrial societies.

state The social institution that holds a monopoly over the legitimate use of force and exercises governing power in a given society.

status Any defined or recognized position within a group or society.

stereotype A preconceived (not based on experience), standardized, group-shared idea about the alleged essential nature of a whole category of persons without regard to the individual differences of those in the category.

stratum In Weber's model, a level in the social hierarchy occupied by individuals of a certain lifestyle.

structural assimilation The acceptance of minority group members into secondary and primary group relationships by members of the majority group.

structural mobility Social movement that results from changes in economic or other social structures.

subcultures Groups that hold norms, values, and patterns of behavior in common with the larger society, but also have their own design for living and world view.

subjective classes In Marx's theory, groups whose members were conscious and aware of their own collective position and interests in the mode of production.

subjective reputation A technique for defining and measuring social class based on other people's evaluations of an individual's position within the class hierarchy.

subjective self-placement A technique for defining and measuring social class based on respondents' perceptions of their own positions within the class hierarchy.

subjectivistic Arguing that people's subjective perceptions and interpretations of reality are of primary importance in shaping their lives and events.

substructure In Marxian theory, the economic system that shaped all other significant material and nonmaterial aspects of societal life, such as political and religious institutions.

superego In Freudian theory, that unconscious part of the human personality representing internalized cultural values and norms.

superstructures In Marxian theory, social or cultural forms like law, politics, and art that derived from and reflected the society's economic substructure.

survey research Type of nonexperimental study in which the researcher asks some defined group a series of questions relating to their behaviors or attitudes.

symbolic interactionism Sociological approach that examines the process by which members of a group or society come to define and assign meaning to their surrounding world, and the consequences or effects of the created world view.

theory A set of logically coherent interrelated concepts that attempts to explain some observable phenomenon or group of facts.

total fertility rate (TFR) A measure of completed fertility, or the total number of children born per 1,000 women.

total institutions Places such as prisons and monasteries, where large numbers of people who are cut off from the larger society have all aspects of their lives planned and controlled by agents of the institution. These total institu-

tions often are the settings in which resocialization takes place.

trading theory Theory of city growth stating that specialists were responsible for producing the surplus food vital for the growth of cities. Traders introduced new seeds and livestock that resulted in improved crops and a successful agricultural revolution. This revolution in turn permitted people to develop occupations other than farming.

traditional authority Weber's term for political rule based on long-standing societal customs.

triad A social group consisting of three members.

typologies Ordering systems that classify individual phenomena into categories or types on the basis of distinguishing characteristics.

unilinear theories of change Theories predicting that societies would undergo a similar (if not identical) set of transformations, resulting in the same end product: the modern industrial state.

urbanization Growth in the proportion of people living in urban areas.

utilitarian organizations In Etzioni's typology, organizations such as corporations or universities that individuals join for some practical, material reason.

vertical mobility Social movement between different levels in the stratification hierarchy.

voluntary mobility Social movement that results from individual efforts.

WASP Acronym for white Anglo-Saxon Protestant, generally regarded as the majority or dominant group in the United States.

world system theory (WST) The perspective that examines the relationship between the developed and developing nations of the world. According to this theory, the developed nations became rich in large measure by systematically exploiting the poor and militarily weak nations of the world.

worldly asceticism As part of the Protestant ethic, the denial of material self-indulgence under the belief that frugality was morally superior to concern for worldly pleasures.

xenophobia The fear and avoidance of foreign people and things.

References

Abadinsky, H. 1989. *Drug Abuse—An Introduction.* Chicago: Nelson-Hall.

Abbot, C. 1987. *The New Urban America— Growth and Politics in Sunbelt Cities.* Chapel Hill, NC: University of North Carolina Press.

Alba, F., and J. E. Potter. 1986. "Population and Development in Mexico Since 1940: An Interpretation." *Population and Development Review* 12(1):47–76.

Alinsky, M. 1977. "Mexico's Population Pressures." *Current History* 86(425):106–131.

———. 1983. "Migration and Unemployment in Mexico." *Current History* 82(488):429–432.

Allinson, G. D. 1984. "Japanese Urban Society and Its Cultural Context," in J. Agnew, J. Mercer, and D. Sopher, eds. *The City in Cultural Conflict.* Boston: Allen and Unwin, pp. 163–185.

Allport, G. W. 1958. *The Nature of Prejudice.* Abridged edition. New York: Doubleday.

Anderson, E. 1978. *A Place on the Corner.* Chicago: University of Chicago Press.

Anderson, K. 1983. "Private Violence." *Time* (September 5): 18–19.

Applebaum, R. P. 1970. *Theories of Social Change.* Chicago: Rand McNally.

Apter, D. E. 1986. *Rethinking Development, Modernization, Dependency and Post-Modern Politics.* Beverly Hills, CA: Sage.

Ashford, N. A. 1974. *Crisis in the Workplace; Occupational Disease and Injury.* Cambridge, MA: M.I.T. Press.

Babbit, B. 1989. "Reviving Mexico." *World Monitor* (March):32–42.

Bahr, H. M., B. A. Chadwick, and J. H. Strauss. 1979. *American Ethnicity.* Lexington, MA: D.C. Heath.

Baker, M. A., C. White Berheide, F. Ross Greckel, L. Carstarphen Gugin, M. J. Lipetz, and M. Texler Segal. 1980. *Women Today: A Multidisciplinary Approach to Women's Studies.* Monterey, CA: Brooks/Cole.

Baltzell, E. D. 1958. *Philadelphia Gentlemen: The Making of a National Upper Class.* Glencoe, IL: Free Press.

Bando, M. S. 1986. *Japanese Women Yesterday and Today.* Tokyo: Foreign Press Center/Japan.

Banfield, E. C. 1974. *The Unheavenly City Revisited.* Boston: Little, Brown.

Bank of Switzerland. 1972. "Japan—Dynamic Force in the Industrial World," pp. 1–56.

Banner, L. W. 1983. *American Beauty.* New York: Knopf.

Barlow, H. T. 1990. *Introduction to Criminology,* 5th ed. Glenview, IL: Scott, Foresman/Little, Brown.

Baron, J. N., and W. Bielby. 1980. "Bringing the Firms Back In: Stratification, Segmentation, and the Organization of Work." *American Sociological Review* 45:736–766.

Barrett, M. J. 1990. "The Case for More School Days." *Atlantic Monthly* (November):78–106.

Barry, K. 1979. *Female Sexual Slavery.* Englewood Cliffs, NJ: Prentice-Hall.

Bartollas, C., and S. Dinitz. 1989. *Introduction to Criminology—Order and Disorder.* New York: Harper and Row.

Basow, S. A. 1986. *Gender Stereotypes.* Pacific Grove, CA: Brooks/Cole.

Bayley, D. H. 1976. *Forces of Order—Police Behavior in Japan and the United States.* Berkeley, CA: University of California Press.

Beaty, J. 1989. "Do Humans Need to Get High?" *Time* (August 21): 58.

Becker, C. B. 1988. "Report from Japan: Causes and Controls of Crime in Japan." *Journal of Criminal Justice* 16:425–435.

Becker, H. S. 1963. *The Outsiders—Studies in the Sociology of Deviance.* New York: Free Press.

Beirne, P., and J. Messerschmidt. 1991. *Criminology.* San Diego, CA: Harcourt Brace Jovanovich.

Bell, A., M. Weinberg, and S. Hammersmith. 1981. *Sexual Preference.* Bloomington, IN: Indiana University Press.

Bellah, R. N. 1988. "Civil Religion in America." *Daedalus* 117:97–118.

Bellah, R. N., R. Madsen, W. G. Sullivan, A. Swidler, and S. M. Tipton. 1985. *Habits of the Heart.* New York: Harper and Row.

Benedict, R. 1946. *The Chrysanthemum and the Sword: Patterns of Japanese Culture.* Cambridge, MA: Houghton Mifflin.

Benjamin, L. 1991. *The Black Elite: Facing the Color Line in the Twilight of the Twentieth Century.* Chicago: Nelson-Hall.

Bennet, N. 1989. "U.S. Man Shortage Is Over, Says Sociology Researcher." *Missoulan,* July 30.

Berger, A. S. 1978. *The City—Urban Communities and Their Problems.* Dubuque, IA: William C. Brown.

Berger, P. L. 1963. *An Invitation to Sociology.* Garden City, NY: Anchor Books.

———. 1967. *The Sacred Canopy: Elements of a Sociological Theory of Religion.* New York: Doubleday.

———. 1977. *Facing up to Modernity.* New York: Basic Books.

Bergeson, A. 1980. "Cycles of Formal Colonial Rule," in T. K. Hopkins and I. Wallerstein, eds. *Processes of the World System.* Beverly Hills, CA: Sage, pp. 119–126.

Bernard, J. 1981. *The Female World.* New York: Free Press.

Berndt, T., and G. W. Ladd, eds. 1989. *Peer Relationships in Child Development.* New York: Wiley.

Bettenson, H. 1974. *Documents of the Christian Church.* London and New York: Oxford University Press.

Biagi, S. 1990. *Media Impact: An Introduction to Mass Media.* Updated first edition. Belmont, CA: Wadsworth.

Bielby, W. T., and J. N. Baron. 1984. "A Woman's Place Is with Other Women," in B. F. Reskin, ed. *Sex Segregation in the Workplace: Trends, Explanations, Remedies.* Washington, DC: National Academy Press, pp. 27–55.

_____. 1986. "Men and Women at Work: Sex Segregation and Statistical Discrimination." *American Journal of Sociology* 91:759–799.

Biemiller, L. 1986. "Asian Students Fear Top Colleges Use Quota Systems." *Chronicle of Higher Education* 23(1):34–35, 37.

Bingham, M. Wall, and S. Hill Gross. 1987. *Women in Japan.* St. Louis Park, MN: Glenhurst Publications.

Black, C. E. 1966. *The Dynamics of Modernization—A Study in Comparative History.* New York: Harper and Row.

Black, J. A., and D. J. Champion. 1976. *Methods and Issues in Social Research.* New York: Wiley.

Blake, J., and K. Davis. 1964. "Norms, Values, and Sanctions," in R. L. Faris, ed. *Handbook of Modern Sociology.* Chicago: Rand McNally.

Blau, P. M., and M. W. Meyer. 1987. *Bureaucracy in Modern Society,* 3rd ed. New York: Random House.

Blau, P. M., and O. D. Duncan. 1967. *The American Occupational Structure.* New York: Wiley.

Blauner, R. 1972. *Racial Oppression in America.* New York: Harper and Row.

Blum, L., and V. Smith. 1988. "Women's Mobility in the Corporation: A Critique of the Politics of Optimism." *Signs* 13(3):528–545.

Blumberg, P. 1981. *Inequality in an Age of Decline.* New York: Oxford University Press.

Blumer, H. 1969. "Symbolic Interactionism," in R. Collins, ed. *Three Sociological Traditions: Selected Readings.* New York: Oxford University Press, pp. 282–299.

Bogue, D. J. 1969. *Principles of Demography.* New York: Wiley.

Bonacich, E. 1972. "A Theory of Ethnic Antagonism: The Split Labor Market." *American Sociological Review* 37(5):547–559.

Bongaarts, J. 1982. "Why Fertility Rates Are So Low," in S. W. Menard and E. W. Mohen, eds. *Perspectives on Population: An Introduction to Concepts and Issues.* New York: Oxford University Press.

Bonhaker, W. 1990. *The Hollow Doll.* New York: Ballantine Books.

Boskind-White, M. 1985. "Bulimarexia: A Sociocultural Perspective," in S. Wiley Emmett, ed. *Theory and Treatment of Anorexia Nervosa and Bulimia—Biomedical, Sociocultural, and Psychological Perspectives.* New York: Brunner/Mazel.

Bourgeois-Pichat, J. 1986. "Comment." *Population and Development Review* 12:243–244.

Bouvier, L. F., and R. W. Gardner. 1986. *Immigration to the United States: The Unfinished Story.* Washington, DC: Population Reference Bureau.

Bowles, S., and H. Gintis. 1976. *Schooling in Capitalist America.* New York: Basic Books.

Braithwaite, J. 1981. "The Myth of Social Class and Criminality Reconsidered." *American Sociological Review* 46:36–47.

Briggs, V. M., Jr. 1985. "Employment Trends and Contemporary Immigration Policy," in N. M. Glazer, ed. *Clamor at the Gates.* San Francisco: Institute for Contemporary Studies.

Brinton, M. C. 1988. "The Social-Institutional Bases of Gender Stratification: Japan as an Illustrative Case." *American Journal of Sociology* 94(2):300–334.

_____. 1989. "Gender Stratification in Contemporary Urban Japan." *American Sociological Review* 54 (August):549–564.

Briseno, O. 1990a. "Hispanics Try to Translate Numbers into Political Clout." *San Diego Union,* May 28.

_____. 1990b. "Baja Orphanages Populated by Children of Working Poor." *San Diego Union,* July 16.

Bromley, R. 1982. "Working the Streets: Survival Strategy, Necessity, or Unavoidable Evil?" in A. Gilbert, J. E. Hardy, and R. Ramirez, eds. *Urbanization in Contemporary Latin America.* New York: Wiley.

Broom, L., and P. Selznick. 1970. *Principles of Sociology.* New York: Harper and Row.

Brown, R. O. 1973. *A First Language: The Early Stages.* Cambridge, MA: Harvard University Press.

Brownmiller, S. 1975. *Against Our Will: Men, Women and Rape.* New York: Simon and Schuster.

Brumberg, J. Jacobs. 1989. *Fasting Girls—The History of Anorexia Nervosa.* New York: New American Library.

Brydon, L., and S. Chant. 1989. *Women in the Third World: Gender Issues in Rural and Urban Areas.* New Brunswick, NJ: Rutgers University Press.

Bryjak, G. J. 1982–1983. India's Urban Catastrophe. *Journal of the Institute for Socioeconomic Studies* (Winter):77–90.

_____. 1985. "The Economics of Assassination: The Punjab Crisis and the Death of Indira Gandhi." *Asian Affairs—An American Review* 12(Spring):25–40.

_____. 1986. "Collective Violence in India." *Asian Affairs—An American Review* 13(Summer):35–55.

_____. 1990. "Reducing Demand Is Our Only Hope." *USA Today,* July, pp. 20–22.

Bryjak, G. J., and M. P. Soroka. 1985. *Sociology: The Biological Factor.* Palo Alto, CA: Peek Publications.

Buckley, R. 1990. *Japan Today,* 2nd ed. Cambridge: Cambridge University Press.

Buckley, W. E., C. E. Yesalis III, K. E. Friedl, W. A. Anderson, A. L. Streit, and J. E. Wright. 1988. "Estimated Prevalence of Anabolic Steroid Use Among Male High School Seniors." *Journal of the American Medical Association* 260(23):3441–3445.

Burgess, E. W. 1925. "The Growth of the City," in R. E. Park and E. W. Burgess, eds. *The City.* Chicago: University of Chicago Press, pp. 47–62.

Burma, I. 1984. *Behind the Mask: On Sexual Demons, Sacred Mothers, Transvestites, Gangsters, and Other Japanese Cultural Heroes.* New York: New American Library.

Bush, R. C. 1988. "Introduction," in R. C. Bush et al., eds. *The Religious World—Communities of Faith.* New York: Macmillan, pp. 1–11.

Butler, E. W. 1976. *Urban Sociology: A Systematic Approach.* New York: Harper and Row.

Calderon, V. 1990. "TV's Border Scene." *San Diego Union,* October 21.

Caldwell, J. C. 1976. "Toward a Restatement of Demographic Transition Theory." *Population and Development Review* 2(3–4):321–366.

_____. 1980. "Mass Education as a Determinant of the Timing of Fertility Decline." *Population and Development Review* 6(2):225–256.

Campbell, D. T., and J. C. Stanley. 1963. *Experimental and Quasi-Experimental Designs for Research.* Chicago: Rand McNally.

Caplow, T. 1968. *Two Against One: Coalitions in Triads.* Englewood Cliffs, NJ: Prentice-Hall.

Carroll, J. B. 1961. *The Study of Language.* Cambridge, MA: Harvard University Press.

Centers, R. 1949. *The Psychology of Social Classes: A Study of Class Consciousness.* Princeton, NJ,: Princeton University Press.

Chase-Dunn, C. 1975. "The Effects of International Dependence on Development and Inequality: A Cross-National Study." *American Sociological Review* 40(December):720–738.

Cherry, K. 1987. *Womansword. What Japanese Words Say About Women.* Tokyo: Kodansha International.

Chirot, D. 1977. *Social Change in the Twentieth Century.* New York: Harcourt Brace Jovanovich.

Chomsky, N. 1965. *Aspects of the Theory of Syntax.* Cambridge, MA: M.I.T. Press, p. 6.

Chown, S. M. 1977. "Morale, Careers and Personal Potentials," in J. E. Birren and K. W. Schaie, eds. *Handbook of the Psychology of Aging.* New York: Van Nostrand Reinhold, pp. 672–691.

Christian Science Monitor. 1984. "Education: Facts for Third World Women." August 9.

Christiansen, K. O. 1977. From lecture at University of Oklahoma.

Christopher, R. 1983. *The Japanese Mind.* New York: Fawcett Columbine.

Chudacoff, H. P. 1981. *The Evolution of American Urban Society.* Englewood Cliffs, NJ: Prentice-Hall.

Cimons, M. 1990. "Paper Calls Child Abuse a National Emergency." *Los Angeles Times,* June 2.

Clammer, J. 1988. "Singapore's Buddhist Chant: A Modern Mantra." *Far Eastern Economic Review* (December 29):27–29.

Cleeland, N. 1990. "Mexican State Legalizes Abortion; Both Sides Stunned." *San Diego Union,* December 20.

_____. 1991. "Gasping in Smoggy Mexico City—Oxygen Kiosk May Prove Helpful." *San Diego Union,* March 9.

Clifford, F. 1991. "Urban Areas Now Home to U.S. Majority." *Los Angeles Times,* February 2.

Clifford, F., and A. C. Roark. 1991. "Big Cities Hit by Census Data Showing Declining Role." *Los Angeles Times,* January 24.

Clifford, F., A. C. Roark, and B. M. Horstman. 1991. "Census Finds Ethnic Boom in Suburbs, Rural Areas." *Los Angeles Times,* February 26.

Clinard, M. B. 1974. *The Sociology of Deviant Behavior.* New York: Holt, Rinehart and Winston.

_____. 1983a. *Corporate Ethics and Crime—The Role of Middle Management.* Beverly Hills, CA: Sage.

_____. 1983b. "Crime in Developing Countries." *Encyclopedia of Crime and Justice* 2:597–601.

Clinard, M. B., and D. J. Abbott. 1977. "Crime in Developing Countries," in Sir L. Radzinowicz and M. E. Wolfgang, eds. *Crime and Justice.* Vol. 1, *The Criminal in Society.* New York: Basic Books, pp. 25–51.

Clinard, M. B., and R. Quinney. 1973. *Criminal Behavior Systems: A Typology.* New York: Holt, Rinehart and Winston.

Clinard, M. B., and P. C. Yeager. 1980. *Corporate Crime.* New York: Free Press.

Coakley, J. J. 1990. *The Sociology of Sport.* St. Louis: C. V. Mosby.

Cohen, R. 1978. "Introduction," in R. Cohen and E. R. Service, eds. *Origins of the State.* Philadelphia: Institute for the Study of Human Issues, pp. 1–20.

Cole, R. 1979. *Work, Mobility, and Participation.* Berkeley, CA: University of California Press.

Coleman, J. S. 1961. *The Adolescent Society.* Garden City, NY: Doubleday.

_____. 1975. *Youth: Transition to Adulthood.* Report of the Panel on Youth of the President's Science Advisory Committee. Chicago: University of Chicago Press.

Coleman, J. W. 1985. *The Criminal Elite: The Sociology of White Collar Crime.* New York: St. Martin's Press.

_____. 1989. *The Criminal Elite: The Sociology of White Collar Crime,* 2nd ed. New York: St. Martin's Press.

Coleman, R. P., and L. Rainwater. 1978. *Social Standing in America: New Dimensions of Class.* New York: Basic Books.

Collier, J. F. 1986. "From Mary to Modern Woman: The Material Basis of Marianismo and Its Transformation in a Spanish Village." *American Ethnologist* 13 (1):100–107.

Collins, R. 1971. "A Conflict Theory of Sexual Stratification." *Social Problems* 19(1):3–21.

_____. 1975. *Conflict Sociology: Toward an Explanatory Science.* New York: Academic Press.

_____. 1979. *The Credential Society: An Historical Sociology of Education and Stratification.* New York: Academic Press.

_____. 1985a. *Sociology of Marriage and the Family—Gender, Love, and Property.* Chicago: Nelson-Hall.

_____. 1985b. *Three Sociological Traditions.* New York: Oxford University Press.

_____. 1988a. *Sociology of Marriage and the Family,* 2nd ed. Chicago: Nelson-Hall.

_____. 1988b. *Theoretical Sociology.* San Diego, CA: Harcourt Brace Jovanovich.

Collins, R., and M. Makowsky. 1984. *The Discovery of Society.* New York: Random House.

Comte, A. 1877. *Early Essays.* London: Longmans, Green.

Conover, T. 1987. *Coyotes.* New York: Random House.

Converse, H. S. 1988. "Hinduism," in R. C. Bush et al., eds. *The Religious World—Communities of Faith.* New York: Macmillan, pp. 52–112.

Conway, M. M. 1991. *Political Participation in the United States,* 2nd ed. Washington, DC: Congressional Quarterly.

Cook, F. 1990. "U.S. Homes Seem like Bargains to Japanese." *San Diego Union,* December 2.

Cooley, C. H. 1902. *Human Nature and the Social Order.* New York: Charles Scribner's Sons.

_____. 1909. *Social Organization.* New York: Charles Scribner's Sons.

Cooper, M. 1983. "Christianity," in vol. 1, *Kodansha Encyclopedia of Japan.* Tokyo: Kodansha, pp. 306–310.

Cornelius, W. A., and A. L. Craig. 1988. *Politics in Mexico: An Introduction and Overview.* La Jolla, CA: Center for U.S.–Mexican Studies, University of California, San Diego.

Coser, L. 1964. *The Functions of Social Conflict.* Glencoe, IL: Free Press.

_____. 1971. *Masters of Sociological Thought.* New York: Harcourt Brace Jovanovich.

Cox, H. 1965. *The Secular City.* New York: Macmillan.

Cox, O. C. 1948. *Caste, Class, and Race: A Study in Social Dynamics.* New York: Modern Reader Paperbacks.

Cressey, D. 1953. *Other People's Money: A Study in the Social Psychology of Embezzlement.* New York: Free Press.

Crompton, R., and M. Mann, eds. 1986. *Gender and Stratification.* Cambridge: Polity Press.

Cuber, J. F., and P. B. Harroff. 1983. "Five Types of Marriage," in A. S. Skolnick and J. H. Skolnick, eds. *Families in Transition.* Boston: Little, Brown, pp. 318–329.

Cubitt, T. 1988. *Latin American Society.* London: Longman.

Curtiss, S. 1977. *Genie: A Psycholinguistic Study of a Modern-Day "Wild Child."* New York: Academic Press.

Dabbs, J. M., Jr., and N. A. Stokes, III. 1975. "Beauty Is Power: The Use of Space on a Sidewalk." *Sociometry* 38(4):551–557.

Dahrendorf, R. 1959. *Class and Class Conflict in Industrial Society.* Stanford, CA: Stanford University Press.

———. 1968. *Essays in the Theory of Society.* Stanford, CA: Stanford University Press.

Daniloff, N. 1982. "For Russia's Women, Worst of Both Worlds." *U.S. News & World Report* (June 28):53–54.

Davies, J. C. 1962. "Toward a Theory of Revolution." *American Sociological Review* 6(1):5–19.

Davis, A., B. B. Gardner, and M. R. Gardner. 1941. *Deep South.* Chicago: University of Chicago Press.

Davis, K. 1940. "Extreme Social Isolation of a Child." *American Journal of Sociology* 45(4):554–565.

———. 1947. "Final Note on a Case of Extreme Isolation." *American Journal of Sociology* 52(5):432–437.

———. 1949. *Human Societies.* New York: Macmillan.

———. 1986. "Low Fertility in Evolutionary Perspective." *Population and Development Review* 12:46–48.

Davis, K., and J. Blake. 1956. "Social Structure and Fertility: An Analytic Framework." *Economic Development and Cultural Change* (April):211–235.

Davis, K., and W. E. Moore. 1945. "Some Principles of Stratification." *American Sociological Review* 10(2):242–249.

Davis, N. 1971. "The Prostitute: Developing a Deviant Identity," in J. H. Henslin, ed. *Studies in the Sociology of Sex.* New York: Appleton-Century-Crofts, pp. 297–322.

de Queiroz, M. I. P. 1989. "Afro-Brazilian Cults and Religious Change in Brazil," in J. A. Beckford and T. Luckman, eds. *The Changing Face of Religion.* Newbury Park, CA: Sage.

Deckard, B. Sinclair. 1983. *The Women's Movement: Political, Socioeconomic, and Psychological Issues,* 3rd ed. New York: Harper and Row.

Decter, M. 1990. "Legitimizing Enslavement Will Not Reduce Its Harm." *Los Angeles Times,* March 20.

Delacroix, J. 1977. "The Export of Raw Materials and Economic Growth: A Cross-National Study." *American Sociological Review* 42(October):795–808.

Denno, D. 1986. In *Biology and Crime—Show No. 17.* Washington, DC: National Institute of Justice Crime File Series.

Diaz-Guerro, R. 1975. *Psychology of the Mexican.* Austin, TX: University of Texas Press.

DiIulio, J. J. 1989. "The Impact of Inner City Crime." *Public Interest* (Summer):28–46.

Dion, K. L. 1979. "Intergroup Conflict and Intragroup Cohesiveness," in W. G. Austin and S. Worchel, eds. *The Social Psychology of Intergroup Relations.* Monterey, CA: Brooks/Cole.

Dobson, E., E. Hindson, and J. Falwell. 1986. *The Fundamentalist Phenomenon,* 2nd ed. Grand Rapids, MI: Baker Book House.

Dogan, M. 1988. "Giant Cities as Maritime Gateways," in M. Dogan and J. Kasarda, eds. *A World of Giant Cities,* vol. 1. Beverly Hills, CA: Sage, pp. 30–55.

Dogan, M., and J. Kasarda. 1988. "How Giant Cities Will Multiply and Grow," in M. Dogan and J. Kasarda, eds. *A World of Giant Cities,* vol. 1. Beverly Hills, CA: Sage, pp. 12–29.

Doi, L. T. 1956. "Japanese Language as an Expression of Japanese Psychology." *Western Speech* 20:90–96.

———. 1973. *The Anatomy of Dependence.* Tokyo: Kodansha International.

Domhoff, G. W., and H. B. Ballard, eds. 1968. *C. Wright Mills and the Power Elite.* Boston: Beacon Press.

Dorr, A. 1986. *Television for Children: A Special Medium for a Special Audience.* Beverly Hills, CA: Sage.

Douglas, J. D. 1967. *The Social Meaning of Suicide.* Princeton, NJ: Princeton University Press.

———. 1976. *Investigative Field Research.* Beverly Hills, CA: Sage.

Durkheim, E. 1933. *The Division of Labor in Society.* New York: Macmillan.

———. 1938. *The Rules of the Sociological Method.* New York: Macmillan.

———. 1951. *Suicide.* New York: Free Press.

———. 1965, original 1915. *The Elementary Forms of the Religious Life.* New York: Free Press.

———. 1966, original 1895. *On the Division of Labor in Society.* G. Simpson, trans. New York: Free Press.

Dye, T. R. 1976. *Who's Running America?: Institutional Leadership in the United States.* Englewood Cliffs, NJ: Prentice-Hall.

———. 1979. *Who's Running America?: The Carter Years,* 2nd ed. Englewood Cliffs, NJ: Prentice-Hall.

———. 1983. *Who's Running America?: The Reagan Years,* 3rd ed. Englewood Cliffs, NJ: Prentice-Hall.

———. 1986. *Who's Running America?: The Conservative Years,* 4th ed. Englewood Cliffs, NJ: Prentice-Hall.

———. 1990. *Who's Running America: The Bush Era,* 5th ed. Englewood Cliffs, NJ: Prentice-Hall.

Dyer, G. 1985. *War.* New York: Crown Publishers.

Earhart, H. B. 1983. "Religion," in vol. 6, *Kodansha Encyclopedia of Japan.* Tokyo: Kodansha, pp. 290–293.

Eccles, J. S. 1987. "Adolescence: Gateway to Gender-Role Transcendance," in D. B. Carter, ed. *Current Conceptions of Sex Roles and Sex Typing.* New York: Praeger, pp. 225–242.

Economist. 1987. "The Proper Way to Behave." July 4, pp. 83–86.

———. 1988a. "The Peons Turn on Mexico's Ever-Ruling Party." March 5, pp. 43–44.

———. 1988b. "Mexico's Ruling Dinosaur." December 3, p. 16.

———. 1989a. "Mexico: From Boom to Bust." February 11, pp. 75–76.

———. 1989b. "Japan and the Koreas: Blind Prejudice." March 11, pp. 37–38.

———. 1989c. "Discomfort Women." November 25, p. 36.

———. 1990. "Japan's Schools: Why Can't Little Taro Think?" April 21.

Edgerton, R. B. 1976. *Deviance: A Cross-Cultural Perspective.* Menlo Park, CA: Cummings.

Elizondo, V. 1983. *Galiliean Journey: The Mexican-American Promise.* Maryknoll, NY: Orbis Books.

Elvy, P. 1987. *Buying Time.* Mystic, CT: Twenty-Third Publications.

Ember, C. R., and M. Ember. 1988. *Anthropology,* 5th ed. Englewood Cliffs, NJ: Prentice-Hall.

Engels, F. 1902, original 1884. *The Origin of the Family.* Chicago: Charles H. Kerr and Company.

England, P., and G. Farkas. 1986. *Households, Employment and Gender.* New York: Aldine.

England, P., G. Farkas, B. Stanek Kilbourne, and T. Dou. 1988. "Explaining Occupational Sex Segregation and Wages: Fndings from a Model with Fixed Effects." *American Sociological Review* 53:544–558.

Erikson, K. T. 1966. *Wayward Puritans.* New York: Wiley.

Escobar, A., M. Gonzales, and B. Roberts. 1987. "Migration, Labour Markets and the International Economy," in J. Eades, ed. *Migrants, Workers and the Social Order.* London: Association of Social Anthropologists, Monograph no. 26, pp. 42–64.

Eshleman, R. J. 1985. *Sociology of Marriage and the Family.* Chicago: Nelson-Hall.

Etzioni, A. 1975. *A Comparative Analysis of Complex Organizations,* rev. and enlarged edition. Glencoe, IL: Free Press.

Evans, P. B., and J. D. Stephens. 1988. "Development and the World Economy," in N. J. Smelser, ed. *Handbook of Sociology.* Newbury Park, CA: Sage, pp. 739–773.

Fagot, B. I., R. Hagan, M. Driver Leinbach, and S. Kronsberg. 1985. "Differential Reactions to Assertive and Communicative Acts of Toddler Boys and Girls." *Child Development* 56:1499–1505.

Falicov, C. J. 1982. "Mexican Families," in M. McGoldrich, ed. *Ethnicity and Family Therapy.* New York: Gardner Press, pp. 134–163.

Falicov, C. J., and B. M. Karrer. 1988. "Cultural Variations in the Family Life Cycle: The Mexican-American Family," in E. Carter and M. McGoldrich, eds., *The Family Life Cycle.* New York: Gardner Press, pp. 383–425.

Fallows, J. 1989. "Containing Japan." *Harpers* (May):62.

Farberow, N. L. 1989. "Suicide," in R. Kastenbaum and B. Kastenbaum, eds. *The Encyclopedia of Death.* Phoenix, AZ: Oryx Press, pp. 227–230.

Featherman, D. L., and R. M. Hauser. 1978. *Opportunity and Change.* New York: Academic Press.

Feingold, A. 1988. "Matching for Attractiveness in Romantic Pictures and Same Sex Friends: Meta Analysis and Theoretical Critique." *Psychological Bulletin* 104:226–235.

Felix, D. 1977. "Income Inequality in Mexico." *Current History* 72 (March):111–136.

Fenwick, C. R. 1982. "Crime and Justice in Japan: Implications for the United States." *International Journal of Comparative Criminal Justice* 6:61–71.

Fewster, S., and T. Gorton. 1987. *Japan: From Shogun to Superstate.* New York: St. Martin's Press.

Finn, P. 1988. "Street People," in *U.S. Department of Justice.* Washington, DC.

Fischer, C. S. 1976. *The Urban Experience.* New York: Harcourt Brace Jovanovich.

Fornos, W. 1987. *Gaining People, Losing Ground: A Blueprint for Stabilizing World Population.* Ephrata, PA: Science Press.

———. 1989. *Letter to Educators.* Washington, DC: Population Crisis Committee.

Foster, L V., and L. Foster. 1986. *Fielding's Mexico 1986.* New York: William Morrow.

Fox, T., and S. M. Miller. 1965. "Inter-Country Variations: Occupational Stratification and Mobility." *Studies in Comparative International Development* 1:3–10.

Frank, I., and R. Hirono. 1974. *How the United States and Japan See Each Other.* New York: Committee for Economic Development.

French, H. F. 1990. "A Most Deadly Trade." *World Watch* (July/August):11–17.

Freud, S. 1930. *Civilization and Its Discontents.* Trans. James Strachey. New York: Norton.

Frey, W. 1990. *Metropolitan America: Beyond the Transition.* Population Bulletin 45(2). Washington, DC: Population Reference Bureau.

Friedan, B. J. 1989. "The Downtown Job Puzzle." *Public Interest* (Fall):71–86.

Fromkin, V., and R. Rodman. 1988. *An Introduction to Language.* New York: Holt, Rinehart and Winston, pp. 375–398.

Fujimoto, K. 1991. "Working Their Way to a Sudden Death." *Japan Times,* January 14–20.

Fukutake, T. 1982. *The Japanese Social Structure: Its Evolution in the Modern Century.* Tokyo: University of Tokyo Press.

Fulwood, S., III. 1990. "California Gains Seven House Seats in Final Census." *Los Angeles Times,* December 27.

Fuse, T. 1983. "Suicide," in *Kodansha Encyclopedia of Japan,* vol. 7. Tokyo: Kodansha, pp. 261–263.

Gagnon, J. H., and W. Simon. 1973. *Sexual Conduct: The Sources of Human Sexuality.* Chicago: Aldine.

Galbraith, J. K. 1979. *The Nature of Mass Poverty.* Cambridge, MA: Harvard University Press.

Gallaway, L., and R. Vedder. 1986. "Inflation, Migration, and Divorce in Contemporary America," in J. R. Peden and F. R. Glahe, eds. *The American Family and State.* San Francisco: Pacific Research Institute for the Public Policy, pp. 285–307.

Galliher, J. F. 1989. *Criminology: Human Rights, Criminal Law, and Crime.* Englewood Cliffs, NJ: Prentice-Hall.

Gans, H. 1962. "Urbanism and Suburbanism as Ways of Life: A Re-evaluation of Definitions," in A. M. Rose, ed. *Human Behavior and Social Process: An Interactional Perspective.* Boston: Houghton Mifflin, pp. 625–648.

———. 1980. *Deciding What's News: A Study of CBS Evening News, NBC Nightly News, Newsweek and Time.* New York: Vintage Press.

Gappert, G. 1987. "Introduction: The Future of Winter Cities," in G. Gappert, ed. *The Future of Winter Cities.* Beverly Hills, CA: Sage, pp. 7–12.

Gardels, N., and M. Berlin Snell. 1989. "Breathing Fecal Dust in Mexico City." *Los Angeles Times Book Review,* April 23, p. 16.

Garfinkel, H. 1956. "Conditions of a Successful Degradation Ceremony." *American Journal of Sociology* 61·420–424.

Garfinkel, P. 1983. "The Best 'Jewish' Mother in the World." *Psychology Today* (September):56–60.

Gelles, R. 1980. "Violence in the Family: A Review of the Research in the Seventies." *Journal of Marriage and the Family* 42:873–885.

Gilbert, A., and P. Ward. 1982. "Low Income Housing and the State," in A. Gilbert, J. E. Hardy, and

R. Ramirez, eds. *Urbanization in Contemporary Latin America.* New York: Wiley, pp. 79–128.

Gill, L. 1990. "Mexico." *Population Today Bulletin* 18(11). Washington, DC: Population Reference Bureau.

Gilly, M. C. 1988. "Sex Roles in Advertising: A Comparison of Television Advertisements in Australia, Mexico, and the United States." *Journal of Marketing* 52(April):75–85.

Gitlin, T. 1985. *Inside Prime Time.* New York: Pantheon Books.

Goetting, A. 1983. "Divorce Outcome Research: Issues and Perspectives," in A. S. Skolnick and J. H. Skolnick, eds. *Family in Transition.* Boston: Little, Brown, pp. 367–387.

Goffman, E. 1961. *Asylums: Essays on the Social Situation of Mental Patients and Other Inmates.* New York: Anchor Books.

Gold, M. E. 1983. *A Dialogue on Comparable Worth.* New York: ILR Press.

Goldwert, M. 1983. *Machismo and Conquest: The Case of Mexico.* Lanham, MD: University Press of America.

Goode, E. 1990. *Deviant Behavior.* Englewood Cliffs, NJ: Prentice-Hall.

Goode, W. J. 1963. *World Revolution and Family Patterns.* New York: Free Press.

Gordon, M. M. 1964. *Assimilation in American Life.* New York: Oxford University Press.

Gortmaker, S. L. 1979. "Poverty and Infant Mortality in the United States." *American Journal of Sociology* 44(2):280–297.

Gould, S. J. 1976. "Biological Potential vs. Biological Determinism." *Natural History* 85(5):12–22.

———. 1981. *The Mismeasure of Man.* New York: Norton.

Gouldner, A. W. 1954a. *Patterns of Industrial Bureaucracy.* Glencoe, IL: Free Press.

———. 1954b. *Wildcat Strike.* Glencoe, IL: Free Press.

Gracey, H. L. 1977. "Learning the Student Role: Kindergarten as Academic Boot Camp," in D. H. Wrong and H. L. Gracey, eds. *Readings in Introductory Sociology,* 3rd ed. New York: Macmillan, pp. 215–226.

Granato, S., and A. Mostkoff. 1989. "The Class Structure of Mexico, 1895–1980," in J. W. Wilkie, ed. *Statistical Abstracts of Latin America,* vol. 27. Los Angeles: UCLA Latin American Center Publications, p. 318.

Grapard, A. G. 1983. "Shinto." *Kodansha Encyclopedia of Japan.* Toyko: Kodansha.

Graven, K. 1990. "Sex Harassment at the Office Stirs Up Japan." *Wall Street Journal,* March 21, pp. B1, B10.

Greeley, A. M. 1989. *Religious Change in America.* Cambridge, MA: Harvard University Press.

Greenberg, J. H. 1968. *Anthropological Linguistics: An Introduction.* New York: Random House.

Griffin, S. 1973. *Rape: The All-American Crime.* Andover, MA: Warner Modular Publications.

Gross, G. 1990. "The Chilango Chill." *San Diego Union,* May 13.

Gusfield, J. 1967. "Tradition and Modernity: Misplaced Polarities in the Study of Social Change." *American Journal of Sociology* (January):351–362.

Gwynne, S. C. 1990. "Up from the Streets." *Time* (April 30): 34.

Hacker, H. 1951. "Women as a Minority Group." *Social Forces* 30:60–69.

———. 1974. "Women as a Minority Group: 20 Years Later," in F. Denmark, ed. *Who Discriminates Against Women?* Beverly Hills, CA: Sage, pp. 124–134.

Hagan, F. E. 1986. *Introduction to Criminology—Theories, Methods, and Criminal Behavior.* Chicago: Nelson-Hall.

Hall, S. 1987. "Little Progress for Mexico's Women." *World Press Review* (May):53–54.

Hanson, R. 1987. "Urban Development in an Advanced Economy," in G. Gappert, ed. *The Future of Winter Cities.* Beverly Hills, CA: Sage, pp. 251–260.

Hardgrave, R. L., Jr., and S. A. Kochanek. 1986. *India—Government and Politics in a Developing Nation.* San Diego, CA: Harcourt Brace Jovanovich.

Harper, C. L. 1989. *Exploring Social Change.* Englewood Cliffs, NJ: Prentice-Hall.

Harris, C. D., and E. L. Ullman. 1945. "The Nature of Cities." *Annals of the Academy of Political and Social Sciences* (November):7–17.

Harris, M. 1983. *Cultural Anthropology.* New York: Harper and Row.

Harris, T. G., and D. Yankelovich. 1989. "What Good Are the Rich?" *Psychology Today* (April):36–39.

Harrison, P. 1984. *Inside the Third World.* New York: Penguin Books.

Hatfield, E., and S. Sprecher. 1986. *Mirror, Mirror: The Importance of Looks in Everyday Life.* Albany, NY: SUNY Press.

Haviland, W. A. 1990. *Cultural Anthropology.* Fort Worth, TX: Holt, Rinehart and Winston.

Hawkes, G. R., and M. Taylor. 1975. "Power Structure in Mexican and Mexican-American Farm Labor Families." *Journal of Marriage and the Family* 37:807–811.

Hawley, A. 1950. *Human Ecology: A Theory of Community Structure.* New York: Rosenthal Press.

Hawton, K. 1986. *Suicide and Attempted Suicide Among Children and Adolescents.* Beverly Hills, CA: Sage.

Heilbroner, R. L. 1980. *An Inquiry Into the Human Prospect.* New York: Norton.

Heise, L. 1989. "The Global War Against Women." *Utne Reader* (November/December):40–45.

Helm, L. 1991. "The Rule of Work in Japan." *Los Angeles Times,* March 17.

Hendry, J. 1987. *Understanding Japanese Society.* London: Croom Helm.

Herrnstein, R. 1986. "Biology and Crime." *National Institute of Justice—Crime File Study Guide.* Washington, DC.

Hess, R., and J. Torney. 1967. *The Development of Political Attitudes in Children.* Chicago: Aldine.

Hiltzik, M. A. 1990. "Africa's Future Riding Train to Nowhere." *Los Angeles Times,* July 17.

———. 1991. "Africa Hit by 'Donor Fatigue.'" *Los Angeles Times,* March 8.

Hinds, H. E., Jr., and C. Tatum. 1984. "Images of Women in Mexican Comic Books." *Journal of Popular Culture* 18(Summer):146–162.

Hiro, D. 1976. *Inside India Today.* New York: Monthly Review Press.

Hirschi, T. 1969. *Causes of Delinquency.* Berkeley, CA: University of California Press.

Hirschi, T., and M. Gottfredson. 1983. "Age and the Explanation Crime." *American Journal of Sociology* 89:552–584.

Hobbes, T. 1881. *Leviathan.* Oxford: James Thornton.

Hodge, R. W., and D. J. Treiman. 1968. "Class Identification in the United States." *American Journal of Sociology* 73:535–547.

Hollingshead, A. B., and F. C. Redlich. 1958. *Social Class and Mental Illness.* New York: Wiley.

Holmstrom, L. Lytle, and A. Wolbert Burgess. 1978. *The Victim of Rape: Institutional Reactions.* New York: John Wesley and Sons.

Hoover, S. M. 1988. *Mass Media Religion.* Newbury Park, CA: Sage.

Hoppenstand, G. 1983. "Yellow Devil Doctors and Opium Dens: A Survey of the Yellow Peril Stereotypes in Mass Media Entertainment," in C. D. Geist and J. Nachbar, eds. *The Popular Culture Reader,* 3rd ed. Bowling Green, OH: Popular Press.

Horton, J., and T. Platt. 1986. "Crime and Criminal Justice Under Capitalism and Socialism: Toward a Marxist Perspective." *Crime and Social Justice* 25:115–135.

Hoselitz, B. F. 1954–1955. "Generative and Parasitic Cities." *Economic Development and Cultural Change* 3:278–294.

Hosken, F. P. 1985. *Academic American Encyclopedia,* vol. 5. Danbury, CT: Grolier, pp. 3–5.

Hoult, T. Ford. 1974. *Dictionary of Modern Sociology.* Totowa, NJ: Littlefield Adams.

Howard, M. C., and P. C. McKim. 1986. *Contemporary Cultural Anthropology.* Boston: Little, Brown.

Hoyt, H. 1939. *The Structure and Growth of Residential Neighborhoods in American Cities.* Washington, DC: Federal Housing Administration.

Hsu, F. K. 1979. "The Cultural Problems of the Cultural Anthropologist." *American Anthropologist* 81:517–532.

"Hunger Myths and Facts." 1989. San Francisco: Institute for Food and Developmental Policy.

Huntington, S. P. 1968. *Political Order in Changing Societies.* New Haven: Yale University Press.

Huth, T. 1989. "The RV Mystique." *Outside* (March): 92–99.

Imhoff, G. 1990. "The Position of U.S. English on Bilingual Education." *Annals of the American Academy of the Political and Social Sciences* 508:48–61.

Impoco, J. 1990. "Motherhood and the Future of Japan." *U.S. News & World Report* (December 24): 56–57.

Impoco, J., and K. Sullivan. 1989. "Sex, Taxes and 'the Madonna Factor.'" *U.S. News & World Report* (August 7):36.

Inciardi, J. A. 1984. *Criminal Justice.* San Diego, CA: Harcourt Brace Jovanovich.

Inkles, A. 1973. "Making Man Modern: On the Causes and Consequences of Individual Change in Six Developing Countries," in A. Etzioni and E. Etzioni-Halvey, eds. *Social Change—Sources, Patterns and Consequences.* New York: Basic Books, pp. 342–361.

Innes, C. A. 1988. *Drug Use and Crime.* Washington, DC: Bureau of Justice Statistics.

Inoue, H. 1990. "As New Leader, Japan Needs to Confront the Past Honestly." *Japan Times,* September 24–30.

Jacklin, C. Nagy. 1989. "Female and Male: Issues of Gender." *American Psychologist* 44(2):127–133.

Jacobs, J. 1990. "Who's Going to Mind the Government Drug Store?" *Los Angeles Times,* March 20.

Jaggar, A. M. 1983. *Feminist Politics and Human Nature.* Totowa, NJ: Rowman and Allanheld.

Jameson, S. 1984. "'Super-Cops' of Japan: The Glow Fades." *Los Angeles Times,* September 4.

———. 1989. "Gingerly, Japanese Open Up." *Los Angeles Times,* October 31.

Japan Times. 1990a. "Education Costs Continue to Zoom." July 21.

———. 1990b. "Life Spans Set New Records." August 13–19, p. 2.

———. 1990c. "Teacher Indicted for Professional Negligence." September 24–30.

Jensen, H., and K. Sullivan. 1989. "Cleaning House: Japan's New Prime Minister Pledges Reforms." *Maclean's* (August 21):31.

Johns, C. J. 1978. "The Triumph of Lawless Force and Lawless Privilege: A Brief History of Mexican Legal Traditions." *International Journal of Comparative and Applied Criminal Justice* 2:49–60.

Johnson, C. 1982. *MITI and the Japanese Miracle: The Growth of Industrial Policy.* Stanford, CA: Stanford University Press.

Johnson, D. P. 1981. *Sociological Theory—Classical Founders and Contemporary Perspectives.* New York: Wiley.

Jones, E., and E. Van Zandt. 1974. *The City: Yesterday, Today and Tomorrow.* Garden City, NY: Doubleday.

Jones, R. S. 1988. "Economic Implications of Japan's Aging Population," in J. K. T. Choy, ed. *Japan—Exploring New Paths.* Washington, DC: Japan Economic Institute of America.

Josephson, W. L. 1987. "Television Violence and Children's Aggression: Testing the Priming, Social Script, and Disinhibition Predictors." *Journal of Personality and Social Psychology* 53(5):882–890.

Kagan, D. 1989. "How America Lost Its First Drug War." *Insight* 20:8–17.

Kaleidoscope: Current World Data. 1988. Santa Barbara, CA: ABC-C1IO.

Kanter, R. Moss. 1983. *The Change Masters: Innovation and Entrepreneurship in the American Corporation.* New York: Simon and Schuster.

———. 1985. "All That Is Entrepreneurial Is Not Gold." *Wall Street Journal,* July 22, p. 18.

Kastenbaum, R., and B. Kastenbaum. 1989. *Suicide. Encyclopedia of Death.* Phoenix, AZ: Oryx Press.

Kepp, M. 1991. "Loss of Land, White Encroachment Cited as Suicides Among Brazil's Indians Rise." *San Diego Union,* May 5.

Kesey, K. 1962. *One Flew Over the Cuckoo's Nest.* New York: Viking Press.

Kessler, R. C., and P. D. Cleary. 1980. "Social Class and Psychological Distress." *American Sociological Review* 45:463–478.

Keyfitz, N. 1986. "The Family That Does Not Reproduce Itself." *Population and Development Review* 12: 139–154.

Kinsey, A. C., W. B. Pomeroy, and C. E. Martin. 1948. *Sexual Behavior in the Human Male.* Philadelphia: W. B. Saunders.

Kirp, D. L., M. G. Yodof, and M. Strong Franks. 1986. *Gender Justice.* Chicago: University of Chicago Press.

Kitsuse, J. I., and A. E. Murase. 1987. "Reform of Education System." *Japan Times,* February 15 and 16.

Kneisner, T. J., M. B. McElroy, and S. P. Wilcox. 1988. "Getting into Poverty Without a Husband, and Getting Out, With or Without." *American Economic Review* 78(2):86–90.

Koch, K. 1974. "Cultural Relativism," in *Encyclopedia of Sociology.* Guilford, CT: Dushkin Publishing Group.

Kohn, M. L. 1976. "Interaction of Social Class and Other Factors in the Etiology of Schizophrenia." *American Journal of Psychiatry* 133(2):179–180.

Konner, M., and C. Worthman. 1980. "Nursing Frequency, Gonadal Function, and Birth Spacing Among Kung Hunter Gatherers." *Science* 207 (February 15): 788–791.

Krishna, R. 1982–1983. In G. J. Bryjak, "India's Urban Catastrophe." *Journal of the Institute for Socioeconomic Studies* VII(4):77–90.

Kuznets, S. 1955. "Economic Growth and Income Inequality." *American Economic Review* (March):178–194.

"Labour and Population." 1977. New York: United Nations Fund for Population Activities.

LaFreniere, P., F. F. Stryer, and R. Gauthier. 1984. "The Emergence of Same-Sex Affiliative Preferences Among Preschool Peers: A Developmental/Ethological Perspective." *Child Development* 55:1958–1965.

Lamb, D. 1984. *The Africans.* New York: Vintage Books.

Landes, J. B. 1979. "Women, Labor and Family Life," in R. Quinney, ed. *Capitalist Society—Readings for a Critical Sociology.* Homewood, IL: Dorsey Press, pp. 214–227.

Lapierre, D. 1985. *The City of Joy.* Garden City, NY: Doubleday.

Larkin, R. P., and G. L. Peters. 1983. *Dictionary of Concepts in Human Geography.* Westport, CT: Greenwood Press.

Lasch, C. 1979. *Haven in a Heartless World.* New York: Basic Books.

Laslett, B., and C. A. B. Warren. 1975. "Losing Weight: The Organizational Promotion of Behavior Change." *Social Problems* 23:69–80.

Lau, A. 1990. "An Epidemic of Hate Crimes Against Asians Is Reported." *San Diego Union,* June 24.

Lauer, J., and R. H. Lauer. 1985. "Marriages Made to Last." *Psychology Today* (June):22–26.

Lauer, R. H. 1982. *Perspectives on Social Change.* Boston: Allyn and Bacon.

Layng, A. 1990. "What Keeps Women 'in Their Place'?" in E. Angeloni, ed. *Anthropology 90/91.* Guilford, CT: Dushkin Publishing Group, pp. 148–151.

Lebra, T. S. 1976. *Japanese Patterns of Behavior.* Honolulu: University of Hawaii Press.

Lebra, T. S., and W. P. Lebra. 1986. *Japanese Culture and Behavior.* Honolulu: University of Hawaii Press.

Leeds, A., and V. Dusek. 1981–1982. "Editors' Note." *Philosophical Forum* 13(2–3):i–xxxiv.

Lemert, E. M. 1951. *Social Pathology.* New York: McGraw-Hill.

Lenski, G. E. 1966. *Power and Privilege: A Theory of Social Stratification.* New York: McGraw-Hill.

Lenski, G. E., and J. Lenski. 1987. *Human Societies: An Introduction to Macrosociology,* 5th ed. New York: McGraw-Hill.

Leslie, G. R., and S. K. Korman. 1989. *The Family in Social Context.* New York: Oxford University Press.

Levine, S. B. 1980. "The Rise of American Boarding Schools and the Development of a National Upper Class." *Social Problems* 28(1):63–94.

Levy, F. 1988. *Dollars and Dreams: The Changing American Income Distribution.* New York: Norton.

Lewis, O. 1960. *Tepoztlan: Village in Mexico.* New York: Holt, Rinehart and Winston.

———. 1961. *Five Families.* New York: Mentor Books.

———. 1966. "The Culture of Poverty." *Scientific American* (October):19–25.

Light, I. 1983. *Cities in World Perspective.* New York: Macmillan.

Lincoln, J. R., and A. L. Kalleberg. 1985. "Work Organization and Commitment." *American Sociological Review* 50:738–760.

Lindquist, D. 1989. "Maquiladoras Draw Pilgrimage of Youth." *Los Angeles Times,* May 28.

———. 1991. "Mexico Attempting to Demystify Business." *San Diego Union,* April 12.

Lindsey, R. 1987. "Colleges Accused of Bias to Stem Asians' Gains." *New York Times,* January 19.

Lipset, S. M. 1963. *Political Man: The Social Bases of Politics.* New York: Anchor Books.

Little, C. B. 1989. *Deviance and Control: Theory, Research, and Social Policy.* Itasca, IL: Peacock.

Lofland, J. 1977. *Doomsday Cult: A Study of Conversion, Proselytization and Maintenance of Faith.* New York: Irvington Publishers.

Lombroso-Ferrero, G. 1972. *Lombroso's Criminal Man.* Montclair, NY: Patterson Smith.

London, B., and B. Williams. 1988. "Multinational Corporate Penetration, Protest, and Basic Needs Provisions in Non-Core Nations: A Cross-National Analysis." *Social Forces* 66:747–773.

Lord, G. F., III, and W. W. Falk. 1982. "Hidden Income and Segmentation: Structural Determinants of Fringe Benefits." *Social Science Quarterly* 63:208–224.

Lorenz, K. 1971. *On Aggression.* Toronto: Bantam Books.

Los Angeles Times. 1990a. "Curing Disease Would Do Little, Add Little to Life Spans, Study Finds." November 2.

———. 1990b. "Mexico Factory Pay Among the Lowest." November 4.

———. 1990c. "Survey: Some Blacks Expect Too Much of Sport." November 15.

Loup, J. 1983. *Can the Third World Survive?* Baltimore and London: Johns Hopkins University Press.

Lowery, S. V. 1990–1991. "Women of the Maquiladoras." *San Diego Business Journal,* pp. 24–25.

Luckenbill, D. F. 1977. "Criminal Homicide as a Situated Transaction." *Social Problems* 25:176–186.

Luckenbill, D. F., and D. P. Doyle. 1989. "Structural Position and Violence: Developing a Cultural Explanation." *Criminology* 27:419–433.

Lutz, W. 1989. *Doublespeak.* New York: Harper Perennial.

Lyon, D. 1988. *The Information Society: Issues and Illusions.* Cambridge: Polity Press.

Maccoby, E. E., and C. Nagy Jacklin. 1974. *The Psychology of Sex Differences.* Palo Alto, CA: Stanford University Press.

———. 1980. "Sex Differences in Aggression: A Rejoinder and Reprise." *Child Development* 51:964–980.

MacDougal, A. K. 1984. "Gap Between Rich and Poor Is Widening." *Los Angeles Times,* October 21.

Macionis, J. 1989. *Sociology.* Englewood Cliffs, NJ: Prentice-Hall.

MacNeill, J. 1989. "Strategies for Sustainable Development." *Scientific American* (September):155–165.

Madge, J. 1962. *The Origins of Scientific Sociology.* New York: Free Press.

Madrid, A. 1990. "Official English: A False Policy Issue." *Annals of the American Academy of the Political and Social Sciences* 508:62–65.

Madsen, C. F., and G. Meyer. 1978. *Minorities in American Society.* New York: D. Van Nostrand, p. 244.

Madsen, W. 1964. *The Mexican-Americans of South Texas.* New York: Holt, Rinehart and Winston.

Magnuson, E. 1981. "The Curse of Violent Crime." *Time* (March 23): 16–21.

Makihara, K. 1990. "Japanese Women: Rewriting Tradition." *Lear's* (February):78–83.

Malinowski, B. 1927. *Sex and Repression in Savage Society.* London: Routledge and Kegan Paul.

Mann, C. C. 1990. The Man with All the Answers. *The Atlantic* (January):45–62.

Maraldo, J. C. 1976. *Buddhism in the Modern World.* New York: Collier Books.

Marciano, T. Donati. 1988. "Families and Religion," in M. B. Sussman and S. K. Steinmetz, eds. *Handbook of Marriage and the Family.* New York: Plenum Press, pp. 285–315.

Marger, M. N. 1987. *Elites and Masses: An Introduction to Political Sociology,* 2nd ed. Belmont, CA: Wadsworth.

Mars, G. 1983. *Cheats at Work—An Anthropology of Workplace Crime.* London: Unwin.

———. 1990. "Cheats at Work—An Anthropology of Workplace Crime," in H. D. Barlow, ed. *Introduction to Criminology,* 5th ed. Glenview, IL: Scott Foresman/Little, Brown.

Marshall, F. R. 1986. Quoted in FAIR (Federation of American Immigration Report) (April).

Martin, R., R. J. Mutchnick, and W. T. Austin. 1990. *Criminological Thought: Pioneers Past and Present.* New York: Macmillan.

Martin, T. Castro, and L. L. Bumpass. 1989. "Recent Trends in Marital Disruption." *Demography* 6:37.

Martindale, D. 1981. *The Nature and Types of Sociological Thought.* Boston: Houghton Mifflin.

Marx, K. 1970, original 1844. *Critique of Hegel's 'Philosophy of Right.'* J. O'Malley, ed. Cambridge: Cambridge University Press.

Marx, K., and F. Engels. 1955, original 1848. *The Communist Manifesto.* S. H. Beer, ed. New York: Appleton-Century-Crofts.

Masao, T. 1968. *Modern Japanese Economy.* Tokyo: Japan Cultural Society.

Massey, D. S. 1987. "Understanding Mexican Migration to the United States." *American Journal of Sociology* 92(6):1372–1403.

Masters, W. H., V. E. Johnson, and R. C. Kolodny. 1988. *Human Sexuality.* Chicago: Scott Foresman/Little, Brown.

Mathews, H. F. 1987. "Intracultural Variations in Beliefs About Gender in a Mexican Community." *American Behavioral Scientist* 31(November–December):219–233.

Matthews, J. 1989. "Rescue Plan for Africa." *World Monitor* (May):28–36.

Maulain, C. O. 1987. *The Radical Right: A World Directory.* Essex, England: Longman Group.

McBee, S. 1984. "Are They Making the Grade?" *U.S. News & World Report* 96(April 2):41–43, 46–47.

McCarthy, K., and R. B. Valdez. 1985. *Current and Future Effects of Mexican Immigration in California.* Santa Barbara, CA: Rand Corporation.

McCord, C., and H. P. Freeman. 1990. "Excess Mortality in Harlem." *New England Journal of Medicine* 322(3):173–177.

McDonnell, P. 1989. "Mexico City Launches Its Boldest Attack Yet on Smog." *Los Angeles Times,* November 23.

McEvedy, C., and R. Jones. 1985. *The Atlas of World Population History.* New York: Penguin Books.

McGuire, S. 1988. "A Compromised Election: Despite Cries of Fraud, Mexico's Ruling Party Claims a Close Victory." *Newsweek* (July 18):36–37.

McKusick, L., W. Horstman, and T. J. Coates. 1985. "AIDS and Sexual Behavior Reported by Gay Men in San Francisco." *American Journal of Public Health* 75:493–496.

McLeod, B. 1986. "The Oriental Express." *Psychology Today* 20(July):48–52.

Mead, G. H. 1934. *Mind, Self, and Society.* Chicago: University of Chicago Press.

Mead, M. 1963, original 1935. *Sex and Temperament in Three Primitive Societies.* New York: William Morrow.

Merrick, T. W. 1986a. "World Population in Transition." *Population Bulletin* 41(2).

———. 1986b. *Population Pressures in Latin America.* Population Bulletin 41(3). Washington, DC: Population Reference Bureau.

Merton, R. 1957. *Social Theory and Social Structure.* New York: Free Press.

———. 1968. *Social Theory and Social Structure,* enlarged edition. New York: Free Press.

Michels, R. 1966, original 1915. *Political Parties.* New York: Free Press.

Middleton, A. 1990. "How Did the Maquiladora Industry Begin?" *San Diego Business Journal,* pp. 4–7.

Milgram, S. 1963. "Behavioral Study of Obedience." *Journal of Abnormal and Social Psychology* 67:371–378.

———. 1965. "Some Conditions of Obedience and Disobedience to Authority." *Human Relations* 18 (February):57–76.

Miller, A. G. 1986. *The Obedience Experiments: A Case of Controversy in Social Science.* New York: Praeger.

Miller, Marjorie. 1989. "Tradition, Poverty Shape Mexico Abortion Debate." *Los Angeles Times,* April 11.

———. 1990a. "Mexico Opposition Party Alleges 56 Political Killings." *Los Angeles Times,* January 30, pp. A1, A15.

———. 1990b. "Ecologists Alarmed as Mexico City's Smog Season Could Be Worst Yet." *Los Angeles Times,* December 18.

Miller, Matt. 1990. "Japan Is Rich, Most Japanese Are Not." *San Diego Union,* December 2.

Miller, R. R. 1985. *Mexico: A History.* Norman, OK: University of Oklahoma Press.

Mills, C. W. 1956. *The Power Elite.* London: Oxford University Press.

Milward, P. 1990. "Humanize Japan's Educational System." *Japan Times,* November 19–25.

Mirowski, P., and S. Helper. 1989. "Maquiladoras: Mexico's Tiger by the Tail?" *Challenge* (May/June):24–30.

Moeran, B. 1986. "Individual, Group and *Seishin:* Japan's Internal Cultural Debate," in T. S. Lebra and W. P. Lebra, eds. *Japanese Culture and Behavior: Selected*

Readings, rev. ed. Honolulu: University of Hawaii Press, pp. 62–89.

Montagu, A. 1980. "Introduction," in A. Montagu, ed. *Sociobiology Examined.* New York: Oxford University Press.

Moore, T. G. 1986. "The Unprecedented Shortage of Births in Europe." *Population and Development Review* 12:3–26.

Muehlenard, C. L., and M. A. Linton. 1987. "Date Rape: Familiar Strangers." *Journal of Counseling Psychology* 34:186–196.

Muller, P. 1981. *Contemporary Suburban America.* Englewood Cliffs, NJ: Prentice-Hall.

Muller, T., and T. J. Espenshade. 1985. *The Fourth Wave: California's Newest Immigrants.* Washington DC: Urban Institute.

Muramatsu, M. 1982. "Japan," in John A. Ross, ed. *International Encyclopedia of Population,* vol. 1. New York: Free Press, pp. 385–390.

Murphy, E. M. 1985. *World Population: Toward the Next Century.* Washington, DC: Population Reference Bureau.

Myrdal, G. 1964. *An American Dilemma.* New York: McGraw-Hill.

Nadelmann, E. 1990. "Challenge Is Not Whether to Decriminalize but How." *Los Angeles Times,* March 20.

Nakamura, H., and J. W. White. 1988. "Tokyo," in M. Dogan and J. Kasarda, eds. *A World of Giant Cities,* vol. 2. Beverly Hills, CA: Sage, pp. 123–156.

Nakane, C. 1984. *Japanese Society.* Tokyo: Charles E. Tuttle.

Nanda, S. 1980. *Cultural Anthropology.* New York: D. Van Nostrand.

———. 1987. *Cultural Anthropology,* 3rd ed. Belmont, CA: Wadsworth.

Nangi, A. 1988. "Islam," in R. C. Bush et al., eds. *The Religious World—Communities of Faith.* New York: Macmillan, pp. 311–356.

Nass, G., and M. Fisher. 1988. *Sexuality Today.* Boston: Towes and Bartlett.

National Institute of Mental Health. 1982. *Television and Behavior: Ten Years of Scientific Progress and Implications of Behavior.* Washington, DC: U.S. Government Printing Office.

National Public Radio. 1991. "Sunday Morning: Report on Brazil." May 12.

Newland, K. 1980. *City Limits: Emerging Constraints of Urban Growth.* Washington, DC: Population Institute.

Newman, K. S. 1988. *Falling from Grace: The Experience of Downward Mobility in the American Middle Class.* New York: Vintage Books.

Newsweek. 1990. "Perspectives." (July 16):17.

Nietschmann, B. 1988. "Third World War: The Global Conflict Over the Rights of Indigenous Nations." *Utne Reader* (November/December):84–90.

Nisbet, E. 1974. *The Sociology of Emile Durkheim.* New York: Oxford University Press.

Nishimura, Y. 1991. "Company Recruits Gear Up for Tough Training Programs." *Japan Times Weekly International Edition,* February 11–17.

Notenstein, F. W. 1945. "Population—The Long View," in T. W. Schultz, ed. *Food for the World.* Chicago: University of Chicago Press, pp. 36–57.

O'Connell, J. 1990. "In More and More U.S. Elections, Apathy Wins." *San Diego Union,* August 12, pp. A1, A10, A11.

Ogburn, W. F. 1950. *Social Change.* New York: Viking Press.

Orcutt, J. A. 1973. "Societal Reaction and the Response to Deviation in Small Groups." *Social Forces* 52:259–267.

Oster, P. 1989. *The Mexicans: A Personal Portrait of a People.* New York: Harper and Row.

Ouchi, W. G. 1981. *Theory Z: How American Business Can Meet the Japanese Challenge.* Reading, MA: Addison-Wesley.

Pacher, S. 1987. "The World According to Lester Brown." *Utne Reader* (September/October):84–93.

Packard, W. 1988. *Evangelism in America.* New York: Paragon House.

Parachini, A. 1986. "Drug Abuse Afflicts U.S. in Cycles." *Los Angeles Times,* July 31.

Parade. 1991. "Japanese Salaries at Record High." January 20.

Parenti, M. 1989. "Imperialism Causes Third World Poverty," in J. Rohr, ed. *The Third World—Opposing View Points.* San Diego, CA: Greenhaven Press, pp. 17–24.

Parker, J. Hill. 1982. *Principles of Sociology.* Lanham, MD: University Press of America.

Parker, L. C., Jr. 1984. *The Japanese Police System Today—An American Perspective.* Tokyo: Kodansha International.

Parrillo, V. N. 1990. *Strangers to These Shores,* 3rd ed. New York: Macmillan.

Parsons, T. 1954. *Essays in Sociological Theory.* New York: Free Press.

———. 1971. *The System of Modern Societies.* Englewood Cliffs, NJ: Prentice-Hall.

Parsons, T., and R. F. Bales. 1955. *Family, Socialization, and Interaction Processes.* New York: Free Press.

Pastor, R. A., and J. G. Castaneda. 1988. *Limits of Friendship—The United States and Mexico.* New York: Vintage Books.

Paz, O. 1961. *The Labyrinth of Solitude: Life and Thought in Mexico.* L. Kemp, trans. New York: Grove Press.

———. 1985. *The Labyrinth of Solitude.* New York: Grove Press.

Pearce, D. 1978. "The Feminization of Poverty: Women, Work, and Welfare." *Urban and Social Change Review* (Winter/Spring):28–36.

———. 1990. "The Feminization of Poverty." *Journal for Peace and Justice Studies* 2(1):1–20.

Peele, S. 1989. *The Diseasing of America—Addiction Treatment Out of Control.* Lexington, MA: D.C. Heath.

Penaiosa, F. 1968. "Mexican Family Roles." *Journal of Marriage and the Family* 30:680–689.

Perrin, R. D. 1989. "American Religion in the Post-Aquarian Age: Values and Demographic Factors in Church Growth and Decline." *Journal for the Scientific Study of Religion* 28(1):75–89.

Perry, J., and E. Perry. 1976. *Face to Face— The Individual and Social Problems.* Canada: Little, Brown.

Peterson, James L., and N. Zill. 1986. "Marital Disruption, Parent-Child Relationships, and Behavior Problems in Children." *Journal of Marriage and the Family* 48:295–307.

Peterson, Janice. 1987. "The Feminization of Poverty." *Journal of Economic Issues* 21(March):329–337.

Pfohl, S. J. 1985. *Images of Deviance and Social Control.* New York: McGraw-Hill.

Phillips, K. 1990a. "In the '80s, the Rich Got a Lot Richer, but with New Taxes That Could Change." *Los Angeles Times,* June 24, pp. M1, M8.

_____. 1990b. *The Politics of Rich and Poor.* New York: Random House.

Pines, M. 1981. "The Civilization of Genie." *Psychology Today* 15(September):28–34.

Popline. 1986. "U.S. Withdraws UNFPA Funding." 8(8).

Population Crisis Committee. 1989. "Population Pressures—Threat to Democracy." Washington, DC: Population Crisis Committee.

Population Institute Report to the 101st Congress. 1988. "A Continent in Crisis—Building a Future for Africa in the 21st Century," pp. 23–24. Special report from the series *Toward the 21st Century.*

Population Reference Bureau. 1986. *Population in Perspective: Regional Views.* Washington, DC: Population Reference Bureau.

Portes, A. 1976. "On the Sociology of Development, Theories and Issues." *American Journal of Sociology* (July):55–85.

Pratt, W. 1984. *Understanding U.S. Fertility: Findings from the National Survey of Family Growth, Cycle III.* Washington, DC: Population Reference Bureau.

Preston, S. H. 1986. "The Decline of Fertility in Non-European Countries." *Population and Development Review* 12:26–47.

Price, S. J., and P. C. McKenry. 1988. *Divorce.* Beverly Hills, CA: Sage.

Queen, S., R. W. Habenstein, and J. S. Quadgno. 1985. *The Family in Various Cultures.* New York: Harper and Row.

Quinney, R. 1970. *The Social Reality of Crime.* Boston: Little, Brown.

_____. 1977. *Class State and Crime—On the Theory and Practice of Criminal Justice.* New York: David McKay.

Ramos, S. 1962. *Profile of Man and Culture in Mexico.* Peter G. Earle, trans. Texas: Texas Pan-American Series.

Rangel, C. 1989. "Imperialism Does Not Cause Third World Poverty," in J. Rohr, ed. *The Third World—Opposing View Points.* San Diego, CA: Greenhaven Press, pp. 25–31.

Raschke, H. J. 1988. "Divorce," in M. B. Sussman and S. K. Steinmetz, eds. *Handbook of Marriage and the Family.* New York: Plenum Press, pp. 597–615.

Raschke, H. J., and V. J. Raschke. 1979. "Family Conflict and Children's Self Concepts: A Comparison of Intact and Single Parent Families." *Journal of Marriage and the Family* 41:367–374.

Reckless, W. C. 1967. *The Crime Problem.* New York: Meredith.

Reeves, R. 1990. "They're Turning to a Minor to Deal with a Major Mess." *Los Angeles Times,* April 19.

Reischauer, E. O. 1988. *The Japanese Today.* Cambridge, MA: Belknap Press of Harvard University Press.

Reskin, B., and H. I. Hartmann, eds. 1985. *Women's Work, Men's Work: Sex Segregation on the Job.* Washington, DC: National Academy Press.

Reynolds, H. 1986. *The Economics of Prostitution.* Springfield, IL: Charles C Thomas.

Richardson, L. 1988. *The Dynamics of Sex and Gender. A Sociological Perspective,* 3rd ed. New York: Harper and Row.

Riding, A. 1989. *Distant Neighbors—A Portrait of the Mexicans.* New York: Vintage Books.

Riesman, D. 1961. *The Lonely Crowd.* New Haven: Yale University Press.

Robbins, T. 1976. In Thomas Robbins et al., eds. "The Last Civil Religion: Reverend Moon and the Unification Church." *Sociological Analysis* 37(2): 111–125.

Robbins, T., D. Anthony, M. Doucas, and T. Curtis. 1976. "The Last Civil Religion: Reverend Moon and the Unification Church." *Sociological Analysis* 37 (2):111–125.

Robertson, R. 1989. "Globalization, Politics, and Religion," in J. A. Beckford and T. Luckman, eds. *The Changing Face of Religion.* Newbury Park, CA: Sage.

Robinson, L., with J. Bussey. 1990. "Can 'Salinastroika' Work?" *U.S. News & World Report* (December 3):51–52.

Rodman, H. 1963. "The Lower Class Value Stretch." *Social Forces* 42(2):205–215.

Roethlisberger, F. J., and W. J. Dickson. 1964, original 1939. *Management and the Worker.* Cambridge, MA: Harvard University Press.

Rogers, A. B. 1988. "Does Biology Constrain Culture?" *American Anthropologist* 90 (December):819–831.

Rohlen, T. P. 1983. *Japan's High Schools.* Berkeley, CA: University of California Press.

_____. 1986. " 'Spiritual Education' in a Japanese Bank," in T. S. Lebra and W. P. Lebra, eds. *Japanese Culture and Behavior.* Honolulu: University of Hawaii Press, pp. 307–335.

Roos, P. A. 1985. *Gender & Work: A Comparative Analysis of Industrial Societies.* Albany, NY: State University of New York Press.

Roos, P. A., and B. F. Reskin. 1984. "Institutional Factors Contributing to Sex Segregation in the Workplace," in B. F. Reskin, ed. *Sex Segregation in the Workplace: Trends, Explanations, Remedies.* Washington, DC: National Academy Press, pp. 235–260.

Rosenberg, H. 1991. "Channel 7 Doesn't Hear the Voices of Dissent." *Los Angeles Times,* February 26.

Ross, E. Alsworth. 1922. *The Social Trend.* New York: Century Company.

Ross, J. A., ed. 1982. *Mexico: The International Encyclopedia of Population.* New York: Free Press.

Rossi, A. 1984. "Gender and Parenthood." *American Sociological Review* 49:1–19.

Rossides, D. W. 1990. *Comparative Societies: Social Types and Their Interrelations.* Englewood Cliffs, NJ: Prentice-Hall.

Rostow, W. W. 1962. *The Process of Economic Growth.* New York: Norton.

Rubenstein, R. 1987. "Japan and Biblical Religion: The Religious Significance of the Japanese Economic Challenge." *Free Inquiry* (Summer):14–20.

Rubinson, R. 1976. "The World Economy and the Distribution of Income Within States: A Cross-National Study." *American Sociological Review* (August):638–659.

Russett, B., et al. 1964. *World Handbook of Political and Social Indicators.* New Haven: Yale University Press.

Sachs, I. 1988. "Vulnerability of Giant Cities and the Life Lottery," in M. Dogan and J. Kasarda, eds. *A World of Giant Cities,* vol. 1. Beverly Hills, CA: Sage, pp. 337–350.

Sachs, S., G. Palumbo, and R. Ross. 1987. "The Cold City: The Winter of Discontent?" in G. Gappert, ed. *The Future of Winter Cities.* Beverly Hills, CA: Sage, pp. 13–34.

Salholz, E. 1987. "Do Colleges Set Asian Quotas?" *Newsweek* 109(February 9):60.

Salholz, E., E. Clift, K. Springer, and P. Johnson. 1990. "Women Under Assault." *Newsweek* (July 16):23–24.

Sanders, W. 1983. *Criminology.* Reading, MA: Addison-Wesley.

San Diego Union. 1989a. "Japan: $43 Billion Aid Package Will Be Offered." July 12.

———. 1989b. "Economic Gain Eludes Majority of Nation's Hispanics in 1980s." December 16.

———. 1990a. "Rich Grew Richer in '80s, but Most Americans Just Treaded Water." January 11, pp. A1, A13.

———. 1990b. "Dramatic Decline Seen in Hispanics, Blacks in College." January 15.

———. 1990c. "Rich Get Richer, Poor Get Poorer, Says new Congressional Tax Study." February 17, p. A15.

———. 1990d. "Japan Sees First Sign of Cocaine Infiltration." April 1.

———. 1990e. "Japanese Court OKs Back Pay in Sex Bias Suit." July 5.

———. 1990f. "Fringe Sects Thrive as Japanese Seek Quick New Spiritual Paths." July 22.

———. 1990g. "Teacher Who Caused Death to Be Fired." July 28.

———. 1990h. "Bias in Promotions at the Very Top Targeted." July 30.

———. 1990i. "Babies in Womb Learn Language, Researcher Says." August 13.

———. 1990j. "Land Crisis Now Reaches Beyond Tokyo." October 21.

———. 1990k. "Japan Boom May Finally Be Slowing." November 22, pp. D1, D2.

———. 1990l. "Economic Gain Eludes Majority of Nation's Hispanics in 1980's." December 16, p. A2.

———. 1991. "Despite Political Gains, Fewer Hispanics Occupy High Elected Offices." January 6.

Satchell, M. 1991. "Poisoning the Border." *U.S. News & World Report* (May 6):33–41.

Savage, D. G. 1990. "Asians, Latinos Surge in U.S. Growth Rates." *Los Angeles Times,* March 2.

Savitch, H. J. 1978. "Black Cities//White Suburbs: Domestic Colonization as an Interpretive Idea." *Annals of the Academy of Political and Social Sciences* (September):118–134.

Savitz, L. D. 1972. "Introduction to the Reprint Edition," in G. Lombroso-Ferrero, ed. *Lombroso's Criminal Man.* Montclair, NY: Patterson Smith.

Sawhill, I. V. 1989. "An Overview." *Public Interest* (Summer):3–15.

Schaefer, R. T. 1990. *Racial and Ethnic Groups,* 4th ed. Glenview, IL: Scott, Foresman/Little, Brown Higher Education.

Schoenberger, K. 1989. "Legal Trap for Japanese." *Los Angeles Times,* April 28.

———. 1990. "U.S. Failing to Close Its Education Gap with Japan." *Los Angeles Times,* January 7.

Schteingart, M. 1988. "Mexico City," in M. Dogan and J. Kasarda, eds. *A World of Giant Cities,* vol. 2. Beverly Hills, CA: Sage, pp. 268–293.

Schwartz, J. 1987. "A 'Superminority' Tops Out." *Newsweek* 109(May 11):48–49.

Scott, W. R. 1987. *Organizations: Rational, Natural, and Open Systems,* 2nd ed. Englewood Cliffs, NJ: Prentice-Hall.

Sewell, W. H., and V. P. Shah. 1967. "Socioeconomic Status, Intelligence, and the Attainment of Higher Education." *Sociology of Education* 40(Winter):1–23.

Shannon, T. R. 1989. *Urban Problems in Sociological Perspective.* Prospect Heights, IL: Waveland Press.

Shapiro, L. 1990. "Guns and Dolls." *Newsweek* (May 28):56–65.

Shaw, D. 1990. "Asian-Americans Chafe Against Stereotype of 'Model Citizen.' " *Los Angeles Times,* December 11.

Shaw, S. 1987. "Wretched of the Earth." *The New Statesman* (March 20):19–20.

Shelley, L. 1981. *Crime and Modernization—The Impact of Industrialization and Urbanization.* Carbondale, IL: Southern Illinois University Press.

Shepard, J. M. 1987. *Sociology.* St. Paul, MN: West Publishing Company.

Shogan, R. 1990. "Poll Finds Rising Cynicism Eroding 2 Parties' Support." *Los Angeles Times,* September 19, pp. A1, A16.

Shur, E. M. 1979. *Interpreting Deviance—A Sociological Introduction.* New York: Harper and Row.

Siegel, L. 1989. *Criminology.* St. Paul, MN: West Publishing Company.

Silver, J. 1990. "Mexico Has Its Own Reform Movement—Salinastroika." *San Diego Union,* October 21, p. C5.

Silver, M., and D. Geller. 1978. "On the Irrelevance of Evil: The Organization and Individual Action." *Journal of Social Issues* 34:125–136.

Simmel, G. 1950, original 1908. *The Sociology of Georg Simmel.* Kurt Wolff, ed. New York: Free Press.

Simon, D. R., and D. S. Eitzen. 1986. *Elite Deviance.* Boston: Allyn and Bacon.

Simons, C. 1987. "They Get By With a Lot of Help from Their *Kyoiku Mamas.*" *Smithsonian* 17(March):44–53.

Simpson, G. E., and J. M. Yinger. 1985. *Racial and Cultural Minorities: An Analysis of Prejudice and Discrimination,* 5th ed. New York: Plenum Press.

Sivard, R. 1985. *Women—A World Survey.* Washington, DC: World Priorities.

———. 1987. *World Military and Social Expenditures.* Washington, DC: World Priorities.

Smelser, N. 1973. "Toward a Theory of Modernization," in A. Etzioni and E. Etzioni-Halvey, eds. *Social Change—Sources, Patterns and Consequences.* New York: Basic Books, pp. 268–284.

Smith, Carol, and C. A. Visher. 1980. "Sex and Involvement in Deviance/Crime: A Quantitative Review of the Literature." *American Sociological Review* 45:691–701.

Smith, Charles. 1990a. "Food for Thought." *Far Eastern Economic Review* (February 1):10–11.

———. 1990b. "Officeless Ladies." *Far Eastern Economic Review* 147(7)(February 15):12–13.

Smith, D. E. 1971. *Religion, Politics, and Change in the Third World.* New York: Free Press.

Smith, L. 1987a. "Divisive Forces in an Inbred Society." *Fortune* (March 30):24–28.

_____. 1987b. "Goodbye Consensus: Divisiveness in Japan." *Current* 297(July/August):30–33.

Soldo, B. I., and E. M. Agree. 1988. *America's Elderly.* Washington, DC: Population Reference Bureau.

Solo, S. 1989. "Japan Discovers Woman Power." *Fortune* (June 19):153–158.

Sowell, T. 1983. "Second Thoughts About the Third World." *Harpers* (November):34–42.

Spates, J., and J. Macionis. 1987. *Sociology of Cities.* New York: St. Martin's Press.

Spradley, J. P., and D. W. McCurdy. 1989. *Anthropology—The Cultural Perspective.* Prospect Heights, IL: Waveland Press.

Sprey, J. 1966. "Family Disorganization: Toward a Conceptual Clarification." *Journal of Marriage and the Family* 28:398–406.

_____. 1969. "The Family as a System of Conflict." *Journal of Marriage and the Family* 31:699–706.

Stark, R., and W. S. Bainbridge. 1979. "Of Churches and Sects: Preliminary Concepts for a Theory of Religious Movements." *Journal for the Scientific Study of Religion* 18:117–133.

Sternlieb, G. 1978. "The City as Sand Box," in E. Gardner, ed. *Saving America's Cities.* New York: McGraw-Hill, pp. 24–32.

Stevens, E. P. 1973. "Marianismo: The Other Face of Machismo in Latin America," in A. Pescatello, ed. *Female and Male in Latin America.* Pittsburgh, PA: University of Pittsburgh Press, pp. 89–101.

Stoddard, E. R. 1987. *Maquiladora Plants in Northern Mexico.* El Paso, TX: Texas Western Press.

Sumner, W. G. 1883. *What Social Classes Owe to Each Other.* New York: Harper and Brothers.

_____. 1960, original 1906. *Folkways.* New York: New American Library.

Sutherland, E. H., and D. R. Cressey. 1970. *Criminology.* Philadelphia: J. P. Lippincott.

Sweet, E. 1985. "Date Rape: The Story of an Epidemic and Those Who Deny It." *Ms./Campus Times* (October):56–59, 84–85.

Sykes, G. M., and D. Matza. 1957. "Techniques of Neutralization: A Theory of Delinquency." *American Sociological Review* 22:664–70.

Szulc, T. 1982. "What Indira Gandhi Wants You to Know." *Parade* (July 25):4–6.

Szymanski, A. 1981. *The Logic of Imperialism.* New York: Praeger.

Tannenbaum, F. 1938. *Crime and the Community.* New York: Ginn.

Tasker, P. 1987. *The Japanese.* New York: Truman Talley Books.

Tavris, C., and C. Wade. 1984. *The Longest War: Sex Differences in Perspective,* 2nd ed. New York: Harcourt Brace Jovanovich.

Theodorson, G. A., and A. Theodorson. 1969. *A Modern Dictionary of Sociology.* New York: Barnes and Noble.

Thio, A. 1988. *Deviant Behavior.* New York: Harper and Row.

Thomas, W. I. 1967, original 1923. *The Unadjusted Girl.* New York: Harper and Row.

Thomas, W. I., with D. Swaine Thomas. 1928. *The Child in America.* New York: Knopf.

Thompson, W. 1929. "Population." *American Journal of Sociology* 34(6):959–975.

Thornton, A. 1985. "Changing Attitudes Toward Separation and Divorce: Causes and Consequences." *American Journal of Sociology* 90:856–872.

Time. 1988. "Slow Count: A Winner and Some Angry Losers in a Historic Race." July 25, p. 50.

Tittle, C. R., W. J. Villemez, and D. A. Smith. 1978. "The Myth of Social Class and Criminality: An Empirical Assessment of the Empirical Evidence." *American Sociological Review* 43:643–656.

"Tobacco's Toll on America." 1989. New York: American Lung Association.

Tobin, J. J., D. Y. H. Wu, and D. H. Davidson. 1989. "How Three Key Countries Shape Their Children." *World Monitor* (April):36–45.

Todaro, M. P., and J. Stilkind. 1981. *City Bias and Rural Neglect: The Dilemma of Urban Development.* New York: Population Council.

Toffler, A. 1990. "Toffler's Next Shock." *World Monitor* (November):33–44.

Tonnies, F. 1963, original 1887. *Community and Society.* New York: Harper and Row.

Treiman, D. J., and P. A. Roos. 1983. "Sex and Earnings in Industrial Society: A Nine-Nation Comparison." *American Journal of Sociology* 89:612–650.

Tuchman, G. 1978. *Making News: A Study in the Construction of Reality.* New York: Free Press.

Tumin, M. M. 1953a. "Some Principles of Stratification: A Critical Analysis." *American Sociological Review* 18(4):387–394.

_____. 1953b. "Reply to Kingsley Davis." *American Sociological Review* 18(6):672–673.

_____. 1957. "Some Unapplauded Consequences of Social Mobility in a Mass Society." *Social Forces* 36(1):32–37.

_____. 1985. *Social Stratification: The Forms and Functions of Inequality,* 2nd ed. Englewood Cliffs, NJ: Prentice-Hall.

Turner, J. H. 1972. *Patterns of Social Organization.* New York: McGraw-Hill.

Turner, J. H., and A. Maryanski. 1979. *Functionalism.* Menlo Park, CA: Benjamin/Cummings.

Turque, B., and R. Hammill. 1989. "A String of Sixty Murders." *Newsweek* (December 4):64.

U.S. Bureau of the Census. 1988. *Current Population Reports,* P-60, no. 161. Washington, DC: U.S. Government Printing Office.

_____. 1989a. *Changes in American Family Life.* Current Population Reports Special Studies, Series P-23, no. 163. Washington, DC: U.S. Government Printing Office.

_____. 1989b. *Households, Families, Marital Status, and Living Arrangements: March 1989.* Current Population Reports, Series P-20, no. 441. Washington, DC: U.S. Government Printing Office.

_____. 1989c. *Studies in Marriage and the Family.* Current Population Reports Special Studies, Series P-23, no. 162. Washington, DC: U.S. Government Printing Office.

_____. 1990. *Statistical Abstract of the United States, 1990.* Washington, DC: U.S. Government Printing Office.

U.S. Department of Health and Human Services. 1989. *Health United States 1989.* Washington, DC: U.S. Government Printing Office.

Useem, M., and J. Karabel. 1986. "Pathways to Corporate Management." *American Sociological Review* 51(2):184–200.

van den Berghe, P. L. 1978. *Race and Racism: A Comparative Perspective,* 2nd ed. New York: Wiley.

van Wolferen, K. 1990. *The Enigma of Japanese Power.* New York: Vintage Books.

Vander Zanden, J. W. 1983. *American Minority Relations,* 4th edition. New York: Plenum Press.

Vasquez, J. M. 1983. "Mexico City—Strangling on Growth." *Los Angeles Times,* December 8.

_____. 1984. "Mexico—A 'Success' on Population." *Los Angeles Times,* September 15.

Vigil, J. D. 1988. *Barrio Gangs—Street Life and Identity in Southern California.* Austin, TX: University of Texas Press.

Vogel, E. F. 1979. *Japan as Number One.* Cambridge, MA: Harvard University Press.

Wacquant, L. J. D. and W. J. Wilson. 1989. "The Cost of Racial and Class Exclusion in the Inner City." *Annals of the American Association of Political and Social Sciences* (January):8–25.

Wagley, C., and M. Harris. 1964. *Minorities in the New World.* New York: Columbia University Press.

Wald, K. D. 1987. *Religion and Politics in the United States.* New York: St. Martin's Press.

Walker, S. 1989. *Sense and Nonsense About Crime—A Policy Guide.* Pacific Grove, CA: Brooks/Cole.

Wallerstein, J. S., and J. Berlin Kelly. 1980. *Surviving the Breakup—How Children and Parents Cope with Divorce.* New York: Basic Books.

Ward, D., and G. G. Kassebaum. 1965. *Women's Prison: Sex and Social Structure.* Chicago: Aldine.

Warner, W. L. 1960. *Social Class in America: The Evaluation of Status.* New York: Harper and Row.

Warner, W. L., and L. Srole. 1945. *The Social Systems of American Ethnic Groups.* New Haven: Yale University Press.

Warner, W. L., and P. S. Lunt. 1941. *The Social Life of a Modern Community.* New Haven: Yale University Press.

Warshaw, S. 1988a. *India Emerges.* Berkeley, CA: Diablo Press.

_____. 1988b. *Japan Emerges.* Berkeley and San Francisco: Diablo Press.

Watanabe, T. 1990. "Ideas? Japanese Buy American, Raising Hackles." *Los Angeles Times,* July 22.

Waud, R. N. 1980. *Economics.* New York: Harper and Row.

Webb, E. J., D. T. Campbell, R. D. Schwartz, and L. Sechrest. 1966. *Unobtrusive Measures: Nonreactive Research in the Social Sciences.* Chicago: Rand McNally.

Weber, M. 1946, original 1919. "Bureaucracy," in H. H. Gerth and C. Wright Mills, eds. *From Max Weber: Essays in Sociology.* New York: Oxford University Press, pp. 196–244.

_____. 1946. "Class, Status, Party," in H. H. Gerth and C. Wright Mills, eds. *From Max Weber: Essays in Sociology.* New York: Oxford University Press.

_____. 1947. *The Theory of Social and Economic Organization.* Edited with an introduction by T. Parsons. New York: Free Press.

_____. 1958, original 1904. *The Protestant Ethic and the Spirit of Capitalism.* New York: Charles Scribner's Sons.

_____. 1978, original 1921. *Economy and Society.* G. Roth and C. Wittich, eds. Berkeley, CA: University of California Press.

Webster. 1983. *Webster's New Twentieth Century Dictionary,* unabridged, 2nd ed. New York: Prentice-Hall.

Weeks, J. R. 1986. *Population: An Introduction to Concepts and Issues.* Belmont, CA: Wadsworth.

Welsh, B. W. W., and P. Butorin. 1990. *Dictionary of Development—Third World Economy, Environment, Society.* New York: Garland Publishing.

Wen, T. E. 1975. *Area Handbook for Mexico.* Washington, DC: U.S. Government Printing Office.

Westerman, M. 1989. "Death of the Frito Bandito." *American Demographics* (March):28–32.

Whalen, J. P. 1971. "The Forging of Christendom," in M. Severy, ed. *Great Religions of the World.* Washington, DC: National Geographic Society, pp. 327–379.

White, M. 1987. "The Virtue of Japanese Mothers: Cultural Definitions of Women's Lives." *Daedalus* 16(Summer):149–163.

Whiting, R. 1989. *You Gotta Have Wa.* New York: Macmillan.

Whyte, W. 1988. *City. Rediscovering the Center.* New York: Doubleday.

Wickman, P. M. 1974. "Social Norms," in *Encyclopedia of Sociology.* Guilford, CT: Dushkin Publishing Group, p. 199.

Wilcox, D. 1984. "El Dia de los Muertos." *American Craft* 44(October–November):40–43.

Wilkie, J. W., and E. Ochoa, eds. 1989. *Statistical Abstract of Latin America,* vol. 27. Los Angeles: UCLA Latin American Center Publications.

Williams, F. P., III, and M. D. McShane. 1988. *Criminological Theory.* Englewood Cliffs, NJ: Prentice-Hall.

Williams, P. W. 1989. *Popular Religion in America,* reprint edition. Urbana, IL: University of Illinois Press.

Williams, R. M., Jr. 1970. *American Values—A Sociological Perspective.* New York: Knopf, pp. 452–502.

Williamson, J. B., A. Munley, and L. Evans. 1980. *Aging and Society.* New York: Holt, Rinehart and Winston.

Willie, C. W. 1978. "The Inclining Significance of Race." *Society* 15(July/August):10, 12–13.

_____. 1979. *The Caste and Class Controversy.* Bayside, NY: General Hall.

Wilson, E. O. 1978a. *On Human Nature.* Cambridge, MA: Harvard University Press.

_____. 1978b. "What Is Sociobiology?" *Society* (September/October): 10–14.

Wilson, J. F., and W. R. Clark. 1989. *Religion: A Preface.* Englewood Cliffs, NJ: Prentice-Hall.

Wilson, J. Q., and R. Herrnstein. 1985. *Crime and Human Nature—The Definitive Study of the Causes of Crime.* New York: Simon and Schuster.

Wilson, S. L. 1989. *Mass Media/Mass Culture: An Introduction.* New York: Random House.

Wilson, W. J. 1978. *The Declining Significance of Race.* Chicago: University of Chicago Press.

_____. 1987. *The Truly Disadvantaged: The Inner City, the Underclass, and Public Policy.* Chicago: University of Chicago Press.

_____. 1989. *The Ghetto Underclass.* Newbury Park, CA: Sage.

Wipf, K. A. 1987. "Mesoamerican Religion: Contemporary Cultures," in *Encyclopedia of Religion.* New York: Macmillan, pp. 428–436.

Wirth, L. 1938. "Urbanism as a Way of Life." *American Journal of Sociology* 44:1–24.

Woodward, K. L., with J. Gordon, N. de la Penna, P. King, M. Peyser, M. Mason, N. Joseph, D. Rosenberg, and R. Hammill. 1990. "A Time to Seek." *Newsweek* (December 17):50–56.

World Development Report. 1988. Washington, DC: The World Bank.

Wright, E. O. 1985. *Classes.* New York: McGraw-Hill.

Wrong, D. H. 1961. "The Oversocialized Conception of Man in Modern Sociology." *American Sociological Review* 26(April):183–193.

Wuthnow, R. 1988. *The Restructuring of American Religion.* Princeton, NJ: Princeton University Press.

Yates, R. E. 1990a. "Japan's Violent Young Rebels 'Fight Back.' " *San Diego Union,* April 8.

———. 1990b. "Overwork Blamed for Deaths of Japanese Businessmen." *San Diego Union,* May 6.

Yoshino, I. R., and S. Murakoshi. 1983. *"Burakumin."* *Kodansha Encyclopedia of Japan,* vol. 1. Tokyo: Kodansha, pp. 216–217.

Yoshio, S. 1983. "Crime," in *Kodansha Encyclopedia of Japan,* vol. 2. Tokyo: Kodansha, pp. 44–46.

Zastrow, C., and L. Bowker. 1984. *Social Problems: Issues and Solutions.* Chicago: Nelson-Hall.

Zausner, M. 1986. *The Streets—A Factual Portrait of Six Prostitutes as Told in Their Own Words.* New York: St. Martin's Press.

Zimbardo, P. G. 1969. "The Human Choice: Individuation, Reason, and Order versus Deindividuation, Impulse, and Chaos," in W. J. Arnold and D. Levine, eds. *Nebraska Symposium.* Lincoln, NE: University of Nebraska Press, pp. 237–307.

Name Index

Subject Index